Studies in Logic

Volume 36

Understanding Vagueness

Logical, Philosophical and Linguistic Perspectives

Studies in Logic Series Editor
Dov Gabbay   dov.gabbay@kcl.ac.uk

Understanding Vagueness

Logical, Philosophical, and Linguistic
Perspectives

Edited by

Petr Cintula,
Christian G. Fermüller,
Lluís Godo

and

Petr Hájek

ISBN 978-1-84890-037-0

College Publications
Scientific Director: Dov Gabbay
Managing Director: Jane Spurr
Department of Informatics
King's College London, Strand, London WC2R 2LS, UK

http://www.collegepublications.co.uk

Original cover design by Laraine Welch
Printed by Lightning Source, Milton Keynes, UK

PREFACE

More than two millennia ago Greek philosophers realized that vagueness poses a challenge to logic: if you remove a single grain of sand from a heap of sand you are still left with a heap of sand, or so it seems. But if this sentence is just as true as the assertion that a million properly arranged sand grains make a heap of sand, then iterative applications of the most basic laws of logic—instantiation and modus ponens—lead us to the conclusion that even a single grain of sand and actually also no sand at all make a heap. This well known sorites paradox does not allude to any strange properties specific to heaps, of course. The same kind of reasoning seduces us to conclude that we are forever young and always old, tall and short, fat and skinny, all at the same time. Just initiate a corresponding sorites series with an innocuous statement referring to a case where the truthful application of the chosen predicate is uncontroversial and add an inductive premise that states that an imperceptible small change in respect to the relevant predicate never turns a true statement into a false one.

The sorites paradox and other phenomena related to the fact that natural language is intrinsically vague have engendered an almost insurmountably large amount of literature on formal models of reasoning with vague language. On our count at least ten monographs and paper collections that focus on theories of vagueness have appeared in the last decade alone. The enterprise that lead to the volume that you are now holding in your hands started in early 2007, when we, a group of logicians and computer scientists in Barcelona, Prague, and Vienna, became aware of a call for project proposals in the programme *Modelling Intelligent Interaction - Logic in the Humanities, Social and Computational Sciences (LogICCC)*, of the European Science Foundation (ESF). Our proposal *Logical Models of Reasoning with Vague Information (LoMoReVI)*, granted in May 2008, was mainly motivated by two insights:

- Contemporary formal logic, in particular, mathematical fuzzy logic, provides a rich toolbox for designing and assembling models of reasoning with vague predicates and propositions.

- Fuzzy logic alone is not sufficient for modeling vagueness at a level that matches the many subtle aspects of vague language use that have emerged from philosophical and linguistic research on this topic.

Correspondingly it has been our aim from the very onset to actively seek interaction with experts on theoretical and empirical aspects of vagueness and related language phenomena. We thus were glad to see that a sister *LogICCC* project *Vagueness, Approximation, and Granularity* would take up mainly linguistic and psychological research challenges related to vagueness.

The majority of the fifteen papers collected in this volume originated with presentations at a conference in Čejkovice, Czech Republic, 14–17 September 2009, that bore the same title as our collaborative research project (CRP): "Logical Models of Reasoning with Vague Information (LoMoReVI)". Incidentally, this event was the first in an impressive series of inter-CRP activities sponsored by ESF to foster the exchange of ideas and collaboration within the Eurocores programme *LogICCC*. A number of additional experts that have not attended the conference have also been invited to contribute. As already mentioned, this book is not the only recent publication on the fascinating topic of vagueness. However, we want to emphasize two features that enhance the attractiveness of this volume.

- In accordance with the broad array of challenges provided by the phenomenon of vagueness, we strive at interdisciplinarity. The list of contributors includes philosophers, linguists, logicians, mathematicians, and computer scientists.

- All papers have not only been peer reviewed, but are accompanied here by comments of other experts. These comments and the replies by the authors document intensive debates at the frontier of contemporary research—in some cases by crossing and reflecting on disciplinary boundaries.

We hope that these features, jointly with the high quality of the papers, render this book interesting and useful beyond merely documenting research related to *LoMoReVI*.

Any project of this kind, in particular when so many people are involved in it, incurs various debts to colleagues, friends, and families. Indeed this book has only been made possible by the generous assistance of many individuals and funding institutions. We are sincerely grateful and hope to be forgiven for not providing a complete list of people we feel indebted to here. However we certainly want to acknowledge explicitly the funding by ESF, that not only supported the *LoMoReVI* project[1] but also provided specific grants for the mentioned *LoMoReVI* conference as well as for this publication. In this context we also thank Dr Eva Hoogland and her team at ESF, who provided impressively effective and always friendly support throughout the whole project. More specific to this publication, we want to express our gratitude to all authors of papers and of comments on papers. All contributions to this volume have been peer reviewed; and while most of the referees also appear as authors, we also want to thank the following additional reviewers: Maria Aloni, Alan Bale, Pilar Dellunde, Alice Kyburg, Jonathan Lawry, George Metcalfe, Carles Noguera, Graham Priest, and Friedrich Slivovsky. Last but not least we wish to thank to Karel Chvalovský, Petra Ivaničová, Eva Pospíšilová, and Jane Spurr for administrative and technical support.

Petr Cintula, Chris Fermüller, Lluís Godo, Petr Hájek
Editors

[1] Via the national funding organisations in Austria (as FWF grant I143-G15), Czech Republic (as GAČR grant ICC/08/E018), and Spain (as MICINN grant FFI2008-03126-E/FILO).

CONTENTS

Fuzzy Logic and Higher-Order Vagueness

NICHOLAS J.J. SMITH[1]

The major reason given in the philosophical literature for dissatisfaction with theories of vagueness based on fuzzy logic is that such theories give rise to a problem of *higher-order vagueness* or *artificial precision*.[2] In this paper I first outline the problem and survey suggested solutions: fuzzy epistemicism; measuring truth on an ordinal scale; logic as modelling; fuzzy metalanguages; blurry sets; and fuzzy plurivaluationism. I then argue that in order to decide upon a solution, we need to understand the true nature and source of the problem. Two possible sources are discussed: the problem stems from the very nature of vagueness—from the defining features of vague predicates; or the problem stems from the way in which the meanings of predicates are determined—by the usage of speakers together with facts about their environment and so on. I argue that the latter is the true source of the problem, and on this basis that fuzzy plurivaluationism is the correct solution.

1 The problem of artificial precision

Each of the following passages—from Haack, Urquhart and Keefe, respectively—gives a nice statement of the problem of artificial precision:[3]

> [Fuzzy logic] imposes artificial precision... [T]hough one is not obliged to require that a predicate either definitely applies or definitely does not apply, one *is* obliged to require that a predicate definitely applies to such-and-such, rather than to such-and-such other, degree (e.g. that a man 5 ft 10 in tall belongs to *tall* to degree 0.6 rather than 0.5). [11, p. 443]

> One immediate objection which presents itself to [the fuzzy] line of approach is the extremely artificial nature of the attaching of precise numerical values to sentences like '73 is a large number' or 'Picasso's *Guernica* is beautiful'. In fact, it seems plausible to say that the nature of vague predicates precludes attaching precise numerical values just as much as it precludes attaching precise classical truth values. [45, p. 108]

[1]Thanks to Libor Běhounek and an anonymous referee for helpful written comments, to audiences at *LoMoReVI* (Čejkovice, 15 September 2009) and AAL (Sydney, 3 July 2010) for helpful discussions, and to the Australian Research Council for research support.

[2]The former term is used more widely in the literature, but the same term is also applied to problems which I regard as being rather different in character from the problem for the fuzzy view under discussion here; I shall therefore use the latter term in this paper.

[3]For further statements of the problem see Copeland [5, pp. 521–2], Goguen [9, p. 332] [10, p. 54], Lakoff [22, pp. 462, 481], Machina [26, p. 187], Rolf [30, pp. 223–4], Schwartz [33, p. 46], Tye [43, p. 11], Williamson [52, pp. 127–8] and Keefe [19, pp. 113–4].

[T]he degree theorist's assignments impose precision in a form that is just as unacceptable as a classical true/false assignment. In so far as a degree theory avoids determinacy over whether a is F, the objection here is that it does so by enforcing determinacy over the *degree* to which a is F. All predications of "is red" will receive a unique, exact value, but it seems inappropriate to associate our vague predicate "red" with any particular exact function from objects to degrees of truth. For a start, what could determine which is the correct function, settling that my coat is red to degree 0.322 rather than 0.321? [18, p. 571]

In a nutshell, the problem for the fuzzy approach is this: it is artificial/implausible/inappropriate to associate each vague *predicate* in natural language with a particular function which assigns one particular fuzzy truth value (i.e. real number between 0 and 1) to each object (the object's degree of possession of the property picked out by that predicate); likewise, it is artificial/implausible/inappropriate to associate each vague *sentence* in natural language with a particular fuzzy truth value (the sentence's degree of truth).

Note that the problem is *not* a problem for pure (mathematical) fuzzy logic: that is, for fuzzy logic *qua* branch of mathematics. It is a problem for theories of vagueness based on fuzzy logic (or more precisely, on fuzzy model theory). Let me explain. Classical logic countenances only two truth values, and classical models are total: every closed well-formed formula (wff) is assigned one or other of these values on each model. This does *not* make it correct, however, to say that it is a commitment of classical logic (model theory) that every statement is either true or false. Such a commitment comes into play only when one seeks to use classical logic to shed light on the semantics of some language (e.g. natural language, or the language of mathematics). It is thus a commitment not of pure classical logic (model theory)—considered as a branch of mathematics—but of model-theoretic semantics (MTS). One who wishes to pursue MTS (in relation to some language), and wishes to make use only of classical model theory, *is* committed to the claim that every statement (made in the language in question) is either true or false.

We therefore need to be careful to distinguish between pure logic (model theory) and MTS. Now note that in order to use classical model theory for the purposes of MTS, one needs to make use of a new notion that does not figure in pure model theory. This is the notion of the *intended model* (or some other notion which plays a similar role— see on). Pure model theory tells us only that a wff is true on this model and false on that one (etc.). In order to obtain a notion of truth *simpliciter*—which is required in MTS—we need a designated model, so that we can say that truth *simpliciter* is truth on the designated model. This is the role played by the intended model.[4] In MTS, my statement 'Bob is tall' is taken to express some wff. This wff is true on some models and false on others. What we want to know, however, is whether it is true *simpliciter*. It is so if it is true on the model which assigns as referent to the singular term which I expressed as 'Bob' the very guy I was talking about when I said 'Bob' and which assigns as extension to the predicate which I expressed as 'tall' the set of things which have the property I was talking about when I said 'is tall'—that is, the intended model.

---

[4]Cf. Lepore [23, p. 181]: "A theory of meaning...is concerned only with a single interpretation of a language, the correct or intended one: so its fundamental notion is that of meaning or truth—simpliciter."

Weiner [50, p. 165] sums up the MTS perspective very nicely: "Natural language (or at least a cleaned up version of a fragment of natural language) is to be understood as a formal language along with an intended interpretation. Truth, for sentences of natural language, is to be understood as truth under the intended interpretation."

Of course, those working in MTS typically do *not* take classical logic and model theory as their starting point. Usually they take some intensional higher-order logic, because they think that this provides the best way of accounting for certain features of natural language. In this paper, we are concerned with those who take fuzzy logic and model theory as their starting point—because they think that this provides the best way of accounting for the *vagueness* of natural language. Now consider the following comment from Hájek [13, p. 368]. The context is a discussion of Shapiro [34]. After mentioning the objection to fuzzy logics from artificial precision and noting Shapiro's response (a version of the logic as modelling approach to be discussed below), Hájek adds (in parentheses): "Let us comment that mathematical fuzzy logic concerns the possibility of sound inference, surely not techniques of ascribing concrete truth degrees to concrete propositions." Quite so: the problem of artificial precision is *not* a problem for mathematical fuzzy logic. But it *is* a problem for fuzzy theories of vagueness—for fuzzy logic-based MTS. Such theories *are* concerned with ascribing concrete truth degrees to concrete propositions. The simplest way for them to proceed is to adopt the idea of an intended model. A proposition will be assigned different degrees of truth on different models; the concrete truth degree of a concrete proposition is the degree of truth assigned to it on the *intended* model. In what follows, when I speak of the '(basic) fuzzy theory of vagueness', what I mean is that version of MTS for natural language which says that a vague discourse is to be modelled as a collection of wffs together with a unique intended fuzzy model. It is *this* view—which is committed to the idea that each vague sentence of natural language has a unique fuzzy truth value, namely its truth value on the intended model—that is threatened by the artificial precision problem.

Summing up: pure/mathematical fuzzy logic does not face the problem of artificial precision, because all models are equal in its eyes. Precisely for this reason, however, it does not (on its own) provide a *theory of vagueness* in the sense of a theory which tells us about the (actual) meaning and truth (simpliciter) of claims made in vague natural language in a way which respects our pre-theoretic intuitions about these matters (e.g. that 'Shaquille O'Neal is tall' is true to degree 1) and reveals what is wrong with sorites reasoning. In order to get such a theory, we need to add to pure fuzzy logic a notion of some model(s) being special or designated in some way: for any vague discourse, amongst all its *possible* models, there are only *some* that are relevant to questions of the (actual) meaning and truth (simpliciter) of statements in the discourse. The simplest approach is to say that there is just one such model: the 'intended model'. This is what I call the 'basic fuzzy theory of vagueness'. It immediately runs into the artificial precision problem. In the next section we examine possible responses to the problem. Some (e.g. fuzzy epistemicism) stick with the basic fuzzy theory of vagueness; some (e.g. fuzzy plurivaluationism) stick with the underlying pure fuzzy model theory, but abandon the notion of a *unique* designated model in favour of a class of such models; some (e.g. blurry sets) abandon the underlying fuzzy model theory in favour of a different kind of pure model theory (while retaining the idea of a unique intended model).

2   Proposed solutions

This section presents six responses to the problem of artificial precision that have been proposed in the literature.

2.1   Fuzzy epistemicism

The fuzzy epistemicist responds to the problem by saying that each vague sentence (e.g. 'Bill is tall') does indeed have a unique fuzzy truth value (e.g. 0.4), but we do not (cannot) know what it is.[5] Our ignorance explains our unease about assigning this or that particular value to a given sentence. Hence the fuzzy epistemicist explains the phenomena behind the objection to the fuzzy view, while defusing the objection: the basic fuzzy theory of vagueness can be retained, complete with the implication that each vague sentence has a unique fuzzy truth value. (Compare the way in which the epistemic account of vagueness would—if it worked—allow us to retain classical MTS for vague natural language.)[6]

2.2   Measuring truth on an ordinal scale

The next response holds that when we assign fuzzy truth values to sentences, the only thing that is meaningful about the assignments is the relative *ordering* of the values assigned. As Goguen puts is:[7]

> We certainly do not want to claim there is some *absolute* [fuzzy] set representing 'short'. ... Probably we should not expect particular numerical values of shortness to be meaningful (except 0 and 1), but rather their *ordering*...degree of membership may be measured by an *ordinal scale*. [9, pp. 331–2]

On this view, while we may assign 'Bill is tall' degree of truth 0.5 and 'Ben is tall' degree of truth 0.6, these are *not* the uniquely correct value assignments: we could just as well assign any other values where the first is less than the second. We can think of this view as follows. Instead of a unique intended fuzzy model, we have a class of acceptable models, closed under a certain sort of transformation of the truth values: any model which can be obtained from an acceptable model by applying an order-preserving (and endpoint-fixing) transformation to the real interval [0,1] is equally acceptable. On this view, then, a vague predicate is *not* associated with a *unique* function which assigns real numbers between 0 and 1 to objects, and a vague sentence is *not* assigned a *unique* fuzzy truth value—and so the objection from artificial precision is avoided.

---

[5]Fuzzy epistemicism is mentioned by Copeland [5, p. 522] and developed in more detail by MacFarlane [25]. Machina [26, p. 187, n.8] could also be interpreted as hinting at such a view when he writes of "difficulties about how to assign degrees of truth to propositions"; Keefe [18, p. 571] [19, p. 115] interprets him in this way and criticises his view on this basis.

[6]Advocates of epistemic theories of vagueness include Cargile [3], Campbell [2], Sorensen [39, ch. 6] [40], Williamson [51] [52, ch's 7–8] and Horwich [16].

[7]See also Sanford [32, p. 29], Machina [26, p. 188], Goguen [10, p. 59], Hájek [12, pp. 162–3], Weatherson [49] and Hyde [17, p. 207].

2.3 Logic as modelling

The most detailed version of this response is Cook's [4].[8] Cook distinguishes *descriptions* from *models*:[9] while descriptions may simplify and approximate, the key feature of models is that some aspects of them are not even *intended* to represent—not even in an approximate or simplified way—an aspect of the thing modelled. Such features of a model are called *artefacts*. Cook gives an example: "a model ship might have, deep in its interior, supports situated where the engine room is located in the actual ship. Although the supports do not represent anything real on the actual ship, they are not necessarily useless or eliminable as a result, since they might be crucial to the structural integrity of the model" [4, p. 236]. Cook then argues that the objection from artificial precision depends on viewing the fuzzy theory of vagueness as providing a *description* of the semantics of vague language. If, on the other hand, we view it as providing a *model*—and if, more specifically, we view the particularity of the fuzzy values assigned (i.e. the fact that one particular value—not any other value—gets assigned) as an *artefact* of the model— then the problem dissolves. The objection to the fuzzy approach turns on the assignment of a unique fuzzy truth value to each vague sentence; if the uniqueness of the assignment is not an aspect of the model which is supposed to correspond to anything about vague language—if it is merely an artefact of the model—then the objection misses the mark.

2.4 Fuzzy metalanguages

The next response is expressed as follows by Williamson:[10]

> If a vague language requires a continuum-valued semantics, that should ap-
> ply in particular to a vague meta-language. The vague meta-language will
> in turn have a vague meta-meta-language, with a continuum-valued seman-
> tics, and so on all the way up the hierarchy of meta-languages. [52, p. 128]

The idea is first to present a semantics for vague language which assigns sentences real numbers as truth values, and then say that the metalanguage in which these assignments were made is itself subject to a semantics of the same sort. So on this view, statements of the form 'The degree of truth of "Bob is tall" is 0.4' need not be simply true or false: they may themselves have intermediate degrees of truth. Thus, rather than exactly one sentence of the form 'The degree of truth of "Bob is tall" is x' being true and the others false, many of them might be true to various degrees. Hence there is a sense in which sentences in natural language which predicate vague properties of objects are *not* each assigned just one particular fuzzy truth value—and so the objection from artificial precision is avoided.

---

[8]For other versions of the response, see Edgington [6, pp. 297, 308–9] and Shapiro [34, ch. 2, §1].

[9]Note that 'model' here is used in the sense it has in, for example, 'model aeroplane' and 'Bohr's model of the atom'. We have hitherto been using the term in a different sense—the one it has in, for example, 'model theory' and 'model of a first-order language'. In order to avoid confusion, we shall use 'model' in Cook's sense in §2.3 and in the part of §3 which discusses the logic as modelling view; in these parts of the paper, we shall use 'structure' in place of 'model' in the other sense. Elsewhere in the paper, we use 'model' in the sense of 'model theory'.

[10]For discussions or mentions of similar or related views see Cook [4], Edgington [6, pp. 297, 310], Field [8, p. 227], Horgan [14, p. 160], Keefe [19, pp. 117–21], McGee and McLaughlin [27, p. 238], Rolf [30, p. 222], Sainsbury [31, p. 260], Tye [41, p. 551] [42, p. 287] [43, p. 16] [44, pp. 219–20], Varzi [47, pp. 7–9] and Williamson [52, p. 130] [53, p. 695].

2.5 Blurry sets

This response—due to Smith [35]—involves a system in which the truth values, rather than being reals in [0,1], are *degree functions*: functions from $[0,1]^*$ to $[0,1]$.[11] Suppose $f : [0,1]^* \to [0,1]$ is the truth value of 'Bob is tall' (B). The idea is that the value which f assigns to the empty sequence—say, 0.5—is a *first approximation* to Bob's degree of tallness/the degree of truth of (B). The values assigned by f to sequences of length 1 then play two roles. First, they rate possible first approximations. The higher the value assigned to $\langle x \rangle$, the better x is as a first approximation to Bob's degree of tallness/the degree of truth of (B). If $f(\langle 0.3 \rangle) = 0.5$, then we say that it is 0.5 true that Bob is tall to degree 0.3; if $f(\langle 0.5 \rangle) = 0.7$, then we say that it is 0.7 true that Bob is tall to degree 0.5; and so on. Second, the assignments to sequences of length 1 jointly constitute a second level of approximation to Bob's degree of tallness/the degree of truth of (B). Together, these assignments determine a function $f_{\langle\rangle} : [0,1] \to [0,1]$. We regard this as encoding a density function over [0,1], and we require that its centre of mass is at $f(\langle\rangle)$ (Figure 1). The same thing happens again when we move to the values assigned

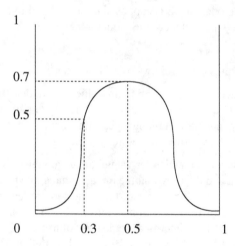

Figure 1. Bob's degree of tallness: second approximation.

to sequences of length 2: these values play two roles. First, they rate possible ratings of first approximations. The higher the value assigned to $\langle x,y \rangle$, the better y is as a rating of x as a first approximation to Bob's degree of tallness/the degree of truth of (B). If $f(\langle 0.5, 0.7 \rangle) = 0.8$, then we say that it is 0.8 true that it is 0.7 true that Bob is tall to degree 0.5; if $f(\langle 0.4, 0.5 \rangle) = 0.3$, then we say that it is 0.3 true that it is 0.5 true that Bob is tall to degree 0.4; and so on. Second, the assignments to sequences of length 2 jointly constitute a third level of approximation to Bob's degree of tallness/the degree of truth of (B). Together, the assignments made by f to sequences $\langle a,x \rangle$ of length 2 whose

---

[11] $[0,1]^*$ is the set of words on the alphabet [0,1]; that is, the set of all finite sequences of elements of [0,1], including the empty sequence $\langle\rangle$.

first member is a determine a function $f_{\langle a \rangle} : [0,1] \rightarrow [0,1]$. This can be seen as encoding a density function, and we require that its centre of mass is at $f(\langle a \rangle)$ (Figure 2). And so

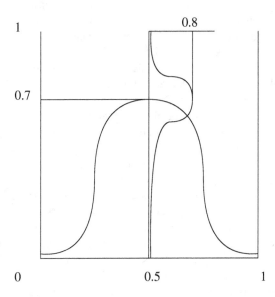

Figure 2. Bob's degree of tallness: third approximation (part view).

the story goes, ad infinitum. Figuratively, we can picture a degree (of truth or property-possession) as a region of varying shades of grey spread between 0 and 1 on the real line. If you focus on any point in this region, you see that what appeared to be a point of a particular shade of grey is in fact just the centre of a further such grey region. The same thing happens if you focus on a point in this further region, and so on. The region is blurry all the way down: no matter how much you increase the magnification, it will not come into sharp focus.

On this view, as on the fuzzy metalanguage view, statements of the form 'The degree of truth of "Bob is tall" is 0.4' need not be simply true or false: they may themselves have intermediate degrees of truth. So rather than exactly one sentence of the form 'The degree of truth of "Bob is tall" is x' being true and the others false, many of them might be true to various degrees. Thus there is a sense in which sentences in natural language which predicate vague properties of objects are *not* each assigned just one particular fuzzy truth value—and so the objection from artificial precision is avoided.

Note that on both the fuzzy metalanguage and blurry set views, we have a hierarchy of statements, none of which tells us the full and final story of the degree of truth of 'Bob is tall'. However there is a crucial difference between the two views. The fuzzy metalanguage view involves a hierarchy of *assignments* of *simple* truth values. The blurry set view involves a *single* assignment of a *complex* truth value—a truth value which has an *internal* hierarchical structure. On the blurry set view, each vague sentence is assigned a unique degree function as its truth value, and these assignments can be described in a classical, precise metalanguage.

2.6   Fuzzy plurivaluationism

In order to explain this response—due to Smith [37]—we must first explain *classical* plurivaluationism. Recall the classical MTS picture outlined at the end of §1: a discourse in natural language is to be modelled as a bunch of wffs together with a unique designated classical model (the 'intended model'); a statement (in a discourse) is true (simpliciter) if it is true relative to the model that is designated (for that discourse). The classical plurivaluationist accepts much of this picture. In particular, she countenances *only* classical models. However she denies that there is always a unique intended model of a discourse. As mentioned in §1, MTS requires some notion additional to those found in pure model theory: for we wish to be able to speak of statements being true or false simpliciter, not merely true on this model and false on that one (with no model being more relevant than any other). One option here is to pick *one* model as uniquely relevant (i.e. the 'intended model'). The plurivaluationist takes a less extreme course, holding instead that sometimes (i.e. for some discourses) there are many acceptable models, none of which is uniquely relevant when it comes to questions of the (actual) meaning and truth (simpliciter) of utterances in the discourse. On this view, when I utter 'Bob is tall', I say *many things* at once: one claim for each acceptable model. Thus we have semantic *indeterminacy*—or equally, semantic *plurality*. However, if *all* the claims I make are true (or false)—that is, if the wff I express is true (or false) on every acceptable model—then we can pretend (talk as if) I make only one claim, which is true (or false). Figuratively, think of a shotgun fired (once) at a target: many pellets are expelled, not just one bullet; but if *all* the pellets go through the bullseye, then we can harmlessly *talk as if* there was just one bullet, which went through.

The plurivaluationist view of vagueness—the view that what is happening when we make vague statements is that we are speaking relative to multiple classical models (the 'acceptable models') as opposed to a single such model (the 'intended model')—is expressed by, amongst others, Lewis and Varzi:

> I regard vagueness as semantic indecision: where we speak vaguely, we have not troubled to settle which of some range of precise meanings our words are meant to express. [24, p. 244,n. 32]

> Broadly speaking, [plurivaluationism][12] tells us two things. The first is that the semantics of our language is not fully determinate, and that statements in this language are open a variety of interpretations each of which is compatible with our ordinary linguistic practices. The second thing is that when the multiplicity of interpretations turns out to be irrelevant, we should ignore it. If what we say is true under all the admissible interpretations of our words, then there is no need to bother being more precise. [48, p. 14]

Note that the classical plurivaluationist view is quite different from a second view, both of which have unfortunately been conflated in the literature under the name 'supervaluationism'. Plurivaluationism trades only in *classical* models; instead of supposing that for each discourse there is *one* model relevant to questions concerning the (actual) meaning and truth (simpliciter) of utterances in the discourse (the 'intended model'), it allows that

---

[12]Varzi actually uses the term 'supervaluationism' here; see below for discussion.

there may be *multiple* such models (the 'acceptable models'). Supervaluationism, properly so-called,[13] involves *one* intended model—which is *non*-classical—and the classical *extensions* of this model. A proposition is true (false) in the intended non-classical model if and only if it is true (false) in every classical extension thereof. The function which assigns truth values to sentences in the non-classical model on this basis is the *supervaluation*. On this view, the classical models are *not* equally-good *interpretations* of the discourse: they do not play the role of specifying what utterances in the discourse *mean* or *pick out*. There is only *one* interpretation: the non-classical model. Its extensions are simply used to *calculate* truth values of sentences in this model. Figure 3 gives a visual representation of the essential differences between plurivaluationism and supervaluationism.

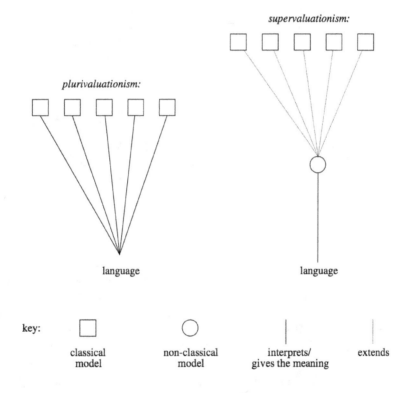

Figure 3. Plurivaluationism and supervaluationism.

Having introduced classical plurivaluationism—and distinguished it from supervaluationism—we can now introduce fuzzy plurivaluationism quite quickly.[14] Fuzzy plurivaluationism is just like classical plurivaluationism except that its models are fuzzy, not

---

[13]I say this because the term 'supervaluation' was introduced by van Fraassen [46] in relation to the view that I am about to describe, which is quite different from plurivaluationism; see Smith [37, pp. 99–102] for further discussion.

[14]For a more detailed presentation and motivation of this theory of vagueness, see Smith [37, §2.5, ch.6].

classical. It stands to the basic fuzzy theory of vagueness—on which a vague discourse is associated with a unique intended fuzzy model—in just the way that classical pluri-valuationism stands to the original classical MTS picture. That is, everything about the original view is retained (so in the classical case, only standard classical models are countenanced, and in the fuzzy case, only standard fuzzy models are countenanced), *except* the idea that each discourse is associated with a unique intended model. The latter idea is replaced with the thought that each discourse is associated with multiple acceptable models.

The situation is summarised in Figure 4. Recall that a system of model-theoretic semantics comprises two ingredients: an underlying system of (pure, mathematical) model theory; and a notion which plays the role of picking out, from amongst all the models countenanced by the underlying model theory, the model(s) relevant to questions of the (actual) meaning and truth (simpliciter) of utterances in a discourse. The table shows two possible choices of first ingredient down the left, and two possible choices of second ingredient across the top. Each of the four possible pairs of choices determines a theory of vagueness: these four theories are shown in the table's body.

ingredient 2 → ↓ ingredient 1	unique intended interpretation	multiple acceptable interpretations
classical model theory	classical MTS	classical plurivaluationism
fuzzy model theory	basic fuzzy theory of vagueness	fuzzy plurivaluationism

Figure 4. Four theories of vagueness.

The upshot of fuzzy plurivaluationism is that there is *not* one uniquely correct as-signment of truth value to 'Bob is tall'. There are multiple, equally-correct assignments: one in each acceptable model. Thus, the objection from artificial precision is avoided.

3   Choosing a solution

We now have six solutions to the artificial precision problem on the table. Which (if any) is the right one? In this section I begin the process of answering this question by arguing that two of the solutions—the logic as modelling and fuzzy metalanguage views—can be ruled out on methodological grounds.

Consider first the fuzzy metalanguage approach. In light of the distinction between pure fuzzy logic and fuzzy MTS, we can distinguish two different ways of understanding this approach—two different ways of fuzzifying the basic fuzzy theory of vagueness: fuzzify pure fuzzy model theory itself; or fuzzify only fuzzy MTS.[15] The first of these

---

[15]To avoid possible misunderstanding: what I mean here is that there are two ways of spelling out the fuzzy metalanguage approach to the problem of artificial precision sketched in §2.4. I am not saying that these are the only two views that could be described using the term 'fuzzy metalanguage'; for example, Běhounek [1] presents a distinct view which some might wish to describe in such terms. Note that Běhounek's view is not intended as a solution to the problem of artificial precision, as presented in §1. (Recall n.2: the term

options involves the idea that the language in which pure fuzzy model theory is presented is vague: the correct semantics for *this* language is fuzzy MTS. The problem with any such approach is well summed-up by Goguen:

> Our models are typical purely exact constructions, and we use ordinary exact logic and set theory freely in their development ... It is hard to see how we can study our subject at all rigorously without such assumptions. [9, p. 327]

We understand pure fuzzy model theory as standard mathematics, presented in the usual precise language of mathematics. If someone were to say at the end of presenting (pure) fuzzy model theory that the language in which he made his presentation was governed by a semantics involving the notions he had just presented—rather than by the standard classical semantics for mathematical language—then we would have to conclude that we had not really understood his presentation after all.[16]

The second option avoids this problem: on this option, the language in which pure fuzzy model theory is presented is the ordinary precise language of mathematics. What *is* vague, on this second option, is that part of the basic fuzzy theory of vagueness which goes beyond pure fuzzy model theory: the notion of the 'intended model'. Sticking to the idea of analyzing vagueness in fuzzy terms, this amounts to the idea that in place of the unique intended fuzzy model posited by the basic fuzzy view, we have a *fuzzy set* of acceptable models: acceptability of a model becomes a graded notion. This view is subject to an immediate difficulty. What are we to say of an utterance which is true to degree (say) 0.7 relative to a model which is acceptable to degree (say) 0.5? That is, how does degree of truth on a model combine with degree of acceptability of that model to yield an absolute (i.e. not model-relative) assessment of an utterance? Perhaps there is something plausible that can be said here (as far as I am aware, no such view has been developed in the literature). In any case, a further problem remains. The view under discussion generalizes fuzzy plurivaluationism: where the latter posits a (crisp) set of acceptable models, the former posits a fuzzy set. As we shall see, however, fuzzy plurivaluationism *solves* the artificial precision problem. Hence, by Ockham's razor, the view under consideration is to be rejected: its added complexity is unnecessary.[17]

Consider next the logic as modelling view. Cook sums up the position as follows:

> In essence, the idea is to treat the problematic parts of the degree-theoretic picture, namely the assignment of particular real numbers to sentences, as mere artefacts. ... If the problematic parts of the account are not intended actually to describe anything occurring in the phenomenon in the first place, then they certainly cannot be *misdescribing*. [4, p. 237]

This seems fine as a defence of the fuzzy view against outright dismissal in the face of the artificial precision problem—but it is essentially a *parry*, a *provisional* defence: matters cannot be left here. For if some parts of the fuzzy view are to be regarded as

---

'higher-order vagueness'—which appears in the titles of both the present paper and [1]—has been applied in the literature both to the problem of artificial precision and to distinct problems.)

[16]For a more detailed argument along these lines, see Smith [37, §6.2.1].

[17]This is not to say that it might not be interesting to explore this view—just that, for purposes of solving the artificial precision problem, we have no reason to adopt it.

representing aspects of the semantics of vague discourse, while others are mere artefacts, then we want to know *which* parts are which. Cook recognises this:

> although sentences do have real verities [i.e. truth values], these verities are not real numbers but are only *modelled* by real numbers...what sorts of objects are they? ... the natural question to ask is which properties of the reals correspond to actual properties of verities and which do not. [4, pp. 239–40]

One answer here would be that only the *ordering* of the reals corresponds to a fact about the verities. This would take us back to the view that truth is measured on an ordinal scale. Cook favours a different response, according to which not only ordering is significant, but also *large* differences between reals—whereas small differences are often (but not always) artefacts. Cook does not spell out this view in a way analogous to the ordinal view: that is, by specifying a kind of transformation of the real interval [0,1] such that a difference between two fuzzy structures is an artefact if and only if one structure can be obtained from the other by such a transformation. Without some such spelling-out, the view remains incomplete: we do not know which aspects of the fuzzy view are artefacts and which are not. With such a spelling-out, the idea that we use fuzzy structures as *models* gives way to the idea that we can fully *describe* the semantics of a vague discourse by associating it not with a fuzzy structure, but with some fully-specified *class* of fuzzy structures which are the same as one another up to the specified kind of transformation (as on the ordinal view). Either way, the logic as modelling view does not—in the final wash-up—make a distinctive contribution. While valuable as an initial parry to the objection from artificial precision, it is essentially a transitory response: it must—if it is to amount to more than hand-waving—eventually give way to a fully-specified system which *can* then be viewed not merely as a model, but as an accurate description of the semantics of vague discourse.[18]

Four proposed solutions remain on the table. How are we to decide which is the right one? In order to do so, we need a clearer idea of the true nature and source of the problem of artificial precision. Consider again the three quotations given in §1, which set out the problem. Haack offers no diagnosis; Urquhart maintains that the *nature of vague predicates* precludes attaching precise numerical values; Keefe asks what could *determine* which is the correct function, settling that her coat is red to degree 0.322 rather than 0.321. I shall argue (§6) that Keefe is on the right track and Urquhart is not: the problem with the fuzzy view turns not on considerations having to do with the nature of vagueness, but rather on considerations having to do with the way in which the meanings of our terms are fixed. In order to make this case, I must first discuss the nature of vagueness (§4) and the question of how meaning is determined (§5).

4   The nature of vagueness

Given some property, object, stuff or phenomenon *P*, we may distinguish between a *surface characterization* of *P*—a set of manifest conditions, possession of which marks out the *P*'s from the non-*P*'s—and a *fundamental definition* of *P*—a statement of the

---

[18]For a more detailed argument along these lines, see Smith [38].

fundamental underlying nature or essence of the P's, which *explains* why they have such-and-such surface characteristics. For example, a surface characterization of *water* says that it is a clear, tasteless, potable liquid which falls as rain, while the fundamental definition says that it is H_2O. In the case of *vagueness* (of predicates), there is a generally accepted surface characterization: vague predicates are those which have borderline cases; whose extensions have blurred boundaries; and which generate sorites paradoxes. What we do *not* have is a fundamental definition of vagueness. Yet before we can say whether something—for example, assignment of a unique fuzzy truth value to each vague sentence—conflicts with the *nature of vagueness*, we need such a fundamental definition: we need to know what *is* the nature of vagueness. In this section I shall briefly discuss some possible definitions of vagueness and explain why they are inadequate, before presenting a definition which I regard as correct.[19]

We might try to define vagueness in terms of possession of borderline cases. This will not do, however, because while it does indeed seem that vague predicates have borderline cases, this is not the *fundamental* fact about them. It cannot be, because we can easily imagine predicates which have borderline cases but which are *not* vague—for example 'is schort', which we define as follows:

1. If x is less than four feet in height, then 'x is schort' is true.

2. If x is more than six feet in height, then 'x is schort' is false.

This predicate has borderline cases, but it does not generate a sorites paradox, nor does its extension have blurred boundaries—hence, it is not vague.

We might try to define vagueness in terms of having an extension that has blurred boundaries—but this characterization is too vague to constitute a fundamental definition.

We might try to define vagueness in terms of sorites susceptibility. This will not do, however, because while it is indeed the case that vague predicates generate sorites paradoxes, this is not the *fundamental* fact about them. It seems clear that vague predicates generate sorites paradoxes *because* they are vague—and so their vagueness cannot *consist in* their generating such paradoxes.

We might try to define vagueness as semantic indeterminacy (of the sort involved in plurivaluationism). Again, however, such indeterminacy cannot be the fundamental fact about vague predicates, because we can easily imagine predicates which exhibit such indeterminacy but which are *not* vague—for example 'gavagai' or 'mass'. If Quine [28, ch. 2] and Field [7], respectively, are right, then these predicates exhibit semantic indeterminacy—but they do not generate sorites paradoxes, nor do their extensions have blurred boundaries: hence they are not vague.

We might—following Wright—try to define vagueness as tolerance, where a predicate F is tolerant with respect to ϕ if there is some positive degree of change in respect of ϕ that things may undergo, which is "insufficient ever to affect the justice with which F is applied to a particular case" [54, p. 334]. The problem with this definition, however, is that given a sorites series for F, F cannot be tolerant, on pain of contradiction. Hence if tolerance is the essence of vagueness, we must either accept true contradictions, or else deny that there are any vague predicates (with associated sorites series).

---

[19] For longer versions of the arguments see Smith [36] or [37, ch. 3].

This brings us to my positive proposal, that F is vague if and only if it satisfies the following condition, for any objects a and b:

Closeness If a and b are very close/similar in respects relevant to the application of F, then 'Fa' and 'Fb' are very close/similar in respect of truth.

The principal advantages of this definition are that it accommodates tolerance intuitions, without contradiction; it yields an explanation of *why* vague predicates have the three characteristic surface features mentioned above; and it accommodates intuitions about higher-order vagueness, within the definition of vagueness itself. For details see Smith [36] and [37, ch. 3]; in what follows I shall assume that Closeness provides the correct fundamental definition of vagueness.

5　The determination of meaning

It is generally agreed that whatever semantic facts there are, they are determined by other facts. For Quine [29, p. 38], these other facts are the publicly accessible facts concerning what people say in what circumstances. Because he thinks that such facts do not determine a unique meaning for 'gavagai', he denies that this sentence *has* a unique meaning. For Kripkenstein [21], the class of meaning-determining facts is wider: it includes dispositional facts, and private mental facts. Nevertheless, he thinks that this wider class of facts still does not determine a unique meaning for 'plus'—and so he denies that 'plus' *has* a determinate meaning.

Turning to vagueness, there is widespread agreement in the literature concerning which facts are relevant to determining the semantic facts:

- All the facts as to what speakers actually say and write, including the circumstances in which these things are said and written, and any causal relations obtaining between speakers and their environments.

- All the facts as to what speakers are disposed to say and write in all kinds of possible circumstances.

- All the facts concerning the eligibility as referents of objects and sets.

(I would also add: all the facts concerning the simplicity/complexity of interpretations.) There is also widespread agreement that if these facts are insufficient to determine (unique) meanings for some utterances, then those utterances have no (unique) meanings. In other words, semantic facts are never primitive or brute: they are always determined by the meaning-determining facts—which are as itemized above.[20]

This generates a constraint on any theory of vagueness: the theory must cohere with the foregoing picture of how meaning is determined. If the theory says that vague predicates have meanings of such-and-such a kind (e.g. functions from objects to classical truth values, or functions from objects to fuzzy truth values), then we must be able to satisfy ourselves that the meaning-determining facts itemized above could indeed determine such meanings for actual vague predicates. To the extent that the meaning-determining facts do *not* appear sufficient to determine meanings for vague predicates of the kind posited by some theory of vagueness, that theory is undermined.

---

[20]For a more detailed discussion of these issues, see Smith [37, §6.1.1].

6 Choosing a solution (continued)

Let us now return to the issue—raised at the end of §3—of the true nature and source of the artificial precision problem. Urquhart maintains that the basic fuzzy theory of vagueness—in particular, the aspect of it which involves assigning a unique fuzzy truth value to each vague statement (i.e. in our terms, its degree of truth on the unique intended fuzzy model of the discourse)—conflicts with the *nature of vague predicates*, while Keefe thinks that the view runs into problems concerning what could *determine* the correct assignment (i.e. in our terms, what could determine *which* model is the unique intended one). Now that we have said something about the nature of vagueness and the issue of the determination of meaning, we are in a position to adjudicate this issue.

First, it will be useful to consider the picture afforded by *classical* MTS, according to which a discourse in natural language is to be modelled as a bunch of wffs together with a unique intended classical model. (As mentioned at the end of §2.1, this is the *semantic* picture underlying *epistemic* theories of vagueness.) This view conflicts with the nature of vagueness. Consider a discourse including some claims of the form 'Point x is red', for points x on a strip of paper which changes colour continuously from red to orange. Given that some points on the strip are definitely red and some definitely not so, on any candidate intended model of the discourse there will be two points on the strip which are very close in respects relevant to the application of 'is red', such that one of them is in the extension of this predicate and the other is not. Hence one of the claims 'k is red' and 'k' is red' (where k and k' are the two points in question) will be true and the other false (Figure 5). This violates Closeness: the classical picture does not allow for the vagueness of 'is red'. The point generalizes to all vague predicates: thus the classical picture conflicts with the nature of vagueness. The classical view *also*

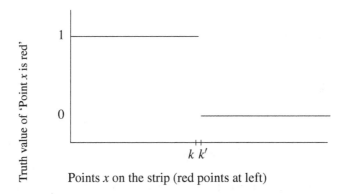

Figure 5. Classical MTS conflicts with the nature of vagueness.

runs into problems concerning the determination of meaning. It seems that the meaning-determining facts itemized in §5 do *not* suffice to pick out a particular height dividing the tall from the non-tall, and so on. Williamson has argued that the classical view is not logically incompatible with the view that usage determines meaning. This is true:

it might just be that the meaning-determining facts are sufficient to determine unique classical extensions for vague predicates (i.e. in our terms, a unique intended classical model for a vague discourse). But we have no idea *how* the trick could be turned—for example, Williamson's own best suggestion fails—and the most reasonable conclusion seems to be to that the meaning-determining facts do *not* suffice to pick out meanings for vague predicates of the kind the classical theory says they have.[21] The classical view of vagueness therefore faces two distinct problems:

1. The *existence* of a sharp drop-off from true to false in a sorites series: this conflicts with the nature of vagueness.

2. The *particular location* of the drop-off: this conflicts with our best views about how meaning is determined.

I refer to these two problems as the *jolt problem* and the *location problem* respectively.

Let us now turn to the view of vagueness based not on classical MTS, but on fuzzy MTS: that is, the view that I have called the 'basic fuzzy theory of vagueness'. Does it conflict with the nature of vagueness (as Urquhart claims)? No! Consider again a discourse including some claims of the form 'Point x is red', for points x on a strip of paper which changes colour continuously from red to orange. Fuzzy model theory has the resources to make available—as candidates for the intended model—models on which 'Point x is red' and 'Point y is red' are always very similar in respect of truth whenever x and y are very similar in respects relevant to the application of 'is red', even though some claims of this form are definitely true and others are definitely false (see Figure 6).

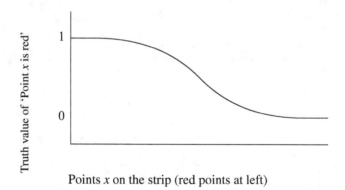

Figure 6. Fuzzy MTS does not conflict with the nature of vagueness.

Hence there is no conflict between the fuzzy view and the nature of vague predicates. Does the fuzzy view run into problems concerning the determination of meaning (as Keefe claims)? Yes! It seems that the meaning-determining facts itemized in §5 do *not*

---

[21] For detailed discussion of these issues—including the critique of Williamson's suggestion alluded to in the text—see Smith [37, §2.1.1].

suffice to pick out a particular function from objects to fuzzy truth values representing the extension of 'is tall' (and similarly for other vague predicates). So the fuzzy view does not face a version of the jolt problem, but it *does* face a version of the location problem. Indeed, we are now in a position to see that its version of the location problem is nothing other than a more fully articulated version of the artificial precision problem with which we began. It is artificial/implausible/inappropriate to associate each vague sentence in natural language with a particular fuzzy truth value *because* doing so conflicts with our best theories about how the meanings of our words are determined.

We turn now to the four proposed solutions to this problem which remain on the table. Fuzzy epistemicism fails to solve the problem. The problem concerns how there could *be* a unique function which is the extension of 'is tall', given that our usage (etc.) does not suffice to pick out a unique such function. Saying that we do not *know* which function it is simply misses the point of the problem.

The proposal that truth is measured on an ordinal scale conflicts with the nature of vagueness. On this view, it *makes no sense* to say that two sentences P and Q are *very close* in respect of truth: it makes sense to say only that one sentence is *truer* than another. (The fact that the two sentences might have truth values which are, in some sense, very close together considered as real numbers—say, 0.8 and 0.8000000000001—is irrelevant: the model on which they have these truth values is interchangeable with any model obtainable from it by an order-preserving and endpoint-fixing transformation of the interval [0,1], and there will be such transformations which take P's truth value arbitrarily close to 0 and Q's arbitrarily close to 1.) But the idea of two sentences being *very close* in respect of truth is at the heart of the Closeness definition—and so a view which makes no room for this notion lacks the resources to distinguish vague predicates (those which satisfy Closeness) from precise predicates (those which violate Closeness).

The blurry set view does not solve the location problem. In just the way that they fail to determine a unique *classical* set (function from objects to classical truth values) or a unique *fuzzy* set (function from objects to fuzzy truth values) as the extension of 'is tall', the meaning-determining facts do not suffice to pick out a unique *blurry set* (function from objects to degree functions) as the extension of 'is tall'.

This brings us to fuzzy plurivaluationism—which *does* solve the location problem. Indeed, it is the *minimal* solution to the problem—for it accepts as its starting point the very idea which constitutes the problem. The problem is that the meaning-determining facts do not suffice to pick out a unique fuzzy model of vague discourse as the intended model. The fuzzy plurivaluationist solution is to abandon the notion of a unique intended model in favour of the idea of multiple acceptable models—where an *acceptable* model is one which is *not* ruled out as *incorrect* by the meaning-determining facts. As the problem is precisely that there is *not* a unique acceptable fuzzy model of vague discourse—because too many models are compatible with the constraints imposed by the meaning-fixing facts—it follows a fortiori that fuzzy plurivaluationism—the view that there are multiple equally correct models—is correct. The upshot of fuzzy plurivaluationism is that 'Bob is tall' does *not* have a uniquely correct degree of truth: it is assigned multiple different degrees of truth—one on each acceptable model—and none of these is more correct than any of the others. This was the desired result: that it was *not* the case on the original fuzzy view was precisely the problem with which we started.

BIBLIOGRAPHY

[1] Libor Běhounek. A model of higher-order vagueness in higher-order fuzzy logic. Typescript (available at http://at.yorku.ca/c/a/s/u/34.dir/casu-34.pdf); abstract of a paper presented at *Uncertainty: Reasoning about Probability and Vagueness*, Institute of Philosophy, Academy of Sciences of the Czech Republic, Prague, 5–8 September, 2006.

[2] Richmond Campbell. The sorites paradox. *Philosophical Studies*, 26:175–191, 1974.

[3] James Cargile. The sorites paradox, 1969. In [20], pages 89–98.

[4] Roy T. Cook. Vagueness and mathematical precision. *Mind*, 111:225–47, 2002.

[5] B. Jack Copeland. Vague identity and fuzzy logic. *Journal of Philosophy*, 94:514–34, 1997.

[6] Dorothy Edgington. Vagueness by degrees, 1997. In [20], pages 294–316.

[7] Hartry Field. Theory change and the indeterminacy of reference. *The Journal of Philosophy*, 70:462–81, 1973.

[8] Hartry Field. Quine and the correspondence theory. *Philosophical Review*, 83:200–28, 1974.

[9] Joseph Goguen. The logic of inexact concepts. *Synthese*, 19:325–73, 1968–69.

[10] Joseph Goguen. Fuzzy sets and the social nature of truth. In Madan M. Gupta, Rammohan K. Ragade, and Ronald R. Yager, editors, *Advances in Fuzzy Set Theory and Applications*, pages 49–67. North-Holland, Amsterdam, 1979.

[11] Susan Haack. Do we need "fuzzy logic"? *International Journal of Man-Machine Studies*, 11:437–45, 1979.

[12] Petr Hájek. Ten questions and one problem on fuzzy logic. *Annals of Pure and Applied Logic*, 96:157–65, 1999.

[13] Petr Hájek. On vagueness, truth values and fuzzy logics. *Studia Logica*, 91:367–82, 2009.

[14] Terence Horgan. Robust vagueness and the forced-march sorites paradox. *Philosophical Perspectives*, 8:159–88, 1994.

[15] Terence Horgan, editor. *Vagueness* (Proceedings of the Spindel Conference 1994), volume 33, Supplement of *Southern Journal of Philosophy*, 1995.

[16] Paul Horwich. *Truth*. Clarendon Press, Oxford, second revised edition, 1998.

[17] Dominic Hyde. *Vagueness, Logic and Ontology*. Ashgate, Aldershot, 2008.

[18] Rosanna Keefe. Vagueness by numbers. *Mind*, 107:565–79, 1998.

[19] Rosanna Keefe. *Theories of Vagueness*. Cambridge University Press, Cambridge, 2000.

[20] Rosanna Keefe and Peter Smith, editors. *Vagueness: A Reader*. MIT Press, Cambridge MA, 1997.

[21] Saul Kripke. *Wittgenstein on Rules and Private Language*. Harvard University Press, Cambridge, MA, 1982.

[22] George Lakoff. Hedges: A study in meaning criteria and the logic of fuzzy concepts. *Journal of Philosophical Logic*, 2:458–508, 1973.

[23] Ernest Lepore. What model theoretic semantics cannot do. *Synthese*, 54:167–87, 1983.

[24] David Lewis. *On the Plurality of Worlds*. Basil Blackwell, Oxford, 1986.

[25] John MacFarlane. Fuzzy epistemicism. In Richard Dietz and Sebastiano Moruzzi, editors, *Cuts and Clouds: Vagueness, Its Nature, and Its Logic*, pages 438–63. Oxford University Press, Oxford, 2010.

[26] Kenton F. Machina. Truth, belief, and vagueness, 1976. In [20], pages 174–203.

[27] Vann McGee and Brian McLaughlin. Distinctions without a difference, 1995. In [15], pages 203–51.

[28] Willard Van Orman Quine. *Word and Object*. MIT Press, Cambridge, MA, 1960.

[29] Willard Van Orman Quine. *Pursuit of Truth*. Harvard University Press, Cambridge, MA, revised edition, 1992.

[30] Bertil Rolf. Sorites. *Synthese*, 58:219–50, 1984.

[31] Mark Sainsbury. Concepts without boundaries, 1990. In [20], pages 251–64.

[32] David H. Sanford. Borderline logic. *American Philosophical Quarterly*, 12:29–39, 1975.

[33] Stephen P. Schwartz. Intuitionism versus degrees of truth. *Analysis*, 50:43–7, 1990.

[34] Stewart Shapiro. *Vagueness in Context*. Clarendon Press, Oxford, 2006.

[35] Nicholas J.J. Smith. Vagueness and blurry sets. *Journal of Philosophical Logic*, 33:165–235, 2004.

[36] Nicholas J.J. Smith. Vagueness as closeness. *Australasian Journal of Philosophy*, 83:157–83, 2005.

[37] Nicholas J.J. Smith. *Vagueness and Degrees of Truth*. Oxford University Press, Oxford, 2008.

[38] Nicholas J.J. Smith. Measuring and modelling truth. *American Philosophical Quarterly*, forthcoming.

[39] Roy Sorensen. *Blindspots*. Clarendon Press, Oxford, 1988.

[40] Roy Sorensen. *Vagueness and Contradiction*. Clarendon Press, Oxford, 2001.

[41] Michael Tye. Vague objects. *Mind*, 99:535–57, 1990.

[42] Michael Tye. Sorites paradoxes and the semantics of vagueness, 1994. In [20], pages 281–93.

[43] Michael Tye. Vagueness: Welcome to the quicksand, 1995. In [15], pages 1–22.

[44] Michael Tye. Fuzzy realism and the problem of the many. *Philosophical Studies*, 81:215–25, 1996.

[45] Alasdair Urquhart. Many-valued logic. In D. Gabbay and F. Guenthner, editors, *Handbook of Philosophical Logic*, volume III, pages 71–116. D. Reidel, Dordrecht, 1986.

[46] Bas C. van Fraassen. Singular terms, truth-value gaps and free logic. *Journal of Philosophy*, 63:481–95, 1966.

[47] Achille C. Varzi. Vague names for sharp objects. In Leo Obrst and Inderjeet Mani, editors, *Proceedings of the KR Workshop on Semantic Approximation, Granularity, and Vagueness*, pages 73–8. AAAI Press, Breckenridge CO, 2000.

[48] Achille C. Varzi. Indeterminate identities and semantic indeterminacy. Typescript (available at http://www.columbia.edu/~av72/papers/Parsons_2003.pdf); text of a talk presented at *The Philosophy of Terence Parsons: Logic, Metaphysics, and Natural Language*, University of Notre Dame, 8 February, 2003.

[49] Brian Weatherson. True, truer, truest. *Philosophical Studies*, 123:47–70, 2005.

[50] Joan Weiner. *Frege Explained: From Arithmetic to Analytic Philosophy*. Open Court, Chicago, 2004.

[51] Timothy Williamson. Vagueness and ignorance, 1992. In [20], pages 265–80.

[52] Timothy Williamson. *Vagueness*. Routledge, London, 1994.

[53] Timothy Williamson. Vagueness in reality. In Michael J. Loux and Dean W. Zimmerman, editors, *The Oxford Handbook of Metaphysics*, pages 690–715. Oxford University Press, 2003.

[54] Crispin Wright. On the coherence of vague predicates. *Synthese*, 30:325–65, 1975.

Nicholas J.J. Smith
Department of Philosophy
Main Quadrangle A14
The University of Sydney
NSW 2006 Australia
Email: njjsmith@sydney.edu.au

Comments on *Fuzzy Logic and Higher-Order Vagueness* by Nicholas J.J. Smith

LIBOR BĚHOUNEK

Smith's article *Fuzzy logic and higher-order vagueness* [12] presents a solution to the problem of artificial precision, encountered in the degree-theoretical semantics of vagueness. The solution is based on fuzzy plurivaluationism, which has been discussed in more detail in Smith's book [11]. Within the degree-theoretical framework, fuzzy plurivaluationism is certainly the appropriate treatment of vague propositions: it has often been implicitly used by formal fuzzy logicians, too—namely, in their modeling of vague concepts by means of formal *theories* over fuzzy logic (see, e.g., [6, 7]). Such theories have (usually infinite) *classes* of models, which directly correspond to Smith's fuzzy plurivaluations. I therefore very much welcome that thanks to Smith, the multi-model fuzzy semantics of vague predicates has been explicitly spelt out in philosophical terms and discussed in the context of the philosophy of vagueness.

For the most part, Smith's article [12] and book [11] only deal with fuzzy (plurivaluationistic) *semantics* of vague predicates, putting aside its logical aspects.[1] Nevertheless, as I try to argue in this Comment, the logical facet of fuzzy plurivaluationism is quite relevant, and it supplements the fuzzy plurivaluationistic picture in important respects. In particular, it can play a rôle in the justification of fuzzy plurivaluationistic semantics, as well as in ascertaining an appropriate characterization of vagueness.

1 Fuzzy plurivaluation as the class of models of a theory over fuzzy logic

In the degree-theoretical semantics of such vague predicates that are based on real-valued quantities (e.g., the predicate *tall,* which is based on the quantity of *height*), the assignment of truth degrees (say, from the $[0, 1]$ interval) to the values of the quantity (here, say, in feet) clearly cannot be uniquely determined in a way that the language users would agree upon. There are no facts connected with the use of language, nor any reasonable meaning postulates for such predicates, that would determine whether a $6'0''$ man should be tall to degree 0.7 or 0.8. In other words, as Smith notes, the meaning-determining facts do not narrow down the set of admissible models of vague predicates to a singleton set; so he rightly concludes that instead of a single "fuzzy" model (constituted by a $[0, 1]$-valued function from feet to degrees), the degree-theoretical semantics of such predicates consists of a whole class of admissible fuzzy models.

Following Quine and 'Kripkenstein', Smith assumes the meaning-determining facts to be primarily based on the linguistic behavior and intentions of the speakers. However,

---

[1] The exception is §5.2 in [11], which puts forward a non-standard definition of logical consequence for fuzzy propositions. The aim of the definition is to maintain classical logic for vague predicates; however, it only works for a restricted set of logical connectives.

the speakers' behavior (including their intentions) is rather non-uniform, and sometimes even inconsistent, especially in the case of vague predicates. For instance, even the same speaker can on different occasions make contradictory statements about the tallness of the same person. The set of fuzzy models that such meaning-determining facts would delimit would therefore be not sharp, as assumed in Smith's fuzzy plurivaluationism, but rather vague and unsharp (in a statistical–probabilistic way).

Smith justifies the assumption of sharpness of the set of fuzzy models, de facto, by Ockham's razor (cf. [11, §6.2.2]): since sharp sets of fuzzy models suffice for the elimination of most paradoxes (including the paradox of artificial precision), there is no need to complicate the account by considering unsharp sets of fuzzy models. Such an explanation is, however, just meta-theoretical: it does not offer a deeper explanation within the theory itself as to why the semantics of vague predicates should be a sharp rather than unsharp set of fuzzy models.

Fuzzy plurivaluationistic semantics with sharp sets of fuzzy models in fact conforms better to a different conception of meaning determination, namely one which identifies the meaning of a word with the set of its *meaning postulates,* i.e., its semantic properties and relations that would be approved by competent speakers,[2] and which therefore have to be satisfied by the predicate's truth conditions (in our case, by the assignment of truth degrees to the values of the underlying quantity). These collectively accepted properties of the predicate can be understood as having been abstracted from the Quinean–Kripkean meaning-determining facts, which thus remain the ultimate factors determining the meaning of words. However, in contrast to the latter non-uniform, inconsistent, vague and variable facts, the derived meaning postulates are artificial extrapolations, thereby made consistent, unified, stable and precise. They are, in fact, the defining properties of the predicate, expressible in the rigorous language of logic, that link the values of the underlying quantities to their associated truth degrees. And since these defining properties are sharp, so is the set of membership functions they delimit.

Consider for example the vague predicate *tall.* In the last instance its meaning is certainly determined by the actual behavior and intentions of the speakers, changing over time and mood, and often contradictory. Nevertheless, from this chaotic evidence (and possibly also from the speakers' reflections on the meaning of the word) it is possible to extract the following condition that the intended usage of the term *tall* is presumed to satisfy:

(1)   If X is tall, and Y is taller than X, then Y is tall as well.

This condition would be approved by a vast majority of competent speakers (even if they occasionally violate it themselves in some situations), and can be regarded as a meaning postulate for the predicate *tall:* those who would not recognize its validity do not understand the word *tall.* Further conditions on the predicate *tall* that would be

---

[2]Apparently, the requirement of the speakers' approval makes the set of such postulates vague again. Nevertheless, the number of generally accepted postulates is much smaller than the unmanageable set of the speakers' individual behaviors and intentions, and so a sharp specification can be defended more easily. Meaning postulates adhered to by only a proportion of the speakers can be seen, for example, as distinguishing between two or more alternative meanings of the vague word, which are still specified by a sharp set of defining properties.

approved by the speakers are, for instance, those related to prototypical cases, e.g.:

(2)   Michael J. Fox is not tall, while

(3)   Christopher Lee is tall.

In the degree-theoretical framework, these meaning postulates for the predicate *tall* can be reformulated as conditions on its membership function. Let us denote the height of an individual x by $h(x)$, and the truth degree of the atomic sentence "x is tall" by Hx. The meaning postulates (1)–(3) then correspond to the following conditions:

(4) $(h(x) > h(y)) \to (Hx \geq Hy)$

(5) $Ha = 0$

(6) $Hb = 1$.

Conditions of this kind have been mentioned by Smith in [11, §6.1.2]. However, it can be furthermore observed that the conditions (4)–(6) constitute the semantics of certain formulae in fuzzy logic.[3] In particular, they are the semantic conditions for (the full truth of) the following formulae:

(7) $(h(x) > h(y)) \to (Hx \to Hy)$,   or equivalently, $Hx \,\&\, (h(x) > h(y)) \to Hy$

(8) $\neg Ha$

(9) Hb.

It can be noticed that the latter three formulae represent a straightforward formalization of the meaning postulates (1)–(3) in fuzzy logic. This fact is not accidental: it is a consequence of the manner in which fuzzy logic expresses relationships between the degrees of gradual predicates. Without going into details here, let us just briefly say that the meaning postulates (1)–(3) can be understood as expressing the axioms of a theory in fuzzy logic, straightforwardly formalized by (7)–(9). The class of (fuzzy) models of this theory then forms the fuzzy plurivaluation that represents the semantics of the predicate *tall*;[4] and this class is sharp, since the axioms (7)–(9) are required to be fully true.[5] A similar pattern can be found in the meaning postulates of other vague predicates.

Smith's plurivaluations are thus exactly the classes of models of formal fuzzy theories that straightforwardly formalize the meaning postulates of vague predicates. Since these meaning postulates do not speak directly about the degrees of truth (cf. (1)–(3)), the degrees are usually underdetermined by the theory, and the semantics of a vague predicate is indeed a sharp multi-element class of membership functions. The logical aspects thus elucidate the nature of Smith's plurivaluations.

---

[3] For detailed information on modern fuzzy logic see [2] or [5].

[4] The meaning postulates for the predicate *tall* are actually more complex than the simplified version (1)–(3) discussed in this Comment. A detailed analysis of the predicate would have to include, i.a., the meaning postulate that "imperceptible changes in height correspond to only negligible changes in the degree of tallness", formalized as the congruence of admissible membership functions w.r.t. a fuzzy indistinguishability relations on heights and degrees of truth (i.e., a certain generalization of Lipschitz continuity); cf. Smith's Closeness principle, [12, §4], discussed below in §2.

[5] Note that in the semantics of fuzzy logic, axioms required to be satisfied to the full degree have always sharp classes of models.

2 Vagueness as semantic indeterminacy, plus optional graduality

In his papers [10, 12] and book [11, ch. 3] Smith gives a definition of vagueness based on the principle of Closeness:

> If a and b are very close/similar in respects relevant to the application of F, then 'Fa' and 'Fb' are very close/similar in respect of truth.

Three objections to this definition have already been raised by Weatherson in [14]. Another problem of this definition can be seen in the fact that it is itself based on the vague terms *very close/similar,* and thus already its application requires an apparatus for handling vagueness. This aspect will be further discussed at the end of this Comment in §4.

As another serious problem with this definition I see its tautologicity: it can be argued that for *all* predicates, similarity in respects relevant to the application of F coincides with similarity in respect of truth—simply because whenever 'Fa' and 'Fb' are dissimilar in respect of truth, then precisely the respects in which a and b differ as regards the application of F are those relevant to its application (and since a and b differ in them, they are dissimilar, too). In other words, the *right* similarity relation that is relevant to the application of F is always the one given by the closeness of truth.[6]

Smith addresses the problem (related to the previous objection) that the Closeness principle is trivially satisfied even by predicates with sharp boundaries or just jump discontinuities by a modification of the Closeness principle [11, §3.3.4], requiring, in essence, the underlying quantity to change gradually at least on a part of the domain. This move, however, binds vagueness by definition to graduality, although their concomitance is not necessary (even if frequent): there are examples of totally bivalent predicates, the assumption of whose graduality would not even make sense, which are still vague: they are susceptible to the sorites paradox and have undecidable (i.e., borderline) cases, including higher-order vagueness. Examples of such predicates are, for instance, bivalent states (such as *pregnant* or *dead*) considered on a time scale several orders of magnitude finer than is the time in which they can change (in the latter cases, e.g., nanoseconds). Even though there is no exact nanosecond in which a woman becomes pregnant, still pregnancy is a bivalent predicate for which no degrees of truth would make sense (not even on the nanosecond scale).[7] Another class of examples are the

---

[6]Consequently, it is not always the one that straightforwardly suggests itself: for instance, the quantity relevant for the application of the predicate "weighs over 1 kg" [11, p. 142] is, in fact, not weight, but only a purely bivalent quantity derived from weight, which can be physically realized, e.g., by triggering a switch by the needle of a balance when setting the object against the Sèvres prototype of the kilogramme. (Similarly for other examples given by Smith, such as *tall* vs. *height* [11, p. 147], etc.) Even though Smith's intuitions on the quantities underlying the application of predicates are understandable, these quantities include, strictly speaking, many aspects that are *not* relevant for the given predicate. Such aspects then do not partake in the "respects relevant to the application of F", and the similarity in them is *irrelevant* for F. They are, nevertheless, relevant for formal fuzzy logic (which can be regarded as the logic of partial truth based on such gradual quantities), and in this looser sense they do underlie gradual vagueness.

[7]Smith would probably consider as relevant to the application of the predicate such aspects as the degree of penetration of a sperm cell into an egg cell, the progress of nidation, the vitality of the embryo, etc., all of which can change gradually. However, since the predicate "pregnant" (when understood as *stipulated* to be bivalent, for instance for legal purposes) cannot change with these parameters continuously, it does not conform to Smith's definition of vagueness.

predicates *determinately P,* which can be understood as bivalent (due to *determinately*), but arguably are still vague (with borderline cases and subject to the sorites).

Plurivaluationism based on fuzzy logic (as opposed to Smith's fuzzy plurivaluation-ism based simply on the $[0, 1]$-valued semantics) offers a partly different perspective on the nature of vagueness, which avoids these difficulties. Since fuzzy logic admits finitely valued or even bivalent models besides the infinite-valued ones, graduality is not, from the fuzzy-logical perspective, an essential feature of fuzzy plurivaluations. It is contin-gent on the semantic postulates for a vague predicate (which constitute a theory over fuzzy logic, see §1 above) whether they admit infinite-valued gradual models only (as with the predicate *tall*),[8] or whether they also admit finitely valued or even bivalent mod-els (perhaps even exclusively, as with the predicate *pregnant*). Rather than graduality, it is the semantic indeterminacy (caused by the character of meaning-determining facts, as discussed in §1) which is essential for vagueness.

From the perspective of fuzzy logic, the essence of vagueness is thus semantic inde-terminacy, only optionally accompanied by graduality.[9] The semantics of vague pred-icates is therefore constituted by classes of models, in general fuzzy (because of the possibility that the predicate is also gradual), but as the case may be, also finitely-valued or even just two-valued. Thus although the degree-theoretical semantics of a vague pred-icate is *in general* a fuzzy plurivaluation, in the special case of bivalent vagueness it is a *classical* plurivaluation. From the viewpoint of fuzzy logic, classical plurivaluation-ism (or the essentially equivalent classical supervaluationism) is just a special case of fuzzy plurivaluationism: a case adequate for *some* of vague predicates (namely the bi-valent ones), though certainly not all of them, as the meaning postulates of many vague predicates allow or even enforce their models to be fuzzy.[10]

As explained in §1, a (fuzzy or classical) plurivaluation is the class of models of a theory over a fuzzy logic (which in the case of classical plurivaluation becomes trivi-alized to classical logic). This theory expresses the constraints on admissible (fuzzy or classical) models, and so is the essence of what in the case of classical super- or plurival-uationism is called the *penumbral connections.* Thus in terms of fuzzy logic, penumbral connections are nothing else but the predicate's meaning postulates, which formalized as the axioms of a theory over fuzzy logic constrain its class of fuzzy models.

---

[8]That is, under the more complex semantic analysis of *tall,* taking into account its continuity with respect to height: see footnote 4 above.

[9]The difference between graduality on the one hand and vagueness as indeterminacy on the other hand is stressed also by Dubois and Prade [4, 3]; cf. also Zadeh quoted in [8, §2] in this volume.

[10]The reader may wonder how the jolt problem, i.e., the supertruth of the existence of a sharp transition point (such as the first nanosecond for the predicate *pregnant;* see [12, §6]) can be eliminated for bivalent vague predicates, considering that the fuzzy-plurivaluationistic solution is based on graduality. For bivalent predicates, however, the problem resides not in the neglect of graduality (which is not present), but rather must reside in a wrong choice of structures employed for modeling the extensions of predicates. Take for instance the predicate *pregnant* on the scale of nanoseconds. If time is modeled by a complete lattice (e.g., as usual, a bounded interval of either real numbers representing time instants or natural numbers representing successive time intervals) and standard sets are taken for extensions of predicates, then every predicate extension, includ-ing that of *pregnant,* necessarily has a first instant (i.e., "the first nanosecond") in every model. However, in non-standard models (formalized, e.g., in Vopěnka's Alternative Set Theory, [13]), subclasses of natural num-bers, though bivalent, need not have first elements. Using such non-standard models of time might therefore avoid the jolt problem for *pregnant* and similar bivalent vague predicates (including *determinately P,* which is subject to the jolt problem even in fuzzy plurivaluationism).

3   Supertruth as deducibility in fuzzy logic

As correctly observed by Smith, fuzzy plurivaluationistic semantics for gradual vague predicates solves the problem of artificial precision. It also provide answers to other frequent objections to degree theories of vagueness and fuzzy logic.

For instance, the linear ordering of the system of truth degrees is frequently criticized, on the basis that for incommensurable pairs of gradual predicates (such as *green* and *big*) it makes no sense to compare their truth degrees (e.g., to say that a ball is more green than big, or vice versa). Even though fuzzy logic does employ linear systems of degrees (most often, the real unit interval), fuzzy plurivaluationism answers the objection in a convincing way (described in [11, §6.1.4], here slightly simplified): since the degrees of both properties vary across admissible fuzzy models, and since the incommensurable predicates are not tied by any meaning postulates (or "penumbral connections"), the sentence p: "a is more P than Q" is true in some models (in which the degree of Pa is larger than that of Qa), but false in others (in which the opposite is true). However, since the semantics of the predicates P and Q is the *whole class* of fuzzy models admitted by their meaning postulates, neither the sentence p nor its negation can be claimed—none of them is *supertrue*. Consequently, the truth status of the sentence p is not semantically determined, and so the properties are indeed incommensurable, even if a linear system of mutually comparable truth values is employed in each fuzzy model.

As seen from this example, for the assessment of (super)truth of sentences involving vague predicates one needs to know which of them are true in all models forming the plurivaluation. However, since the plurivaluation is the class of models of a fuzzy theory that formalizes meaning postulates, the latter question is equivalent to asking which sentences are true in all fuzzy models of this theory; in other words, which are its *consequences in fuzzy logic*. As a matter of fact, the consequence relation of fuzzy logic and the corresponding deduction rules have literally been *designed* to determine the supertruth of sentences of fuzzy plurivaluationism.[11]

4   Plurivaluations taken seriously

Smith's analysis of meaning-determining facts suggests that plurivaluations, be they fuzzy or classical, are to be taken seriously. The meaning of a vague predicate is the *whole* class of (fuzzy or classical) models, and there is nothing that would determine the meaning more narrowly. As already discussed in the previous paragraph, the only semantically grounded statements about such predicates are therefore the "supertrue" sentences—i.e., those valid in *all* fuzzy models admitted by the meaning postulates.

These facts are often overlooked, and *single* membership functions are frequently taken for the semantics of vague predicates (especially in the fuzzy literature, e.g., [15]). This not only contradicts the arguments pointing to fuzzy plurivaluationism, but also leads to inadequate models that retain graduality (which is just accidental to vagueness) while indeterminacy (which is substantial for vagueness) has been removed. Consequently, what is modeled are no longer vague, but artificially precisified gradual predicates. The artificial precisification can be an expedient simplification in technical practice. It should be, however, kept in mind that the precisification is in most cases com-

---

[11]From the perspective of fuzzy logic, however, exactly the converse is the case: fuzzy plurivaluationism is just the semantic representation of what derivations in fuzzy logic are about.

pletely arbitrary, and that taking a slightly different membership function can lead to radically different results.[12] Unless the choice of a particular membership function is justified by some aspect of the technical application, the results may be just artifacts of the choice and have little in common with the original vague predicates modeled.

In some cases, the neglect of the plurivaluationistic nature of vague predicates is subtler, but still casts a shadow of doubt on the meaningfulness of the model. At the very least, the use of specific membership degrees in these models calls for explanation.

Consider, for example, the use of a fixed (though arbitrary) threshold r in Cerami and Pardo's r-semantics for counterfactuals (see [1, §5] in this volume). Justification of its meaningfulness would require clarification of the notion of possible world used in the definition: if the meaning of a vague predicate in a possible world (e.g., the meaning of *tall* in a world in which I measure $6'4$ instead of my actual height) is a fuzzy plurivaluation, then a sentence (e.g., "I am tall") may exceed the fixed threshold r in only some of the models from the fuzzy plurivaluation; exceeding the threshold is then a semantically meaningless criterion. A fixed threshold could only be meaningful if possible worlds were comprised of precisified membership functions; however, it remains to be clarified whether such a conception of possible worlds is reasonable (this question is loosely connected with the problem whether vagueness is in the world or only in language).

Similarly it should be made clear what is the meaning of specific truth degrees assigned by the speakers to vague propositions in Sauerland's study ([9, §2.2] in this volume), considering that the semantics of a vague predicate is in fact a fuzzy plurivaluation, and so the truth degrees of such propositions are only determined up to certain limits. A more careful analysis would probably find out that rather than degrees of *truth* (which are not uniquely determined), Sauerland actually studies (something like) the degrees of the speakers' subjective agreement with statements (which, on the other hand, might be unique and ascertainable). It is then no wonder that the degrees do not follow the patterns of fuzzy logic, as they represent a completely different (most probably even non-truth-functional) modality than that studied by fuzzy logic.

Finally, the plurivaluationistic nature of vague predicates poses another problem for Smith's definition of vagueness, or rather for its coherence with fuzzy plurivaluationism. As noted in §2 of this Comment, the Closeness principle is based on the vague notion of "very close/similar". According to fuzzy plurivaluationism, the meaning of this term is a *class* of fuzzy models of the closeness or similarity relation, rather than a single such model. Across these models, there may be considerable differences in the truth value of the sentence "a and b are very close/similar in respects relevant to the application of F", as well as the sentence " 'Fa'and 'Fb' are very close/similar in respect of truth". Whether the condition of the Closeness principle for F is satisfied therefore can (and for many vague predicates F probably also will) vary across the models in the plurivaluation that represents the meaning of the principle; yet no fact determining the meaning of this

---

[12]For instance, the truth value of $Ax \to Bx$ in standard Gödel fuzzy logic is 1 if the truth values of Ax and Bx both equal 0.4, but drops to as low as 0.39 if the value of Bx is decreased by just 0.01. The truth value of the proposition can thus be radically different even for very close membership functions (here, differing just by 0.01). A similar effect can occur even in standard Łukasiewicz logic despite the continuity of truth functions of all its propositional connectives, as the truth functions of more complex formulae can grow very rapidly and yield large differences for negligible changes in degrees.

principle can decide between these models. Consequently, the proposition "F is vague" is itself vague, and its truth status is for many predicates F undetermined, being neither supertrue nor superfalse in the plurivaluation that represents its meaning.

Even if one does not adopt fuzzy plurivaluationism as the theory of vagueness that should apply to the Closeness principle, still the undeniable semantic underdeterminacy of the expression "very close/similar" makes any application of this definition problematic and calls for an explanation. The conception sketched above in §2, which identifies vagueness with the very indeterminacy of meaning (and only optional graduality), on the other hand, does not refer to the vague concept of closeness/similarity, and therefore does not suffer from this problem.

These arguments notwithstanding, it should be stressed that the Closeness-based definition of vagueness is not central to Smith's degree-theoretical approach, nor to the fuzzy-plurivaluationistic solution to the problem of artificial precision. In [11] and [12] it in fact only plays a rôle of a supporting argument, from which the rest of the theory is essentially independent. From the perspective of fuzzy logic, Smith's fuzzy plurivaluationism represents adequate degree-theoretical semantics for gradual vagueness. As I tried to hint here, fuzzy logic might contribute to its picture by elucidating the nature of fuzzy plurivaluations (as the models of meaning postulates formalized in fuzzy logic), proposing a different definition of vagueness, and supplementing the picture with classically plurivaluational, bivalent (or finite-valued) vagueness.

BIBLIOGRAPHY

[1] Cerami M., Pardo P.: Many-valued semantics for vague counterfactuals. *This volume*, 2011.
[2] Cintula P., Hájek P., Noguera C. (eds.): *Handbook of Mathematical Fuzzy Logic*. College Publications, to appear in 2011.
[3] Dubois D.: Have fuzzy sets anything to do with vagueness? *This volume*, 2011.
[4] Dubois D., Prade H.: Gradual elements in a fuzzy set. *Soft Computing* 12: 165–175, 2008.
[5] Hájek P.: *Metamathematics of Fuzzy Logic*. Kluwer, 1998.
[6] Hájek P., Novák V.: The sorites paradox and fuzzy logic. *International Journal of General Systems* 32: 373–383, 2003.
[7] Novák V.: A formal theory of intermediate quantifiers. *Fuzzy Sets and Systems* 159: 1229–1246, 2008.
[8] Prade H., Schockaert S.: Handling borderline cases using degrees: an information processing perspective. *This volume*, 2011.
[9] Sauerland U.: Vagueness in language: the case against fuzzy logic revisited. *This volume*, 2011.
[10] Smith N.J.J.: Vagueness as closeness. *Australasian Journal of Philosophy* 83: 157–183, 2005.
[11] Smith N.J.J.: *Vagueness and Degrees of Truth*. Oxford University Press, 2008.
[12] Smith N.J.J.: Fuzzy logic and higher-order vagueness. *This volume*, 2011.
[13] Vopěnka, P.: *Mathematics in the Alternative Set Theory*. Teubner, 1979.
[14] Weatherson B.: Three objections to Smith on vagueness. Manuscript, published online at http://brian.weatherson.org/totsov.pdf (accessed October 2011), 2004.
[15] Zadeh L.: Fuzzy logic and approximate reasoning. *Synthese* 30: 407–428, 1975.

Libor Běhounek
Institute of Computer Science
Academy of Sciences of the Czech Republic
Pod Vodárenskou věží 2
182 07 Prague 8, Czech Republic
Email: behounek@cs.cas.cz

Reply to Libor Běhounek's Comments on *Fuzzy Logic and Higher-Order Vagueness*

NICHOLAS J.J. SMITH

I am extremely grateful to Libor Běhounek for his very interesting and valuable comments on my paper. In what follows, I shall try to respond to his objections. As will be evident from the fact that it frequently directs the reader to [1] for longer discussions of issues and more detailed presentations of arguments, my paper is not fully self-contained: at a number of places, it stands in need of the further support provided by the longer work [1]. Accordingly—and because I have very limited space here—these replies will sometimes take the form of indicating where in [1] considerations which address the objection under discussion are presented.

1 What determines the set of acceptable models?

According to fuzzy plurivaluationism, which is the view defended in my paper (and originally proposed, and defended at greater length, in [1]), a vague discourse is associated not with a single correct or intended fuzzy model, but with multiple acceptable fuzzy models. Běhounek is sympathetic with this general idea, but proposes a different mechanism by which the class of acceptable models is determined.

On my view (see §5 of my paper, and [1, §§6.1.1–6.1.2]), the main (but not the only) meaning-determining facts are speakers' usage dispositions, and the acceptable models of a discourse are those that meet all the constraints imposed by the meaning-determining facts. Such constraints include paradigm case constraints (if speakers would all unhesitatingly apply the predicate 'tall' to the object a in normal conditions, then any acceptable model must assign 'tall' a function which maps a to 1), ordering constraints (if persons a and b are of the same sex and roughly the same age, and a's height is greater than b's, then any acceptable model must assign to the predicate 'is tall' a function which maps a to a value greater than or equal to the value to which it maps b), and so on. Běhounek expresses a worry about this way of picking out the acceptable models, and proposes an alternative. The worry is that the set of acceptable models so determined will not be sharp. I offer my reply to this concern in [1, §6.2.2].[1] The alternative proposal is that the acceptable models are those on which certain axioms are fully true. These axioms are thought of as formalisations in fuzzy logic of meaning postulates for vague predicates.

---

[1] Běhounek refers to this section of my book, writing "Smith justifies the assumption of sharpness of the set of fuzzy models, de facto, by Ockham's razor... Such an explanation is, however, just meta-theoretical: it does not offer a deeper explanation within the theory itself as to why the semantics of vague predicates should be a sharp rather than unsharp set of fuzzy models." I disagree with this characterisation of my reply: I do try to offer an 'internal' reason why the set of acceptable models should be sharp; see in particular the discussion at [1, pp. 312–313].

I have a concern of my own about the alternative proposal. Let us say that a set S of models is axiomatisable if there is a set F of formulas such that S includes all and only the models on which every formula in F is fully true. I certainly agree that if the set of acceptable models of a discourse is axiomatisable, then approaching it via its axioms can be beneficial, allowing us to bring to bear useful logical tools. However, I see no reason to think that the set of acceptable models of a discourse will always be axiomatisable. To give the flavour of the kind of concern I have in mind here, consider for a moment classical first order logic. It seems to me that it could be part of the meaning of a certain predicate P—common knowledge to speakers—that there can be only finitely many P's. However, as is well known, there is no set F of wffs (of first order logic) such that on every (classical) model on which all the wffs in F are true, the extension of P is a finite set.

So much for giving the general flavour of my worry about Běhounek's proposal that "Smith's plurivaluations are thus exactly the classes of models of formal fuzzy theories that straightforwardly formalize the meaning postulates of vague predicates"— let's turn now to a second example, of more direct relevance to the discussion of fuzzy approaches to vagueness. As already mentioned, one form of constraint on acceptable interpretations concerns paradigm cases. For example, Běhounek gives the examples:

- Michael J. Fox is not tall.

- Christopher Lee is tall.

He suggests that these can be axiomatized as $\neg Ha$ and Hb, respectively. But there is a problem here: there are models that make Hb true on which the name b does not refer to Christopher Lee. Thus, the following two constraints on models are not equivalent:

1. Ensure that Christopher Lee (i.e. the man himself) is (fully) in the extension of H on the model.

2. Ensure that the formula Hb is (fully) true on the model.

To satisfy the second condition, we need only ensure that the referent of b—whatever it is on the model in question—is in the extension of H on the model. To satisfy the first condition, we have to ensure that Christopher Lee himself is in the extension of H on the model.

This issue cannot be resolved simply by adding more axioms which constrain the interpretation of the name b: for as is well known, if some propositions (in this case the expanded set of axioms) are all true in a model $\mathfrak{M}$, then they are likewise all true in any model which is isomorphic to $\mathfrak{M}$. The best that a set of axioms can do is fix its models up to isomorphism. But it seems that the set of *acceptable* models of a discourse need not be closed under isomorphism. Suppose we have an acceptable model of a vague discourse which includes the word 'tall'. In this model, Christopher Lee is in the extension of the predicate 'tall'. Now consider an isomorphic model, whose domain contains only (say) numbers. It would seem that this is *not* an acceptable model of the original vague discourse.

If we formulate meaning postulates for some of the vague terms in a discourse, then we know that the acceptable models of the discourse will be *among* the models of the theory whose axioms formalise those meaning postulates. This is certainly useful knowledge. What is not clear, however, is that given a vague discourse, we can always find a set of axioms such that the models of those axioms are *precisely* the acceptable models of the discourse. Whether or not we can do this depends, of course, on the discourse, and on the chosen logic. The general worry, however, is as follows. For a given logic, there will be a kind of transformation of models such that the class of models of any set of axioms will be closed under such transformations. (For example, in the case of classical predicate logic, models of a theory are closed under isomorphisms; in the case of certain modal logics, models are closed under bisimulations [2, ch. 3]; and so on.) The worry is that the set of acceptable models of a discourse will *not* be closed under such transformations. If so, then the set of acceptable models cannot be specified as the set of models of certain axioms. It is for this reason that I prefer my way of specifying the acceptable models—as those not ruled out as incorrect by the constraints on models generated by the meaning-fixing facts (which comprise, inter alia, the usage dispositions of speakers)—to the alternative way proposed by Běhounek.

2 Vagueness, closeness and semantic indeterminacy

In my paper, I propose that F is vague if and only if it satisfies the following condition, for any objects a and b:

Closeness If a and b are very close/similar in respects relevant to the application of F, then 'Fa' and 'Fb' are very close/similar in respect of truth.

Běhounek makes a number of objections to this definition of vagueness. First, he says that "it is itself based on the vague terms *very close/similar*, and thus already its application requires an apparatus for handling vagueness". However, as explained at [1, p. 145], the relation of absolute closeness or similarity, as it features in Closeness, is to be regarded as *precise* (even if the *ordinary* notion of absolute similarity in F-relevant respects is vague, for some predicates F; see [1, p. 145, n. 30]). Second, Běhounek objects that the definition is trivially true, on the basis of the suggestion that "similarity in respects relevant to the application of F coincides with similarity in respect of truth". I argue against this suggestion at [1, pp. 179–80]. Third, Běhounek argues that there are counterexamples to the definition: predicates which are vague, but which do not conform to Closeness. The only example discussed at any length is that of "the predicate 'pregnant' (when understood as *stipulated* to be bivalent, for instance for legal purposes)". I agree that this predicate does not count as vague according to the Closeness definition—but I find it hard to understand why Běhounek thinks that it is *intuitively* vague. This may well be related to the point to be discussed next (where, it seems, there is a terminological dispute between us over the meaning of the term 'vague').

Běhounek suggests: "Rather than graduality, it is the semantic indeterminacy ... which is essential for vagueness." I disagree. I argue that standard examples of vague predicates—'tall', 'bald' and so on—exhibit two distinct features: they conform to

Closeness (they exhibit graduality, in Běhounek's terms); and they have multiple accept-able extensions—one on each acceptable model (they exhibit semantic indeterminacy). I attach the term 'vagueness' to the first feature (see [1, §6.1.3]). It seems that Běhounek wants to attach it to the second feature. This may seem like a trivial terminological dispute—but actually I think that there are good reasons for going my way here, not Běhounek's. I take it as a datum that the term 'vague' should be applied to predicates which exhibit three features: they admit of borderline cases; they generate Sorites para-doxes; and they have blurred boundaries. (If someone did not agree with *this*, then that *would* I think be a mere terminological dispute of no deep interest.) I argue that if a predicate satisfies Closeness, then it will exhibit these three features [1, §§3.5.2–3.5.4]. I also argue that if a predicate is semantically indeterminate, then it need *not* exhibit these three features [1, p. 137]. Hence, we should, in the first instance, attach the term 'vague' to predicates which conform to Closeness—not (contra Běhounek) to predicates which merely exhibit semantic indeterminacy.

BIBLIOGRAPHY

[1] Nicholas J.J. Smith. *Vagueness and Degrees of Truth*. Oxford University Press, Oxford, 2008.
[2] Johan van Benthem. *Modal Logic for Open Minds*. CSLI, Stanford, 2010.

Comments on *Fuzzy Logic and Higher-Order Vagueness* by Nicholas J.J. Smith

FRANCESCO PAOLI

This interesting and well-written paper is an attempt to provide a solution to the long-standing problem of higher-order vagueness, or artificial precision, which has so far undermined the plausibility of the fuzzy perspective on vagueness. After reviewing other approaches to the problem, the author contends that the proper way out of this quandary is what he terms *fuzzy plurivaluationism*. The arguments advanced by the author in favour of his viewpoint are clear and well-articulated, while the paper contains a survey of the state of the art on this ongoing debate that stands out for its commendable completeness. In what follows, therefore, I will not dwell on the undeniable merits of the paper, but I will rather attempt to explain why I remain unconvinced by Smith's reasoning to the effect that fuzzy plurivaluationism is really the way to go.

Smith is right when he claims that any serious bid to tackle the issue of vagueness should offer not only a recipe to solve the sorites paradox and the like, but also a general view on the nature of the phenomenon itself. We must distinguish "between a *surface characterization* of P—a set of manifest conditions, possession of which marks out the P's from the non-P's—and a *fundamental definition* of P—a statement of the fundamental underlying nature of the P's, which explains why they have such-and-such surface characteristics" (pp. 12–13). Features like the presence of borderline cases or blurry boundaries, or sorites susceptibility, may constitute a surface characterization of vagueness (of predicates), but none of these marks counts, according to Smith, as a fundamental definition of the concept. The latter is given instead by what he calls the *Closeness principle*: "If a and b are very close/similar in respects relevant to the application of F, then 'Fa' and 'Fb' are very close/similar in respect of truth".

This is all well and good insofar as we confine ourselves to *dimensional* predicates ('tall', 'old'), which come with a naturally associated metrics. It is crystal clear what it means for a and b to be very close/similar in respects relevant to the application of 'tall', for we can conveniently rephrase our statement in terms of the *measures* of a's and b's heights. But there is more to vagueness (of predicates) than dimensional predicates have to offer, although their sorites susceptibility (and the circumstance that the sorites paradox is ubiquitous in discussions about vagueness) has turned them by and large into the prototypical examples of the concept. Evaluative predicates ('beautiful', 'clever') are more difficult to get a hold of, given that they lack an obvious metrics (as Max Cresswell [4, p. 281] vividly puts it: "Must we postulate the kalon as a degree of beauty or the andron as a degree of manliness?") and are typically multidimensional. Still, they are uncontentiously considered as vague, given their possession of several traits collectively associated with vagueness—they are intrinsically gradable; they are compatible with hedges; they admit a nontrivial comparative; they have borderline cases of application; they normally come in antonymous pairs. It remains to be seen whether the Closeness principle makes sense when F is an evaluative predicate. What does it mean for a and b to be very close/similar in respects relevant to the application of 'clever'?

I may agree with Smith that the presence of borderline cases does not provide a fundamental definition of vagueness—perhaps borderline cases are just the surface manifestation of some more basic property still waiting to be unveiled. Yet, I am not completely persuaded by his claim that it fails to be a necessary and sufficient condition for vagueness of predicates. Smith cites the example of a predicate, 'schort', having the same associated metrics as 'short', but whose domains of application and non-application (relative to the given metrics) are separated by sharp cut-off points from a no man's land where 'a is schort' is neither true nor false. The example is admittedly artificial, and I believe that its artificiality could divert from its controversial character. It makes perfectly sense to say that 'a is short' in case a is a borderline case for a short person. More than that: a necessary condition for a to be a borderline case for F is that F is actually *defined* for a (no one would say that clothes-pegs make borderline cases for flirtatious girls simply because the corresponding sentence is nonsensical, hence neither true nor false). Here, on the other hand, the definition reads as though 'schort' makes sense exactly of those people who are either less than four feet or more than six feet tall. Maybe I am wrong on that score, but what I would like to see is an example of a natural language predicate (not an artificial one) that exhibits the behaviour alluded to by the author.

Fuzzy plurivaluationism is, in my opinion, plagued by a further problem. One of the central questions about vagueness is whether it is due e.g. to the way we use language, to our lack of knowledge regarding certain aspects of reality, to some intrinsic features of the world around us. All the main competing theories take a stand about this issue. For instance, vagueness can be seen either as a matter of ignorance (epistemicism), or a semantic phenomenon due to ambiguity (super- or plurivaluationism), or an ontological phenomenon intrinsic to the nature of vague properties (this view seems to be at least implicit in some basic fuzzy theories). It is unclear to me how we should assess fuzzy plurivaluationism under this respect. On p. 8, when discussing classical plurivaluationism and its denial of a unique intended model, the source of vagueness is ascribed to "semantic *indeterminacy*—or equally, semantic *plurality*", but in view of the remarks on p. 9 ("Fuzzy plurivaluationism is just like classical plurivaluationism except that its models are fuzzy") it looks like we can safely assume that the picture also holds for its fuzzy variant. That stands to reason, given the fact that fuzzy plurivaluationism is, indeed, a form of plurivaluationism. However, it does not seem to sit well with the adoption of a fuzzy semantics of *any* sort. Fuzzy semantics assigns a truth value in between 0 and 1 to 'Bob is tall' whenever Bob has the property to some intermediate degree. In the standard fuzzy perspective, we do not say many things at once: we say just one thing about a property which neither definitely applies nor definitely fails to apply. On this hybrid approach, on the other hand, vagueness would seem to depend from the latter phenomenon as much as from semantic indeterminacy. On the basis of what Smith says, I do not have sufficient evidence to assess whether this is the correct interpretation. If so, perhaps this concurrence calls for more substantial justification.

Smith carefully distinguishes between the problem of artificial precision and other related, but different, meanings that the phrase 'higher-order vagueness' has in the literature. On one of such readings, you have this problem if your semantics provides for a sharp drop-off between the region of definitely positive (or negative) instances of a predicate and its borderline cases. Traditional classical plurivaluationism and basic fuzzy semantics are generally believed to suffer from this problem. If fuzzy plurivaluationism has to establish itself as one of the prominent options about vagueness in the next future (and I believe it can), such concerns should be addressed. One of these is due to Williamson [5, p. 156 ff.]. Take a sorites series from orange to red. It is hopeless, Williamson contends, to look for the first shade which is definitely red—i.e. that it is red in every acceptable model. Here we have fuzzy models rather than classical models; but what prevents Williamson's objection from going into effect? More precisely: what is the first shade which has the property 'red' to degree 1 in every acceptable model?

Finally, I have the impression that the fuzzy metalanguage approach has been dismissed too quickly. Fuzzy class theory ([2, 3]), briefly mentioned in the paper, has been used [1] in an attempt to frame this position into the precise language of fuzzy mathematics, rather than classical mathematics. This would seem to defuse Goguen's objection quoted on p. 10.

The fact that I disagree with its main thesis, of course, does not imply that I did not enjoy this paper, or that I did not value its worth. I hope that giving a thought to these small observations will help its author to polish a perspective that is likely to gain increasing resonance in the next years.

BIBLIOGRAPHY

[1] Běhounek L., "A model of higher-order vagueness in higher-order fuzzy logic", *Uncertainty: Reasoning about Probability and Vagueness*, Prague, September 5–8, 2006, http://atlas-conferences.com/cgi-bin/abstract/casu-34.
[2] Běhounek L., Cintula P., "Fuzzy class theory", *Fuzzy Sets and Systems*, 154, 1, 2005, pp. 34–55.
[3] Běhounek L., Cintula P., "From fuzzy logic to fuzzy mathematics: a methodological manifesto", *Fuzzy Sets and Systems*, 157, 5, 2006, pp. 642–646.
[4] Cresswell M.J., "The semantics of degree", in B. Partee (Ed.), *Montague Grammar*, Academic Press, New York, 1976, pp. 261–292.
[5] Williamson T., *Vagueness*, Routledge, London, 1994.

Francesco Paoli
Department of Philosophy
University of Cagliari, Italy
Via Is Mirrionis 1
09123 Cagliari, Italy
Email: paoli@unica.it

Reply to Francesco Paoli's Comments on
Fuzzy Logic and Higher-Order Vagueness

NICHOLAS J.J. SMITH

I am extremely grateful to Francesco Paoli for his very interesting and valuable comments on my paper. In what follows, I shall try to respond to his objections. As will be evident from the fact that it frequently directs the reader to [2] for longer discussions of issues and more detailed presentations of arguments, my paper is not fully self-contained: at a number of places, it stands in need of the further support provided by the longer work [2]. Accordingly—and because I have very limited space here—these replies will sometimes take the form of indicating where in [2] considerations which address the objection under discussion are presented.

1 Multidimensional predicates and closeness

In my paper, I propose that F is vague if and only if it satisfies the following condition, for any objects a and b:

Closeness If a and b are very close/similar in respects relevant to the application of F, then 'Fa' and 'Fb' are very close/similar in respect of truth.

Paoli objects that while this definition is adequate for predicates such as 'tall' and 'old' which are associated with natural metrics, it does not seem to extend to multidimensional predicates such as 'beautiful' and 'clever' which lack obvious metrics. He asks "What does it mean for a and b to be very close/similar in respects relevant to the application of 'clever'?"

I offer a response to this sort of worry in [2, p. 145, n. 31]. The example considered there is the predicate 'table', but the idea applies just as well to 'clever'. The basic thought is that a and b are very close/similar in respects relevant to the application of a multidimensional predicate such as 'clever' iff they are very close along each dimension considered individually.

Of course it will often be difficult to specify the dimensions. In the case of cleverness, for example, it is clear that height is not a relevant respect (the fact that Bill is tall and Ben short has no bearing on the question whether each is clever) while speed and accuracy at mental arithmetic is relevant (the fact that Bill can quickly and accurately add two digit numbers in his head, while Ben cannot, does have a bearing on the question whether each is clever)—but these observations still leave us far from a complete analysis of the respects relevant to application of the predicate 'clever'. However, competent speakers surely have an implicit grasp of which factors are relevant to the application of multidimensional predicates: otherwise they would not be able to use these predicates successfully.

In any case, the key point here is that we can say what it *means* for a and b to be very close/similar in respects relevant to the application of a multidimensional predicate such as 'clever'—it means that they are very close along each dimension considered individually—even if we cannot (without a great deal of difficulty) make explicit exactly what the relevant dimensions are in any given case. Difficulties in specifying the dimensions—which are certainly real (even though, as competent speakers, we must have some implicit grasp of which factors are relevant)—do not translate into a problem with the very idea of applying Closeness to multidimensional predicates.

2   Vagueness and borderline cases

I argue in my paper, using as an example the made-up predicate 'is schort', that having borderline cases is not sufficient for being vague. Paoli objects to the example as follows:

> a necessary condition for a to be a borderline case for F is that F is actually *defined* for a... Here, on the other hand, the definition reads as though 'schort' makes sense exactly of those people who are either less than four feet or more than six feet tall.

We need to distinguish two senses in which a predicate might not be defined for certain objects. First, there is the sense Paoli is using: a predicate F is not defined for an object a if Fa is nonsense (a 'category mistake'). The relationship between 'schort' and persons between four and six feet in height is meant to be different, however. The predicate is 'not defined' for these cases in a quite different sense: namely, we have *said nothing at all* about whether the predicate applies to these cases—and what we have said (that it applies to objects less than four feet in height, and does not apply to objects more than six feet in height) has no implications regarding these remaining cases. In other words, the definition of the predicate is *silent* regarding these cases. That is why they are borderline cases: they are cases where we do not know what to say (which is quite different from cases for which a predicate is not defined in the *first* sense: here we know *not* to apply the predicate). At the same time, the sharp delineation of these cases prevents the predicate from being vague. Hence the claim that a predicate can have borderline cases without being vague.

Paoli asks for a natural language predicate—not an artificial one—that has borderline cases but is not vague. It is hard to think of such a predicate, precisely for the reason that it would have to possess two features:

1. there are cases regarding which the definition of the predicate is simply silent (i.e. says nothing, one way or the other, regarding the application of the predicate)

2. this range of cases is sharply delineated

There are plenty of naturally occurring predicates with the first feature. For example, when terms are defined in the rules of sports or games (e.g. 'fault' in tennis) certain situations are simply *not envisaged at all*, and so nothing is said about them, one way or the other. (For example, if the tennis ball *passes through* the net without the ball or the net being disrupted in any way—perhaps due to some sort of quantum effect—is this a fault?) However, the set of cases about which the definition remains silent is not generally sharply bounded. (If it were, it would be natural to complete the definition by saying something about these cases, one way or the other.)

Nevertheless, I think that the clear *possibility* of a predicate (such as 'is schort') whose definition says nothing either way about some sharply-bounded set of cases is enough to show that having borderline cases is insufficient for vagueness. It does not seem to me that a naturally occurring example of such a predicate is required to make this point.

3   Worldly vagueness and semantic indeterminacy

Paoli writes:

> In the standard fuzzy perspective, we do not say many things at once: we say just one thing about a property which neither definitely applies nor definitely fails to apply. On [Smith's] hybrid approach, on the other hand, vagueness would seem to depend from the latter phenomenon as much as from semantic indeterminacy. On the basis of what Smith says, I do not have sufficient evidence to assess whether this is the correct interpretation. If so, perhaps this concurrence calls for more substantial justification.

It is correct that my view—fuzzy plurivaluationism—combines semantic indeterminacy (of the sort found in classical plurivaluationism) and (as I call it) worldly vagueness (of the sort found in the standard fuzzy picture). I make a detailed case for this combination of features in [2]. However, I do not think that *vagueness* depends on semantic indeterminacy: in my view, as explained in detail in [2, §6.1.3], I regard semantic indeterminacy as a separate phenomenon, distinct from vagueness.

4   Higher-order vagueness

Paoli raises a version of one problem that has often gone under the heading 'higher-order vagueness'—the problem of "a sharp drop-off between the region of definitely positive (or negative) instances of a predicate and its borderline cases"—asking "what is the first shade which has the property 'red' to degree 1 in every acceptable model?" This is a significant objection to fuzzy plurivaluationism, which requires a detailed reply. I have given such a reply in [2, §6.2.2].

5   Fuzzy metalanguages

In my paper, I describe two different views, both of which could be described as proposing a 'fuzzy metalanguage'. I object to the first on grounds summed up in a quote from Goguen, and to the second on different grounds. Paoli writes:

> I have the impression that the fuzzy metalanguage approach has been dismissed too quickly. Fuzzy class theory, briefly mentioned in [Smith's] paper, has been used [1] in an attempt to frame this position into the precise language of fuzzy mathematics, rather than classical mathematics. This would seem to defuse Goguen's objection.

I quite agree that Běhounek's view [1] is not subject to Goguen's objection. However, as I say briefly in the paper (n. 15), Běhounek's view is not the same as either of the two versions of the 'fuzzy metalanguage' view which I criticise, and it is not—unlike those two views—intended as a solution to the problem of artificial precision (as presented in §1 of my paper). If my aim had been to say that there is no good view that can reasonably be described as involving a 'fuzzy metalanguage', then it would be quite correct to say that I had not made the case: that the fuzzy metalanguage approach had been dismissed too quickly. However, my aim was more modest: to reject two particular versions of the 'fuzzy metalanguage' approach as solutions to the problem of artificial precision (as presented in §1 of my paper). As things stand, I still believe that such rejection is warranted.

BIBLIOGRAPHY

[1] Libor Běhounek. A model of higher-order vagueness in higher-order fuzzy logic. Typescript (available at http://at.yorku.ca/c/a/s/u/34.dir/casu-34.pdf); abstract of a paper presented at *Uncertainty: Reasoning about Probability and Vagueness*, Institute of Philosophy, Academy of Sciences of the Czech Republic, Prague, 5–8 September, 2006.

[2] Nicholas J.J. Smith. *Vagueness and Degrees of Truth*. Oxford University Press, Oxford, 2008.

Inconstancy and Inconsistency

DAVID RIPLEY[1]

In everyday language, we can call someone 'consistent' to say that they're reliable, that they don't change over time. Someone who's consistently on time is *always* on time. Similarly, we can call someone 'inconsistent' to say the opposite: that they're change-able, mercurial. A student who receives inconsistent grades on her tests throughout a semester has performed better on some than on others.

With our philosophy hats on, though, we mean something quite different by 'consis-tent' and 'inconsistent'. Something consistent is simply something that's not contradic-tory. There's nothing contradictory about being on time, so anyone who's on time at all is consistently on time, in this sense of 'consistent'. And only a student with an unusual teacher can receive inconsistent grades on her tests throughout a semester, in this sense of 'inconsistent'.

In this paper, I'll use 'consistent' and 'inconsistent' in their usual philosophical sense: to mark the second distinction. By contrast, I'll use 'constant' and 'inconstant' to mark the first distinction. And although we can, should, and do sharply distinguish the two distinctions, they are related. In particular, they have both been used to account for some otherwise puzzling phenomena surrounding vague language. According to some theorists, vague language is inconstant. According to others, it is inconsistent.

I do not propose here to settle these differences; only to get a bit clearer about what the differences amount to, and to show what it would take to settle them. In §1 I'll give a brief overview of theories of vagueness that crucially invoke inconstancy, and theories that crucially invoke inconsistency. (I'll also briefly mention inconsistency's twin, incompleteness.) In §2, I present a formal framework (along the lines of that in [9]) for inconstancy and inconsistency. This will clarify just how the target theories of vagueness differ. §3 summarizes one strain of experimental research on speakers' use of vague predicates: research into claims like 'Man x is both tall and not tall', when man x is a borderline case of 'tall'. Such phenomena invite explanation in terms of inconstancy or inconsistency, and I'll explore explanations of both sorts. These explanations will lead me to revisit the formal framework in §4, and prove that, in a certain sense to be clarified there, inconstancy and inconsistency are deeply related; each can do everything the other can do. Finally, §5 offers some lessons to be drawn from the preceding discussion, and points out ways around the equivalence result proved in §4. The overall lesson is this: only with a theory of context in hand can we distinguish inconstancy from inconsistency.

[1]Research supported by the Agence Nationale de la Recherche, Project "Cognitive Origins of Vagueness", grant ANR-07-JCJC-0070. This paper has benefited greatly from discussions with Emmanuel Chemla, Paul Égré, Patrick Greenough, Joshua Knobe, Graham Priest, Diana Raffman, François Recanati, Greg Restall, Robert van Rooij, Laura Schroeter, and Zach Weber, as well as the comments of two anonymous referees.

1 Setting the scene

This discussion will operate broadly within the framework of [9]. Although it is familiar, I'll recount it briefly here. It's a story about how expressions come to have extensions, and so how predicates come to be associated with things that do or don't satisfy them, how names come to be associated with their bearers, how sentences come to be associated with truth-values, &c. Each (disambiguated) expression is first of all associated with a *character*. From character to extension, there is a two-step process. First, the character, together with the context of use, determines a *content*. For simplicity, I'll identify characters with functions from contexts of use to contents. Second, the content, together with circumstances of evaluation, determines an *extension*. Again for simplicity, I'll take contents to be functions from circumstances of evaluation to extensions. Note that this is so far terribly silent about what extensions, contexts, and circumstances of evaluation *are*. That's good; we'll be considering a few different hypotheses as we go along, but much of the discussion will stay at this abstract level.

1.1 Inconstant characters

I'll say that a character C is *inconstant* when there are contexts of use c_1, c_2 such that $C(c_1) \neq C(c_2)$. The classic examples of expressions with inconstant characters are indexicals. Consider the character of the indexical 'I'; call it I. If c_1 is a context of use in which I utter 'I', and c_2 is a context of use in which Napoleon utters 'I', $I(c_1)$ is a function that takes any circumstance of evaluation to me, and $I(c_2)$ is a function that takes any circumstance of evaluation to Napoleon.[2] Since I am not Napoleon, I is an inconstant character. Similar examples show that other indexicals, like 'here', 'now', 'three months ago', &c, have inconstant characters as well.

Indexicals, though, are not the only expressions with inconstant character. Demonstratives as well have inconstant character: the content determined by 'that' in one context of use (where one thing is demonstrated) can differ from the content determined by 'that' in another context of use (where something else is demonstrated).

Some (e.g. [20]) have alleged that vague words have inconstant character as well. (In fact, Soames takes vague words to *be* indexicals.) On these views, uses of the same vague predicate in distinct contexts of use can determine distinct contents. Thus, if context of use varies in the appropriate ways, two different occurrences of the same vague sentence might be used to claim different things. Here's an example. Let's consider a flea named Maximilian, and suppose that Maximilian is particularly large for a flea. In a context where we're categorizing fleas by size, Carrie might say 'Maximilian is huge', and thereby express that Maximilian is very large for a flea. By contrast, in a case where we're categorizing animals by size, Carrie might say 'Maximilian isn't huge', and thereby express that Maximilian isn't very large for an animal. In these two occurrences, 'huge' is expressing two distinct contents. In the first case, it expresses the property of being very large for a flea, and in the second case, it expresses the property of being very large for an animal.

---

[2]This makes some irrelevant assumptions for concreteness; maybe 'I' doesn't determine a constant function at all! But we don't need to worry about that here; it's an example of how the framework might operate.

This is an example of a particular sort of context-dependence: dependence on con-textually-determined comparison class. It is relatively uncontroversial that vague words exhibit this sort of context-dependence. But this is not *why* they are vague. For one thing, some precise predicates depend on comparison class as well. Maximilian is larger than average, if the comparison class is the class of fleas, and he's not larger than aver-age, if the comparison class is the class of animals. But 'larger than average' is perfectly precise. For another, dependence on comparison class does not exhaust vagueness; even once we fix a particular comparison class, say the class of fleas, it can still be a vague matter whether some particular flea is huge (relative to that comparison class). Contex-tualists like Soames acknowledge this, and propose that inconstant character can be used to account for the remaining vagueness as well.

On their view, there are no vague contents; the vagueness is in the character only. The inconstant character determines a range of possible contents, depending on the con-text of use. (Some aspects of the context of use might determine a comparison class, but let's suppose that the comparison class is fixed, so as to focus on vagueness in particu-lar.) Take the example 'huge', and suppose our comparison class is fixed to the class of animals. In some contexts of use, this might determine a content *bigger than 1000 kg*; in other contexts of use, a content *longer than 20 m*. But on every content determined by 'huge' with respect to this comparison class, a full-grown blue whale counts as huge, and a wasp does not. Clear cases and countercases of 'huge' are things that have or lack the content in question *no matter which content it is*. Borderline cases, on the other hand, have some of the contents and lack others.

This is entirely neutral about just which aspects of a context of use matter for the content determined by vague characters. Of course, individual theorists need not remain neutral in this way, and may well disagree with each other. I won't get into those differ-ences here; an inconstant-character theorist simply takes *some* aspect of context of use to matter.[3]

1.2 Inconstant contents

I'll say that a content C is *inconstant* when there are circumstances of evaluation c_1, c_2 such that $C(c_1) \neq C(c_2)$. Most contents are typically taken to be inconstant. Any con-tent that has different extensions at different possible worlds, for example, is inconstant. If we take at least some time-relativity to occur in the step from content to extension (as e.g. [9] does), then there will be contents that have different extensions at different times. These, too, will be inconstant. Even precise contents, then, are often taken to be inconstant.

But worlds and times are not the only factors alleged to matter for inconstant con-tents. For example, [10] takes instances of so-called 'faultless disagreement' to involve inconstant content. On their view, when Jack and Jill disagree about whether avocado is tasty (say Jack thinks it is and Jill thinks it isn't), they are not talking past each other be-cause there is a single content involved. That content (call it AT) maps world/time/judge triples to truth values. Jack and Jill are faultless because from Jack's point of view, the relevant triple is $w/t/Jack$ (for some w,t), where $AT(w,t,Jack)$ is true, and from Jill's

---

[3]In the formal framework of [9], contexts of use are taken to determine at least an agent, time, position, and world, but factors besides these might be relevant as well.

point of view the relevant triple is $w/t/Jill$ (for the same w,t), where $AT(w,t,Jill)$ is false. On this view, the content AT is inconstant, and indeed its inconstancy is sensitive to the judge parameter contributed by circumstances of evaluation. (Other inconstant contents, like 'is over a meter in height' might have different extensions at different worlds or times, but will not depend on the judge parameter.)

A theory of vagueness based on inconstant contents (as offered in e.g. [5]) allows for vague contents; once character and context have determined a content, there's still more to the vagueness story. These theories have a similar structure to inconstant-character theories, but deployed between content and extension, rather than between character and content. Thus, for an inconstant-content theorist, clear cases of a vague content C are in all of its extensions, clear countercases of C are in none of its extensions, and borderline cases of C are in some extensions and out of others.

Again, this is strictly neutral as to which aspects of a circumstance of evaluation matter. It's also neutral as to what a circumstance of evaluation is, and as to how (or whether) a sentence's context of use affects which circumstances of evaluation are relevant for judging it. Again, individual theorists are not neutral about these issues, but I won't enter into these debates here, except to point out that world- or time-dependence alone don't seem to suffice for vagueness. Because of this, below I will sometimes take inconstant content-views to suppose that vague contents determine distinct extensions *given* a world and time.[4] I think this is fair to every extant inconstant-content theorist of vagueness.

1.3 Inconsistent extensions

Let's call a pair of a context of use and a circumstance of evaluation a *total parameter*. Then, given a total parameter, a character determines a single extension. On the Kaplanian picture, there is no room for an extension to be inconstant. An extension does not determine anything else that might vary. However, the picture so far is neutral on just what sort of thing an extension ought to be. Let's stick to predicates for the moment; although their extensions are typically taken to be sets, all that's vital is that they be the sorts of things that objects can be *in* or *out* of. Pa is true in a total parameter iff a is in P's extension relative to that total parameter; and $\neg Pa$ is true in a total parameter iff a is out of P's extension relative to that total parameter.

I'll say that an extension is *inconsistent* when some things are both in it and out of it. If we are using a classical metalanguage, we are barred from simultaneously doing all of: 1) taking extensions to be sets, 2) taking 'in' to be set membership, and 3) taking 'out' to be set non-membership. In a paraconsistent set theory (like those described in [12] or [24]), we could do all of 1)–3). I think the most natural exposition of an inconsistent-extension view would adopt a paraconsistent metalanguage, and do just that. But it's not required, and here I'll stick to a classical metalanguage. There's a familiar way to do this:[5] an extension is a pair $\langle I,O \rangle$ of (classical) sets. The members of I are in the extension, and the members of O are out of it. An inconsistent extension, on this understanding, is one in which I and O overlap.[6]

---

[4]The formal framework of [9] does not allow for this.

[5]See [2] or [13] for more details.

[6]Sometimes I is called an 'extension' and O an 'antiextension'. This is clearly a different use of 'extension'

Inconsistent extensions, like inconstant characters and contents, have found application outside of vagueness. For example, [12] takes the predicate 'true', w/r/t some (perhaps all) total parameters, to have an inconsistent extension. Some sentences are both in and out; they are both true and not true. For example, the sentence 'this sentence is not true' is both true and not true, according to Priest. This is, of course, inconsistent.

Vague predicates have also been taken to have inconsistent extensions, in e.g. [25, 14, 17]. (None of these papers explicitly relates inconsistency to Kaplan's framework, but I take the idea of an inconsistent extension to be faithful to what all three authors propose.) For these authors, a vague predicate P, relative to a particular total parameter, determines an inconsistent extension. On this picture, vagueness persists at the level of extensions. Clear cases of a vague extension E are in its extension, clear countercases of E are out of its extension, and borderline cases of E are both in and out of its extension.

1.4   Incomplete extensions

This also gives us a way to understand *incomplete extensions*. An extension is incomplete iff there is something neither in it nor out of it. Given our pair-of-sets modeling of extensions, this is easy to capture. Simply take a pair $\langle I, O \rangle$ such that $I \cup O$ does not exhaust the domain.

Incomplete extensions have been taken to play an important role in understanding vagueness by a number of different authors, including [6], [20], [23], &c. I won't have much to say about them here. As we'll see, the core phenomenon I'm interested in exploring is one much more easily explained in terms of inconstancy or inconsistency than incompleteness. This doesn't at all rule out incompleteness's playing a role in a full theory of vague language.[7] It just won't occupy center stage in this paper.

2   A model theory

DEFINITION 1   *A model is a tuple* $\langle D, C_1, C_2, I \rangle$ *such that:*

- *D is a domain: a set of objects,*

- *C_1 is a set of contexts of use,*

- *C_2 is a set of circumstances of evaluation, and*

- *I is an* interpretation function*:*

   - *For every singular term a in the language, $I(a) \in D$,[8] and*

   - *for every predicate P in the language, $I(P)$ is a function from members of C_1 to (functions from members of C_2 to (pairs $\langle E_I, E_O \rangle$ of subsets of D)).[9]*

---

than the one at play in the Kaplanian tradition. My 'extension' follows the Kaplanian tradition, and so picks out 'extension'/'antiextension' pairs, in the other sense.

[7] Indeed, I think incompleteness should play such a role, and have argued in [3] for a theory of vagueness that integrates inconsistency with incompleteness.

[8] These models thus don't allow for inconstancy in which thing a singular term picks out. It would be easy to allow for, but since it will play no role here, I keep it simple.

[9] The pairs here are extensions; they tell us what is in (their first member) and what is out (their second). Thus, the functions from C_2 to the pairs are contents, and the functions from C_1 to contents are characters. This clause tells us: I must assign a character to every predicate.

Abbreviations: It will be handy to talk about total parameters in what follows; as above, a total parameter is a pair of a context of use with a circumstance of evaluation. I'll write T_M for the set of total parameters included in a model M. That is, where $M = \langle D, C_1, C_2, I \rangle$, $T_M = C_1 \times C_2$. Also, it'll be handy to think of a predicate P's extension in a total parameter t: let's use $I(P)(t)$ for the whole extension (a pair), $I_I(P)(t)$ for the set of things *in* the extension (the pair's first member), and $I_O(P)(t)$ for the set of things *out* of it (the pair's second member). If we need to be more explicit, we can separate out the context of use from the circumstance of evaluation: where c_1 is a context of use and c_2 is a circumstance of evaluation, $I(P)(c_1)(c_2)$ is a whole extension, $I_I(P)(c_1)(c_2)$ is what's in it, and $I_O(P)(c_1)(c_2)$ is what's out of it.

We can now recursively define a notion of *satisfaction*. Note that a model does not satisfy a sentence simpliciter. It does so only with respect to a total parameter.

DEFINITION 2 *For a model $M = \langle D, C_1, C_2, I \rangle$ and a total parameter $t \in T_M$:*

- $M, t \vDash Pa$ iff $I(a) \in I_I(P)(t)$

- $M, t \vDash \neg Pa$ iff $I(a) \in I_O(P)(t)$

- $M, t \vDash A \wedge B$ iff $M, t \vDash A$ and $M, t \vDash B$

- $M, t \vDash \neg(A \wedge B)$ iff $M, t \vDash \neg A$ or $M, t \vDash \neg B$

- $M, t \vDash \forall x A$ iff every x-variant M' of M is such that $M', t \vDash A$

- $M, t \vDash \neg \forall x A$ iff some x-variant M' of M is such that $M', t \vDash \neg A$

An x-variant of a model M is defined in the obvious way; $\vee$ and $\exists$ can be defined similarly to the above or taken to be abbreviations. Definition 2 has the effect of taking compound sentences, in the presence of inconsistent or incomplete extensions, to be governed by the system FDE described in e.g. [2, 13]. For arguments that this truth-functional way of treating inconsistency and incompleteness is superior to its subvaluationist and supervaluationist relatives, see e.g. [7, 17]; I won't argue the point here.

We now have a formal framework within which to understand the various hypotheses considered above about vague language. The hypotheses considered here can all take our language to have a unique, 'intended' model. (That is, nothing in their treatment of vagueness prohibits such a hypothesis. This is unlike, say, [19]'s 'plurivaluationism', which crucially rejects this hypothesis.) Call this intended model $M_@ = \langle D_@, C_{1_@}, C_{2_@}, I_@ \rangle$.

A predicate P in our language has inconstant character iff there are $c, d \in C_{1_@}$ such that $I_@(P)(c) \neq I_@(P)(d)$. A predicate P has inconstant content in a context of use $c \in C_{1_@}$ iff there are $e, f \in C_{2_@}$ such that $I_@(P)(c)(e) \neq I_@(P)(c)(f)$. A predicate P has an inconsistent extension in a total parameter $t \in T_{M_@}$ iff $I_{@_I}(P)(t) \cap I_{@_O}(P)(t) \neq \emptyset$. And a predicate P has an incomplete extension in a total parameter $t \in T_{M_@}$ iff $I_{@_I}(P)(t) \cup I_{@_O}(P)(t) \neq D_@$.

Since features of our language are reflected in features of the intended model, we can view hypotheses about our language as hypotheses about the intended model. For example, if a theorist takes our language to be fully consistent, she will think that the intended model never assigns an inconsistent extension to any predicate, in any total parameter.

Call a model *consistent* iff it never assigns an inconsistent extension to any predicate in any total parameter, and *inconsistent* otherwise. Similarly, call a model *complete* iff it never assigns an incomplete extension to any predicate in any total parameter, and *incomplete* otherwise. (That is, consistency or completeness of a model requires absolute overall consistency or completeness of its extensions; a single inconsistent or incomplete extension results in an inconsistent or incomplete model.) Finally, call a model *classical* iff it is both consistent and complete.

So far, this model theory serves merely to systematize and clarify the issues at hand. But in §4, it will be used to show that inconsistency and inconstancy are more intimately related than one might at first suspect. First, though, let's get clearer on the contrast between them, by looking at their distinct explanations of some recent empirical work.

3 Experimental results

In this section, I briefly present data from two studies of speakers' responses to vague sentences. The studies are reported more fully in [18] and [1] respectively.

In [18], I report and discuss the results of an experiment conducted at the University of North Carolina at Chapel Hill. In this experiment, participants were shown several pairs of shapes. Each consisted of a circle and a square at some distance from each other. The distances ranged from quite far (as far as could be displayed on the projectors used) to quite close (touching). Each participant was randomly assigned to one of four groups, and a different sentence was assigned to each group. Participants were asked to indicate their level of agreement or disagreement with their assigned sentence as applied to each pair in turn, by choosing a number from 1 to 7, where 1 was labeled 'Disagree' and 7 labeled 'Agree'. The sentences were:

- The circle is near the square and it isn't near the square.

- The circle both is and isn't near the square.

- The circle neither is near the square nor isn't near the square.

- The circle neither is nor isn't near the square.

A majority of participants (76/149) gave responses that fit a hump pattern: the maximum level of agreement occurred for some pair(s) at intermediate distance, with agreement decreasing towards clear cases of 'near' or clear countercases of 'near'. Indeed, the maximum responses were significantly higher than the responses to the extreme cases.[10] This result held across sentences; there was no significant difference among sentence types in the frequency of responses fitting the hump pattern,[11] or in level of maximum response.[12]

---

[10]Maximum responses: mean 5.3, standard deviation 1.9. Extreme cases: mean 2.4, standard deviation 1.7. $t = 19.4$, dof = 148, $p < .001$. Restricted to responses that fit the hump pattern, the results are even more extreme: Maximum responses: mean 5.3, standard deviation 1.4; extreme cases: mean 1.2, standard deviation .5; $t = 25.4$, dof = 75, $p < .001$. The crucial number here is p; it gives the probability of seeing a difference this extreme in the data if there were really no underlying difference. A probability less than .001 is very small—if there were no underlying difference, the observed data would be extremely unlikely.

[11]$\chi^2(3, N = 149) = 4.3, p = .23$.

[12]$F(1, 148) = .62, p = .6$; restricted to hump responses, $F(1, 75) = 1.41, p = .25$.

Moreover, participants did not just tend to agree *more* with these sentences in the middle cases; they tended to agree *simpliciter*. Although different participants gave their maximum responses to different pairs, the mean of these maxima was significantly above the middle response of 4.[13]

In [1], the authors report and discuss a similar experiment. In this experiment, participants were shown a picture of five men of varying heights, from quite tall to quite short, and asked to judge four sentences about each man, for a total of twenty judgments; questions were randomly ordered. For man number n, participants judged the sentences:

- #n is tall

- #n is not tall

- #n is tall and not tall

- #n is neither tall nor not tall

Unlike the previous study, in this study participants were asked not for a degree of agreement, but for a simple categorical judgment. The possible responses for each sentence were: 'True', 'False', and 'Can't tell'.

Again, participants tended to agree more with the 'both' and 'neither' sentences for men of middling height.[14] Because of the way Alxatib & Pelletier report their data, it is impossible to tell how many participants agree with 'both' or 'neither' sentences for some man or other in the middle ground. The best we can do is to tell how many participants agreed for the man in the exact center. This is a less informative measure, since some participants may not have taken the exact center man to be the best borderline case. We see that participants exhibit no clear preference about either the 'both' or the 'neither' sentence, as applied to the exact center man.[15] However, even this lack of clear preference is a phenomenon to be explained. On many theories of language, there is simply no room for these sentences *ever* to be true.

How can we explain these patterns of judgments? There are a large number of available options, each of which makes its own predictions about what would happen in further experiments. The way in which I'll proceed is to consider the options we began with—inconstant character, inconstant content, and inconsistent extensions— explore how they would explain the existing results, and draw out such predictions. I'll argue that inconstant-character explanations have trouble explaining the results in [18], but that inconstant-content and inconsistent-extension explanations can do better. Of course, there are many more possible explanations of the above data than just these three. Here, I take a narrow focus. (For discussion of a number of other options, see [18].)

---

[13] $t = 8.15$, dof = 148, $p < .001$; restricted to hump responses, $t = 8.15$, dof = 75, $p < .001$.

[14] For 'both' sentences: 44.7% of participants agreed for the man of median height, as opposed to 14.5% for the shortest and 5.3% for the tallest. For 'neither': 53.9% agreed for the man of median height, as opposed to 27.6% for the shortest and 6.6% for the tallest.

[15] From 76 participants, Alxatib & Pelletier report 34 'True' responses and 31 'False' responses to the 'both' sentence. Measured by a sign test, $p = .80$; the data show no significant preference. For the 'neither' sentence, they report 41 'True' responses and 32 'False'. Here, $p = .35$; still no significant preference.

3.1 Inconstancy explanations

The two varieties of inconstancy explanation have much in common; I'll use our notion of total parameter to ignore the differences between them until §3.2. Consider familiar cases of inconstancy: indexicals like 'I' and 'today'. In different total parameters, these take on different extensions. This can happen even within a single sentence; e.g., the following sentence does not have to be contradictory: 'Jim's birthday is today, but it's not today'. After all, midnight may have passed while the sentence was being uttered. The two occurrences of 'today' can pick out different days because they *occur* at different times. The total parameter changes in between the occurrences, and it changes in a way that matters for the extension assigned to 'today'. The same can happen for 'I'. Here, what matters about the total parameter is who is speaking. Consider a sentence begun by one person and finished by another: 'I'm sleepy today, but I'm not'. Again, the sentence need not be contradictory, so long as total parameter shifts during its utterance in an appropriate way. (It's important that the two tokens of 'I' be uttered by different people.)

A theorist who takes vagueness to consist in inconstancy thus has a *prima facie* explanation for the results of the above experiments. According to this explanation, participants who agreed with the claim that a certain man was both tall and not tall, or that a certain pair of shapes was both near and not near, were not actually agreeing to a contradiction, but simply saying that the man is tall relative to one total parameter, but not relative to another. Since we know (from examples like those above) that total-context changes within the utterance of a sentence can affect the extensions determined by the sentence's predicates, this would explain why participants might agree to the sentences in question. Similarly, when participants agreed with the claim that a certain man was neither tall nor not tall, or that a certain pair of shapes was neither near nor not near, total-context shifts within the utterance could explain their response.

Of course, this is not in itself a complete explanation. We need to know more. In particular, we need to know why it is that total parameter shifts in just the right way to secure such agreement, especially since it must shift in different ways for different sentences. That is, for participants to agree to 'both', they must first take the man to be tall and then not tall, while to agree to 'neither', they must first take the man to be not tall and then tall. We also need some story about what the relevant aspect of total parameter is. What is it that changes when total parameter changes? Finally, we would need to know why it is that total parameter only shifts so as to allow such agreement in borderline cases, but not in clear cases.

Here's part of a potential explanation: suppose there is a range of extensions a vague predicate can determine, and some extensions that are ruled out. For example, perhaps 'tall' can determine an extension that draws the line (for adult males, say) at 180 cm, or an extension that draws the line at 181 cm, but cannot determine an extension that draws the line at 210 cm. Someone 210 cm tall, then, will count as tall no matter which extension the character determines, but someone 181 cm tall will be in some extensions and out of others. This is plausible enough, and is broadly in line with much thinking, contextualist and otherwise, about vagueness. Then we could explain why agreement to 'both' and 'neither' sentences doesn't occur as much in extreme cases; in clear cases and clear countercases, the various possible extensions are all agreed.

This would tell us why participants don't agree to 'both' and 'neither' sentences in clear cases, but it wouldn't yet tell us why they *do* agree in borderline cases, just why they *could*. Here as well, it's worth some care. One plausible thought is that participants will agree with sentences proposed to them as much as possible. That is, we might suppose that they have a bias towards 'agree' and 'true' responses. This would allow us to predict agreement from the possibility of agreement. But it does not seem to be a thought that can apply in full generality to the above results. Alxatib & Pelletier, recall, also asked their subjects about atomic sentences: 'Man *n* is tall' and 'Man *n* is not tall'. Here, though, they found that participants tended *not* to call the sentences true when man *n* was a borderline case. This casts doubt on the thought that participants simply want to agree as much as possible. If there is indeed an extension available that allows participants to call the sentence true (as there must be in borderline cases, on an inconstancy explanation), then a bias toward agreement would predict agreement with atomic sentences in borderline cases. But this is not what is observed. But for our purposes here, let's suppose that an explanation for these results in terms of inconstancy can be found. We've got other fish to fry.

3.2   Character, content, and occurrences

So much for the similarities. The inconstant-character theorist faces a particular problem that her inconstant-content relatives don't seem to. The problem is this: our other examples of inconstant character—indexicals and demonstratives—exhibit a particular feature that vague predicates lack. Although an inconstant character can determine two different contexts within a single sentence (as we've seen), it can only do this when the word at issue occurs *twice*.

Return to our earlier examples. Although 'Jim's birthday is today, but it's not today' can be about two different days if its utterance is timed right, 'Jim's birthday is today, but it's not' is about only *one* day, no matter how its utterance is timed. Although 'I'm sleepy, but I'm not sleepy' can be about two different people, if uttered by them in the appropriate way, 'I'm sleepy and not sleepy' is about only *one* person, no matter how it is uttered. Demonstratives work the same way. Although 'Mary's buying that, unless Joan buys that' can be about two different things (picked out by the different occurrences of 'that', perhaps along with two overt demonstrations), 'Mary's buying that, unless Joan does' can only be about *one* thing, no matter how many overt demonstrations accompany it. The pattern is quite general (see [22]).

An inconstant-character explanation of the vagueness data should thus predict a striking difference between 'The circle is near the square and it isn't near the square' and 'The circle both is and isn't near the square', as well as between 'The circle neither is near the square nor isn't near the square' and 'The circle neither is nor isn't near the square'. After all, the first sentence in each pair has two occurrences of 'near'; this allows for context shifts to matter, resulting in two distinct contents within each sentence. But the second sentence in each pair should not allow for this, since there is only one occurrence of 'near', and as we've seen, we can only get one content out of one occurrence of an inconstant character, no matter how context does or does not shift. But this prediction is not borne out. In fact, there is no significant difference in maximum response for the sentences within either pair.[16] Neither is there a significant difference in maximum response overall between the two-'near' sentences and the one-'near' sentences.[17] An inconstant-character explanation should not predict this, and could account for it only at the cost of supposing that although vague predicates have inconstant characters, they do not behave in their inconstancy like other expressions with inconstant character. That would be ad hoc, to say the least.

Inconstant-content explanations do better when it comes to this fact. The reason is this: it may well be, for all we know, that a single occurrence can determine a single content that is then evaluated with respect to two distinct circumstances of evaluation. We do not, as we did for inconstant characters, have evidence to the contrary. Thus, all inconstant-content theorists need suppose is that this is indeed so, and I see no reason to begrudge them this assumption. Thus, inconstant-content theorists have an available explanation for the above data.

3.3 Inconsistent extensions

Of course, inconsistent-extension explanations also have an available explanation for the data, and a quite different one. On such an account, there is no need for variation at all. The vague predicates, relative to a particular total parameter, determine an inconsistent extension, and the borderline cases are simply both in that extension and out of it. When participants agree to 'both' sentences, they are simply reporting this fact. It might at first seem that participants' agreement to 'neither' sentences tells against this hypothesis, but that's not so. If something is both P and not P, then it is indeed neither P (since it's not P) nor not P (since it's not not P).[18] Thus, an inconsistent-extension approach predicts the observed responses to the 'both' sentences and the 'neither' sentences.[19]

So inconsistency views can explain the observed data, as can inconstancy views. Where one sees a single inconsistent extension, the other sees distinct consistent extensions. As far as the data collected in [18] and [1] shows, either of these explanations can work. Is there any data that could tell between them?

4 An equivalence

This section will suggest that there is not, at least given our current level of abstraction. As we've seen, inconstancy explanations for the above data crucially invoke *multiple* total parameters to do their work. If we suppose that each sentence is judged in a single total parameter, inconstancy explanations lose all grip on the data. This suggests that our earlier model-theoretic notion of satisfaction is too restrictive to understand the incon-

---

[16]For conjunction: $t = .35$, dof = 82, $p = .73$; for disjunction, $t = 1.2$, dof = 63, $p = .24$.

[17]$t = .55$, dof = 147, $p = .59$.

[18]This relies on one De Morgan law and a double-negation inference; both are valid in the logic—LP—recommended by the inconsistent-extension authors cited above, as well as the logic—FDE—of the (possibly-incomplete) models in §2.

[19]And indeed to the atomics, if the pragmatic hypothesis of [12, p. 291] is taken as part of an inconsistent-extension view. Priest proposes that a Gricean implicature can be generated in some contexts by the assertion of p: if the speaker believed both p and $\neg p$, an assertion of either one would be misleadingly incomplete, so the hearer is entitled to conclude that the speaker does not believe both. This could explain, if participants believe that borderline cases are both P and not P, why they might be reluctant to agree to either atomic claim in isolation.

stancy theorist's predictions; it needs to be liberalized. We need the idea of a sentence being satisfied by a model together with a *set* of total parameters.

DEFINITION 3 *For a model* $M = \langle D, C_1, C_2, I \rangle$ *and a set* $\{t_i\} \subseteq T_M$ *of total parameters:*

- $M, \{t_i\} \vDash Pa$ *iff* $I(a) \in I_I(P)(t)$, *for some* $t \in \{t_i\}$

- $M, \{t_i\} \vDash \neg Pa$ *iff* $I(a) \in I_O(P)(t)$, *for some* $t \in \{t_i\}$

- $M, \{t_i\} \vDash A \wedge B$ *iff* $M, \{t_i\} \vDash A$ *and* $M, \{t_i\} \vDash B$

- $M, \{t_i\} \vDash \neg(A \wedge B)$ *iff* $M, \{t_i\} \vDash \neg A$ *or* $M, \{t\} \vDash \neg B$

- $M, \{t_i\} \vDash \forall x A$ *iff every x-variant* M' *of M is such that* $M', \{t_i\} \vDash A$

- $M, \{t_i\} \vDash \neg \forall x A$ *iff some x-variant* M' *of M is such that* $M', \{t_i\} \vDash \neg A$

What is it for a sentence to be satisfied by a *set* of total parameters? It is for there to be some way of deploying these total parameters in the course of the sentence's interpretation that results in the sentence being satisfied.

FACT 4 *From Definition 3 we can prove the following by induction on formula construction:*[20]

- *This definition subsumes Definition 2 as a special case:* $M, t \vDash \phi$ *iff* $M, \{t\} \vDash \phi$, *for any* M, t, ϕ, *as can be shown by induction on* ϕ*'s construction.*

- *Where* $\{t_j\} \subseteq \{t_i\}$, $\{\phi : M, \{t_j\} \vDash \phi\} \subseteq \{\phi : M, \{t_i\} \vDash \phi\}$.

When experimental participants agree to 'The circle both is and isn't near the square', the inconstancy theorist takes them to do so only relative to a *set* of total parameters. In (at least) one total parameter in the set, the circle is in the (consistent) extension of 'near the square', and in (at least) one other total parameter in the set, the circle is out of the (different, still consistent) extension of 'near the square'. Since a conjunction, relative to a set of total parameters, may have its conjuncts evaluated in different total parameters, the overall sentence can be true.

(An inconstancy theorist need not, of course, accept this claim about conjunction. She might think that conjunctions are only ever evaluated in a single total parameter. Then she would reject Definition 3; but she would at the same time lose any explanation for the observed results. It is crucial to the inconstancy theorist's explanation that the conjunctions evaluated as true by the participants are evaluated as true only because their conjuncts are evaluated in different total parameters.)

Relative to a set of total parameters, then, some sentences that look like contradictions can be true, *even in a classical model*. They only 'look like contradictions'; since the model is fully classical, nothing inconsistent is in play here.

It's fair to ask at this point: just how much of the behavior of inconsistent models can be simulated by inconstant models? Or vice versa: how much of the behavior of

---

[20]Appropriate restrictions should be made throughout: M is a model, $\{t_i\} \subseteq T_M$, where M is the model in question, &c.

inconstant models can be simulated by inconsistent models? The short answer to both questions: *all of it.*[21]

FACT 5 *For any model $M = \langle D, C_1, C_2, I \rangle$, there is a consistent model $M' = \langle D', C_1', C_2', I' \rangle$ such that: for any total parameter $t \in T_M$ there is a set $\{t_i\} \subseteq T_{M'}$ of total parameters such that: for all sentences ϕ, $M, t \vDash \phi$ iff $M', \{t_i\} \vDash \phi$. (Where M is complete, there is a classical M' that fits the bill.)*

Proof Here's one such M':[22]

- $D' = D$

- $C_1' = C_1$

- $C_2' = \{\langle c, i \rangle : c \in C_2 \text{ and } i \in \{0, 1\}\}$

- $I'(a) = I(a)$, for singular terms a

- Where $t = \langle c_1, \langle c_2, 0 \rangle \rangle$, $I'(P)(t) = \langle \{d \in D' : d \in (I_I(P)(c_1)(c_2) - I_O(P)(c_1)(c_2))\},$
  $\{d \in D' : d \in I_O(P)(c_1)(c_2)\} \rangle$

- Where $t = \langle c_1, \langle c_2, 1 \rangle \rangle$, $I'(P)(t) = \langle \{d \in D' : d \in I_I(P)(c_1)(c_2)\},$
  $\{d \in D' : d \in (I_O(P)(c_1)(c_2) - I_I(P)(c_1)(c_2))\} \rangle$

The basic idea is simple, although it takes a few brackets to spell out: Any extension is split into two consistent 'shadow extensions'. One shadow (tagged with a 0 above) is such that something's out of it iff it's out of the original extension, and in it iff it's in the original extension *and not also* out of the original extension. The other shadow (tagged with a 1) is such that something's in it iff it's in the original extension, and out of it iff it's out of the original extension *and not also* in the original extension. If the original extension is consistent, its shadows are identical to each other, and to the original extension. The machinery only matters where the original extension is inconsistent.

Note that M' is consistent. Any total parameter t is of the form $\langle c_1, \langle c_2, i \rangle \rangle$, where $i \in \{0, 1\}$. Where $i = 0$, something is in $I'(P)(t)$ iff it's in $I_I(P)(c_1)(c_2)$ *and not also* in $I_O(P)(c_1)(c_2)$. Something is out of $I'(P)(t)$ iff it's in $I_O(P)(c_1)(c_2)$. Nothing can meet both these conditions; it'd have to be both in and out of $I_O(P)(c_1)(c_2)$, and I've stipulated that our metalanguage is fully classical; that can't happen. Similar reasoning shows that where $i = 1$, $I'(P)(t)$ must be consistent as well.

What's more, where $t = \langle c_1, \langle c_2, i \rangle \rangle$, something is either in or out of $I'(P)(t)$ iff it's either in $I_I(P)(c_1)(c_2)$ or in $I_O(P)(c_1)(c_2)$. Since $D = D'$, it quickly follows that M' is complete iff M is. Since M' is consistent, we know M' is classical iff M is complete.

The last part of the proof speaks to the equivalence between the two models, and works by induction on the construction of ϕ. For any total parameter $t = \langle c_1, c_2 \rangle \in T_M$, let $t_i = \langle c_1, \langle c_2, i \rangle \rangle$, where $i \in \{0, 1\}$; so $\{t_i\} = \{\langle c_1, \langle c_2, i \rangle \rangle : i \in \{0, 1\}\}$. Obviously $\{t_i\} \subseteq T_{M'}$. Base cases:

---

[21] The following facts owe much to remarks in [11].

[22] Here, I use inconstant content to mimic inconsistent extension. Inconstant character, or some mix between the two, would work equally well formally, but inconstant content is more philosophically satisfying for the task at hand, for reasons given in §3.2.

$M,t \vDash Pa$ iff $M', \{t_i\} \vDash Pa$: $M,t \vDash Pa$ iff $I(a) \in I_I(P)(t)$ iff $I'(a) \in I'_I(P)(t_1)$ iff
$$M', \{t_i\} \vDash Pa.$$

(For the last step RTL direction: note that $M', \{t_i\} \vDash Pa$ iff $M', t_i \vDash Pa$ for some $t_i \in \{t_i\}$. But we know there are only two such t_i: t_1 and t_0. Reflection on the definition of I' reveals that $I'_I(P)(t_0) \subseteq I'_I(P)(t_1)$; so if $M', t_0 \vDash Pa$, then $M', t_1 \vDash Pa$; so if $M', \{t_i\} \vDash Pa$, then $M', t_1 \vDash Pa$, and so $I'(a) \in I'_I(P)(t_1)$.)

$M,t \vDash \neg Pa$ iff $M', \{t_i\} \vDash \neg Pa$: $M,t \vDash Pa$ iff $I(a) \in I_O(P)(t)$ iff $I'(a) \in I'_O(P)(t_0)$ iff
$$M', \{t_i\} \vDash \neg Pa.$$

(The last step RTL direction is justified in the same way as the previous parenthetical indicates, mutatis mutandis.)

The inductive cases follow immediately from Definitions 2 and 3, given the inductive hypothesis.   □

FACT 6 *For any consistent model M, there is a model M' such that: for any set of total parameters $\{t_i\} \subseteq T_M$, there is a total parameter $t \in T_{M'}$ such that: for all sentences ϕ, $M, \{t_i\} \vDash \phi$ iff $M', t \vDash \phi$. (Where M is classical, there is a complete M' that fits the bill.)*

Proof Here's one such M':

- $D' = D$

- It doesn't matter what C'_1 is (so long as it's nonempty)

- $C'_2 = \wp(T_M)$

- $I'(a) = I(a)$, for singular terms a

- $I'(P)(c_1)(c_2) = \langle \{d \in D : d \in I_I(P)(t)$ for some $t \in c_2\}$,
$\{d \in D : d \in I_O(P)(t)$ for some $t \in c_2\}\rangle$

Here, we take each set of total parameters in M to a single circumstance of evaluation in M'. Contexts of utterance in M' simply don't matter; we let circumstances of evaluation do all the work. (Note that c_1 doesn't appear on the right hand of the '=' in the definition of $I'(P)(c_1)(c_2)$.)[23] M assigns to P a set E of extensions in a set of total parameters. That set of total parameters determines a single circumstance of evaluation in M', and in M' P gets as its extension, in any total parameter involving this circumstance of evaluation, a blurring of all the extensions in E. Something is in the blurred extension iff it's in any member of E, and out of the blurred extension iff it's out of any member of E. (In fact, this technique doesn't rely on M being consistent; it works just as well for arbitrary M. We can show that M' is complete iff M is, and that the stated equivalence holds.)

The equivalence between M and M' is shown as in the proof of Fact 5, by induction on formula construction. Let t be some total parameter in M' whose second member is $\{t_i\}$. Then $M, \{t_i\} \vDash \phi$ iff $M', t \vDash \phi$. Base cases:

$M, \{t_i\} \vDash Pa$ iff $M', t \vDash Pa$: $M', t \vDash Pa$ iff $I'(a) \in I'_I(P)(t)$ iff $I(a) \in I_I(P)(t')$ for some $t' \in \{t_i\}$ iff $M, \{t_i\} \vDash Pa$.

---

[23] As before, this is formally arbitrary. Here, it's philosophically arbitrary as well. But it does the job.

$M, \{t_i\} \vDash \neg Pa$ iff $M', t \vDash \neg Pa$: $M', t \vDash \neg Pa$ iff $I'(a) \in I'_O(P)(t)$ iff $I(a) \in I_O(P)(t')$ for some $t' \in \{t_i\}$ iff $M, \{t_i\} \vDash \neg Pa$.

As before, the remainder of the induction follows from Definitions 2 and 3. □

Facts 5 and 6 show us that inconstancy can stand in for inconsistency, and vice versa. Whenever an inconsistent-extension theorist supposes that an assertion of a seemingly-contradictory sentence happens in a single total parameter, an inconstancy theorist can claim that the assertion happens across multiple contexts. Fact 5 shows that this strategy will always work. Similarly, when an inconstancy theorist supposes that an assertion happens across multiple contexts, an inconsistency theorist can claim that the assertion happens within a single context. Fact 6 shows that *this* strategy will always work.

For all that, though, inconstancy and inconsistency are quite different hypotheses. In the next section, I consider some ways we might try to tell between them, despite the equivalence demonstrated here.

5 How to discriminate

We've been supposing throughout this paper that inconstancy and inconsistency are empirical hypotheses. Typically, empirical hypotheses are judged by their consequences, but we've just seen that differences in predictions will be hard to come by in this case. It will not be impossible, though; in §5.2 I'll discuss ways to find empirical differences between inconstancy theories and inconsistency theories.

But first, it might be thought that there's an easier way to settle the issue. After all, if we require consistency of our theories, then an inconsistent-extension approach is simply a non-starter; so even if it were predictively equivalent to an inconstancy theory, we ought to prefer the inconstancy theory, simply because it is not inconsistent.

5.1 Consistency as a theoretical requirement

To stop there would be to flatly beg the question against certain inconsistent-extension views, of course. Some might decide, with [11], that begging the question is simply the thing to do when faced with inconsistency. That would be a mistake in this case; it would offer us no reason to accept an inconstancy view over an inconsistency view. Rather, it would be to concede that no such reason is offerable.

Of course, rather than simply begging the question, one might attempt to offer such reason. Maybe there are compelling arguments against inconsistent theories in general, or inconsistent theories as they apply to vague language. These are more general issues than there is room to consider here. I do not believe, however, that any such arguments are convincing. For a thorough consideration of the issue, see [12] (for the general case) or [8] (for the application to vagueness).

But even if we suppose that consistency is absolutely required of any theory we offer, this still does not rule out inconsistent-extension theories per se. The inconsistent-extension theorist can avoid contradicting herself, if she so chooses. She cannot avoid supposing that language users contradict themselves when it comes to borderline cases of vague predicates. But so long as she takes them to be *mistaken*, she can stay totally consistent. There is room here for an error theory of a certain type. In its structure, it would be reminiscent of theories offered in [21] and [4]. They take speakers to be led into error with vague predicates by their linguistic competence. As pointed out in [18], Sorensen and Eklund do not predict that speakers believe contradictions about borderline cases; they predict very different errors. But someone could offer a theory that takes speakers to assign inconsistent extensions to their vague predicates *in error*.

As far as I know, nobody has offered such a theory. Certainly the inconsistent-extension theories cited above—those in [25], [14], and [17]—*are* inconsistent. *They* would be ruled out by an absolute consistency constraint on theories. But theories much like these can remain consistent while explaining the present data in the same way. So consistency as a theoretical virtue isn't going to help us decide between inconstancy and inconsistency theories.

5.2   Different predictions

The real key to the decision is going to have to come from empirical predictions. In the light of Facts 5 and 6, these are going to be tricky to come by, but it's not impossible. There is a way to get inconstancy theories to make different predictions from inconsistency theories: develop rich empirical theories of *total parameter*. Here, I'll give a toy example that shows how this could be done, then point out that my earlier argument against inconstant-character theories fits this mold, and finally turn to an empirical theory of context offered in [15].

First, a silly example. Suppose we all agree (for whatever reason) that the only way for total parameter to change is for the speaker to be in a different room. If the speaker is in the same room in two total parameters, then they are in fact the same total parameter. Now suppose that speakers tend to agree with 'Man x is both tall and not tall' when man x is a borderline case, and that they do so *without moving from one room to another*. Given our supposition, speakers cannot be using two different total parameters in evaluating the sentence; there is only one context involved. Thus, the inconstancy theorist would have no available explanation for the (supposed) data, while the inconsistency theorist would.

It's easy to see how this gets around Fact 5: the proof of Fact 5 relied on playing fast and loose with contexts. If we have some understanding of what a context is and (more importantly) when it must be constant, the construction in the proof of Fact 5 can't get off the ground. This silly example is enough to break the proof.

In fact, we've already seen a less silly example of this same phenomenon: I argued in §3.2 than an inconstant-character theory could not explain the experimental data, since we should take a single occurrence of a vague predicate to be evaluated in at most one context of use, and that's where an inconstant-character theory has to allow for variation to explain the data. Again, this is an example of relating an empirical phenomenon (one occurrence of a vague predicate) to a constraint on total parameters (no shifting the context-of-use part). As we saw, this allows us to get some empirical bite on our theories.

Finally, I turn to an example in the literature of a possible empirical constraint on total-context-shifting. In [15], two types of context are distinguished: *internal* and *external*. External context involves the full setting in which a judgment takes place: its location and time, along with other factors relevant for the judgment in question. For example, if the judgment in question is a color-judgment, lighting and background conditions are vitally important. Internal context, on the other hand, is a matter of the judger's psychology. Raffman gives an example of a subject being marched from red to orange along a sorites sequence, and imagines homunculi battling in the judger's head: one for a judgment of red, one for a judgment of orange. (Nothing hangs on the homunculus-talk being taken literally.) At first, she says, the red homunculus is the clear winner, but as the colors being judged move towards orange, the competition gets closer and closer. Eventually, the orange homunculus wins the day. This shift—from the red homunculus dominating to the orange homunculus dominating—is a shift in internal context. This shift will affect the judger's judgments, and since (according to Raffman) vague predicates are judgment-dependent, the effect on judgments will amount to an effect on the extensions of 'red' and 'orange'.

We don't need to worry about which aspects of Raffman's contexts (internal or external) correspond to which aspects of our total parameter (context of use or circumstance of evaluation). We can simply suppose that internal and external context together are enough for total parameter.

If this were all we had, it would still not be enough to derive any experimental predictions. We still need to know more about the conditions under which this total parameter changes, and the effects of such a change. Raffman provides us with just what we're after. She predicts that internal context shifts are *sticky*. That is, she thinks it is easier for the currently dominant homunculus to stay on top than it is for another homunculus to depose it. Now empirical predictions are forthcoming:

> Once [an automatic] car has shifted to a new gear, it will continue to use that gear as long as possible, even if it slows to a speed previously handled by a lower gear. For example, if the car has shifted from second to third gear at 30 mph, it will remain in third even if it slows to 25 mph, a speed previously handled by second. (Shifting gears is hard work.) Analogously, once the competent speaker has shifted from 'red' to 'orange', if asked to retrace his steps down the series he will now call some patches 'orange' that he formerly called 'red'. The "winning" homunculus always strives to maintain her control as long as she can [15, p. 179].

If total parameters are sticky in this way, it's hard to see how to use a shift in total parameter to explain the data in §3. The inconstancy explanation crucially turned on rapidly varying total parameters; supposing stickiness is in play blocks that rapid variation.

Of course, a different empirical theory of context could well yield a different result. This in no way impugns the prospects of an inconstancy theory that can account for the data. But it makes a point clearer: inconstancy theories differ from inconsistency theories only insofar as they differ from each other. There is always an inconstancy theory to match any inconsistency theory, and vice versa; but the matching theories will differ about how total parameter works. If we have good reason to suppose that total parameter is constrained in some way or other, we can get at real differences between inconstancy and inconsistency. If we do not, we cannot.

6 Conclusion

In this paper, I've argued that inconstancy and inconsistency are closer relatives than one might think at first glance. To show this, I've pointed out experimental data that they both seem well-suited to explain, and proved a formal result showing that either phenomenon can simulate the other. But the simulation, as we've just seen, can happen only if we have no constraints on the notion of context. So the lesson here is for inconstancy theorists and inconsistency theorists alike: *get clear on what context is*. The difference between inconstancy and inconsistency just doesn't matter otherwise.

BIBLIOGRAPHY

[1] Sam Alxatib and Jeff Pelletier: The psychology of vagueness: borderline cases and contradictions. *Mind and Language* 26 (2011), 287–326.

[2] Jc Beall and Bas van Fraassen: *Possibilities and Paradox: An introduction to modal and many-valued logic*. Oxford University Press, 2003.

[3] Pablo Cobreros, Paul Égré, David Ripley, and Robert van Rooij: Tolerant, classical, strict. *Journal of Philosophical Logic*. Forthcoming.

[4] Matti Eklund: What vagueness consists in. *Philosophical Studies* 125 (2005), 27–60.

[5] Delia Graff Fara: Shifting sands: An interest-relative theory of vagueness. *Philosophical Topics* 28 (2000), 45–81. (Originally published under the name "Delia Graff").

[6] Kit Fine: Vagueness, truth, and logic. *Synthese* 30 (1975), 265–300.

[7] Dominic Hyde: The prospects of a paraconsistent approach to vagueness. In R. Dietz, S. Moruzzi (eds.) *Cuts and Clouds: Vagueness, its Nature and its Logic*. Oxford University Press, 2010.

[8] Dominic Hyde and Mark Colyvan: Paraconsistent vagueness: Why not? *Australasian Journal of Logic* 6 (2008), 107–121.

[9] David Kaplan: Demonstratives. In J. Almog, J. Perry, H. Wettstein (eds.) *Themes from Kaplan*. Oxford University Press, 1989.

[10] Peter Lasersohn: Context dependence, disagreement, and predicates of personal taste. *Linguistics and Philosophy* 28 (2005), 643–686.

[11] David Lewis: Logic for equivocators. *Noûs* 16 (1982), 431–441.

[12] Graham Priest: *In Contradiction (2nd edition)*. Oxford University Press, 2006.

[13] Graham Priest: *An Introduction to Non-classical Logic: From if to is*. Cambridge University Press, 2008.

[14] Graham Priest: Inclosures, vagueness, and self-reference. *Notre Dame Journal of Formal Logic* 51 (2010), 69–84.

[15] Diana Raffman: Vagueness and context-relativity. *Philosophical Studies* 81 (1996), 175–192.

[16] Diana Raffman: How to understand contextualism about vagueness. *Analysis* 65 (2005), 244–248.

[17] David Ripley: Sorting out the sorites. In F. Berto, E. Mares, K. Tanaka (eds.) *Paraconsistency: Logic and Applications*. Springer, forthcoming.

[18] David Ripley: Contradictions at the borders. In R. Nouwen, R. van Rooij, U. Sauerland, H.-C. Schmitz (eds.) *Vagueness in Communication*. Springer, pp. 169–188, 2011.

[19] Nicholas J. J. Smith: *Vagueness and Degrees of Truth*. Oxford University Press, 2008.

[20] Scott Soames: Replies. *Philosophy and Phenomenological Research* 65 (2002), 429–452.

[21] Roy Sorensen: *Vagueness and Contradiction*. Oxford University Press, 2001.

[22] Jason Stanley: Context, interest-relativity, and the sorites. *Analysis* 63 (2003), 269–280.

[23] Michael Tye: Sorites paradoxes and the semantics of vagueness. *Philosophical Perspectives* 8 (1994), 189–206.

[24] Zach Weber: Transfinite numbers in paraconsistent set theory. *Review of Symbolic Logic* 3 (2010), 71–92.

[25] Zach Weber: A paraconsistent model of vagueness. *Mind* 119 (2011), 1025–1045.

David Ripley
Department of Philosophy
University of Melbourne
Old Quad, Parkville
Victoria 3010, Australia
Email: davewripley@gmail.com

Comments on *Inconstancy and Inconsistency* by David Ripley

NICHOLAS J.J. SMITH

Overview

In this very interesting paper, David Ripley brings together formal work on the semantics of vague predicates with experimental work on speakers' reactions to statements involving such predicates. Working within a broadly Kaplanian framework—in which predicate expressions have characters, which together with contexts determine contents, which together with circumstances determine extensions—Ripley distinguishes three positions on the semantics of vague predicates [§1–§2]:

1. A vague predicate P has an inconstant character: there are contexts c_1 and c_2 and circumstance i such that the extension of P relative to c_1 and i is not the same as the extension of P relative to c_2 and i.

2. A vague predicate P has an inconstant content: there is a context c and circumstances i_1 and i_2 such that the extension of P relative to c and i_1 is not the same as the extension of P relative to c and i_2.

3. A vague predicate P has an inconsistent extension: there is a context c, circumstance i and object x such that x is both in and out of the extension of P relative to c and i.

Ripley then describes two experiments—both reported in more detail elsewhere—in which speakers were asked to respond to statements involving vague predicates (the two-place predicate 'is near' and the one-place predicate 'is tall') [§3]. Finally, Ripley assesses the three semantic theories, in light of the experimental results.

The assessment phase proceeds as follows. Ripley first argues that inconstant character views cannot provide a good explanation of the experimental data, while inconstant content and inconsistent extension views can explain the data [§3.1–§3.3]. He then addresses the question whether there could be data which distinguish these two views: data which only one of the views can explain. Here, Ripley first shows that given an assertion of an apparent contradiction involving a vague predicate (e.g. 'The circle both is and isn't near the square'), an inconstant content explanation can always be constructed to match an inconsistent extension explanation of the assertion, and vice versa [§4]. Nevertheless, Ripley argues that inconstant content and inconsistent extension views are potentially empirically distinguishable. The former explain the data via the idea that the circumstance shifts; the latter do not. If we had an empirical theory which placed constraints on when circumstances can shift, we could in theory rule out inconstant content explanations by setting up experimental situations in which the circumstance is held fixed [§5].

In this commentary, I shall first make a general point about the current states of the theoretical and experimental literatures on vagueness, before making two more specific points about Ripley's assessment of inconstant content and inconsistent extension views.

General point

The general point is that, when reading Ripley's paper, one is struck by the discrepancy between the highly-developed theoretical literature and the fledgling empirical literature. In light of existing work in logic, model theory and formal semantics, Ripley is able, in just a few pages, to set up an elaborate and sophisticated set of distinctions amongst different theoretical positions on vagueness. When it comes to the empirical work, however, the body of evidence strikes one as extremely limited. This is not a complaint against Ripley: he is one of those actively working to increase the body of available evidence. The point is that we should keep in mind that the sophistication of the theories being discussed—their level of formal complexity and the subtlety of the distinctions between them—far outweighs the level of detail to be found in the data in light of which these theories are to be assessed. One is reminded of a circus elephant balancing on a tiny stool. The idea that the sum total of experience does not determine a unique choice of physical theory is a familiar one. The problem—in this case, of choosing a theory of vagueness—is that much worse when the data are so meagre.

The simple response to this observation would be to say that we should do more experiments and gather more data. However, there is an essential difficulty here. We are all competent in the use of vague predicates in their clear areas of application and in the areas in which they clearly do not apply. Different theories of vagueness, however, typically say different things about the borderline regions—not about the areas of clear application and clear non-application. In these areas, however, reliable data are very hard to obtain. This is because our standard practice is to *avoid* the borderline areas—and when, for one reason or another, we are forced to consider them, the typical response is to coin a new predicate: either a precise version of the original vague one, or a new vague predicate whose clear area of application coincides with the borderline region of the original vague predicate.

Consider, for example, the classification of humans into 'children', 'adolescents' and 'adults'. These three terms are vague. Suppose someone is forced to consider the borderline region between adolescents and adults—say, for purposes of deciding who can vote, or who can purchase alcohol. A standard response is to introduce a new predicate: 'legal adult'. This is a precisified version of the original vague predicate 'adult'. It has no borderline cases. Or suppose someone is compelled to consider the borderline region between children and adolescents—say, for purposes of finding new target markets. A standard response is to introduce a new predicate: 'tween'. This is a vague predicate, whose area of clear application is the borderline region between the clear areas of application of the vague predicates 'child' and 'adolescent'.

We are, then, uncomfortable in borderline regions: we try to avoid them, and when we cannot, we typically shift to new terms, which either have no borderline regions, or have borderlines somewhere else. Now think about experiments in which speakers are asked to respond to statements, made using vague predicates, about objects in the borderline regions of those predicates. Speakers have very little experience operating with these predicates *in these regions*—and when we ask people to do things that they generally try to avoid doing, and hence with which they have little experience, it is likely that the results will be noisy. That makes it hard to draw stable conclusions from the results of the experiments.

Consider the following analogy. Someone is doing some research in which they show subjects photographs of various persons and ask the subjects to rate the extent to which they find the persons physically attractive. Now suppose the experimenter puts into the mix photos of the subject's family members. We simply do not think of our family members in these terms—hence it is entirely unclear what conclusions the experimenter could legitimately draw from the results of the experiment, whatever the results were. Similarly in the case of vagueness. When you ask subjects to consider terms used in situations in which they generally go out of their way to avoid using such terms, it is not clear what conclusions you may draw from the results—whatever the results turn out to be.

We may put the point this way. The experiments are supposed to elicit responses from the subjects which flow from the subjects' *competence* in using vague predicates. The problem is that competence with vague predicates requires an ability to use them in their clear areas of application, and an ability to *identify* their borderline regions—but it does not require an ability to *use* vague predicates in their borderline regions. In fact, the latter is something we generally do not do. Thus, it is not clear that subjects' responses to the experiments flow from their pre-existing competence with vague predicates—for they are being asked to do something new: to perform a kind of task with which they have little or no experience.

In sum, not only is there a need for more data, there may well be a need for a different kind of data: data based not on asking subjects what they think of various statements made, using vague terms, about objects in the borderline regions of those terms—but rather arrived at in more sophisticated and subtle ways. What these ways might be is not something I am in a position to settle here: this is a large topic that requires extensive discussion. My aim here is not to preempt that discussion but to put it on the agenda.

Specific comments

I turn now to more specific comments. More particularly, there are a couple of places where Ripley seems to overstate the case in favour of inconsistent extension views as against inconstant content views.

First, Ripley writes:

> inconsistent-extension explanations also have an available explanation for the data... The vague predicates... determine an inconsistent extension, and the borderline cases are simply both in that extension and out of it. When participants agree to 'both' sentences, they are simply reporting this fact. It might at first seem that participants' agreement to 'neither' sentences tells against this hypothesis, but that's not so. If something is both P and not P, then it is indeed neither P (since it's not P) nor not P (since it's not not P). Thus, an inconsistent-extension approach predicts the observed responses to the 'both' sentences and the 'neither' sentences. [p. 51]

This is fine up until the last sentence: but I disagree that the inconsistent extension approach predicts the observed responses to 'neither' sentences. Consider an analogy. Suppose you have a theory according to which most people think that there are seven oceans. Your theory predicts that when you ask people whether the number of oceans is seven, they will say 'Yes'. It does not predict that when you ask people whether the number of oceans is $147/21$, they will say 'Yes'—even though $147/21 = 7$. For, to give the answer 'Yes' to the latter question, the subject has to work out that $147/21 = 7$. As not everyone can be expected to perform this calculation quickly and accurately, one's theory would predict fewer 'Yes' responses to the second question than to the first. Similarly in the present case. If x is P and not P, then by reasonably basic logical reasoning, it follows (as Ripley says) that x is neither P nor not P. However, not everyone can be expected to carry out such reasoning quickly and accurately, so it seems that the inconsistent extension view should predict less agreement to 'neither' sentences than to 'both' sentences. Moreover, it should predict an increasing discrepancy between the two kinds of sentences as the background cognitive load on subjects is increased.

Second, Ripley writes:

> If total parameters are sticky in this way, it's hard to see how to use a shift in total parameter to explain the data... The inconstancy explanation crucially turned on rapidly varying total parameters; supposing stickiness is in play blocks that rapid variation. [p. 57]

I do not see that stickiness threatens the inconstancy explanation. As Ripley says, the inconstancy explanation turns on rapid variation of total parameter—but stickiness says nothing about the possible rapidity of variation: stickiness means that changes are *asymmetrical*; it does not mean that they are *slow*. Consider Raffman's example, as quoted by Ripley [pp. 56–57]:

> Once [an automatic] car has shifted to a new gear, it will continue to use that gear as long as possible, even if it slows to a speed previously handled by a lower gear. For example, if the car has shifted from second to third gear at 30 mph, it will remain in third even if it slows to 25 mph, a speed previously handled by second. (Shifting gears is hard work.)

The point here is that the shift does not occur in the same place on the way up as on the way down: there is an asymmetry. The point is not that shifts cannot occur quickly. Imagine a control device within some piece of high-speed equipment. It might be asymmetrical—sticky—in precisely the same way as the automatic gear-change mechanism: and yet it might make thousands of shifts every second.

Nicholas J.J. Smith
Department of Philosophy
Main Quadrangle A14
The University of Sydney
NSW 2006 Australia
Email: njjsmith@sydney.edu.au

Reply to Nicholas Smith's Comments on *Inconstancy and Inconsistency*

DAVID RIPLEY

Smith's comments on "Inconstancy and Inconsistency" are clear and valuable, and there is a great deal in them that I agree with. For maximum entertainment value, of course, I'll focus on the bits I disagree with. First, I'll defend judgment-based experimental methodologies against Smith's worries. Then, I'll argue that the specific arguments I make in the main paper stand despite Smith's objections to them.

1 Reason for hope

Smith begins by pointing out the gulf between our philosophical and logical theories of vagueness on the one hand and the data we have on the other; and there is indeed a dearth of data (for now) about judgments of compound sentences, particularly the seemingly-contradictory compound sentences I've discussed, in borderline cases. For the most part, psychologists have been much more interested in other sorts of judgments, particularly simple judgments. Despite this lack of data, philosophical and logical work has proceeded at a brisk pace; we have a variety of frameworks that make a variety of predictions here. As a result, data collected here should have considerable theoretical payoff. Smith is right: we need more.

Smith seems to claim, though, that there is little research even on simple categorization judgments in borderline cases, and this is just not so. There is, in fact, a great deal of experimental research on just the phenomena Smith points to, mostly reported in the literature on the psychology of categorization. Examples range from the classic [McCloskey and Glucksberg, 1978] to the much more recent [Hampton, 2007]. Nor are the results just noise: there is often surprising and intricate texture to judgments in this middle ground. For an example of particularly interesting data, see [Hampton et al., 2011]; this paper reports experiments that seem to provide evidence against epistemicism precisely due to the texture of judgments in borderline cases.

Moreover, the obstacles Smith envisions to such research do not in fact create a great deal of difficulty; really, they are the very object of the research. There is no a priori reason to expect experiments in which participants are comfortable with the task they are asked to perform to produce more reliable data than experiments in which participants are uncomfortable. Further, if the data being sought is data about the form that discomfort takes, there is every reason in the world to expect the reverse. (To build on Smith's analogy, if we wanted to study how judgements of attractiveness interact with the incest taboo, we might well follow a methodology like the one he dismisses. Indeed, the experiments reported in [Fraley and Marks, 2010] are not so far off.)

But this is just our situation: data about clear cases of vague predicates are not theoretically important. Almost all going theories will agree on them. It's data about borderline cases that we need. Since the goal is to learn about borderline cases, diving in and asking participants about borderline cases is an important source of data. It cannot be dismissed as unreliable on the grounds of participants' discomfort; that discomfort is itself part of the phenomenon to be studied. This sort of methodology has resulted in considerable success when it comes to simple categorization judgments, and there is no reason to expect it to be less reliable when it comes to compound judgments.

Of course, other data is available too. We shouldn't restrict ourselves to methodology based on eliciting judgments; Smith is absolutely right that we should explore other options as well.[1] But I think he shouldn't give up on judgment-based methodology so hastily, in view of its history of successful applications.

2   Inconsistent theories and 'neither'

Smith argues that I am too quick to allow that inconsistent theories predict agreement to 'neither' sentences in borderline cases. He points out that we cannot expect participants to carry out logical reasoning quickly or accurately. *If* participants can arrive at the conclusion that something is neither P nor not P only by starting from the premise that it is both P and not P, we should not expect every participant who reaches the starting point to make it to the finish line. They may get lost along the way. As such, we should expect fewer positive responses to 'neither' sentences than to 'both' sentences. We should expect this all the more, he says, if participants are under cognitive load.

I agree with this as far as it goes—but notice the 'if'. I don't agree that an inconsistent-extension theorist is committed to the claim that participants can arrive at the 'neither' conclusion only via reasoning from a 'both' premise. Nor do I see a reason that an inconsistent-extension theorist should accept this principle. Rather, the 'neither' judgment can be reached compositionally, in the same way that a 'both' judgment can be reached. We merely need to suppose that, when asked to check whether something is neither A nor B, participants check whether it is A and whether is is B and then combine those checks in an appropriate way. This way need not involve 'and' at all. In symbols: there is no need to get to $\neg(A \vee \neg A)$ *from* $A \wedge \neg A$. Both can be reached from judgments of A and $\neg A$, which are then combined in the appropriate ways.

The reasoning from 'both' to 'neither' I make in the initial paper, and which Smith quotes, is reasoning intended to show *us* that the inconsistent theory in fact predicts 'neither' sentences to be true. It's meta-level reasoning, and not to be attributed to experimental participants. The point is quite general: a formal semantic theory ought to make predictions, and we, as theorists, must reason about it to see what predictions it makes. (Less-familiar theories, like inconsistent ones, call for quite careful reasoning here.) Whether those predictions are correct or not does not depend on whether speakers in fact conduct reasoning that parallels ours.

There is something in the area, though, that seems worth mentioning: it might well be easier to combine individual judgments with 'and' than it is to combine them with 'neither...nor'. That seems like a plausible hypothesis on its own, and data in [Geurts

---

[1] Corpuses!

and van der Slik, 2005] is at least friendly to the idea. If this is so, we might expect some differences between 'both' and 'neither' sentences, particularly under cognitive load. It's not clear to me, however, that we should expect *lower* agreement to 'neither' than to 'both'; it depends on the details of the differences between 'and' and 'neither'.

3   Stickiness

Finally, I think things are worse for the stickiness-based inconstancy hypothesis of [Raffman, 1996] than Smith supposes. While I agree with Smith that stickiness on its own involves no commitments to any particular speed, only to some asymmetry, Raffman's particular use of the stickiness hypothesis does involve a commitment to some particular speed. Smith includes only the first half of the quote I used from Raffman's paper, but the very next sentence is crucial: "Analogously, once the competent speaker has shifted from 'red' to 'orange', if asked to retrace his steps down the series he will now call some patches 'orange' that he formerly called 'red' [Raffman, 1996, p. 179]. That is, the stickiness, on Raffman's theory, ought to be sticky enough to influence participants' responses to multiple future stimuli. It's this that causes trouble for a switching-in-the-middle theory of judgments about single stimuli. I agree with Smith that it would be possible to develop a theory on which context shifts are sticky that still succeeds in explaining the observed responses. However, in allowing for context shifts rapid enough to do the job, it would give up the prediction Raffman makes (and for which she provides some evidence in [Raffman, 2012]).

Every one of these issues deserves more discussion than there is space to give it here. Many thanks are due to Smith for raising these issues, and to the editors of this volume for giving us an opportunity to discuss them.

BIBLIOGRAPHY

[Fraley and Marks, 2010] Fraley, R.C. and Marks, M.J. (2010). Westermarck, Freud, and the incest taboo: Does familial resemblance activate sexual attraction? *Personality and Social Psychology Bulletin*, 36(9): 1202–1212.

[Geurts and van der Slik, 2005] Geurts, B. and van der Slik, F. (2005). Monotonicity and processing load. *Journal of Semantics*, 22:97–117.

[Hampton, 2007] Hampton, J.A. (2007). Typicality, graded membership, and vagueness. *Cognitive Science*, 31:355–383.

[Hampton et al., 2011] Hampton, J.A., Aina, B., Andersson, J.M., Mirza, H.Z., and Parmar, S. (2011). The Rumsfeld effect: The unknown unknown. *Journal of Experimental Psychology: Learning, Memory, and Cognition*. To appear.

[McCloskey and Glucksberg, 1978] McCloskey, M.E. and Glucksberg, S. (1978). Natural categories: Well-defined or fuzzy sets? *Memory and Cognition*, 6(4):462–472.

[Raffman, 1996] Raffman, D. (1996). Vagueness and context-relativity. *Philosophical Studies*, 81:175–192.

[Raffman, 2012] Raffman, D. (2012). *Unruly Words: A Study of Vague Language*. Oxford University Press, Oxford. To appear.

Vagueness: A Mathematician's Perspective

THOMAS VETTERLEIN[1]

Overview

I comment on the question of how to deal appropriately with vague information by formal means. I am critical of attempts to endow vague concepts with semantics in analogy to crisp concepts that refer to a mathematical structure. I argue, to the contrary, that vagueness pertains to the variability of the models associated with a particular mode of perception; the crucial point from my perspective is that we may choose between structures of differing granularity.

I see the primary challenge as finding a solution to the problem of reasoning simultaneously at different levels of granularity—a problem to which a canonical solution is unlikely to exist. The idea of modelling vague concepts by fuzzy sets is defended, and additionally, two logical calculi of possible practical value are suggested.

1 Introduction

There are many different ways of interpreting vagueness in natural language—too many, it seems. There is little hope of overcoming the conceptual differences. Epistemicism, supervaluationism, contextualism, degree theory: each of these keywords refers to one or more of a variety of competing approaches to accounting for vagueness of expressions in natural language. Becoming familiar with even a single approach is a demanding task; a treatment of the topic may cover whole books. For the beginner, the diversity of the approaches and the sheer volume of material can easily be discouraging. Some efforts to systematise the field have recently been made; I refer to [18] for a compact and systematic presentation of presently important lines of research. A convergence to a generally accepted and easily comprehensible position cannot be observed.

A common goal of several approaches to vagueness is to find the correct way of arguing on the basis of vague concepts, ideally with the same preciseness and correctness with which we argue about crisp concepts in mathematical proofs. The question is posed: which propositions involving vague concepts are as undoubtedly correct as, say, the fact that for every natural number there is a number that is larger by one? The problem of an appropriate semantics is closely related. The question is raised: what semantics are as natural for vague concepts as natural numbers are for Peano arithmetic?

I doubt that developing a formalism to reason about vague concepts *correctly* is a reasonable goal. Our chances of finding a formalism for reasoning in the presence of vagueness are much better when our efforts focus on *adequacy* instead. Such for-

---

[1]The author acknowledges support of the Eurocores-LogICCC ESF project LoMoReVI. Furthermore, he would like to thank Ingrid G. Abfalter for her help improving the linguistic quality of this contribution.

malisms are already available. Several reasoning methods are of practical relevance and not subject to the requirement to be in any sense correct. For example, below I mention two logics that can serve specific purposes in the context of vagueness. The formalisms developed for practical purposes are flexible, undogmatic, subject to improvement, and thus not of the same type as the formalisms suggested within a particular approach to vagueness. Since a range of pragmatic, practical approaches exists, we have little reason not to accept the situation as it is and to pursue ideal theoretical solutions of questionable feasibility. The goal of correctness does not even make sense.

The paper is organized as follows. In order to explain my point of view, I begin by looking further into the context of the problem and discuss topics that might, at first sight, seem unrelated. Vagueness concerns particular fundamental issues in which, in my opinion, progress must be made to allow progress in the discussion about vagueness.

Section 2 centres around a common characteristic of discussions about the nature of statements containing vague concepts. Often, utterances about properties of objects are dealt with on the one hand, and the characterisation of what these objects are actually like is treated on the other hand. The way we characterise external objects in natural language utterances and the actual nature of these objects are often treated separately and as two different topics. It is assumed that we speak about something that exists anyway. I oppose this *realistic* point of view with a sharply contrasting one: a purely *perception-based* account of reality that is restricted to the more fundamental aspect of perception and that rejects the idea that objects can be described, at least in principle, in full detail and fully correctly without taking into account the process of their observation.

Section 3 addresses three current approaches to vagueness: epistemicism [19], supervaluationism [5], and contextualism [16]. I devote particular attention to the position each approach adopts regarding the two afore-mentioned contrasting ways of understanding reality. In Section 4, I make my critical stance against the realistic point of view explicit. I do not reject realism completely; my criticism refers to the vagueness debate. A critical reflection on the three considered approaches to vagueness follows in Section 5. The criticism is extensive, but it does not affect each approach in its entirety.

In Section 6, an alternative approach is developed. I argue as follows. From the perception-based standpoint, viewing reality as the totality of what is around us is part of our thinking model. Indeed, this totality need not be regarded as determined by forces beyond the human scope. When using familiar mathematical structures to describe states or processes involving particular kinds of object, we just employ the thinking model associated with these states or processes. The structures representing properties of objects are assumed to reflect the ways in which we perceive objects, that is, how we are able to speak about an object at all. There is no obvious reason to assume that these structures have any status of existence other than being associated with our means of observation. As a consequence, the structures can be seen as something flexible, changing with the way we refer to an object under different conditions rather than being bound to an object in some absolute manner. In particular, different levels of granularity may give rise to different descriptions, and different descriptions lead to different models. I argue that a formal treatment of vagueness must face the challenge of providing a single formalism that copes with a variety of models differing in granularity, for instance, a coarse-grained level in combination with a fine-grained level model.

I show that defining a generally applicable theoretical framework is not a reasonable aim and stress the value of pragmatic approaches dealing with vagueness, of which I provide two examples. In Section 7, I defend Zadeh's well-known model of vague concepts [21] and mention fuzzy sets as a possible—and surely not the worst—approach. In Section 8, I present further alternatives: I will outline two logics based on the idea that reasoning should be stable under small changes: the Logic of Approximate Entailment [15, 2, 6] and the Logic of Strong Entailment [3].

2   Two contrasting understandings of reality

The ongoing discussion about vagueness has reached a stage clearly beyond the simple initial observation that numerous expressions in natural language do not allow sharp delimitation of their meaning when we consider the full range of objects to which they might refer. Early contributions to the modern discussion, such as by M. Black [1], were far from the intricate analyses offered at present. However, reading [1] already leads to non-trivial questions, and navigating the labyrinth of recent contributions is surely an even greater challenge.

A reasonable systematisation of the problems involved and the solutions proposed is desirable. In this section I specify a—somewhat uncommon—guiding criterion for examining approaches to vagueness. I do not start with the Sorites paradox and examine which of the apparently contradictory statements is kept and which is rejected. I also do not follow Smith's classification [18, Ch. 2], which relates directly formal mathematics and natural language and which cannot capture approaches that reject this procedure. The question that I find most significant and which additionally serves to delineate my own opinion is how comprehensively the notion of reality is taken.

I pick out two contrasting points of view regarding reality, but do not claim that these are the only possible ones. The positions do not originate from the discussion about theories of reality, to which I do not intend to contribute. They represent two extremes that exclude each other but are both characterised by a high degree of coherence. I must add that I am probably not capable of a fair presentation, because, naturally, I propagate only one point of view in the present context. Nevertheless, I do not want to claim that the other point of view is generally inappropriate; it has its applications. Its popularity, either in the pure form discussed here or in a weakened form, is, however, an obstacle to the discussions about vagueness.

On the one hand, reality can be understood in a comprehensive way: the number of facts considered as real can be extended to the maximum possible. This probably leads to what is called naive realism, which states that the world as we see and feel it exists independently of us; everything, except ourselves and what we actively influence, would have the same status of existence in our absence. In particular, a unique flow of history is assumed. This means, for instance, that everything that research has derived about the time before and after the existence of life on earth is taken literally. Furthermore, the role of an observer entering the world is to describe what exists and happens around him. Accordingly, an observer can make true judgements about the world. His observations are not considered as observations relative to him, and—provided that no errors occur—the content of the observations has a status of absoluteness.

I do not suggest that this view be labelled "naive"; I simply call this understanding of reality the *realism-based* viewpoint. Its main characteristic is that two constituents are distinguished and kept separate: the world and its observation by us.

On the other hand, we may confine ourselves solely to the latter constituent: the aspect of observation, or—more generally—of perception. This leads to a minimalist understanding of reality hereafter called the *perception-based* viewpoint. Only the very fact that we are capable of perception and of relating perceptions made at different times is considered as real. The world is then identified with the totality of experienced perceptions. This view of reality does not encompass everything that ever happened or will happen in the future but can, if we want, be related to a single individual. The role of the former constituent, the "world", is modified accordingly. The reference to objects, their properties, and their development is understood as our way of describing what we perceive.

Both views of reality suggest a particular understanding of the role of natural language and a particular understanding of mathematical logic. Let us extend both the realism-based and the perception-based viewpoint in order to include a suitable characterisation of natural and formal language. I do not claim that the additional elements are implied by necessity; I assume only that we are led to a coherent picture in both cases.

In this contribution, natural language is understood as just the part of language that refers to what we perceive as being and happening in the world. According to the realism-based viewpoint, natural language serves to tell what the world is like. It enables us to make judgements about an existing structure that can be true or false, determined by facts associated with properties of the world and accordingly called "extralingual". It is then natural to draw a close analogy between natural language and the formal languages used in mathematics. Also the latter usually refer to a certain structure and allow statements about it that can be true or false. The difference between the two types of language, however, is well known. Mathematical propositions are, with reference to a model, either true or false; and exactly one of these possibilities applies. The inability of natural language to provide the same conceptual clarity as mathematics is sometimes considered a deficiency.

According to the perception-based viewpoint, the significance of utterances in natural language is restricted. Language is assumed to enable us to systematise, and thus express, our perceptions. Language is not assumed to inform about independently holding properties of the objects it describes. Furthermore, descriptions are typically realised by comparison, by pointing out similarities or differences. Natural-language concepts serve to identify or distinguish different situations in a specific respect; natural language enables us to communicate perceptible similarities or differences.

Next, let us consider formal reasoning methods; let us examine how logic, as the foundation of mathematics, may be characterised when adopting one of the two basic points of view outlined above. According to the realism-based viewpoint, mathematics serves to develop systematically theories of the structures that appear in reality. In this sense, mathematics is a tool for describing the structure of the world. Logic provides the methodology for deriving knowledge in a proper way. In logic, the laws of truth are investigated: logic shows how to derive from one truth something else that is equally true.

Following these ideas, formal statements can be related directly to facts, and, in contrast to natural language, the clean logical foundation helps us to avoid imprecise statements and prevents us from erroneous conclusions. The exact relationship between natural and formal languages certainly calls for clarification; vagueness causes a problem that needs to be tackled.

The perception-based viewpoint has a different understanding of mathematics, and in particular logic. When choosing a formal language and axioms, we begin with a specific aspect under which a particular kind of situation can be described by perceptual means, for instance, the spatial extension of an object or the temporal extension of a process. In order to formalise reasoning, we do not choose a formal language and axioms by means of a straightforward translation of the corresponding natural-language statements. To apply the mathematical method, we take an indirect route: we first determine a model associated with the considered aspect. It is this model to which the formal language, the axioms, and derivation rules refer. The base set of the model represents circumstances that differ only in the selected aspect. Furthermore, the model includes the mutual relationships between these circumstances with respect to the selected aspect. Accordingly, a model is a finite first-order structure, or a method to construct successively an increasingly larger finite first-order structure, leading to a countably infinite structure.

Thus, constructing a mathematical model means compiling systematically all possible variations of a situation with respect to the considered aspect. In particular, the procedure relies on a perceptual ability of ours. In the case of an infinite construction, the possible variations are enumerated systematically, our capacity to imagine being necessarily involved as well.

As a basic example, let us consider the spatial extension as an aspect with respect to which objects can differ observably. Considering "size" just as the notion that distinguishes the smaller from the larger leads to a dense linear order that has a lower and no upper bound. The formal language and axioms to reason about "size" may then refer to this structure, and our derivation rules must be sound with respect to it.[2]

This concludes the specification of the two extreme poles with respect to which I intend to position my own approach and particular existing ones to vagueness.

3   Epistemicism, supervaluationism, and contextualism

The key question is how to deal formally with vague statements. In the absence of a satisfactory solution, it is not surprising that no standard approach exists and that different approaches are usually incompatible. Let us outline the characteristic features of three well-known lines of research.

Epistemicism clearly belongs to the best-known approaches to vagueness. Timothy Williamson is one of its proponents; his position is described in [20], and a comprehensive treatment can be found in [19].

In [20], the reader is asked to consider an example of a vague property, namely the property of a person to be "thin". Following Williamson, this property divides, under given circumstances, humans into two groups: those who are thin and those who are not. A "thin" person is said to be a member of the former group. Thus, "thin" divides

---

[2]Incidentally, we may of course define equally well a structure without reference to any perception. Mathematics can be done on the basis of arbitrary axioms which a priori do not refer to any known structure. Indeed, in very few areas of mathematics proper understanding of the results is thus impossible. However, the value of such research is questionable.

the entities in question into two parts. Epistemicism places great emphasis on this fact, which is referred to as bivalence.

Williamson considers thinness to be dependent on a person's waist size compared to the average waist size of the rest of the population. However, this measure varies continuously, and no point of division is identifiable. Indeed, it may happen that a person, for example "TW" (the author of [19, 20]), cannot be categorised as belonging to either of the two groups. The dilemma of vagueness becomes apparent: if we assume that "TW is thin" and "TW is not thin" are both false statements, we are faced with a contradiction, given that the two statements "TW is thin" and "TW is not thin" suggest a bivalent classification.

The specific feature of epistemicism is that the picture of the two groups into which humans are divided by the property "thin" is not revised when it comes to borderline cases; bivalence is preserved at all costs. The trick is to distinguish two levels: at the first level we find what we as humans may observe, or in some way conclude, and thus know; at the second level we have what remains hidden to us, what can by no means be revealed and thus remains, as a matter of principle, unknown to us. Epistemicism claims that, depending on the context, a hard cutoff between the thin and non-thin people exists but that we have no means of finding it. An explanation for this ignorance is also provided: our ability to conclude something requires a margin for error. What applies can be detected only if it could also be detected under slightly changed circumstances. This is why we can in fact conclude and state correctly less than actually applies. In particular, "TW" is either thin or not thin, but nobody knows; in fact nobody can know.

It is not difficult to tell which understanding of reality fits best with epistemicism. The fact that the realism-based viewpoint, together with its above-outlined extension with regard to natural language and mathematics, fits perfectly signifies the one and only advantage of this approach: its great coherence. If the world is given and fixed, and if language serves to specify what is and what happens in the world, each property denoted by a natural-language expression should have an actual, though possibly not experienceable, meaning in the sense that the property should apply or not apply in all circumstances. Otherwise, the expression would be without definite reference or even constitute, as Williamson puts it when considering a strict view, "mere noise" [20, Sec. 1].

Kit Fine's paper [5] led to the so-called supervaluationist approach. Like epistemicism, supervaluationism also seeks to save bivalence when reasoning in the presence of vagueness. In contrast to epistemicism, however, so-called truth-value gaps are allowed; a vague property may apply, not apply, or does not possess a truth status. Thus, in the associated formal setting, a vague proposition is assigned "true", "false", or no truth value. In supervaluationism, the pursuit of bivalence does not lead to the claim that vague properties are actually crisp, but to the consideration of all possibilities to "sharpen" the property in an acceptable way. In particular, not one specific crisp property is singled out, but all acceptable sharpenings are considered. "Truth" is finally identified with "supertruth", which roughly means that a statement is true under all the acceptable sharpenings. As a particular argument in favour of this approach, the formalism is claimed to deal properly with so-called penumbral connections; for instance, the statement "K. is tall or K. is not tall" is assigned "true" even if K. is a borderline case for "tall".

The supervaluationist approach does not suggest an answer to the question of which theory of reality is appropriate. An incompatibility with the perception-based viewpoint, as regards the understanding of natural language, can nevertheless be detected. A precisification associates a natural-language expression with a fine-grained scale of distinctions and specifies a region on this scale. This procedure leaves the realm of what the expression has to say. In fact, a precisification does not model the natural-language expression itself but goes declaredly beyond it. This idea is not in line with the perception-based viewpoint; rather, a model of a natural-language expression is required to represent the corresponding perception. If the expression offers a rough classification, then its model must also be based on this rough classification. Finer distinctions require information which is not specifiable by means of the expression; hence, its use is inappropriate.

A remarkable counterpoint to the preceding two theories is Stewart Shapiro's contextualism, which is summarised in [17] and explained in detail in [16]. According to this approach, and as in supervaluationism, formalised vague statements are in one of three states—true, false, or undetermined. Partial evaluations arise, but—unlike in supervaluationism—they are not to be extended into total evaluations. Furthermore, the evaluations are bound to a given moment of a conversation. Thus, unlike both in supervaluationism and in epistemicism, the context does not arise as an element that must be taken into account additionally and increases the complexity of the approach, but is the core of the theory. The evaluations assign truth values only to as many properties as can be discussed at a time by humans, and it is then no problem to postulate a tolerance principle, according to which practically indistinguishable circumstances must be judged the same way.

According to a complaisant interpretation, contextualism is in accordance with the perception-based viewpoint outlined above. In fact, the question whether a vague property applies or not is asked only for a specific utterance of a specific speaker. Furthermore, the truth status of a proposition is kept flexible; it can change at any moment, depending on how the conversation proceeds. However, according to Shapiro, the decision on the applicability of a vague property is not made spontaneously on the basis of the speaker's impression. The decision is rather thought of as a function of everything that could be associated with a context, for instance, the state of the conversation, example cases, and contrasting cases. A further incompatibility is the fact that Shapiro uses his model to solve the Sorites paradox by means of a so-called forced march, which forces speakers to decide on truth or falsity in borderline cases, that is, in cases where by definition the perception suggests neither possibility.

Contextualism does not depend on a definite position on the question of how to understand reality. We cannot say that it exhibits elements of the realism-based viewpoint, provided that we leave [16, Ch. 7] out of consideration. An interpretation in a framework of a perception-based approach would be possible. However, this possibility is not taken into consideration.

4   The realism-based viewpoint: an obstacle

I now return to the general level at which I started the discussion and reconsider the two contrasting understandings of reality. This section identifies the problems we face when adopting the extreme form of realism which I called realism-based viewpoint. I propagate the perception-based viewpoint as the line to be followed. My considerations affect all three approaches discussed in the preceding section and lead to basic criticism, although to a different degree in each case. I confine myself here to general arguments; critical points that are specific to each approach follow in the next section.

Note that, in this contribution, I only address the vagueness debate, and I do not claim that a broad interpretation of the notion of reality is bad in principle. To give an example where it is appropriate, I may mention any of the attempts to systematise parts of natural language. By insisting on a perception-based view these attempts might become unnecessarily complicated. For example, terminologies used in specific scientific fields have been reviewed systematically within the framework of so-called realism-based ontology [12]. Among its underlying principles we also find those that do not appear in the best light in the present contribution. The different scope given, the approach can be seen as appropriate though.

The current discussions on vagueness involve more basic issues than those considered by the proponents of realism-based ontology. At the latest when addressing the often-posed question of where the "source" of vagueness is located, general features of language and of "the world" must be considered.

To be able to argue as flexibly as possible, we should consider the smallest number of facts necessary as unchangeably fixed. In particular, we should consider not more than the absolute minimum as part of reality. The realism-based viewpoint represents the opposite. There is probably an infinite number of possibilities to model human perceptions. There is, moreover, the standard way of doing so. The standard model is the basis of natural language and assumes an observer-independent world consisting of objects whose properties change over time. The realism-based viewpoint takes the standard model for granted. Owing to this limitation, all flexibility is relinquished when we consider our existence not from our everyday perspective but from a meta-level, as is done in discussions about vagueness.

Let us recall the effect of a realism-based view on the interpretation of natural language. It is often stated—possibly with a negative undertone—that natural language does not allow the same kind of semantics as a formal language. In particular, it is stated that natural language lacks the precision we find in mathematics. It is, however, interesting to imagine what precision in natural language would actually mean. Assume that "K. is tall", stated in the context of a conversation, means that K.'s height is lower-bounded by some precise value. This interpretation is odd simply because there is no way of making the associated observation. Not even the best instruments would help, and, at a certain level of preciseness, such statements are even unreasonable in the context of modern physical theories. Even without reference to possible methods of measurement, the interpretation of "tall" in terms of precise values is odd; we would express more than we can tell by looking at K. and estimating her height.

Some authors go so far as to claim that vagueness reflects a kind of deficiency of language. It might be beyond doubt that not all our perceptions can be expressed to others by means of language. However, the converse idea that language could be such that we can express more than we perceive has no basis—simply because we do not have anything more than our perceptions. Williamson's statement that words in natural language mean that something holds true or not but we have no way of knowing is an assumption whose meaning is void.

The weakness of the realism-based viewpoint becomes evident when we consider the relationship between natural and formal language. The realist understanding puts emphasis on analogies. In fact, a property expressed by natural language is regularly called a "predicate"—a notion which, in my opinion, should better remain the preserve of mathematical logic. A predicate in first-order logic refers to a formal language that is interpreted in a formal structure. A vague property refers to a way of expressing what we observe. Even if both these aspects are related, they are definitely not the same. I criticise the tendency to treat natural and formal languages analogously. The point is of general significance: the problem of inappropriate use of formal reasoning techniques is present in all three approaches mentioned above.

The analogous treatment of natural and formal language becomes obvious when a statement is translated "into symbolic form" without specifying the formal framework; both language and derivation rules are either tacitly understood or a matter of discussion, and the semantics is regularly neglected. Williamson's article [20, Sec. 1] is an example of such a style of reasoning; a particularly extreme case is an article by G. Evans [4].

Generally, there are two acceptable approaches to logic—a syntactic and a model-theoretic one. The syntactic approach views a logic as a calculus that specifies how formal statements can be derived from other formal statements. If the content of the formal statements is unclear, one certainly must take care not to do anything more than recombine strings of symbols.

A logical calculus contributes to a better understanding of a problem in a particularly transparent way if we start with its semantics. In this case, it is ensured that we know how to interpret the results derived by formal means. The relationship between formal propositions and the addressed situation is mediated by the structure on which the semantics is based.

Both approaches to logic may be justifiable. The former is presently more popular, although the latter is definitely of higher value. It is, however, unacceptable that in many cases neither of these lines is followed, as in the examples mentioned above.

By adopting the perception-based viewpoint I follow the principle of assuming not more than necessary in any case. Not even allowing perceptions to be part of reality would mean denying that anything can be taken for real; such an absurd position would block the current discussion and probably others as well.

From the minimalist perspective, we easily observe that considerations that depend on a wide notion of reality are susceptible to encountering pseudo-problems. A problem statement can either be rendered precise or lacks content. We can only make a question precise if we can reduce it to the domain of perceptions, that is, if we can reformulate it in terms of notions ultimately related to perceptions. This principle is seldom applied in discussions about vagueness.

Consider, for example, the common question of what the "source of vagueness" is like. Unless the epistemicist's answer is accepted, an argumentation may proceed as follows. The set of objects to which a specific property expressed in natural language applies is typically not sharply delimitable. This suggests that vague properties are actually not suitable to express facts about the world; at least they are not capable of doing so in the same neat way as predicates in mathematics. The question is then why; it is not obvious where this problem originates. Since it is assumed that there is the world on the one hand and our natural-language statements about it on the other hand, the reason must apparently be located in exactly one of these domains. Hence, either the world is, in some mysterious sense, the carrier of vagueness, or the so-called semantics of natural language has features different from usual first-order semantics. Unless the former possibility is taken seriously, vagueness is understood as the problem of associating semantics with natural-language expressions, in analogy to predicates of a first-order language. As language is assumed to express true facts, there should moreover exist a canonical solution rather than a variety of equally acceptable ones: the correct semantics are to be discovered.

This train of thought may sound so convincing that we might immediately want to start the search for the one and only semantics. However, we should not be dazzled by arguments that cannot even be subjected to criticism because they are void. The distinction between the "world" and our statements about it is not unreasonable by itself; it is well applicable, provided that we identify the "world" as an overall model of our sensual experiences. However, general statements about the "world" then refer to a model. Such statements can not necessarily be reformulated in terms of what gives rise to the model, that is, in terms of our sensual experiences. A statement for which a reformulation is impossible does not tell us anything; it just reveals the arbitrariness of our model.

Examples in which a reduction to the level of perceptions is impossible can be found in the above considerations. In particular, we cannot state precisely what it means to locate the source of vagueness, what it means that the world itself is vague, or what it means that natural language could be not vague. At least I do not see a way of doing so. Arguments based on such questions or assumptions lack content.

5   Three untenable theories of vagueness

Let us now examine the three mentioned approaches to vagueness individually in a critical way.

In a framework based on the perception-based view there is certainly no hope of keeping any feature of epistemicism. To make clear that the differences are irreconcilable, I just mention Williamson's use of the notion "knowledge". He maintains that opponents of his theory say that in borderline cases of a property there is nothing to know concerning the question whether the property applies or not. I go one step further and claim that talking of knowledge is generally inadequate, not only in borderline cases. If I say "K. is tall", I express my impression that most people I have seen before are smaller, and there is no relationship to knowledge. Williamson's understanding of "knowledge" and "ignorance" is pre-empiricist and thus unacceptable.

Although supervaluationism seems to be based on less arbitrary assumptions, the approach is also not acceptable. I have already commented that the very idea of a precisification is not well compatible with the perception-based viewpoint. Moreover, the overall motivation is questionable: to cope with what Fine calls penumbral connections. Fine claims that "K. is tall" and "K. is not tall" are exhaustive statements. Yes, they are—at the moment at which they are made because then we have a two-element scale in mind, and we classify people into just two groups. However, we no longer do so when considering somebody who does not fit into the scheme. The existence of penumbral connections is doubtful. Compare also the criticism of Smith [18, Sec. 2.4].

Contextualism is an approach with potential. However, if it is taken as a means to model the mechanism through which we come to the conclusions "tall" or "not tall", its best features are overlooked. The dynamic character of language as regards the fluctuating distinction between "tall" and "not tall" is well taken into account. However, the dynamic character of language as regards spontaneous introduction of new concepts in order to adapt dynamically the view on some topic, to integrate new details, and, in particular, to increase precision is not considered, or at least not systematically.

Finally, in all three approaches we find the idea that vague statements express truths about the world in the sense of the realism-based viewpoint. Accordingly, all three approaches do not separate cleanly the formal from the informal level of argumentation but follow the unfortunate practise of identifying natural language directly with a formal language. Williamson argues explicitly in this way. Fine begins his paper [5] with the questions "What is the correct logic of vagueness?" and "What are the correct truth conditions for a vague language?" Shapiro's realistic understanding of natural language becomes evident at the latest when he discusses in length the question whether vagueness originates from language or from the world [16, Ch. 7].

Asking for truth conditions easily leads to unfounded argumentation. Sometimes the formal language is extended by a meta-language containing a so-called truth predicate. Lacking any kind of semantics or proof system, reasoning in this pseudo-formal construct may become prone to erratic speculation. In [20, Sec. 1], for instance, the so-called T-scheme is used but then found to require a verbose justification; classical logic is used, but then specific laws are called into question; the idea that we might do better with intuitionistic logic is proposed. The overall impression is that not even the author takes a result derived from such an unstable basis seriously.

6 Shifting granularities

What is implied when I say "the blackboard is flat"? Understanding this statement as a description of what the world is like at a specific location at a specific time indeed requires truth conditions. Note that truth conditions are loaded with meaning: they tell whether the statement in question applies or does not apply under all possible circumstances, possibly including all places in the world and any time in history and in the future. My statement, if found true, would then reveal that an evaluation of the truth conditions leads to a positive result. Is this the implication of my saying "the blackboard is flat"?

No. When I utter this sentence, I do not refer, consciously or unconsciously, to a universe of possible circumstances. Giving this sentence a meaning does not require a sophisticated theory. The utterance is based on my image of a flat surface as opposed to a curved one. I call the blackboard flat because I observe that it is flat, and this in turn means that my observation fits with the picture of flatness that I have in mind. As a result, the utterance evokes a corresponding picture in the imagination of the person to whom I speak.

My impression can, of course, change later; on closer inspection I may find that the blackboard actually has a dent and is thus not flat. This discovery does not imply that my first statement was wrong; the two statements just report two successive impressions which do not agree. In particular, the "world" and its properties need not be involved to understand what it means to communicate that something is "flat". To develop a theory of "flatness" does not mean to analyse the "world" but to analyse impressions differing in definite respects.

The viewpoint I propagate considers human utterances as expression of perceptions in an absolute or relative way, and not as descriptions of how the world "really is". My approach to a formal treatment of vague information incorporates this idea and thus relies entirely on the perception-based viewpoint. It is little surprise that there is no associated canonical formal framework. Vagueness concerns the very process of defining a formal framework, and the approach can just offer general guidelines of how to use formal techniques to reason about vague properties.

Restricting reality to perceptions leads to a three-part picture: (i) our perceptions, (ii) the models we associate with selected types of perceptions, and (iii) the statements referring to the models. The world as it is then understood is a world of perceptions and is not directly accessible by the statements about it: a model lies in between.

Let a specific way of viewing a certain situation be given, for instance, a set of persons distinguished by size. Recall that the perception-based viewpoint is incompatible with direct translation of content to be modelled into a formal language. Instead, we must first associate a structure with the considered situation, then we can think of a way to reason about this model. When creating a model, we may observe that there is no canonical way to proceed; a certain amount of freedom is given. In case of "size", we must decide how fine the distinctions reflected in the model should be.

From mathematical practise, we are used to putting everything into a model that is imaginable with respect to a specific way of looking at things. Our model is in this case typically the result of an unbounded process and hence infinite. In particular, to model the notion of "size" it is common to use the set of positive rationals or reals. Whereas the construction method is based on a type of perception, not all elements of the result, the finished model, correspond to particular perceptions. In fact, we cannot distinguish between arbitrarily close sizes. The models we typically use in mathematics are finer than anything distinguishable.

In contrast, a natural-language expression such as "tall" is not appropriately modelled within an infinite structure but within a structure containing only what is distinguishable at the moment at which it is uttered. The utterance "K. is tall" could well refer to the structure consisting just of "small", "medium-sized", and "tall" and be endowed, so to say, with the natural order. The perception-based viewpoint does not regard the statement "K. is tall" as a consequence of the absolute fact that K. has a specific height. Rather, it is understood as the description of an observation relative to other observations. The speaker might refer to the many people he has seen before, he might consider a specific group of people, and one or more persons might be particularly weighted in this group: according to his impression, K. is considerably taller than the middle-sized people he has in mind. We are led to the three-element linear order as the appropriate model of "size" in this case.

I conclude that there need not be a unique model associated with a particular type of perception. Various alternatives might exist, and if there is a choice, one cannot claim that a particular choice describes the situation sufficiently or even correctly.

Freedom in formalisation even applies at the propositional level. Consider classical propositional logic (CPL). Sometimes CPL is viewed as the unquestionable basis of everything. However, CPL is the logic of true and false, no more or less. In everyday life, CPL is fundamental because it is the standard way of bringing structure into a variety of actual or possible situations; we choose properties that hold in some and do not hold in the other cases. When applying CPL, the reference of the yes-no propositions is essential for interpreting the results. The insight into the given problem that is achieved depends directly on the assignments made. However, these assignments may well be subject to modification, and modified assignments could well lead to different insights.

There need not arise a unique structure in a given context: in particular, different levels of granularity are possible. Vagueness reflects the fact that different points of view of the same object may lead to different structures, to coarser or to finer ones. The process of modelling is generally flexible, so in particular we can choose models of different granularity. Combining the associated structures into a single model may be seen as an uncommon, but certainly not an unfeasible, task in mathematical modelling.

Developing a formalism is not a challenge but just usual mathematical work if limited to one level of granularity. When regarding "tall" as "distinctly taller than middle-sized", we can model this property by the top element of a three-element linear order, and its vagueness is irrelevant. If the three categories chosen are found sufficient to describe the persons in question, no problem arises. In fact, it does not even make sense to classify "tall" as vague in this case because "vague" is a relative notion, and a finer level of perception must necessarily be specified. The mathematical theory of a three-element linear order does not cause problems. In the case of the finest level of granularity, the relevant theory can be that of rational numbers, which is less straightforward but well developed.

Vagueness comes into play when we switch from a given level of granularity to finer ones. Whenever a borderline-tall person comes up in a conversation about small and tall persons, the speakers are forced to refine the scale. The interesting question is then how the entities of the previous scale translate into those of the new one or—more formally speaking—how the old scale is embedded in the new one. I presume that, after switching to the finer scale, the role of "tall" is narrower than before because "tall" is now understood as not applying to the borderline-tall person. However, examining how the transition works exactly is not a case for speculation but for empirical tests in the field of experimental psychology.

A particularly interesting question is how the coarse model, such as the three-element one, relates to the finest possible model that is usually used in mathematics. This question is most closely related to what discussions on vagueness usually focus on. It is a special case of the challenge of formalising reasoning under vagueness: how to reason simultaneously on a coarse level and the finest possible one.

We conclude by considering the Sorites paradox:

> If n grains of sand form a heap, then so do $n - 1$.
>
> 10,000 grains form a heap.
>
> Consequently, one single grain forms a heap.

Let us try to determine, on the basis of the perception-based viewpoint, what the problem is.

It is assumed that there is a collection of grains in front of us. For reasoning, an aspect is chosen with respect to which the situation is described. The Sorites paradox deals with the size of the collection of grains; this is the chosen aspect.

There are, possibly among others, two different ways of describing the grains in this respect. On the one hand, two collections of grains may differ by exactly one grain. This observation lets us realise that the grains can be counted. Thus, we may state that there are exactly n grains in front of us, where n runs, say, from 1 to 10,000. On the other hand, we may simply ponder whether the grains in front of us form a heap or not. In the first case we distinguish between 10,000 situations, in the latter case between two. A model for the first case may be the natural numbers from 1 to 10,000 endowed with the successor relation; for the latter case we may choose the two-element Boolean algebra.

For each of the two choices, we may now speak and make conclusions about the set of grains. The quality of our statements will differ. In the first case, we may address questions depending on single grains, for instance, whether the totality of grains can be divided into seven collections of equal size. In the second case, we may address questions concerning the totality of grains, for instance, whether an ant crawling behind the grains can be seen or not.

The Sorites argument makes simultaneous use of both ways of describing the situation. Two models are referred to at the same time, and elements from distinct models are put into relation. Moreover, all elements of the models are taken into account.

However, if we want to consider both situations together in a consistent manner, we must provide a common model: we must merge the two structures. We need to define a common refinement: the coarser structure—heap, non-heap—needs to be embedded in the finer one—1, ..., 10,000. Consistency can be expected only by reference to one structure; the entanglement of references to two different structures causes the paradox.

The embedding can probably be achieved by a variety of methods. One possibility of saving the notion "heap"/"non-heap" and making it accessible to the fine scale, is extending it by adding a degree [8].

This is the "solution" to the paradox. The question why we are "taken in" by the paradox can be answered as follows. Saying that a specific number of grains form a heap evokes a picture of a heap in our mind. The exact number does not matter because it is not part of the image. Furthermore, the picture does not change when removing a single grain, and so we agree with the first statement. On the other hand, the number 10,000 seems so large to us that putting together that many grains presumably results in a heap. Finally, a single grain does not evoke a picture of a heap.

According to the perception-based view, coping with vagueness essentially requires combining models. Generally applicable solutions to the problem of how to deal formally with vagueness, however, are not obvious.

7   Fuzzy sets

The last two sections present specific models of situations in which vagueness is to be taken into account. Neither are they "theories of vagueness" nor do they claim to be. They address selected aspects and are of practical rather than dogmatic quality.

Degree-based approaches, although of some practical relevance, seem to be of limited popularity in discussions on vagueness; an exception is [18]. From the perception-based viewpoint, the idea is reasonable.

When the vagueness of a property denoted by an expression in natural language is problematic, at least two levels of granularity are involved. Recall the previous example. When calling somebody "tall" or "short", we make the distinction between, say, short, middle-sized, and tall persons; formally speaking, we use the three-element linear order. Alternatively, when we intend to distinguish between any two people who differ in size, we are led to a structure such as the rational numbers, based on an infinite iteration of the idea that lengthy objects of given sizes can be concatenated and split into equal parts. The tricky question is how to treat both levels of granularity in a single formal calculus.

Let us focus on the common special case: we intend to include one coarse level and the finest possible level in the analysis. To each level we may associate a structure; I hereafter refer to them simply as the coarse and the fine model, respectively. The task is to interrelate them, that is, to describe how an element of one structure relates to an arbitrary element of the other one. This equates to the question of how well two such elements fit to each other, taking into account the content they represent.

Thus, we must specify how an entity from the finest possible level, such as a precise size, fits to an entity of the coarse level, such as "tall". There are several degrees of fit, and the set of degrees is a bounded linear order. As the transition between the two extremes, *not fitting at all* to *perfectly fitting*, is smooth, the linear order should be dense. Using the real unit interval $[0, 1]$ as a set of truth degrees—the usual choice in fuzzy set theory—is thus reasonable, although the rational unit interval would be more appropriate.

We should then ask which significance individual degrees have. In particular, $[0, 1]$ is not only a linear order but also an additive structure. Recall that notions such as "tall" are used when directly observing the object in question, and the speaker's opinion is the determining factor. A speaker using "tall" or "not tall" decides spontaneously that "tall" fits well or does not fit at all; the obvious cases, modelled by 0 and 1, are determined by a speaker's rough impression. In borderline cases, a speaker would use neither "tall" nor "not tall". The question is then whether any specific intermediate truth degree reflects the situation appropriately, and the answer depends on whether the speaker is able to decide spontaneously on a number between 0 and 1.

We see that the relationship between the coarse and the fine model does not stand on firm ground, and nothing can be done about it because the speaker's spontaneity is involved. Judgements such as "tall" and "middle-sized" might even not be reproducible by the same speaker. It is moreover unclear if the intermediate truth values can be used to measure a degree to which some property applies. If we are pedantic, we may add that the relationship of our fine scale to the object in question is also not clear because the former is over-precise. As the fine scale we may, for instance, use the positive rationals; the size of a given person can, however, not be associated with a precise number in a well-defined way.

The effect of the last point is, of course, tiny compared to the remaining uncertainties and can thus be neglected. Furthermore, the question whether real numbers are a suitable choice for truth degrees can only be clarified in experiments. Probably the earliest investigation in this direction is described in [9]. The result is amazing and confirms that the very idea of using fuzzy sets to model natural-language expressions is reasonable; the participants in the experiments assigned truth degrees in a largely consistent way. Experiments of this kind suggest the overall conclusion that the fuzzy set model is an appropriate choice as a model of vague concepts.

Accepting this conclusion, I find that the degree-based approach to vagueness is well in line with the standpoint propagated in this contribution. It is, however, important to remark that the justification of the fuzzy set model strongly relies on its flexibility. A particular fuzzy set may be justified as a model of an expression used by a speaker in a particular context in a particular conversation. A general model of the same expression is subject to indeterminateness, which can be reduced if the context is well specified, but never eliminated. However, this indeterminateness need not be seen as a serious drawback; it is a natural consequence of our task of combining two levels of granularity. On the one hand, we deal with the content of utterances and not with measurement results. On the other hand, we use a model whose base set consists of entities that are even more precise than any measurement device.

Criticisms of degree-based approaches to vagueness may be rooted in the fact that fuzzy sets are not as rigidly connected to anything tangible as, say, real numbers. From the realism-based viewpoint, it is natural to require that a fuzzy set be uniquely determined. From the perception-based viewpoint, this is, however, unfeasible and contradicts the role of a fuzzy set as a model of a natural-language expression. A unique fuzzy set associated with a concept such as "tall" would imply a definite relationship between this concept and the underlying fine model. If it were possible to assign a particular role to the value 0.666 in the image of a fuzzy set modelling "tall", it would be possible to define a particular role for the precise size mapping to this particular value. Thus, the absurd consequence would be that "tall" determines the role of specific elements of the fine structure.

I have argued in favour of the classical fuzzy set model; indeed, fuzzy sets are useful tools for embedding a coarse model in a fine one. My defence ends here. The development of fuzzy set theory has been motivated by more ambitious aims than modelling individual natural-language expressions. It is another issue how to use fuzzy sets to formalise reasoning under vagueness. In this respect, results are not yet convincing.

Although fuzzy logics in the sense of [7] can be regarded as logics of fuzzy sets, and although a very prosperous research field has developed around fuzzy logics, it remains unclear how fuzzy logic relates to vagueness. Much has been written on this topic; I will add one example that offers both hope and disappointment. The idea of defining a logic of a collection of fuzzy sets with pointwise defined logical operations is defendable. A further result presented in [9] suggests that when connecting expressions referring to "size" by "or" or "not", the corresponding fuzzy sets connect like the pointwise maximum or the pointwise standard negation, respectively. This result is encouraging. However, it does not support Gödel logic with standard negation. Apart from the fact that [9] shows only that fuzzy sets referring to the same aspect, namely "size", can be combined, the question of the role of the residual implication remains open.

We conclude that fuzzy sets are a natural tool for interrelating coarse and fine concepts. However, when formalising reasoning under vagueness, the methodology of fuzzy logic, in particular of fuzzy logic in the sense of [7], has limited value. From the perception-based viewpoint, the problem is easily determined: for inference at the coarse level the fine model should play no role. If we are to formalise reasoning as we ourselves do it, the fine model is out of place; contrary to a common claim [22], fuzzy sets are of little help in emulating what we conclude ourselves from statements involving vague concepts. If we are to reason about concepts that belong to a coarse level, reasoning should also take place at this coarse level. An appropriate approach should offer an inference with respect to coarse structures, which should, however, be allowed to vary in granularity.

8 Logics for reasoning with tolerance

Methods to cope with vagueness have been developed on the basis of practical needs in several fields. A controlling device based on vague specifications, a clinical guideline based on vague conditions, an expert system based on vague notions—in all these cases the duality of a rough and a fine scale appears and a practical solution is required to master the inconvenient side of vagueness.

It is certainly regrettable that methods are often chosen ad hoc and are not justified on the basis of clear principles. However, as far as vagueness is concerned, we cannot expect to be able to develop a logic dealing with vagueness under all circumstances and in the only appropriate way. The problem must be faced for each application separately and can hardly be solved once and for all. There is no difficulty in using different approaches for different applications; and when dealing with a specific problem it is not a deficiency to be unable to single out a single ideal formalism.

This section describes two logics that address one particular aspect arising in connection with vagueness: they are, in a certain sense, tolerant with regard to small changes. These approaches can of course not generally compete with fuzzy set theory. They are quite application-specific, but with regard to the problem considered they are rather satisfying.

We deal with crisp properties, but a similarity relation allows expressing that two properties, although otherwise generally unrelated, resemble each other. A formalism for approximate reasoning was originally proposed by E. Ruspini [15], and a variety of associated logics were subsequently studied [2, 6]. I mention two logics that arose from this line: the Logic of Approximate Entailment (LAE) [14] and the Logic of Strong Entailment (LSE) [3]. I define them semantically. Axiomatisations of these, or closely related, logics can be found in the referenced articles.

LAE is a propositional logic. Our model reflects the fine level; a system of yes-no properties is modelled by a Boolean algebra $\mathscr{B}$ of subsets of a set W. Furthermore, W is endowed with a similarity relation, that is, with a mapping $s \colon W \times W \to [0,1]$ such that, for any $p,q,r \in W$, $s(p,q) = 1$ iff $p = q$, $s(p,q) = s(q,p)$, and $s(p,r) \geq s(p,q) \odot s(q,r)$, where $\odot$ is a fixed t-norm. For $d \in [0,1]$, we define the d-neighbourhood of an $A \in \mathscr{B}$ as $U_d(A) = \{p \in W : s(p,q) \geq d \text{ for some } q \in A\}$.

The language of LAE comprises variables $\varphi_1, \varphi_2, \dots$ and constants $\top, \bot$, and propositions are built up from the atoms by means of the operations $\wedge, \vee, \neg$. An implication is a triple consisting of two propositions α, β and a value $d \in [0,1]$, denoted by

(1) $\alpha \overset{d}{\rightarrow} \beta$.

Propositions are evaluated by elements of $\mathscr{B}$ such that connectives are preserved. An implication (1) is satisfied by an evaluation v if $v(\alpha) \subseteq U_d(v(\beta))$. The notion of semantic entailment of an implication by a set of implications is defined in the expected way.

LSE is defined similarly, but an implication is denoted by

$$\alpha \overset{d}{\Rightarrow} \beta$$

and is satisfied by an evaluation v if $U_d(v(\alpha)) \subseteq v(\beta)$.

Both logics deal with "tolerance". Intuitively speaking, in LAE, $\alpha \overset{d}{\rightarrow} \beta$ means that α implies β only approximately; there is a proposition α' that is similar to α to a degree $\geq d$ and implies β. Furthermore, if a proposition α'' is similar to α to a degree $\geq e$, the conclusion is possible that $\alpha \overset{d \odot e}{\rightarrow} \beta$. In LSE, $\alpha \overset{d}{\Rightarrow} \beta$ means that α implies β and that this is even the case for all propositions α' that are similar to α to a degree $\geq d$.

The embedding of a coarse structure in a fine one, which is necessary to deal formally with vague properties, is not fixed a priori and, in particular, tolerant of small changes. This latter aspect is taken into account by the two logics mentioned. LAE and LSE are no candidates for the ultimate logic of vagueness, but they take a relevant aspect into account.

9   Conclusion

The discussion about vagueness has become complicated; there are several competing research lines that can hardly be combined into a single one. Issues at increasingly fundamental levels are addressed. The modern discussion might have begun with some general considerations about natural language and formal methods, but nowadays, ideas such as "genuinely vague objects" appear in serious arguments.

I have sought to develop a view of the topic in which questions such as "Why is language vague?" do not play a role. Posing the question why natural language is vague makes no sense, simply because language cannot be different from what it is. In particular, I have argued that it is inappropriate to view vagueness as something originating from a deficiency. Instead, I have stressed the clear difference between a formal and a natural language.

I have reviewed the situation from a perspective which I originally adopted to cope with difficulties in a different field—the foundational debate in quantum physics. Although even quantum physicists express their results in terms of moving particles as little balls, quantum physics is best understood the minimalist way, that is, by means of purely statistical interpretation. The mechanistic perspective has, in my opinion, become obsolete since quantum theories emerged. The traditional point of view according to which the observer steps into the world to make observations of what is there independently, is outdated: the observation is the basis, and the observed object depends on its observation. This perspective reduces the role of mathematics to providing tools for developing formal models that fit the observations as well as possible, rather than tools for reasoning correctly about facts of the world.

I have widened this perspective to address not only specific physical phenomena but anything expressible in natural language. If we consider anything at all as part of reality, the set of perceptions experienced during our lives, is the bare minimum. Our language describes these perceptions, relating them to each other. Surely, a notion such as "size" gives rise to a formal structure; "size" can be represented by a linear order. Nevertheless, we use expressions such as "tall" to distinguish between different sizes or to identify similar sizes. The very reason for calling somebody "tall" is to communicate the impression that the person is taller than most other people considered in the given situation.

I have argued that vagueness reflects the fact that objects can be classified according to, say, their size at different levels of granularity. Vagueness is a relative notion; it concerns the problem that a rough classification cannot be refined in a canonical way. The expression "tall" is used to distinguish from "middle-sized"; the expression "1.8 m tall" is used to distinguish from "smaller than 1.75 m or taller than 1.85 m". The challenge is to deal with the two or more levels of granularity in a combined formalism.

There are several possibilities to do this practically, and specific solutions are typically undogmatic and imperfect. In fact, when evaluating a particular method, we must take into account that we deal with utterances in natural languages rather than with reproducible physical measurements; the evaluation is a task for experimental psychology.

The discussions on vagueness have developed their own dynamics, and presumptions are often made that are difficult to discern. It is my standpoint that the decision whether a topic is well defined depends on the possibility to reduce the problem to the level of perception. As long as the topic ultimately concerns perceptions, arguments can be discussed. If, however, a style is predominant in which speculation dominates, it is difficult to believe that the results are meaningful.

BIBLIOGRAPHY

[1] M. Black, Vagueness: An exercise in logical analysis, *Philosophy of Science* 4 (1937), 427–455. Shortened reprint in [11].

[2] D. Dubois, H. Prade, F. Esteva, P. Garcia, L. Godo. A logical approach to interpolation based on similarity relations, *Int. J. Approx. Reasoning* 17 (1997), 1–36.

[3] F. Esteva, Ll. Godo, R. O. Rodríguez, T. Vetterlein, On the logics of similarity-based approximate and strong entailment, Actas del XV Congreso Español Sobre Tecnologías y Logica Fuzzy (Proceedings of the 15th Spanish Congress on Fuzzy Logic and Technology) (Huelva 2010); 187–192.

[4] G. Evans, Can there be vague objects?, *Analysis* 38 (1978), 208; reprinted in [11].

[5] K. Fine, Vagueness, truth and logic, *Synthese* 30 (1975), 265–300; reprinted in [11].

[6] Ll. Godo, R. O. Rodríguez, Logical approaches to fuzzy similarity-based reasoning: an overview, in: G. Della Riccia et al. (eds.), "Preferences and similarities", Springer-Verlag, Wien 2008; 75–128.

[7] P. Hájek, "Metamathematics of Fuzzy Logic", Kluwer Acad. Publ., Dordrecht 1998.

[8] P. Hájek, V. Novák, The sorites paradox and fuzzy logic, *Int. J. Gen. Syst.* 32 (2003), 373–383.

[9] H. M. Hersh, A. Caramazza, A fuzzy set approach to modifiers and vagueness in natural language, *Journal of Experimental Psychology: General* 105 (1975), 254–276.

[10] R. Keefe, "Theories of Vagueness", Cambridge University Press, Cambridge 2000.

[11] R. Keefe, P. Smith (eds.), "Vagueness: a reader", MIT Press, Cambridge 1999.

[12] K. Munn, B. Smith, "Applied Ontology. An Introduction", Ontos-Verlag, Frankfurt-Heusenstamm 2009.

[13] T. Placek, J. Butterfield, "Non-Locality and Modality", Proc. of the NATO Advanced Research Workshop on Modality, Probability, and Bell's Theorem (Cracow, 19.–23.8.2001), Kluwer Acad. Publ., Dordrecht 2002.

[14] R. O. Rodríguez, "Aspectos formales en el Razonamiento basado en Relaciones de Similitud Borrosas", Ph.D. Thesis, Technical University of Catalonia, 2002.

[15] E. Ruspini, On the semantics of fuzzy logic, *International Journal of Approximate Reasoning* 5 (1991), 45–88.

[16] S. Shapiro, "Vagueness in Context", Oxford University Press, Oxford 2006.

[17] S. Shapiro, Reasoning with slippery predicates, *Stud. Log.* 90 (2008), 313–336.

[18] N. J. J. Smith, "Vagueness and Degrees of Truth", Oxford University Press, Oxford 2008.

[19] T. Williamson, "Vagueness", Routledge, Abingdon 2005.

[20] T. Williamson, Vagueness and ignorance, *Proc. of the Aristotelian Society, Supp.* 66 (1992), 145–162; reprinted in [11].

[21] L. A. Zadeh, Fuzzy sets, *Information and Control* 8 (1965), 338–353.

[22] L. A. Zadeh, Fuzzy logic = computing with words, *IEEE Trans. Fuzzy Syst.* 4 (1996), 103–111.

Thomas Vetterlein
Department of Knowledge-Based Mathematical Systems
Johannes Kepler University
Altenberger Straße 69, 4040 Linz, Austria
Email: Thomas.Vetterlein@jku.at

Comments on *Vagueness: A Mathematician's Perspective* by Thomas Vetterlein

CHRISTIAN G. FERMÜLLER

Thomas Vetterlein calls his reflections on the vagueness discourse "a mathematician's perspective", but he actually does not shy away from entering a perennial *philosophical* debate by referring to two distinct understandings of reality, contrasting a "realism-based viewpoint" with a "perception-based viewpoint". Mathematicians often foster a Platonistic view of the nature of mathematical entities and frequently favor realist interpretations of application scenarios, which seems to differ markedly from a perception-based view. Therefore it is very interesting to see a mathematician explicitly arguing in favor of the latter position, dismissing a "realism-based" approach to vagueness.

Let me right away emphasize that I strongly disagree with some essential assertions in the paper, but that I nevertheless deem it a very refreshing, well-informed, and spiritedly argued view on some important aspects of the philosophical discourse on vagueness. Moreover, Vetterlein highlights some aspects of vague language that are often neglected and arguably deserve more attention. In what follows I will first indicate my discontents, and only then briefly refer to what I take to be the most valuable contributions of the paper.

This comment is clearly not the right place to contribute to the philosophical debate on realism versus anti-realism, however I feel impelled to recall some well-known problems for a thoroughly "perception-based viewpoint" of language and reasoning. Any position that maintains that when people speak about tables, students, and motorcycles they actually do not really refer to furniture, persons, and vehicles but rather to *perceptions* runs into great troubles in explaining the meaning of (vague or non-vague) words and propositions. What are these "perceptions" anyway, if we cannot simply say that they are perceptions *of* objects, persons, etc.? I claim that I can, in all usual circumstances, very well distinguish between, say, a table and my perception of a table. I do not wish to deny that in attributing properties to tables I often, but certainly not always, *partly* rely on perceptions. However I always rely on semantic knowledge too: I know—and have to know sufficiently well to be able to communicate successfully—in which contexts it is adequate to call an object "a table" and when to call it "small" or "big". Philosophers and linguists speak of truth conditions here. Vetterlein seems to strongly dislike this terminology, but he does not show us how we can dispense with it in any theory about the meaning of words and sentences. Of course, one may follow no less than the late Wittgenstein and deny the possibility of coherent semantic theories of natural language altogether. Indeed, some of Vetterlein's remarks seem to point into that direction. However, the price to pay for this move is huge. Not only does it entail the dismissal of a substantial body of contemporary philosophical and linguistic research, but it also severs the links between traditional theories of language—based on the syntax/semantics/pragmatics triangle—and their and engineering applications that call for more than just an *ad hoc* account of information processing in natural language.

Leaving fundamental semantic skepticism aside, I maintain, probably along with the vast majority of contemporary philosophers and linguists, that the attempt to systematically reconstruct statements about chairs, people, the weather, etc., as expressing just perceptions is doomed to failure. Based solely on perceptions how can we even start to explain in a systematic manner what happens if a speaker successfully informs a hearer by uttering an ordinary statement like "This table is somewhat small, but there should be a much bigger one in the next room"? Perceptions are notoriously unreliable, subjective, constantly in flux, and therefore hard to tie in any systematic manner to our actual or idealized use of language. In other words: how can one hope to find in perceptions the *robustness* that seems to be a precondition for a coherent theory of meaningful talk about physical objects, their size, color, temperature, etc.; not to speak of ordinary statements about luck, worries, hope and other not directly perceivable, but nevertheless very real phenomena, which ordinary language allows us to refer to effortlessly. Vetterlein's paper does not tell us how, in explaining successful communication with vague language, reasoning about perceptions could replace a realist, truth condition based semantics. By the latter term I mean any account of language that maintains that a speaker truthfully asserts "Peter is tall" if and only if the context of the utterance singles out a person P and a range of heights H, such that the height of P is within H, *independently* of whether the speaker (or anyone else) has certain perceptions.[1]

As witnessed by perennial philosophical debates, realist positions, whether "naive", "scientific", "internal", or of any other variety are beleaguered by their own deep problems. Nevertheless I contend that any successful model of vague language should at least remain compatible with a realist frame; i.e., it should allow to take speakers at face value, when they assert that certain objects *really* have certain properties and are not just *perceived* to have those properties. In particular, the model should not rely on a translation or re-interpretation of ordinary assertions like "Maria is young" in terms of perceptions.[2]

To sum up my criticism, I am convinced that the reference to perceptions is neither sufficient nor in general necessary to explain the nature of vague language. To use the same strong, but admirably clear language that Vetterlein employs in the title of Section 5 of his essay ("Three untenable theories of vagueness") I claim that any essentially perception-based theory of vague language is untenable: it simply does not get off the ground in explaining why and how we are able to convey information by uttering ordinary, and therefore often vague, sentences.

---

[1]Note that realist semantics, in this sense, does not preclude possible refinements of the above condition that are based on the idea that "truthfulness" as well as "falling in a range" (i.e., set membership in mathematical parlor) may come in degrees. Whether and when such refinements are *adequate* is another matter, of course, that is the subject of other papers in this volume.

[2]For illustration, consider a leisurely conversation with my wife about, say, kids with parents of our own generation. Suppose I utter in this context "[My boss's daughter,] Maria, is young" without being able to ground my assertion on any relevant perception. I have never seen Maria; but I know that she still attends elementary school. I infer from this and from my knowledge about the meaning of the word "young" that, in the given context, it is adequate to call Maria young. I doubt that any theory that only refers to perceptions, rather than to (real) ages of (real) people can successfully explain what I am informing my wife about.

In spite of my misgivings about the feasibility of a perception-based theory of the meaning and use of (vague) language, I think that the paper contains a number of valuable insights that are seldom explicitly mentioned in the vast literature on vagueness. I recapitulate just three items, in the hope to thus draw further attention to them.

1. Vetterlein emphasizes that the discourse on vagueness has become winded and complex and that a rather wide range of approaches are discussed as competing 'theories of vagueness'. Philosophers hardly ever seem to doubt that at most one of those theories can be "correct". I agree with Vetterlein that this attitude is inadequate for the problem at hand. The idea that vagueness is a phenomenon about which our theoretical accounts are right or wrong in a sense comparable to theories about, say, the early universe, or the evolution of reptiles, is highly problematic. However, in contrast to Vetterlein, I do not think that a "realism-based" rather than "perception-based" attitude is primarily responsible for the widespread inclination to evaluate theories about the use and meaning of (vague) language in analogy to theories in natural science. But, whatever the roots of this situation may be, my sympathies are with Vetterlein's call for a pragmatic methodology that is prepared to create and adapt models of communication with vague language as triggered by an open and diverse range of application scenarios.

2. Related to the previous point, Vetterlein sketches a view of the role of mathematics and, in particular, mathematical logic that might explain why discussions on theoretical accounts of vagueness between philosophers (and linguists) on the one hand side, and mathematicians, logicians, and computer scientists on the other hand side, often seem to be afflicted by fundamental misunderstandings about the aims and nature of the whole endeavor. He points out that mathematics provides a rich toolbox for the construction of flexible models that can be adapted to varying applications, without committing the user of these tools to any position regarding "the real logic" of vagueness. This in particular also applies to the seemingly contentious use of fuzzy logic: routine applications of fuzzy logic and related formal machinery do not presuppose that there is a fixed, objective degree of truth associated with each vague proposition. Rather those degrees serve as formal counterparts of quickly shifting, spontaneous, and tentative judgments referring to highly context-dependent and often purely imaginary reference scales. To claim that such models are only of interest in the context of certain engineering tasks, but have no relevance for systematic investigations into the nature of vague language, reveals not only a problematic approach to vagueness, but also indicated a rather narrow and unimaginative view on scientific and philosophical investigations in general.

3. Finally, and probably most importantly, Vetterlein highlights a concrete feature of vagueness that seems to be largely ignored by philosophers: namely that frequently a switch between *different levels of granularity* of reference scales and measures is involved in the use of vague language. He not only draws attention to this fact, but insists on its centrality in getting to grips with vague language. He also indicates how the sorites paradox may be "solved" by reference to shifting granularities. Moreover, some concrete "logics for reasoning with tolerance" are briefly described in the final part of the paper. I sincerely hope that this line of research will be continued and finds wider attention. As a side remark, let me mention that Manfred Krifka and some of his collaborators in *LoMoReVI*'s sister project *VAAG* (Vagueness, Approximation, and Granularity) do actually investigate shifting levels of granularity from a linguistic perspective. It would be nice to see some connections between these two lines of research emerge in future.

After having declared in the first part of these comments that I strongly disagree with some basic tenets of Vetterlein's paper, I could leave it at the above conciliatory and sympathetic comments. However, I trust to have Thomas's approval when I rather opt for formulating a challenge, that must appear quite provocative to him: I claim that an appropriate model of vague language that focuses on shifting levels of granularity is perfectly compatible with a realist approach to semantics. Nothing in the indicated model precludes the assumption that we are actually referring to objective, mind-independent entities when using expressions like "small table" in the relevant manner. The reason that I would like to see a "realism-based" account of vagueness that involves shifts between differently fine reference scales worked out in detail is that I am convinced that it will tie in nicely with recent linguistic research on vagueness, mentioned in the previous paragraph. Moreover, it were certainly a pity if linguists and philosophers (including, in this context, Vetterlein himself!) remain under the false impression that one has to forsake straightforward talk of reference to mind-independent objects and of truth conditions to obtain useful models of important features of vague language.

Christian G. Fermüller
Vienna University of Technology
Favoritenstr. 9–11/E1852
A-1040 Wien, Austria
Email: chrisf@logic.at

Reply to Christian Fermüller's Comments on
Vagueness: A Mathematician's Perspective

THOMAS VETTERLEIN

Once, mathematicians discussed intensely the foundations of their field, but awareness of the underlying problems has largely disappeared. Today hardly any mathematician spends much time contemplating what mathematics actually is; we are satisfied with the belief that we examine things in great generality and with great precision. In our daily work, the question of what it means to model something by formal means is in fact rarely important. Sometimes, however, the lack of insight into the process of mathematical modelling leads to problems. Philosophers have traditionally dealt with all sorts of fundamental questions. However, if they are unable to provide satisfactory advice, we (mathematicians) must ourselves take the initiative, though we then risk compromising ourselves. We may easily come into conflict with achievements established in philosophy or elsewhere.

My concern has been the formal treatment of vague properties. In search of a reasonable basis for my work on vagueness, I learned that the path I chose ignores substantial recent achievements in philosophy and linguistics. Who would have expected that the harmless-sounding topic "vagueness" would lead to conflicts of this magnitude?

I appreciate that Chris Fermüller's comments are formulated in a way that indicates tolerance. Still, he rejects my argument almost entirely. Fermüller suggests that there is no hope of basing a reasonable theory of natural language upon the approach that I have called perceptionalism a conviction he shares with the vast majority of contemporary philosophers. Thus, I must accept the fact that I am not in line with the experts in fundamental matters. Moreover, Fermüller points out that my arguments also conflict with principles upheld in linguistics.

I am open to new ideas. From these sobering conclusions, however, hardly anything follows. Philosophers have not provided a convincing and commonly understandable solution to the problem addressed, let alone a solution with practical impact. Moreover, the friction between linguists' work and my standpoint concerns, presumably, natural language processing technologies, a very productive field, but one in which, I dare say, achievements lag behind original expectations. For instance, it is at present not possible to infer automatically and reliably from a medical report whether a given diagnosis is confirmed or excluded.

Let me review the matter of content. If Fermüller conjectures that I reject the possibility of finding a uniform and all-encompassing formal approach to natural language such as a universal calculus that is at our disposal to formalize any kind of linguistic situation, he is right. In particular, I do not value first-order theories referring to a fixed model of the world, allowing, for instance, quantification over "all" existing objects of a certain kind. Work in this style might be of some particular use, but its applicability is restricted for reasons of principle. By means of a first-order theory, we can explore only a specific abstract structure; mathematics does not really have a wider scope. In natural language, in contrast, we deal with dynamically changing structures; as we speak, models are continuously created, modified, revised, rejected and replaced. This is the relevant topic. In mathematics, we must—and we can—systematically check all relevant possible behaviours of a property, and we are then capable of making general statements. Language instead deals with the typical circumstances in which a property holds; we make statements in terms of similarities and differences, and to check systematically all related circumstances is neither possible nor required. Fermüller hints at a critical attitude of mine towards the syntax-semantics-pragmatics triangle. Separation of these three areas is, without doubt, possible; priorities, however, are often chosen in a somewhat peculiar way. To assign the main role to syntax blurs the fundamental distinction between natural and formal language.

Fermüller's criticism culminates in the claim that a theory of natural language based on the pure notion of perception would be untenable. All I can set against these doubts is an explanation of how a formalization of natural language based on perceptionalism would look. Note that my actual contribution focussed on the formal treatment of vagueness in the case when new mathematical methods are required, and, as usual, I considered the case in which a coarse and the finest possible level of granularity are to be combined. Formalizing natural language in general is a different matter; we then deal with coarse levels only. To explain in a single paragraph the implications of the perception-based viewpoint is, however, impossible; I restrict myself to some key points.

The crucial role is not played by perceptions in isolation; such an approach might indeed be untenable; the link between perceptions made at different times would be missing. The crucial role is played by the models which systematize these perceptions.

Accordingly, perceptionalism puts emphasis on models rather than on formal statements. A natural-language utterance (where "natural language" is understood in the same restricted way as in the main text) evokes a picture in a person's mind, and it is this picture, against the background of pictures imagined before, that is to be modelled. A model is a finite first-order structure that captures selected aspects of the situation in question in comparison with other situations. This idea contrasts sharply with the common procedure of directly creating formulas according to the syntactical structure of the sentence. Moreover, a picture can be more or less detailed. By default, we do not choose the finest available model associated with a situation, but one that includes just enough details to represent the situation adequately. The finest possible model is the limit of a sequence of increasingly fine-grained models and is generally not relevant; the converse standpoint that a coarse model arises from blurring a fine model is rejected. Finally, the role of the "world" as the totality of what we observe around us is identified with the systematics according to which we endow pictures with structure. The "world model" offers generally applicable structural features including, in particular, our everyday experiences.

Fermüller argues that we can easily distinguish between an object and its perception. A theory of language that does not account for this difference would indeed be of limited use. To see how this aspect can be included in our considerations, we must clarify what the distinction actually means. When referring to the object itself, we associate with it all its actual and possible properties known or predictable from experience; when referring to its perception, we mean merely the fact that we observe it, even if it is a mirage. Thus, in one case we deal with all the consequences implied by integrating the object into the associated model; in the other case, we deal with one observation.

It is my own firm conviction that questions refer ultimately to perceptions or else they are meaningless; problems may just *appear* to be problems. To ask whether objects are mind-independent is to leave the realm of perceptions; the question is meaningless. Accordingly, we cannot associate with an object anything other than tactual and possible experiences involving it. We see that this restriction does not conflict with the requirement to treat objects and their perceptions in different formal ways.

However, this restriction does conflict with Fermüller's demand to model sentences such as "Peter is tall" independently of perceptions. This utterance is made when, among the people the speaker has in mind, Peter sticks out due to his height. To ask for independent criteria of "tallness" does not make sense.

Fermüller claims that a realist frame is a prerequisite for natural language modelling. This claim is intended to oppose my standpoint that the realism-based viewpoint cannot reasonably account for vagueness. However, I was referring to an extreme form of realism, on the basis of which the notion of vagueness cannot even be properly characterized. The word "real" is part of our language and thus has a role. We can ask what "real" means within the model that describes circumstances specified in natural language: it means conforming to the model. Consequently, a frame for natural language must indeed be realist, namely in the sense that it can deal with the statement that something is in line with generally accepted expectations.

Understanding reality relative to a model in fact brings us close to a methodology for which I have indicated tolerance: "realism-based ontology". Its proponents might strongly deny any parallels with my approach. However, I consider that, when it comes to practical work, the main principles are shared. In particular, it is essential for both approaches that statements can be made from different perspectives, in particular at different levels of granularity, and that no perspective is *a priori* superior to others. Furthermore, in both approaches, theories are never considered as fixed and definite, but as subject to revision whenever necessary.

Fermüller evaluates the idea of shifting levels of granularity positively, and he predicts "provocatively"—that an elaboration of this idea will bring us close to a realist frame. I have indicated the sense in which he is, in fact, right. Still, the prediction is surprising. Realists seem to think in terms of precise facts; all coarse notions are assumed to possess an interpretation at the one and only finest possible level. If we rely on perceptionalism, there simply will not be any fine level: unless somebody uses a ruler, lengths will not be modelled in centimetres. The fact that shifting levels of granularity involves ambiguity will, for the realists, remain an unsolved problem.

Personally, I take the—no less provocative—opposite viewpoint: whatever can be achieved within a framework based on naive realism can a fortiori be achieved within a framework based on perceptionalism.

Vagueness Through Definitions

Michael Freund[1]

Overview

At the basis of categorization theory stands the difference between *sharp* and *vague* concepts. Sharp concepts are those for which categorial membership is an all-or-nothing matter: a given object falls or does not fall under a sharp concept, and no intermediate state is conceivable. For vague concepts, on the contrary, intermediate states are possible, and categorial membership becomes a matter of degree. This definition of vagueness as opposed to sharpness conceals the fact that this notion is by no means a uniform one, and that different types of vagueness coexist. The treatment of vague concepts therefore depends of the type of vagueness these concepts instantiate. In this paper, we restrict our attention to the family of concepts that are learnt and known through a list of defining features. Partial membership to the corresponding category then results from partial membership relative to its defining features. In this elementary type of vagueness, we show that the categorization process is fully accounted for by the construction of a membership order among the objects at hand, which, naturally defined for simple concepts, can be easily extended to compound concepts, thus providing an interesting solution to the problem of compositionality.

1 Introduction

In categorization theory, different models have been proposed to account for the notion of concept. The classical model, formalized by Frege [2], identified concepts with functions whose values were truth values. In this model, objects *falling* under a concept, that is, objects the concept term is true of, form a mathematical set, called the *category* or the *extension* of the concept. Membership to this set is in consequence given by a simple two-valued truth function, and set theory is viewed as the adequate tool to deal with categorization. The inadequacy of this rudimentary model to capture phenomena like the *typicality effect* inside a category, or the existence of a *borderline* between membership and non-membership was pointed out by the work of Eleanor Rosch [14] and her followers, who showed in particular the existence of *vague* concepts for which membership cannot be an all-or-nothing matter. This led to several theories proposing different

---

[1]The main results of this paper were exposed at the conference LoMoReVI, held in Čejkovice, Czech Republic, in September 2009. I wish to thank the organizers, and especially Lluís Godo, for having given me the opportunity of talking about my work. I also thank the anonymous referees whose numerous remarks and suggestions greatly helped me to improve this paper. Thanks are also due to Brahim Djioua and Daniel Lehmann who helped me a lot formatting the final LaTeX version in the suitable text style.

models aiming at a correct representation of the major domains of categorization theory like categorial membership, typicality or resemblance.

In order to deal with the problem of vagueness, as early as 1965, Zadeh [18] introduced fuzzy logic as a way to handle concepts for which membership could not be decided on a simple IS-A procedure. Membership functions taking continuous or discrete values in the unit interval were consequently substituted to the two-valued characteristic function primitively associated with a category. Some drawbacks and counterintuitive results pointed out by Osherson-Smith [11] and Kamp-Partee [5] led the researchers to revise the initial fuzzy model and to look for alternative fuzzy logics displaying models more suitable to represent membership relative to vague concepts (see [1] or [7] for a an overview on the most recent work in this area).

For several reasons which will be explained in the next section, we shall depart from the general framework in which categorization theory has progressed in recent years. This paper will only focus on a very specific kind of concepts, and no general theory will be elaborated. We shall circumscribe our work to a very particular area, being quite aware that no generalization of our results is to be expected outside of the domain we choose. This domain is restricted both to a specific family of concepts and to a specific aspect of categorization theory: the class of concepts we are interested in, which we will call *definable*, consists of the concepts that come to the knowledge of an agent through a *definition*, that is with the help of simpler features; the categorization problem we are interested in is restricted to that of *categorial membership* in the concerned class. The solution we shall propose is therefore a particular one: we will show that, for definable concepts, it is possible to account for categorial membership by means of a qualitative ordering that compares the way the same concept may apply to different objects. This ordering can then be extended to compound concepts in a way that fully conforms with the intuition.

2 The notion of vagueness

The treatment of vague concepts suffers from an important drawback, which is its (default) assumption that vagueness is a uniform notion, and therefore bound to receive a uniform treatment. This attitude is quite disputable, though, as the same term covers different phenomena. For instance we may consider on the one hand concepts like *to-be-a-heap*, *to-be-tall*, *to-be-rich*, and on the other hand, concepts like *to-be-a-cause*, *to-be-beautiful*, *to-be-a-lie*. All these are vague concepts, but vagueness in the first group stems from *quantitative* considerations, whereas these considerations are meaningless for concepts of the second kind, which rather deserve to be qualified as *qualitatively* vague. It is thus natural to expect a numerical treatment of membership in the first case while looking for a different model in the second one.

The question then naturally arises whether we could use a criterion to characterize these two kinds of concepts, and whether other distinctions could be made inside the family of vague concepts. We observe however that, at this stage, we do not even have at our disposal a clear way of distinguishing between vague and sharp concepts. Several attempts have been conducted in the last decades to provide a strict definition of vagueness. To say that '*vagueness occurs whenever it is impossible to determine the limit between membership and non-membership to the concerned category*' only leads to the conviction that vagueness itself is a vague notion. In [8], Lupu proposed to define vagueness through membership functions: thus, a concept α would be vague if and only if there existed objects x for which the sentence 'x *falls under the concept* α' was not a Boolean proposition. It is interesting to note that this characterization does not imply by itself the impossibility of deciding between membership and non-membership. At any rate, we notice that the proposed definition implicitly assimilates vagueness with fuzziness as it treats this notion as a quantitative magnitude. A slight improvement in this proposal could consist in considering as vague every concept α for which there exists at least three objects to which α applies differently: this simple characterization would avoid implicitly using membership functions that have not been themselves first defined.

These considerations tend to show that a general theory of vagueness is doomed to fail. On the contrary, a study of the different kinds of vagueness together with the search for an appropriate framework for each family of vague concepts constitute at this stage a more promising approach. For this reason, we have chosen to focus our study on a particular family of concepts that can be easily circumscribed, and whose treatment appears possible and effective, without the need of any purpose-built complex formalism.

3 Definable concepts

The family we have chosen to study includes concepts whose meaning—as grasped by a given agent—can be learnt and understood with the help of simpler concepts that are already part of the agent's knowledge. We shall call these concepts '*definable*'. Such are for instance scientific concepts, (a *mammal* is a 'warm-blooded vertebrate that secretes milk', a *Banach space* is a 'complete normed vector space', a *bird* is a 'vertebrate with beak, wings and feathers'...). Note that for each of these examples, it is possible to find more than two objects to which the concept applies differently: being a vertebrate, a fish, for instance, has more *mammalhood* than a worm, and less than a cow; a normed (incomplete) vector space is not quite a Banach space but it is closer to it than, say, the set of odd numbers; a bat, finally, has somehow more *birdhood* than a mouse although it is definitely not a bird. Thus, following the avatar of Lupu's definition proposed in the preceding section, we see that these concepts should be considered as *vague*. Of course, it may seem paradoxical to call *vague* a mathematical or a scientific concept. More generally, we have the feeling that a precise definition should exclude vagueness rather than create it. However, in the absence of any satisfying definition of vagueness, we do not see any contradiction in considering definable concepts as constituting a specific subfamily of vague concepts. In any case, our goal in this paper is not to argue for or against the vagueness of a certain class of concepts, but to provide a suitable framework to study their categorization properties.

Definable concepts may be considered as constituting the heart of the so-called *attributional view* advocated by some authors in the late seventies [16] and [15], which gave rise to the so-called *binary model* [10]. Following this theory, class membership relative to a concept is accounted for by a set of *defining features*, while all questions regarding typicality are taken care of through a (different) set of *characteristic features*. It is only the former set that will retain our attention in the present paper, since our aim is actually to provide a framework for categorial membership.

The attributional view linked categorization problems relative to a concept with categorization relative to its defining features. For example, for a given agent, the concept *to-be-a-bird* may be seen as a definable concept, being defined trough the concepts *to-have-a-beak*, *to-have-feathers*, and *to-have-wings*. For this agent, the *birdhood* of a given item x will be consequently analyzed through its membership relative to the three mentioned defining concepts. Namely, the agent will estimate to what extent x may be considered as having a beak, having feathers and having wings. Similarly, to quote an example of Putnam [13], the *meaning* of the term *tiger* will be captured by reference to the terms *yellow feline, fierce, black stripes,* and *jungle*: the defining features associated with the concept *to-be-a-tiger* then consist of the concepts *to-be-a-yellow-feline, to-have-black-stripes, to-live-in-the jungle* and *to-be-fierce*. The word *tiger* applies to an item in as much as this item is a feline that is yellow with black stripes, fierce and lives in the jungle.

The defining features of a concept constituted a set of (necessary and sufficient) conditions that an item had to fullfil to be considered as a plain exemplar of this concept; at the same time they provided information on items that only partly fell under it, attributing to them an intermediate *membership degree* based on the number of defining features they possessed. However research in this direction was soon abandoned because of the few uncontroversial examples proposed by the theory: concepts cannot be generally learnt through a simple list of key-words. As we shall see, however, some improvement in the treatment of definable concepts generates a technique for membership evaluation that can be carried over to a more general and much representative family of concepts. This justifies our interest for this theory.

An interesting point with the theory of definable concepts is that it implicitly supposes a complexity hierarchy between the target concept and the sources that are used in the defining process. Indeed, a definition is effective only on condition that the terms used in the explanation or the description of a new concept are themselves already part of the agent's knowledge. In this sense, associating with a particular concept a set of features that help understanding it evokes the process of a dictionary or an encyclopedia, which renders theoretically possible the construction of complex concepts from a well-defined set of primitive ones. In principle, we could thus introduce the notion of concept *constructibility*: choosing once and for all a set of *primitive* concepts, the family of constructible concepts can be iteratively enumerated by requiring that

1) primitive concepts are constructible

2) any concept presented with a defining set of constructible features is constructible

3) there are no other constructible concepts than those obtained through 1) or 2).

Such 'constructible' concepts were partly studied in [3] under the additional hypothesis that primitive concepts on which the construction was based were *sharp* concepts. We shall come back later to this notion of conceptual dictionary.

If a definable concept takes all its meaning and properties from its defining features, its associated categorial membership must be inherited from the categorial membership associated with these defining features. This raises the problem of determining whether and how a model could account for this passage from the extensional properties of the defining features to those of the newly defined concept. But before addressing this problem, we first need to explain our position concerning the mathematical formalism that we think is best adequate for the study of categorial membership.

Categorial membership relative to a concept measures how strongly this concept applies to the different objects that an agent has at his disposal. In general, the human mind disposes of no tool to directly evaluate this magnitude: even though differences in membership may be felt—one undoubtedly agrees for instance that a conventional bomb would be more a *weapon of mass destruction* than a machine-gun—it is impossible, except in some limit cases, to assign a precise number that would exactly measure the membership or the non-membership degree of a given item. When directly questioned what membership degree should be attributed to a machine-gun considered as a *weapon of mass destruction*, an agent will be generally unable to provide a sensible answer: what indeed could be the meaning of a sentence like 'a machine-gun is a *weapon of mass destruction* up to degree .35'? Similarly, an agent may be unable to assign a precise membership degree to a sink as a *piece of furniture*, while being fully ready to decide that this sink is 'more' a piece of furniture than a heat-pipe, and 'less' a piece of furniture than a window.

As a matter of fact, the only thing the human mind is capable of concerning membership evaluation is to *compare* two objects and decide which one, if any, falls 'more' under the concerned concept. Thus, the concept *to-be-a-weapon-of mass-destruction* will be generally considered as applying *more* to a machine-gun than to an arquebus, and *less* to a spear than to an arquebus. Clearly, this judgement shows the existence of a basic ordering induced by the concept *to-be-a-weapon-of mass-destruction* in the universe of discourse, but this ordering is by no means a consequence of a supposed degree assignment that the agent has set *a-priori* on the objects at his disposal. Naturally such an assignment may be established by him once the collection of objects of his universe has been displayed before him and comparison has been made between the items of this collection. For instance, a non-decreasing ranking like *bludgeon* $\leq$ *sword* $\leq$ *crossbow* $\leq$ *arquebus* $\leq$ *gun* $\leq$ *machine-gun* $\leq$ *flamethrower* $\leq$ *conventional bomb* $\leq$ *scud* $\leq$ *atomic bomb* may yield *a posteriori* a membership degree of the concerned items, which can be readily visualized on their position on a [0,1] scale: thus, an *atomic bomb* will be considered as being 100% a WMD, a *scud* as 90%, a *conventional bomb* as 80% and so on. The point is that these numerical values will appear as a consequence of a pre-recognized order among the different weapons that are part of the agent's universe: they won't be at the origin of it.

Ordering relations therefore appear to provide the most adequate model to account for categorial membership as perceived by a cognitive agent. Appealing systematically to relations of this type whenever it is possible avoids the drawbacks, shortcomings or counter-intuitive results that may result from the application of more sophisticated theories. It is true that in some cases, order relations may be insufficient to fully treat categorial membership. Such will be for instance the case for *fuzzy concepts*, or for vague concepts of a continuous type: for these concepts, interesting theories have been developed in different domains—fuzzy set theory, geometrical spaces, quantum mechanics. But for the specific class of concepts studied in this paper, that of '*definable concepts*', the family of order relations is sufficiently wide to perfectly model the problem of categorial membership.

With this in mind, the problem of determining how membership is transmitted to a concept from its defining features transforms itself into that of understanding how the different membership orders associated with the source features can melt into a single target membership order.

The construction of such an order has already been proposed in [3] for the family of concepts that can be recursively built out of a set of sharp primitives. We shall propose a simplified construction for elementary definable concepts, that will then be extended to compound concepts as well as to arbitrary definable concepts. But first a remark is necessary.

As we mentioned, the theory of definable concepts suffers from an important drawback, which is its lack of convincing examples. Concepts tend to be not easily definable: *birdhood* may be defined by a certain set of features that will be collectively possessed by birds and only by birds, but this is not so for *fishhood*: naturalists failed to propose a list of features that would apply to and only to fish. One may also think of the term *knowledge*, classically defined as *justified true belief* and thereafter subjected to numerous criticisms. Moreover, definitions rarely boil down to a simple list of words: disjunctions are frequently used, as well as negations, analogies or, even, examples. Thus, natural kind concepts and usual artifacts are seldom, if ever, defined by a simple enumeration of their most representative features, and the latter, when they exist, cannot be systematically considered as simpler than the target concept. Nominal concepts may be introduced through definitions—this is indeed the case for scientific concepts like mathematic definitions or entities classifiers—but the items that intervene in this definition are organized in a dynamical sequential way, allowing a term to act on another, and making use of constructors and modifiers. For this reason, it will be necessary to adapt the apparatus used in the case of elementary definable concepts to a larger class that will include non trivial examples of concept definitions. As we shall see, this task can be achieved by translating the dynamical structure of a definition into an ordered sequence of compound concepts built out through a determination operator, and to which we can apply the construction elaborated in the case of elementary definitions.

4   Categorial membership for definable concepts

Before treating the general case of concepts introduced through a definition, we examine the elementary case where both the structure of the definition and the defining terms used in it are of the simplest form.

4.1   Elementary definable concepts

The family of elementary concepts that are part of the universe of an agent covers the concepts that are brought to his knowledge through the help of several elementary (that is non compound) concepts, which are already part of the agent's knowledge. An elementary concept α is thus present in the agent's mind together with a finite set $\Delta(\alpha)$ of *defining features* that are supposed to be simpler than α. From the point of view of the agent, this set includes all the features that explain or illustrate α, helping to differentiate it from its neighboring concepts. For instance, the meaning of *tent* may be explained to a child through the definition: *tent = shelter made out of cloth*; in the child's mind, the corresponding set $\Delta(\alpha)$ would then consist of the concepts *to-be-a-shelter, to-be-made-of-cloth*. Similarly, the defining feature set associated with the concept *to-be-a-bird* may be the set {*to-be-a-vertebrate, to-be-a-oviparous to-have-a-beak, to-have-feathers*}, and that associated with the concept *to-be-carnivorous* may consist in the concepts *to-be-an-animal* and *to-eat-meat*. The *definition* of α is of an elementary type, consisting of a simple list, and the elements of $\Delta(\alpha)$ are elementary concepts that are supposed to be *less complex* than the target concept α.

Our basic assumption concerning the concepts of $\Delta(\alpha)$ is that they are part of the agent's knowledge, and that they are sufficient to enable him to acquire full knowledge of the categorial membership associated with α.

From these two requirements, we see that the categorization process of a definable concept results from the categorization process associated of its defining features. For instance, to judge if a given object *x* is a *bird*, defined as *a vertebrate that is oviparous, has beak, wings and feathers*, we have to evaluate its *being a vertebrate*, its *being oviparous*, its *having a beak* and its *having feathers*.

Note at this point that the terms 'concept' and 'feature' cover different notions. Formally, concepts are most often introduced through the auxiliary *to-be* followed by a noun: *to-be-a-bird, to-be-a-vector-space, to-be-a-democracy*. Features may be presented through a verb (*to-fly*), the auxiliary *to-have* followed by a noun (*to-have-a-beak*), or the auxiliary *to-be* followed by an adjective (*to-be-tall*). While concepts appear as unary predicates, this condition is no more necessary for features, which may take arbitrary forms. On the ground level, we know that features, like concepts, apply to the objects at hand but, contrary to these latter, they borrow part of their significance from the concept they are attached to. Properties like *to-be-tall, to-be-rich*, or *to-be-red* take their full meaning only in a given context, that is when qualifying well-defined entities. Even simple verbal forms like *to-fly, to-run, to-live-in-water, to-be-made-of-metal* need a principal referent concept to fully seize the strength with which they apply to different items. To summarize, we would say that the meaning of a feature depends on the context in which this feature is used, contrary to the meaning of a concept which exists by itself.

It is true that, strictly speaking, features cannot be considered as concepts in the sense of Frege. It is for this reason that they did not call the attention of researchers in such different logical approaches of categorization theory like Fuzzy Logics, Formal Concept Analysis and Description Logics. In these approaches indeed, concepts are implicitly or not, assimilated to unary predicates, that are introduced through a noun (*to-be-a-bird*), a verb (*to-fly*) or an adjective (*to-be-yellow*). In Description Logics binary predicates characterize the *roles* of the language, which are used to express relationship between the concepts [9]. Thus, *to-be-a-tree* will be a concept, expressible by a single symbol *A*, but *to-have-green-leaves* is a 'role', expressed by a formula of the type '$\forall$ hasLeaves.Green'. This distinction renders impossible the treatment of membership for concepts defined by two-place predicates. In this paper, we shall nevertheless consider that all features that are used to define or characterize a concept can be themselves treated as concepts.

Any feature defining a concept α will therefore be considered as inducing a membership order among the objects at hand that is meant to reflect the strength with which the feature, *taken in the context of* α, applies to the items of the universe of discourse. Note that in most cases, this strength can be measured through a *total* preorder that ranks the objects of the universe on a finite scale. This is clearly true for fuzzy features like *to-be-tall*, *to-be-rich* or *to-be-warm*, since the measure of their applicability is always approximative (to an inch, a cent or a degree); this is even truer in the general process of categorization: in the context of a given concept α, ranking the objects relatively to a feature only yields a small number of non equivalent classes. To determine, for instance, to which extent a flower may be considered as a *poppy*, one evaluates very roughly its redness, its shape and the size of its petals. Comparison with other real or fictitious objects shows only a finite number of ordered non equivalent classes of reds between the color of that particular flower and that of an ideal poppy. Thus, in the context of a *poppy*, there exists only a small number of possible degrees of *redness*.

Let us now come back to the notion of definable concepts. The feature sets associated with this kind of concepts cannot be totally arbitrary, because all the features that define α must have 'something in common'—namely the fact that they qualify a well defined concept. We shall therefore assume as a basic property of the set $\Delta(\alpha)$ that all its elements apply together on at least one object: as we shall see, this will guarantee the existence of objects that fully fall under α.

4.2   A social choice problem for membership inheritance

How precisely does a concept inherit its category membership from that of its defining features ? For the reasons evoked above, the categorial membership induced by a concept α will be best accounted for by a partial preorder, that is a reflexive and transitive relation $\preceq_\alpha$, which can be used as a comparison tool between the objects at hand. The expression '$x \preceq_\alpha y$' will translate the fact that 'the concept α applies at least as much to object y as to object x'. We shall denote by $\prec_\alpha$ the corresponding strict partial order, that is the irreflexive and transitive relation defined by $x \prec_\alpha y$ iff $x \preceq_\alpha y$ and not $y \preceq_\alpha x$. This relation can be used to translate the fact that α applies better (or more) to y than to x.

Our assumption is that the defining features of the concept α are part of the agent's knowledge; this means that the agent knows, for every concept γ of $\Delta(\alpha)$, the structure of the associated membership preorder $\preceq_\gamma$. As we noticed, this latter is supposed to be *connected* (total): given two items x and y, either $x \preceq_\gamma y$, or $y \preceq_\gamma x$. The requirement that the knowledge of the $\preceq_\gamma$'s is sufficient to acquire knowledge of the target order relation $\preceq_\alpha$ shows that $\preceq_\alpha$ should be naturally deduced from the $\preceq_\gamma$'s.

It is interesting to observe that the problem of determining $\preceq_\alpha$ from the orders $\preceq_\gamma$'s is closely related with that encountered in *social choice theory*: there indeed, one tries to aggregate individual votes concerning a certain number of candidates into a general ranking $\leq$ of these candidates that would best approach the individual rankings $\leq_1, \leq_2, \ldots, \leq_n$ proposed by the voters. Our situation is somewhat similar: having to decide if the definable concept α applies more to the item x than to the item y, we may consider each of the defining features γ of α as a *voter*, examine successively if this feature applies more to x than to y, and eventually use a decision procedure to conclude. Some differences however deserve to be pointed out: the first one is that, in social choice theory, the preference relations $\leq_i$ as well as the resulting relation $\leq$ are supposed to be total (connected) relations. On the contrary, from our point of view, and unlike what happens in most categorization theories, we accept that the resulting α-membership of two items may be incomparable. For instance, an agent may consider that the '*birdhood*' of a tortoise cannot be compared with that of a bat, for the reason that tortoises, contrary to bats, share with birds the fact they lay eggs and have a beak, while bats, contrary to tortoises, share with birds their having wings and being warm-blooded. No comparison should therefore be made between these two items, as far as birdhood is concerned. A second difference is that, in categorization theory, one looks for a membership order that best models a known fact, namely the behavior of an intelligent agent while, in social choice, one tries to determine an abstract and general procedure for aggregating votes under some well defined constraints—an impossible task in the general case, as shown by Arrow's famous theorem. Note also that the constraints we are dealing with are different from those encountered in social choice: for instance, the fact that all defining features of a definable concept should apply simultaneously to at least one object would impose that, in all elections, there should be one candidate on which all voters agree.

Of course, the simplest way to build the relation $\preceq_\alpha$ from the relations $\preceq_\gamma$, $\gamma \in \Delta(\alpha)$, would be to take their intersection, simply setting $\preceq_\alpha = \cap_{\gamma \in \Delta(\alpha)} \preceq_\gamma$. This would amount to considering that the concept α applies no more to x than to y if such is the case for every defining feature of α. An alternative to this skeptical approach would consist in 'counting the votes', and set $x \preceq_\alpha y$ if the number of defining features γ such that $x \preceq_\gamma y$ is at least as great as the number of defining features δ such that $y \preceq_\delta x$: this non-transitive relation leads to the so-called Condorcet method. However, the fact that in these approaches, the defining features of α are all given equal importance forbids their adoption, not mentioning the side drawbacks that these procedures may carry. In categorization theory indeed, the defining features of a concept are rarely considered by an agent as equivalent. Thus, each of the sets $\Delta(\alpha)$ is usually presented with a *salience* relation between its elements, which is adequately translated by a strict partial order on $\Delta(\alpha)$. For instance, a particular agent may associate with the concept *to-be-a-bird* the defining set {*to-be-a-vertebrate, to-be-oviparous, to-have-feathers, to-habe-a-beak, to-have-wings*}, considering furthermore that *having wings* is a more important feature for birdhood than *having a beak*. For this agent consequently, a bat would be given more birdhood than a tortoise.

We therefore have to deal with the presence of voters whose voices have different importance. When this difference is quantifiable, that is, when it can be translated by a natural number that corresponds to an importance rank, it can be accounted for by a simple perequation: the voice of a voter of rank i will weigh i times that of an 'ordinary' voter. Alternatively, it is also possible to attach to each defining feature of α its *cue validity* probability: given a defining feature $\beta \in \Delta(\alpha)$, its cue validity is the probability $P(\alpha/\beta)$ that an object x falls under α, knowing that it has the feature β. Then, the membership degree of an object x, defined as the probability that x falls under α, can be computed as the sum $\Sigma_\beta P(\alpha/\beta)P(\beta)$. However, in our case, there is no reason why the defining features of a concept should be attributed such a numerical rank of importance or such a degree of probability: again, an agent may be quite able to compare the relative salience of two features of a concept without being able to associate a degree to these saliences. Apart from this pragmatic inability, salience may be simply not expressible by a gradation. For instance, taking again the concept *to-be-a-bird* and its defining set {*to-be-a-vertebrate, to-be-oviparous, to-have-feathers, to-have-a-beak, to-have-wings*}, suppose we equip this set with an order that renders *having-wings* more salient than *having-a-beak*, all other features being incomparable. Clearly, any grading function on $\Delta(\alpha)$ consistent with this order would attribute a greater rank to the feature *having-wings* than to the feature *to-be-oviparous*, thus making these two features comparable in $\Delta(\alpha)$, which they were not supposed to be.

Except for some specific cases, we therefore have to work with a completely arbitrary salience relation on $\Delta(\alpha)$. We will only assume that this salience is translated by a strict partial order in $\Delta(\alpha)$. Our task is to build a voting procedure that takes into account the relative importance of the voters, so that, in case of conflict, the voice of a subordinate can be overruled by that of a hierarchical superior. This may be done through the simple following idea which simplifies the construction proposed in [3]: a candidate y will be declared at least as good as a candidate x if for any voter that prefers x to y there exists a more important voter that prefers y to x. Formally this yields the relation:

$$x \preceq_\alpha y \text{ iff for each feature } \gamma \in \Delta(\alpha) \text{ such that } y \prec_\gamma x \text{ there exists a feature } \delta \in \Delta(\alpha),$$
$$\delta \text{ more salient than } \gamma, \text{ such that } x \prec_\delta y.$$

This relation $\preceq_\alpha$ is clearly reflexive; its transitivity follows from the connectedness of the membership preorders $\preceq_\gamma$.

The corresponding strict partial order is then defined by

$$x \prec_\alpha y \text{ if and only if } x \preceq_\alpha y \text{ and there exists a feature } \gamma \in \Delta(\alpha) \text{ such that } x \prec_\gamma y.$$

EXAMPLE 1 Let α be the concept *to-be-a-bird*, with associated defining feature set $\Delta(\alpha) = \{$*to-be-an-animal, to-have-two-legs, to-lay-eggs, to-have-a-beak, to-have-wings*$\}$, all features being considered as sharp by the agent. Suppose that the salience order is given by the Hasse diagram, to be read bottom-top:

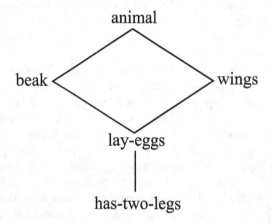

Let us compare the relative birdhood of a *sparrow,* a *mouse,* a *tortoise,* a *bat,* a *dragonfly* and a *plane,* respectively denoted by s, m, t, b, d and p.

In order to determine the induced membership order, we build the following array:

	two-legs	lay-eggs	beak	wings	animal
sparrow	★	★	★	★	★
mouse					★
tortoise		★	★		★
bat	★			★	★
plane				★	
dragonfly		★		★	★

We readily check that $d \prec_\alpha s$, $m \prec_\alpha t$, and $m \prec_\alpha b$. Note that we have $b \preceq_\alpha d$, since the concept *to-have-two-legs* under which the bat falls, contrary to the dragonfly, is dominated by the concept *to-lay-eggs* that applies to the dragonfly and not to the bat. On the other hand, we do not have $d \preceq_\alpha b$, as nothing compensates the fact that the dragonfly lays eggs and the bat does not. This yields $b \prec_\alpha d$. Similarly, we have $p \prec_\alpha m$. We also remark that the tortoise and the bat are incomparable, that is, we have neither $b \preceq_\alpha t$, nor $t \preceq_\alpha b$.

The strict α-membership order induced on these six elements is therefore given by the following diagram:

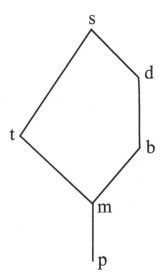

The construction of the (pre)order $\prec_\alpha$ we presented in this section is simpler and more intuitive than that proposed in [3]. It renders possible a computation of the target membership order directly from the membership orders induced by the defining features. It successfully takes care of the salience order on $\Delta(\alpha)$ even in the cases where this order cannot be expressed by a degree or a rank of importance among the defining features of α. However, in some situations, the results this order leads to may seem disputable: this happens in particular in the case where the concept α is defined by a significant number of features that are all equally salient except for a particular one, which is more salient than all others. Then if this particular attribute applies less to x than to y, we will have $x \prec_\alpha y$, even in the case where every other defining feature δ applies more to x than to y. The situation is analogous to an election where, because of his rank, a single individual could dictate his preferences to everybody.

Although it is rarely the case that $\Delta(\alpha)$ consists of a single salient feature opposed to a bunch of non salient ones, it may be useful to consider an alternative to the above construction so as to take into account the *number* of voters that prefer a candidate to another one. This can be done by requiring that a candidate y cannot be preferred to a candidate x unless, for any group of voters that prefer x to y, there exists an equally numerous group of more salient voters that prefer y to x. In other words we consider now the relation $\leq_\alpha$ defined by:

> $x \leq_\alpha y$ if for each sequence of distinct elements $\kappa_1, \kappa_2, \ldots \kappa_n$ of $\Delta(\alpha)$ such that $y \prec_{\kappa_i} x$, there exists a sequence of distinct elements $\gamma_1, \gamma_2, \ldots \gamma_n$ of $\Delta(\alpha)$, γ_i more salient than κ_i, such that $x \prec_{\gamma_i} y$.

In this situation, each voter may see his decision overruled by a personally attached direct superior, but the voice of a single voter, be it the most important of all, cannot overrule more than one voice.

The relation $\leq_\alpha$ is clearly reflexive. It is not in general transitive. We shall denote by $\leq_\alpha^*$ its transitive closure. This latter yields the desired new membership preorder. Note that we have $\preceq_\alpha^* \subseteq \preceq_\alpha$ and similarly $\prec_\alpha^* \subseteq \prec_\alpha$. When the salience order on $\Delta(\alpha)$ is empty, both membership orders $\preceq_\alpha$ and $\preceq_\alpha^*$ boil down to the intersection $\cap_{\gamma \in \Delta(\alpha)} \preceq_\gamma$.

4.3 Defining membership through membership orders

It is now possible to precisely define the notion of (full) *membership*: we shall say that an object x 'falls under the concept α' if x is $\prec_\alpha$-maximal among the objects that form the universe of discourse, that is if there exists no object y such that $x \prec_\alpha y$. This is equivalent to saying that x is $\prec_\alpha$-maximal in this set. When this is the case, x will be said to be an *instance* or an *exemplar* of α. This definition by means of maximal membership conforms with the intuition: an object x (fully) falls under a concept α if α cannot apply more to an object y than to x. It has as a consequence that, whatever salience order is set on $\Delta(\alpha)$, an object falls under the definable concept α if and only if it falls under each of its defining features.[1] We find thus again the classical characterization of a defining feature set as a set of features that are 'individually necessary and jointly sufficient to ensure membership relative to α'. We shall denote by $Ext\,\alpha$ the set of all objects that fall under α; this set forms the *extension* or the *category* associated with α.

---

[1] We use here the assumption made at the end of Section 4.1 that there exists at least one object that falls under all the features of α.

Contrary to full membership, partial membership cannot be directly defined from the membership orders $\prec_\alpha$ or $\prec_\alpha^\star$. However, it is possible to introduce the notion of a *membership distance*, which can be used to measure 'how far' an object x stands from falling under α (see [3] for details). For this purpose, it is enough to consider the number of objects that can be possibly inserted between x and an exemplar of α: more precisely, the $\prec_\alpha$-membership distance μ_α of an object x is defined as the maximal length of a chain $x \prec_\alpha x_1 \prec_\alpha x_2 \prec_\alpha \cdots \prec_\alpha x_n$. Such a chain must necessarily end up with an element of $Ext\,\alpha$ since, given any object x not falling under α, it holds $x \prec_\alpha z$ for any exemplar z of α.

EXAMPLE 2 Let us consider the preceding example and denote by μ_{bird} the membership distance of an object x to the category *birds*. Then we have $\mu_{bird}(t) = 1$ because, except birds themselves, there exists no oviparous animal with beak that would have two legs or that would have wings. Similarly, we have $\mu_{bird}(d) = 1$, since there exists no animal x such that $d \prec_{bird} x \prec_{bird} s$. Since the bat falls under three out of the five elements of Δ_{bird} we have necessarily $\mu_{bird}(b) < 3$, and the inequality $b \prec_{bird} d \prec_{bird} s$ then yields $\mu_{bird}(b) = 2$. As for the mouse, we have $m \prec_{bird} b \prec_{bird} d \prec_{bird} s$, but this is not a chain of maximal length. For instance, noting that men have two legs, we also have the chain $m \prec_{bird} k \prec_{bird} b \prec_{bird} d \prec_{bird} s$, where k denotes a man. This shows that $\mu_{bird}(m) \geq 4$, and thus $\mu_{bird}(m) = 4$ since, among the animals, only four features are sufficient to define a bird (we recall that all these features are supposed to be sharp). As a consequence, we have $\mu_{bird}(p) = 5$.

Note that an object falls under α if and only if its membership distance is null. Clearly, given two objects x and y with $x \prec_\alpha y$, the membership distance of y will be smaller than that of x. The converse is generally not true, though: y may be closer to $Ext\,\alpha$ than x without being comparable with it. In this sense the information provided by the membership distance is not as precise as that provided by membership functions. However, it is interesting to observe that the membership distance provides a *threshold* for categorial membership: if x has membership distance equal to 1, and y falls more than x under α, then it must be the case that y is an exemplar of α. In the above example, any object that has more birdhood than a tortoise is necessarily a bird.

5   The case of compound concepts

Elementary concepts give rise to compound ones through different combinations. The simplest one is the ordinary conjunction, &, which corresponds to a simple juxtaposition of terms, as in *(to-be-green)&(to-be-light)*. Theoretically, it should be possible to consider also logical operations like concept negation or concept disjunction, but the pseudo-concepts to which these operations lead may end up into meaningless notions, e.g. concepts with no prototypes, or concepts with empty extensions.

We shall therefore only examine concept conjunction, and moreover restrict ourselves to the case where the resulting pseudo concept $\alpha\&\beta$ has a non-empty extension: that is, we suppose given two concepts α and β such that $Ext\,\alpha \cap Ext\,\beta \neq \emptyset$. The membership order on the conjunction $\alpha\&\beta$ is set by considering the (fictitious) associated defining feature set $\Delta(\alpha\&\beta) = \{\alpha, \beta\}$, which we equip with an empty salience order.

We have therefore $x \preceq_{\alpha\&\beta} y$ iff $x \preceq_\alpha y$ and $x \preceq_\beta y$; similarly we define the relation $\preceq^\star_{\alpha\&\beta}$ by $x \preceq^\star_{\alpha\&\beta} y$ iff $x \preceq^\star_\alpha y$ and $x \preceq^\star_\beta y$: thus, the membership order of the conjunction is just the intersection of the membership orders of its components. For instance, given two individuals x and y, x is considered as no more a *physician-and-a-Parisian* than y if x is no more a physician than y and at the same time no more a Parisian than y. Note that we have $\preceq_{\alpha\&\alpha} = \preceq_\alpha = \preceq^\star_{\alpha\&\alpha}$.

Let us define the *extension* of $\alpha\&\beta$ as the set of all $\prec_{\alpha\&\beta}$-maximal elements. The hypothesis made on $Ext\,\alpha$ and $Ext\,\beta$ implies that this set is also the set of all $\prec^\star_{\alpha\&\beta}$-maximal elements. We easily check that full membership is compositional in the sense that $Ext\,\alpha \cap Ext\,\beta = Ext\,\alpha\&\beta$.

It is interesting to observe that the relations $\preceq_{\alpha\&\beta}$ and $\preceq^\star_{\alpha\&\beta}$ can be directly recovered by assigning to the concept $\alpha\&\beta$ a defining feature set equal to the disjoint union of $\Delta(\alpha)$ and $\Delta(\beta)$. More precisely, let $\widetilde{\Delta}(\alpha)$ be the set $\{(\gamma,\alpha); \gamma \in \Delta(\alpha)\}$ equipped with the salience order that makes (γ,α) more salient than (δ,α) if and only if γ is more salient than δ. Similarly set $\widetilde{\Delta}(\beta) = \{(\delta,\beta); \delta \in \Delta(\beta)\}$ with the same corresponding salience order. The structure of these sets emphasizes the fact that features are in general dependent of the concept they apply to. Consider now the set $\widetilde{\Delta}(\alpha\&\beta) = \widetilde{\Delta}(\alpha) \cup \widetilde{\Delta}(\beta)$ with the salience order that extends those of $\widetilde{\Delta}(\alpha)$ and $\widetilde{\Delta}(\beta)$ and is empty elsewhere. The membership order induced by the concept $\alpha\&\beta$ with associated defining feature set $\widetilde{\Delta}(\alpha\&\beta)$ is then exactly the order $\preceq_{\alpha\&\beta}$.

More interesting than the simple conjunction of two concepts is, in the framework of categorization theory, the modification or the determination of a concept by another one. In [3] we have introduced a specific connective called the *determination operator*, that can be used to account for the *modification* of a principal concept α by a modifier β. This determination, denoted by $\beta \star \alpha$, is most often translated by the combination of an adjective or an adjectived verb with a noun (e.g. the concepts *to-be-a-carnivorous-animal, to-be-a-flying-bird, to-be-a french-student, to-be-a-red-apple*), but it can also be rendered by a noun-noun combination (eg. *to-be-a-pet-fish, to-be-a-barnyard-bird*). Typically, in the compound concept $\beta \star \alpha$, the main concept α is defined through a predicate of the type *to-be-x*, while the accessory concept β is of the form *to-have-the-property-y*.

It is important to keep in mind that we consider only the conceptual combinations that are *intersective*: the objects that fall under the composed concept $\beta \star \alpha$ are exactly those that both fall under α and under β. Thus, and to mention the best known examples, the determination connective cannot be used to form complex concepts like *to-be-a-brick-factory, to-be-a-criminal lawyer* or *to-be-a-topless-district*: indeed, a brick factory need not be a factory that is made out of bricks, a criminal lawyer not a lawyer that is a criminal, and a topless district not a district that is topless (see [5] for the distinction between intersective and non-intersective modifiers). Note also that the intersection condition forbids us to consider a concept like *to-have-green-leaves* as the determination of the concept *to-have-leaves* by the concept *to-be-green*.

Some determinations that are not properly intersective may nevertheless benefit from our treatment of concept determination. Consider for instance a concept like *to-be-a-good-violinist*. We do not have intersection properly here, since a good violinist is not somebody that is good and that is violinist. However, we have to remember that features take part of their meaning from the concepts they are used with. Here the feature used as a modifier, *good*, takes the meaning *to-play-well*, and a good violinist is a violinist that plays well. Thus, setting α for the principal concept *to-be-a-violinist* and β for the modifier *to-play-well-the-violin* we can consider that the meaning of the concept *to-be-a-good-violinist* is correctly translated by the composition $\beta \star \alpha$.

Modified concepts are generally not definable, and they are not brought to the agent's knowledge with the help of a defining features set. It is not difficult however to extend the order $\preceq_\alpha$ defined in the preceding paragraph to this family of concepts. The construction of the membership order induced by $\beta \star \alpha$ is obtained by attaching to this concept the (fictitious) set of features $\Delta(\beta \star \alpha) = \{\beta, \alpha\}$ equipped with an order that makes α more salient than β. We have thus $x \preceq_{\beta\star\alpha} y$ iff $x \preceq_\alpha y$ and either $x \prec_\alpha y$, or $x \preceq_\beta y$. This construction yields a preorder that takes into account the predominance of the principal concept α. In this model, the concept *to-be-a-flying-bird* will be considered as applying more to a penguin than to a bat. Note that we have again $\preceq_{\alpha\star\alpha} = \preceq_\alpha = \preceq^*_{\alpha\star\alpha}$.

As in the case of the conjunction, we observe that the relation $\preceq_{\beta\star\alpha}$ may be d through the disjoint union of $\Delta(\alpha)$ and $\Delta(\beta)$, equipped with an order that extends their respective salience orders, making furthermore any element of $\Delta(\alpha)$ more salient than any element of $\Delta(\beta)$.

5.1 Structured defining sets

As we already mentioned, the defining set associated with a (definable) concept cannot be simply described by means of a list of features. Rather, these features are most often articulated through some operators or constructors. The description of a term can also make use of locutions like *on which, through which*, etc. The key words that intervene in the definition of a concept are at any case constituted by a certain number of nouns, verbs, and modifiers, to which an apparatus consisting of auxiliary verbs, pronouns, locutions and ingredient markers provides the final *Gestalt*.

Similarly, a conceptual dictionary cannot be expressive if it does not propose, together with its set of primitive concepts, a structure or a *grammar* that helps extending the meaning of an enumeration of defining features. This fact has already been underlined by Ray Jackendoff [4] and Anna Wierzbicka [17]. In particular, in her research on a *Natural Semantic Metalanguage* (NSM), Wierzbicka and her followers proposed, together with a list of conceptual primitives, a list of conceptual elementary structures that constitute the syntax of this (meta)language (For an introduction to Wierzbicka work, see [12] or [6]).

Categorial membership clearly becomes more difficult to evaluate when the definition by which is introduced the target concept rests on a non-trivial subjacent grammar. As an example of the problems encountered in this situation, let us consider the following (structured) definition of *maple*:

'*a tall tree growing in northern countries, whose leaves have five points, and the resin of which is used to produce a syrup*'.

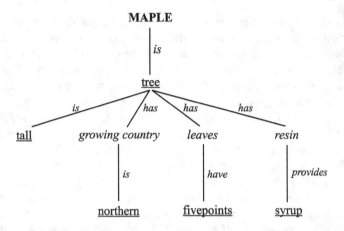

Figure 1. Definition tree for *maple*.

Among the features listed in this definition, only that of *tree* directly applies to the target concept *maple*. All the other ones are linked with some secondary concepts: thus, *tall* refers to *tree*, *to-have-fivepoints* refers to *leaves*, *northern* refers to *country*, and *syrup* refers to *resin*. The key features that intervene in this definition are the concepts *tree, tall, northern, fivepoints, syrup.* The apparatus is encapsulated by the sequence: is a + *key-feature*, that is + *key-feature*, whose growing country is + *key-feature*, whose shape of leaves is + *key-feature*, whose resin produces + *key-feature*. We can formalize the whole definition by a tree in which the edges translate the verbs used in the definition process, and where the nodes underlined in roman letters stand for the key features and those in italics indicate the auxiliary concepts used in the *Gestalt* (Figure 1).

It is clear that the membership of an object *x* relatively to the concept *to-be-a-maple* not only depends on its own membership relative to the concept *to-be-a-tree*, but also depends on the membership of other objects (the leaves of *x*, the resin of *x*) relative to auxiliary concepts (*to-have-five-points, to-provide-a-syrup*): it is not the object *x* itself that may be qualified as *having fivepoints* but the auxiliary object 'leaves of *x*'. We see in this example an important difference with the simple defining features sets used in the preceding section, where the membership of an object relative to the target concept was directly evaluated through the membership of *this same object* relative to the defining features.

The problem is now that the auxiliary objects that correspond to the auxiliary concepts may simply not exist for the chosen item *x* whose membership is to be evaluated: thus, it may be the case that *x* is not a tree, or that *x* is a pine-tree and has no leaves, in which case it is meaningless to pretend to evaluate the membership of *its* leaves relative to the concept *to-have-fivepoints*. This observation seems to ruin any attempt to evaluate an item's membership through the elementary key-features that intervene in its definition when the defining feature set is not presented as a simple list.

Fortunately, in a great number of cases, we can still use the (complex) auxiliary features, provided we do not systematically try to break them down into elementary components. Let us take again the *maple* example: we may interpret its definition by saying that an object x is a maple if *it is a tree* that *is tall*, if *it has a growing country* that *is northern* and if *it has resin* that *produces syrup*. This translation enables us to consider the membership of the same single object, x, relative to the four compound concepts *(to-be-tall)⋆(to-be-a-tree), to-have-a-((northern)⋆(growing-country)), to-have((five points) ⋆(leaves)), to-have-a-((producing syrup)⋆(resin))*. The first concept—*(to-be-tall)⋆(to-be-a-tree)*—is obtained through a determination, and its application to any object will be evaluated from that of the concepts *to-be-a-tree* and *to-be-tall*, as shown in Section 5. As for the other ones, we have to consider them as complex indecomposable concepts: there exists indeed no way to compute their associated membership through that of their constituents: similarly, the concept *to-eat-a-red-apple* cannot be simply formed through the concepts *to-eat, to-be-an-apple* and *to-be-red*. We find here again the difference of treatment between one-place and two-place predicates.

In order to compare the respective *maplehood* of two items, we will therefore have to compare their respective memberships relative to each of these four concepts. Note that this again amounts to associating with the target concept *to-be-a-maple* a set of defining features: this set simply consists of the concepts: *to-have-a-(producing syrup)⋆(resin), (to-be-tall)⋆(to-be-a-tree), to-have-a-(northern)⋆(growing-country), to-have(five points) ⋆(leaves)*, on which a salience order may be set as in the elementary case.

These observations show that, in the general case, it is possible to account for the categorial membership associated with any definable concept whose structured definition can be modelled by an ordered set of simple or compound concepts. For such a concept α we will simply define the membership order $\prec_\alpha$ as one of the orders defined in paragraph 4.2.

As we see, the evaluation of the categorial membership order relative to a much larger family of concepts than those that can be elementarily definable is now possible.

5.2   Conceptual dictionaries

In this final section, we examine the theoretical case of concepts that can be recursively defined from a fixed set of primitive concepts. Formally, we suppose given a fixed set of concepts $\mathscr{C}$ together with a *defining function* Δ from $\mathscr{C}$ into the set $\wp_0(\mathscr{C})$ of all finite subsets of $\mathscr{C}$: this function associates with every concept α of $\mathscr{C}$ a subset $\Delta(\alpha)$ that, when non empty, gathers the defining features of α. The elements of $\mathscr{C}$ whose image by Δ is the empty set are the *primitive* concepts of the *dictionary* constituted by the pair $(\mathscr{C}, \Delta)$. Primitive concepts are characterized by the fact that they cannot be learnt through other concepts: they have no defining features, they are presented as a whole. The defining function Δ is supposed to be effective and non-redundant, in the sense that a finite number of operations should be sufficient to define any concept of $\mathscr{C}$ from the primitive ones. To be more precise, we require the following condition of *Finite Delta Sequences* to be satisfied by the dictionary:

(FDS):   any sequence $\alpha_0, \alpha_1, \ldots, \alpha_{n-1}, \alpha_n, \ldots$ with $\alpha_i \in \Delta(\alpha_{i-1})$ is finite.

Let $\alpha <_\Delta \beta$ be the relation on $\mathscr{C}$ defined as:

$\alpha <_\Delta \beta$ if there exists a sequence $\alpha = \alpha_0, \alpha_1, \ldots, \alpha_{n-1}, \alpha_n = \beta$ such that for all
$i < n-1$, $\alpha_i \in \Delta(\alpha_{i+1})$.

The relation '$\alpha <_\Delta \beta$' may be read as 'α is *simpler* than β': indeed, it translates the fact that α intervenes in the definition of β, and thus must be more accessible to the agent.

The (FDS) condition readily implies the following properties:

- The graph determined by the function Δ is acyclic

- $<_\Delta$ is a strict partial order

- Every $<_\Delta$-descending chain is finite

- The $<_\Delta$-minimal elements are the primitive elements of $\mathscr{C}$.

Given a concept α of $\mathscr{C}$, a *defining chain* for α is a descending chain from α that has maximal length. By condition (FDS) such a chain necessarily ends up with a primitive concept, which can be considered as a *root* of α. Its length measures the *complexity* of the concept α.

The membership order associated with a concept α of the dictionary depends on the membership orders associated with all the elements β that intervene in its definition, that is all the elements β such that $\beta <_\Delta \alpha$. Using the construction proposed in the preceding paragraph, it is theoretically possible to compute the α-membership order from the orders associated with all the primitive elements γ such that $\gamma <_\Delta \alpha$. However, the procedure is complex because it requires to take into account the salience orders of all the sets $\Delta(\beta), \beta <_\Delta \alpha$. It is only in the particular case where these salience orders are empty that the membership order associated with α can be directly computed from its roots.

Things are simpler if we restrict ourselves to the problem of determining the *extension* of α, that is the set of all objects that fall under α: we have indeed the equality $Ext\,\alpha = \bigcap Ext\,\gamma$, where the intersection is taken over all the roots of α. An object therefore falls under a concept of the dictionary if and only if it falls under all its roots. Full membership can be thus totally evaluated at the ground level.

6   Conclusion

Concept definitions through defining features provide an interesting and effective tool for the study of problems linked with categorization theory. They render possible the construction of a purely qualitative membership order that enables to compare the membership of two objects relative to a given concept. This order, that takes into account the relative salience of the different features by which a concept is defined, can be extended to complex concepts built through juxtaposition or determination. It enjoys compositional properties and yields the extension of a composed concept as the intersection of the extensions of its components. These results can be extended to concepts whose definition requires the use of a simple subjacent structure, and provide an interesting insight on the extensional properties of conceptual dictionaries. However, one has to be aware that this study only concerns the family of concepts for which exists a definition, which is not the case for all concepts. Also, categorial membership in itself is not sufficient to account for problems that go beyond the extensional treatment of concepts: in particular, problems linked with prototype or resemblance theory need more sophisticated tools than those provided in this work.

BIBLIOGRAPHY

[1] D. Dubois, F. Esteva, L. Godo, and H. Prade. An information-based discussion of vagueness. In Cohen and Lefebvre, editors, *Handbook of Categorization in Cognitive Science*, pages 892–913. 2005.

[2] G. Frege. *Begriffsschrift, eine der arithmetischen nachgebildete Formelsprache des reinen Denkens*. Halle, 1879.

[3] M. Freund. On the notion of concept I. *Artificial Intelligence*, 172:570–590, 2008.

[4] R. Jackendoff. *Patterns in the mind: language and human nature*. New York Harvester Wheatsheaf, 1993.

[5] H. Kamp and B. Partee. Prototype theory and compositionality. *Cognition*, 57:129–191, 1995.

[6] A. Koselak. La semantique naturelle d'Anna Wierzbicka et les enjeux interculturels. *Questions de communication*, 4:83–95, 2003.

[7] J.W.T. Lee. Ordinal decomposability and fuzzy connectives. *Fuzzy sets and systems*, 136:237–249, 2003.

[8] M. Lupu. Concepts vagues et categorisation. *Cahiers de linguistique française*, 25:291–304, 2003.

[9] D. Nardi and R.J. Brachman. An introduction to description logics. In Franz Baader, editor, *The Description Logic Handbook*, pages 1–44. Cambridge University Press, 2003.

[10] D. Osherson and E.E. Smith. Gradedness and conceptual combination. *Cognition*, 12:299–318, 1982.

[11] D. Osherson and E.E. Smith. On the adequacy of prototype theory as a theory of concepts. *Cognition*, 11:237–262, 1981.

[12] B. Peeters and C. Goddard. The natural semantic metalanguage (nsm) approach: An overview with reference to the most important Romance languages. *In B. Peeters (ed.), Semantic primes and universal grammar. Empirical evidence from the Romance languages*, 19:13–88, 2006.

[13] H. Putnam. The meaning of meaning. In *Mind, language and reality*, pages 115–120. Cambridge University Press, 1975.

[14] E. Rosch. Cognitive representations of semantic categories. *Journal of Experimental Psychology*, 104:192–233, 1975.

[15] E.E. Smith and DL Medin. *Categories and concepts*. Harvard University Press, Cambridge, 1981.

[16] E.E. Smith, E.J. Shoben, and L.J. Rips. Structure and process in semantic memory: a featural model for semantic decisions. *Psychological Review*, 81:214–241, 1974.

[17] A. Wierzbicka. *Semantics. Primes and Universals*. Oxford University Press, 1996.

[18] L.A. Zadeh. Fuzzy sets. *Information and Control*, 8:338–353, 1965.

Michael Freund

Institut D'Histoire et de Philosophie des Sciences et des Techniques

13 rue du Four

75006 Paris, France

Email: micfreund@gmail.com

Comments on *Vagueness Through Definitions* by Michael Freund

PAUL ÉGRÉ[1]

Most theories of vagueness characterize the phenomenon by reference to the extension of our concepts: the vagueness of a predicate is usually described by the existence of borderline cases, namely cases for which the predicate neither clearly applies, nor clearly fails to apply. A lot remains to be said about the relation between the existence of borderline cases and structural aspects of the meaning of vague predicates from which that existence could analytically derive. The first originality of Michael Freund's approach to vagueness in this regard is the connection sought between vagueness and the *intension* or definition of our concepts. What Freund examines in his paper are the defining features of complex concepts, namely the various criteria that enter into the decision of whether or not to apply the concept to a given object.

A second and related originality of Freund's account is the emphasis put on *multidimensionality*. Vagueness is generally looked at from a one-dimensional perspective. For instance, when discussing the vagueness of gradable adjectives such as "bald", "tall" or "young", we generally consider a single dimension of comparison for whether or not an object should fall under the concept. For "bald", membership is typically presented as a function of the number of hairs, for "tall", as a function of height, for "young", as a function of age. However, vagueness is also characteristic of complex concepts expressed by common nouns, such as "car", "bird" or "vegetable". In order to determine whether an object is a car or not, we cannot rely on a unique nor obvious scale of comparison. Rather, as stressed by Freund in his account, the application of such concepts to particular objects involves the consideration of distinct and separable features that can vary independently.

A very important insight of Freund's contribution to this volume is that one source of vagueness lies in the existence of multiple respects of comparison, at least for an important class of predicates, namely definable predicates expressible by common nouns. For instance, when we apply a concept such as "car" to an object, there are several defining features that we need to check for, but also that we need to weigh against each other. From Freund's account, both aspects are responsible for vagueness. An object may instantiate more of the defining features of a concept than some other object. But possibly,

[1]Thanks to M. Freund for helpful discussion, and to E. Chemla and P. Schlenker for unrelated joint work, but with serendipitous impact on aspects of this research. The research leading to these results has received funding from the Agence Nationale de la Recherche (grant ANR-07-JCJC-0070), and the European Research Council under the European Community's Seventh Framework Programme (FP7/2007-2013) / ERC grant agreement no. 229 441-CCC.

though an object might instantiate fewer of the defining features of a concept than some other object, it might instantiate features that have more weight for the application of that concept.

I should say at the outset that I find Freund's account of the vagueness of definable concepts both very convincing and very insightful. In this commentary, I would like to question two aspects of his account. The first concerns the grounds for his opposition between qualitative and quantitative vagueness, and the question of whether those really are two heterogenous phenomena. My sense is that the opposition is more adequately phrased in terms of one- vs multi-dimensional vagueness, and that his account suggests a promising unified theory, one that could account for how we deal with vagueness and comparison for distinct lexical classes. In relation to that, the second aspect of his account I wish to discuss concerns Freund's construction of an ordering relation for definable concepts. As I understand Freund's account, a concept will be vague whenever that concept can be applied *partially* to an object, or *to some degree*. A very interesting aspect of his account is that Freund does not take degrees as given, but rather, shows how to construct them from an underlying ordering relation. In so doing, Freund's paper is also a contribution to the general theory of the relation between vagueness and measurement, namely to the study of how numerical scales are obtained for vague predicates. One aspect I shall particularly focus on concerns the link proposed by Freund between multidimensional predicates and the notion of a partially ordered scale.

1   Qualitative and quantitative vagueness

At the beginning of his paper, Freund opposes two kinds of vague concepts: concepts such as "heap", "tall" or "rich", and concepts such as "cause", "beautiful" or "lie". His suggestion is that the former may be grouped under the heading of 'quantitative vagueness', whereas the latter may be grouped under the heading of 'qualitative vagueness'. Because of the apparent heterogeneity between the two classes, Freund suggests that a general theory of vagueness is probably 'doomed to fail'. I believe his own project suggests a more optimistic outlook.

First of all, Freund's account of vagueness remains compatible with the idea that vagueness involves a duality between clear cases and borderline cases. For instance, for the 'qualitatively' vague predicates he considers, a clear case is one that instantiates all of the defining features of a concept, while a borderline case would be one that instantiates only some of the defining features of the concept. Secondly, for Freund the hallmark of vagueness appears to be gradability. To use his example, in the same way in which we can say that 'John is taller than Mary', we can say, even in the nominal domain, that 'a machine-gun is more of a weapon of mass destruction than an arquebus'.

Further remarks can be made about the dichotomy proposed by Freund. Firstly, his distinction is orthogonal to a distinction between lexical categories. For instance, "beautiful" is a gradable adjective, just like "tall", but the latter is viewed as quantitative, and the former qualitative. Likewise, "heap" is a noun, just like "lie", but the latter is called qualitative, and the former quantitative. Reflecting on the grounds for Freund's distinction, the main difference really seems to concern whether the predicate in question comes with a unique salient scale of comparison, or whether it involves several respects of comparison. Consider the case of "beautiful". It is doubtful whether "beautiful" is a definable concept in the sense intended by Freund, simply because there may not be more elementary concepts in terms of which "beautiful" can be defined. However, it is very plausible that "beautiful" comes with the equivalent of what Freund calls "defining features". Consider what we might mean by "a beautiful house". To judge whether a house is beautiful, we may need to assess whether it has a beautiful garden, a beautiful architecture, a beautiful furniture, and so on. Each of those aspects may in turn require the consideration of specific features. Thus, although there may be no analytic definition of "beautiful", we see that the application of the predicate depends on several respects of comparison that constitute an analogue of Freund's defining features.

Freund's central claim, however, is that unlike for "tall" or "heap", for concepts such as "car" or "weapon of mass destruction", we find no obvious numerical scale upon which to order the objects for comparison. This is undeniably correct, but I believe Freund's central thesis, which is that the assignment of numerical degrees from predicates to objects supervenes on a qualitative ordering between them, can be applied across the board.[2] As discussed in several recent theories about vagueness and the grammar of comparison (in particular van Rooij 2011, Sassoon 2010, Solt this volume, Burnett 2011), for a predicate like "tall", comparison depends on a *ratio* scale, one that encodes both information about position in the ordering, but also about differences and about ratios between intervals. For instance, we can say "Sam is taller than Jim" (ordinal information), but also "Sam is 2 cm taller than Jim" (interval information), and finally "Sam is twice as tall as Jim" (ratio information). For some predicates that Freund would call 'quantitative', however, like "heap", the information encoded is not as fine-grained as that provided by a ratio scale. For instance, it seems we cannot say "this is twice as much a heap as that" (even when the number of grains for heap 1 is twice as much the number of grains for heap 2). Or for an adjective like "bald", there is no obvious sense in which one might say "Sam is twice as bald as Jim" (even if Sam has half as much hair on his head). Turning to Freund's definable concepts, note that although one can say "a machine-gun is more of a WMD than an arquebus", without explicit stipulations one could hardly say "a machine-gun is twice as much of a WMD than an arquebus", or even just specify the precise amount to which a machine-gun is more of a WMD than an arquebus. This suggests that for concepts like "WMD" or "car", one might expect comparison to be encoded by an ordinal scale.

Because of that, my sense is that Freund's distinction between 'qualitative' and 'quantitative' vagueness could be cast as follows: the predicates Freund calls qualitative likely include all predicates involving either several defining features (like "car", "vegetable", "blue jacket"), or several respects of comparison (like "beautiful", "intelligent", "healthy"), predicates that can be characterized as multidimensional for that matter. Reciprocally, the predicates Freund calls 'quantitative' can be characterized as one-dimensional, namely predicates for which a unique most salient scale of comparison is relevant. Importantly, however, talk of 'quantitatively' vague predicates obscures the fact that predicates in that class can come with different measurement scales (like "tall", coming with a ratio scale, and "bald", coming with an interval scale). Nevertheless, the difference between 'qualitatively' vague and 'quantitatively' vague predicates may still

---

[2]The relation between relational scales and numerical scales is the object of representation theorems in measurement theory. See Roberts (1985) for an overview.

have a correlate in terms of the structure of the underlying scales. A possibility might be that all one-dimensional predicates encode information at least about intervals (see Sassoon 2010), and that multidimensional predicates basically encode at most ordinal information.[3] For multidimensional predicates, Freund's own thesis is that the default is a partially ordered scale.

2 Multidimensionality and partially ordered scales

The problem Freund deals with in the second half of his paper is the following: given a multidimensional predicate—such as "car", "bird", "blue jacket"—and a series of objects, to construct an integrated scale of comparison in order to determine how much an object is a car, a bird or a blue jacket.

Note that there are at least three degrees of freedom in this problem, and therefore three potential sources of vagueness in how we actually deal with multidimensional predicates. The first concerns the problem of determining the position of the object relative to each of the concept's dimensions or features. Take a complex concept like "blue jacket": in order to determine whether something is a blue jacket, one needs to determine how blue it is, and how much of a jacket it is. There is room for vagueness within each of the dimensions. The second degree concerns the problem of fixing the relative weight of the dimensions. For instance, a green jacket may, arguably, be more of a blue jacket (or closer to a blue jacket) than a blue sock, if we assume that the dimension of the modifier weighs less than that of the modified concept in this example. There is room for vagueness also at this stage, since in some cases the relative weight of the dimensions may be hard to determine. Finally, even supposing these two steps to be precisely resolved, the third degree concerns the integration of the dimensions into one. As Freund points out in his paper, there are several methods, just as for the aggregation of preferences in social choice theory, and a third source for vagueness concerns the potential indeterminacy of the method itself.

The main interest of Freund's paper is that he offers a canonical scaling method for multidimensional predicates, intended to show how we actually compare objects relative to several dimensions. Freund makes two assumptions to that effect: one is that objects can be completely ordered within each dimension (so vagueness is taken to be resolved at that level), and the other is that dimensions are partially ordered. The output of Freund's integrative construction is a partially ordered scale. Freund's emphasis on partially ordered scales is particularly noteworthy, for it relates to a foundational issue in measurement theory, which concerns the adequacy of totally ordered scales to deal with multidimensional integration. Standard scales since Stevens (1946) are completely ordered scales. However, some psychologists have argued that partially ordered scales could be needed precisely to deal with multidimensionality. This was done in particular by Coombs (1951), who points out that partially ordered scales "fall between nominal and ordinal scales".

---

[3]Sassoon's view is in fact the following: "Most plausibly, the majority of positive adjectives denote measures with all the properties of interval-scales in the first place, and sometimes, but not always, also properties of ratio-scales". Even for one-dimensional adjectives, however, more fine-grained differences need to be taken into account. See in particular Burnett's 2011 account of scale structure for relative vs. absolute gradable adjectives.

A questionable aspect, however, concerns the link between such partially ordered scales and the derivation of a membership degree for an object relative to the concept. In Freund's Example 1 for how various animals can be ordered relative to the concept 'bird', we see that the bat and tortoise are incomparable in the resulting ordering, basically because both differ on features that are incomparable. Nevertheless, Freund's definition of membership distance assigns a higher degree of 'birdhood' to the tortoise than to the bat. This points to a mismatch between the induced partial order and the complete order intended by the membership distance. The tortoise and dragonfly, for example, though also incomparable, eventually receive the same membership degree.

As I see it, a variant on Freund's construction could consist in first extracting a canonical weak order from the finite partial ordering for features, so that incomparable features with the same rank in the initial partial ordering could be assumed to have equal weight. Under that assumption, features would be completely ordered, so as to directly derive a consistent ordinal scale for what Freund calls membership distance. For example, a compromise between Freund's method and the Condorcet method would be to generalize the notion of *lexicographic ordering* as follows: say that x strictly precedes y (relative to a set of weakly ordered defining features) iff either x has more features of rank 1 than y, or x and y have an identical number of features or rank 1 but x has more features of rank 2, or they have an identical number of features of rank 1 and of rank 2 but x has more features of rank 3, $\ldots$, or x and y have an identical number of features of rank 1 to $n-1$, but x has more features of rank n. For instance, in the bat and tortoise case, this method would predict that the tortoise has more birdhood than the bat, directly in agreement with Freund's membership ranking. It would still assign the same position to the tortoise and dragonfly in the ordering, consistently with that ranking.[4]

Ultimately, it is unobvious to me whether, as Coombs and Freund claim on similar grounds, it matters for multidimensional scaling to keep incomparable elements, or whether it is more appropriate to resolve incomparabilities into ties of the appropriate kind to obtain an ordinal scale. This is the difference between considering that two students are incomparable in how good they are in mathematics, because one is very good at geometry, and average in arithmetic, while the other is very good in arithmetic, but

---

[4] Let us illustrate this. Each animal in Freund's table can be identified by a sequence of 1 and 0, one for each feature, corresponding to whether it has that feature or not. Assume that features are weakly ordered in accordance to their depth in the initial partial order, so that 'animal' has rank 1, 'beak' and 'wings' have equal rank 2, 'lay-eggs' has rank 3, and 'has two-legs' rank 4. Mapping Freund's table from right to left, the bat is representable by the sequence $(1_1, 1_2, 0_2, 0_3, 1_4)$ and the tortoise by $(1_1, 0_2, 1_2, 1_3, 0_4)$.

From our definition, $(1_1, 0_2, 1_2, 1_3, 0_4) < (1_1, 1_2, 0_2, 0_3, 1_4)$, that is tortoise and bat have an identical number of features of rank 1 and of rank 2, but on rank 3 the tortoise has a feature the bat does not have. The tortoise and dragonfly have the same degree of birdhood, since $(1_1, 0_2, 1_2, 1_3, 0_4) = (1_1, 1_2, 0_2, 1_3, 0_4)$ (in all ranks, they instantiate the same number of features). Freund's method would make the same predictions for those two cases under the same assumptions, if we replaced "more salient" by "at least as salient" in his definition on pg. 104. However, that modified definition would make different predictions in general. For instance, it would predict that $(1_1, 1_2, 0_2, 0_2) = (1_1, 0_2, 1_2, 1_2)$, whereas we would predict that $(1_1, 0_2, 1_2, 1_2) < (1_1, 1_2, 0_2, 0_2)$.

Nevertheless, as pointed out to me by Freund, we are back to the original problem that motivates his approach if we try to generalize our definition to cases in which features are satisfied to some degree only. For in the general case "x has more features of rank i than y" may be taken to mean that there are strictly more features γ_i of the same rank i for which $x \leq_{\gamma_i} y$ than such features for which $y \leq_{\gamma_i} x$. This definition gives rise to familiar intransitivities (Condorcet cycles) when features are no longer assumed to be either fully satisfied or fully failed, as they are in the foregoing example.

average in geometry. Likely, we may consider them to be incomparable, but there is also a legitimate sense in which they should be given the same grade at the end of term, by giving arithmetic and geometry equal weights. For Coombs (1951: p. 486), incidentally, the example of course grades is precisely an example of "summative" integration between dimensions, to which he opposes cases in which features 'do not compensate each other'. Coombs however does not entertain lexicographic orderings, which can offer a non-additive way to integrate dimensions into a complete order. Our own suggestion above is actually a mix of compensatory and noncompensatory integration between dimensions, since we assume features of equal rank to compensate each other, but that features of lower rank cannot compensate features of higher rank.

BIBLIOGRAPHY

H. Burnett (2011). The Puzzle(s) of Absolute Adjectives: On Vagueness, Comparison, and the Origin of Scale Structure. *UCLA Working Papers in Linguistics*. UCLA.

C.H. Coombs. (1951). Mathematical Models in Psychological Scaling. *Journal of the American Statistical Association*, 46 (256):480–489.

F. Roberts (1985). *Measurement Theory*. Encyclopedia of Mathematics and its Applications. Cambridge University Press.

R. van Rooij (2011). Vagueness and Linguistics. In G. Ronzitti (Ed.), *Vagueness: A Guide*, Springer, pp. 123–170. Dordrecht: Springer.

G. Sassoon (2010). Measurement Theory in Linguistics. *Synthese*, 174:151–180.

S. Solt (2011). Vagueness in Quantity. *This volume*.

S.S. Stevens (1946). On the Theory of Scales of Measurement. *Science*, 103: 677–80.

Paul Égré
Institut Jean-Nicod
Département d'Etudes Cognitives
Ecole Normale Supérieure
29, rue d'Ulm, 75005 Paris
E-mail: paul.egre@ens.fr

Reply to Paul Égré's Comments on *Vagueness Through Definitions*

MICHAEL FREUND

The remarks made by Paul Égré show the necessity of emphasizing the distinction between concepts and features as well as the difference of treatment this distinction leads to. Features, as such, borrow their sense from the context they are used in: it is only in the shadow of this context that their meaning can be grasped. When a feature is considered relatively to a given concept, like 'to have wings' in the context of being an animal, or 'to be red' in the context of being an apple, the resulting sharpening of its meaning renders possible the use of ordered scales to measure the strength with which this feature applies to the objects of the universe. On the contrary, it is meaningless to attribute a numerical degree or a rank to evaluate the categorial membership attached to a vague concept when this vagueness is qualitative. A consequence of this fact is that the categorial membership order associated with a vague concept is generally not total, even when this concept is grasped through a set of defining features.

However the temptation of quantitatively evaluating categorial membership is great, as it offers the possibility of using the whole apparatus of numerical calculus to treat problems linked with Perception and Cognitive Psychology. In this perspective, it may appear desirable to have at one's disposal a way of transforming membership comparison into membership evaluation. The notion of membership distance μ_α, evoked in Section 4.3, provides an answer to this problem, but this solution has to be taken as a fair approximation of a agent's judgment. Other solutions exist, like the Condorcet method evoked by Égré, or the Borda-Hampton method, which attributes to an object x the membership degree $\sum \rho(\gamma)\delta_\gamma(x)$ in which $\rho(\gamma)$ denotes the rank of the feature γ and $\delta_\gamma(x)$ the strength with which this feature applies to x. These solutions, though, present several drawbacks. In particular, they all consider that the salience order among the features is *ranked,* so that a degree of importance can be attributed to each defining feature of a concept. This is not the perspective I have adopted in this paper, working on the more general case of an arbitrary strict partial salience order.

Altogether, and except for the case of quantitatively vague concepts, no numerical tool can adequately account for categorial membership. In a sense, this negative result is reassuring: it illustrates the fact that there exists some categories for which the notion of membership degree is simply meaningless.

Comparison of Complex Predicates:
and, or and *more*

GALIT W. SASSOON[1]

Are complex predicates—in particular, negated (e.g., not expensive), conjunctive (e.g., expensive and time consuming) and disjunctive predicates (e.g., tall or bald)—associated with a graded structure, namely a mapping of entities to degrees? On the one hand, most up to date semantic theories of gradability and comparison in natural language disregard this question. On the other hand, contemporary fuzzy logical theories provide compositional rules to construct a degree function for a complex expression based on the degree functions of its constituents. These composition rules have been found useful for a variety of practical applications. The question is then whether these rules can correctly represent the interpretation of complex natural language expressions and its relation to the interpretation of their constituents. The relevance of this question is enhanced by recent findings from a variety of studies (Ripley 2011; Serchuk et al., 2010; Alxatib and Pelletier 2011), according to which high percentages of subjects count contradictory predicates such as tall and not tall as true of borderline cases (neither short nor tall entities). While these findings stand in sharp contrast to predictions of vagueness-based theories of adjectives, they are in accord with the predictions of a fuzzy analysis, as extensively argued by Kamp and Partee (1995). Given these new findings, then, the fact that fuzzy analyses allow for non-zero truth values to contradictions can no longer count against them (for a more detailed discussion see Sauerland, this volume). It is therefore increasingly important to test other predictions of applications of fuzzy analyses to natural language conjunctions and disjunctions. To this end, this paper discusses preliminary results based on a questionnaire eliciting judgments from 35 Hebrew speakers. The results suggest that, counter the predictions of fuzzy analyses, comparative and equative morphemes cannot apply to conjunctions and disjunctions of gradable adjectives.

---

[1]This work was made possible by the Orgler Scholarship (Tel Aviv University, 2004–2007) as well as the project 'On vagueness – and how to be precise enough', funded by the Netherlands Organization for Scientific Research (NWO 360-20-201). This paper has benefitted a lot from comments by Uli Sauerland, as well as an additional anonymous reviewer and from Petr Cintula's help with the typesetting. Any remaining mistakes are all mine. I warmly thank my special friends and colleagues in Tel Aviv who helped me carrying out the experimental study for this paper, including Ido Ben Tzvi, Uriel Cohen Priva, Aynat Rubinstein, Tal Keidar, Meira Marom, Aya Meltzer, Tal David, Lior Laks, Julie Fadlon, Eytan Kidron, Sefi Potashnik, Iddo Greental, Eugenia Berger, Hillel Taub-Tabib, Lena Fainleib, Lustigman Lyle, Bracha Nir-Sagiv, Aviad Eilam, Shai Cohen, Dafna Heller, Aldo Sevi, Ziva Wijler, Nirit Kadmon, and Adar Weidman.

1 Introduction

Part 1 of this paper briefly surveys prominent semantic analyses of natural language comparison constructions (Section 1.1) and coordination constructions (Section 1.2). Part 2 presents an empirical study of the two constructions, focusing on comparisons of conjunctions and comparisons of disjunctions. Part 3 concludes with the implications this study has concerning the theoretical debates presented below.

1.1 The comparative morpheme

Linguistic theories of gradability and comparison can be divided into two main approaches, 'ordinal' and 'numerical' (cf. Sassoon 2010a). The ordinal approach attempts to reduce the interpretation of comparative morphemes such as more and as to ordering relations between individuals or between their ordinal degrees in predicates P, i.e., $>P$ and $\geq P$, respectively (cf. Sapir 1944; Creswell 1977; Moltmann 2006; Bale 2008). In particular, in vagueness based gradability theories the ordering relations $>P$ and $\geq P$ are derived based on facts pertaining to membership in P's denotation, rather than based on fine grained numerical measurements. On these theories, an entity is more P than other entities iff it falls under P relative to more delineations (possible boundary specifications for vague predicates P; cf. Lewis 1970, 1979; Kamp 1975; Fine 1975; Klein 1980; Landman 1991; van Rooij 2011).

In opposition, the numerical approach provides a unified analysis of comparative morphemes with and without numerical modifiers. This approach characterizes gradable adjectives as associated with numerical degree functions, i.e. mapping of entities $x \in D_x$ to a set of degrees isomorphic to the real numbers $r \in \mathfrak{R}$ (Russell 1905; Bartsch and Venneman 1972; Klein 1991; Kamp and Partee 1995; Kennedy 1999; Heim 2000; Schwarzschild and Wilkinson 2002; Landman 2005; Sassoon 2010). Assuming a λ-categorial language in the style of Heim and Kratzer (1998), with basic types x for individuals, t for truth values, and r for numerical degrees, and basic semantic domains D_x, D_t, and $D_r = \mathfrak{R}$ (sets of individuals, truth values, and numerical degrees, respectively). Gradable adjectives are interpreted as follows:

(1) Let T_c stand for a set of indices, the worlds (or completions) consistent with a background context c (cf. Stalnaker, 1978; Kamp 1975).

(2) For any context c, for any $t \in T_c$ and any gradable adjective P :

   (a) $f_{P,t} \in \mathfrak{R}^{D_x}$ is *the degree function of P in t* (a function from entities x in the domain D_x to real numbers r in $\mathfrak{R}$)

   (b) P holds true of an object $x \in D_x$ in t iff x's value exceeds P's cutoff point: $f_{P,t}(x) > cutoff(P, t)$ (Kennedy, 1999).

In particular, theories in this approach tend to assume that gradable predicates map arguments to degrees for which *plus, difference* and *ratio* operations are applicable (von Stechow 1984a,b). The numerical approach is prevalent in the literature, as it provides straightforward semantic accounts of expressions whose interpretation is mediated by the application of operations on numbers (identity, multiplication, difference, etc.), such as, e.g., numerical modifiers like *2 meters tall*, ratio predicates like *twice as happy as*

Sam, and difference predicates like *2 meters shorter than Sam*. In these theories, the interpretation of *more* and *as* involves the application of a difference operation, as demonstrated in (3), with $r_{m,t}$ being the degree of height of the meter in t (von Stechow 1984a; Schwarzschild and Wilkinson 2002; Kennedy and McNally 2005; Schwarzschild 2005; Kennedy and Levin 2007:17; Sassoon 2010a).

(3)   a. [[Dan is *2 meters taller* than Sam]]$_t$ = 1 iff $f_{tall,t}([[Dan]]_t) - f_{tall,t}([[Sam]]_t)$
$= 2r_{m,t}$
b. [[Dan is *happier* than Sam]]$_t$ = 1 iff $\exists r > 0 : f_{happy,t}([[Dan]]_t) - f_{happy,t}$
$([[Sam]]_t) = r$.

Thus, despite differences in detail between analyses, all in all, a widely employed view is that, e.g., *Dan is taller than Sam (by 2 meters)* holds true in an index *t* iff the difference between Dan and Sam's degrees in *t* is a positive real number (twice the degree of a meter unit object in *t*).

The basic interpretation of phrasal *er* as a difference operation is, then, roughly, $\lambda r_2 \in \mathfrak{R}.\lambda M_{\langle r,t \rangle}.\lambda r_1 \in \mathfrak{R}.M(r_1 - r_2)$, where the variable M has to be saturated by a degree predicate like *two inches* (Schwarzschild and Wilkinson 2002; Landman 2005; Sassoon 2010b) and the interpretation of *as* is $\lambda r_2 \in \mathfrak{R}.\lambda r_1 \in \mathfrak{R}.[[er]](r_2, \lambda r.r \geq 0, r_1)$, which reduces to: $\lambda r_2.\lambda r_1.r_1 - r_2 \geq 0$. Given the latter, the use of the comparative, rather than the equative, normally excludes the possibility that M is $\lambda r.r \geq 0$; i.e., in the absence of an overt numerical degree modification, M is thought to be saturated by the predicate $\lambda r \in \mathfrak{R}.r > 0$ ('somewhat'), implying that $r_1 - r_2 > 0$ (cf. Schwarzschild and Wilkinson 2002; Landman 2005; Sassoon 2010b), as illustrated below. Finally, when *er* combines with an adjective as in *taller*, interpretation type shifts to an individual level: $\lambda f \in \mathfrak{R}^{D_x}.\lambda x_2 \in D_x.\lambda M.\lambda x_1 \in D. [[er]] (f(x_2))(M)(f(x_1))$, which reduces to $\lambda f \in \mathfrak{R}^{D_x}.\lambda x_2 \in D_x.\lambda M.\lambda x_1 \in D_x.M(f(x_1) - f(x_2))$.

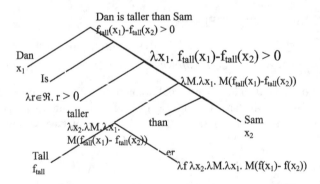

On both the vagueness-based and numerical approach, a comparative or equative morpheme applies to one predicate at a time, e.g. *The table is taller than the chair is wide* is a comparison of the table's status (degree or denotation membership) with respect to a single predicate (*tall*), and the chair's status with respect to a single predicate (*wide*). An open question, then, regards the interpretation of combinations of comparison morphemes with complex predicates, as in, for instance, *more honest and intelligent* and *equally expensive and time consuming*. How are such statements interpreted?

The next section discusses two different possible answers, a fuzzy and a Boolean one. Section 2 presents an empirical investigation whose goal is to decide between the two. Implications to the numerical versus vagueness-based debate are addressed.

1.2   The interpretation of coordination constructions

Sentences with conjunctions and modified-nouns in predicate position usually entail the sentences resulting from dropping some of the constituents or changing the constituent ordering. For example, (5a) entails (5b,c) and (6a) entails (6b,c). In addition, (5a) and (6a) are equivalent to (5d) and (6d) respectively. Such entailment-patterns form the basis for the intersective analysis of modified-nouns and conjunctions, whereby they denote the intersection of their constituents' denotations, as stated and illustrated in (7) (Kamp and Partee 1995; Landman 2000; Heim and Kratzer 1998). The intersection-rule in (7) directly predicts the fact that an item is classified as, for instance, *a four legged animal* or *an animal which is four legged* iff it is classified as *an animal* and it is classified as *four legged*.

(5) a. Tweety is brown and big

    b. Tweety is brown

    c. Tweety is big

    d. Tweety is big and brown

(6) a. Tweety is a four legged animal

    b. Tweety is four legged

    c. Tweety is an animal

    d. Tweety is an animal and is four legged

(7) $\forall t \in T : [[P \text{ (and) } Q]]_t = [[P]]_t \cap [[Q]]_t$

    a. $[[\text{brown and big}]]_t = \lambda x \in D_x.brown(x) \wedge big(x) = [[\text{brown}]]_t \cap [[\text{big}]]_t$

    b. $[[\text{brown apple}]]_t = \lambda x \in D_x.brown(x) \wedge apple(x) = [[\text{brown}]]_t \cap [[\text{apple}]]_t$

The same basic facts hold in the verbal domain, too. For example, the entailments from (8a) to (8b–e) are instances of intersective inference patterns in modified verbs. These additional facts form the basis for the Davidsonian intersective analysis of modified verbs ((9); Landman 2000).

(8) a. Dan ate quickly with a knife

    b. Dan ate with a knife

    c. Dan ate quickly

    d. Dan ate

    e. Dan ate with a knife quickly

(9) $\exists e \in E : [[\text{eating}]]_t(e) \wedge Agent(e) = [[\text{Dan}]]_t \wedge \exists x \in D_x,$
    $Instrument(e) = x \wedge [[\text{knife}]]_t(x)\ldots$

Using the intersection rule, most up to date semantic theories of gradability and comparison in natural language do not associate complex predicates (e.g., negated, conjunctive and disjunctive ones) with graded structures (say, a mapping of entities to numerical degrees). However, fuzzy logical theories can be used to do precisely that (cf. Hájek, 2009). Fuzzy logic is a form of multi-valued logic, whereby propositions may have as a truth value any number in the real interval [0,1]. The disjunction, conjunction and negation operators of Boolean logic exist in fuzzy logic and are usually defined as the maximum, minimum, and complement, respectively (Zadeh 1965); when they are defined this way, they are called the *Zadeh operators*. So for the fuzzy propositions $P(x)$ and $Q(y)$:

(10) a. $[[\neg P(x)]]_t = 1 - [[P(x)]]_t$

   b. $[[P(x) \wedge Q(y)]]_t = \min([[P(x)]]_t, [[Q(y)]]_t)$

   c. $[[P(x) \vee Q(y)]]_t = \max([[P(x)]]_t, [[Q(y)]]_t)$

Other definitions exist for conjunctive and disjunctive expressions that are not based merely on a selection of one of the constituents' degrees; rather, these definitions make use of functions t_{and} and t_{or} (often called *t norms and t-conorms* for conjunctions and disjunctions, respectively) to compute a value for the complex expression based on the values of both of its constituents, as follows:

(11) a. $[[\neg P(x)]]_t = t_{not,t}([[P(x)]]_t)$

   b. $[[P(x) \wedge Q(y)]]_t = t_{and,t}([[P(x)]]_t, [[Q(y)]]_t)$

   c. $[[P(x) \vee Q(y)]]_t = t_{or,t}([[P(x)]]_t, [[Q(y)]]_t)$

There are multiple choices for the fuzzy conjunction and disjunction operators. A common choice is the algebraic product for fuzzy conjunction and algebraic sum for fuzzy disjunction, but there are an infinite number of other choices (Yen, 1999; Hájek, 2009). Rather than the definitions of (or axioms constraining) the *t*-functions, the very possibility that such functions may be relevant to natural language coordination constructions is the focus of interest of this paper. Recall that *more* is analyzed as denoting a difference modifier, e.g., *Dan is taller than Sam* is true in c iff $f_{tall,c}([[\text{Dan}]]_c) - f_{tall,c}([[\text{Sam}]]_c) > 0$ (cf. Section 1.1). According to this analysis, *more* cannot apply to the interpretations of two predicates—two degree functions—simultaneously. However, if natural language semantics is 'fuzzy', i.e. conjunctive and disjunctive predicates are systematically associated with composed degree functions, *more* should be capable of accessing these functions and operating on them. Let $f_{P\text{-}and\text{-}Q,t}$ be the function $\lambda x \in D_x. t_{and}(f_{P,t}(x), f_{Q,t}(x))$ and $f_{P\text{-}or\text{-}Q,t}$ be the function $\lambda x \in D_x. t_{or}(f_{P,t}(x), f_{Q,t}(x))$. A fuzzy natural language semantic theory predicts the following interpretations for expressions of the form *more P and Q* and *more P or Q*.

(12) A fuzzy natural language semantic theory:

   1. a. $[[\text{more } P \text{ and } Q]]_t = \lambda x_2 \in D_x. \lambda x_1 \in D_x. f_{P\text{-}and\text{-}Q,t}(x_1) - f_{P\text{-}and\text{-}Q,t}(x_2) > 0$

   2. b. $[[\text{more } P \text{ or } Q]]_t = \lambda x_2 \in D_x. \lambda x_1 \in D_x. f_{P\text{-}or\text{-}Q,t}(x_1) - f_{P\text{-}or\text{-}Q,t}(x_2) > 0$

On the one hand, psychological findings pertaining to modified nouns seem to support a fuzzy semantic analysis of complex natural language expressions. Psychological theories associate concepts (typically, nominal ones) with functions corresponding to the mean of entities in a variety of dimensions. Hampton (1987; 1988a; 1997a,b) has analyzed ratings of goodness of example (typicality) of a list of entities in modified-nouns of the form 'Ps which are Qs' (such as, for instance, *pets which are birds*) and in their constituents (e.g. *pets* and *birds*). The following patterns emerged.

First, for any item x, it is possible to predict x's typicality rating in a modified-noun, $f_{P\text{-}and\text{-}Q}(x)$, from x's ratings in the constituents, $f_P(x)$, and $f_Q(x)$, by an equation like (13a). W_P and W_Q represent the constituents' weights and $W_{P\times Q}$ represents the weight of the constituents' interaction (the product $f_P(x) \times f_Q(x)$). For example, the values for *pets which are birds* were: $W_{pets} = .30$, $W_{birds} = .78$, and $W_{pets\times birds} = .10$.

Second, the typicality ratings in modified-nouns with negated constituents, i.e. $f_{P\text{-}and\text{-}not\text{-}Q}(x)$, are predicted by adding a negative sign to the weight of the negated constituent $(-W_Q)$. The interaction term is also negative when significant (13b). For example, for *pets which are not birds* the weights were: $W_P = .32$, $W_Q = -.75$, and $W_{P\times Q} = -.11$. Why? Because the better an item is as an example of Q, the worse it is as an example of not-Q.

Third, given the logical connections between disjunction, conjunction and negation $(P \vee Q = \neg(\neg P \wedge \neg Q))$, and the fact that negation affects the equation by changing the coefficient sign, Hampton predicted that the typicality ratings in disjunctions like *hobbies or games*, deg $f_{P\text{-}or\text{-}Q}(x)$, would be given by adding a negative sign to the interaction term $(-W_{P\times Q})$. Why? The value $f_{P\text{-}or\text{-}Q}(x)$ ought to be identical to $f_{\neg(\neg P \wedge \neg Q)}(x)$, which, in turn, should be given by an equation in which a negative sign is added to the weight of each negated-constituent (namely by the equation: $-(-W_P f_P(x) - W_Q f_Q(x) + W_{P\times Q}(f_P(x) \times f_Q(x)))$). After the elimination of double negative-signs, this equation reduces to the one in (13c), with the negative interaction-weight. And indeed, using (13c), Hampton (1988b) could predict the typicality ratings in disjunctions from the ratings in the disjuncts.

(13) a. $f_{P\text{-}and\text{-}Q}(x) = W_P f_P(x) + W_Q f_Q(x) + W_{P\times Q}(f_P(x) \times f_Q(x))$.

    b. $f_{P\text{-}and\text{-}not\text{-}Q}(x) = W_P f_P(x) - W_Q f_Q(x) - W_{P\times Q}(f_P(x) \times f_Q(x))$.

    c. $f_{P\text{-}or\text{-}Q}(x) = W_P f_P(x) + W_Q f_Q(x) - W_{P\times Q}(f_P(x) \times f_Q(x))$.

On the other hand, the constituent-'based equations in (13) seem to be too coarse-grained. Negated constituents, for instance, sometimes have a decreased weight, because some dimensions are treated as characterizing both the predicate and its negation. For example, *animate* often characterizes both birds and entities that are not birds, and *bird-hood* characterizes both robins and non-robins. In general, the typicality ratings in modified-nouns are better fitted by a composite-prototype representation, wherein the weight of each dimension is adjusted by a special function.

More importantly, these findings may not extend to adjectival conjunctions and disjunctions. The graded structure of adjectival predicates is rather different in nature from that of nominal ones. The interpretation of adjectives like *tall* and *expensive*, for example, directly relate to conventional measurements of height and cost, rather than to

a weighted mean in a set of dimensions. For one, these adjectival degree functions are unbounded from above. In addition, while adjectives can combine with *more* (or *er*) to create within-predicate comparisons (as in, e.g., *two meters taller*), nouns and noun phrases do not combine with *more*, as illustrated by the infelicity of, for example, **Tweety is more a bird/birder than Tan*, **x is (a) more **midget giant** than y* and **x is (a) more **fat bald man** than y*. When licensed, the comparative morpheme either associates with the modifier most adjacent to it alone, as in *x is a fatter bald man than y*, or has to be modified by *of*, as in *x is more of a midget giant than y*. The latter statement is interpreted as if the noun phrase is modified with *typical*, as in *x is more typical of a midget giant than y*, where the adjective *typical* forms the argument of *more* and the noun phrase only provides typicality dimensions for *typical* to bind. In opposition, combinations of *more* with conjunctions or disjunctions of adjectives are fine. For example, *x is more expensive and elegant than y* is perfectly grammatical, and so is '*x yoter shamen ve kerea'x*' ('x is more fat and bald than y') in Hebrew and similar languages, whereby the comparative morpheme always surfaces as an independent word (*yoter*; 'more') and never as a dependent morpheme similar to English *er*.

Moreover, rather than to relate to a unique graded structure of the conjunctive concepts in question, intuitively, these phrases seem to convey '**more** expensive and **more** elegant' and 'fat**ter** and bald**er**', respectively. The same phenomenon pertains also to conjunctive multi-dimensional adjectives, like *typical with respect to flying and singing* or *healthy with respect to blood pressure and pulse*.

Thus, gradability is different in nouns and adjectives. While nominal functions may be correctly described using some sort of fuzzy semantics, it is questionable whether adjectival functions can be so described. Perhaps adjectival conjunctions and disjunctions, such as *tall and/or fat*, are not systematically associated with degree functions at all. If so, *more* should not be capable of combining with conjunctive or disjunctive predicates directly; rather, in constructions of the form *more P and Q* or *more P or Q*, the Boolean operators *and* and *or*, respectively, should take wide scope with respect to *more*, so that *more* would modify each conjunct/ disjunct separately, operating on one basic degree function at a time (Sassoon 2007; Bale 2007). Such a non-fuzzy, classically 'Boolean' natural language semantic theory predicts the following interpretations for expressions of the form *more P and Q* and *more P or Q*.[2]

(14) A Boolean natural language semantic theory:

   a. $[[\text{more } P \text{ and } Q]]_t = [[\text{more } P \text{ and more } Q]]_t$

   $= \lambda x_2 \in D_x . \lambda x_1 \in D_x . \ (f_{P,t}(x_1) - f_{P,t}(x_2) > 0) \wedge (f_{Q,t}(x_1) - f_{Q,t}(x_2) > 0)$

   b. $[[\text{more } P \text{ or } Q]]_t = [[\text{more } P \text{ or more } Q]]_t$

   $= \lambda x_2 \in D_x . \lambda x_1 \in D_x . \ (f_{P,t}(x_1) - f_{P,t}(x_2) > 0) \vee (f_{Q,t}(x_1) - f_{Q,t}(x_2) > 0)$

---

[2] The requirement for a unique dimension in the use of a comparative morpheme can only be abandoned in between-predicate comparisons. Conjunctive and disjunctive concepts seem to be felicitous and to receive interpretations with the connective in narrow scope in such comparisons (cf. i.–iii.), though more systematic future research needs to carve out the precise set of interpretations that may be assigned to such statements.

　i. This is more a kitchen utensil than an electronic device.

　ii. This is more a piece of furniture and a game than a kitchen utensil or an electronic device.

　iii. Dan is more fat, bald and unhappy than good-looking, energetic and funny.

While linguists belonging to the numerical degree approach (cf. Section 1.1 above) such as Kennedy (1999) sometimes argue that this approach resembles fuzzy logic, they never, to the best of my knowledge, actually study the question of whether conjunctions and disjunctions of morphologically gradable adjectives are also morphologically gradable, i.e. felicitously licensing *more*. A basic way to test whether the interpretation of expressions of the form *more P and/or Q* is fuzzy (cf. (12)) or non-fuzzy (cf. (14)), is by presenting subjects with pairs of entities differing along one conjunct/ disjunct (say *P*) but otherwise identical (equally *Q*), and asking them whether these pairs stand in the relations (i) *more P and Q*, (ii) *less P and Q* and/or (iii) *equally P and Q* , and (iv) *more P or Q*, (v) *less P or Q* and/or (vi) *equally P or Q*. A non-fuzzy analysis predicts that such pairs stand in none of the three conjunctive relations (i)–(iii) (because they stand in none of the relations *more P and more Q, less P and less Q* and *equally P and equally Q*) and in the two disjunctive relation (iv) and (vi) (because they stand in the relations *more P or more Q* and *equally P or equally Q*). In sharp contrast, a fuzzy analysis does not allow for these possibilities; pairs of entities ought to stand in one and only one conjunctive relation and disjunctive relation, depending on their composed $t_{P\text{-}and\text{-}Q}$ and $t_{P\text{-}or\text{-}Q}$ degrees, respectively. Entity pairs standing in no relation or in more than one relation are at least not straightforwardly accounted for by a fuzzy analysis.

A small questionnaire was designed to examine what the facts actually are, i.e. whether they are more easily fitted by a fuzzy analysis such as the one provided in (12) or by a Boolean analysis such as the one in (14).

2 *And, or*, and *more*, a general judgments questionnaire

2.1 Method

Subjects The subjects were 35 native speakers of Hebrew, 21 females and 14 males, in the age range 20–40 with three exceptions of ages 41, 44 and 59 (average age 31) and with academic education of at least one year (17 graduate students).

Design and material The subjects received a written questionnaire. An opening paragraph included general instructions. This opening paragraph, translated from Hebrew to English for the purpose of presentation in this paper, is as follows:

> The goal of this questionnaire is to understand the way people think and the way they use certain words. Hence, there are no right and wrong answers. For each question provide the answer which on your opinion is the most reasonable and accurate. A slot for comments follows each section. We will be happy with any comment pertaining to the reasons for which you choose to answer the way you do or to uncertainty you might have. Filling in the comment slot is not obligatory. While some sections look alike, it is very important that you relate to each one of them separately. While the questions in this questionnaire are given in masculine forms, they are addressed to both genders. Many thanks in advance for your patience in filling in the questionnaire.
>
> On every section, draw a circle around the answer you select.

The questionnaire included 13 sections, 5 of which are relevant for the present research. Each section included a short paragraph with a brief description of two characters consisting of their values or relative status in two gradable properties. The paragraph was followed by either yes-no questions (followed by Yes/No), or two-valued questions, followed by two names (for instance, Dan/Sam). The yes/no questions asked whether the two characters stand in a certain comparison relation with respect to a given predicate; the two valued questions asked which entity ranks higher in asymmetric comparison relations. The questions can be divided to various different conditions depending on the type of *comparison relation* and the type of *predicate*.

Predicate types included basic gradable adjectives such as *tall,* conjunctions and disjunctions of gradable adjectives such as *bald and/or tall,* and nominal constructions modified by gradable adjectives, such as *bald tall [one].* Notice that adjectives stand alone (with no overt noun phrase to modify) significantly more easily in Hebrew than in English, as is apparent from the translations of some of the questions below. Therefore, some material that did not occur in the original questionnaire has been added in square brackets to enhance clarity of the English translation (e.g. [*one*] in the nominal example given above).

Comparison types included simple comparisons (as in, e.g., *taller, less tall,* and *equally tall*) and complex comparisons, mainly of ease of classification (as in *easier/ less easy/equally easy to determine that Moshe is tall than that Danny is tall*) and difficulty of classification (*harder, less hard / equally hard to determine...*), but also, on few sections, comparisons of *typicality* (as in *more typical of a tall person*), *fitness* (as in *fits more to be a subject in a scientific experiment studying properties of tall people*) and *certainty* (as in *if Danny fits, Moshe definitely fits*). Asking questions with different forms of comparison can reveal whether different ways to relate to the relative ordering of entities along dimensions like height produce similar or different answers. At the same time they may serve to test reliability. Notice that comparative adjectives like *taller* in Hebrew are construed of two separate words: *yoter gavoha* ('more tall'; 'taller'), thus the data below is presented in the Hebrew way, e.g. using *more fat* rather than *fatter,* even where English speakers would prefer the latter.

For example, on section 1 the subjects read the following description of two characters called Moshe and Danny: "Assume Moshe weighs 100 kg and Danny weighs 90 kg and they are alike in other things (for instance, height)." The questions following this paragraph include simple comparison, as well as comparison of ease and difficulty of classification, but only in relation to a basic adjective (*fat*), for this section was introductory in nature, with the goal to check whether subjects understand the general logic of the questions in the questionnaire:

(15) Section 1, the questions:

The basic condition, simple comparison

a. Is Moshe more <u>fat</u> than Danny?   Yes/No

The basic condition, complex comparison

b. Is it easier to determine that Moshe is <u>fat</u> than that Danny is <u>fat</u>?   Yes/No

c. Is it harder to determine that Danny is <u>fat</u> than that Moshe is <u>fat</u>?   Yes/No

On section 3, the subjects read the following description: "Assume Moshe weighs 100 kg and he is 195 cm tall, and Danny weighs 70 kg and is he is 195 cm tall." (i.e., Moshe is fatter than Danny, but they are equally tall). The questions included both basic (fat, tall) and conjunctive adjectives (fat and tall), as well as simple and complex comparisons. If natural language semantics is generally fuzzy, subjects should regard *fat* and *tall* as assigning Moshe and Danny degrees in a bound interval isomorphic to the real interval [0,1]. Then, based on these degrees, subjects should try to compute Moshe and Danny's degrees in *fat and tall*, thereby judging either Moshe or Danny as *more fat and tall*.

In opposition, if natural language semantics is not generally fuzzy (the 'Boolean' hypothesis), subjects would not have access to degrees in complex predicates like *fat and tall*; rather they will interpret *more fat and tall* with *and* scoping over *more*; i.e. they will try to determine whether it is Moshe or Danny that is *more fat and more tall* (i.e. *fatter and taller*). Since neither one is *fatter and taller,* nor are they *equally fat and tall* in the sense of being *equally fat* and *equally tall*, subjects are expected to say that (i) Moshe is **not** more "*fat and bald*"; (ii) Danny is **not** more "*fat and bald*" and (iii) They are **not** equally "*fat and bald*".

Three measures where taken in order to bias subjects **against** such 'Boolean' answers with wide scope for *and/or* with respect to *more*, and towards 'fuzzy' answers, whereby degrees and ordering relations are construed for complex predicates. First, the following introductory comment preceded the questions of section 3:

(16) Section 3, introductory comment:

An important comment regarding sections in the questionnaire of the form:

(1) Is Moshe more tall and fat than Danny?

(2) Is Moshe more tall or fat than Danny?

The intention is not to ask whether Moshe is more tall and/or whether Moshe is more fat; rather, the intention in (1) is to ask whether Moshe exemplifies better the complex property fat and tall. The intention in (2) is to ask whether Moshe exemplifies better the complex property fat or tall."

Second, in each and every section, the adjectival conjunctions and disjunctions were underlined in all the questions under concern, so that they will be processed as relating to a single unified property.

Third, section 9 presented the two figures as equally fat and one balder than the other (i.e. the same pattern as in section 3); however, this section begins with 9a directly asking whether Moshe is both more fat and more bald than Danny is (an unambiguously wide-scope *and/or* question) and immediately continued by asking whether Moshe is more fat and Bald than Danny is (9b). On this setup, subjects are expected to try to interpret 9b as asking for something different than 9a, thereby interpreting *and* within the scope of *more*. Likewise, sections 3 and 4 begin by asking who is *more fat* and who is *more tall/bald*, except in two separate subsections (3a,c and 4a,b) rather than in a conjoined question.

Finally, section 4 presented characters in inverse relations (Aharon *fatter* and Danny *balder*) and section 7 involved a conjunctive typicality adjective referencing two typicality features; this adjective translates roughly to *typical of a flying and calling creature*. A

complete presentation of the relevant sections (1, 3, 4, 7 and 9) is found in the appendix (see also the tables in the result section below).

Procedure The subjects have received the questionnaire by email. They were asked to fill it in themselves and not to consult with anyone but me if they have questions. When they were undecided, they were encouraged to nonetheless select the answer that fits best their opinion. They have received as much time as they needed to fill in answers and were encouraged to add comments on each section.

2.2 Results

The results of sections 1, 3 and 4 are presented first, divided to results of basic conditions (atomic predicates), followed by conjunctive, disjunctive and modifier-position conditions.[3] Only then are the results of sections 9 and 7 presented, which appear to reflect mainly the effect of repetition of judgments on all conditions.

2.2.1 Judgments for atomic ('basic') predicates

Simple comparison The answers pertaining to basic predicates confirmed expectations: on sections 1 and 3 Moshe was generally judged fatter, with 89% and 94% agreement when his 100 kgs were compared to Danny's 90 kg and 70 kg, respectively. Apparently, the bigger weight difference in 3a vs. 1a explains the higher percentage of agreement in 3a.

The judgments of the few subjects that did not agree to say that Moshe is fatter (even in the 30 kg difference condition) are probably explained by the fact that (as often mentioned in the comment sections throughout the questionnaire) ordering judgments in adjectives like *fat* (as well as *tall*) may be based on both weight and height as well as on general look (since mere weight may reflect muscles rather than fat).

On 3c subjects generally did not agree that any one of the 195 cm tall characters is taller than the other (6% agreement). On section 4, subjects' answers to 4a,b unequivocally indicate that they agree that Aharon is fatter (100%) and Danny is balder (97%), as expected given that Aharon is 30 kg fatter than Danny, but is not bald, respectively.

Complex comparison The same pattern is found with comparison of ease of classification (e.g., *easier to determine that x is fat than that y is*), but with smaller percentages of agreement (69% vs. 89% in 1b and 3b, respectively). Using comparison of difficulty of classification in 1c (e.g., *harder to determine that y is fat than that x is*), yields even smaller percentage (60%). One comment regarding 1b indicates that it is easy to determine that both are fat. Apparently, this yields the use of *easier to determine* less appropriate than the use of *fatter*; it yields the use of *harder to determine* even less appropriate.

Also, given that subjects' negative answer to (3c) implies that the characters are equally tall, most (25) subjects ignored question 3d concerning whether it is easier to determine that one of them is tall; however, four of the 35 subjects (12%) did agree that tallness is easier to determine for one than for the other, justifying their answers by assigning a role to their very different weights.

---

[3]The results for complex comparisons are basically the same as the results for simple ones, except somewhat weaker. However, as discussed below, they appear to have been affected by a methodological problem. Thus, these results are presented separately from those for simple comparisons; readers that are only interested in the main question the paper asks can skip the paragraphs pertaining to complex comparisons and still capture the main findings.

Section 1 Moshe – 100 kg; Danny – 90 kg	%**'Yes'**	'No' answers	'Yes' answers
a. Is Moshe more <u>fat</u> than Danny?	89%	4	31
b. Is it easier to determine that Moshe is <u>fat</u> than that Danny is <u>fat</u>?	69%	11	24
c. Is it harder to determine that Danny is <u>fat</u> than that Moshe is <u>fat</u>?	60%	14	21

Section 3a–d Moshe – 100 kg; Danny – 70 kg; both – 195 cm tall	%**'Yes'**	'No' answers	'Yes' answers
a. Is Moshe more <u>fat</u> than Danny?	94%	2	33
b. Is it easier to determine that Moshe is <u>fat</u> than that Danny is <u>fat</u>?	89%	4	31
c. Is one of them more <u>tall</u> than the other?	6%	30	2
d. Is it easier to determine that he is <u>tall</u>?	40%	6	4

Section 4a,b Aharon – 100 kg; Danny – 70 kg; Aharon – not bald; Danny – bald	% **'Danny'**	'Aharon'	'Danny'
a. Who is more <u>fat</u>	0%	33	0
b. Who is more <u>bald</u>	97%	1	32

Table 1. The basic conditions:

(i) Given his higher weight, Moshe is generally judged fatter (sections 1,3; same with Aharon in 4); (ii) given Moshe and Danny's equal heights, none is judged taller (sections 1 and 3) and (iii) given their inverse classification as bald and not bald, Danny is judged to be balder (section 4).

2.2.2   Judgments for conjunctive predicates

Simple comparison   The answers to the conjunctive questions in sections 3 and 4 are generally supportive of the Boolean theory. Recall that on section 3, the characters were equally tall but Moshe was 30 kg fatter. Despite this difference on one of the conjuncts, Moshe was generally judged neither *more fat and bald* nor *less fat and bald* than Danny, with 6% and 0% agreement in 3e and 3f, respectively. Obviously, the two characters are not equally <u>fat and bald</u> (cf. the results for question 4e below). Thus, this result suggests that the questions tend to be interpreted with *and* scoping over *more*, i.e. subjects try to determine whether Moshe is *more fat and more tall* in 3e and whether he is *less fat and less tall* in 3f. The latter is clearly not the case (testified by across-the board disagreement); the former is not the case because the characters are equally tall. Counter the prediction of a fuzzy semantic theory, then, subjects did not judge Moshe *more fat and tall*, presumably because they did not compose a degree function for the conjunctive concept *fat and tall*.

Concerning section 4, recall that subjects' answers to 4a,b unequivocally indicate that they agree that Aharon is fatter (100%) and Danny is balder (97%). Probably precisely because of that, counter the prediction of a fuzzy theory, subjects did not appear to compute degrees for the conjunctive concept *fat and bald;* rather, in line with the Boolean hypothesis, the answers to 4a–f unequivocally indicate that subjects agree to say neither that any of the two characters is more <u>fat and bald</u> (0% agreement to 4c), nor that they are equally <u>fat and bald</u> (9% agreement to 4e). This suggests that these questions are interpreted with *and* scoping over *more*; subjects were trying to determine whether Aharon is *more fat <u>and</u> more bald* or whether he is *less fat <u>and</u> less bald* in 4a (both are clearly not the case) and whether Aharon and Danny are equally fat <u>and</u> equally bald in 4c (which again is clearly not the case).

In sum, counter the prediction of a fuzzy theory, subjects did not judge any character to be *more fat and bald*, and at the same time judged them not to be *equally fat and bald*. This seems to indicate that they did not compose a degree function for the conjunctive concept *fat and bald*.[4]

Section 3e–f			
Moshe – 100 kg; Danny – 70 kg; both – 195 cm tall	%'**Yes**'	'No'	'Yes'
e. Is Moshe more <u>fat and tall</u> than Danny?	6%	33	2
f. Is Moshe less <u>fat and tall</u> than Danny?	0%	32	0
g. Is it easier to determine that Moshe is <u>fat and tall</u> than that Danny is?	38%	21	13
h. Is it harder to determine that Moshe is <u>fat and tall</u> than that Danny is?	12%	30	4

Table 2. The first conjunction condition:
Despite a 30 kg weight difference (all other things being equal), Moshe is generally not judged *more fat and tall*.

Section 4c–f			
Aharon – 100 kg; Danny – 70 kg; Aharon – not bald; Danny – bald	%'**Yes**'	'No'	'Yes'
c. Is any of them more <u>fat and bald</u> than the other?	0%	34	0
d. Is it easier to determine that one of them is <u>fat and bald</u> than that the other is?	3%	34	1
e. Are they equally <u>fat and bald</u>?	9%	31	3
f. Is it equally easy to determine that they are <u>fat and bald</u>?	6%	31	2

Table 3. The second conjunction condition:
When Aharon is *fatter* and Danny *balder*, generally, neither is judged *more fat and bald*.

---

[4]To the best of my understanding, product based t-norms and sum based t-conorms cannot account for these data, except perhaps by virtue of a residua given an assumption of interaction between, e.g., *fat* and *bald*. But such an assumption is not justified, for *fat* and *bald* are (intuitively) independent.

Complex comparison The pattern of results with comparisons of ease of classification (e.g., *easier to determine that x is fat and tall*) is similar to the pattern found with direct comparison (e.g. *more fat and bald*), except for larger percentage (almost 40%) of agreement to say, on section 3g, that it is easier to determine that Moshe is more <u>fat and tall</u>. At any rate, most subjects still disagree to rank Moshe higher.

Two points reveal that the results concerning ease of classification should be taken with a grain of salt.

First, subjects commented that Danny is obviously **not** fat and tall (because he is by no means fat), rendering this comparison inappropriate; again, we see evidence supporting the hypothesis that comparisons of the form *easier to determine that x is P than that y is P* are only appropriate if it is possible to determine that both *x* and *y* are *P*, but it isn't too easy to do so or to reject doing so (*P*-hood is somewhat uncertain or dubious, but is definitely a live option). But if classification as, *P*, not *P* or undetermined is the main issue at stake in ease-of-classification comparisons, their acceptance is compatible with a Boolean theory; hence, these comparisons are not ideal means to distinguish between fuzzy and boolean interpretations.

Second, probably subjects would have been more willing to say that it is easier to determine *whether* Moshe is <u>fat and tall</u> than whether Danny is. This issue is left for future research to resolve. Notice, however, that reinterpretation of *that* as *whether* may explain the unexpected 12% (rather than 0%) agreement to 3h (it is harder to determine that [≅ whether] Moshe is <u>fat and tall</u>), since it is very easy to determine that Danny falls outside this conjunction (because he is by no means fat), while Moshe's classification is uncertain. Indeed, some subjects commented that they could only have answered the questions positively if *easier to determine that* would have been substituted for *easier to determine whether* and others said that they have answered *as if* the question included a *whether-*, rather than a *that*-complementizer.

At any rate, the results pertaining to section 4 are pretty clear. Subjects agree to say neither that for any of the two characters it is easier to determine that he is <u>fat and bald</u> (3% agreement to 4c), nor that for both this is equally easy to determine (6% agreement to 4f). This suggests that these questions are interpreted with *and* scoping over *more*; subjects were trying to determine whether, e.g. for Aharon, it is *easier to determine that he is fat <u>and</u> easier to determine that he is bald* or whether it is *less easy to determine that he is fat <u>and</u> less easy to determine that he is bald* in 4b (both are clearly not the case) and whether for Aharon and Danny it is *equally easy to determine that they are fat <u>and</u> equally easy to determine that they are bald* in 4d (which again is clearly not the case).

2.2.3   Judgments for disjunctive predicates

Simple comparison The answers to the disjunctive questions confirmed the Boolean theory's predictions, although to a lesser extent.

Notice that if subjects were to construct a degree function for *fat or bald*, their answers to 4e–g should have been that none is *more <u>fat or bald</u>*, for both characters have a high degree in one disjunct and a low degree in the other disjunct, rendering their degrees in *<u>fat or bald</u>* more or less equal. However, first, we have already seen that they are not judged equally fat and bald (cf. Table 3, 4e, f). Second, the answers to 4g indicate that $3/4$ of the subjects agree that one of the two characters is more <u>fat or bald</u>

(74% agreement in 4g). Third, importantly, less than half of the subjects (46%) were willing to provide a single name indicating who is more fat or bald, Danny or Aharon (only 16/35 answers for 4h).

Thus, first and foremost, the 19 subjects (54%) not providing an answer to this question indicate that they interpreted *more fat or bald* as *more fat or more bald*, classifying both characters as such. In other words, these subjects interpreted *or* as scoping over *more*, trying to determine whether Aharon is *more fat or more bald* and whether Danny is *more fat or more bald*; both are clearly the case as Aharon is fatter and Danny balder, rendering 4g true and at the same time making it impossible to choose one answer to 4h.

Second, of the 16 answers, the majority (10, which make 63%) selected Danny as their candidate, explaining that Danny is clearly bald and hence fat or bald, while Aharon is not clearly fat, thus not clearly fat or bald. Thus, these subjects were using a Boolean union rule for classification under disjunctions. The remaining 6 subjects did not indicate why they selected Aharon.

Third, one could argue that the 16 subjects answering 4h were using fuzzy disjunctive degrees; however, had this been the case, these 16 subjects would have agreed to consider one of the characters as *more fat and bald* in the second conjunctive condition, but they did not (cf. 0% and 3% agreement to 4c,d, Table 3). Thus, these results do not indicate fuzzy reasoning.[5]

Section 4g–j Aharon – 100 kg; Danny – 70 kg; Aharon – not bald; Danny – bald	%'**Danny**' %'**Yes**'	'Aharon'/ 'No'	'Danny'/ 'Yes'
g. Is one of them more <u>fat or bald</u> than the other?	74%	9	25
h. Who is more <u>fat or bald</u>	63%	6	10
i. Is it easier to determine that one of them is <u>fat or bald</u> than that the other is?	68%	11	23
j. For whom is it easier to determine that?	77%	5	17

Table 4. The first disjunction condition:
When Aharon is *fatter* and Danny *balder*, generally, both are judged *more fat or tall*.

Complex comparison Similar patterns are found in the ease of classification questions. Most subjects agree to say that for one of the two characters it is easier to determine that he is <u>fat or bald</u> (68% agreement in 4i), and 77% of the 22 subjects that provided an answer to 4j have selected Danny. Danny is clearly bald and hence <u>fat or bald</u>, while Aharon is not clearly fat, thus not clearly <u>fat or bald</u>. For this reason, it is easier to determine that Danny is fat or bald, assuming a union classification-rule for disjunctions.

---

[5]The use of product and sum functions for *and* and *or* cannot account for these data, as it predicts, for any pair of entities standing in the relation "equally P and Q", that in order to also stand in the relation "more P or Q", their P values should both be greater than both their Q values (or vice versa). This condition is not satisfied in the present scenario, since Danny's degree in *bald* exceeds Aharon's degree in *fat* (Danny is definitely bald, but 100 kg is not definitely fat), but Aharon's degree in *bald* doesn't (Aharon is 'maybe not bald'). Similarly, Aharon's degree in *fat* exceeds his degree in bald, but not Danny's.

Moreover, 13 subjects did not give an answer to this question, indicating that they probably classified both as ones for whom is *easier to determine fat or bald,* as predicted by the Boolean theory. They have probably interpreted these questions with *or* scoping over *more,* trying to determine whether for Aharon it is *easier to determine that he is fat or easier to determine that he is bald* or whether for Danny it is *easier to determine that he is fat or easier to determine that he is bald;* both are clearly the case (as Aharon is fatter and Danny balder), making it impossible to choose one answer.

Also, the results of 4s–w with fitness comparisons and certainty comparisons support reliability. On 4s, 92% of the subjects agree that Danny fits more to an experiment for which fat or bald subjects are needed. Likewise, on 4t, 82% refused to rank Aharon higher (to say that if Danny fits, Aharon definitely fits), while on 4w, 61% agreed to rank Danny higher (if Aharon fits, Danny definitely does).

Section 4s–w Aharon – 100 kg; Danny – 70 kg; Aharon – not bald; Danny – bald	% **'Danny'** % **'Yes'**	'Aharon'/ 'No'	'Danny'/ 'Yes'
s. <u>Fat or bald</u> subjects are needed to fill in a questionnaire for a scientific experiment. Who fits more?	92%	2	22
t. It is true that if Danny fits Aharon definitely fits?	18%	27	6
w. It is true that if Aharon fits Danny definitely fits?	61%	13	20

Table 5. The second disjunction condition:

When Aharon is *fatter* (100 kg vs. 70 kg) and Danny is *balder,* generally, Danny 'fits more' and is 'more definitely classified in' the category *fat or tall.*

2.2.4   Judgments for predicates in modifier position

On this condition the adjectives occur with no overt coordination marker; rather, they are in a modifier position of a null noun (perhaps the rightmost adjective functions as a noun in this construction). On 4o–r, it is *bald* that is more adjacent to the empty noun head (or perhaps itself functions as a noun), whereas in 4k–n *fat* is in the more 'nominal' position. At any rate, subjects could not take *more* in the modified noun condition to refer only to the adjective not adjacent to (or not itself functioning as) the head noun (trying to determine whether any of the characters is a *fatter bald man* in 4k–n or a *balder fat man* in 4o–r), because for this interpretation to occur in Hebrew the comparative morpheme and the adjective it modifies should follow the noun they modify rather than precede it.

The results on this condition are similar to the results on the conjunction condition, though a bit weaker. The majority of the subjects refused to agree that any of the characters is more *fat bald [person]* (13% agreement in 4k) and *bald fat [person]* (23% agreement in 4o), with less than a third of the subjects—9 and 11 answering the questions 'which one is' in 4l and 4p, of which 89% and 91% respectively selected Danny. This suggests that most subjects interpreted these questions with a Boolean conjunctive operator scoping over *more,* as explained above for *more bald and fat.*

The results for the ease of classification comparisons are similar but slightly weaker, as in previous sections, suggesting that the subjects answered reliably. Most subjects refused to say for any of the two characters that it is easier to determine that he is <u>fat bald</u> (27% agreement in 4m) or that he is <u>bald fat</u> (25% agreement in 4q), with about a third of the subjects—11 and 14 answering the questions 'which one is' in 4n and 4r, of which 82% and 100% respectively selected Danny to be better in the modified construction.

The selection of Danny rather than Aharon by subjects in 4l,n,p,r may be merely due to Danny's description as bald and Aharon's description as maybe not bald, as opposed to the absence of direct descriptions of their status in *fat*. Still, it seems puzzling that 70 kg counts as fat here. Thus, the order of conditions may have affected the results. The present condition directly followed the disjunction condition, whereby Danny ranked higher for obvious reasons (cf. Section 2.2.3).

Section 4k–r Aharon – 100 kg; Danny – 70 kg; Aharon – not bald; Danny – bald	%'**Danny**' %'**Yes**'	'Aharon'/ 'No'	'Danny'/ 'Yes'
k. Is any of them more <u>fat bald</u> than the other?	13%	27	4
l. Who is more fat bald?	89%	1	8
m. Is it easier to determine that one of them is <u>fat bald</u> than that the other is?	27%	24	9
n. For whom is it easier to determine that?	82%	2	9
o. Is any of them more <u>bald fat</u> than the other?	23%	23	7
p. Who is more <u>bald fat</u>?	91%	1	10
q. Is it easier to determine that one of them is <u>bald fat</u> than that the other is?	25%	24	8
r. For whom is it easier to determine that?	100%	0	14

Table 6. The modifier-position condition:

When Aharon is *fatter* (100 kg vs. 70 kg) and Danny is *balder*, generally, neither is more [of a] fat bald [person] and neither is more [of a] bald fat [person]; but if one is selected, Danny is.

We see that, as in previous sections, the results support a Boolean theory rather than a fuzzy theory for complex concepts, over and above the fact that complex concepts where underlined and an explicit comment asked subjects to consider the whole concept rather than each constituent separately (cf. section 2.1). We can, therefore, conclude that the results for sections 1,3 and 4 support the existence of a Boolean bias, whereby Boolean operators (conjunction or disjunction) are interpreted in wide scope with respect to comparative morphemes (or phrases).

2.2.5   Judgments for section 9—the 'repetition' conditions

To overcome this Boolean bias, section 9 begins by directly asking whether Moshe is both <u>more fat</u> and <u>more bald</u> (9a) versus whether Moshe is more <u>fat and Bald</u> than

Danny (9b). The idea is that on this setup, subjects will try to interpret 9b as asking for something different than 9a, thereby interpreting *and* within the scope of *more*. Recall that on section 9, the characters were equally fat (100 kg) but Moshe was balder. This setup is, then, very similar to the one in section 3. The results, however, are different.

Subjects generally disagreed to answer 9a positively (9% agreement); however, while most subjects still disagreed to answer 9b positively, much fewer did (43% agreement). These results indicate that an alternative fuzzy interpretation may be accessed, although it is not the preferred or natural interpretation for contexts such as those given in the questionnaire.

Even more striking is the 91% and 79% agreement to it being easier to determine that Moshe is fat and bald (9c) and bald and fat (9d) than that Danny is, respectively. As in previous sections, replacing direct comparison with comparisons of ease of classification facilitates agreement to rank Moshe higher, but this time facilitation is extreme.[6]

Nonetheless, two problems in the experimental design make it impossible to conclude that under the conditions specified above (when sentences such as 9b are adjacent to sentences such as 9a) speakers generally tend to interpret *and* within the scope of *more*, i.e. to compute a graded structure—degrees and/or ordering—for conjunctions, in line with a fuzzy semantic theory.

The first problem is that the order of presentation of sections and questions was one and the same for all subjects. Thus, the high percentages in 9b–d may also result from an effect of repetition of the same sort of questions, together with a desire on the part of the subjects to be cooperative, i.e., to answer positively, a desire that was repressed by virtue of the Boolean bias. But having answered more than 20 conjunctive/disjunctive questions before getting to section 9 (4 questions on section 3 plus 19 questions on section 4), subjects' tendency to disagree that *and/or* can scope under *more* may have slowly diminished. Perhaps, then, repetition in itself facilitates the composition of a unified degree function or ordering for the complex category.

The second problem regards an additional difference between section 3 and section 9. If both characters of section 9 are considered possibly fat (100 kg) and either definitely or possibly bald, this may have facilitated positive answers. Recall that on section 3 subjects commented that Danny is *obviously not* fat and tall, and that, for this reason, comparison of ease/difficulty of classification under these concepts is inappropriate; it may well be the case, then, that on question 9 more subjects were willing to accept the use of *easier to determine that* because no character was *obviously not* fat and *obviously not* bald. Furthermore, it may well be that more subjects answered *as if* the relevant questions included *whether* instead of *that* on section 9 than on section 3, due to the fact that 9 occurred after 3. But if it is only the status of entities as *bald* or *not bald* (or *undetermined*) that matters, the interpretation, in both cases, could be Boolean (supplemented by a representation of epistemic ignorance and/or vagueness, cf. part 3), with wide-scope for *and* with respect to the comparison phrase, as discussed earlier.

The same considerations apply to the modified noun conditions in 9e–h and even more so to the disjunction conditions, as seen in 9i–o.

---

[6]Recall that on section 3 Moshe was generally judged neither *more fat and tall* nor *less fat and tall* than Danny, with 6% and 0% agreement respectively, and that less than 40% agreed to say that *it is easier to determine that Moshe is more fat and tall*.

Section 9a–d

Moshe is bald; Danny is less bald (maybe not bald); Both – 100 kg	%'**Danny**' %'**Yes**'	'Moshe'/ 'No'	'Danny'/ 'Yes'
a. Is Moshe both <u>more fat</u> and <u>more bald</u>?	9%	32	3
b. Is Moshe more <u>fat and Bald</u> than Danny?	43%	20	15
c. Is it easier to determine that Moshe is <u>fat and bald</u> than that Dan is <u>fat and bald</u>?	91%	3	32
d. Is it easier to determine that Moshe is <u>bald and fat</u> than that Dan is <u>bald and fat</u>?	79%	7	27

Table 7a: The 'repetition' condition—conjunction.

e. Is Moshe more <u>fat bald</u> than Danny is?	55%	15	18
f. Is it easier to determine that Moshe is <u>fat bald</u> than that Danny is <u>fat bald</u>?	71%	10	25
g. Is Moshe more <u>bald fat</u> than Danny is?	54%	16	19
h. Is it easier to determine that Moshe is <u>bald fat</u> than that Danny is <u>bald fat</u>?	70%	10	23

Table 7b: The 'repetition' condition—modifier-position.

i. Is Moshe more <u>fat or Bald</u> than Danny?	100%	0	35
j. Is it easier to determine that Moshe is <u>fat or bald</u> than that Danny is?	91%	3	31
k. Is Moshe more <u>Bald or fat</u> than Danny?	100%	0	35
l. Is it easier to determine that Moshe is <u>bald or fat</u> than that Dan is?	97%	1	32
m. <u>Fat or bald</u> subjects are needed to fill a questionnaire for a scientific experiment. Who fits more?	7%	28	2
n. It is true that if Danny fits Moshe definitely fits?	77%	8	27
o. It is true that if Moshe fits Danny definitely fits?	15%	29	5

Table 7c: The 'repetition' condition—disjunction.

The answers to section 7 were basically Boolean in nature. Subjects were presented with two creatures not satisfying the first conjunct (*flying*) and differing along the second (*calling*), the latter being more typical of a calling creature than the former (non-calling creature). In this case, both creatures obviously do not satisfy the conjunction and the former obviously does not satisfy the disjunction. Most subjects disagreed about the latter being more typical of the modified noun *flying calling* [creature] (29% agreement for 7a) and conjunction *flying and calling* [creature] (37% agreement for 7b). Conversely, most subjects agreed about it being more typical of the disjunction *flying or calling* [creature] (80% agreement for 7c).

The results on section 7 are somewhere in between those of section 3 and those of section 9. This supports the hypothesis that the results on section 9 are explained by the two above mentioned problems, i.e. an effect of repetition, together with characters not obviously violating any of the constituents of the complex predicates in section 9.

Section 7 Two non-flying creatures; The first one doesn't call; The second one is more typical of a calling creature	% **'Yes'**	'No'	'Yes'
a. Is the second more typical of a flying calling [creature]?	29%	25	10
b. Is the second more typical of a flying and calling [creature]?	37%	22	13
c. Is the second more typical of a flying or calling [creature]?	80%	7	28

Table 7d: The 'repetition' condition—general.

3   General discussion

We have seen that Hebrew speakers tend to dislike ordering entities under conjunctive or disjunctive concepts when the two entities do not stand in one and the same ordering relation (e.g. *more*) in all the constituents. The subjects have taken care to make this point clear in their comments, stating that questions that ask them to do so are impossible to answer, are inappropriate, that the complex (conjunctive or other) comparison will not be used by a person sensitive to the language in such circumstances and so on. One subject has written that these questions are of the same type as questions such as *is a cucumber more long or more green*. We cannot tell. In fact answering the latter is impossible for precisely the same reasons; two properties that are not easily comparable are involved. They are not easily comparable precisely because they do not consist of mappings of entities to degrees on a bound interval isomorphic to the real interval between 0 and 1.

In accordance with these comments, the results presented in part 2 show that a truly compositional interpretation, i.e. a degree function (or ordering) of a conjunction/disjunction of properties, composed based on the degree functions (or ordering relations) of the constituents, is hardly ever occurring naturally in the absence of a particularly encouraging context. Evidence for this is, for example, the fact that in section 3, the two characters are described as *equally tall* (195 cm), but Moshe is 30 kg *fatter*, but still most subjects refuse to say that either Moshe or Danny is *more fat and tall* (3e–h). These results suggest that speakers are, more often than not, unwilling to interpret *and* inside the scope of *more*, i.e. *more P and Q* is interpreted as *more P and more Q*, not as *More (P and Q)*. The same holds for *or*. These results are in line with a Boolean analysis more than with a fuzzy one. However, these preliminary findings are restricted to contexts of the nature the questionnaire examined. Other types of contexts should be investigated in the future, as well as the effect of repetition on interpretation. In addition, other languages should be studied.[7]

The results are also consistent with the hypothesis that a use of a truly compositional degree function (or ordering) may be facilitated by repetition of discussion and processing of the interpretation of complex concepts such as *fat and bald* (cf., the results of section 9). Also, mentioning a conjunctive comparison, e.g. *more fat and bald*, following a conjunction of comparisons, e.g. *more fat and more bald*, may trigger such an interpretation. Therefore, it may be useful to test such contexts in the future, separating the two variables (repetition and conjunction of comparisons) from one another.[8]

Another variable affecting the results is whether the ranked entities obviously violate one of the atomic concepts in question or not. That membership or non-membership in the categories in question plays an important role in judgments of ordering is in line with vagueness based accounts of gradability in natural language. According to theories in this approach, an entity pair $\langle x, y \rangle$ is classified as *more P* iff, roughly, either x is P but y not necessarily P, or alternatively y is not P but x is not necessarily not P (Kamp 1975; Fine 1975; Klein 1980; van Rooij 2011). The present study shows that when subjects are forced to give a comparative judgment about the degrees of instances with respect to conjunctions or disjunctions, judgments seem to be determined by the characters' likelihood of classification in the positive or negative denotations of the conjunction or disjunction.

For example, when Moshe weighed 100 kg and Danny only 70 kg (Moshe was *fatter*), but Danny was *bald* and Moshe was *not bald* (Danny was *balder*), according to the few subjects that selected one character to be *more fat and/or bald* than the other, Danny scored much better than Moshe relative to *fat or bald* (questions 4), because it is easier to determine that Danny is *fat or bald* (Danny is *bald*, while Moshe is not *bald* and is not necessarily *fat*); also, Danny scored much better than Moshe relative to *fat bald / bald fat,* because it is easier to determine that Moshe is <u>not</u>: *fat and bald* (because Moshe is not *bald*), while Danny might still be *fat and bald*. A similar pattern occurred in other scenarios as well. When the two characters were *equally tall* (195 cm), but Moshe was *fatter* (100 kg as opposed to Danny's 70 kg), among those who answered the question, Moshe was regarded as *more fat and tall* than Danny (section 3). When the characters where *fat*, and *equally fat* (100 kg), but Moshe was *balder*, 90%–100% of the subject agreed that Moshe is more *fat or bald* than Danny (section 9). Future research may, then, profit from asking what happens when knowledge about denotation membership is more uncertain.

A different issue raising many questions yet to be examined regards different sorts of ways to refer to ordering relations with adjectives (e.g., *more* versus *less* comparatives, as well as simple versus complex comparison). Different ways to refer seem to differ in a variety of respects, one of which is the extent to which they raise the expectation

---

[7]Novel findings (currently in process) suggest that English is similar to Hebrew in that conjunctive and disjunctive predicates such as *expensive and time consuming* appear incompatible with gradable morphology and interpretation.

[8]Novel findings (currently in process) strongly support the assumption that it is repetition, rather than conjunction of comparisons, that facilitates fuzzy interpretations.

that the ordered entities are predicate members; this expectation may also be stronger for the subject or for the object (Sassoon 2007). These issues call for further empirical investigation.

The phenomenon this paper investigates pertains also to conjunctive multi-dimensional adjectives, like *typical with respect to flying and singing* or *healthy with respect to blood pressure and pulse*, when these are combined with *more*. Our results suggest that, by and large, *and* takes wide scope, and *more* combines with a single function at a time (per a conjunct); e.g., we understand *healthier with respect to blood pressure and pulse* to mean *healthier with respect to blood pressure and healthier with respect to pulse*.

An important open question is to what extent ordering in conjunctive predicates can be based on the entities' weighted mean in the constituents, in context in which information about weights is made available. If, for example, I compare a patient with cancer to a patient with the flu, I may weigh the cancer as more important, and judge the former patient as having a higher degree of sickness with respect to the conjunction of these dimensions. When context does not tell us how the conjuncts are to be weighed (for instance, if I compare a patient with cancer to a patient with serious heart problems), this strategy might fail. When it fails, we are left with a wide-scope interpretation like *healthier with respect to cancer and healthier with respect to the heart*, and we are likely to be reluctant to say about any of the patients that he is healthier (in the given conjunction of respects). Thus, another open question for the future is to examine the effect of constituents with variable weights.

An alternative strategy for construing an ordering relation for conjunctive and disjunctive adjectives is by using the mean in the typicality dimensions of the modified nouns corresponding to them. Any adjective can modify a trivial noun such as *object, individual, one*. Like other noun phrases, the noun phrase *healthy entity* is linked with a set of typicality dimensions such that entities whose mean degree in these dimensions is high are classified as members in the denotation (cf. Murphy 2002's review of data concerning basic nouns and Hampton's 1997a,b review of data concerning nouns modified by a nominal relative clause, such as *birds which are pet*); examples of dimensions typical of *healthy people* include *calm, does not smoke, does not drink, does not eat fat, eats fruit and vegetables, is regularly involved in sport activities*, etc. Such dimensions may be directly linked to modified nouns such as *healthy person*, but only indirectly related to the adjective *healthy* itself, for otherwise we would expect ordering judgments in conjunctions and disjunctions of adjectives to be as easy as the typicality judgments are in nouns modified by a nominal relative clause or in noun-noun compounds. The study presented in this paper suggests that this is not the case.

In sum, compositionality of the ordering of conjunctions and disjunctions, fails more often than not. The ordering of many pairs of entities in a conjunction (or a disjunction) cannot be predicted from their ordering in the constituents. Thus, while a fuzzy analysis could have been considered a natural extension of the numerical approach (Kennedy 1999), this no longer seems a viable option. Rather, ordering relations for conjunctions and disjunctions need to be learnt directly based on whether entities are classified in their intersective and union-based denotations or not, as well as, perhaps, on the constituent weights and typicality features. However, information about the latter is often not available. Thus, conjunctions and disjunctions tend not to license gradable morphology.

Last but not least, what are the implications for the numerical versus vagueness-based debate? On the one hand, the fact that conjunctive and disjunctive predicates do not appear gradable is surprising given a vagueness-based approach, for if we use denotations (rather than numerical measurements) to systematically build ordering relations, why aren't we able to systematically use the denotations of conjunctive and disjunctive concepts to do so? After all, these predicates are at least as vague as their constituents are. The numerical approach fairs better over here; since *and* and *or* are merely Boolean, conjunctive and disjunctive predicates denote entity sets, not degree functions, which explains why they are non-gradable. On the other hand, we have seen that when we do make gradable judgments in relation to complex predicates, they do seem to go along the line suggested by vagueness based theories. This is probably the case because no other option (no unified numerical degree function) is available.

Hence, the general moral to draw from all the above must be in favor of a combined approach. Both measurement-based degree functions and vagueness-based ordering relations play a role in the semantics of natural language expressions (for a discussion and a detailed model see Sassoon 2007). In addition, different predicate types may be associated with different types of degree functions (e.g., numerical versus ordinal; cf. Sassoon 2010a).

BIBLIOGRAPHY

Alxatib, Sam and Pelletier, Francis Jeffry (2011). The psychology of vagueness: Borderline cases and contradictions. *Mind and Language* 26(3):287–326.

Bale, Alan C. (2007). Boolean AND and the semantic correlates of gradable adjectives. *International Conference on Adjectives. Lille* (France), 13–15, September, 2007.

Bale, Alan C. (2008). A universal scale of comparison. *Linguistics and Philosophy* 31(1):1–55.

Bartsch, Renate and Venneman, Theo (1972). *Semantic structures: A study in the relation between semantics and syntax.* Athenäum-Skripten Linguistik 9, Frankfurt am Main: Athenäum.

Cresswell, Maxwell John (1977). The semantics of degree. In Barbara Partee (ed.), *Montague grammar*, New York: Academic Press, pages 261–292.

Fine, Kit (1975). Truth, vagueness and logics. *Synthese* 30:265–300.

Hampton, James (1987). Inheritance of attributes in natural concept conjunction. *Memory and Cognition* 15(1):55–71.

Hampton, James (1988a). Overextension of conjunctive concepts: Evidence for a unitary model of concept typicality and class diagnosticity. *Journal of Experimental Psychology: Learning, Memory & Cognition* 14:12–32.

Hampton, James (1988b). Disjunction of natural concepts. *Memory & Cognition* 16(6):579–591.

Hampton, James (1997a). Conceptual combination: Conjunction and negation of natural concepts. *Memory & Cognition* 25(6):888–909.

Hampton, James (1997b). Conceptual Combination. In Koen Lamberts and David Shanks (eds.), *Knowledge, Concepts and Concepts*. Cambridge, MA: The MIT Press, pages 135–162.

Hájek, Petr (2009). Fuzzy logic. In Edward N. Zalta (ed.), *The Stanford Encyclopedia of Philosophy*. Spring 2009 edition.

Heim, Irene (2000). Degree operators and scope. *Proceedings of SALT X*. Ithaca, NY: CLC Publications.

Heim, Irene and Kratzer, Angelika (1998). *Semantics in Generative Grammar*. Malden, Oxford: Blackwell Publishers.

Kamp, Hans (1975). Two theories about adjectives. In Edward Keenan (ed.), *Formal semantics for natural language*, Cambridge: Cambridge University Press, pages 123–155.

Kamp, Hans and Partee, Barbara (1995). Prototype theory and compositionality. *Cognition* 57:129–191.

Kennedy, Christopher (1999). *Projecting the adjective: The syntax and semantics of gradability and comparison*. New York: Garland (1997 UCSC Doctoral dissertation).

Kennedy, Christopher (2001). Polar opposition and the ontology of degrees. *Linguistics and Philosophy* 24(1):33–70.

Kennedy, Christopher and Levin, Beth (2007). Measure of change: The adjectival core of degree achievements. In Louise McNally and Christopher Kennedy (eds.), *Adjectives and adverbs: Syntax, semantics and discourse*. Oxford: Oxford University Press, pages 156–182.

Kennedy, Christopher and McNally, Louise (2005). Scale structure and the semantic typology of gradable predicates. *Language* 81:345–381.

Klein, Ewan (1980). A semantics for positive and comparative adjectives. *Linguistics and Philosophy* 4:1–45.

Klein, Ewan (1991). Comparatives. In Arnim von Stechow and Dieter Wunderlich (eds.), *Semantik/semantics, an international handbook of contemporary research*, Berlin, NY: Walter de Gruyter, pages 673–691.

Landman, Fred (1991). *Structures for semantics*. Dordrecht: Kluwer.

Landman, Fred (2000). *Events and plurality*, Dordrecht: Kluwer.

Landman, Fred (2005). *An almost (but not quite) naïve theory of measures*. Manuscript, Tel Aviv Uni.

Lewis, David K. (1970). General semantics. *Synthese* 22:18–67. Reprinted In David K. Lewis (1983). *Philosophical Papers* volume 1, New York: Oxford University Press, pages 189–229.

Lewis, David K. (1979). Scorekeeping in a language game. *Journal of Philosophical Logic* 8:339–359. Reprinted In David K. Lewis (1983). *Philosophical Papers* volume 1, New York: Oxford University Press, pages 233–249.

Moltmann, Friederike (2006). *Comparatives without degrees. A new approach*. A manuscript for the workshop on scalar meaning, University of Chicago.

Murphy, Gregory L. (2002). *The big book of concepts*. Cambridge, MA: The MIT Press.

Ripley, David (2011). Contradictions at the borders. In Rick Nouwen, Uli Sauerland, Hans-Christian Schmitz, and Robert van Rooij (eds.), *Vagueness in Communication*, LNCS 6517/2011. Heidelberg: Springer, pages 169–188.

Russell, Bertrand (1905). On denoting. *Mind* 14:479–493. Reprinted from *Essays in Analysis* by Russell, B., 1973, London: Allen and Unwin, pages 103–119.

Sapir, Edward (1944). Grading: A study in semantics. *Philosophy of Science* 11:93–116.

Sassoon, Galit W. (2007). *Vagueness, gradability and typicality, a comprehensive semantic analysis*. Doctoral Dissertation, Tel Aviv University.

Sassoon, Galit W. (2010a). Measurement theory in linguistics. *Synthese* 174(1):151–180.

Sassoon, Galit W. (2010b). The degree functions of negative adjectives. *Natural language semantics* 18(2):141–181.

Sauerland, Uli (2011). Vagueness in language: The case against fuzzy logic revisited. *This volume*.

Schwarzschild, Roger (2008). The semantics of comparatives and other degree constructions. *Language and Linguistics Compass, 2.2*, 308–331.

Schwarzschild, Roger and Wilkinson, Karina (2002). Quantifiers in comparatives: A semantics of degree based on intervals. *Natural Language Semantics* 10:1–41.

Serchuk, Phil, Hargreaves, Ian, and Zach, Richard (2010). Vagueness, logic and use: Four experimental studies on vagueness. Forthcoming in *Mind and Language*.

Seuren, Peter (1978). The structure and selection of positive and negative gradable adjectives. In *Papers from the Para-session on the Lexicon. 14th Regional Meeting of the Chicago Linguistic Society* Chicago: CSL, pages 336–346.

Stalnaker, Robert (1978). Assertion. In Peter Cole (ed.), *Syntax and semantics 9: Pragmatics*, New York: Academic Press, pages 315–332.

van Fraassen, Bas C. (1969). Presuppositions, supervaluations and free logic. In K. Lambert (ed.), *The logical way of doing things*, New Haven: Yale University Press, pages 67–91.

van Rooij, Robert (2011). Vagueness and linguistics. In Giuseppina Ronzitti (ed.), *Vagueness: A guide,* vol. 19 of Logic, Epistemology, and the Unity of Science Series. Dordrecht: Springer, pages 123–170.

Veltman, Frank (1984). Data semantics. In Jeroen Groenendijk, Theo Janssen and Martin Stokhof (eds.), *Truth, interpretation and information proceedings of the 3rd Amsterdam colloquium*, pages 43–64.

von Stechow, Arnim (1984a). Comparing semantic theories of comparison. *Journal of Semantics* 3:1–77.

von Stechow, Arnim (1984b). My reaction to Cresswell's, Hellan's, Hoeksema's and Seuren's comments. *Journal of Semantics* 3:183–199.

Yen, John (1999). Fuzzy logic—A modern perspective, *Transactions on Knowledge and Data Engineering* 11(1):153–165.

Zadeh, Lotfi A. (1965). Fuzzy sets. *Information and Control* 8(3):338–353.

Appendix

On section 1 the subjects read the following description of characters called Moshe and Danny: "Assume Moshe weighs 100 kg and Danny weighs 90 kg and they are alike in other things (for instance, height)." Here are the questions that followed the paragraph.

(17) Section 1, the questions:

The basic condition

a. Is Moshe more <u>fat</u> than Danny?   Yes/No

b. Is it easier to determine that Moshe is <u>fat</u> than that Danny is <u>fat</u>?   Yes/No

c. Is it harder to determine that Danny is <u>fat</u> than that Moshe is <u>fat</u>?   Yes/No

On section 3, the subjects read the following description: "Assume Moshe weighs 100 kg and he is 195 cm tall, and Danny weighs 70 kg and is he is 195 cm tall." (i.e., Moshe is fatter than Danny, but they are equally tall).

(18) Section 3, the questions:

The basic condition

a. is Moshe more <u>fat</u> than Danny?   Yes/No

b. Is it easier to determine that Moshe is <u>fat</u> than that Danny is <u>fat</u>?   Yes/No

c. is one of them more <u>tall</u> than the other?   Yes/No

d. Is it easier to determine that he is <u>tall</u>?   Yes/No

The conjunction condition

e. Is Moshe more <u>fat and tall</u> than Danny?   Yes/No

f. Is Moshe less <u>fat and tall</u> than Danny?   Yes/No

g. Is it easier to determine that Moshe is <u>fat and tall</u> than that Danny is?   Yes/No

h. Is it harder to determine that Moshe is <u>fat and tall</u> than that Danny is?   Yes/No

i. Comments: [three empty lines]

On section 4, the subjects read the following description of characters called Aharon and Danny: "Assume Aharon weighs 100 kg and he is not bald, and Danny weighs 70 kg and is bald. They are alike in other respects." Thus, in this scenario Aharon is *fatter* and Danny is *balder*.

(19) Section 4, the questions:

The basic condition

a. Who is more fat?   Aharon/Danny

b. Who is more bald?   Aharon/Danny

The conjunction condition

c. Is any of them more <u>fat and bald</u> than the other?   Yes/No

d. Is it easier to determine that one of them is <u>fat and bald</u> than that the other is?

Yes/No

e. Are they equally <u>fat and bald</u>?   Yes/No

f. Is it equally easy to determine that they are <u>fat and bald</u>?   Yes/No

The disjunction condition

g. Is one of them more <u>fat or bald</u> than the other?   Yes/No

h. Who is more <u>fat or bald</u>?   Aharon/Danny

i. Is it easier to determine that one of them is <u>fat or bald</u> than that the other is?
                                                                               Yes/No

j. For whom is it easier to determine that?   Aharon/Danny

The modifier condition

k. Is any of them more <u>fat bald</u> than the other?   Yes/No

l. Who is more fat bald? Aharon/ Danny

m. Is it easier to determine that one of them is <u>fat bald</u> than that the other is?
                                                                               Yes/No

n. For whom is it easier to determine that?   Aharon/Danny

o. Is any of them more <u>bald fat</u> than the other?   Yes/No

p. Who is more <u>bald fat</u>?   Aharon/Danny

q. Is it easier to determine that one of them is <u>bald fat</u> than that the other is?
                                                                               Yes/No

r. For whom is it easier to determine that?   Aharon/Danny

The disjunction condition—continued

s. <u>Fat or bald</u> subjects are needed to fill a questionnaire for a scientific experiment.
Who fits more?   Aharon/Danny

t. It is true that if Danny fits Aharon definitely fits?   Yes/No

w. It is true that if Aharon fits Danny definitely fits   Yes/No

u. Comments: [3 lines]

Section 9 began with the following description: "Assume Moshe and Danny both weigh 100 kg and also that Moshe is bald and Danny is less bald (maybe even isn't bald at all)." Thus, here Moshe and Danny are equally fat, but Moshe is balder (the same pattern as in section 3). They are alike in other respects."

(20) Section 9, the questions:

The conjunction condition

a. Is Moshe both <u>more fat</u> and <u>more bald</u>?   Yes/No

b. Is Moshe more <u>fat and Bald</u> than Danny?   Yes/No

c. Is it easier to determine that Moshe is <u>fat and bald</u> than that Dan is <u>fat and bald</u>?
                                                                               Yes/No

d. Is it easier to determine that Moshe is <u>bald and fat</u> than that Dan is <u>bald and fat</u>?
                                                                               Yes/No

The modifier condition

e. Is Moshe more <u>fat bald</u> than Danny is? Yes/No

f. Is it easier to determine that Moshe is <u>fat bald</u> than that Danny is <u>fat bald</u>?
Yes/No

g. Is Moshe more <u>bald fat</u> than Danny is? Yes/No

h. Is it easier to determine that Moshe is <u>bald fat</u> than that Danny is <u>bald fat</u>?
Yes/No

The disjunction condition

i. Is Moshe more <u>fat or Bald</u> than Danny? Yes/No

j. Is it easier to determine that Moshe is <u>fat or bald</u> than that Danny is? Yes/No

k. Is Moshe more <u>Bald or fat</u> than Danny? Yes/No

l. Is it easier to determine that Moshe is <u>bald or fat</u> than that Dan is? Yes/No

m. <u>Fat or bald</u> subjects are needed to fill a questionnaire for a scientific experiment. Who fits more? Moshe/Danny

n. It is true that if Danny fits Moshe definitely fits? Yes/No

o. It is true that if Moshe fits Danny definitely fits Yes/No

p. Comments: [3 lines]

On section 7 the subjects read a description of two creatures differing only on whether they call or not: "Imagine two creatures that do not fly; also, the first one does not call, while the second is more typical of a calling creature than the first".

(21) Section 7, the questions:

The multidimensional, conjunctive adjective condition

a. Is the second more typical of a <u>flying calling</u> [creature]? Yes/No

b. Is the second more typical of a <u>flying and calling</u> [creature]? Yes/No

c. Is the second more typical of a <u>flying or calling</u> [creature]? Yes/No

d. comments [3 lines]

Galit W. Sassoon
Institute for Logic, Language and Computation
Universiteit van Amsterdam
P.O. Box 94242
1090 GE Amsterdam, the Netherlands
Email: galitadar@gmail.com

Comments on *Comparison of Complex Predicates: 'and', 'or' and 'more'* by Galit W. Sassoon

DAVID RIPLEY

In "Comparison of complex predicates: *and, or,* and *more*", Galit W. Sassoon reports the results of a survey involving complex predicates such as 'fat and tall' and 'fat or bald'. Respondents were asked to compare a variety of characters with regards to these complex predicates, for example to say whether or not one is more *fat and tall* than another.

The experimental exploration of compound predicates is in its infancy, and Sassoon has significantly expanded the range of data we now have available. This is important and valuable work.

Sassoon interprets her data as posing a difficulty for certain fuzzy-logic-based theories of vague predication. In this note, I want to suggest that her data, if robust, would cause difficulty for a wider range of fuzzy- and fuzzyish-logic-based theories than those she considers. I also want to urge caution about some of the conclusions Sassoon draws from her data.

1 Linear order and partial order

One crucial piece of data Sassoon appeals to in her argument against fuzzy approaches to these comparisons of complexes can be seen in §2.2.2, where she discusses responses to questions 4c ('Is any of them more *fat and bald* than the other?') and 4e ('Are they equally *fat and bald*?'). These questions are asked about the characters Aharon and Danny, where Aharon weighs 100 kg and is not bald, and Danny weighs 70 kg and is bald. To both questions, the answer 'No' predominates. Sassoon suggests that degree functions cannot account for this pattern of judgments.

Indeed, no assignment of degrees from a *linearly ordered* set could account for this data. If Aharon and Danny bear degrees of *fat and bald* from a linearly ordered scale, then either Aharon's degree is greater than Danny's, Danny's degree is greater than Aharon's, or the two degrees are equal—this is exactly the linear order condition. Sassoon's introduction to degree theories in §1.2 suggests that she assumes that the degree theorist is committed to this linear order condition: "Fuzzy logic is a form of multi-valued logic, whereby propositions may have as a truth value any number in the real interval [0, 1]". Note that the real interval [0, 1] is linearly ordered: given any two numbers x and y in the interval, either x is greater than y, y is greater than x, or $x = y$.

However, a number of degree theorists have advanced theories on which the degrees are *not* linearly ordered, but rather only partially ordered. For example, the theories advanced in [Slaney, 1988, Paoli, 1999, Weatherson, 2005] all have this feature. NB: I'm not too fussed about terminology here: maybe these approaches count as 'fuzzy' and maybe they don't. What's interesting, I think, is to explore the ways in which these theories can and cannot account for Sassoon's data. As it turns out, I think these theories all face difficulties here, suggesting that Sassoon may well be able to use her data to rule out, or at least cause trouble for, a wider range of logical approaches than she considers.

1.1   Partially ordered degrees

The theories advanced in [Slaney, 1988, Paoli, 1999, Weatherson, 2005] are importantly different from each other in a number of respects, which I hereby declare my intention to ignore. The important features for our purposes here are shared by all three approaches. I use $\leq$ for the partial order on degrees.

First, all three approaches allow for degrees c and d that violate linear order; that is, such that $c \not\leq d$ and $d \not\leq c$. This feature seems to allow them to accommodate Sassoon's data in 4c and 4e: if respondents assign Aharon and Danny such degrees for *fat and bald*, then their responses are just what we should expect. Neither is greater than the other, nor are they equal.

1.2   Conjunction and monotonicity

The trouble threatens, rather, when we look to section 3, particularly questions 3a ('Is Moshe more *fat* than Danny?') and 3e ('Is Moshe more *fat and tall* than Danny?'). In this section, Moshe weighs 100 kg and is 195 cm tall, and Danny weighs 70 kg and is also 195 cm tall. Respondents overwhelmingly chose 'Yes' as a response to question 3a, and 'No' as a response to question 3e.

In what follows, I need to make two assumptions about responses to questions that Sassoon, unfortunately, did not ask participants. Neither is terribly risky, I don't think. The first is that respondents would overwhelmingly answer 'Yes' to the question whether Moshe and Danny are *equally* tall, or the question whether they are *as tall as* each other. If we assume linear order, respondents' 'No' answers to 3c ('Is one of them more *tall* than the other?') would settle this, but here we are precisely *not* assuming linear order, so this becomes a separate question. However, since both Moshe and Danny are 195 cm tall, it would be very surprising if respondents did not judge them to be equally tall. The second assumption is perhaps more controversial, but I think also relatively secure: we need to know what respondents think of the question whether Moshe and Danny are *equally* fat and bald. I assume the answer is 'No'; this seems quite plausible, but is not supported by any data.

With these two assumptions in hand, we have enough to put pressure even on the partially-ordered approaches to degrees cited above. All three take conjunction (which I'll write $\wedge$) to be *monotone*.[1] ([Paoli, 1999] offers a logical system with two distinct conjunctions, but both are monotone.) But let f_M and f_D be Moshe's and Danny's respective degrees of fatness, and let t_M and t_D be their respective degrees of tallness (in all cases, as attributed by respondents). By the first assumption, $t_D = t_M$. By the responses to 3a, $f_D \leq f_M$. Thus, by the monotonicity of conjunction, $f_D \wedge t_D \leq f_M \wedge t_M$. However, responses to 3e rule out Moshe's being *more* fat and tall than Danny, and the second

---

[1] Where $\leq$ is the partial order on degrees, a binary connective $\cdot$ is *monotone* iff $c \leq c'$ and $d \leq d'$ imply $c \cdot d \leq c' \cdot d'$.

assumption rules out their being *equally* fat and tall. Something, then, has gone wrong. If the assumptions and the data are all sound, then the trouble is with the assumption that conjunctions are monotone. Even partially-ordered approaches, then, may well face trouble in the area.

This trouble is not exclusive to partially-ordered theories, though. All t-norms are monotone; thus, all fuzzy logics that interpret conjunction as a t-norm—including the vast majority of linearly-ordered fuzzy logics—will face this difficulty as well.

2   Disjunction

It seems a good bet that this trouble with the conjunctive data might have an echo in the disjunctive data. After all, all three above theories predict disjunction to be monotone as well, as does any fuzzy theory that analyzes disjunction with a t-conorm (again, the vast majority of linearly-ordered fuzzy logics). If the disjunctive data reproduce the pattern of the conjunctive data, the same problem ought to appear.

Unfortunately, things here are much less clear. The most basic data about comparative judgments of disjunctions comes from questions 4g ('Is one of them [ie Aharon or Daniel] more *fat or bald* than the other?') and 4h ('Who is more *fat or bald*?'). Here, most respondents (74%) answered 'Yes' to 4g, but only 46% of respondents answered 4h at all. (Of these, 63% said 'Danny'.)

Sassoon interprets this as follows: since Aharon is more fat than Danny and Danny is more bald than Aharon, each of them is either more fat or more bald than the other. If respondents interpret 'more *fat or bald*' as 'more fat or more bald', then we should expect them to judge that each of Aharon and Danny is more fat or bald than the other, leading to a 'Yes' response to 4g. However, since each is more fat or bald than the other, when respondents are asked to identify which one is more fat or bald in 4h, they cannot, and as a result do not answer the question.

This is plausible enough as far as it goes, but I think it cannot yet be taken as established. When Sassoon says 'the 19 subjects (54%) not providing an answer to [4h] indicate that they interpreted 'more *fat or bald*' as 'more fat *or* more bald', classifying both characters as such', she overstates the case. There are any number of reasons why a respondent might fail to answer any particular question. If the reason is indeed the one Sassoon hypothesizes, this should be easy enough to get better evidence for. First and foremost, one could simply expand the answer space, allowing respondents to answer 'Both' to 4h. Sassoon's explanation for the non-responses would predict respondents to be strongly drawn to the 'Both' answer; presumably competing explanations would not.

Sassoon goes on to interpret the responses of the 16 respondents who do answer 4h, I think far too hastily. She says: '[O]f the 16 answers, the majority (10, which make 63%) selected Danny as their candidate, explaining that Danny is clearly bald and hence *fat or bald*, while Aharon is not clearly fat, thus not clearly *fat or bald*. Thus, these subjects were using a Boolean union rule for classification under disjunctions'. But this is a nonsequitur, even if all 10 respondents provided this exact reasoning, because the very same reasoning would be predicted by a wide variety of fuzzy and other theories as well. Any logic of disjunction validating the inference from A to $A \lor B$ will do. Thus, the reasoning in favor of 'Danny' offered by Sassoon's respondents to 4h does very little to support her Boolean hypothesis.

Sassoon seems to realize this, and briefly considers the possibility that those respondents that answered 4h were able to do so via their use of a fuzzy disjunction. She argues against this as follows: '[H]ad this been the case, these 16 subjects would have agreed to consider one of the characters as *more fat and bald* in the second conjunctive condition, but they did not ... Thus, these results do not indicate fuzzy reasoning'. This assumes that conjunction and disjunction will be *uniform* in their fuzziness: either both fuzzy or neither. This does not seem like a warranted assumption. Moreover, if Sassoon is willing to make such an assumption, it's unclear why she considers disjunctive responses at all. The argument she offers that conjunctions are not interpreted fuzzily ought to have settled the issue.

Once we allow for the possibility that conjunctions are not interpreted fuzzily but disjunctions are, however, we see that some separate argument is needed for the claim that disjunctions are not interpreted fuzzily. I should flag: Sassoon may well be right that they are not. In fact, I see no better explanation for the lack of responses to 4h than the one she offers. But if her explanation is right, it should not be hard to find better evidence for it than this.

In sum, I take Sassoon's data to show, in some respects, more than she gives it credit for. Linear order is not the only trouble with fuzzy logics; theories taking conjunction to be monotone will have trouble as well. This covers not only the usual linearly-ordered fuzzy theories, but also their best-known partially-ordered relatives. On the other hand, her data regarding judgments of disjunctions is not as compelling as she takes it to be. More caution, and more data, is required.

BIBLIOGRAPHY

[Paoli, 1999] Paoli, F. (1999). Comparative logic as an approach to comparison in natural language. *Journal of Semantics*, 16(1):67–96.
[Slaney, 1988] Slaney, J. K. (1988). A logic for vagueness. The Australasian Journal of Logic 8:100–134.
[Weatherson, 2005] Weatherson, B. (2005). True, truer, truest. *Philosophical Studies*, 123(1):47–70.

David Ripley
Department of Philosophy
University of Melbourne
Old Quad, Parkville
Victoria 3010, Australia
Email: davewripley@gmail.com

Reply to David Ripley's Comments on *Comparison of Complex Predicates: 'and', 'or' and 'more'*

GALIT W. SASSOON

I agree with Ripley that additional theories and theoretical approaches should be considered in light of the findings discussed in my paper. I am particularly grateful for his remark concerning theories taking conjunction to be monotone. In a similar vein, joint work with Frank Veltman (in preparation), resulted in arguments against several dominant approaches to the analysis of vagueness and comparison, including the supervaluationist approach (Kamp 1975) and the Kleinean approach (Klein 1980). The basis for these arguments comes from the inference form highlighted by the reported experiment—Premise: *x* is more *P* and *Q* than *y*; Conclusion: *x* is more *Q* than *y*—which these theories fail to capture. Additional approaches (and inference patterns) should be considered in the future.

At the same time, I wholeheartedly agree with Ripley that more data is required before any solid conclusions can be drawn regarding the generality of my results, in particular in the case of disjunctions. The research reported in the paper is preliminary, and to be continued. Let me mention, in this context, that an ongoing experimental study of complex comparisons in English supports the hypothesis that the interpretation of comparisons with conjunctions of concrete one dimensional adjectives, such as *expensive and time consuming,* is Boolean. At the same time, that new study shows that disjunctions, as well as conjunctions of more abstract and multidimensional adjectives, such as *experienced and successful,* are more complex to understand.

This is not surprising. Disjunctions are notorious for posing a variety of semantic-pragmatic challenges to language researchers, such as free choice interpretations. For example, utterances of *Take an apple or a pear* normally convey that the addressee may take an apple (but not a pear), AND he or she may take a pear (but not an apple). Thus, disjunctions of offers and in particular of commands normally convey a conjunction of offers or commands. Somewhat similar effects show up in the context of disjunctive comparisons, e.g., many speakers interpret *equally experienced OR successful* on a par with *equally experienced AND successful.*

As for multidimensional adjectives, consider, for example, the adjective *successful.* One can be successful in some respects, but not successful in others (cf. Klein 1980). The set of respects that count for a truthful application of this adjective is highly context dependent. The considerations governing the selection of respects, and the operations that integrate them into a single, unified adjectival sense are poorly understood (conjunctions? disjunctions? Boolean? Fuzzy? etc.) Finally, to the best of my knowledge, the interactions between these operators and those denoted by natural language modifiers of gradability and comparison (*more, very, most,* and so on) have rarely been investigated so far. The main conclusion to draw is, therefore: more experimentation is needed!

The paper and comments illustrate the relevance of descriptive, empirical work to the study of formal semantics in linguistics, philosophy of language and logic. Formal theoretical work might progress through the study of inference forms—their robustness among language users, and their generality across lexical items. My hope is that the complexity of the data will inspire logicians to develop new systems, particularly suited to natural language semantics.

BIBLIOGRAPHY

Kamp, Hans (1975). Two theories about adjectives. In Edward Keenan (ed.), *Formal semantics for natural language*, Cambridge: Cambridge University Press, pages 123–155.

Klein, Ewan (1980). A semantics for positive and comparative adjectives. *Linguistics and Philosophy* 4:1–45.

Vagueness in Quantity:
Two Case Studies from a Linguistic Perspective

STEPHANIE SOLT[1]

1 Introduction

Much work on vagueness has focused on adjectives such as *thin, bald* and *red* as the paradigm case of the phenomenon. But vagueness is prevalent also in many other domains of natural language, and it is one of these other domains—namely expressions of quantity—that is the focus of the present paper. Quantificational expressions present a diverse range of examples of vagueness, imprecision and underspecification. Some quantifiers, such as *many, few, much* and (as will be seen below) *most*, are inherently vague. Others have definite but underspecified truth conditions; for example, *some dogs* must be at least two, but does not specify the number further. Vagueness in quantity may be signaled explicitly via modifiers such as *roughly* (*roughly 50 books*) and *approximately* (*approximately 1000 residents*). And even without modification, seemingly precise expressions such as number words may be interpreted approximately; for example, *'there were 100 people in the audience'* is typically understood to mean 'roughly 100'.

In this paper, I examine two case studies of vagueness within the realm of quantity expressions: the vague quantifiers *many, few, much* and *little*, which pattern in some respects with gradable adjectives, but also show some illuminating differences; and the quantifier *most*, which along with *more than half* provides a minimal pair of a vague and a non-vague expression with otherwise overlapping semantics.

My goal in delving into this topic for a contribution to a volume on reasoning with vague information is first of all to explore what we can learn about vagueness by examining its manifestation in the expression of quantity. I hope to show in what follows that facts from this general area are able to shed some new light on approaches and mechanisms that have been applied to the analysis of vagueness.

But secondly, as I am a linguist, my contribution necessarily comes from the perspective of that field. Perhaps the most central goal of linguistics is to account for the (mostly unconscious) linguistic knowledge of native speakers of a language. This includes, among other things, knowledge about whether a string of words is or is not a grammatical sentence of the language, and about the interpretation(s) that a grammatical sentence can receive. A variety of data sources can be brought to bear on these questions, including the linguist's own intuitions, judgments elicited from other speakers, attested

[1]I would like to thank the two anonymous reviewers, whose comments helped me greatly in clarifying my thinking on several points. Work on this project was funded by the European Science Foundation (ESF) and the Deutsche Forschungsgemeinschaft (DFG) under the auspices of the EuroCORES programme LogICCC.

examples of speech or writing, and performance by subjects on structured experimental tasks. In this paper, I also aim to illustrate what the careful examination of linguistic data such as these can tell us about the nature and the proper treatment of vagueness.

For a preview of what is to come, the first of the two case studies discussed below will strengthen the case for the relevance of comparison classes in the interpretation of vague, gradable expressions (though suggesting that the traditional notion of a comparison class must be broadened somewhat). The second raises the possibility that vagueness is, in at least some cases, associated with a less informative underlying scale structure than that typically assumed in degree-based semantic analyses.

2   How many is *many*?

For the first case study, I consider the so-called 'vague quantifiers' or 'vague numerals' *many* and *few*, and their mass counterparts *much* and *little*:

(1)   a. <u>Many</u> people I know like jazz.

        b. <u>Few</u> students came to the lecture.

        c. I don't have <u>much</u> money.

        d. There's <u>little</u> water left in the bucket.

Many and *few* are quantifiers that combine with plural countable nouns, expressing roughly 'a large number of' and 'a small number of'. *Much* and *little* occur with non-countable (mass) nouns, and correspondingly express something like 'a large amount of' and 'a small amount of'. But what is meant by a large or small amount or quantity is of course vague.

It can readily be shown that words of the *many* class pattern in a variety of respects with the better-studied class of vague gradable adjectives such as *tall*, *thin*, and *expensive*. As seen in (2) and (3), they have comparative and superlative forms, and combine with a range of degree modifiers (the defining characteristics of gradable expressions):

(2)   a. Betty has <u>many</u> friends/<u>more</u> friends than Sue/<u>the most</u> friends.

        b. Betty has <u>few</u> friends/<u>fewer</u> friends than Sue/<u>the fewest</u> friends.
            (cf. tall/taller/tallest)

(3)   a. Fred drank <u>too much</u> wine.

        b. Barney drank <u>very little</u> wine.

        c. Betty read <u>as many</u> books <u>as</u> Wilma.

        d. I'm surprised Wilma read <u>that few</u> books.
            (cf. too tall, very tall, as tall as, etc.)

Beyond this, their interpretation is context sensitive, just as in the case of gradable adjectives. For example, the number of students in attendance that would suffice to establish the truth of (4) depends among other things on the context or situation of utterance: Are we, for example, talking about an in-class lecture in a university seminar, or a campus-wide lecture by a prominent and popular figure such as Bill Clinton? And even with the context fixed, the boundaries for *many* and its counterparts remain fuzzy, resulting in borderline cases. We might consider 1000 students attending Clinton's lecture to be a clear case of *many*, and 5 in attendance to be a clear case of *not many*, but what about 50? 100?

(4) <u>Many</u> students attended the lecture.

These patterns—context dependence and fuzzy borders/borderline cases—are just what is observed with gradable adjectives. For example, the truth or falsity of *Fred is tall* depends on the context (is Fred an adult man? an 8-year-old boy? a professional basketball player?), and for any context, some cases will seem to fall into a grey area.

Finally, as with other instances of vague predicates, these words give rise to the Sorites paradox. For example, the two reasonable-sounding premises in (5a,b) seem to lead to the unquestionably false (5c):

(5) a. 1000 students attending Clinton's lecture counts as *many*.

  b. If *n* students attending Clinton's lecture counts as *many*, then $n - 1$ students attending also counts as *many*.

  c. 3 students attending Clinton's lecture counts as *many*.

In light of this long list of parallels between gradable adjectives on the one hand and the *many* class on the other, it is desirable that whatever analysis is developed for the former case be extendable to the latter. That is my goal here.

As an aside, the reader might at this stage wonder why, if words like *many* behave so similarly to gradable adjectives, we don't simply conclude that they <u>are</u> ordinary gradable adjectives, and thus require no special treatment. In [1], I show that there are a number of significant distributional differences between the two classes, which give reason to think that they belong to distinct semantic types. As one example, words of the *many* class can occur as modifiers in comparatives (6a,b). Ordinary gradable adjectives cannot (6c); even the adjective *numerous*, which otherwise has much the same semantic content as *many*, is extremely awkward in this position (6d):[2]

(6) a. <u>Many</u> more than 100 students attended the lecture.

  b. John is <u>much</u> taller than Fred.

  c. *John is <u>tall</u> taller than Fred.

  d. ?<u>Numerous</u> more than 100 students attended the lecture.

In [1], I argue that differences of this sort can be accounted for by analyzing *many* and like words as predicates over scalar intervals (sets of degrees), in contrast to ordinary gradable adjectives, which are analyzed as predicates over individuals (I refer the reader to that work for further justification of this claim, and for details of the implementation). For present purposes, however, we can abstract away from this distinction.

---

[2]Here I follow the linguist's convention of using a star (*) to mark a sentence that is ungrammatical, in the sense of not being a possible sentence in the language, and a question mark (?) to mark a sentence that is degraded but not outright ungrammatical.

Let us turn now to the semantic analysis of vague predicates such as these. A long tradition holds that sentences involving vague adjectives, such as those in (7), should be analyzed with reference to a **comparison class** that in some way serves to provide a frame of reference or standard of comparison (see especially [2, 3, 4, 5, 6, 7]; though see [8] for an opposing position). On this approach, (7a) would be interpreted as saying that Fred's height exceeds the standard for some set of individuals of which Fred is a member (adult American men, 8-year-old boys, basketball players, etc); (7b) is true if the cost of Sue's apartment exceeds the standard for some relevant set of apartments; and so forth.

(7)   a. Fred is <u>tall</u>.

        b. Sue's apartment is <u>expensive</u>.

This view is made more plausible by the fact that the comparison class may be made overt via a *for*-phrase, as in (8):

(8)   a. Fred is <u>tall</u> for a jockey.

        b. Sue's apartment is <u>expensive</u> for a place on this street.

A comparison class analysis can be implemented in a variety of ways. On the delineation-based approach developed by Klein [4], gradable adjectives are taken to introduce a partitioning of the comparison class into three sets, a positive extension, a negative extension and an extension gap. Sentences of the form in (7) and (8) are true if the subject falls in the positive extension (with respect to the comparison class), false if he or she falls into the negative extension, and undefined otherwise. Alternately, a comparison class analysis can be given a degree-based implementation (see e.g. [6]), according to which gradable adjectives are analyzed as expressing relations between individuals and degrees on the scale associated with some dimension of measurement. Sentences such as (7) and (8) are then true if the degree associated with the subject exceeds some standard degree (or set of degrees) derived from the comparison class.

Putting aside for now a discussion of the relative strengths and weaknesses of these two approaches, and provisionally adopting the latter option, examples such as (8a) can be analyzed as having the following truth conditions:

(9) $[\![\text{Fred is tall for a jockey}]\!] = 1$ iff $HEIGHT(fred) > R_{Std}$.

(10) $[\![\text{Fred is short for a jockey}]\!] = 1$ iff $HEIGHT(fred) < R_{Std}$,

        where $R_{Std} = median_{x:jockey(x)}(HEIGHT(x)) \pm n$, for some value n.

Here *HEIGHT* is a measure function that associates individuals with their degree of height. On this view, the standard of comparison R_{Std} is a range around the median value in the comparison class, whose width is determined by the value n. The effect is that 'tall for a jockey' receives the interpretation 'taller than most jockeys', and 'short for a jockey' is correspondingly 'shorter than most jockeys'; this seems to correctly capture our intuitions. Note that it is necessary to define the standard as a range rather than a single point to account for the acceptability of sentences such as *'Fred isn't tall for a jockey, but he isn't short either'*. In [9], I argue that the value n, and thus the width of the standard range, is actually a function of the degree of dispersion within the comparison class. As evidence, speakers tend to agree that the truth or falsity of a sentence such as (8b) is dependent not just on the average price for apartments on this street, but also on how prices are distributed. If most apartment prices are clustered closely around the average, then a price only moderately above that price would count as expensive; but if there is a broader range of variation in apartment prices, the standard for what counts as expensive (for an apartment on this street) shifts upward. For the sake of simplicity, I will not represent this here, and will just use the value n.

With the formulation in (9), we have a framework for expressing (if not an actual explanation for) both the context sensitivity of words such as *tall* as well as the existence of borderline cases. Context sensitivity derives from the possibility of selecting different sets for the comparison class; this may be specified via a *for* phrase, or may be left to the context. Borderline cases arise as a result of the underspecification of the value n.

Let us turn now to words of the *many* class. There have been a number of attempts to capture their interpretive variability (see especially [10, 11, 12, 13, 14, 15, 16, 17]), but as discussed further below, these typically capture some but not all of the readings available to them. That they, too, should be analyzed with reference to a comparison class is suggested by the fact that they also occur with *for*-phrases:

(11)   a. Fred has <u>many</u> friends.

      b. For a politician, Fred has <u>many</u> friends.

This can be captured with essentially the same approach as was applied to the case of *tall* above, simply by replacing the function *HEIGHT* by the function *NUMBER*, which associates sets of individuals with their cardinality:[3]

(12) $[$For a politician, Fred has many friends$] = 1$ iff
$$NUMBER(Fred's\ friends) > R_{Std},$$
where $R_{Std} = median_{x:politician(x)}(NUMBER(x's\ friends)) \pm n.$

It appears, then, that the comparison class analysis of gradable predicates meets the desired goal of being extendable to the case of words such as *many*. But now consider examples such as the following, where there is no subject whose characteristics may be considered in relation to a comparison class:

(13)   <u>Few</u> students attended the lecture.

Here, it helps to consider a little more closely the interpretations that a sentence like this may receive. As has often been noted in the literature (see e.g. [12]), examples such as (13) tend to have multiple distinct readings, which can be brought out by different continuations, as in (14). One possible reading is that the number of students who attended the lecture is smaller than the number of members of some other group(s) who did so (cf. (14a)); a second is that the number of students attending the lecture is smaller than

---

[3]This is what we need for *many* and *few*, where the dimension in question is cardinality. In the case of *much* and *little*, which occur with non-countable nouns, we require a function that associates entities with their measure on some other dimension, e.g. volume, weight, etc.

the number of students who participated in other activities (cf. (14b)). (Below, I will consider some further possibilities beyond these two.)

(14)   a. Few students attended the lecture, as compared to the number of faculty members there.

   b. Few students attended the lecture, as compared to the number who went to the football match.

This suggests that the comparison class invoked is a set of alternatives to the domain of quantification, or to the sentential predicate. For example, the two readings of (13) noted above might be analyzed with reference to the following comparison classes:

(15)   a. $C = \{students, faculty members, townspeople, \ldots\}$.

   b. $C = \{went to the lecture, went to the football match, studied, \ldots\}$.

The proposal that some uses of words of the *many* class must be analyzed with reference to some such sets of alternatives is found for example in the work of Lappin [12]. My proposal here is that we can view this as a variant of a comparison class based analysis. But note that in doing so, we have extended the notion of a comparison class from a set of individuals (as needed for examples such as (7) and (11)) to include also sets of sets of individuals.

   Note also that the approach proposed here is similar in some respects to those under which words of the *many* class are analyzed with respect to alternatives generated via focus (e.g. [14, 16]). The difference is that here, the set of alternatives (i.e. the comparison class) plays a direct role in setting the standard of comparison, rather than contributing to the logical form of the sentence, or having a purely pragmatic effect.

   A further possibility is suggested by the following example:

(16)   There are few cars in the parking lot today.

What comparison class might be involved here? Again, consider what would be conveyed by an utterance of (16). On its most natural interpretation, (16) does not seem to mean that the number of cars in the lot is smaller than the number of most other types of things in the lot, or smaller than the number of cars in most other places (though both of these readings are at least marginally possible, particularly with stress on *cars* and *parking lot*, respectively). Rather, it seems to me that the preferred interpretation is that the number of cars in the parking lot today is smaller than the number there at most other relevant times. This suggests that we have a comparison class over times.

   The possibility that we have comparison classes of times in addition to comparison classes of individuals is supported by the fact that *for*-phrases can refer explicitly to times (17a). Furthermore, this possibility is not limited to words like *many* (17b), though this option seems to be more readily available with this class than with ordinary gradable adjectives.

(17)   a. For a Sunday, there are few cars in the parking lot.

   b. For a Sunday, the parking lot is crowded.

The comparison class approach developed up to this point can be extended to capture these cases as well, by assuming, as is standardly done, that the logical forms corresponding to sentences of natural language include an argument or interpretation parameter that ranges over times. The truth conditions of a relevant example can then be expressed as follows (where t is a variable that ranges over times, and t^* is the time of utterance):

(18)   [For a Sunday, there are few cars in the parking lot] = 1 iff
$$NUMBER(cars\ in\ the\ lot\ at\ t^*) < R_{Std},$$
where $R_{Std} = median_{t:Sunday(t)}(NUMBER(cars\ in\ the\ lot\ at\ t)) \pm n.$

By this means, the comparison class analysis is able to capture a further interpretation available to words of the *many* class.

Consider now the following variant of an earlier example:

(19)   <u>Few</u> students attended the lecture today.

A moment's introspection will show that this sentence also has a variety of readings. It can be interpreted as saying alternately: the number of students who came to the lecture was smaller than the numbers of students who participated in most alternative activities; smaller than the number of members of most other groups who came to the lecture; or smaller than the number who came to corresponding lectures at most other times. As discussed above, these readings could be modeled in terms of comparison classes consisting of alternatives to 'came to the lecture', alternatives to 'students', or alternatives to 'today'. But (19) also has another reading, perhaps the most salient one, according to which it expresses that the number of students who came to today's lecture is smaller than the speaker expected.

To capture this last reading, it is necessary to introduce some notion of alternate possible situations, or ways the world might have been. But this is of course nothing particularly unusual in semantic analysis. The necessary step is to move from an extensional to an intensional semantics, and introduce a variable or interpretation parameter that ranges over possible worlds. This is the same step that is typically taken, for example, in the analysis of modals such as *must* and *can*.

The truth conditions of (19) on this reading can then be formalized as follows (where w^0 is the actual world):

(20)   [Few students attended the lecture] = 1 iff
$$NUMBER(students\ who\ attended\ the\ lecture\ in\ w^0) < R_{Std},$$
where $R_{Std} = median_w(NUMBER(students\ who\ attended\ the\ lecture\ in\ w)) \pm n.$

It seems, then, that in addition to comparison classes over individuals, sets of individuals and times, we also need comparison classes over worlds.

In fact, the approach represented in (20) is very close to a well known intensional analysis of *many* proposed by Fernando & Kamp [15]. Starting from the basic insight that n C's count as many iff the number of C's 'could well have been' less than n, these authors propose an interpretation for *many* that involves a probability function over worlds:

(21)   n-IS-MANY$_x(\chi)$ iff "it is probable that" $(\exists_{<n}x(\chi))$
                iff $p(\{w : |\{x : \chi\ in\ w\}| < n\}) > c.$

This same insight is captured in (20), which introduces the more specific requirement
that the number must be lower in most relevant worlds. Thus the intensional analysis
can be derived as a special case of a more general comparison class approach.

A further special case of comparison classes is illustrated by examples such as the
following:

(22)   <u>Few</u> faculty children attended the departmental picnic.

As has been pointed out numerous times in the literature, and discussed in particular by
Partee [13], examples such as these are ambiguous between two distinct interpretations,
which have come to be known as 'proportional' and 'cardinal'. On the proportional
reading, the sentence means that a small proportion of all faculty children attended the
picnic. On the cardinal reading, it means that the number of faculty children who attended was small in the absolute sense, regardless of what proportion of all faculty children this group makes up. These two interpretations are truth conditionally distinct: If
it is the case that there <u>are</u> only a small number of faculty children, and they all attended
the picnic, (22) is false on the proportional reading but true on the cardinal reading.

As evidence that this ambiguity is not just a dramatic instance of context sensitivity, note that the availability of one or the other of these interpretations is grammatically
constrained. With a certain class of predicates that express more or less permanent properties (so-called individual-level predicates), only the proportional reading is available.
For example, (23a) must mean that a small proportion of the lawyers I know are honest
(the proportional reading); if I know only two or three lawyers and they are all honest,
the sentence is false. Conversely, sentences with predicates of existence strongly favor
the cardinal reading. Thus (23b) means that there <u>are</u> only a small number of two-headed
snakes, not that of all the two-headed snakes, only a small proportion exist.

(23)   a. <u>Few</u> lawyers I know are honest.

            b. <u>Few</u> two-headed snakes exist.

The factors responsible for the pattern exemplified in (23a), whereby certain contexts allow only the proportional reading, have been the subject of considerable discussion in the linguistics literature (see e.g. [18]). My goal here is not to delve into this
matter, but rather to show that the proportional interpretation of words of the *many* class
can also be handled by a variant of the comparison class analysis. Specifically, for a
sentence of the form in (24a), let the comparison class C be a set of subsets of the set
denoted by the noun phrase sister of *many/few*, as in (24b):

(24)   a. Many/few A B

            b. $C = (A \cap B) \cup \{X : X \subset A \wedge X \cap (A \cap B) = \emptyset\}$

Then when the comparison class analysis developed above is implemented, *many A* will be interpreted as a large proportion of the *As*, and *few A* will be interpreted as a small proportion of the *As*. For example, (25) receives the interpretation that the set of honest lawyers I know is smaller than most other (non-overlapping) sets of lawyers I know:[4]

(25) $[\![$*Few lawyers I know are honest*$]\!]$ = 1 iff

$$NUMBER(honest\ lawyers\ I\ know) < R_{Std},$$

where $R_{Std} = median_{X \in C}(NUMBER(X)) \pm n$ and
$C = \{honest\ lawyers\ I\ know\} \cup \{X : X \subseteq \{dishonest\ lawyers\ I\ know\}\}$.

Interestingly, Klein [10] proposes an analysis very much along these lines as the basic semantics for *many* and *few*. I would suggest that such an analysis is too narrow, in that a comparison class of the specific form in (24) is not able to capture the time- and world-based readings of these words. But the preceding discussion shows that this interpretation can be derived as a special case of a more general comparison class analysis, which is also able to handle these other types of interpretations.

To summarize the main theme of this case study, investigating patterns in the interpretation of words of the *many* class provides further support for the role of comparison classes in the semantics of vague predicates. To be sure, we have seen that the notion of a comparison class must be expanded from how it is typically understood: Not only do we have comparison classes whose members range over individuals, but also those whose members range over sets of individuals, times and worlds. But with this broader view, we are able to capture a range of readings available to words such as *many*, in doing so subsuming several more specific analyses of their meaning under a single more general framework. While I do not claim to have provided evidence that all uses of *many* words (or vague predicates in general) should be analyzed with respect to a comparison class, a case can be made for the central importance of this construct.

3   A tale of *most Americans*

For the second case study, I consider a word that is not generally categorized as vague, namely the quantifier *most*. In this section, I will show that *most* does in fact exhibit a classic hallmark of vagueness, namely a fuzzy boundary, and that it furthermore gives us an insight into the properties that distinguish a vague expression from an otherwise equivalent precise expression.

If we were to consult an introductory semantics textbook (e.g. [20]), we might find that a sentence of the form in (26a) was given a logical form along the lines of (26b), where $|X|$ is the cardinality of the set X:

(26)   a. Most Americans have broadband internet access.

         b. $|Americans\ with\ broadband\ internet\ access|$ >

                           $|Americans\ without\ broadband\ internet\ access|$

---

[4]The restriction to non-overlapping sets in (24) and (25) is necessary to set the cut-offs for *many* and *few* at the appropriate proportions. If we instead considered all subsets of the domain set A, then *many* would be restricted to proportions over 50%, i.e. equivalent to *most*, which is not consistent with speakers' intuitions. The present definition sets the cut-off lower (how low depends on *n*). See [21] for another case where truth conditions must be stated in terms of non-overlapping subsets of a set, this one involving the quantifier *most*.

With the semantics given here, *most* has a precise lower bound at 50%, such that any proportion greater than 50% counts as *most*. But this is at odds with the usual intuition of native speakers that a narrow majority is not sufficient to establish the truth of a sentence involving *most*. That is, speakers commonly judge that *most* is more than 'more than 50%'.

The following example provides nice illustration of the intuition that proportions just slightly over 50% do not support the use of *most*. It is a fact about the U.S. population that it has a slightly female skew (in 2008, the figures were 50.7% female versus 49.3% male). But the following sentence is not at all a felicitous way to describe this situation:

(27) <u>Most</u> Americans are female.

It is not entirely clear whether (27) should be considered false in the present situation, or true but in some way pragmatically deviant. But in either case there is nothing about the analysis represented in (26) that explains its oddness.

If *most* isn't lower bounded at 50%, what is its lower bound? The answer is that a precise value cannot be given: While the intuition seems to be that the minimum standard for *most* must be somewhat greater than 50%, there is no value n such that speakers judge any proportion over n% to be *most*, while proportions less than or equal to n% are not *most*. Thus *most* has a fuzzy boundary, just as is observed in the case of vague adjectives such as *tall (for a jockey)*. We can imagine this giving rise to a version of the Sorites paradox as well (if n% does not count as *most*, then $(n+0.01)$% also does not count as *most*; and so forth).

Interestingly, English has another way of expressing a proportion greater than 50%, namely the complex quantifier *more than half*. The difference is that in this case the lower bound is sharp, not fuzzy. For example, (28a) is true if just slightly more than 50% of (relevant) Americans have broadband, and (28b) is, in the actual situation, clearly true.

(28) a. <u>More than half</u> of Americans have broadband internet access.

  b. <u>More than half</u> of Americans are female.

It is perhaps not entirely appropriate to characterize *more than half* as precise, in that it specifies a range of proportions rather than a single value. But the extent of that range can be specified precisely, and in this respect we have a clear contrast to *most*.

Thus in *most* and *more than half* we have a pair of expressions with essentially overlapping semantics, but which differ in that one is vague (in the sense of having a fuzzy boundary) while the other is precisely defined. I would like to propose that in examining the behavior of this pair, we have the opportunity to uncover other properties that might distinguish vague from non-vague expressions more generally. This is the goal of this section. (Note that at the end of the section, I will suggest that there is another class of pairs that exhibit the same contrast, and that point to a similar conclusion.)

In examining this topic, I draw on attested examples of the use of *most* and *more than half*, sourced from the Corpus of Contemporary American English (COCA) [19], a 410+ million word (approximately 20 million words per year for the years 1990–2010) corpus equally divided among spoken language, fiction, popular magazines, newspapers, and academic texts.

As of mid 2009, there were 432,830 occurrences of *most* and 4857 occurrences of *more than half* in COCA. In what follows, I focus on the use of *most* and *more than half* as quantifiers, as in examples (26) and (28). I put aside the so-called relative proportional use of *most* (e.g. *Anna read the most books*) and its use in adjectival superlatives (e.g. *Anna is the most diligent student*), as well as the adverbial use of *more than half* (e.g. *Our work is more than half finished*).

A look at the corpus data demonstrates deep distributional differences between *most* and *more than half*.

First, the corpus data substantiates the intuition that *more than half* is felicitously used for proportions just slightly greater than 50%, while *most* is not. Of course, in the majority of corpus examples involving the use of a quantifier, it is not possible to determine what the actual proportion is. However, there is one particular type of example, found quite commonly in the reporting of survey data, where a quantifier is used in conjunction with an exact percent; this usage gives us the sort of data we need to investigate the proportions which are described by the two quantifiers in question. In (29) and (30) we see typical examples of this sort for *most* and *more than half*, respectively. Note that the cited percentages are considerably higher in the former than the latter case.

(29) a. The survey showed that <u>most</u> students (81.5%) do not use websites for math-related assignments.   (Education, 129(1), pp. 56–79, 2008)

   b. <u>Most</u> Caucasian grandparents were married (67%), had attained an education level above high school (64%), and lived on an annual household income above $20,000 (74%).
                (Journal of Instructional Psychology, 24(2), p. 119, 1997)

   c. <u>Most</u> respondents (92.6 percent) had completed high school.
                (Journal of Environmental Health, 69(5), pp. 26–30, 2006)

(30) a. <u>More than half</u> of respondents (55%) say that making money is more important now than it was five years ago.   (Money, 21(3), p. 72, 1992)

   b. <u>More than half</u> of the respondents (60%) earned Ph.D. degrees.
                (Physical Educator, 53(4), p. 170, 1996)

   c. Booz Allen Hamilton, a technology consultancy, concluded in a study that <u>more than half</u> of new hires (51 per cent) were found through the Internet.
                (Christian Science Monitor, 2000)

This pattern is confirmed quantitatively. Figure 1 tallies all of these numerical examples found in the corpus for *more than half*, and the corresponding examples, involving the same nouns, for *most*. These data show that *more than half* is typically used for proportions between 50% and 65%; in over a third of cases, the percentage in question is less than 55%. By contrast, *most* is rarely used for proportions below 60%, and quite common up to over 90%.

What is interesting is that this difference in the range of proportions conveyed goes hand-in-hand with several other more fundamental differences in the distribution of *most* and *more than half*.

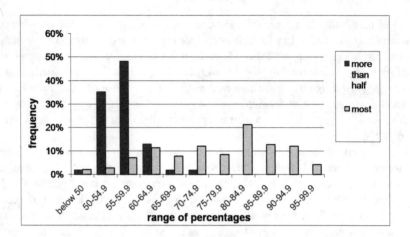

Figure 1. Percentages associated with *most* and *more than half*.

Plural nouns and generic interpretations As seen in the corpus examples in (31), *most* can readily be followed directly by a plural noun phrase, and in this case tends to take on a generic interpretation. (31a), for example, says something about the behavior of people in general; (31b) tells us something about teens in general.

(31)   a. <u>Most</u> people follow the moral judgments of those around them.

                              (Writer, 121(7), pp. 30–33, 2008)

       b. <u>Most</u> teens want to fit in with their peers.   (CNN YourHealth, 31/8/2002)

By contrast, *more than half* has a very different feel. As illustration, when *most* in natural examples of this sort is replaced by *more than half*, as in (32), the results are decidedly odd, and the generic flavor is lost entirely. Rather, to the extent that the resulting sentences are acceptable, they have what might be termed a 'survey results' interpretation; (32b), for example, seems to report on some sort of survey conducted among teens.

(32)   a. ?<u>More than half</u> of people follow the moral judgments of those around them.

       b. ?<u>More than half</u> of teens want to fit in with their peers.

Numerically, it is actually rare that *more than half* is followed directly by a plural noun, this occurring in only 8% of cases (68 out of 860 randomly selected tokens), compared to 57% of cases for *most* (516 out of 909 tokens). Instead, *more than half* usually (79% of cases) occurs in a partitive construction, followed by a definite description or pronoun:

(33)   a. <u>More than half of the tornadoes in November</u> were produced on the 27th by a line of strong thunderstorms that stretched from northeast Oklahoma to northern Illinois.   (Weatherwise, 44(2), p. 19, 1991)

       b. Dumars scored 31 points and made <u>more than half of his shots</u> in a 102-94 victory over the Bucks.   (New York Times, 17/2/1999)

c. In Illinois, the organ bank reports nearly 4,000 people on the organ transplant waiting list—<u>more than half of them</u> waiting for kidneys.

(Chicago Sun Times, 11/8/1999)

What ties together the examples in (33) is that the noun phrases following *more than half* (e.g. *the tornadoes in November*; *his [i.e. Dumars'] shots*) denote sets of individuals or entities localized in space and time. Furthermore, this generalization carries over to the minority of cases where *more than half* is followed directly by a plural noun. While (32b) is odd, (34) is perfectly felicitous; the difference is that while *teens* in (32b) is most readily interpreted as referring to teens in general, *teens surveyed* in (34) denotes a particular group of teens.

(34)   <u>More than half of teens surveyed</u> said they are "not too careful or not at all careful" to protect their skin.   (Todays Parent, 23(7), p. 154, 2006)

Supporting data The intuition that *more than half* (in contrast to *most*) has a 'survey results' interpretation is corroborated by examining the degree to which some sort of data is cited to support the use of the two quantifiers. To assess this, six plural nouns were selected that occurred multiple times in the corpus with *more than half*; for each, the proportion of cases was tallied in which there was mention of some sort of supporting data in the immediate context. For comparison, the same analysis was done for the first 100 occurrences of each of the the same six nouns with *most*.[5] As seen in Table 1, the difference is dramatic: In 80% of cases with *more than half*, there is some reference to supporting data; but this is true for just 19% of the cases with *most*. To put this differently, *more than half* is typically used when actual numerical data is being reported; *most* is not.

Table 1. Presence of supporting data.

	Cases with supporting data mentioned	
	More than half	Most
Americans	5/12	13/100
Men	4/6	5/100
Women	4/5	7/100
Students	5/5	36/100
Patients	5/5	39/100
Families	1/2	11/100
TOTAL	28/35	111/600
	80%	19%

Uncountable domains A further, and particularly intriguing, difference between *most* and *more than half* relates to the sort of domains over which they quantify. Consider corpus examples such as the following:

(35)   a. But like <u>most</u> things, obesity is not spread equally across social classes.

(Mens Health, 23(7), p. 164, 2008)

---

[5]The restriction to 100 tokens per noun was necessitated by the very large number of occurrences of *most* with these nouns, e.g. over 2000 occurrences of *most Americans*.

    b. <u>Most</u> beliefs, worries, and memories also operate outside awareness.

                                (Science News, 142(16), 1992)

    c. But he had enough material on his truck to handle <u>most</u> problems.

                             (Contractor, 47(4), p. 30, 2000)

All of these sentences are entirely felicitous, but when one stops to think about it, there is something quite odd here. To take (35a) as an example, the 'things' whose distribution across social classes is mentioned do not seem to be the sort of entities that we could put on a list and count. The same could be said about 'beliefs, worries and memories' and the 'problems' faced by contractors. Yet quantification with *most* is nonetheless acceptable.

The same cannot be said about *more than half*. When *most* in the attested examples is replaced by *more than half*, as in (36), the result is once again peculiar:

(36)   a. ?But like <u>more than half of things</u>, obesity is not spread equally across social classes.

       b. ?<u>More than half</u> of beliefs, worries, and memories also operate outside awareness.

       c. ?But he had enough material on his truck to handle <u>more than half</u> of problems.

The source of the oddness is the implication of enumerability that results: (36a), for example, seems to imply that we have in fact made a list of 'things', and gone down that list to count how many are spread equally across social classes. Thus *more than half* requires a domain that is enumerable; *most*, apparently, does not.

The examples given in (35) involve plural nouns, and the dimension in question is number. A similar contrast is observed in the mass domain, where another dimension of measurement is involved. The felicitous corpus example (37a) contrasts with the awkward (37b); the issue here is that racism is not something that can be quantitatively measured. On the other hand, *more than half* is acceptable in examples such as (38), the difference being that energy use can receive a numerical measure (expressed e.g. in kilowatt hours).

(37)   a. But black activists acknowledge that <u>most</u> racism is not so blatant.

                           (Associated Press, 16/9/1991)

       b. ?But black activists acknowledge that <u>more than half</u> of racism is not so blatant.

(38)   <u>More than half</u> of home energy use goes to space heating and cooling.

                       (Popular Mechanics, 184(6), p. 79, 2007)

As the preceding discussion shows, *most* and *more than half*—despite their superficially similar meanings—are used very differently by speakers. There is a common thread that connects the three contrasts discussed above. All have something to do with number and countability or measurability. *More than half* is restricted to quantifying over domains that are enumerable (i.e. whose members can be individuated and counted) or otherwise measurable. It typically combines with noun phrases denoting sets that are spatially and temporally bounded, and thus countable or measurable, and its use is frequently supported by some sort of numerical data. These restrictions do not apply to *most*. To put it differently, the felicitous use of *more than half* rests in some way on the possibility, at least in principle, of assigning numerical measures to the entities or groups in question, while that of *most* does not.

Thus the distinction between a precise boundary (*more than half*) and a vague or fuzzy boundary (*most*) goes hand-in-hand with a second distinction, that between a requirement for numerical representability and the lack of such a requirement. I would like to propose that these two patterns are in fact related, and that the second provides a clue to the first.

In implementing this idea, I build on a proposal by Hackl [21], who argues that *most* and *more than half* have distinct logical forms that, while truth-conditionally equivalent, give rise to different verification strategies in sentence processing. In somewhat generalized form, Hackl's logical forms are the following:

(39)   a. $[\![$*more than half*$]\!](A)(B) = 1$ iff $\mu_{DIM}(A \cap B) > \mu_{DIM}(A)/2$.

        b. $[\![$*most*$]\!](A)(B) = 1$ iff $\mu_{DIM}(A \cap B) > \mu_{DIM}(A - B)$.

Here μ_{DIM} is a measure function, that is, a function that associates an entity or set with a degree on the scale associated with some dimension of measurement *DIM*.

But while both the formulae in (39) are based on μ_{DIM}, there is an important difference in the structure of the measurement scale that is assumed in the two cases. In (39a), μ_{DIM} must yield a value that can be meaningfully divided by two. To borrow a concept from measurement theory (see especially [22]), this means that here μ_{DIM} encodes measurement at the ratio level, and thus that the underlying numerical scale is a ratio scale, featuring a fixed zero point and a fixed unit of measure. Examples of ratio scales include weight measured in pounds or kilograms, length measured in meters or feet, or set cardinality represented via the natural numbers, all familiar cases of quantitative measurement. Thus by virtue of its logical form, the felicitous use of *more than half* presupposes measurement at the ratio level. From this follows the requirement that the domain of quantification be enumerable or otherwise quantitatively measurable.

The logical form for *most* in (39b), on the other hand, places much weaker requirements on the structure of the scale that serves as the range of μ_{DIM}. For example, suppose that we start with a simple qualitative ordering of individuals or sets, one which could be represented numerically by assigning whole numbers to those individuals/sets in an order-preserving manner (similar to assigning place numbers to finishers in a race, without recording their actual finishing times). In measurement-theoretic terms, this is ordinal level measurement. An ordinal-level measure function μ_{DIM} is sufficient to support the evaluation of the formula in (39b), which will come out as true if the rank order assigned to $A \cap B$ precedes or exceeds that assigned to $A - B$. To return to an earlier example, even if the problems faced by contractors are not enumerable or countable in a traditional sense, (35c) could be evaluated as true if the problems the individual in question could handle were ranked above those he couldn't with respect to a qualitative (i.e. ordinal) ranking of sets or entities. Put differently, *most*, unlike *more than half*, does not presuppose something as informative as ratio-level measurement, and thus may be felicitously used in situations where *more than half* is not supported.

Furthermore, even ordinal level measurement is not necessary. Imagine that we start with a 'tolerant' ordering of individuals based on a 'significantly greater than' relationship. By this, I mean an ordering where the difference relationship $\succ$ is transitive but the indifference relationship $\sim$ is not, such that we might have $x \sim y$ and $y \sim z$ but $x \succ z$. In formal terms, such an ordering relationship is a semi-order (see [23, 7]). A tolerant ordering can be given a numerical representation via a measure function μ_{DIM} that assigns each set or entity a range of values rather than a single point, with the 'greater than' relationship $>$ holding between two degrees (i.e. ranges) only if there is no overlap between them. Such a measure function is sufficient to support the logical form in (39b), which will hold true if $A \cap B$ has a 'significantly' greater measure with respect to the relevant dimension than $A - B$. But as discussed above, this is precisely the situation when *most* is used, namely when the number or measure of As that are B is significantly greater than the number/measure of As that are not B. That is, the absence of a sharp lower bound for *most* can be related to the possibility for its interpretation relative to a tolerant ordering.

There is in fact considerable support for the psychological reality of the encoding of cardinalities and other measures as ranges of a sort, whose difference is a function of their degree of (non-)overlap. Findings from the psychology of number cognition (see especially [24]) demonstrate that in addition to the ability to represent precise number, humans (and other animals) possess a separate and more primitive approximate number system (ANS). In the ANS, numerical magnitudes are thought to be encoded as ranges of activation on the equivalent of a mental number line. The representations generated by the ANS support simple arithmetic and, importantly for the present case, the comparison of quantities. In this function, its operation is ratio-dependent: Two numbers can be reliably distinguished via the ANS only if the ratio between them is sufficiently large, that is, if the overlap between their ranges is sufficiently small (cf. the above discussion of tolerant orderings).

A connection between the ANS and the semantics of *most* has been made previously by Pietroski et al. [25], who show that verification of sentences with *most* exhibits a characteristic pattern of ratio dependence, and Halberda et al. [26], who demonstrate that young children who lack full numerical competence may still be able to evaluate *most* approximately. The present discussion suggests that it is the logical form of *most* that allows its evaluation via the ANS. Furthermore, since the ANS is the more basic of humans' two systems for processing number (emerging evolutionarily and developmentally before the ability to represent precise number), it is reasonable to assume that it serves as the default option in the interpretation of *most*. In this way we can account for the tendency for *most* to be used in an imprecise manner even when precise number is available.

The picture that emerges is the following. The precise *more than half* encodes a comparison of points on a ratio scale (an aspect of its meaning that also restricts its use to cases where ratio-level measurement is possible). The vague *most*, on the other hand, assumes a less informative scale structure, perhaps one based on a tolerant ordering (which accounts for both its broader distribution relative to *more than half*, as well as its essentially fuzzy lower bound). In this case, then, precision versus vagueness corresponds to a difference in what level of measurement, and thus what sort of scale structure, is involved.

One wonders whether this distinction might characterize precision versus vagueness more generally. Here, it is helpful to consider another sort of example. The contrast in interpretation between *more than half* and *most* has a parallel in the contrast between so-called explicit and implicit comparatives, as exemplified in (40):

(40)   a. John is taller than Fred.   **Explicit**

        b. John is tall compared to Fred.   **Implicit**

As discussed in particular by Kennedy [8], (40a) but not (40b) supports crisp comparisons. That is, if John is only very slightly (say, 1 cm) taller than Fred, the explicit comparative (40a) is true, but the implicit comparative (40b) is false. This recalls the acceptability of *more than half*, but not *most*, for proportions just slightly greater than 50%. Van Rooij [7] proposes that while explicit comparatives such as (40a) can be modeled via weak orders (which include ratio-level scales as a special case), implicit comparatives such as (40b) should be modeled via semi-orders, just as is proposed above for *most*. Thus once again, the vague member of the pair is associated with a tolerant ordering structure.

Importantly, the claim here is not that dimensions such as height, number and so forth <u>cannot</u> be measured at the ratio level. This is obviously not the case. Rather, the idea is that these dimensions can also be measured at a less informative level, specifically relative to a semi-ordered scale structure of the type discussed above, and it is this level of measurement that is assumed by vague expressions that reference these dimensions (including the quantifier *most*, and perhaps gradable adjectives in implicit comparatives).

If such a generalization can be established more generally, the implication would be that the formal modeling of vague expressions should make reference to other types of degree structures than the totally ordered scales often assumed in degree semantics. I leave this more general possibility as a topic for further investigation.

4 Concluding remarks

The goal of this paper was to take a close look at linguistic data relating to vagueness in the expression of quantity, with a view to exploring what this less studied area might be able to tell us about the nature and proper treatment of vagueness more generally. Most of the discussion above has focused on particular lexical items in English: words of the *many* class in the first case study, the quantifier *most* in the second. But both of these case studies suggest some broader implications for the formal analysis of vagueness, the first reinforcing the relevance of comparison classes in the interpretation of vague expressions, the second raising the possibility that vagueness is, in at least some cases, associated with a tolerant scale structure.

In closing, I would like to suggest that similar insights may be available through the in depth investigation of vagueness as it occurs in other domains of natural language, including in particular vague nouns, as well expressions of temporal and spatial relationships such as prepositions.

BIBLIOGRAPHY

[1] Solt, Stephanie (2009). The semantics of adjectives of quantity. Ph.D. Dissertation, City University of New York.

[2] Bartsch, Renate and Theo Vennemann (1972). *Semantic structures*. Frankfurt: Athenäum.

[3] Cresswell, Maxwell J. (1977). The semantics of degree. In Barbara H. Partee (ed.), *Montague grammar*, 261–292. New York: Academic Press.

[4] Klein, Ewan (1980). A semantics for positive and comparative adjectives. *Linguistics and Philosophy*, 4, 1–45.

[5] von Stechow, Arnim (1984). Comparing semantic theories of comparison. *Journal of Semantics*, 3, 1–77.

[6] Fults, Scott (2006). The structure of comparison: An investigation of gradable adjectives. Ph.D. Dissertation, University of Maryland.

[7] van Rooij, Robert (2011). Implicit and explicit comparatives. In Paul Égré and Nathan Klinedinst (eds.), *Vagueness and language use*, 51–72. New York: Palgrave Macmillan.

[8] Kennedy, Christopher (2007). Vagueness and grammar: The semantics of relative and absolute gradable adjectives *Linguistics and Philosophy*, 30, 1–45.

[9] Solt, Stephanie (2010). Notes on the comparison class. In Rick Nouwen, Robert van Rooij, Uli Sauerland and Hans-Christian Schmitz (eds.), *Vagueness in communication* (ViC2009), LNAI 6517, 189–206. Berlin, Heidelberg: Springer Verlag.

[10] Klein, Ewan (1981). The interpretation of adjectival, nominal, and adverbial comparatives. In Jeroen Groenendijk, Theo Janssen and Martin Stokhof (eds.), *Formal methods in the study of language*, 381–398. Amsterdam: Mathematical Center Tracts.

[11] Westerståhl, Dag (1985). Logical constants in quantifier languages. *Linguistics and Philosophy*, 8, 387–413.

[12] Lappin, Shalom (1988). The semantics of 'many' as a weak determiner. *Linguistics*, 26, 977–998.

[13] Partee, Barbara H. (1989). Many quantifiers. In Joyce Powers and Kenneth de Jong (eds.), *Proceedings of the 5th Eastern States Conference on Linguistics*, 383–402. Columbus, OH: Ohio State University.

[14] Büring, Daniel (1996). A weak theory of strong readings. In Teresa Galloway and Justin Spence (eds.), *Proceedings of Semantics and Linguistic Theory* (SALT) 6, 17–34. Ithaca, NY: CLC Publications.

[15] Fernando, Tim and Hans Kamp (1996). Expecting Many. In Teresa Galloway and Justin Spence (eds.), *Proceedings of Semantics and Linguistic Theory* (SALT) 6, 53–68. Ithaca, NY: CLC Publications.

[16] Herburger, Elena (1997). Focus and weak noun phrases. *Natural Language Semantics*, 5, 53–78.

[17] Lappin, Shalom (2000). An intensional parametric semantics for vague quantifiers. *Linguistics and Philosophy*, 23, 599–620.

[18] Diesing, Molly (1992). *Indefinites*. Cambridge, MA: MIT Press.

[19] Davies, Mark (2008–). The Corpus of Contemporary American English (COCA): 410+ million words, 1990–present. Available online at http://www.americancorpus.org.

[20] Chierchia, Gennaro and Sally McConnell-Ginet (2000). *Meaning and grammar*, 2nd Edition. Cambridge, MA: MIT Press.

[21] Hackl, Martin (2009). On the grammar and processing of proportional quantifiers: *Most* versus *more than half*. *Natural Language Semantics*, 17, 63–98.

[22] Kranz, David H., R. Duncan Luce, Patrick Suppes and Amos Tversky (1971). *Foundations of measurement: Additive and polynomial representations*. New York: Academic Press.

[23] Luce, R. Duncan (1956). Semiorders and a theory of utility discrimination. *Econometrica*, 24, 178–191.

[24] Dehaene, Stanislas (1997). *The number sense: How the mind creates mathematics*. Oxford: Oxford University Press.

[25] Pietroski, Paul, Jeffrey Lidz, Tim Hunter and Justin Halberda (2009). The meaning of 'most': Semantics, numerosity, and psychology. *Mind and Language*, 24(5), 554–585.

[26] Halberda, Justin, Len Taing and Jeffrey Lidz (2008). The development of "most" comprehension and its potential dependence on counting-ability in preschoolers. *Language Learning and Development*, 4(2), 99–121.

Stephanie Solt
Zentrum für Allgemeine Sprachwissenschaft (ZAS)
Schützenstraße 18
10117 Berlin, Germany
E-mail: solt@zas.gwz-berlin.de

Comments on *Vagueness in Quantity* by Stephanie Solt

PAUL ÉGRÉ[1]

Overview

There is a very active trend of research in linguistics at the moment about the right way to interpret vague expressions of quantification such as "many", "few" and "most". In this note I would like to focus my discussion on the second part of Solt's exciting paper, regarding the meaning difference between the two determiner expressions "most" and "more than half". The problem of the relation between those expressions has been addressed in a number of recent works, in particular by M. Ariel (2003, 2004), M. Hackl (2009) and by P. Pietroski et al. (2009). Like Solt, these authors give empirical evidence for the view that "most" and "more than half" make different contributions to the meaning of the sentences in which they occur. Importantly, however, they tend to agree that the truth conditions for complete sentences of the form "most *As* are *Bs*" and "more than half of *As* are *Bs*" are logically equivalent.[2] Solt's main emphasis in her paper is slightly different. It rests on the idea that "more than half" and "most" manipulate different scales of measurement, corresponding to different levels of informativeness. Because I find myself in agreement with most of Solt's account in her paper (not to say more than half of it), in this commentary I would like first to adduce further evidence in favor of her semantic analysis of "most", in particular concerning the need for measure functions. I then discuss the status of the entailment relations between "most" and "more than half" and some tentative counterexamples to either direction of implication between the two determiners.

"Most" and measure functions

At least two sets of facts have been presented in the literature to suggest that "most" and "more than half" might have different meanings. The first, investigated in particular by Ariel (2003, 2004), is that "most" typically receives "larger majority interpretations than 'more than half' " (Ariel 2003). This is illustrated by Solt's example "most Americans are female", a sentence which seems less appropriate to use than "more than half of Americans are female" to describe the proportion of 50.7% of female among Americans. The second set of observations concerns the fact that the determiner "most", which rests on superlative morphology (see Hackl 2009), does not specify an explicit comparison

[1]Thanks to the ANR program ANR-07-JCJC-0070 for support related to this research, and to Marie-Auxille Denis, Orin Percus, David Ripley, Philippe Schlenker and Benjamin Spector for helpful conversations.

[2]This is not exactly so for Ariel, who considers that "most" semantically excludes "all", unlike "more than half". For her, "most students attended the party" must therefore be false when "all students attended the party" is true, whereas "more than half of the students attended the party" still counts as true. Unlike Ariel, I consider this difference as pragmatic rather than semantic. I shall not say more about it here though.

point for the minimum proportion of As that is needed to say that "most As are Bs". In contrast to that, "more than half", which uses the comparative "more", fixes a precise lower threshold by means of the proportional expression "half". This morphological difference plays a central part in Hackl's decompositional theory of the determiner "most" in particular. Besides those two sets of observations, Solt in her paper puts particular emphasis on a third contrast, which concerns the fact that "most" can quantify over domains that are not enumerable, or otherwise for which no obvious measure is available, whereas "more than half" appears to require either enumerability, or a scale of measurement with clear measurement units. An illustration of this phenomenon is given by Solt concerning the combination of "most" with mass nouns, as in the pair "most racism is not so blatant" vs. "(?) more than half of racism is not so blatant".

The first aspect of Solt's paper on which I wish to dwell concerns precisely the idea that the semantics of "most" must involve a measure function in order to take account of quantification over domains that are not enumerable. On her account, "most$(A)(B)$" means that the measure of things that are A and B is greater than the measure of things that are A and not B. Interestingly, the idea that the semantics of "most" requires a measure function has been put forward independently by Schlenker (2006) and by Chierchia (2010: p. 138, fn. 44), each time in the context of broader considerations about mass nouns. Schlenker, for instance, points out that a sentence like "most of the water in the room is poisoned" can only be judged true or false depending on how water is measured (for instance it will depend on whether it is the overall volume, the number of water containers in the room, and so on). Similarly, Chierchia points out that we can meaningfully judge the following sentence about numbers to be true:

(1)   Most numbers are not prime.

despite the fact that the set of prime numbers and the set of composite numbers have equal cardinality.

It is worth lingering on that particular example, because prima facie, it gives a direct counterexample to the standard cardinality analysis of "most" given in generalized quantifier theory, and moreover because it lends further support to Solt's analysis. Indeed, on the standard analysis, "most As are Bs" should mean that the cardinality of the set AB is greater than the cardinality of the set $A\overline{B}$. However, since there are as many prime numbers as there are natural numbers, this predicts that (1) should be false in that case. There is a legitimate sense in which we can utter (1) truly, however. Interestingly, it seems odd to say:

(2)   (?) More than half of the natural numbers are not prime.

In this case the oddness does not appear to originate from the fact that the sentence would be false. For it would be equally odd to say that "(?) exactly half of the natural numbers are not prime", in order to mean that "there are as many primes as there are nonprimes". Moreover, the oddness cannot result from the fact that the natural numbers are not enumerable, since they are. Rather, the problem seems to be exactly related to the fact that the scale of cardinal numbers is no longer a ratio scale once we reach infinite cardinals, in agreement with Solt's remarks. Indeed, although there is an absolute zero point on the scale of cardinal numbers, this scale is no longer a ratio scale for infinite cardinalities, since on a ratio scale, when $\mu(A) = a$ and $\mu(B) = 2 \cdot a$, one can meaningfully say that "there are twice as many Bs as As", and infer "there are more Bs than As". At the very least, infinite cardinalities do involve a departure from the idea that the concatenation of an interval of a given size with an interval of the same size will yield a larger interval, as happens for measures defined over the real numbers.

The situation is different with (1). As suggested by Chierchia, we likely accept this sentence in relation to a measure of the frequency of prime numbers among natural numbers. Let us elaborate on this: we know from the prime number theorem that the number of prime numbers less or equal to n tends to $n/\log(n)$ as n tends to infinity (see e.g. Jameson 2003). This entails that the probability for a number less or equal to n drawn at random to be prime can be approximated by $1/\log(n)$. Hence, the larger the initial segment of natural numbers we consider, the lower the probability will be that a given number in that segment is prime. When n tends to infinity, this probability tends to 0, and the probability for a number not to be prime tends to 1. This can be seen as one way to associate a measure to the set of prime numbers. Whether we actually understand a sentence such as (1) in relation to that measure is open to discussion. Maybe what we have in mind when we utter (1) is something related, but simpler, like the following: for any n sufficiently large, we can observe that the number of prime numbers less or equal to n is strictly less than the number of nonprime numbers less or equal to n. That is, any initial segment of the natural numbers that is sufficiently large contains more composite numbers than prime numbers. Possibly, therefore, we may be using a standard cardinality measure to check the meaning of (1), but restricting cardinality comparison to arbitrarily large segments.

Could "more than half" fail to entail "most"?

Besides the emphasis on measure functions, another aspect of Solt's discussion concerns the idea that "most" is used "when the number or measure of As that are B is *significantly greater* than the number/measure of As that are not B" (emphasis mine). By contrast, "more than half" will be true even if the number or measure of As that are B is just above a half on the relevant scale. One aspect Solt does not make entirely explicit is whether the notion "significantly greater" should then be part of the truth conditions of sentences with "most", or whether it is only pragmatically relevant. Supposing it were part of the truth conditions for "most", this would directly explain that "most" gets larger majority interpretations than "more than half". On the other hand, it would predict that a sentence like "most Americans are female" should be judged false for majority proportions such as 50.7%, that are only slightly above 1/2.

Solt leaves open whether this should be so, or whether we only have a pragmatic preference for using "more than half" in that case. As I understand Solt's account, however, the notion of significant difference should likely *not* be part of the truth conditions of "most". It appears to be relevant primarily in relation to our analogical representation of magnitudes in order to check that the measure of AB is greater than the measure of $A\overline{B}$. The reason I see for this is that we can still use "most" in cases in which we can rely on precise measurement for the comparison of the set AB with the set $A\overline{B}$. For instance, Pietroski et al. in their study point out that even though subjects use "most" in accordance with the laws of psychophysics to estimate whether there are more yellow dots than non-yellow dots in a visual display, "one extra yellow dot suffices (up to the stochastic limits of the ANS to detect this difference) for judging that most dots are yellow". This means that whenever "more than half$(A)(B)$" can be judged true, "most$(A)(B)$" should also be true, at least if the same dimension of comparison is used each time.

On the other hand, if dimensions of comparison can vary for "most" and "more than half", judgments may come apart, but only as a result of pragmatic ambiguity. For instance, imagine a jar filled with 100 very small black marbles at the bottom, and 20 big red marbles on top of them, and suppose that the 100 black marbles fill a fifth of the volume of the jar, while the 20 red left occupy the rest of the jar's volume. In the cardinality sense, "more than half of the marbles in the jar are black" is true. However, I could easily imagine people to judge that "most of the marbles in the jar are red" (and therefore not black), making use of some form of coercion, to mean "most marbles are red *in proportion to the jar's volume*" (consistently with Solt's remarks about "many").[3] It would be interesting to see if one can say in the same sense: "[in proportion to the jar's volume] more than half of the marbles in the jar are red".

As I see Solt's theory, the entailment from "more than half" to "most" is semantically robust, and the fact that larger majority interpretations are assigned for "most" calls for a pragmatic explanation. Regarding the converse entailment, from "most$(A)(B)$" to "more than half of$(A)(B)$", I wonder if an appropriate way to describe Solt's view may not be in terms of Strawson-entailment (von Fintel 1999). That is, "most$(A)(B)$" will entail "more than half$(A)(B)$" only if the presuppositions of "more than half" are satisfied, that is, only when a common ratio scale can be used for both expressions. Solt's example "most racism is not so blatant" is an example of that sort: the entailment to "more than half of racism" only fails because no obvious ratio scale is available for the latter to be used felicitously.

Relative majorities

Could there be, however, reasons to think that "most" and "more than half" need not entail each other either way, even when the same scale can be used for both? One tentative example I can think of concerns the case of relative or qualified majorities. Consider an election in which the rule is that a proposal will be accepted only if it gets a majority of at least 60% of the votes, and consider a case in which the proposal gets only 54% of the votes. Plausibly, one should be willing to say that "more than half of the people voted for the proposal". But it might be judged false that "most people voted for the proposal", if "most" in that case is evaluated against the minimum of 60%. This would be a case where in order for the set of AB to be counted as greater than the set of $A\overline{B}$, the proportion of AB simply must exceed 60%. Conversely, even when the majority rule is set at 50%, one may find occurrences of "most people voted for candidate A" even as the proportion of people who voted for candidate A is less than 50%, provided A is the candidate with the largest number of votes, and with a significant relative majority in comparison to other candidates (viz. 40% for A vs. less than 4% for each of 15 competitors).

Such examples are not conclusive against the entailment relations between "most" and "more than half", however. For the first example, my intuitions easily change if

---

[3]I believe actual experiments have been made on examples of that sort, which I remember G. Chierchia to mention in a lecture. Unfortunately, I can no longer track the references for this example.

the majority rule is set at 75%, and exactly 70% voted for the proposal. In that case, it seems fine to me to say that "although most people voted for the proposal, the majority was not reached". For the second example, a more natural determiner expression precisely seems to be "a majority" rather than "most". Ariel (2004: pp. 696–97) considers actual election cases with reports such as "Yosifov was elected by a majority of 41.6%". While use of "a majority" is perfectly appropriate, it is unclear to me whether one could say "most people voted for Yosifov" in that case, except maybe for a situation in which Yosifov would have gotten an overwhelming proportion of votes in comparison to each alternative candidate. If so, it may be that "most" is used for comparison to subsets of the whole domain, namely to mean "most people voted for Yosifov *in comparison to any other candidate they could vote for*". That is, the sentence may be judged true by comparing the proportion of people who voted for Yosifov to the distribution of votes among other candidates (that is, to the respective proportion of each other candidate), assuming the resulting ratio to be high each time. If such uses of "most" exist, consequently, I believe that they remain entirely compatible with the measure-theoretic analysis of "most" outlined in Solt's paper.

BIBLIOGRAPHY

Ariel M. (2003). Does *most* mean 'more than half'? *Berkeley Linguistics Society* 29:17–30.

Ariel M. (2004). Most. *Language* 80(4):658–706.

Chierchia G. (2010). Mass nouns, vagueness and semantic variation. *Synthese* 174:99–149

von Fintel K. (1999). NPI licensing, Strawson entailment, and context dependency. *Journal of Semantics* 16(2):97–148.

Hackl M. (2009). On the grammar and processing of proportional quantifiers: *Most* versus *more than half*. *Natural Language Semantics* 17:63–98

Jameson G.J.O. (2003). *The Prime Number Theorem*. Cambridge University Press.

Pietroski P., J. Lidz, T. Hunter, and J. Halberda, (2009). The meaning of 'most': Semantics, numerosity, and psychology. *Mind and Language* 24(5):554–585.

Schlenker P. (2006). Ontological symmetry in language: a brief manifesto. *Mind and Language* 21(4):504–539.

Solt S. (2011). Vagueness in quantity: Two case studies from a linguistic perspective. *This volume*.

Paul Égré
Institut Jean-Nicod
Département d'Etudes Cognitives
Ecole Normale Supérieure
29, rue d'Ulm, 75005 Paris
E-mail: paul.egre@ens.fr

Reply to Paul Égré's Comments on *Vagueness in Quantity: Two Case Studies from a Linguistic Perspective*

STEPHANIE SOLT[1]

I would first of all like to thank Paul Égré for his thorough and thoughtful reading of my paper, and for the further evidence he puts forward in favor of the proposals therein. Égré raises a number of interesting points, and I won't be able to address all of them here, but I would like to offer some fairly open-ended remarks on some specific aspects of his comments.

I'll focus first on the very interesting facts relating to infinite domains. As Égré notes, there seems to be a contrast in acceptability in pairs such as the following:

(1)   a. Most of the natural numbers are composite.
        b. ?More than half of the natural numbers are composite.

And indeed one finds naturally occurring examples of the form in (2), but corresponding *more than half* examples are absent even from the enormous Google 'corpus' (and replacing *most* with *more than half* in (2) leads to the same oddness as in (1b)).

(2)   A paradoxical situation arises because, on the one hand, it seems evident that most natural numbers are not perfect squares ...[2]

Égré argues that contrasts of this sort are predicted by my analysis, and I concur, though I might frame the source of the contrast in slightly different terms. According to the logical forms I adopt (repeated below), calculating the truth value of (1b) would involve assigning the totality of natural numbers a measure that can be meaningfully divided by two—which of course is not possible. On the other hand, establishing the truth of (1a) requires merely establishing a relationship of 'greater than' between the sets of composite and prime numbers. This might be done in any number of ways. One of those proposed by Égré strikes me as particularly natural, namely, generalizing over finite segments of the number line of the form $[1, n]$, as it can readily be verified that for any sufficiently large n, the required relationship will hold.

(3)   a. $[\![$more than half$]\!](A)(B) = 1$ iff $\mu_{DIM}(A \cap B) > \mu_{DIM}(A)/2$.
        b. $[\![$most$]\!](A)(B) = 1$ iff $\mu_{DIM}(A \cap B) > \mu_{DIM}(A - B)$.

[1]I would like to thank the editors of this volume for the opportunity to include this reply, and again acknowledge the support I have received from the European Science Foundation (ESF) and the Deutsche Forschungsgemeinschaft (DFG) under the auspices of the EuroCORES Programme LogICCC.

[2]http://lofi.forum.physorg.com/Galileo%26%2339%3Bs-Paradox_25289.html

I would very much like to leave it at this, as this would indeed represent a nice argument in favor of my proposal. I fear, however, that the facts are more complicated. The problem is that the relevant *more than half* examples don't seem to be quite as deviant as this analysis would predict—not as bad, for instance, as the examples with non-enumerable domains discussed in my paper. Related examples of the form in (4a) are, to me, fairly acceptable, although here too it should be necessary to establish a measure for the totality of natural numbers and divide that value by 2. And (1b) also improves with the addition of a modifier, as in (4b). This suggests that the real source of the infelicity of (1b) might be that it is wildly underinformative—our naive intuition is that the proportion of composites among the natural numbers is far greater than 50%.

(4)   a.   Exactly half of the natural numbers are divisible by two.
       b.   Far/way/vastly more than half of the natural numbers are composite.

Égré relates the felicity of (1a) to the possibility of interpreting *most* with respect to a measure function other than a cardinality measure. But then the (at least marginal) felicity of the (4) examples suggests that something similar must be available in the case of *more than half*. This is not in itself incompatible with my proposal, in that (3a), like (3b), does not encode cardinality as a measure; but it is more difficult to see what the measure function in question might be, in that it must relate entities to points on a ratio scale.

In short, when we turn to infinite domains such as the natural numbers, the facts do not line up quite as predicted either by my measure function analysis or a more traditional one. I suspect that the underlying issue here is that we as humans aren't really equipped to deal with infinity. When faced with (fairly abstract) examples such as those discussed above, we somehow make them manageable—perhaps by reducing the domain to a finite one, perhaps by generalizing over a set of such finite domains. But how exactly we might do this, and what this could tell us about the semantics of expressions like *most* and *more than half*, are questions I will have to leave to the future.

I'll turn now from a very complex issue to a somewhat more straightforward one. Égré raises the possibility that *most* might fail to entail *more than half*, or put differently, that *most* might be felicitously used for proportions less than 50%. Some speakers do in fact allow this, as evidenced by naturally occurring examples such as the following (which are quite easy to find):

(5)   Most respondents (43 per cent) were renters, 28 per cent lived in public housing, five per cent were paying off mortgages and 18 per cent were homeless.[3]

What is involved in cases such as this is the comparison of some contextually provided set of proportions; for example, in (5), the proportion of renters among respondents is compared to a salient set of alternatives, namely the proportions of mortgage payers, homeless, etc. (see also [1] for experimental evidence for the existence of this sort of reading).

---

[3]http://news.theage.com.au/breaking-news-national/women-and-singles-suffer-on-poverty-line-20090626-cz95.html

As written, the logical form in (3b) does not account for examples such as these, but I suspect they could be handled by a generalized version of this formula, in which the measures of three or more sets or entities are compared. I leave this, too, for further investigation.

Finally, Égré points out that I am not entirely explicit about whether I consider the 'significantly greater than 50%' component of *most*'s meaning to be truth-conditional or pragmatic in nature. He is correct in inferring that I see this as a pragmatic effect, the result of a preference for interpreting the logical form in (3b) relative to a 'tolerant' or semi-ordered scale, whose structure reflects our innate approximate numerical abilities. I discuss this in greater depth in [2]. Regarding the entailment relationship between *most* and *more than half*, the parallel to cases of Strawson entailment is a nice one, and I thank Égré for it.

BIBLIOGRAPHY

[1] Kotek, Hadas, Yasutada Sudo, Edwin Howard, and Martin Hackl. To appear. *Most* meanings are superlative. In *Syntax and Semantics 37: Experiments at the interface,* ed. Jeff Runner. New York: Academic Press.
[2] Solt, Stephanie. Submitted. On measurement and quantification: the case of *most* and *more than half.* Submitted to *Language.*

Vagueness in Language:
The Case Against Fuzzy Logic Revisited

ULI SAUERLAND[1]

Introduction

When I started interacting with logicians, I was surprised to learn that fuzzy logic is still a big and active field of basic research. This surprise stemmed from my experience with fuzzy logic in my own field, linguistic semantics: In semantics, fuzzy logic was explored in the analysis of vagueness in the early seventies by Lakoff [10], but has been regarded as unsuitable for the analysis of language meaning at least since the influential work of Kamp in 1975 [8], which I summarize below. Therefore, I held the belief that fuzzy logic, though it has been useful in technical applications—I once possessed a Japanese rice-cooker that was advertised to use fuzzy logic—, was not useful for the analysis of vagueness. As I have learned since, I was just ignorant of a big chunk of modern mathematical logic, and fuzzy logic is in fact a lively paradigm of research on vagueness. The lack of interaction between linguists and logicians that my experience illustrates seems to be a more general phenomenon: From the interaction with logicians, I have learned that many fuzzy logicians also do not seem to be aware of current work in linguistics on vagueness. The different attitudes towards fuzzy logic in linguistics and in logic are, of course, most likely rationally justified on the basis of the different goals of the two fields. However, historical accidents can also happen in the development of a field of science, in which case the different traditions in two fields may turn out to have no rational basis. So, which is it in the case of fuzzy logic and linguistics?

In this paper, I revisit the arguments against the use of fuzzy logic in linguistics (or more generally, against a truth-functional account of vagueness). In part, this is an exercise to explain to fuzzy logicians why linguists have shown little interest in their research paradigm. But, the paper contains more than this interdisciplinary service effort that I started out on: In fact, this seems an opportune time for revisiting the arguments against fuzzy logic in linguistics since three recent developments affect the argument. First, the formal apparatus of fuzzy logic has been made more general since the 1970s, specifically by Hájek [6], and this may make it possible to define operators in a way to make fuzzy logic more suitable for linguistic purposes. Secondly, recent research in philosophy has examined variations of fuzzy logic ([18, 19]). Since the goals of linguistic semantics

[1] I am very grateful to Sam Alxatib, Stephanie Solt, Hans Kamp, Chris Fermüller, and Libor Běhounek for comments that helped me to substantially improve this paper. I also thank the audience of the 2010 LoMoReVI conference at Čejkovice for inspiring discussion of the issues discussed here. This work was made possible by the financial support of the DFG grants SA 925/1 and SA 925/4, the latter within the ESF Eurocore LogiCCC project VAAG. All remaining errors are of course my responsibility.

seem sometimes closer to those of some branches of philosophy of language than they are to the goals of mathematical logic, fuzzy logic work in philosophy may mark the right time to reexamine fuzzy logic from a linguistic perspective as well. Finally, the reasoning used to exclude fuzzy logic in linguistics has been tied to the intuition that p *and not p* is a contradiction. However, this intuition seems dubious especially when p contains a vague predicate. For instance, one can easily think of circumstances where *'What I did was smart and not smart.'* or *'Bea is both tall and not tall.'* don't sound like senseless contradictions. In fact, some recent experimental work that I describe below has shown that contradictions of classical logic aren't always felt to be contradictory by speakers. So, it is important to see to what extent the argument against fuzzy logic depends on a specific stance on the semantics of contradictions. In sum then, there are three good reasons to take another look at fuzzy logic for linguistic purposes.

After recognizing that the argument against fuzzy logic in linguistics needs to be updated, I provide such an update in this paper. I conclude, however, that the conclusion reached by Kamp [8] and others still stands: For capturing vagueness in linguistic semantics, fuzzy logic or any other purely truth-functional theory doesn't provide a suitable mathematical formalism. As I already mentioned, this conclusion of course doesn't say anything about the intellectual merits of fuzzy logic in itself, but only shows that the interests of fuzzy logicians and linguists diverge: Linguists are interested in formulating specific formal models that can be used to account for linguistic phenomena. Logicians explore classes of formal models that have interesting mathematical properties and sometimes also have applications.

The paper is structured as follows. In the first section, I start off with summarizing work by Kamp [8] and others that effectively dissuaded linguists from looking at fuzzy logic for the last 35 years. As I show, the assumption that contradictions are contradictory has been central to this argument. In Section 2, I then examine the argument in the light of recent developments. Specifically I summarize recent experiments on the acceptability of contradictions. The new experimental study I report tests whether any truth-functional, fuzzy logic could provide an account of linguistic vagueness if the acceptability of contradictions is integrated into linguistic semantics. As I report, the study shows that a truth functional, fuzzy logic alone could not model vagueness in language successfully. In the conclusion, I mention formal theories of vagueness that seem better suited for the account of vagueness in language in light of the data in Section 2.

1   The classical argument

The argument that I summarize in this section, has been made by several people and I am actually not sure of its origin. Most influential in linguistics have been the presentations by Kamp [8] and Fine [4]. Kamp points out that the argument can be already found in work by Rescher [16]. But, Rescher's presentation seems to not have had the same effect as the later ones in dissuading linguists from applying fuzzy logic, since Lakoff still applied fuzzy logic in linguistics in 1973 [10], while I am not aware of any serious applications since then: There has been considerable work on vagueness in linguistics since 1973, just little of it makes use of fuzzy logic.[2] I summarize here mostly the work

---

[2]Fuzzy logic has been discussed by linguists more recently 1975, but only to dismiss its account for vagueness. There is also some work within fuzzy logic that addresses natural language (e.g. [15, 3], which I was

of Kamp [8] and to a lesser extent that of Fine [4].

In fuzzy logic, propositional expressions have a numerical value between 0 and 1 as their meaning, and negation and conjunction are interpreted as functions mapping a single such numerical value for negation or a pair of them for conjunction to another value between 0 and 1. Kamp [8, p. 131] raises the question what the truth value of conjunction should be if each conjunct has truth value $\frac{1}{2}$. I quote the relevant paragraph in full:

> What value would $F(\wedge)$ assign to the pair of arguments $(\frac{1}{2}, \frac{1}{2})$? It is plausible that the value should be $\leq \frac{1}{2}$. For how could a conjunction be true to a higher degree that one of its conjuncts? But which value $\leq \frac{1}{2}$? $\frac{1}{2}$ seems out because if $[\![\phi]\!]_M^{\mathcal{M}} = \frac{1}{2}$ then, if we accept our definition of $F(\neg)$, $[\![\neg\phi]\!]_M^{\mathcal{M}} = \frac{1}{2}$. So we would have $[\![\phi \wedge \neg\phi]\!]_M^{\mathcal{M}} = \frac{1}{2}$, which seems absurd. For how could a logical contradiction be true to *any* degree? However, if we stipulate that $(F(\wedge))(\frac{1}{2}, \frac{1}{2}) = 0$, we are stuck with the even less desirable consequence that if $[\![\phi]\!]_M^{\mathcal{M}} = \frac{1}{2}$, $[\![\phi \wedge \phi]\!]_M^{\mathcal{M}} = 0$. And if we choose any number between 0 and $\frac{1}{2}$, we get the wrong values for both $\phi \wedge \neg\phi$ and $\phi \wedge \phi$. [8, p. 131]

A few explanatory notes may be necessary to understand fully Kamp's presentation. Kamp assumes a two stage formalism that assigns to sentences of ordinary English their semantic value following Montague [13]. The semantic value is assumed by linguists to form the basis for semantic judgments of speakers like whether a sentence is true in particular scenario or whether one sentence entails another. Since Montague was a mathematician trained in model-theory, the semantic evaluation procedure bears many similarities to Tarskian model theory. In particular, the scenario in which a sentence is evaluated is represented as a set of parameters of the evaluation procedure. In Kamp's formal system these are the indices M and $\mathcal{M}$ that occur as super- and subscripts on the evaluation function $[\![-]\!]$. Since Kamp adopts Montague's two stage interpretation, the natural language expression *and* is first translated to the formal symbol $\wedge$, which is then interpreted model-theoretically. F is the function that assigns the value to logical constants in the second stage of the semantic evaluation procedure. For conjunction, the first question in the quotation is really about how the natural language expression *and* is interpreted, though $\wedge$ is also the symbol used also by logicians to represent conjunction in a logical system. Similarly, Kamp assumes that natural language negation (*not* or *it is not the case that*) is translated by the symbol $\neg$ in the intermediate representation, but here Kamp assumes that $F(\neg)$ maps p to $1 - p$. With these notes, Kamp's argument can be fully appreciated.

Kamp's argument is independent of the specific formalism he adopted, some of which like the two-stage interpretation procedure are no longer used in the field. In essence, the narrow point is that for sentences of the form *A and not A* we would want the semantic value 0, but for sentences of the form *A and A* we would want the semantic value of *A* itself. But, if there is an *A* with semantic value 0.5 and if the negation of *A*

---

unfortunately unable to access while writing this paper. But, note that these papers weren't published in linguistic journals, but in a fuzzy logic journal, so I ask to be forgiven for disregarding them. Furthermore, the proposal of [11] resembles fuzzy logic, but Lasersohn doesn't address standard logical expressions like negation in his account.

then also had semantic value 0.5, it is impossible to provide a semantic value for *and* that has the desired results. So, three concrete assumptions underlying the argument are that 1) there is a formula A with semantic value 0.5, 2) that for A, $\neg A$ also has semantic value 0.5, and 3) that $A \wedge \neg A$ has truth value 0.

As I already mentioned, Kamp points out that the argument is not original to his work, but can be already found in [16]. Furthermore, at the same time as Kamp, Fine [4] presents essentially the same arguments against multi-valued approaches to vagueness. Specifically, Fine (p. 270) also proclaims that *'Surely P & −P is false even though P is indefinite.'*[3] This quote also makes clear that the contradictory nature of a sentence of the form *A and not A* is essentially self-evident for Fine just as for Kamp—a point, we will come back to in the next section.

Beyond the specifics of the presentation of the argument, there's also a broader question that the argument highlights: whether a truth-functional logical system is appropriate for capturing vagueness in linguistics. In a subsequent paragraph of his paper, Kamp summarizes his argument as follows: *'the truth value of a complex formula—say $\phi \wedge \psi$— should depend not just on the truth values of the components—i.e. ϕ and ψ—but also on certain aspects of these formulae which contribute to their truth values but cannot be unambiguously recaptured from them.'* This broader question is based on one of the central concerns of linguistic semantics: Compositionality. Linguists are very interested in the fact that we humans can combine the meanings of individual words to yield sentence meanings, and want to account for people's linguistic intuitions for sentences such as *A and A* or *A and not A* as a function of the semantic value of *A*. The broader question is whether this can be done truth-functionally if *A* contains a vague expression. After investigating critically the three concrete assumptions Kamp used in his presentation in the following, we will return to this broader question, and will present empirical evidence that truth-functionality does not obtain in language when vague predicates are involved.

1.1 Initial discussion

The argument by Kamp and Fine discussed in the previous section has been widely accepted in linguistics: As already mentioned, I am not aware of serious work on vagueness in linguistics in the last 35 years that is based on fuzzy logic. Nevertheless, I mentioned reasons for reexamining the argument at this point of time in the introduction already. From my perspective, the main motivation to reexamine the argument is evidence that speakers don't perceive contradictions of classical logic to be contradictory when it comes to borderline cases. The acceptance of borderline contradictions may be taken to argue that such contradictions don't have semantic value 0 as assumed by Kamp and Fine. In the following section, I investigate a truth-functional theory that assigns to borderline contradictions a semantic value greater than 0. However, this move is by no means necessary: It may also be that contradictions have semantic value 0, but that our intuitions are affected by factors other than the semantic value. Semantic values are after all only a theoretical concept within a complex semantic-pragmatic-psycholinguistic theory of human intuitions about sentence meaning. In the remainder of this section, I argue that if contradictions are taken to have semantic value 0, the argument Kamp and Fine presented still goes through even given developments in fuzzy logic since 1975.

---

[3]The &-sign represents conjunction and the −-sign negation in Fine's article.

First, one may ask whether the sentences used in the argument shouldn't just be excluded: The relevant sentences for the argument are of the form *A and not A* on the one hand and *A and A* on the other in the presentation of Kamp [8]. Such conjunctions can be excluded by design in technical applications of logic like my rice-cooker, but this cannot be done in linguistic semantics: They are both instantiated by grammatical sentences and native speakers of English do have judgments on their truth or falsity. In the case, of *A and A* the linguistic status perhaps warrants some further comment since utterances such as *It's raining and raining* or *I am bored and I am bored* are likely to be very rare. However, to explain the rarity of *A and A*-type utterances, we have to rely on the assumption that *A and A* has the same semantic value as *A*. Then it follows from widely accepted linguistic theories such as the pragmatics of Grice [5], that the extra effort of saying *A and A* rather than just *A* should not be undertaken by speakers unless there is a specific rhetorical effect speakers aim to accomplish by the repetition. So, Kamp is justified to assume that *A and A* has the same semantic value as *A*. In sum, a semantic theory that does not provide semantic values for *A and not A* as well as *A and A* would be incomplete from a linguistic perspective.

Second, one may ask whether *and* couldn't be ambiguous. Lexical ambiguity is after all a frequent phenomenon in natural language, and if there were two words *and* that could overcome Kamp's problem. In the case of *A and not A*, we could assume that we make use of the word *and*$_1$ that assigns to the pair $(0.5, 0.5)$ the semantic value 0. When we are looking at *A and A*, however, we make use of *and*$_2$ and we get 0.5 for the pair $(0.5, 0.5)$. But, this account would clearly be *ad hoc* and would need to be supplemented with an explanation of why *and*$_1$ cannot be made use of in *A and A*, while *and*$_2$ cannot be used in *A and not A*. In fact, for *A and B* probably a third *and*$_3$ would need to be postulated when *B* is neither *A* nor $\neg A$.

Third, fuzzy logic seems to have undergone tremendous progress. As an outsider, I cannot fully appreciate all the changes since the time of Kamp's and Fine's writing (1975). From my superficial understanding, it seems one change has been that different versions of the operators representing conjunction and negation are being considered in systematic ways. Since the argument as presented by Kamp and Fine relies on assumptions about the interpretation of conjunction and negation, it is worthwhile to look whether novel variations of fuzzy logic can overcome the problems set out by Kamp and Fine.

I use two conventions in the following three paragraphs: 1) I use the abbreviation *V* for the set of sentences with semantic value other than 0 and 1. 2) I use lower case letters as variables ranging over $[0, 1]$.

I furthermore strengthen one assumption concerning semantic value 0 in addition to the assumption that classical contradictions have truth value 0. Namely, I assume in addition that, if a complex formula *F* has truth value 0, then either a basic formula occurring in *F* has truth value 0 or 1 or *F* is a classical contradiction. So, for example $a \wedge \neg b$ may only have truth value 0 if either a is 0, b is 1, or a is equal to b. This assumption is necessary for the following argument because, for example, a fuzzy logic that assigns to $a \wedge b$ 1 if and only if $a = b = 1$ and 0 otherwise doesn't lead to linguistic problems of the type Kamp and Fine point out–it behaves just like classical logic with respect to classical contradictions of the type Kamp and Fine discuss. As Fermüller (p.c.) points out, though, the assumption I just introduced excludes two widely discussed types of fuzzy logic; namely, the Gödel-logic and product logic, which both define the negation of any positive truth value as 0 [7]. However, systems where *tall* is vague, but derived predicates such as *not tall* or *short* are not, are of lesser interest for linguistic purposes.

As I understand from Hájek's non-technical summary [7], modern fuzzy logic generalizes the conjunction to be any binary operator $*$ on $[0, 1]$ that is a *T-norm*, which is defined as a commutative, associative, non-decreasing, (i.e. $a \leq b$ and $c \leq d$ then $a * c \leq b * d$) function where 1 is the unit element (i.e. $1 * a = a$).[4] As we saw above, Kamp already leaves it open how to interpret conjunction *and*. His point is that there can be no single function resulting in the correct interpretation for both *A and not A* as well as *A and A*. For negation, however, Kamp only considers one possibility, namely the Łukasiewicz negation defined by $\neg a = 1 - a$. In Hájek's work, negation is assumed to be a any non-increasing (i.e. if $a \leq b$, then $\neg a \geq \neg b$) function with $\neg 0 = 1$ and $\neg 1 = 0$.[5] Obviously, the three concrete assumptions of Kamp's argument mentioned above are not guaranteed in such a more general system, specifically there maybe no A with $[\![A]\!] = 0.5$ or it may be that $\neg 0.5 \neq 0.5$. In the next two paragraphs, I show that Kamp's argument still goes through with this more general notion of negation.

First, assume that negation has a fix-point that is instantiated by a sentence A, i.e. there is a sentence A in V such that the semantic values of A and $\neg A$ are identical. Then it follows that $A \wedge \neg A$ must have the same semantic value as $A \wedge A$. But since only $A \wedge \neg A$ is a classical contradiction, this entailment contradicts our assumption that, of all complex sentences, all and only classical contradictions have semantic value 0. So, it cannot be that case that negation has a fix-point that is instantiated by a sentence. Note that this is already somewhat unexpected since negation represents some cognitive operation humans perform on the number scale. Intuitively it seems such an operation should be continuous and therefore should have a fix-point by Brouwer's theorem. Then the fix-point must not be instantiated by a sentence—i.e. be a gap in the space of possible truth-values. Concretely that entails that the mapping from a X to the semantic value '*A guy of height X is tall*' cannot be continuous. But, that runs counter an intuition underlying applications of fuzzy logic: that vagueness is captured by a continuous mapping of some perceptual quality (here: height) to truth values: intuitively, there shouldn't be any jumps in semantic value as height goes up.

Secondly, for argument's sake assume only that there is at least one pair A and B of logically independent (i.e. neither sentence entails the other and they also don't contradict each other) sentences in V with the same semantic value. This assumption is different from the previous one that A and $\neg A$ have the same truth value. Technically even the new assumption is not necessarily satisfied since the set of sentences of a language is only countably infinite while the set $[0, 1]$ has a higher cardinality. Hence it may be technically possible to define a mapping from sentences to $[0, 1]$ where no two sentences are mapped to the same value and Hájek's axioms are satisfied. However, linguistically

---

[4]In addition, continuity (or at least, continuity in the left argument) is often required of $*$. But this doesn't play a role in the following.

[5]Modern fuzzy logic often assumes additional constraints on negation, specifically concerning its interaction with conjunction. Since these are not important for the following argument though, I will not discuss them at this point.

the application of fuzzy logic wouldn't make any sense unless some generalization is achieved. And a generalization is only achieved if the initial assumption is satisfied: there are logically independent sentences A and B with the same truth value. But then it follows that $A \wedge \neg A$ must have a different truth value from $B \wedge \neg A$ since the former is a classical contradiction with semantic value 0, while the latter isn't, and therefore by assumption has a semantic value greater than 0.

In sum, this section showed that, as long as we maintain that of the complex sentences made up from basic ones that don't have truth value 0 nor 1, only the contradictions of classical logic have semantic value 0, fuzzy logic doesn't provide a useful model for vagueness in language. The argument was essentially already presented by Kamp, Fine and others more than 35 years ago as I summarized here. In the last few paragraphs, I provided some generalizations of this argument to cover more recent developments in fuzzy logic. As I have noted occasionally, my argument concerns linguistic utility not mere logical possibility: It is could be technically possible to define functions $*$ and $\neg$ that satisfy the axioms of fuzzy logic and don't lead to the contradictions noted above. But such functions if they exist would be linguistic monstrosities, and therefore I don't consider them seriously. However, there is still a serious candidate which I consider in the next section: a semantics based on fuzzy logic where classical contradictions do not necessarily have truth value 0.

2   The dialethic argument

The most controversial aspect of the argument summarized in Section 1 is the assumption that sentences A *and not* A should have semantic value 0. As I already quoted above, Kamp [8] and Fine [4] regarded it as evident that classical contradictions should have semantic value 0. Fine pronounces another semantic value to be *absurd*, while Kamp states that *surely* 0 must be the semantic value of a contradiction. Since the relevant sentences are contradictions in classical logic, the certainty of Kamp and Fine seems initially justified.

However, linguistic intuitions often stand in conflict to classical logic. And as noted above already, sentences such as *'What I did was smart and not smart.'* or *'Bea is both tall and not tall.'* sound not as non-sensical as classical logic would predict—following Ripley [17] I refer to such examples as *Borderline Contradictions*. In this section, I first summarize two pieces of experimental evidence from recent papers that show that people do find such borderline contradictions quite acceptable. This seems to undercut the argument against fuzzy logic as presented in the previous section (though see [9] for a defense). So, it raises the question whether actual linguistic intuitions on contradictions are in line with fuzzy logic. This question I address with a new experiment in the second subsection below. Specifically, I set up a comparison between $A \wedge \neg A$ and $B \wedge \neg A$, where B is logically unrelated to A, but has the same semantic value. Fuzzy logic predicts the contradiction $A \wedge \neg A$ and the conjunction $B \wedge \neg A$ to have the same semantic value if A and B have the same semantic value because of $\wedge$'s truth-functionality. But, my experimental results indicate that $A \wedge \neg A$ is significantly more acceptable than $B \wedge \neg A$. So I conclude that the amount of agreement to borderline contradictions is so high, that it cannot be accounted for directly by fuzzy logic (nor by classical logic).

2.1 Experimental evidence for dialetheism

In this section, I summarize two recent experiments, one by Alxatib and Pelletier [1] and the other by Ripley [17], that show that many speakers indeed regard sentences of the form *A and not A* as informative and accept them under the right set of circumstances.

Alxatib and Pelletier's experiment Alxatib and Pelletier [1] primarily set out to argue against the account of truth value gaps by Bonini *et al.* [2]; however, their result is also of interest for our purposes. Their result confirms the intuition that borderline contradictions are most acceptable for borderline cases.

Alxatib and Pelletier [1] made subjects evaluate sentences as descriptions of a picture. They presented subjects a picture of five men drawn in the style of an American police line-up. Behind the men, a height scale is visible so in addition to their relative height, also the absolute heights are known. The five men are 5′4″, 5′7″, 5′11″, 6′2″, and 6′6″ tall. Alxatib and Pelletier asked their subjects to judge sentences as true or false given the picture, and offered also a third, *can't tell* response choice. In addition to the sentences '*X is tall*' and '*X is not tall*', they also included the sentence (1), which is of primary interest to us:

(1)   *X* is tall and not tall.

Sentence (1) is, of course, a contradiction in classical logic. However, Alxatib and Pelletier report that 44.7% of their subjects judge (1) to be true for the borderline case, the 5′11″ man, and only 40.8% judge (1) to be false in that case. The amount of agreement is lower for all the other heights.

It is noteworthy that the subjects in Alxatib and Pelletier's study regard sentence (1) to be true more frequently than either of its conjuncts: This is clearly the case for '*X is not tall*', which is judged true by 25.0% and false by 67.1% of subjects for the 5′11″ tall man. '*X is tall*' is judged true by 46.1% and false by 44.7% for the 5′11″ tall man. So, *X is tall* is judged true more frequently than (1), but it is also judged false more frequently. By comparing the percentage of agreement among those subjects indicating either agreement or disagreement (i.e. not the *can't tell*-option), Alxatib and Pelletier argue that (1) at 52.3% is more frequently judged true than '*X is tall*' at 50.8%.

Ripley's experiment Ripley [17] reports an experiment he conducted on contradictory sentences. Ripley's experiment uses graded acceptability judgments rather than just a binary true/false-choice. Ripley also confirms the intuition that borderline contradictions are most acceptable for borderline cases, and furthermore shows that this intuition holds across the following four different ways to express a borderline contradiction.

(2)   a. The circle is near the square and it is not near the square.
        b. The circle is and is not near the square.
        c. The circle neither is near the square nor is not near the square.
        d. The circle neither is nor isn't near the square.

Participants were assigned to one of these four conditions, so that each subject would only see one of the sentences in (2). They were then asked to indicate for seven different pictures whether they agreed with the sentence. Specifically, they were asked to indicate agreement on a scale from 1 to 7 (disagree to agree).

Ripley classifies subjects by distinct response patterns. The most frequent pattern Ripley refers to as the hump pattern, and describes it as follows: The maximum degree of agreement is indicated for one of the middle pictures, and agreement slopes down monotonically to both sides. This pattern is exhibited by more than 50% of the subjects in Ripley's experiment and corroborates the Alxatib and Pelletier finding just reported that borderline contradictions are most acceptable for borderline cases. Ripley describes furthermore that only about 10% of subjects indicate uniform disagreement to the contradictory statement in all conditions. This shows that Kamp's and Fine's intuition that classical contradictions should *surely* be judged wrong are not reflected directly in most speakers' intuitions, but only in the judgments of a small minority.

Moreover, Ripley reports the average amount of agreement: The maximum amount of agreement is 4.1, slightly above the midpoint of Ripley's 1 to 7 scale. The picture with this amount of agreement is one of the middle pictures, and the average amount of agreement also exhibits the hump patterns that the majority of individuals exhibit.

Finally, Ripley compares the four different conditions in (2) that he used in his experiment. Ripley reports that in his study there was no significant difference between the versions a and c without ellipsis and the b and d versions with ellipsis. This result, as Ripley points out, is important in evaluating proposals that trace back contradiction tolerance to an ambiguity in the vague term involved like the one of Kamp and Partee [9]. A second comparison, Ripley reports is between the conjunctive version a and b and the disjunctive ones in c and d. In this comparison, as well, the differences are not significant.

Discussion Both summarized papers confirm the intuition that borderline contradictions are generally found to be quite acceptable. The highest degree of agreement is found for the borderline cases. We could probably still attribute this agreement to classical contradictions entirely to pragmatics (*pace* Ripley [17]), but *prima facie* it provides support for a non-classical logic where at least some contradictions are acceptable. If we accept that, the argument against fuzzy logic presented in Section 1 doesn't go through any longer.

Does this mean that now we can adopt fuzzy logic for language interpretation? While this is mostly an open question, there is some indication in the data above already that indicated that borderline contradictions are actually still a problem for fuzzy logic. Not because their semantic value is 0 as in the classical argument, but because now their semantic value is higher than predicted by fuzzy logic. Specifically, I noted that agreement to $A \land \neg A$ is greater than agreement to either A and $\neg A$ in Alxatib and Pelletier's results, though only marginally so. At the same time, I would not expect agreement to a conjunction $A \land B$ to be higher than that of either conjunct (i.e. clear non-monotonicity) unless A and B stand in some logical or pragmatic relation to each other. In the following section, I report on a new experiment that confirms this intuition.

2.2 Dialetheism and fuzzy logic: an experimental test

My main goal in this section is to examine, whether fuzzy logic is suitable for linguistic purposes if dialetheism is accepted as the basis for data like those reported in the previous section. The experimental results by Alxatib and Pelletier [1] and Ripley [17] show that the argument against fuzzy logic for linguistic semantics by Kamp [8] and Fine [4]

pair	A/B	sentence
1	A	A 5′10″-guy is tall.
	B	A guy with $100,000 is rich.
2	A	A car driving at 70 mph is fast.
	B	A 250 page book is thick.
3	A	A 83 degree Fahrenheit day is hot.
	B	A town 45 miles away is far.
4	A	A 2 hour flight is long.
	B	A 50 year old guy is old.
5	A	A 3280-foot mountain is high.
	B	A 10 day vacation is long.

Figure 1. Basic Borderline Statements.

is less clear-cut that it was previously made out to be. Given that there is some experimental support for dialetheism that option needs to be considered, and Kamp and Fine failed to do so.

A crucial prediction fuzzy logic makes is truth-functionality of conjunction. I.e. if a and b have the same truth value, $a \wedge \neg a$ and $b \wedge \neg a$ have the same truth value too. However, intuitively this is not how borderline contradictions seem to behave in language: If we are talking about a 5′10″-guy with kind-of-blondish hair, I find *'He's a tall blond guy.'* much more difficult to swallow than *'He's both tall and not tall.'* Here *tall blond* may receive a non-intersective interpretation, but imagine being in New York and then compare *'Boston is large and far away.'* with *'Boston is large and not large.'*—the latter seems more acceptable to me. I now describe an experiment I conducted to confirm this intuition experimentally. Specifically, my goal was to investigate the case where A, B, $\neg A$, and $\neg B$ are agreed to at the 50% level. My expectation was that the borderline contradictions $A \wedge \neg A$ and $B \wedge \neg B$ would be more acceptable than the crossed conjunctions $A \wedge \neg B$ and $B \wedge \neg A$.

Pre-test To confirm the intuitions just mentioned experimentally, the main problem is that the ideal test would require two sentences judged true to exactly the same degree. But it is not realistic to find such sentences. I decided to settle for sentences in the 40% to 60% range. I decided to start with using a greater set of sentences than just two, and only use those in the analysis that satisfy the identity of truth value requirement. So, we need several statements at the borderline. To determine suitable borderline values, I conducted a pre-test. The test was conducted over the internet using the Amazon MTurk platform. 50 subjects participated and each received 10 cents for the participation. The subjects read a short instruction, part of which told them people are often not strictly logical. Then subjects were asked to answer twelve questions such as *How tall is a guy who is tall and not tall? (in inches)*. It was assumed that the median response would represent a borderline value for the respective predicate. The sentences shown in Figure 1 were constructed from the result as basic borderline propositions. For example, the median response to the question mentioned above was 70. From this the basic borderline proposition in the first line (i.e. pair 1, sentence A) of Figure 1 was derived: *'A 5′10″*

ba-	*A*	A 5′10″-guy is tall.
sic	*B*	A guy with $100,000 is rich.
nega-	¬*A*	A 5′10″-guy isn't tall.
tions	¬*B*	A guy with $100,000 isn't rich.
contra-	*A* ∧ ¬*B*	A 5′10″-guy is tall and a guy with $100,000 isn't rich.
dictions	*B* ∧ ¬*A*	A guy with $100,000 is rich and a 5′10″-guy isn't tall.
conjunc-	*A* ∧ ¬*A*	A 5′10″-guy is tall and a 5′10″-guy isn't tall.
tions	*B* ∧ ¬*B*	A guy with $100,000 is rich and a guy with $100,000 isn't rich.

Figure 2. Sample conditions used in the main experiment (pair 1).

(i.e. 70 inches) guy is tall.'. In Figure 1, the propositions are furthermore grouped into pairs of *A* and *B*, which play a role in the construction of the main experimental items as described in the following section.

Subjects, method, and materials quad The main experiment also was conducted over the internet using the Amazon MTurk platform. 100 subjects participated, and the only selection criterion used was that their HIT-acceptance rate as reported by the Amazon system be greater than 50%.[6] Subjects' gender, native language, and country of residence were reported, but not used as exclusion criteria.

The experiment used eight conditions per pair of items, which are illustrated in Figure 2. The example conditions in 2 are drawn from the pair 1 of borderline values of Figure 1. The other conditions were created in the same manner out of each of the subsequent pairs of lines of Figure 1. The conditions were created to test both the agreement to individual conjuncts, as well as to the conjunctions. In particular, both the borderline assertions *A* and *B* and their negations ¬*A* and ¬*B* were tested because the comparison of the conjunctions would be relevant for my goals only if all four of these received truth value 0.5. The crucial comparison then is between the two classical contradictions *AnA* and *BnB* on the one hand and the non-contradictions *AnB* and *BnA* on the other. Note that the conditions were designed so as to make sure that all conditions would have a negation in the second conjunct. This was done so that all four of these conditions would have comparable grammatical and logical complexity.

Five different questionnaires were created from the experimental items. This was done to make sure that each subject would see each basic item *A* or *B* only once in the experiment, either on its own or as part of a more complex sentence. Recall that there were five pairs (*A*, *B*) of the basic borderline assertions created from Figure 1. So, then for example one questionnaire may have contained *A* and *B* of pair 1, ¬*A* and ¬*B* of pair 2, *A* ∧ ¬*B* of pair 3, *B* ∧ ¬*A* of pair 4, and *A* ∧ ¬*A* and *B* ∧ ¬*B* of pair 5. Each questionnaire therefore contained eight experimental items. In addition, twelve filler sentences were added to each questionnaire. The order of sentences was randomized individually in each questionnaire.

The subjects were divided into five groups of twenty. Each group was assigned one of the questionnaires. Subjects were instructed that the questionnaire was not a math

---

[6]Work conducted within the MTurk platform is always reviewed by the requesters and then either accepted or rejected. The HIT-acceptance rate indicates how often an individual's work has been accepted in the past.

test, but one of how true they felt the sentences are. Furthermore, they were given some examples of such intermediate truth, namely 95% for *'The Earth is round'* since it is not perfectly round, 50% for *'Mammals are furry'*. Subjects were then asked to indicate for each of the test items how true they felt it was.

Results and Discussion All values given by the subjects were in the 0 to 100 range, even though there were no restrictions on the input implemented in the html-code—i.e. a subject could have entered any alphanumeric string. So, that all responses were in range shows that subjects had paid attention to the instructions. Some subjects skipped single questions, but only 4 of 2000 data points were missing.

The average relative agreement to A, B, $\neg A$, and $\neg B$ was never exactly 50%. However, it had been decided to consider those items further where the relative agreement for each of A, B, $\neg A$, and $\neg B$ was between 40% and 60%. Only pair 1 of the conditions satisfied this requirement. The means for eight conditions in the four excluded conditions are shown in Figure 3.[7] The data in Figure 4 shows the average relative agreement (mean) and the standard error (SE) for each of the eight conditions of pair 1:

pair	A	$\neg A$	B	$\neg B$	$A \wedge \neg A$	$B \wedge \neg B$	$A \wedge \neg B$	$B \wedge \neg A$
2	54.6	47.1	**34.8**	59.9	52.5	42.3	53.1	42.4
3	47.9	**22.1**	59.8	**70.3**	51.6	54.9	50.6	46.4
4	**30.3**	**18.7**	54.6	69.8	27.5	72.0	43.1	56.2
5	**63.5**	**34.8**	55.2	49.9	45.6	49.3	60.8	43.8

Figure 3. Mean agreement in % for excluded pairs (violations marked by boldface).

	borderline				contradiction		conjunction	
	A	$\neg A$	B	$\neg B$	$A \wedge \neg A$	$B \wedge \neg B$	$A \wedge \neg B$	$B \wedge \neg A$
mean	45	42	45.75	47.25	48.15	46.5	43.2	25.65
SE	(6.7)	(6.0)	(7.0)	(7.0)	(4.3)	(6.1)	(4.3)	(5.4)

Figure 4. Mean agreement in % and standard error (SE) for pair 1.

The agreement to $A \wedge \neg A$ and $B \wedge \neg B$ is lower than we expected given that the basic propositions were borderline. To compare borderline propositions, A, B, $\neg A$, and $\neg B$, with the classical contradictions, $A \wedge \neg A$ and $B \wedge \neg B$, a Welch two sample t-test was computed. The difference was shown to not be significant at the $p < 0.05$ level $(t(103.4) = -0.50, p = 0.62)$. This is, however, in line with the findings Ripley [17], who attributes the low agreement to borderline contradictions to cultural influence. Another reason may have been the greater grammatical and logical complexity of the contradiction items compared to the basic borderline propositions.

The more telling comparison is that between borderline contradictions and non-contradictory conjunctions. We find 47.3% agreement to the contradictions, $A \wedge \neg A$

---

[7] As Libor Běhounek (p.c.) points out, the comparison of sentence A of pair 2 and sentence B of pair 4 indicates that truth functionality more generally doesn't hold for graded truth judgments: Though the basic formulas are judged the same in the mean, the derived formulas ¬A and ¬B respectively are judged differently (with the difference likely to be significant, though I haven't tested this).

and $B \wedge \neg B$, compared to only 34.4% agreement to the non-contradictory conjunctions, $A \wedge \neg B$ and $B \wedge \neg A$. A Welch two sample t-test was computed to compare the two conditions. The test showed that subjects agreed to the borderline contradictions significantly more frequently than to the non-contradictory conjunctions at the $p < 0.05$ level ($t(77.0) = 2.60, p = 0.011$). The result shows an account of agreement levels based on fuzzy logic would not make the right prediction for conjunctions of borderline cases.

The experimental result therefore disconfirms the predictions of an account of speakers' graded truth judgments based solely on fuzzy logic.

3   Conclusions

The main point of this paper argues that fuzzy logic cannot provide a complete model for linguistic semantics of vagueness: Though speakers have no problems assigning intermediate truth values to sentences, the truth values assigned to complex sentences aren't systematic in a way that a fuzzy logic would predict. Therefore, adopting a fuzzy logic instead of a classical one doesn't provide a better approach to vagueness. In both cases, the account of truth-value judgments for complex sentences containing vague predicates cannot be that of the logical system, but needs to be relegated to pragmatics.

For the most part, I discussed the semantics of borderline contradictions such as *'She is tall and she is not tall.'* . Specifically I showed experimentally that the truth-functionality assumed by fuzzy logic fails. This finding holds regardless of whether we take the classical position that borderline contradictions are really contradictory (i.e. semantic value 0) or the dialethetist position where the semantic value of borderline contradictions is assumed to be the one speakers' intuitions actually assign to it, i.e. some truth value greater than 0. The specific problems the two positions give rise to are different though: For the classical position, the problem is simply that, if two logically unrelated A and B have the same semantic value, $A \wedge \neg A$ is less true than $B \wedge \neg A$ is judged to be. For the dialethetist position, the problem is the data I show above: When two logically unrelated A and B that have essentially the same semantic value, $A \wedge \neg A$ is judged more true than $B \wedge \neg A$ is. So, either way we cannot derive the semantic value of $A \wedge \neg A$ by applying a T-norm * to the semantic values of A and $\neg A$ that we would also apply to in evaluating $B \wedge \neg A$. This cannot be captured by a truth-functional logic, including a fuzzy one.

The results have implications for the account of vagueness in language beyond being problematic for classical and fuzzy logic. Fuzzy logic specifically cannot account for the data discussed because it builds vagueness directly into the logical composition. The data discussed speak instead for a separation of vagueness and logical composition, i.e. systems with the following two components: 1) a parameter of evaluation relating to vagueness and 2) a not fully truth-functional logic. Such parametric systems include epistemic approaches as well as sub- and super-valuation, and even ones such as fuzzy pluri-valuationism of Smith [19] where their non-vague logic is a fuzzy logic. The parametric approaches differ with respect to the nature of the paramater of evaluation and also with respect to the nature of the non-vague logic. The semantic value of a sentence is then determined from the results of evaluating the sentence relative to one or more parameter settings—in the case of vague expressions, typically more than one parameter setting would need to be considered. Specifically, if we have a probabilistic measure $\int$ on the parameter space P, truth judgments on sentences could be related to $\int_{p \in P} f(p) \partial p$ as is done, for instance, by Lassiter [12].

While our main result doesn't tell us much about the nature of the parameters, the experimental results discussed in Section 2—specifically the new finding showing that borderline contradictions are of higher acceptability than conjunctions of two unrelated propositions—tell us something about the non-vague logic used. Namely, none of these results are straightforwardly predicted if the logic used is completely classical. I think it is still possible to maintain a classical logic and allow the evaluation parameters to be shifted quite freely in the course of the evaluation of a sentence. But, a non-classical logic together with a parameter for vagueness provides a more straightforward account of the data.

BIBLIOGRAPHY

[1] Sam Alxatib and Jeffrey Pelletier. On the psychology of truth-gaps. In Nouwen et al. [14], pages 13–36.

[2] Nicolao Bonini, Daniel Osherson, Riccardo Viale, and Tim Williamson. On the psychology of vague predicates. *Mind and Language*, 14:377–393, 1999.

[3] Antonín Dvořák and Vilém Novák. Formal theories and linguistic descriptions. *Fuzzy Sets and Systems*, 143(1):169–188, 2004.

[4] Kit Fine. Vagueness, truth, and logic. *Synthese*, 30:265–300, 1975.

[5] Paul Grice. *Studies in the Way of Words*. Harvard University Press, Cambridge, Mass., 1989.

[6] Petr Hájek. *Metamathematics of Fuzzy Logic*. Springer, 1998.

[7] Petr Hájek. Fuzzy logic. In Edward N. Zalta, editor, *The Stanford Encyclopedia of Philosophy*. Spring 2009 edition, 2009.

[8] Hans Kamp. Two theories of adjectives. In Edward Keenan, editor, *Formal Semantics of Natural Languages*, pages 123–155. Cambridge University Press, 1975.

[9] Hans Kamp and Barbara H. Partee. Prototype theory and compositionality. *Cognition*, 57:129–191, 1995.

[10] George Lakoff. Hedges: A study in meaning criteria and the logic of fuzzy concepts. *Journal of Philosophical Logic*, 2:458–508, 1973.

[11] Peter Lasersohn. Pragmatic halos. *Language*, 75:522–551, 1999.

[12] Daniel Lassiter. Vagueness as probabilistic linguistic knowledge. In Nouwen et al. [14].

[13] Richard Montague. The proper treatment of quantification in ordinary English. In R.H. Thomason, editor, *Formal Philosophy: Selected Papers of Richard Montague*, pages 247–270. Yale University Press, New Haven, Conn., 1974[1970].

[14] Rick Nouwen, Robert van Rooij, Uli Sauerland, and Hans-Christian Schmitz, editors. *Vagueness in Communication*. Springer, Heidelberg, Germany, 2011.

[15] Vilem Novák. Antonyms and linguistic quantifiers in fuzzy logic. *Fuzzy Sets and Systems*, 124(3): 335–351, 2001.

[16] Nicholas Rescher. *Many-Valued Logic*. McGraw-Hill, New York, N.Y., 1969.

[17] David J. Ripley. Contradictions at the borders. In Nouwen et al. [14], pages 169–188.

[18] Stephen Schiffer. Vagueness and partial belief. *Philosophical Issues*, pages 220–257, 2000.

[19] Nicholas J. J. Smith. *Vagueness and Degrees of Truth*. Oxford University Press, USA, 2009.

Uli Sauerland

Zentrum für Allgemeine Sprachwissenschaft (Center for General Linguistics)

Schützenstr. 18

10117 Berlin, Germany

Email: uli@alum.mit.edu

Comments on *Vagueness in Language: The Case Against Fuzzy Logic Revisited* by Uli Sauerland

CHRISTIAN G. FERMÜLLER

Uli Sauerland's contribution to this volume is very important indeed, since it addresses a question of central relevance to anyone interested in logical approaches to reasoning in face of vagueness: why has fuzzy logic been so thoroughly discarded, and consequently neglected, by linguists as a possible tool for modeling vague language? The main "culprit" is quickly identified to be Hans Kamp's seemingly very influential paper "Two theories of adjectives" from 1975. (We refer to Sauerland's paper for precise references.) Clearly it is time for revisiting Kamp's arguments, variations of which, as Sauerland points out, can actually be found in a number of other places as well, including Rescher's classic monograph on many-valued logic. Of course one may and should also ask why engineers, mathematicians, and logicians who propagate fuzzy logic as a tool for handling vague propositions and predicates have largely ignored the work of semanticists of natural language. I think that an analysis of Kamp's arguments is a good starting point for answering that latter question too. However, my own assessment is somewhat different from Sauerland's. In particular I think that a number of implicit, but essential methodological assumptions, that separate natural language semantics from mathematical fuzzy logic, are largely to be blamed for the mutual disinterest if not outright dismissal. This would hardly be of much interest, if it were not the case that both disciplines claim that "models of vague language" are important items on their respective research agenda.[1]

Sauerland recapitulates Kamp's argument in a clear and succinct manner, that nicely assists its analysis from a contemporary point of view. I do not want to go into all components of the argument here, but rather want to focus on three aspects that may serve to illustrate what I mean by implicit underlying methodological principles that I think are relevant here: (1) logical contradictions, (2) ambiguity of logical connectives, and (3) truth-functionality.

1. Kamp claims that it is "absurd" to assign the value $\frac{1}{2}$, or in fact any other value but 0, to a sentence of the form $\phi \wedge \neg\phi$, asking rhetorically "how could a logical contradiction be true to *any* degree?" I find it interesting that seemingly only quite recently linguistic research has been conducted that confirms an intuition that not only in fuzzy logics,

---

[1] The situation is considerably complicated by the fact that the term "fuzzy logic" is used to label quite distinct areas of engineering, mathematics, and more recently mathematical logic, as pointed out at many places of this volume. However for the purpose of this short comment we may ignore these complications and focus on the question whether the family t-norm based fuzzy logics is of potential relevance in the context of formal models of reasoning with vague propositions and concepts.

but also, e.g., in paraconsistent logics is taken for granted. Namely that competent speakers are quite ready to accept—at least to some degree—sentences of the indicated contradictory form if vague predicates are involved. One can of course maintain that an acceptance of an utterance like "He is nice and not nice" indicates that it has to be read as "He is nice in one respect but not so in another respect". But the experiments by Alxatib/Pelletier and by Ripley, that Sauerland comments on, indicate considerable agreement to sentences where the involved gradable predicates make it very difficult to argue that they are not of the logical form $\phi \wedge \neg\phi$.

Of course, fuzzy logicians are quick to point out that acceptability is routinely a matter of degree, anyway. According to their approach the acceptability of ϕ and $\neg\phi$ to *equal degree*, rather than spelling logical disaster, only indicates the presence of a clear borderline case. There is no need to advertise here the benefits of such an approach, e.g., in dealing with sorites series. However fuzzy logicians often show little understanding of a methodological principle that seems to be implicit in almost all relevant linguistic literature: treat acceptability as a bivalent category; i.e., truth-conditions should be formulated in a manner that allows one to decide whether they apply or not, once the context is fixed and all relevant ambiguities are sorted out. I presume—and even think to understand myself well enough—that there good reasons for adhering to this principle in linguistics. In fact I submit that fuzzy logicians mostly respect an analogous principle themselves: treat validity and logical consequence as bivalent categories. Of course, there is also work on graded consequence and other forms of "fuzzification" of the meta-level. However even there, on pain of violating well established scientific standards, one better remains grounded in good old classical (bivalent) mathematics at the appropriate level of investigation. But of course working in classical mathematics (on the meta-level) does not prevent one to study non-classical models.

2. A standard reply of fuzzy logicians to the charge that a sentence of the form "*A* and not *A*" should receive the value 0 is to point out that in Łukasiewicz logic (and in many other logics for that matter) one can choose between two different forms of conjunction: strong conjunction (t-norm conjunction), with $\phi \& \neg\phi$ always yielding 0, and weak conjunction (lattice conjunction), where $\phi \wedge \neg\phi$ may receive any value between 0 and $\frac{1}{2}$. This of course triggers the question whether "and" could be ambiguous. To a logician this question may seem naive, since from the viewpoint of modern logic the answer is obvious: of course we can and should distinguish different forms of conjunction, i.e., different meanings of "and"! One of the hallmarks of the important area of substructural logics is the distinction between "additive" and "multiplicative" versions of connectives like conjunction. But also other logics, like some that are successfully applied in software verification, demonstrate the need to distinguish between different forms of conjunction in particular contexts. T-norm based fuzzy logics are certainly in good company here: in fact there are strong analogies between the weak/strong distinction in (e.g.) Łukasiewicz logic and the additive/multiplicative distinction in (e.g.) Girard's linear logic.

The fact that contemporary logic, for the most part, wholeheartedly embraces pluralism not only at the level of different logical systems but frequently also differentiates forms of conjunction within a single system, does not answer the question whether the word "and" is ambiguous in standard English (disregarding its extensions to specific mathematical and technical vocabularies). I presume that many linguists will disagree with my conviction that the latter question is unanswerable empirically. After all well accepted methods, in particular the ellipsis test, seem to be available for testing for ambiguity. But I have never seen any of these tests applied successfully to words that correspond to logical connectives and I strongly doubt that it can be done at all. Sauerland dismisses the idea that "and" might be lexically ambiguous as "clearly *ad hoc*" without presenting further arguments. However this only confirms my conviction that not clear empirical facts, but rather certain methodological presuppositions are at play here. From conversations with linguists I have learned that to support the idea that "and" might be ambiguous one should at least be able to point to languages where the allegedly different forms of conjunctions are indeed expressed by different words. It so happens that I currently struggle to learn a bit of Khmer (Cambodian). I was quite surprised to be exposed already in the first two lessons of my textbook[2] to three different Khmer expressions that are all translated simply as "and" there, but that seemingly are not used fully interchangeably http://www.english-khmer.com/ returns two distinct Khmer words for "and"). Note that I do not claim to have found a language that witnesses the ambiguity of conjunction. In fact, I can think of various alternative explanations for having different words in a language that all roughly correspond to the English "and". I only want to emphasize that if, on the one hand, logicians and computer scientists have good reasons to distinguish between distinct forms of conjunctions and, on the other hand, linguists find good reasons to insist that there is only one core meaning of the word "and", then this is not because one of the two disciplines got it all wrong. It rather indicates that the question what the word "and" means and, in particular, whether it is ambiguous cannot be answered satisfactorily without subscribing to a whole package of theoretical and methodological assumptions that reflect different research goals and traditions.

3. As recognized by Sauerland (see his footnote 3 on a corresponding observation by Libor Běhounek) the main problem with a "naive" attempt to use fuzzy logic to model the meaning of vague language, as derived from observable behavior of competent speakers, is its insistence on truth-functionality.[3] But again, I think that a quite fundamental methodological confusion is sometimes impeding discussions about "models of reasoning with vague language" in logics and linguistics, respectively. The particular confusion that I have in mind, however, seems to be easily resolvable by pointing out the ambiguity of the word "model" here. Whereas linguists aim for a systematic *description* of observable linguistic behavior—or so the story goes—logicians prefer their formal models to be interpreted *prescriptively*, as tools for successful reasoning, in particular in scenarios where the degree of nesting of logical operators transcends levels commonly observed in natural language use. Truth-functionality is a good case in point. In fact we need not focus on fuzzy logic to understand the issue. Already for classical logic it is clear that the principle of truth-functionality is not well reflected in the actual behavior of human agents in face of logically complex reasoning tasks. Nor is the actual use

---

[2]Richard K. Gilbert, Sovandy Hang: "Cambodian for Beginners", Paiboon Publishing, 2004.

[3]In this short comment, I have to remain silent on the various fuzzy logic based models (in a wider sense) that are decidedly not truth-functional. Didier Dubois's contribution to this volume discusses some of them. But he also emphasizes that fuzziness and vagueness are to be treated as two distinct features anyway.

of simple natural language phrases of the form "If A then B", "A and B", etc., always directly conforming to the corresponding classical truth tables. Yet it is hard to deny that imposing truth-functionality is a very useful methodological principle for (a certain type of) "models of reasoning". A familiar analogous case is probabilistic reasoning: while psychologists point out that human reasoners hardly adhere to the mathematical laws of probability theory, one can also demonstrate in which sense and under which circumstances they actually *should* do so.

The issue about using truth-functional logics for modeling observable linguistic behavior is often taken to be fully settled by the above remarks: logics (including fuzzy logics) are prescriptive tools, but linguists strive for formal descriptions of natural language features as reflected in empirical data. However I think that this plea for non-interference is definitely too quick. First of all, the heavy use of logical machinery (largely of higher order classical and intensional logics) witnesses the fact that formal logic is not just a prescriptive tool, but undoubtedly useful also in defining complex descriptive models, if not handled too naively. The latter qualification is meant to emphasize the well known fact that, whatever we mean by the "logical form" of a sentence in natural language, we can hardly expect it to be obvious or always easily and uniquely determined. Secondly, I maintain that not only logicians, but also semanticists of natural language, abstract away considerably from "naked" empirical data when constructing their models. As we know well from philosophy and history of science: observations are always theory-laden; and that is not a defect, but rather a constructive hallmark of scientific reasoning. On the other hand, fuzzy logicians cannot credibly claim that they do not care at all about natural language use, but only aim at purely prescriptive models that provide examples of interesting mathematical artifacts. Such claims clearly contradict the manner in which the considerable amount of research on "fuzzy linguistic variables", "linguistic hedges", "fuzzy quantifiers", etc., is motivated and explained.

It is probably still too early to judge whether an interaction between mathematical fuzzy logic and natural language semantics that is profitable for both sides is worthwhile and feasible. I think that the work of Uli Sauerland and a number of his colleagues in linguistics justifies cautious optimism: it witnesses a level of interest in contemporary fuzzy logics that, with hindsight, renders the all too brief encounter between the two fields in the 1970s a rather unhappy historical fact. Needless to say that I eagerly hope for more awareness of contemporary linguistic research on vagueness on the side of fuzzy logic as well. In any case, I am convinced that a better mutual understanding of the often quite different aims, methods, and theoretical as well as cultural background of the two research fields will prove to be profitable well beyond attempts to simply combine techniques originating in different corners of expertise about the multi-faceted phenomenon of vagueness.

Christian G. Fermüller
Vienna University of Technology
Favoritenstr. 9–11/E1852
A-1040 Wien, Austria
Email: chrisf@logic.at

Reply to Christian Fermüller's Comments on *Vagueness in Language: The Case Against Fuzzy Logic Revisited*

ULI SAUERLAND[1]

Two of the linguistic papers in this volume—the one by Galit Sassoon and my own—though outwardly critical, seek a dialog with fuzzy logic. Thankfully, Chris Fermüller has taken up the dialog and the discussion has already been fertile—more on this later. Mainly though, this note is about the nature of idealization in linguistic research in general and in the specific case of *and*.

Idealization is a necessity in linguistic research. Verifiable theories in all empirical sciences rest on idealizations: point masses, perfect vacuums in physics, complete purity or homogenous mixture in chemistry, homogenous populations of species in biology. If anything, linguistics must rely even more so on idealization since linguistic data are extremely rich: the ways in any individual can relate to even a short sequence of words (or even made up word-like sound sequences) go far beyond acceptance and are affected by a multitude of factors. The *systematic description of observable linguistic behavior*, therefore, only plays only a supporting role in linguistic research as Fermüller also hints. Linguists idealize at various levels depending on their theoretical goals. In many cases, indeed, a successful research strategy has been to maximize idealization as much as possible up to almost loosing any relation to empirical observation (e.g. the minimalist program in syntax of Chomsky [2]).

The drive for idealization perhaps explains the linguists' attraction to the classical semantics of *and* even more so than the argument of Kamp I review. Two relevant layers of idealization for the semantics of *and* are the distinction between competence and performance and that between semantics and pragmatics. The competence/performance distinction involves many factors, but for example whether we ask for a rash judgment or a more considered one. The semantics/pragmatics distinction assumes a separation between a bare, rather abstract sentence meaning perhaps just consisting of truth conditions and principles of sentence use that apply to the sentence meaning in a conversation scenario. Pragmatics is where most linguists would suspect the reason for the high acceptability of some sentences of the form $\phi \wedge \neg \phi$ lies while performance factors contribute additional noise. This presumption explains why there has been limited linguistic interest in such phenomena. Because of the nature of empirical research, data can only be evaluated against an interdependent network of theories that are, in the case of linguistics, at best partially understood. Assuming classical *and* as the semantics is attractive because it makes it easier to figure out some of the other components of the theory.

[1] I acknowledge again the financial support of the DFG grants SA 925/1 and SA 925/4, the latter within the ESF Eurocore LogiCCC project VAAG. In addition, this work was supported by the Bundesministerium für Bildung und Forschung (BMBF) (Grant Nr. 01UG0711). All errors are solely my responsibility.

The special role of classical *and* in cognition further motivates its status as the ideal for linguistic theory to adhere to. Fermüller mentions that at the meta-level even fuzzy logicians assume a classical (bivalent) semantics. I find it plausible that classical *and* is a conceptual universal in a broader sense like a platonic ideal though I am ignorant of relevant research on the matter. I suspect though that all of us, even a person fully ignorant of mathematics, will find it easy to adopt the concepts of bivalent propositional calculus including the meaning of *and*. Fuzzy logics with its variety of conjunction operators (of course, all converging on the classical *and* in a bivalent system) don't share this status. It's even worse that the system with $a \wedge b = \min(a, b)$ and $\neg a = 1 - a$ that is of attractive simplicity to linguists (e.g. the one Kamp discusses) doesn't have the properties mathematicians desire most.

How would we know idealization has been taken to far? I should mention that some linguists (though not me) have even tried to subsume constituent coordination as in *John and Mary are married* under classical logical meaning of *and* [5]. I think the Khmer facts Fermüller mentions make it difficult to maintain this view: A recently published grammar of Khmer describes it a follows: "The par excellence use of *nwng* is to signal constituent coordination, while that of *haeuj* is to signal clause coordination." [3, p. 407]. Also Japanese and another 124 languages [4] have two distinct words for constituent and clause coordination like Khmer. But even such evidence isn't unequivocal and one needs to more carefully consider the Khmer data.

In recent work of mine and others [1], we actually advocate a theory that assumes that intermediate truth values are part the semantics of natural language. For conjunction, we propose a new semantics that is not truth-functional with respect to the extensions (i.e. the truth values), but applies to the intensions of its conjuncts. So, this is fuzzy logic with a slight modification. We think this enables us to account a little better for speakers' intuitions concerning examples of the $\phi \wedge \neg \phi$ type including those discussed in my main paper in this volume. Our work, in my own opinion, moves dangerously far away from the ideal of classical *and*. The example of fuzzy logic has given us the courage to propose this system, but the jury is still out whether the gain is worth adding anything to the classical system.

BIBLIOGRAPHY

[1] Sam Alxatib, Peter Pagin, and Uli Sauerland. Acceptable contradictions: Pragmatics or semantics? a reply to Cobreros et al. Submitted.
[2] Noam Chomsky. *The Minimalist Program*. MIT Press, Cambridge, Mass., 1995.
[3] Jon Haiman. *Cambodian: Khmer*. John Benjamins, 2011.
[4] Martin Haspelmath. Nominal and verbal conjunction. In Matthew S. Dryer and Martin Haspelmath, editors, *The World Atlas of Language Structures Online*. Max Planck Digital Library, Munich, 2011.
[5] Yoad Winter. *Flexibility principles in Boolean semantics: The interpretation of coordination, plurality, and scope in natural language*. The MIT Press, Cambridge, Mass., 2001.

Vagueness, Tolerance and Non-Transitive Entailment

ROBERT VAN ROOIJ[1]

1 Tolerance and vagueness

Vagueness is standardly opposed to precision. Just as gradable adjectives like 'tall' and a quantity modifier like 'a lot' are prototypically vague expressions, mathematical adjectives like 'rectangular', and measure phrases like '1.80 meters' are prototypically precise. But what does it mean for these latter expressions to be precise? On first thought it just means that they have an exact mathematical definition. However, if we want to use these terms to talk about observable objects, it is clear that these mathematical definitions would be useless: if they exist at all, we cannot possibly determine what are the existing (non-mathematical) rectangular objects in the precise geometrical sense, or objects that are exactly 1.80 meters long. For this reason, one allows for a margin of measurement error, or a threshold, in physics, psychophysics and other sciences. The assumption that the predicates we use are observational predicates gives rise to another consequence as well. If statements like 'the length of stick S is 1.45 meters' come with a large enough margin of error, the circumstances in which this statement is appropriate (or true, if you don't want the notion of truth to be empty) might *overlap* with the appropriate circumstances for uttering statements like 'the length of stick S is 1.50 meters'. Thus, although the predicates 'being a stick of 1.45 meters' and 'being a stick of 1.50 meters' are inconsistent under a precise interpretation, the predicates might well be applicable to the same object when a margin of error is taken into account, i.e., when the predicates are interpreted tolerantly.[2] Thus, although the standard, i.e. precise, semantic meanings of two predicates might be *incompatible*, when one or both of these observational predicates are more realistically interpreted in a tolerant way, they might well be *compatible*.

[1]The main ideas of this paper were first presented in a workshop on vagueness at Pamplona, Spain in June, 2009. Paul Égré acted as a commentator on this paper and soon 'joined' the project. Shortly after, Pablo Cobreros and Dave Ripley joined the project as well, and thanks to them I now have a much better understanding of what I was actually proposing in Section 4 of this paper. I thank them for this, but in this paper I tried to stay as close as possible to my original contribution to the Pamplona workshop. Nevertheless, I still got rid of some needless complications, and used already some terminology that is used in our joint work as well (published as 'Tolerant, classical, strict' in the Journal of Philosophical Logic). The original idea of Section 4 came up during a talk of Elia Zardini, when I was trying to understand in my own terms what he was proposing. I would like to thank the anonymous reviewers for helpful comments and suggestions and Inés Crespo for checking my English.

[2]I don't want to suggest that 1.45 meters does not have a precise meaning, but just that if you want to make it meaningful in measurement, it cannot be as precise as one might hope. I will suggest that measurement error is closely related with what we call vagueness (see also Section 6.2). Wheeler (2002) rightly argues, in my opinion, that allowing for measurement errors is perhaps the most natural way to motivate paraconsistency in logic.

A traditional way of thinking about vagueness is in terms of the *existence of border-line cases*. If the sentence 'John is a tall man' is neither (clearly) true nor (clearly) false, then John is a borderline case of a tall man. As a result, predicates like 'tall' and 'bald' do not give rise to a two-fold, but rather to a three-fold partition of objects: the positive ones, the negatives ones, and the borderline cases. Authors like Dummett (1975), Wright (1975), Kamp (1981), and others have argued that the existence of borderline cases is inadequate to characterize vagueness. Instead, what we have to realize is that these pred-icates are *observational predicates* that give rise to *tolerance*: a vague predicate is insen-sitive to very small changes in the objects to which it can be meaningfully predicated.

If being tolerant to small changes is indeed *constitutive* to the meaning of vague predicates, it seems that most approaches to vagueness went wrong. Consider the Sorites paradox: from (i) a giant is tall, (ii) a dwarf is not, and (iii) if a is tall and not significantly taller than b, b must be tall as well (the inductive premise), we derive a contradiction, if we consider enough individuals with enough different lengths. Trying to account for this paradox, most approaches claim that the inductive premise is false. But it is exactly this inductive premise stating that the relevant predicate is tolerant. In this paper I argue, instead, that the tolerance principle is valid with respect to a natural notion of truth and consequence. What we should give up is the idea that this notion of consequence is transitive. In this paper I will first introduce semi-orders and non-transitive similarity relations in Section 2. In terms of that, I discuss traditional approaches to vagueness in Section 3 before I introduce my own account in Section 4. In Section 5 I show that my analysis is still closely related to other analyses. In the last section I will connect my analysis to more general theories of concept-analysis in cognitive theories of meaning.

2   The Sorites and semi-orders

Consider a long series of people ordered in terms of their height, from tallest to shortest; however the variance between any two adjacent people is indistinguishable (even though one is taller than the other in the precise sense, one cannot tell in practice which one is smaller). Of each of them you are asked whether he or she is tall. Let's suppose that you judge the shortest one to definitely be short (hence, not tall). Now consider the tallest person. If you decide that this person is tall, it seems only reasonable to judge the second individual to be tall as well, since you cannot distinguish by observation their heights. But, then, by the same token, the third person must be tall as well, and so on indefinitely. In particular, this makes also the last person tall, which is in contradiction with what we have assumed before.

This so-called Sorites reasoning is elementary, based only on our intuition that the first individual is tall, the last short, and the following inductive premise, which seems unobjectable:

> **(P)**   If you call one individual tall, and this individual is not visibly taller
> than another individual, you have to call the other one tall too.

Our above Sorites reasoning involved the predicate 'tall', but that was obviously not essential. Take any predicate P that gives rise to a complete ordering 'as P as' with respect to a domain of objects D. Let us assume that '$\sim_P$' is the indistinguishability, or indifference, relation between individuals with respect to predicate P. Now we can state the inductive premise somewhat more formally as follows:

(**P**)   For any $x, y \in D$: $(Px \wedge x \sim_P y) \rightarrow Py$.

If we assume that it is possible that $\exists x_1, \ldots, x_n$: $x_1 \sim_P x_2 \wedge \cdots \wedge x_{n-1} \sim_P x_n$, but Px_1 and $\neg Px_n$, the paradox will arise. It immediately follows that the relation $\sim_P$ cannot be an equivalence relation. It is natural to define the indifference relation $\sim_P$ from an ordering relation 'P-er than', $\succ_P$. For many purposes it is natural to let the relation $\succ_P$ be a strict weak order:

DEFINITION 1 A *strict weak order* is a structure $\langle D, R \rangle$, with R a binary relation on D that is irreflexive (IR), transitive (TR), and almost connected (AC):

(IR) $\forall x$: $\neg R(x, x)$
(TR) $\forall x, y, z$: $(R(x, y) \wedge R(y, z)) \rightarrow R(x, z)$
(AC) $\forall x, y, z$: $R(x, y) \rightarrow (R(x, z) \vee R(z, y))$

If we now define the indifference relation, '$\sim_P$', as follows: $x \sim_P y$ iff$_{def}$ neither $x \succ_P y$ nor $y \succ_P x$, it is clear that '$\sim_P$' is an equivalence relation. But this means that strict weak orders cannot be used to derive the relevant indifference relation for vagueness.

Fortunately, there is a well-known ordering that does have the desired properties: what Luce (1956) calls a *semi-order*. Semi-orders were introduced by Luce in economics to account for the intuition that the notion of 'indifference' is not transitive:

> A person may be indifferent between 100 and 101 grains of sugar in his coffee, indifferent between 101 and 102, ..., and indifferent between 4999 and 5000. If indifference were transitive he would be indifferent between 100 and 5000 grains, and this is probably false. (Luce, 1956)

Luce's argument fits well with Fechner's (1860) claim, based on psychophysics experiments, that our ability to discriminate between stimuli is generally not transitive. Of course, the problem Luce discusses is just a variant of the Sorites paradox. Luce (1956) introduces semi-orders as an order that gives rise to a non-transitive similarity relation. Following Scott & Suppes' (1958) (equivalent, but still) simpler definition, a structure $\langle D, R \rangle$, with R a binary relation on D, is a semi-order just in case R is irreflexive (IR), satisfies the interval-order (IO) condition, and is semi-transitive (STr).[3]

DEFINITION 2 A *semi-order* is a structure $\langle D, R \rangle$, with R a binary relation on D that satisfies the following conditions:

(IR) $\forall x$: $\neg R(x, x)$
(IO) $\forall x, y, v, w$: $(R(x, y) \wedge R(v, w)) \rightarrow (R(x, w) \vee R(v, y))$
(STr) $\forall x, y, z, v$: $(R(x, y) \wedge R(y, z)) \rightarrow (R(x, v) \vee R(v, z))$

---

[3] Any relation that is irreflexive and satisfies the interval-order condition is called an *interval order*. All interval orders are also transitive, meaning that they are stronger than strict partial orders.

It is important to see that if we interpret the relation '$\succ_P$' as a semi-order, it is irreflexive and transitive, but it need not be almost connected. Informally, this means that according to this ordering the statement '$x \succ_P y$' means that x is *significantly* or *noticeably P*-er than y (if 'P' is 'tall', '*noticeably P*-er than' could be '2 cm taller than', for instance, see the role of ε below). The fact that semi-orders are irreflexive and transitive but not almost connected, is important for us. The reason is that in terms of '$\succ_P$' we can define our desired similarity relation '$\sim_P$' as follows: $x \sim_P y$ iff neither $x \succ_P y$ nor $y \succ_P x$. The relation '$\sim_P$' is reflexive and symmetric, but need not be transitive. Thus, '$\sim_P$' does not give rise to an equivalence relation. Intuitively, '$x \sim_P y$' means that there is no significant, or noticiceable, difference between x and y. I believe semi-orders capture most of our intuitions about vagueness.[4] Semi-orders can be given a measure-theoretical interpretation in a weak sense. '$x \succ_P y$' is true iff there is a real-valued function f_P and some fixed (small) real number ε (the *margin of error*) such that $f_P(x) > f_P(y) + \varepsilon$ (see Luce, 1956). Thus, if we fix the margin of error to 2 cm, for instance, it would mean that x is significantly taller than y iff x is at least 2 cm taller than y. In the same way '$x \sim_P y$' is true if the difference in P-ness between x and y is less than or equal to ε, $|f_P(x) - f_P(y)| \leq \varepsilon$. In case $\varepsilon = 0$, i.e., if there is no margin of error, the semi-order is a strict weak order.

3 Solving the Sorites by weakening (P)

The standard reaction to the Sorites paradox is to say that the argument is valid, but that the inductive premise (**P**) (or one of its instantiations) is *false*. The question that arises then is why it *seems* to us that the inductive premise is true. It is here that the different proposals to solve the Sorites paradox differ.

According to supervaluation theory, (**P**) seems true because none of the instantiations of its negation is supertrue. According to proponents of degree theories such as fuzzy logic, the inductive premise, or *principle of tolerance* seems true because it is *almost* true.

Many linguists and philosophers do not like the fuzzy logic approach to vagueness, for one thing because it is not really clear what it means for a sentence to be true to degree $n \in [0,1]$. For another, the approach seems to over-generate. This is certainly the case if one seeks to account for comparative statements in terms of degrees of truth. First, it has been argued that an adjective like 'clever' is multidimensional, and thus that the 'cleverer than'-relation gives rise only to a partial order. But fuzzy logicians have to say it gives rise to a strict weak, or linear order.[5] Second, if all sentences have a degree of truth, it remains unclear why 'The temperature here is much higher than Paul is tall' is so hard to interpret.[6] The treatment of vagueness and the Sorites paradox in supervaluation theory is not unproblematic either, however. The selling point of supervaluation theory

---

[4]Kamp (1981), Pinkal (1984), Veltman (1987), van Deemter (1995), and Gaifman (1997) all make implicitly or explicitly use of semi-orders. I argue in van Rooij (2011a) that Graff (2000) does the same. Also Williamson's (1994) accessibility relation between worlds, used to represent epistemic indistinguishability, can be defined in terms of a corresponding semi-order relation R between these worlds.

[5]A linear order is a strict weak order that is also connected. R is connected iff $\forall x, y\colon R(x,y) \vee R(y,x) \vee x = y$.

[6]Linguists and philosophers have given many other reasons why they don't like a fuzzy logic approach to vagueness. I have to admit that I don't find most of these reasons very convincing.

is that it preserves all classical validities. Thus, it is claimed that logically speaking there is no difference between classical logic and supervaluation theory. But the non-standard way of accounting for these validities still comes with its *logical price*. Proponents of supervaluation theory hold that although there is a cutoff-point—i.e. the formula $\exists x,y$ $[Px \wedge x \sim_P y \wedge \neg Py]$ is supertrue—, still, no one of its instantiations itself is supertrue. This is a remarkable logical feature: in classical logic it holds that $A \vee B \models A,B$ (meaning that at least one of A and B must be true in each model that verifies $A \vee B$). In supervaluation theory this doesn't hold anymore; $\exists x: Px \not\models_{supv} Px_1,\ldots,Px_n$. Thus, contrary to what is sometimes claimed, supervaluation theory does not preserve all classical validities.[7] Another problem is of a more conceptual nature. Supervaluation theory makes use of complete refinements, and supervaluation theory assumes that we *can* always make sharp cutoff-points: vagueness exists only because in daily life we are *too lazy* to make them. But this assumption seems to be wrong: vagueness exists, according to Dummett (1975), because we *cannot* make such sharp cutoff-points even if we wanted to.[8]

For a while, the so-called 'contextualist' solution to the Sorites paradox was quite popular (e.g., Kamp, 1981; Pinkal, 1984; Veltman, 1987; Raffman, 1996; Van Deemter, 1995; Graff, 2000). Kamp (1981) was the first, and perhaps also the most radical contextualist. He proposed that each instance of the conditional '$(Px \wedge x \sim_P y) \rightarrow Py$' is true, but that one cannot put all these conditionals together into a true universal statement. Most proponents of the contextualist solution follow Kamp (1981) in trying to preserve (most of) (**P**), and by making use of a mechanism of *context change*.[9] They typically propose to give up some other standard logical assumption. One way of working out the contextual solution assumes that similarity depends on context, and that this context changes in a Sorites sequence. The similarity relation can be made context dependent by turning it into a *four*-place relation. One way to do so is to assume that the similarity relation is of the form '$\sim_P^z$', and that $x \sim_P^z y$ is defined to be true iff $x \sim_P z$ and $y \sim_P z$ (and defined only in case either $x \sim_P z$ or $y \sim_P z$). Notice that $x \sim_P y$ iff $x \sim_P^x y$ iff $x \sim_P^y y$, and that the paradox could be derived as usual in case (**P**) would be reformulated as $\forall x,y: (Px \wedge x \sim_P^x y) \rightarrow Py$. Thus, this principle is still considered to be false, though almost all of its instantiations are considered to be true. How, then, is the paradox avoided? Well, observe that $\sim_P^z$ is an equivalence relation, and thus that the relation is transitive after all. Notice that if the contextual tolerance principle (**P**$_{c1}$) is formulated in terms of a fixed '$\sim_P^z$' relation,

(**P**$_{c1}$) $\forall x,y: (Px \wedge x \sim_P^z y) \rightarrow Py$.

it is unproblematic to take the principle to be valid. As a consequence it has to be assumed, however, that $x \sim_P^z y$ is false for at least one pair $\langle x,y \rangle$ for which $x \sim_P y$ holds: in contrast to '$\sim_P$', '$\sim_P^z$' gives rise to a clear cutoff-point. Thus, (**P**$_{c1}$) is a weakening of (**P**). However, the idea of contextualists is that this unnatural fixed cutoff-point is

---

[7]Of course, proponents of supervaluation theory (e.g., Fine, 1975; Keefe, 2000) claim that there is a good reason for this, but that is another matter.

[8]Other problems show up if we want to account for higher-order vagueness in terms of a definiteness operator. See Williamson (1994) and Varzi (2007) for discussion of the problem, and Keefe (2000) and Cobreros (2008) for replies.

[9]For a discussion of this mechanism of context change, see Stanley (2003) and papers that followed that. See also Keefe (2007).

avoided, because in the interpretation of a Sorites sequence the relevant individual z that determines the similarity relation changes, and the extension of P with it. Thus, although every context gives rise to a particular cutoff-point, context change makes it so that we are unable to find the cutoff-point between P and $\neg P$.

A somewhat more general way to work out the contextualist idea is to assume that similarity is context-dependent because similarity depends on a contextually given *comparison class* c (cf. Veltman, 1987; van Deemter, 1995). Say that $x \sim_P^c y$ iff $\neg \exists z \in c$: $x \sim_P z \succ_P y$ or $x \succ_P z \sim_y y$. Thus, x and y are similar with respect to comparison class c if x and y are not (even) *indirectly* distinguishable w.r.t. elements of c.[10] The inductive premises are reformulated in terms of the new context-dependent similarity relation. The idea is that c contains only the individuals mentioned before, and in the sentence itself. Notice that this is fine if one just looks at specific conditionals of the form '$(P(x,c) \wedge x \sim_P^c y) \rightarrow P(y,c)$': c consists just of $\{x, y\}$. However, a major problem of this approach (and shared by the original contextual solutions of Kamp, 1981; Pinkal, 1984) shows up when we look at the inductive premise as a quantified formula:

$$(\mathbf{P}_{c2}) \quad \forall x, y \colon (P(x,c) \wedge x \sim_P^c y) \rightarrow P(y,c).$$

In this case, c must be the set of all individuals, some of which are considered to have property P and some which are considered not to have it. Notice that the relation $\sim_P^c$ is an equivalence relation. Hence, it gives rise to a fixed cutoff-point for what counts as P. Notice that $(\mathbf{P}_{c2})$ is again a weakening of $(\mathbf{P})$. Thus, contextualists succeed in making a weakened version of $(\mathbf{P})$ valid, but do so for a surprising reason: $(\mathbf{P}_{c2})$ is valid because for some x and y for which $x \sim_P y$, it holds that the antecedent of $(\mathbf{P}_{c2})$ is false because $x \not\sim_P^c y$.[11]

How good is the contextualist solution to the Sorites? As we saw, it comes with two proposals: (i) the inductive premise of the Sorites seems to be valid, because a close variant of it, i.e., $(\mathbf{P}_{c1})$ or $(\mathbf{P}_{c2})$ is valid, and (ii) context change. Both proposals have been criticized. The first because the 'natural' notion of similarity is replaced by an unnatural notion of indirect distinguishability (see, e.g. Williamson, 1994). The contextualist realizes this unnaturalness, and claims that she can avoid the unnatural consequences of making use of this indirect notion by an appeal to context change. But either context change is pushed up until the last pair in a Sorites sequence, and we have a contradiction after all, or it stops at one point, and we still have an unnatural cutoff-point (a cutoff-point between x and y, even though $x \sim_P y$).

A more recent contextual solution to the paradox was proposed by Gaifman (1997/ 2010) (see also Pagin, 2011; van Rooij, 2011a, 2011b).[12] The idea is that it only makes sense to use a predicate P in a context—i.e., with respect to a comparison class—if it helps to clearly demarcate the set of individuals that have property P from those that do not. Thus, c can only be an element of the set of *pragmatically appropriate* comparison

---

[10] This notion was defined previously by Goodman (1951) and Luce (1956).

[11] Still, Graff (2000) claims that this is the way it should be. According to her, c would (or could) rather say that c just contains those individuals focussed on. Suppose we have the following ordering: $v \sim_P w \sim_P x \sim_P y$ such that $v \succ_P x$ and $w \succ_P y$. Suppose now that $c = \{v, y\}$. In that case, she would claim, it is natural that the cutoff-point between P and $\neg P$ occurs between w and x.

[12] In van Rooij (2011a, 2011b) it is claimed (based on textual 'evidence' given to me by Frank Veltman) that the solution is actually very much in the spirit of the later philosophy of Wittgenstein.

classes C_A just in case the gap between the last individual(s) that have property P and the first that do(es) not must be between individuals x and y such that x is clearly, or significantly, P-er than y. This is not the case if the graph of the relation '$\sim_P$' is closed in $c \times c$. Indeed, it is exactly in those cases that the Sorites paradox arises. Notice that also Gaifman's solution comes down to weakening inductive hypothesis (**P**). This time it is by quantifying only over the *appropriate* comparison classes:

$(\mathbf{P_g})$ $\quad \forall x,y \in D, c \in C_A : (P(x,c) \wedge x \sim_P y) \to P(y,c).$

Another solution is closely related with recent work of Raffman (2005) and Shapiro (2006).[13] Shapiro states it in terms of three-valued logic, and Raffman in terms of pairs of contrary antonymns. The idea is that a predicate P and its antonyms $\overline{P}$ do not necessarily partition the set D of all objects, and there might be elements that neither (clearly) have property P nor property $\overline{P}$, but are somewhere 'in the middle'. Once one makes such a move it is very natural to assume that the inductive principle (**P**) is not valid, but a weakened version of it, $(\mathbf{P_s})$, is. This weakened principle says that if you call one individual tall, and this individual is not visibly, or relevantly, taller than another individual, you will or should not call the other one short or not tall.

$(\mathbf{P_s})$ $\quad \forall x,y : (Px \wedge x \sim_P y) \to \neg \overline{P}y.$

Of course, principle $(\mathbf{P_s})$ can only be different from the original (**P**) if $\neg \overline{P}y$ does not come down to the same as Py. Thus, a gap between the sets of P- and $\overline{P}$-individuals is required. Notice that the Sorites paradox can now be 'solved' in a familiar way: Px_1 and $\overline{P}x_n$ are true, and modus ponens is valid, but the inductive hypothesis, or (all) its instantiations, are not. However, since we adopt $(\mathbf{P_s})$ as a valid principle of language use, we can explain why inductive hypothesis (**P**) *seems* so natural. To illustrate, if $D = \{x,y,z\}$, it might be that $I(P) = \{x\}, I(\overline{P}) = \{z\}$, and $x \sim_P y \sim_P z$. Notice that such a models satisfies $(\mathbf{P_s})$ but not (**P**).

A final proposal I will discuss here was made by Williamson (1994). It is well-known that according to Williamson's epistemic approach, predicates do have a strict cutoff-point, it is just that we don't know it. As in other approaches, also for Williamson it is clear that adopting (**P**) immediately gives rise to paradox. To explain why we are still tempted to accept it, Williamson (1994) offers the following weakening of (**P**) that doesn't give rise to paradox:

$(\mathbf{P_\square})$ $\quad \forall x,y \in D : (\square Px \wedge x \sim y) \to Py$

Thus, if x is *known* to have property P, and x is similar to y, y will actually have property y. Notice that this is also a weakening of (**P**) because the $\square Px$ entails Px. Williamson's proposal is closely related to the 'three-valued' one discussed above. Suppose we redefine the objects that do not have property $\overline{P}$ as the objects that might have property P (in model M): $M \models \Diamond Px$ iff$_{df}$ $M \not\models \overline{P}x$. In that case, $(\mathbf{P_s})$ comes down to $(\mathbf{P_{s'}})$ $\forall x,y \in D : (Px \wedge x \sim y) \to \Diamond Py$. If '$\Diamond$' is the dual of '$\square$', this, in turn, comes down to $(\mathbf{P_\square})$. The notion of duality will play an important role in the following section as well.

---

[13] Shapiro (2006) argues that his solution is closely related to Waismann's (1945) notion of 'Open Texture'. For what it is worth, I believe that Waismann's notion is more related to the previously discussed 'solution' of the Sorites.

4   Tolerance and non-transitive entailment

In the previous section we have seen that it is standard to tackle the Sorites paradox by weakening the inductive premise (**P**) in some way or other. But there exists an interesting alternative, which perhaps goes back to Kamp (1981), and has recently been defended by Zardini (2008). According to it, the tolerance principle is true, but the Sorites reasoning is invalid because the *inference relation* itself is not transitive. Zardini's way of working out this suggestion into a concrete proposal is rather involved. In this section I work out the same suggestion in a simpler and more straightforward way. My aim in this section is to make this rather non-standard approach more plausible on independent grounds. In Section 5 I will try to seduce proponents of other views by showing that this solution is actually closely related to (some of) the approaches discussed in the previous section.

Let us start with a semi-order $\langle D, \succ_P \rangle$ for each vague predicate P holding in all models; this gives rise to a similarity relation '$\sim_P$' that is reflexive, symmetric, but not transitive. I would like to propose now that given this similarity relation, we can interpret sentences in at least two different ways: in terms of '$\models$' as we normally do, but also in a *tolerant* way in terms of '$\models^{t'}$'. Take a standard first order model $\langle D, I \rangle$ extended with a fixed semi-order relation $\succ_P$ (for each P), $M = \langle D, I, \succ_P \rangle$, and define (i) $x \sim_P y$ as before and (ii) '$\models^{t'}$' (and '$\models$') recursively as follows (for simplicity I use the substitutional analysis of quantification and assume that every individual has a unique name):

$M \models \phi$ defined in the usual way.

$M \models^{t'} P(\underline{a})$ iff $\exists d \sim_P a \colon M \models P(\underline{d})$, with $\underline{d}$ as name for d.

$M \models^{t'} \neg\phi$ iff $M \not\models^{t'} \phi$.

$M \models^{t'} \phi \wedge \psi$ iff $M \models^{t'} \phi$ and $M \models^{t'} \psi$.

$M \models^{t'} \forall x \phi$ iff   for all $d \in I_M \colon M \models^{t'} \phi[^x/\underline{d}]$.

Now we can define two *tolerant* entailment relations, '$\models^{tt}$' and '$\models^{ct}$', as follows: $\phi \models^{tt} \psi$ iff $[\![\phi]\!]^{t'} \subseteq [\![\psi]\!]^{t'}$, and $\phi \models^{ct} \psi$ iff $[\![\phi]\!] \subseteq [\![\psi]\!]^{t'}$, where $[\![\phi]\!]^{(t')} = \{M \mid M \models^{(t')} \phi\}$. We will say that ϕ is tolerance-valid iff $M \models^{t'} \phi$ in all models M with an indistinguishability relation. Although the first tolerant entailment relation is defined rather classically, I will be mostly interested in the second entailment relation. This second entailment relation is *not transitive*: from $\phi \models^{ct} \psi$ and $\psi \models^{ct} \chi$ it doesn't follow that $\phi \models^{ct} \chi$. Assume, for instance, that for all models $a \sim_P b \sim_P c$, but that $a \succ_P c$. Now $P(\underline{a}) \models^{ct} P(\underline{b})$ and $P(\underline{b}) \models^{ct} P(\underline{c})$, but not $P(\underline{a}) \models^{ct} P(\underline{c})$: there might be a model M such that $I_M(P) = \{a\}$.

Material implication doesn't mirror '$\models^{ct}$', but we can define a new conditional connective, i.e. '$\to ct$', that does. Say that $M \models \phi \to^{ct} \psi$ iff$_{def}$ if $M \models \phi$, then $M \models^{t'} \psi$. Notice that (**P$_t$**) $\forall x, y \colon (P(x) \wedge x \sim_P y) \to^{ct} P(y)$ is classically valid. This is not problematic to account for the Sorites, because the hypothetical syllogism is not valid when formulated in terms of '$\to^{ct}$'.[14] Instead of reinterpreting implication, it is also possible to interpret negation differently. I will show that with negation defined in this way, (**P**) itself is tolerance-valid.

---

[14] A similar story would hold for conditionals like '$\to^{sc}$' and '$\to^{st}$'.

In the following I will define the meaning of negation used to interpret tolerance-truth (from now on '$\models^t$') in terms of a new notion of *strict* truth: '$\models^s$'. In fact, we have to define '$\models^t$' and '$\models^s$' simultaneously.

$M \models^t P(\underline{a})$ iff $\exists d \sim_P a : M \models P(\underline{d})$.

$M \models^t \neg \phi$ iff $M \not\models^s \phi$.

$M \models^t \phi \wedge \psi$ iff $M \models^t \phi$ and $M \models^t \psi$.

$M \models^t \forall x \phi$ iff $\forall d \in I_M, M \models^t \phi[^x/_{\underline{d}}]$.

$M \models^s P(\underline{a})$ iff $\forall d \sim_P a, M \models P(\underline{d})$.

$M \models^s \neg \phi$ iff $M \not\models^t \phi$.

$M \models^s \phi \wedge \psi$ iff $M \models^s \phi$ and $M \models^s \psi$.

$M \models^s \forall x \phi$ iff $\forall d \in I_M, M \models^s \phi[^x/_{\underline{d}}]$.

The connectives '$\vee$' and '$\rightarrow$' are defined in terms of '$\neg$' and '$\wedge$' as usual. Notice that $P(\underline{a}) \vee \neg P(\underline{a})$ is tolerant-valid, can be strictly true, but is not a strict-tautology. $P(\underline{a}) \wedge \neg P(\underline{a})$, on the other hand, cannot be strictly true, but can be tolerantly true.[15] For each predicate P we can add a P-similarity relation to the language. For convenience,[16] I will simply denote it in the same way as it should be interpreted: '$\sim_P$'. We will assume that the similarity relation should be interpreted in a fixed way, and cannot have a separate strict or tolerant reading: $M \models a \sim_P b$ iff $M \models^s a \sim_P b$ iff $M \models^t a \sim_P b$ iff $I(a) \sim_P I(b)$. The most appealing fact about this system is that the original tolerance principle, **(P)** $\forall x, y[(Px \wedge x \sim_P y) \rightarrow Py]$ is tolerance-valid! This is easy to see because for this sentence to be tolerance-true in M it has to be the case for any a and b such that $a \sim_P b$ that $M \models^t Pa \rightarrow P\underline{b}$, or equivalently $M \models^t \neg P\underline{a} \vee P\underline{b}$. Hence, given the analysis of negation, either $\exists d \sim_P a : M \not\models P(\underline{d})$ or $\exists d' \sim_P b : M \models P(\underline{d'})$. But this is always the case. Thus, on the present analysis we can say that the original **(P)** is, though not classically valid, still tolerantly valid. Notice that **(P)** is neither classically nor strictly valid.[17]

Thus, what we have now, finally, is a notion of validity according to which the original **(P)** is valid. This does not give rise to the prediction that all objects have property P in case the entailment relation is $\models^{tt}$. For that relation, modus ponens is not valid. However, we have opted for entailment relation $\models^{ct}$ (with t' replaced by t everywhere) according to which modus ponens *is* valid. Still, no reason to worry, because this relation is non-transitive. We can conclude that it does not follow that all objects have property P.[18]

---

[15] Dave Ripley (p.c.) pointed out that my notions of tolerant and strict truth in fact correspond with the notions of truth in Priest's (1979) logic of paradox (LP) and Kleene's system K3, respectively. These connections are proved and explored in Cobreros et al. (2011).

[16] Though perhaps confusing for the formally inclined.

[17] It was also not valid in our earlier formulation of tolerant truth, $\models^t$.

[18] Although it is widely acknowledged that one can 'solve' the Sorites by assuming that the entailment relation is non-transitive, it is hardly ever seriously defended (if at all). The reason for this, it seems, is Dummett's (1975) claim that one cannot seriously deny the ability to chain inferences, because this principle is taken to be essential to the very enterprise of proof. To counter this objection, in Cobreros et al. (2011) we provide a proof theory that corresponds to $\models^{ct}$ (and, in fact, many other non-classical inference relations). For completeness, in Cobreros et al. (2011) the non-transitive entailment relation that is actually preferred is '$\models^{st}$' rather than '$\models^{ct}$' that I originally proposed (in this paper). See Cobreros et al. (2011) for motivation.

5   Comparison with other approaches

Although our approach seems rather non-standard, it is closely related with other approaches. Consider, for instance super- and subvaluationalism.[19] There exists a close relation between our notions of strict and tolerant truth with the notions of truth in supervaluationalism, and subvaluationalism (Hyde, 1997), respectively. Notice in particular that subvaluationalism is paraconsistent, just like our notion of tolerant truth: $P\underline{a}$ can be both true *and* false, without giving rise to catastrophic consequences. Indeed, these theories, just like supervaluationalism and our notion of strict truth, are very similar when we only consider atomic statements: in both cases we define truth in terms of existential and universal quantification, respectively. Moreover, in both cases the two notions are each other's duals. But the analogy disappears when we consider more complex statements.

The reason is that we make use of this quantificational interpretation at the *local level*, while they only do so only at the *global* level. Although looking at the global level means to give up on the idea that interpretation goes compositional, interpreting globally instead of locally still seems to be advantageous. This is so because as a result, both $P(\underline{a}) \vee \neg P(\underline{a})$ and $P(\underline{a}) \wedge \neg P(\underline{a})$ are validities, while for us the former can be strictly false, and the latter can be tolerantly true.

Moreover, the idea of interpreting globally is crucial for Fine's (1975) analysis of penumbral connections. We have already seen that supervaluationalism is not so classical after all, once one does not limit oneself to single-conclusion arguments. Something similar holds for subvaluationism, as already observed in the original article, and stressed by Keefe (2000). Hyde (1997) makes non-classical predictions once one does not limit oneself to single-premise arguments: $\phi, \psi \nvDash_{subv} \phi \wedge \psi$. In Cobreros et al. (2011) we argue that there is much to say in favor of our notions of truth and entailment. In particular, $\phi, \psi \vDash^{ct} \phi \wedge \psi$ and $\phi \vee \psi \vDash^{ct} \phi, \psi$. As for penumbral connections, we admit that $\neg P(\underline{a}) \wedge P(\underline{b})$ can be tolerantly true even if $a \succeq_P b$. In Cobreros et al. (2011) we argue that as far as semantics is concerned, this is, in fact, not a problem. What has to be explained, though, is why it is pragmatically *inappropriate* to utter a statement saying '$\neg P(\underline{a}) \wedge P(\underline{b})$'. The explanation is that without any further information, a hearer of this utterance will conclude from this that $b \succ_P a$, because this is the only way in which the statement can be true if the statement is interpreted in the strongest possible way.[20] If the speaker knows that $a \succeq_P b$ it is thus inappropriate to make such a statement. See Alxatib & Pelletier (2011) for a very similar move to solve the very similar problem of why contradictory attributed can sometimes truthfully be attributed to the same borderline object.

For another comparison, consider Williamson's approach. Recall that he wanted to 'save' the intuition of tolerance by turning $(\mathbf{P}_\square)$ $(\forall x, y: (\square Px \wedge x \sim_P y) \to Py)$ into a validity. Similarly for our reformulation of the tolerance principle of Shapiro: $(\mathbf{P}_s)$ $(\forall x, y: (Px \wedge x \sim_P y) \to \Diamond Py)$. I will show now that by re-interpreting '$\square$' and '$\Diamond$' in terms of our similarity relation, there exists an obvious relation between these approaches and mine. The redefinition goes as follows:

$$M \vDash \square\phi \quad \text{iff} \quad M \vDash^s \phi \qquad \text{and} \qquad M \vDash \Diamond\phi \quad \text{iff} \quad M \vDash^t \phi$$

---

[19]This connection is made much more explicitly in Cobreros et al. (2010).

[20]Interpreting sentences that semantically allow for different interpretations in the strongest possible way is quite standard in pragmatics. Of course, this kind of pragmatic interpretation can be overruled by further information—it behaves non-monotonically—, in our case that $a \succeq b$.

Notice that $\Diamond P(\underline{a}) \wedge \Diamond \neg P(\underline{a})$ is possible, but $\Diamond P(\underline{a}) \wedge \neg \Diamond P(\underline{a})$ is impossible; $\Diamond P(\underline{a}) \vee \neg \Diamond P(\underline{a})$ and $\Box P(\underline{a}) \vee \neg \Box P(\underline{a})$ are tautologies; $\Box P(\underline{a}) \wedge \neg \Box P(\underline{a})$ is impossible, just as $\Diamond P(\underline{a}) \wedge \Box \neg P(\underline{a})$. Observe also that it now immediately follows that $\neg \Box \neg \phi \equiv \Diamond \phi$ and $\neg \Diamond \neg \phi \equiv \Box \phi$: '$\Box$' and '$\Diamond$' are duals of each other. Notice that both $\forall x, y \colon \Box Px \wedge x \sim_P y \to Py$ and $\forall x, y \colon Px \wedge x \sim_P y \to \Diamond Py$ are valid, and are equivalent to each other. The fact that (**P**) is tolerantly valid is actually *weaker* than either of them: the reformulation of (**P**) would be $\forall x, y \colon \Box Px \wedge x \sim_P y \to \Diamond Py$. For Williamson (1994) it is only natural to assume that if ($\mathbf{P}_w$) holds, agents *know* that it holds. The corresponding strengthening of (**P**) in our case, however, doesn't seem natural. Indeed, it is certainly not the case that $\Box \forall x, y [(Px \wedge x \sim_P y) \to \Diamond Py]$ is valid. Before I suggested to account for a notion of vague inference as follows: $\phi \models^{ct} \psi$ iff $[\![\phi]\!]^c \subseteq [\![\psi]\!]^t$. Alternatively, we could do something else, which sounds equally natural: $\phi \models^{sc} \psi$ iff $[\![\psi]\!]^s \subseteq [\![\phi]\!]^c$. In terms of our 'modal' system, these inference relations can be incorporated into the object-language as follows: $\phi \models^{ct} \psi$ iff for all M, $M \models \phi \to \Diamond \psi$, and $\phi \models^{sc} \psi$ iff for all M, $M \models \Box \phi \to \psi$. These notions do not exactly coincide.

Consider, finally, the contextualist solution. Recall that according to Kamp (1981), each instance of the conditional $(Px \wedge x \sim_P y) \to Py$ is true, it is just that we cannot put all these conditionals together to turn them into a true universal statement. Our solution is similar, though we don't talk about truth of conditional statements but of valid inferences: each inference step is (*ct*)-valid, but we cannot chain them together to a (*ct*)-valid inference. As a second connection, observe that our introduced conditional '$\to^{ct}$' is very similar to the conditional introduced by Kamp (1981). As a last point of contact, consider the notion of meaning change proposed in contextualist solutions. Contextualists typically say that the meaning of predicate P changes during the interpretation of the Sorites sequence. It is almost immediately obvious in terms of our framework how this meaning change takes place: first, it has to be the case that $M \models P\underline{a}$. At the second step, the meaning of P changes, and we end up with a new model M' such that $M' \models P\underline{b}$ iff $M \models \Diamond P\underline{b}$ (or $M \models^t P\underline{b}$). At the third step, the meaning of P changes again, and we end up with a new model M'' such that $M'' \models P\underline{c}$ iff $M' \models \Diamond P\underline{c}$ (or $M' \models^t P\underline{c}$). And so on, indefinitely. But do we really need to go to new models every time? We need not, if we can iterate modalities, as we will see in the subsequent section.

6 Similarity and borderlines

Traditional approaches of vagueness start with borderlines. To account for higher-order vagueness, one then needs a whole sequence of higher-order borderlines. In this section I suggest two ways to represent higher-order borderlines: one in terms of iteration of 'modalities'; another in terms of fine-grainedness.

6.1 Iteration, and higher order vagueness

Let $\mathbf{B}\phi$ be an abbreviation of $\neg \Box \phi \wedge \neg \Box \neg \phi$. Thus, $\mathbf{B}P(\underline{a})$ means that a is a borderline case of P. Our system allows for first-order borderline cases, but it makes it impossible to account for higher-order borderlines, and thus cannot account for higher-order vagueness. But why don't we just say that a is a second-order borderline case of P if $\neg \Box \Box P(\underline{a}) \wedge \neg \Box \Box \neg P(\underline{a})$. This sounds right, but the problem is that we cannot yet interpret these types of formulas, because we haven't specified yet how to make sense of

'$M \models^s \Box\phi$' or '$M \models^t \Box\phi$'. So let us try to do just that. What we need to do is to interpret formulas with respect to a (perhaps empty) *sequence* of s's and t's, like $\langle s,s,t\rangle$ or $\langle t,t\rangle$. We will abbreviate a sequence by 'σ', and if $\sigma = \langle x_1,\ldots,x_n\rangle$, then '$\sigma t$' will be $\langle x_1,\ldots,x_n,t\rangle$ and 'σs' will be $\langle x_1,\ldots,x_n,s\rangle$. σ^* will just be the same as σ except that all t's and s's are substituted for each other. Thus, if $\sigma = \langle s,s,t\rangle$, for instance, then $\sigma^* = \langle t,t,s\rangle$. Furthermore, we are going to say that if σ is the empty sequence, '$\langle\rangle$', $M \models^\sigma \phi$ iff $M \models \phi$.

$$M \models^\sigma \Box\phi \qquad \text{iff} \qquad M \models^{\sigma s} \phi \text{ and } M \models^\sigma \Diamond\phi \text{ iff } M \models^{\sigma t} \phi.$$

$$M \models^{\sigma t} P(\underline{a}) \qquad \text{iff} \qquad \exists d \sim_P a\colon M \models^\sigma P(\underline{d}).$$
$$M \models^{\sigma t} \neg\phi \qquad \text{iff} \qquad M \not\models^{\sigma^* s} \phi.$$
$$M \models^{\sigma t} \phi \wedge \psi \qquad \text{iff} \qquad M \models^{\sigma t} \phi \text{ and } M \models^{\sigma t} \psi.$$
$$M \models^{\sigma t} \forall x\phi \qquad \text{iff} \qquad \forall d \in I_M\colon M \models^{\sigma t} \phi[^x/_{\underline{d}}].$$

$$M \models^{\sigma s} P(\underline{a}) \qquad \text{iff} \qquad \forall d \sim_P a\colon M \models^\sigma P(\underline{d}).$$
$$M \models^{\sigma s} \neg\phi \qquad \text{iff} \qquad M \not\models^{\sigma^* t} \phi.$$
$$M \models^{\sigma s} \phi \wedge \psi \qquad \text{iff} \qquad M \models^{\sigma s} \phi \text{ and } M \models^{\sigma s} \psi.$$
$$M \models^{\sigma s} \forall x\phi \qquad \text{iff} \qquad \forall d \in I_M\colon M \models^{\sigma s} \phi[^x/_{\underline{d}}].$$

To see what is going on, let us assume a domain $\{u,v,w,x,y,z\}$ such that $u \sim_P v \sim_P w \sim_P x \sim_P y \sim_P z$ and $u \succ_P w$, $v \succ_P x$, $w \succ_P y$, and $x \succ_P z$ together with the assumption that '$\succ_P$' is a semi-order. Let us now assume that $I_M(P) = \{u,v,w\}$. If we build the complex predicate '$\Box P$' and say that this holds of a in M iff $M \models \Box P(\underline{a})$, it follows that $I_M(\Box P) = \{u,v\}$, and $I_M(\Box\Box P) = \{u\}$. Similarly, it follows that $I_M(\Box\neg P) = \{y,z\}$, and $I_M(\Box\Box\neg P) = \{z\}$. The first-order borderline cases of P, $\mathbf{B}^1 P$, are those d for which it holds that $\neg\Box^1 P(\underline{d}) \wedge \neg\Box^1 \neg P(\underline{d})$. Thus, $I_M(\mathbf{B}^1 P) = \{w,x\}$. Similarly, $I_M(\mathbf{B}^2 P) = \{d \in D \mid M \models \neg\Box^2 P(\underline{d}) \wedge \neg\Box^2 \neg P(\underline{d})\} = \{v,w,x,y\}$ and $I_M(\mathbf{B}^3 P) = \{u,v,w,x,y,z\}$.[21]

Our analysis of higher-order vagueness is similar to Gaifman's (1997/2010) treatment. Both start with a standard two-valued logic and build higher-order vagueness in terms of it. What would happen if our basic logic were not two-valued, but three-valued instead? Very little, except that n-order borderlines are now defined 'one step behind'. Suppose we take the same domain as above, giving rise to the same semi-order, but assume that $I_M(P) = \{u,v\}$ and $I_M(\overline{P}) = \{y,z\}$. One proposal would be to say that $I_M(\mathbf{B}^n P) = \{d \in D \mid M \models \neg\Box^{n-1} P(\underline{d}) \wedge \neg\Box^{n-1} \overline{P}(\underline{d})\}$. Thus $I_M(\mathbf{B}^1 P) = D - (I_M(P) \cup I_M(\overline{P})) = \{w,x\}$, while $I_M(\mathbf{B}^2 P) = \{v,w,x,y\}$ and $I_M(\mathbf{B}^3 P) = \{u,v,w,x,y,z\}$. Perhaps more in accordance with tradition would be to define $I_M(\mathbf{B}^n P)$ as follows:

$$I_M(\mathbf{B}^n P) = \{d \in D \mid M \models \neg\Box^{n-1} P(\underline{d}) \wedge \neg\Box^{n-1} \overline{P}(\underline{d}) \wedge \neg\mathbf{B}^{n-1} P(\underline{d})\}.$$

But to make sense of this, we have to know what things like $M \models^t BP(\underline{d})$ mean. A natural definition goes as follows:

$$M \models \mathbf{B}P(\underline{d}) \qquad \text{iff} \qquad d \notin I_M(P) \cup I_M(\overline{P}).$$
$$M \models^{\sigma s} \mathbf{B}P(\underline{d}) \qquad \text{iff} \qquad \forall d' \sim_P d\colon M \models^\sigma \mathbf{B}P(\underline{d'}).$$

---

[21] Alternatively, we might define the nth order borderline cases of P as those d for which it holds that $\neg\Box^n P(\underline{d}) \wedge P(\underline{d}) \wedge \Diamond^n P(\underline{d})$. In that case, $I_M(\mathbf{B}^1 P) = \{w\}$, $I_M(\mathbf{B}^2 P) = \{v,w\}$ and $I_M(\mathbf{B}^3 P) = \{u,v,w\}$.

$M \models^{\sigma t} \mathbf{B}P(\underline{d})$ iff $\exists d' \sim_P d : M \models^{\sigma} \mathbf{B}P(\underline{d'})$.

Shapiro's (2006) weakened version of (**P**), i.e. (**P**$_s$), could now perhaps best be stated as follows: $\forall x, y : (\Box^n Px \wedge x \sim_P y) \rightarrow (\Box^n P(y) \vee \mathbf{B}^{n+1} P(y))$.

6.2 Borderlines and fine-grainedness

In natural language we conceptualize and describe the world at different levels of granularity. A road, for instance, can be viewed as a line, a surface, or a volume. The level of granularity that we make use of depends on what is relevant (cf. Hobbs, 1985). When we are planning a trip, we view the road as a line. When we are driving on it, we view it as a surface, and when we hit a pothole, it becomes a volume to us. In our use of natural language we even employ this fact by being able to describe the same phenomenon at different levels of granularity within the same discourse. Thus, we sometimes explicitly shift perspective, i.e., shift the level of granularity to describe the same situation. This is perhaps most obviously the case when we talk about time and space: "It is two o'clock. In fact, it is two minutes after two." In this sentence we shift to describe a time-point in a more specific way. Suppose that we consider two models, M and M' that are exactly alike, except that they differ on the interpretation of a specific ordering relation, such as 'earlier than', or 'taller than'. When can we think of the one model, M', as being finer-gained than the other, M? The only reasonable proposal seems to be to say that M' is a refinement of M with respect to some ordering $\geq$, $M \sqsubseteq M'$, only if $\forall x, y, z \in D$: if $M' \models x \geq y \wedge y \geq z$ and $M \models x \sim z$ (with $x \sim y$ iff $x \not\succ y$ and $y \not\succ x$), then $M \models x \sim y \wedge y \sim z$. This follows if we define refinements as follows: M' is a refinement of M with respect to $\geq$ iff $V_M(>) \subseteq V_{M'}(>)$.

In the special case that the ordering relation is a weak order, this way to relate different models in terms of a coarsening relation makes use of a standard technique. Recall, first, that the relation $\sim$ is in that case an equivalence relation. In a coarser-grained model M we associate each equivalence class in the finer-grained model M' via an homomorphic function f with an equivalence class of the coarse grained model M, and say that $M \models x > y$ iff $\forall x' \in f^{-1}(x), y' \in f^{-1}(y) : M' \models x' > y'$. But observe that only a slight extension of the method can be used for other orders as well, in particular for semi-orders (recall that a weak order is a special kind of semi-order). Thus we say that M' is a refinement of M with respect to $\succ$ iff $V_M(\succ) \subseteq V_{M'}(\succ)$. Notice that if $V_M(\succ) \subset V_{M'}(\succ)$, it means that in M more individuals are $\sim$-related than in M'. In measure theoretic terms, it means that the margin of error ε is larger in M than it is in M', which is typically the case if in M' more is at stake.[22] Similarly, we say that $M \models x \succ y$ iff $\forall x' \in R(x), \forall y' \in R(y) : M' \models x' \succ y'$, where R is a relation between elements of M and M' that preserves $\succ$.[23] Suppose that the ordering is '(observably) P-er than'. Notice that at M it only makes sense to say that $Px \wedge \neg Py$ in case $M \models x \succ_P y$. Suppose that in M the last individual in the extension of P is x, while y is the first individual in its anti-extension. Does that mean that we have a clear cutoff-point for the extension of P? It does not, if we are allowed to look at finer-grained models, where the domain of such a finer-grained model might be bigger than the domain of M.

---

[22]I believe that much of what Graff (2000) discusses as 'interest relative' can be captured in this way.

[23]Meaning that if $M \models x \succ y$, then $\forall x' \in \{z \in D_{M'} \mid xRz\}$ and $\forall y' \in \{z \in D_{M'} \mid yRz\} : M' \models x' \succ y'$.

One can image a whole sequence of refinements of a model M_0: $M_0 \sqsubseteq M_1 \sqsubseteq \cdots \sqsubseteq$ $M_n \ldots$[24] It terms of it, we might define a *definiteness* operator to account for higher-order vagueness.[25] Say that $M_i \models \mathbf{D}Px$ iff $\forall x' \in \{y \in D_{M_j} \mid xR_{ij}y\}$: $M_j \models Px'$ (where M_j is the immediate refinement of M_i, and R_{ij} is a relation with domain M_i and range M_j respecting the ordering relations $\succ$ in their respected models). Similarly, we might define a to be a borderline-case of P in M_i, $M_i \models \mathbf{BP}\underline{a}$, if it holds that $M_i \models \neg\mathbf{D}P\underline{a} \wedge \neg\mathbf{D}\neg P\underline{a}$. Similarly for higher-order borderline cases.

Recall that $M_i \models^s P\underline{a}$ iff $\forall d \sim_P a$: $M_i \models Pd$. Observe that there exists a relation between $P\underline{a}$ being *stricty* true in M_i, and $P\underline{a}$ being *definitely* true in in M_i: $M_i \models^s P\underline{a}$ iff $M_i \models \mathbf{D}P\underline{a}$ iff $\forall d \in \{x \in D_{M_i} \mid aR_{ij}x\}$: $M_j \models Pd$. Similarly, $M_i \models^t P\underline{a}$ iff $M_i \models \mathbf{D}P\underline{a} \vee \mathbf{BP}\underline{a}$, i.e., if $\exists d \in \{x' \in D_{M_j} \mid aR_{ij}x'\}$: $M_j \models Pd$. Notice that $M_i \not\models^s P\underline{a}$ does not correspond with $M_i \models \neg\mathbf{D}P\underline{a}$, but rather with $M_i \models \mathbf{D}\neg P\underline{a}$.

7 Clusters, prototypes, and defining similarity

In Section 2 we started with an ordering relation and defined a similarity relation in terms of it. But this is obviously not crucial for thinking about similarity, or resemblance. Suppose we start out with a primitive similarity relation, $\sim$, that is reflexive and symmetric, but not necessarily transitive. We can now think of a *similarity class* as a class of objects S such that $\forall x, y \in S$: $x \sim y$. A maximal such similarity class might be called a *cluster*.[26] Clusters hardly play a role in categorization when starting out with one-dimensional ordering relations like 'taller than', or 'earlier than'. But they play a crucial role in categorization when more dimensions are at stake. Clusters can be tolerant, or strict. Let us say that a cluster is tolerant in case $C^t =_{df} \{x \in D \mid \exists y \in C: x \sim y\} \neq C$, and strict otherwise. If predicate P is interpreted by cluster C_P, it holds that $M \models^t P\underline{a}$ iff $a \in C_P^t$. We can also define the strict version of a cluster, $C_P^s =_{df} \{x \in C_P \mid \forall y \in D: y \sim x \to y \in C_P\}$. It follows immediately that $M \models^s P\underline{a}$ iff $a \in C_P^s$. Notice that if C_P is strict, $C_P = C_P^s$. In general, the classical interpretation of P, $[\![P]\!] = C_P$, should be such that $C_P^s \subseteq [\![P]\!] \subseteq C_P^t$. Notice that by definition it holds that $C_P^t \subseteq C_Q$ iff $C_P \subseteq C_Q^s$, which is again an interesting relation between our dual concepts.

In terms of a similarity relation and a cluster, we can define a notion of a prototype. First, define '$\preceq$' as follows: $x \preceq y$ iff$_{df}$ $\{z \in D \mid z \sim x\} \subseteq \{z \in D \mid z \sim y\}$.[27] Now suppose that for a cluster C, there exists an element $x \in C$ such that $\forall y \in C$: $x \preceq y$. In such a case it makes sense to call this element a *prototype* of C. Notice that it is well possible that a cluster C has more than one prototype. It is useful to have such prototypes, because it is taken to be much more effortful to represent meanings in terms of their extensions than in terms of their prototypes. There need not be any loss involved: in Gärdenfors' (2000) geometrical approach to meaning, for instance, the extension of a (set of) term(s) can be derived from the prototype(s). But if a cluster has a prototype, something similar (actually, something stronger) can be done here as well: the cluster C associated with

---

[24]Perhaps there is no most fine-grained model.

[25]For what it is worth, I feel that this is in the spirit of what is proposed by Fine (1975) and Keefe (2000).

[26]This definition of clusters follows the pattern of quasi-analysis proposed in Carnap (1961). I will ignore Goodman's (1951) well-known imperfect community problem of this construction in this paper.

[27]Notice that if we define $x \approx y$ as true iff $x \preceq y$ and $y \preceq x$, it immediately follows that '$\approx$' is an equivalence relation, and, in fact, the *indirect* indistinguishability relation as defined by Goodman (1951) and Luce (1956).

prototype x_C is determined as *the* unique cluster such that x is an element of it. Notice that being a prototype is something special, because there might well be two clusters, C_1 and C_2, such that $\exists x \in C_1, \exists y \in C_2: x \sim y$, i.e., $C_1' \cap C_2 \neq \emptyset$ (or equivalently, $C_1 \cap C_2' \neq \emptyset$).

'Similarity' is not an absolute notion: one pair of objects can be more similar to each other than another pair. In geometrical models of meaning, similarity is measured by the inverse of a distance measure d between two objects. In Tversky's (1977) contrast model, the similarity of two objects is determined by the primitive features they share, and the features they differ on. Say that object x and y come with sets of primitive features X and Y. If we only consider the features they share, the similarity of x and y can be measured in terms of $X \cap Y$: x is more similar to y than v is to w iff $f(X \cap Y) > f(V \cap W)$, with f some real valued function monotone on '$\supseteq$'.[28] Clusters as determined above now depend on when we take two objects similar enough to be called 'similar'. If we fix this, we can determine what a cluster is, and what a tolerant cluster is. If C is a cluster, there still might be some elements in C that are more similar to all other elements of C than just 'similar'. Following Tversky, we can measure the prototypicality of each $x \in C$ as follows: $p(x, C) = \sum_{y \in C} f(X \cap Y)$. A prototype of C is then simply an element of C with the highest p-value.

Note that until now I started with a specific notion of similarity, perhaps explained in terms of measurement errors, or a primitive idea of what counts as a relevant difference. But Tversky's model suggests that we can explain our similarity relation in terms of shared features. Take any arbitrary n-ary partition Q of the set D of all individuals. Which of those partitions naturally classifies those individuals? Take any element q of Q, and determine its *family resemblance* as follows: $FR(q) = \sum_{x,y \in q} f(X \cap Y)$. Categorization Q can now be called 'at least as good' as categorization Q' (another partition of D) just in case $\sum_{q \in Q} FR(q) \geq \sum_{q' \in Q'} FR(q')$. With Rosch (1973) we might now call X a 'basic category' just in case X is an element of the best categorization of D. What is interesting for us is that a best categorization Q can determine a level of similarity to be the 'basic' one, i.e., to be '$\sim$'. But first let us assume that a basic categorization is 'nice' in case $\forall q, q' \in Q: \min\{f(X \cap Y) \mid x, y \in q\} \approx \min\{f(X \cap Y) \mid x, y \in q'\}$.[29] With respect to such a 'nice' categorization Q, we can define the similarity relation as follows: $x \sim y$ iff$_{df}$ $f(X \cap Y) \geq \min\{f(V \cap W) \mid v, w \in q\}$, for any $q \in Q$.

8 Conclusion

In this paper I argued that vagueness is crucially related with tolerant interpretation, and that the latter is only natural for observational predicates. Still, most approaches dealing with the Sorites in the end give up the principle of tolerance. I argued, instead, that once tolerance plays a role, the entailment relation need not be transitive anymore. It was shown how to make sense of this proposal by virtue of a paraconsistent language and semantics, and how it relates to some of the standard analyses. Finally, I related our analysis to some analyses of concepts in cognitive science.

---

[28] Tversky's model is much more flexible than this; who allows for x to be more similar to y than y is to x.

[29] If we assume that $\forall q, q' \in Q: \min\{f(X \cap Y) \mid x, y \in q\} > \max\{f(X \cap Z) \mid x \in q, z \in q'\}$, categorization is clearly analogous to Gaifman's treatment to avoid the Sorites paradox. In fact, this principle is behind most of the hierarchical structuring models: If one starts with a difference measure, one can show that if for all x, y, z: $d(x, y) \leq d(x, z) = d(y, z)$, then the set of objects give rise to a hierarchically ordered tree (cf. Johnson, 1967).

BIBLIOGRAPHY

Alxatib, S. and J. Pelletier (2011), 'The psychology of vagueness: Borderline cases and contradictions', *Mind and Language*. 26: 287–326.

Carnap, R. (1961), *Der Logische Aufbau der Welt*, Meiner, Hamburg.

Cobreros, P. (2008), 'Supervaluationism and logical consequence: a third way', *Studia Logica*, 90: 291–312.

Cobreros, P., P. Égré, D. Ripley, and R. van Rooij (2010), 'Supervaluationism and mixed consequence in a super-/sub-valuationist setting', in X. Arrazola and M. Ponte (eds.), *LogKCA-10. Proceedings of the second ILCLI international workshop on Logic and Philosophy of Knowledge, Communication and Action*, University of the Basque Country Press. pp. 157–175.

Cobreros, P., P. Égré, D. Ripley, and R. van Rooij (2011), 'Tolerent, classical, strict', *Journal of Philosophical Logic*, DOI: 10.1007/210992-010-9165-z.

Deemter, K. van (1995), 'The Sorites fallacy and the context-dependence of vague predicates', in M. Kanazawa, et al., *Quantifiers, Deduction, and Context*, CSLI Publications, Stanford, Ca., pp. 59–86.

Dummett, M. (1975), 'Wang's paradox', *Synthese*, 30: 301–324.

Dechner, G.T. (1860), *Elemente der Psychophysics*, Breitkopf und Härtel, Leipzig.

Fine, K. (1975), 'Vagueness, truth and logic', *Synthese*, 30: 265–300.

Gaifman, H. (2010), 'Vagueness, tolerance and contextual logic', *Synthese*. (The paper was originally written in 1997, and available ever since.)

Gärdenfors, P. (2000), *Conceptual Spaces. The Geometry of Thought*, MIT Press.

Goodman, N. (1951), *The structure of appearance*, Bobbs-Merill Publ.

Graff, D. (2000), 'Shifting sands: An interest relative theory of vagueness', *Philosophical Topics*, 28: 45–81.

Hobbs, J. (1985), 'Granularity', *Proceedings of the International Joint Conference on Artificial Intelligence (IJCAI-85)*, pp. 432–435.

Hyde, D. (1997), 'From heaps and gaps to heaps and gluts', *Mind*, 106: 641–660.

Johnson, S.C. (1967), 'Hierarchical clustering schemes', *Psychometrika*, 32, 241–254.

Kamp, H. (1975), 'Two theories of adjectives', in E. Keenan (ed.), *Formal Semantics of Natural Language*, Cambridge University Press, Cambridge, pp. 123–155.

Kamp, H. (1981), 'The paradox of the heap', in U. Mönnich (ed.), *Aspects of Philosophical Logic*, D. Reidel, Dordrecht, pp. 225–277.

Keefe, R. (2000), *Theories of Vagueness*, Cambridge University Press, Cambridge.

Keefe, R. (2007), 'Vagueness without context change', *Mind*, 116: 275–292.

Klein, E. (1980), 'The semantics of positive and comparative adjectives', *Linguistics and Philosophy*, 4: 1–45.

Luce, R.D. (1956), 'Semiorders and a theory of utility discrimination', *Econometrica*, 24: 178–191.

Pagin, P. (2011), 'Vagueness and domain restriction', in N. Clinedinst and P. Égré (eds.), *Vagueness and Language Use*, Palgrave MacMillan.

Priest, G. (1979), 'Logic of paradox', *Journal of Philosophical Logic*, 8: 219–241.

Raffman, D. (1996), 'Vagueness and Context-Relativity', *Philosophical Studies*, 81: 175–192.

Raffman, D. (2005), 'Borderline cases and bivalence', *Philosophical Review*, 114: 1–31.

Ripley, D. (ms), 'Sorting out the Sorites', Institut Jean-Nicod, ENS, Paris.

Rooij, R. van (2011a), 'Vagueness and linguistics', in Ronzitti (ed.), *Vagueness: A Guide*, Springer, pp. 123–170.

Rooij, R. van (2011b), 'Implicit versus explicit comparatives', in N. Clinedinst and P. Égré (eds.), *Vagueness and Language Use*, Palgrave MacMillan.

Rosch, E. (1973), 'On the internal structure of perceptual and semantic categories', in T.E. Moore (ed.), *Cognitive development and the acquisition of language*, New York, Academic Press.

Scott, D. and P. Suppes (1958), 'Foundational aspects of theories of measurement', *Journal of Symbolic Logic*, 23: 113–128.

Shapiro, S. (2006), *Vagueness in Context*, Clarendon Press, Oxford.

Stanley, J. (2003), 'Context, interest relativity, and the Sorites', *Analysis*, 63: 269–281.

Tversky, A. (1977), 'Features of similarity', *Psychological Review*, 84: 327–352.

Varzi, A. (2007), 'Supervaluationism and its logic', *Mind*, 116: 633–676.

Veltman, F. (1987), *Syllabus Logische Analyse 2: Vaagheid*, Universiteit van Amsterdam.

Waismann, F. (1945), 'Verifiability', *Proceedings of the Aristotelian Society*. Supplementary Volume 19: 119–150.

Wheeler, G. (2002), 'Kinds of inconsistency', in W. Carnieli, M. Coniglio and I.M.L. D'Ottaiano (eds.), *Paraconsistency: the logical way to the inconsistent*, LNPAM, New York.

Williamson, T. (1994), *Vagueness*, Rootledge, London.

Wright, C. (1975), 'On the coherence of vague predicates', *Synthese*, 30: 325–365.

Zardini, E. (2008), 'A model of tolerance', *Studia Logica*, 90: 337–368.

Robert van Rooij
Faculteit der Geesteswetenschappen
Institute for Logic, Language and Computation
Universiteit van Amsterdam
P.O. Box 94242
1090 GE Amsterdam, the Netherlands
Email: r.a.m.vanrooij@uva.nl

Comments on *Vagueness, Tolerance and Non-Transitive Entailment* by Robert van Rooij

ONDREJ MAJER

Robert van Rooij presents an original framework dealing with the formalization of vague predicates. His solution is based on a non-classical entailment, which he calls tolerant entailment. The author thoroughly discusses the relation of his solution to the major approaches to vagueness (supervaluationism, contextualism, epistemic approaches, ...) and gives an analysis of higher order vagueness.

The paper discusses several topics related to the analysis of vagueness. We shall not comment on all of them but instead concentrate on the notion of tolerant truth and its connections to modal logic.

1 Tolerance

In the beginning of the paper the author introduces the notion of tolerance, which according to him is a property constitutive to the meaning of vague predicates. Formally the tolerance principle is expressed as:

(P)   For any $x, y \in D$: $(Px \wedge x \sim_P y) \to Py$.

The tolerance principle is responsible for the most famous problem related to vague predicates—the Sorites paradox.

The author argues that an adequate formalization of vague predicates should allow (at least in some weak sense) for a truth of the tolerance principle (as it is constitutive), but that on the other hand it should block the Sorites paradox.

The author starts his analysis with a discussion of the notion of gradable predicates (like bald, tall, ...) and introduces a relation which is supposed to order individuals in the given domain with respect to the degree in which they obey the property P (the author calls it "P-er than" and denotes $<_P$). The author assumes it is natural $<_P$ to be a strict weak order (irreflexive, transitive and almost connected) and shows that the corresponding indifference relation is an equivalence and so is potentially open to the Sorites series.

It might be worth discussing in more detail in which sense the properties of the relation $<_P$ are natural (e.g. why not something weaker like partial order) as the author himself does not use it. He instead introduces a relation of semiorder and argues that it is the central notion in his approach to vagueness.

Van Rooij mentions an interesting characterization of semi-orders in the terms of a function f_P assigning to an individual a real number which can be understood as a degree in which the individual possesses the property P:

$x <_P y$ is true   iff   there is a real-valued function f_P and some fixed (small) real number ε (the margin of error) such that $f_P(x) > f_P(y) + \varepsilon$.

The corresponding indifference relation is not equivalence (it is not transitive) and can be interpreted in the terms of a margin of error:

$$x \sim_P y \quad \text{iff} \quad |f_P(x) - f_P(y)| \leq \varepsilon.$$

Though the author does not use this characterization in the rest of the article, it might be interesting to reformulate his system in terms of the "measurement function" f_P and to see if there can be found some resemblances to the degree-theoretic approach (although van Rooij shares some objections against it).

2 Non-classical entailment

Robert van Rooij proposes a framework dealing with vague expressions based on a non-classical notion of entailment which is non-transitive. He starts with a classical first order language with unary vague predicates. The corresponding models are however non-classical—each model is equipped with a relation $<_P$ (and consequently with a similarity relation $\sim_P$) for each vague predicate P. This relation strongly resembles the accessibility relation in the standard Kripkean semantics for modal logics and allows the definition of a non-classical notion of satisfaction. While formulae without a vague predicate (if any) are defined in a standard way, an atomic formula Pa is *tolerantly true* in M iff there is an individual d indistinguishable from a, such that Pd.

$M \models^t Pa \quad$ iff $\quad M \models Pd$ for some individual d such that $\mathbf{a} \sim_P \mathbf{d}$.
($\mathbf{a}$ is the individual corresponding to the name a)

The author defines two notion of entailment based on the notion of tolerant satisfaction:

(tt) $\phi \models^{tt} \psi$ iff $M \models_t \phi$ implies $M \models_t \psi$ for all models M

(ct) $\phi \models^{ct} \psi$ iff $M \models \phi$ implies $M \models_t \psi$ for all models M.

Let us note that strictly speaking the satisfaction relation should be indexed by the class of models in question as "all models" in the definition cannot mean all the first order models, but the first order models equipped by a relation of similarity for each vague predicate contained in the language.

Then the author provides an alternative definition of (possibility like) tolerant truth and the corresponding dual notion of (necessity like) strict truth. Tolerant truth in a model is defined like before, except for the clause for negation:

$M \models^t Pa \quad$ iff $\quad M \models Pd$ for some individual d such that $\mathbf{a} \sim_P \mathbf{d}$
$M \models^t \neg\phi \quad$ iff $\quad M \not\models^s \phi$.

Where the strict truth is defined as:

$M \models^s Pa \quad$ iff $\quad M \models Pd$ for all individuals d such that $\mathbf{a} \sim_P \mathbf{d}$
$M \models^s \neg\phi \quad$ iff $\quad M \not\models^t \phi$.

Finally the similarity relation $\sim_P$ is added to the language (with the classical interpretation under all notions of truth), allowing the Tolerance principle to be explicitly expressed in the language. It turns out that it is tolerance valid, i.e.

$$M \models^t \forall x, y((Px \land x \sim_P y) \to Py) \text{ for all models } M.$$

It also nicely deals with the problem of cutoff points (points a, b such that $a \sim_P b, Pa$, but $\neg Pb$) as

$$M \not\models^s (Pa \land \neg Pa), \text{ for all } M, \text{ but } M \models^t (Pa \land \neg Pa) \text{ for some } M.$$

The author then compares his solution with the main approaches to vagueness and argues that some sort of non-classical entailment is implicitly or explicitly used in the majority of them. The solution is certainly impressive and seems to solve the majority of problems connected to the formal approach to vagueness. There are still, however, some additional questions to be asked.

Which one of the tolerant consequences shall we use? The author prefers (ct) consequence, but admits also (sc). Are there any reasons to choose one rather then the other? Or any non-transitive consequence would do? Shall we use classical consequence for crisp predicates and the tolerant for the vague ones?

3   Modal reformulation

As mentioned above, the notions of strict and tolerant truth are modal by nature (at least for a logician) and seem to correspond straightforwardly to necessity and possibility. The author discusses a 'modal' reformulation of his approach, but the modalities are just shortcuts for the notions defined before. It might seem trivial, but we think it is worth trying to take the modal approach literally and check to see how straightforward the correspondence is. The attractiveness of this approach is that we keep a standard notion of consequence in a modal frame and the modal attribution of vague properties to objects is made explicit.

Let us assume we have a standard modal frame consisting of a universe W, of points $a, b, \ldots \in W$ and an accessibility relation $\sim_P$ defined on $W \times W$. Our language consists only of one propositional symbol P which (maybe a bit unusually) represents some vague property. The fact that an individual a has the property P is then represented as $a \models P$ (we shall abbreviate it as a_P, if convenient). The tolerant (strict) truth of a formula Pa in a first order model with a similarity relation corresponds to the truth of a modal formula in a frame:

(t) $a \models \Diamond P$ iff there is an $b, a \sim_P b$ such that $b \models P$

(s) $a \models \Box P$ iff for all $b, a \sim_P b$ it holds that $b \models P$.

In the modal formalization the tolerance principle is not expressible in the object language, but only on the meta-level:

(P)   for any $a, b \in W$ if $a \models P$ and $a \sim_P b$ then $b \models P$.

This condition says that truth is preserved along the accessibility relation (persistence) and is just valid for a certain class of frames. So in this form the tolerance principle does not hold in general. On the other hand, their modal versions, which as the author mentions correspond to Williamson's epistemic approach and Shapiro's contextualist approach, follow from the standard definition of necessity/possibility and are valid in all modal frames:

(PW)   for any $a, b \in W$ if $a \models \Box P$ and $a \sim_p b$ then $b \models P$

(PS)   for any $a, b \in W$ if $a \models P$ and $a \sim_p b$ then $b \models \Diamond P$.

These versions of the principle hold independently of the properties of the similarity relation. If we rewrite van Rooij's tolerant version of the tolerance principle, we obtain:

(PR)   for any $a, b \in W$ if $a \models \Box P$ and $a \sim_p b$ then $b \models \Diamond P$.

Which is equivalent to: for any $a, b \in W, a \sim_p b$ it holds that $a \not\models \Box P$ or $b \models \Diamond P$. This is valid for all frames, where the accessibility relation corresponds to semi-order:

– either $a \models P$ and then $b \models \Diamond P$ (from the symmetry of $\sim_P$)

– or $a \not\models P$ hence $a \models \Diamond \neg P$ (from the reflexivity of $\sim_P$).

In fact (PR) holds for all frames with reflexive and symmetric accessibility relation.

Tolerant and strict entailment in the modal setup

Tolerant entailment in van Rooij's system is defined on a class of classical first order models equipped with a similarity relation satisfying some properties; namely, those following from the fact that it is based on a semiorder. Its modal translation will be defined on a class of modal frames, again with a certain kind of accessibility relation.

Tolerant entailment (tt) says, that ϕ tolerantly entails ψ (in a class $\mathscr{F}$ of modal frames) iff $F, a \models \Diamond \phi$, implies $F, a \models \Diamond \psi$ for all $a \in F$ and all $F \in \mathscr{F}$ which we can rewrite as

(tt) $\phi \models^{tt}_{\mathscr{F}} \psi$ iff $F \models \Diamond \phi \rightarrow \Diamond \psi$ for all $F \in \mathscr{F}$.

Similarly, ϕ (ct)-entails ψ (in a class of modal frames $\mathscr{F}$) iff $F, a \models \phi$, implies $F, a \models \Diamond \phi$ for all $a \in F$ and all $F \in \mathscr{F}$ which we can rewrite as

(ct) $\phi \models^{ct}_{\mathscr{F}} \psi$ iff $F \models \phi \rightarrow \Diamond \psi$ for all $F \in \mathscr{F}$.

The last entailment author discusses is (sc), which is equivalent to $F, a \models \Box \phi$, implies $F, a \models \psi$ for all $a \in F$ and all $F \in \mathscr{F}$ which we can rewrite as

(sc) $\phi \models^{sc}_{\mathscr{F}} \psi$ iff $F \models \Box \phi \rightarrow \psi$ for all $F \in \mathscr{F}$.

There is no room here to develop this idea further, let us just suggest some (possible) advantages of this approach:

- the non-standard notion of tolerant truth/entailment is replaced by the standard notion of truth/validity in a modal frame about which there are good intuitions and which is well studied

- it might be interesting to observe if different sorts of non-standard entailment can be forced by different conditions on accessibility relations in modal frames, in particular if there is any other relation than the similarity based on a semi-order satisfying the conditions of tolerant entailment

- higher-order vagueness would be represented as a standard embedding of modalities and does not need a special treatment

There are obviously some disadvantages that should be mentioned. Unlike in the original article the tolerance principle is not formulated in the object language but only in the metalanguage. This, however, should not be a big problem as the principle itself is about reasoning with vague predicates. For some it might also seem unintuitive or at least not straightforward to model vague properties as propositions rather than predicates.

The presented proposals do not suggest that the framework introduced in the original article should be completely reformulated. Rather, they represent an attempt to see this framework from a slightly different point of view which might show some interesting connections with standard, well developed logical frameworks.

Ondrej Majer
Institute of Philosophy
Academy of Sciences of the Czech Republic
Jilská 1
110 00 Prague 1, Czech Republic
Email: majer@flu.cas.cz

Reply to Ondrej Majer's Comments on
Vagueness, Tolerance and Non-Transitive Entailment

ROBERT VAN ROOIJ

In the paper I suggested that for many predicates P, the 'P-er than' relation is a strict weak order. Ondrej Majer asks why I assume that, given that I concentrate myself later in the paper on semi-orders. Well, in case the ordering relation can be made more precise by means of measurement phrases, there is no choice but to use a strict weak order. In fact, speaker's intuitions about a relation like 'taller than' very much correspond with that of strict weak orders. Having said that, I realize very well that there are many comparative relations which have only weaker properties (for instance only a partial order), 'smarter than' is arguably one of them. My point for introducing strict weak orders was not so much to claim that most comparative relations are of this type, but rather that if this is assumed, it can hardly be explained why the Sorties paradox is a problem. I believe that the Sorites paradox only arises because the way *we* normally observe *tallness*, for instance, the *observably taller than*-relation should be a semi-order, rather than a strict weak one.

Can the use of degrees in the measurement of semi-orders not be used to formulate a degree-based analysis of vagueness?, Ondrej Majer wonders. Perhaps, I didn't try out, and I invite Majer to work out this interesting thought. But I agree with Ondrej that there exists a certain similarity between the approach I favor and fuzzy logic-based analyses of logic. In contrast to most standard logicians and semanticists I am not impressed by the standard objections that formulas like $Pa \wedge \neg Pa$ and $Pa \vee \neg Pa$ are not predicted to be contradictions and tautologies, respectively, if P is a vague predicate. In fact, this is at it should be (see Atxatib and Pelletier, 2011 and Ripley, 2011), and my notions of strict and tolerant satisfaction account for this. Moreover, I believe that the most natural notion of consequence that can be formulated using using fuzzy logic is a non-transitive one. Having said that, I don't believe that we need as many values of truth that fuzzy logicians standardly assume: three or four can do a whole lot.

Ondrej Majer correctly observes that given the semantics I propose, there are a number of tolerant (non-transitive) consequence relations that can be formulated. In the paper I suggest to use consequence relation ct (according to which the conclusion should be (at least) tolerantly true, if all the premises are (at least) classically true), and Majer reasonably asks why? In fact, in Cobreros et al. (2011) we use the same semantics but propose a different notion of logical consequence: st-consequence, according to which the conclusion should be (at least) tolerantly true, if all the premises are (at least) strictly true. The preference for this consequence relation is motivated by the following observation: st-consequence is the only consequence relation that validates the tolerance principle, the deduction principle, and modus ponens.

Ondrej Majer wonders whether I would like to use classical consequence for crisp predicates and tolerant consequence for vague ones. This is certainly one possibility, but perhaps not the most natural one. I assumed that for vague predicates there is a difference between strict, classical, and tolerant satisfaction. It is natural to assume, however, that such a distinction does not exist for crisp predicates. In that case, my tolerant notion of consequence comes down to classical consequence, and I don't need two distinct notions of consequence. I believe this is a natural way to treat crisp predicates. This is perhaps especially the case because there seems to exist predicates that have both crisp and tolerant readings, like *bald*. It is perhaps more natural to assume two distinct readings of *bald* than two ways of reasoning with it.

If ones observes a problem with a logic to describe some phenomena, there are at many times two strategies available. Either you change the logic, or you reformulate the sentences, or the principles you wanted to model. In fact, this was in a sense the point of the paper: Williamson (1994) and others wanted to model vagueness, and the tolerance-principle that governed it. However, many of them relied very much on classical logic. They thus had to reformulate the tolerance-principle. Similarly, Ondrej Majer proposes to reformulate the sentences that talk about vagueness in terms of modal statements. Instead of using this strategy, I proposed to reformulate the logic. Now, it was already well-known that the Sorites paradox could be solved by giving up on transitivity of inference, but it was generally agreed that this was a no-go, because entailment is transitive, isn't it? Well, no, it doesn't have to (in exceptional circumstances)! Except for logical conservatism, I don't see any good reason to stick to this old notion of consequence. Moreover, there is nothing wrong with a non-transitive notion of consequence: it has a clear semantics, and later work by me and co-workers (Pablo Cobreros, Paul Égré, and David Ripley) shows that this logic also has a very natural proof-theory and can be used to solve a number of other paradoxical phenomena as well (such as the liar paradox). Furthermore, this framework is arguable a more natural description of some empirical observations made by Atxatib and Pelletier (2011) and Ripley (2011) than a modal one as suggested by Ondrej Majer. Thus, I like the reformulation of Ondrej to give a modal reformulation of my model, but no, I am not going to follow it.

BIBLIOGRAPHY

Alxatib, S. and J. Pelletier (2011), 'The psychology of vagueness: Borderline cases and contradictions', *Mind and Language*. **26**: 287–326

Cobreros, P., P. Égré, D. Ripley, and R. van Rooij (2011a), 'Tolerent, classical, strict', to appear in *Journal of Philosophical Logic*, DOI: 10.1007/210992-010-9165-z.

Cobreros, P., P. Égré, D. Ripley, and R. van Rooij (2011b), 'Supervaluationism and mixed consequence in a super-/sub-valuationist setting', to appear in *Studia Logica*.

Cobreros, P., P. Égré, D. Ripley, and R. van Rooij (2011c), 'Reaching transparent truth', submitted.

Ripley, D. (2011), 'Contradictions at the borders', in R. Nouwen, R. van Rooij, U. Sauerland, and H. Schmitz (eds.), *Vagueness in Communication*, Springer, pp. 169–188

Williamson, T. (1994), *Vagueness*, Rootledge, London.

Comparing Context Updates in Delineation and Scale Based Models of Vagueness

CHRISTOPH ROSCHGER[1]

1 Introduction

Although there exists a multitude of different approaches to vagueness in linguistics, there seems to be a general agreement that vagueness involves one or another kind of context dependence. E.g. Lewis [17] gives a high level overview of the use of contexts in natural language and illustrates that they are essential for modeling the shifting of vague standards. Therefore a vague sentence cannot be interpreted in isolation from the rest of a discourse; instead its truth conditions depend on—implicit or explicit—assumptions made by the conversationalists so far. Models of vagueness can be roughly divided into two groups: scale based and delineation models. Whereas scale based models explicitly model vague standards as cut off points on some appropriate scale, delineation models take another route. Vague adjectives are treated as boolean predicates whose extension crucially is context dependent. Scale based models are nowadays more popular in linguistics; there is much work going on in exploring connections between the scale structure of gradable adjectives and their use in natural language. Delineation models, on the other hand, have their roots in the philosophy of vagueness and typically make use of supervaluation [5].

The general aim of this contribution is to compare these two kinds of approaches in terms of their ability to model the notions of context and context update and to elucidate where their particular strengths and weaknesses lie in this respect. For this purpose, two concrete models are picked, namely Barker [3] as an example for a scale based approach and Kyburg and Morreau [15] as an example for a delineation based approach. Finally also Shapiro's [19] account of vagueness in context is presented and we point out how to combine it with Kyburg and Morreau's approach. Shapiro himself is not a linguist, but his model explicitly refers to conversationalists taking part in a conversation during which vague standards are shifted. The main result is to show in which situations Barker's and Kyburg and Morreau's approaches make the same predictions and which aspects cannot be modeled properly in either model. As an example Kyburg and Morreau's model is clearly superior when the hearer is confronted with new information which requires the shifting of vague standards such that previously established information has to be retracted. Barker however does not consider such situations; once vague information is added to the current context it is never invalidated. On the other hand, Barker's model provides more flexibility when it comes to predicate modifiers such as

---

[1] Supported by Eurocores-ESF/FWF grant I143-G15 (LogICCC-LoMoReVI)

very, *definitely*, or *clearly* and can straightforwardly handle more complex comparisons including degrees, such as '*Jack is 2 cm taller than John*".

The paper is structured as follows: in Section 2 we give a short overview highlighting some examples of how contexts are modeled in linguistics for other purposes than vagueness. In Section 3 we present Barker's, Kyburg and Morreau's, and Shapiro's approaches in more detail. Finally, Section 4 first points out how to combine Shapiro's approach with Kyburg and Morreau's and then explores the mentioned connections between Barker's and Kyburg and Morreau's approaches. This done by first defining a simple intermediate representation for contexts such that both types of contexts as defined by Barker and by Kyburg and Morreau can be translated into this representation. Then we show that, if a situation is modeled twice, one time as defined by Barker's scale based approach and one time as defined by Kyburg and Morreau's delineation approach, the same intermediate representation is reached in both models.

2   Contexts in Linguistics

Vagueness is not the only motivation for explicitly modeling context in linguistic formal semantics. Contexts are also most prominently employed for resolving anaphoric relations (see e.g. [7, 6]) or for modeling (existential) presuppositions [8] in a compositional way. In these cases contexts are identified with (sets of) possible assignments of objects to variables. The main point of these so-called *dynamic semantics* is that the meaning of a proposition is identified with its ability to update the context, its *context change potential*. Typically contexts are modeled as sets of possible worlds. Deciding if a proposition is *true* in a given context C then amounts to updating C accordingly and checking if the resulting context is empty or not.

As an example consider the text "*A man walks. He whistles.*" Assume, for the sake of simplicity, that the domain of all men under consideration consists of just three ones, men $\sharp 1$, $\sharp 2$, and $\sharp 3$, the predicate *walks* is true for both men $\sharp 1$ and $\sharp 2$, and the predicate *whistles* is true only for man $\sharp 2$. Moreover, assume that previous analysis has already yielded that *He* refers to *man*, therefore the text can be annotated as "*A man$_1$ walks. He$_1$ whistles.*" The semantic analysis of "*A man$_1$ walks*" first introduces a new discourse referent—Heim uses file cards as a metaphor—such that the individual referred by 1 is a man and walks. Thus the intermediary context is $\{\{1 \mapsto \sharp 1\}, \{1 \mapsto \sharp 2\}\}$. Similarly, "*He$_1$ whistles.*" filters out the first assignment since man $\sharp 1$ does not whistle in our little model resulting in the final context $\{1 \mapsto \sharp 2\}$. More complex ways of updating the context arise when taking into account relative clauses, quantifiers, or negation.

3   Contexts and Vagueness

When dealing with vagueness richer structures than just possible assignments from variables to individuals are required. In this section we outline three different approaches to that purpose: Barker [3] as an example of a scale based[2] account of vagueness, Kyburg

---

[2]In linguistics scale based approaches are also called *degree based*. In order to avoid confusion with other degree based approaches to vagueness such as fuzzy logic, we use the name *scale based* here. This is to stress that degrees only occur on certain scales corresponding to vague adjectives (such as degrees of height, of weight, or of color) but not as degrees of truth.

and Morreau's approach as an account of a delineation based one, and Shapiro's approach which is also delineation based.

Whereas scale-based accounts of vagueness map vague predicates to degrees on an adequate scale, delineation accounts treat predicates like *tall* as boolean predicates whose extension is context dependent. Specific scales can then be modeled by non-vague propositions constraining the space of possible precifications.

Barker's and Kyburg and Morreau's approaches may not be the most prominent examples of scale and delineation based linguistic accounts of vagueness. For example, other more popular approaches are Kennedy's [11, 10] and Klein's [12, 13, 14]. However, in this contribution the focus is at comparing how the context, and therefore the interpretations of vague predicates, are updated dynamically during a conversation, and in this respect both Barker's and Kyburg and Morreau's approaches are more explicit than e.g. Klein's and Kennedy's. Barker himself also gives this as a motivation for his approach [2]: *"However, what is still missing [...] is an explicit account of precisely how the context change potential of an expression depends on the compositional meaning of the expression."* Finally, Shapiro motivates his contextual approach to vagueness very elaborately, but more from a philosophical point of view than from a linguistic one. Nevertheless, as described below, his model lines up very nicely Kyburg and Morreau's.

3.1 Barker's approach

As an example of a scale based approach, Chris Barker [3] defines a context C as a set of possible worlds w where in each world $w \in C$ a vague predicate has a precise threshold value and each relevant object a precise (maximal) degree to which it possesses the predicate in question. Barker's running example is the vague predicate *tall*; the meaning of this predicate is denoted as $[\![tall]\!]$. Although many vague predicates such as *tall* or *heavy* intuitively correspond to a set of linearly ordered degrees, this is not the case for predicates like *stupid* or *clever*. Barker therefore only assumes that the set of degrees is partially ordered and obeys monotonicity, i.e. if *John* is *stupid* to degree d, he is also stupid to each degree smaller than d.

Formally there is a delineation function $\mathbf{d}$ which maps gradable adjective meanings to degrees locally for each possible world; for example $\mathbf{d}(w)([\![tall]\!])$ denotes the (vague) standard of tallness in the world w. For a degree d and a vague predicate α, let $w[d/\alpha]$ denote a possible world which is exactly like w except for setting $\mathbf{d}(w)(\alpha)$ to d. Moreover, for each vague predicate there exists a corresponding constant relation in the object language, e.g. **tall**, where $\mathbf{tall}(d,\mathbf{j})$ gives all possible worlds where the individual denoted by $\mathbf{j}$ is tall *at least* to the degree d. Other scale based approaches, e.g. that of Kennedy [11], favor another more transparent formalization instead, where each individual is assigned a single degree of height. Deciding if *John* is *tall* at least to degree d then amounts to comparing d with John's degree of height. However, this is not sufficient without further restrictions on the scale structure, namely if the scale is not linearly ordered. For linear scales Kennedy notes that such a formalization is equivalent to Barker's one. In this case, *John*'s degree of height in the possible world w can be expressed as $\max\{d : w \in \mathbf{tall}(d,\mathbf{j})\}$ using Barker's definitions.

As argued by Klein [12] vague adjectives always have to be interpreted relative to a comparison class: while John may be tall in some context, he may not be a tall basketball player. Even, if the adjective occurs without the noun (i.e. basketball player) this comparison class is seen as contextually determined. This can easily be incorporated into Barker's model by defining different threshold values for each relevant comparison class, effectively treating e.g. *"tall for a basketball player"* and *"tall for a man"* as different vague predicates with the all possible worlds w satisfying that $\mathbf{d}(w)(\llbracket tall_{basketball\,player}\rrbracket)$ $\geq \mathbf{d}(w)(\llbracket tall_{man}\rrbracket)$.

Initially a large context C stands for ignorance.[3] If, e.g., only the individuals *John* and *Eve* and the vague predicate *tall* are under consideration (and we do not yet know anything about *John*'s and *Jack*'s tallness), C consists of all potential combinations of threshold values for *tall* as well as John's and Eve's degrees of height. If we then hear the utterance *"John is tall"*, all possible worlds in C are filtered out where John's degree of height is higher than the threshold for tallness resulting in a new context C'. Thus, the evaluation of such simple sentences is made locally in each possible world under consideration. The meaning of *tall* therefore is defined by Barker as[4]

$$\llbracket tall\rrbracket(x)(C) = \{w \in C : w \in \mathbf{tall}(\mathbf{d}(w)(\llbracket tall\rrbracket),x)\}.$$

So, $\llbracket tall\rrbracket(x)$ denotes a function which takes a context C as argument and returns all possible worlds in C, where the individual denoted by x exceeds the (local) standard of tallness denoted by $\mathbf{d}(w)(\llbracket tall\rrbracket)$. The new context C' is then obtained by applying $\llbracket tall\rrbracket$ to the original context C:

$$C' = \llbracket tall\rrbracket(\mathbf{j})(C)$$

with $\mathbf{j}$ referring to *John*. If we then hear *"Jack is taller than John"*, again worlds in C' are filtered out by comparing Jack's and John's degrees of height there. In this case, automatically only possible worlds are left in the final context where Eve is regarded as tall as well (due to monotonicity of the scale structure).

Barker's approach allows one to model so-called *predicate modifiers* such as *very*, *definitely*, or *clearly*. Like for simple predicates such as *tall*, *very tall* operates separately on each possible world under consideration: An individual is considered as *very* tall, if she is not only *tall*, but *tall* by some margin. The exact size of this margin is again subject to vagueness and may differ between possible worlds (note that the first argument α is the meaning of a predicate, e.g. $\llbracket tall\rrbracket$):

$$\llbracket very\rrbracket(\alpha)(x)(C) =_{\mathrm{DEF}} \{w \in \alpha(x)(C) : \exists d.(w[d/\alpha] \in \alpha(x)(C)$$
$$\wedge \mathbf{very}(\mathbf{d}(w)(\llbracket very\rrbracket),\mathbf{d}(w)(\alpha),d)\}$$

where $\mathbf{d}(w)(\llbracket very\rrbracket)$ denotes the (local) margin imposed by *very* in world w; and **very** is a relation over degrees such that $\mathbf{very}(s,d,d')$ holds exactly if the difference between d' and d is larger than s.

---

[3]It seems reasonable to assume the context to be finite due to some level of granularity enforced by our perceptual and cognitive capabilities.

[4]Barker, in common linguistic tradition, gives all his definitions in lambda-notation, e.g. as $\llbracket tall\rrbracket = \lambda x\lambda C.\{w \in C : w \in \mathbf{tall}(\mathbf{d}(w)(\llbracket tall\rrbracket),x)\}$. Here, we chose a syntax more familiar to non-linguists. Moreover, note the use of $\llbracket tall\rrbracket$ inside its own definition. This circularity is of a harmless type as the usage of $\llbracket tall\rrbracket$ inside of $\mathbf{d}(w)(\llbracket tall\rrbracket)$ is only to refer to the function's name as a marker.

Other more complicated predicates like *definitely tall* do not operate on each world locally, but depend on the overall structure of the context. Let C be a context and $w \in C$ a possible world. Then "*John is definitely tall*" is true in w if and only if John is tall in all worlds u where John is as tall as in w, i.e. the local degree of John's height in u is compared to all possible standards for tallness adequate for this specific height. Thus, the predicate modifier $[\![definitely]\!]$ can be defined as follows:

$$[\![definitely]\!](\alpha)(x)(C) =_{\text{DEF}} \{w \in \alpha(x)(C) : \forall d.(w[d/\alpha] \in C) \to w[d/\alpha] \in \alpha(x)(C)\}.$$

Similarly to the predicate modifiers *definitely* and *very* Barker also gives precise truth conditions for *clearly*, which is a combination of both very and definitely. The comparative form *taller* can also be formalized using Barker's framework as a predicate modifier: $[\![-er]\!]$ takes as first argument the meaning of a predicate such as $[\![tall]\!]$ and returns a function for comparing two individuals with respect to *tallness*. Barker proposes different different ways of defining the comparative based on different treatments of the comparative in linguistic literature. One of them is:

$$[\![-er]\!](\alpha)(x)(y)(C) =_{\text{DEF}} \{w \in C : \exists d.(w[d/\alpha] \in \alpha(y)) \land (\neg w[d/\alpha] \in \alpha(x))\}.$$

Using this formulation an individual **a** is *taller* than an individual **b** if and only if there is a degree d such that **a** is at least that tall, but **b** is not. The important point here is that no matter which formulation is used the comparative does not depend on the (local) standard of *tallness*; and neither does an utterance of the form "**a** *is taller than* **b**" have any sharpening update effect on this standard.

Although not considered by Barker, also negation can be easily formulated as a predicate modifier. The possible worlds where an individual **a** is *not tall* are exactly those filtered out when updating with the information that **a** is *tall*:

$$[\![not]\!](\alpha)(x)(C) =_{\text{DEF}} C \backslash [\![\alpha]\!](x)(C).$$

As Barker explains, context update can account for two different kinds of statements, namely descriptive and meta-linguistic ones. Consider as an example the sentence "*For an American Feynman is tall.*": in a descriptive reading this statement can be uttered to inform a hearer (vaguely) about Feynman's height. But if the exact height of Feynman is known to both conversationalists (e.g. because he is standing next to them), the sentence can be used to tell the hearer about one's usage of the word *tall*, i.e. about the general tallness of people in America.

In general, the further the conversation proceeds and the more sentences are uttered, the smaller and the more precise the context gets. According to Barker, possible worlds are never added to the context during the conversation. This seems consistent with other dynamic linguistic approaches modeling e.g. anaphoric relations or existential presuppositions as explained in Section 2. There, possible worlds consist of assignments of variables to individuals instead of containing threshold values and so on. However the contexts do not necessarily get smaller the more the conversation proceeds, but this is due only to the fact that new variables may be introduced during a conversation. As Barker requires that all relevant individuals and vague adjectives are a priori present in the initial context, this situation does not occur here.

3.2 Kyburg and Morreau's approach

An alternative approach has been introduced by Kyburg and Morreau [15]. In contrast to many other linguistic theories of vagueness this one does not employ degrees and scales nor threshold values for vague standards. For vague predicates such as *tall* Barker's approach is straightforward, since for deciding whether a person is tall we take into account only her height, which can be measured in a natural way. There are, however, other predicates like *clever* for which there exists no such natural scale. For example, we can say that some person is *clever* in some respect but not in some other respect.

According to Kyburg and Morreau therefore a context is modeled as a set of sentences over a "vague language". They employ the metaphor of a blackboard where the common knowledge and shared presuppositions are written visible to all participants. The vague language is standard first order predicate logic augmented with a sentential operator D. In contrast to classical logic, however, predicates may be decided only partially for vague predicates.

Thus a model is a partial interpretation of the vague predicates together with possible (consistent) ways of making them precise; the so-called *precification space*. At each precification point in such a space, an object can belong to the extension of a vague predicate or to the anti-extension or to none of these. Consistency of precification points requires that no object is both in the extension and in the anti-extension of a vague predicate at the same time.

This is formalized as follows: a model is defined as a quadruple $\langle \mathcal{U}, \mathcal{P}, \leq, l \rangle$ where $\mathcal{U}$ denotes the domain of relevant individuals, $\mathcal{P}$ denotes a set of abstract precification points, and l denotes a partial interpretation function. Therefore, l assigns to each predicate symbol R and each precification point $p \in \mathcal{P}$ two disjoint subsets of $\mathcal{U}$, namely $l^+(R,p)$ and $l^-(R,p)$, i.e. the extension and anti-extension of R at p.[5] The interpretation l must respect the partial ordering $\leq$ with minimal point @ in the sense that for all points $p, q \in \mathcal{P}$, if $p \leq q$ then $l^+(R,p) \subseteq l^+(R,q)$ and $l^-(R,p) \subseteq l^-(R,q)$.

Not every consistent precification does make sense in a conversation. If we have two people, *John* and *Jack*, where *John* is taller than *Jack*, we must not judge *Jack* as *tall* and *John* as *not tall*. Such restrictions on the structure of the precification space are called *penumbral connections*.

Another requirement on the precification space is that for each precification point p there is a further complete refinement q of p. A precification point is complete if each object is either in the extension or the anti-extension of the vague predicates in question. This requirement directly refers to supervaluationist theories of vagueness [5]. As in other (linguistic) theories, e.g. [16] and [9] supervaluation then is used for evaluating truth at a precification point. A formula is true or false at a given precification point, if it is true or false, respectively, for all possible complete precifications; evaluation at a complete point is classical. Truth in a model is identified with truth at the root @.

The notions of *determinate truth* and *borderline* cases are defined as follows: A proposition ϕ is called *determinately true* or *determinately false*, denoted as $D(\phi)$ and $D(\neg\phi)$, if it is true or false, respectively, in all possible precification points in the whole context space $\mathcal{P}$, i.e. possible contexts. If there exist both such precification points

---

[5]For n-place relation symbols the extension and anti-extension consist of subsets of $\mathcal{U}^n$.

in $\mathscr{P}$, then ϕ is called *indeterminate*, denoted as $I(\phi)$. Note that a proposition of the form $D(\phi)$ or $I(\phi)$ is not vague anymore since it is evaluated on the whole space of contexts no matter which one is the current one. If α is a vague predicate and x an object then x is called a borderline case of α if $I(\alpha(x))$ holds. Therefore, in distinction to Barker, it is possible to have a precification point where both $I(tall(x))$ and $tall(x)$ are available signifying that x is a borderline case of *tallness*, but the current conversation has established that x is to be regarded as *tall*.

For example, the penumbral connection indicated above can be formalized as

$$D((\text{taller-than}(John, Jack) \wedge \text{tall}(Jack)) \rightarrow \text{tall}(John))).$$

Kyburg and Morreau use *belief revision theory* [1] to describe context updates. Belief revision is a well studied topic in knowledge representation. It is based on the definition of a *revision operator* $*$ for adding new information to a knowledge base (and thus possibly invalidating old one). A knowledge base is a set of sentences closed under deduction. The idea is to view the context as a knowledge base and to perform a context update by revising the current context with the new information. While belief revision operates on the set of sentences known to be true at a point in a conversation, an update with consistent information can be regarded as moving alongside a branch in the precification space in an adequate model. If vague information is invalidated, i.e. if the new information is inconsistent with previously established information, then this can be regarded as a jump to another branch in the precification space.

When performing a context update with a set of propositions, it seems reasonable to treat vague and non-vague propositions differently: Take the new information as a starting point. Then simply add the non-vague sentences of the prior context. Thus, non-vague sentences thus are never invalidated, so the resulting context may be inconsistent if the new information contradicts some non-vague sentence in the old knowledge base. Kyburg and Morreau argue that in this case inconsistency appropriately models the resulting context, because even a human agent is at least puzzled when faced with non-vague contradictory information. In the following we assume that new non-vague information is never inconsistent. For the vague sentences Kyburg and Morreau give examples, such as *accommodation*, where human agents do invalidate former sentences in order to maintain consistency. As an example a pig may be referred to as *"the fat one"* in one situation if it stands next to another skinny pig. In the next situation, where it stands next to an even fatter one, *"the fat one"* designates the other pig. This process is called *accommodation*, the shifting of vague standards. Therefore, after adding the non-vague sentences, just add as many sentences from the original context while retaining consistency. By this procedure a new precification point in the space $\mathscr{P}$ is reached, since the penumbral connections belong to the non-vague sentences which are not invalidated.

Kyburg and Morreau's way of updating ensures that the new information will be present in the resulting context, only old vague sentences are invalidated. More complex situations arise if there are several distinct ways to form the new context. Consider, e.g., a context C includes two vague propositions ϕ and ψ. When updating with the proposition $\neg\phi \vee \neg\psi$, there are several possibilities: either invalidate ϕ, or ψ, or invalidate both. The last one may seem as the only canonical solution in this situation, but both other possibilities are superior in the sense that less information is invalidated.

The solution offered by belief revision (in short) is the following: one defines an operator $*$ for revising a knowledge base with new information, where a knowledge base is identified with a set of sentences closed under modus ponens. Such an operator is characterized by the so-called AGM postulates.

Let C be a consistent, deductively closed knowledge base and s a sentence. Then $*$ is a belief revision operator if it satisfies the following rules:

Closure $C * s$ is a deductively closed set of formulas,

Success $s \in C * s$,

Inclusion $C * s \subseteq C + s$, where $C + s$ is the deductive closure of $C \cup \{s\}$,

Vacuity if $\neg s \notin C$ then $C * s = C + s$,

Consistency $C * s$ is consistent, if s is consistent, and

Extensionality if s and t are logically equivalent then $C * s = C * t$.

These postulates ensure that a revision operator "behaves well" in the sense that the new information is guaranteed to be present in the resulting context C (Success), no superfluous unrelated information is added to C (Inclusion), enough information is invalidated in order to retain consistency (Consistent), and the update is independent of the syntactic representation of s (Extensionality). Whatever can be proved using the AGM-postulates will then hold for *any* way of updating the context. The theory on belief revision is well developed and there are alternative characterizations of the revision operator giving more concrete choices for devising such operators.

Following Kyburg and Morreau, suitable operators discard as little information as possible when confronted with new inconsistent data. Otherwise, a trivial revision operator would be to discard the whole knowledge base C when confronted with new inconsistent information s. As Kyburg and Morreau argue, such a behavior is not desirable, as only as little information as possible inconsistent with s will invalidated by a human. However, this is not always an unambiguous prescription as illustrated by the following example. It can be shown that the definition of a suitable revision operator boils down to the definition of a so-called *selection function* which chooses one knowledge base out of a set of (maximal consistent) ones.

Consider two men, John and Jack standing next to each other, where Jack is taller and has more hair than John and consider *"John is not tall"*, and *"Jack is not bald"* as vague propositions which have already been uttered during the conversation. Now assume that a speaker mentions *"the tall and bald guy"*. The resulting context then has to designate exactly one of these two men as tall and bald, but without revoking either *"John is not tall"* or *"Jack is not bald"* this will not happen. In the first case John's status of tallness is not added to the resulting context. We then can infer that John is the man referred to and hence also is regarded as tall. On the other hand we can as well revoke Jack's status of baldness, ultimately picking him as referent.

A corresponding selection function thus has to choose one out of the two (maximal) information sets, where either John is not regarded as tall or Jack is not regarded as bald. Which one of these will be taken is beyond Kyburg and Morreau's account of vagueness.

3.3 Shapiro's approach

Shapiro's approach to vagueness [19, 20] shares many features with supervaluation, but also some fundamental differences. A common criticism of supervaluation focuses on the completability requirement [4]. Arguably, in some cases such complete precifications may not exist, as for example in typical Sorites situations; instead they are artifacts of the model.

As a running example Shapiro uses a Sorites situation as follows: assume, 10000 men are lined up ordered according to their amount and arrangement of hair where the first man has no hair at all and the last one has full hair. A group of conversationalists is asked to judge whether man $\sharp 1$ is bald, then man $\sharp 2$ and so on, where all conversationalist must establish one judgment for each man $\sharp i$. The principle of *tolerance* then dictates that we cannot judge a man $\sharp i$ to be bald, when at the same time judging man $\sharp i + 1$ not to be bald, considering that the amount and arrangement of hair of these men differ only marginally. However, this implies that there exist no complete precifications consistent with the facts that the first and the last men are bald and not bald, respectively, and therefore the principle of tolerance cannot be seen as a penumbral connection with the completability requirement in force.

On the technical side, Shapiro's approach is obtained by dropping the completability requirement. Instead it is allowed at each precification point to leave the baldness of some men unjudged. This way, by distinguishing between ϕ *is false at a further precification point* and ϕ *is not true at all further precification points* he obtains more fine-grained notions of truth than in a supervaluationist framework, where these two propositions coincide. Most notably, the tolerance principle can be formulated for Sorites situations as a penumbral connection requiring that there are no complete precifications.

Shapiro introduces the notion of *forcing*. A proposition ϕ is forced at a precification point P if for each refinement Q of P there is a further refinement Q' of P such that ϕ is true at Q'. He argues that a formula ϕ being forced at each precification point is an adequate characterization of determinate truth as described above for supervaluationist approaches. Note that both these notions coincide if we enforce the completability requirement.

There is also a further, more conceptual, difference between supervaluation and Shapiro's approach: supervaluation entertains the slogan *'Truth is supertruth'* implying that truth is not to be interpreted locally with respect to a single precification point but globally for the whole precification space. Accordingly, precification points themselves only serve as technical vehicle for determining truth. According to Shapiro, however, truth is always relative to some precification point and as a conversation proceeds, the current point may and will change. In the next section we will explain why this point of view is arguably more adequate for linguistic contextual models of vagueness than the supervaluation approach, because precification points do indeed correspond to (intermediary) contexts; both notions, *truth in a context* and *determinate truth* are of interest.

In the beginning of a conversation only the externally determined non-vague facts are known to the hearer. As the conversation proceeds and sentences are uttered more and more judgments are made resulting in new contexts which are refinements of the initial one. This means that typically propositions which are true or false remain true or false, respectively, only (some) yet unsettled cases are decided. Shapiro therefore models the context space as a tree structure with the initial context at the root and demonstrates that context update basically consists of moving alongside this tree's branches. However, when it comes to Sorites situations, Shapiro carefully argues that at some point a jump to another branch in the tree will occur, invalidating propositions which have already been true in a former context. So, when going through a Sorites series as above, at some point j, the speaker will eventually switch from *bald* to *not bald*. Then not only man $\sharp j$ is added to the anti-extension of *bald*, instead the last few men judged previously are removed from the extension of *bald*. This is necessary in order for tolerance to remain in force. Shapiro does not, however, give any clue on how actually to determine how many men are affected from this context jump.

4 Comparison of contextual approaches to vagueness

In this section we compare the three different accounts of vagueness presented above. We point out how to combine Shapiro's and Kyburg and Morreau's approaches and why this indeed makes sense.

For Barker's and Kyburg and Morreau's approaches we show how a conversational context can be translated from one approach into the other one and to what respect predictions made differ between these approaches. Moreover we elucidate differences in the expressiveness of the approaches, i.e. in which situations which approach is superior to the other one.

4.1 Shapiro - Kyburg/Morreau

Shapiro's and Kyburg and Morreau's accounts of vagueness are both delineation-based, but whereas the latter one makes use of supervaluation, Shapiro presents his approach as an alternative to supervaluation.

A context according to both approaches amounts to a partial interpretation of the (vague) predicates in question. Therefore a context as in Kyburg and Morreau has essentially the same structure as a context according to Shapiro. However, the space of possible contexts, and therefore the way how connectives (and modifiers such as *definitely*) are interpreted in a context may differ. A model according to Kyburg and Morreau is also a model according to Shapiro, but not the other way round as both are partial interpretations, but Shapiro does not require that the completability requirement is in force, i.e. that each partial interpretation can be extended to a complete interpretation; there it is possible for penumbral connections to constrain the context space further than with that requirement in force. Therefore, it may be the case that a complete assignment in a model according to Kyburg and Morreau is not available there. This occurs especially in Sorites situations as explained in the previous section where the penumbral connections forbid complete sharpenings:

Using supervaluation as suggested by Kyburg and Morreau, the sentence "*Man $\sharp i$ is bald, but man $\sharp i + 1$ is not*" is not predicted to be (determinately) false (for $1 \leq i < 10000$), instead it is indeterminate which, arguably, goes against intuition. Moreover, the sentence "*There exists an i such that man $\sharp i$ is bald and man $\sharp i + 1$ is not*" turns out to be determinately true! Shapiro, however, argues that by the principle of tolerance there exist no complete interpretations in such situations and therefore predicts both sentences as expected. He also notes that his formal definitions of definite truth coincide with the ones given by supervaluation in situations where all partial interpretations can indeed be extended to compete ones.

Shapiro's account of vagueness may seem incompatible with Kyburg and Morreau's one when it comes to context update at the first glance. Shapiro does not explicitly write about context update, but rather of moving from one point in the precification space to another one.

Since, however, in Shapiro's approach the non-vague facts—including also penumbral connections—are guaranteed to hold at all precification points, we can interpret a context update as described by Kyburg and Morreau simply as a jump to another precification point. This way, Kyburg and Morreau's way of updating contexts can be regarded as a refinement of Shapiro's, describing the update more precisely by means of belief revision theory.

As noted in the last section Shapiro's notion of truth at a context arguably fits Kyburg and Morreau's model more than supervaluation. Whereas the latter one promotes (super)truth relative to the whole context space, Kyburg and Morreau very much agree with Shapiro in regarding partial interpretations as concrete contexts in conversations which change over time, and with truth being relative to such a context. Therefore a version of Kyburg and Morreau's approach with Shapiro's account of vagueness instead of supervaluation seems fruitful. Technically this allows one to disregard the completability requirement when modeling context spaces.

4.2   Kyburg/Morreau - Barker

Barker's and Kyburg and Morreau's accounts of vagueness may seem completely different and incompatible to each other at the first glance, as the first one treats vague predicates by assigning degrees to individuals and comparing these degrees with some threshold value locally for a possible world. Nevertheless, we show that for both accounts contexts (or models of context, respectively) can be identified with sets of classical worlds:

DEFINITION 1 *Let $\mathcal{U}$ be the set of individuals and $\mathcal{R}$ the set of vague predicates under consideration. Then a classical world s is a complete interpretation of all the predicates in $\mathcal{R}$ formalized as a set of literals such that for all $R \in \mathcal{R}$ and for all $u \in \mathcal{U}$ either $R(u) \in s$ or $\neg R(u) \in s$.*

DEFINITION 2 *Let $s \in S$ be a complete interpretation, $R \in \mathcal{R}$ a predicate, and $\mathcal{U}$ be the universe of discourse. Then the positive and negative extensions of R at s are defined as $l^+(R,s) =_{DEF} \{u \in \mathcal{U} : R(u) \in s\}$ and $l^-(R,s) =_{DEF} \mathcal{U} \setminus l^+(R,s)$, respectively.*

There is a subtle difference between Kyburg and Morreau's and Barker's approaches to vagueness. Whereas Kyburg and Morreau explicitly model the precification space $\mathcal{P}$ and points $p \in \mathcal{P}$ in this space, Barker does not directly make this distinction. For him the initial context C_0 also determines all other possible contexts, the context space there consists of all subsets of C_0. Penumbral connections are only implicitly given by the contents of the possible worlds and the scale structures for the vague adjectives in question and not modeled explicitly.

More than that, Kyburg and Morreau's notion of context as a set of sentences does not directly correspond to a point in a precification space; instead several models may be adequate for a context. As we will see below a context as in Barker directly corresponds to a set of complete interpretations, therefore Barker's contexts are less general than Kyburg and Morreau's. Consider e.g. the proposition $D(P(a)) \lor D(\neg P(a))$, adequate models in Kyburg and Morreau's framework may either have a in the extension of P at all precification points or in the anti-extension, a situation which is not straightforwardly expressible in Barker's approach. When comparing both accounts of vagueness we therefore contrast Barker's notion of a context with Kyburg and Morreau's notion of a context's model. It is however crucial to keep in mind that a context as in Kyburg and Morreau may have several distinct models and thus this framework is more powerful in the sense that contexts are seen as something more general than by Barker.

In the following we will describe how both Kyburg and Morreau's and Barker's notions of contexts can be translated to the intermediate representation defined above as well as the inverse; given an intermediate representation obtained from some context we need to be able to reconstruct the corresponding contexts in either approach. For Kyburg and Morreau's approach there are two different ways to interpret a model as a set of classical worlds: Initially, one might be tempted to identify a partial interpretation with all its complete extensions. This method, however, is not fruitful as seen in the following example: assume two vague predicates *tall* and *heavy* with the penumbral connections stating that nobody can be both tall and not heavy (or not tall but heavy) at the same time (but can be tall with his state of heaviness left undecided, nevertheless), formalized as

$D(\forall x \neg (\textbf{tall}(x) \land \neg \textbf{heavy}(x))$ and
$D(\forall x \neg (\neg \textbf{tall}(x) \land \textbf{heavy}(x))$.

Furthermore, assume that one individual denoted by **a** is under consideration. Then the according precification space $\mathscr{P}$ has the following structure:

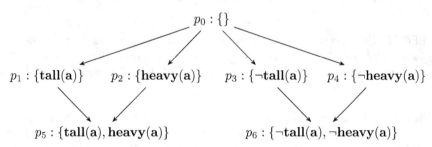

Now, if we identify a partial interpretation with all of its complete extensions, p_1 and p_2 are both identified with p_5 (and the same for p_3, p_4, and p_6), thus losing information about the original partial interpretation. Because of this loss of information we cannot distinguish between situations where e.g. **a** is tall, but his status of heaviness is undecided, or **a** is heavy, but his status of tallness is undecided, or **a** is both tall and heavy. However, as it is our aim to directly compare the expressiveness of Barker's and Kyburg and Morreau's approaches, it is required that each representation of a context as a set of classical worlds corresponds to exactly one context as in Kyburg and Morreau.

Therefore we take another, even simpler, road: identify a partial interpretation with *all* classical extensions, not necessarily present in $\mathscr{P}$. If, e.g. somebody's status of heaviness is undecided at p_1, ensure that p_1 translation to complete interpretations includes one where she is heavy and one where she is not, regardless of any penumbral connections:

DEFINITION 3 *Let $\mathscr{P}$ be a precification space, $p \in \mathscr{P}$ a partial interpretation, and $\mathscr{U}$ the (finite) universe of discourse. Then the translation from p to a set of classical worlds, denoted as $T_{km}p$, is defined as*[6]

$$T_{km}p =_{\text{DEF}} \bigcirc_{R \in \mathscr{R}} \bigcirc_{u \in \mathscr{U}} \phi(R, u, p) \text{ where}$$

$$\phi(R, u, p) = \begin{cases} \{R(u)\} & \text{iff } u \in l^+(R, p) \\ \{\neg R(u)\} & \text{iff } u \in l^-(R, p) \\ \{R(u), \neg R(u)\} & \text{otherwise} \end{cases}$$

for all $R \in \mathscr{R}$.

This definition ensures that, if $R(u)$ is true (or false) at p then $R(u)$ will be true (or false, respectively) at all classical worlds in $T_{km}p$ and otherwise there will be worlds where $R(u)$ is true and worlds in $T_{km}p$ where $R(u)$ is false.

The transformation also works the other way round: given a set of complete interpretations the according partial one can be reconstructed. For each vague predicate, let its extension and anti-extension be the intersections of its extensions (and anti-extensions, respectively) in all complete interpretations under consideration.

PROPOSITION 4 *Let $\mathscr{P}$ be a precification space and S a set of complete interpretations. Then a partial interpretation $p \in \mathscr{P}$ is identified with S, denoted $p = T_{km}^{-1}S$, if and only if for all $R \in \mathscr{R}$ both*

$$l^+(R, p) = \bigcap_{s \in S} l^+(R, s) \qquad \text{and} \qquad l^-(R, p) = \bigcap_{s \in S} l^-(R, s)$$

hold, thus $T_{km}(T_{km}^{-1}S) = S$.

Proof For any $p \in \mathscr{P}$, $R \in \mathscr{R}$, and $u \in \mathscr{U}$: if $u \in l^+(R, p)$ then $\phi(R, u, p) = \{R(u)\}$, thus $R(u) \in s$ for all $s \in T_{km}p$ and therefore $l^+(R, p) \subseteq \bigcap_{s \in S} l^+(R, s)$. If $u \notin l^+(R, p)$ then $\phi(R, u, p) = \{\neg R(u)\}$ or $\phi(R, u, p) = \{R(u), \neg R(u)\}$ and, thus, there exists $s \in T_{km}p$ such that $R(u) \notin s$. Therefore $l^+(R, p) = \bigcap_{s \in S} l^+(R, s)$ and completely analogously for $l^-(R, p)$. □

---

[6]We use the operator $\bigcirc$ to denote the concatenation of sets: let $A = A_1, \ldots, A_n$ be a family of sets. Then $\bigcirc_A$ is defined as

$$\bigcirc_A =_{\text{DEF}} \{\{a_1, a_2, \ldots, a_n\} : a_1 \in A_1, a_2 \in A_2, \ldots, a_n \in A_n\}.$$

Mote that in general for an arbitrary S the partial interpretation $T_{km}^{-1}S$ need not exist in $\mathscr{P}$, if it is excluded by some penumbral connection. Likewise, it may be the case that $T_{km}p = S$, and thus $p = T_{km}^{-1}S$, but also $p = T_{km}^{-1}S'$ with $S \neq S'$. Consider the vague predicates *tall*, two individuals denoted by **a** and **b**, and a partial interpretation p where both **a**'s and **b**'s states of tallness is undecided: $l^{+}(\textbf{tall}, p) = l^{-}(\textbf{tall}, p) = \{\}$. Then $T_{km}p = S = \{\{\textbf{tall(a)}, \textbf{tall(b)}\}, \{\textbf{tall(a)}, \neg\textbf{tall(b)}\}, \{\neg\textbf{tall(a)}, \textbf{tall(b)}\}, \{\neg\textbf{tall(a)}, \neg\textbf{tall(b)}\}\}$ and $T_{km}^{-1}S = p$, but also $T_{km}^{-1}\{\{\textbf{tall(a)}, \neg\textbf{tall(b)}\}, \{\neg\textbf{tall(a)}, \textbf{tall(b)}\}\} = p$.

On the other hand, a context as in Barker can be easily seen as a set of classical worlds: consider a set C of possible worlds according to Barker and a possible world $w \in C$. Thus, e.g. for the vague predicate *tall* the expression $\textbf{d}(w)(\llbracket tall \rrbracket)$ denotes the local standard of tallness in world w, and an individual **a** is *tall* in w if and only if $w \in \textbf{tall}(\textbf{d}(w)(\llbracket tall \rrbracket), \textbf{a})$. Each world w can then straightforwardly be identified with a complete interpretation by evaluating the relevant predicates:

DEFINITION 5 *Let C be a context according to Barker. Then the translation of C to complete interpretations T_bC is defined as*

$$T_bC = \{s(w) \mid w \in C\} \text{ where } s(w) \text{ is the smallest set such that}$$
$$R(u) \in s(w) \text{ if } w \in \textbf{R}(\textbf{d}(w)(R), u) \text{ and}$$
$$\neg R(u) \in s(w) \text{ if } w \notin \textbf{R}(\textbf{d}(w)(R), u)$$

for all individuals $u \in \mathscr{U}$ and $R \in \mathscr{R}$.

Translating a set of complete interpretations back to a model as in Barker without any further information, however, is not feasible: one would have to fix arbitrary degrees for the cutoff points of the vague predicates, for the degrees to which individuals possess these predicates and, moreover, the scale of these degrees. However, if we assume a fixed initial context C_0 as the "most indefinite" context, i.e. the context at the beginning of a conversation, we can view the power set of C_0 as a context space. We can then find the appropriate subset C of C_0, i.e. a "less indefinite" context, given a set of complete interpretations S just by taking those possible worlds in C_0 which are sanctioned by some interpretation $s \in S$:

PROPOSITION 6 *Let S be a complete interpretation, C_0 a fixed context as defined by Barker. Then a context $C \subseteq C_0$ can be determined such that $T_bC = S$ by setting*

$$T_b^{-1}S = \{w \in C_0 : \exists s \in S.\forall u \in \mathscr{U}.\forall R \in \mathscr{R}.w \in \textbf{R}(\textbf{d}(w)(R), \textbf{u}) \leftrightarrow R(u) \in s\}.$$

This way, given a precification space $\mathscr{P}$ of partial interpretations and an initial context C_0 one can switch between Barker's and Kyburg and Morreau's notions of context: let $p \in \mathscr{P}$ be a partial interpretation. Then $C = T_b^{-1}T_{km}p$ denotes the corresponding context according to Barker and, vice versa, given C we can find p as $p = T_{km}^{-1}T_bC$ as described by Definitions 3 and 4 and Propositions 1 and 2. Moreover, this ability to switch back and forth between both notions of context ensures that no information is lost during this process which is crucial for our aim of comparing the expressiveness of both approaches. At this point the question naturally arises, to which extent these two models are equivalent in the sense that they make the same predictions given such contexts C and p.

One subtle difference between both approaches is the treatment of scale structure: Barker simply stipulates that degrees range over an appropriate scale. There are few restrictions on the scale—it must be a partial order obeying monotonicity—but its exact type is not described *inside* the model. For all of his examples Barker uses linear scales, like people's height. Contrarily, for Kyburg and Morreau there is a priori no such externally defined scale structure, instead it can be defined inside the model itself by the means of penumbral connections. Let us use *tall* as an example for an adjective denoting a degree on a linear scale. Other weaker scale structures, however, can be modeled completely analogously. The binary predicates **taller_than** and **as_tall_as** and the unary vague one **tall** can be can be characterized as:

(NV_1) $D(\forall x \forall y.(\textbf{as\_tall\_as}(x,y) \vee \neg\textbf{as\_tall\_as}(x,y))$

(RE_1) $D(\forall x.\textbf{as\_tall\_as}(x,x))$

(TR_1) $D(\forall x \forall y \forall z.(\textbf{as\_tall\_as}(x,y) \wedge \textbf{as\_tall\_as}(y,z))$
           $\rightarrow \textbf{as\_tall\_as}(x,z))$

(SY_1) $D(\forall x \forall y.(\textbf{as\_tall\_as}(x,y) \rightarrow \textbf{as\_tall\_as}(y,x))$

(NV_2) $D(\forall x \forall y.(\textbf{taller\_than}(x,y) \vee \neg\textbf{taller\_than}(x,y))$

(TR_2) $D(\forall x \forall y \forall z.(\textbf{taller\_than}(x,y) \wedge \textbf{taller\_than}(y,z))$
           $\rightarrow \textbf{taller\_than}(x,z))$

(TI_2) $D(\forall x \forall y.\textbf{taller\_than}(x,y) \vee \textbf{taller\_than}(y,x) \vee \textbf{as\_tall\_as}(x,y))$

(i) $D(\forall x \forall y.(\textbf{tall}(x) \wedge \textbf{taller\_than}(y,x)) \rightarrow \textbf{tall}(y))$

(ii) $D(\forall x \forall y.(\neg\textbf{tall}(x) \wedge \textbf{taller\_than}(x,y)) \rightarrow \neg\textbf{tall}(y))$

Properties (NV_1) and (NV_2) here ensure that both **as_tall_as** and **taller_than** are non-vague; at each partial interpretation any pair of individuals is either in their extension or anti-extension. This goes in accordance with Barker [3] arguing that comparative clauses like *taller than* do not involve any vagueness. Properties (RE_1), (SY_1), and (TR_1) ensure that **as_tall_as** is indeed an equivalence relation by postulating reflexivity, symmetry, and transitivity. Similarly, properties (TR_2), (TI_2) ensure that **taller_than** is a strict total order by postulating that it is transitive and trichotomous. Finally, properties (i) and (ii) ensure that the vague predicate **tall** respects this total ordering. Rooij [18] also gives similar axiomatizations for other orderings motivated by taking the positive adjective, e.g. *tall*, as a starting point and observing how *tall* behaves with respect to comparison classes. These orderings can be characterized by penumbral connections completely analogously as described here for a linear ordering.

Assume now that a situation is modeled twice: one time using a scale based model in the sense of Barker and another time using a delineation model in the sense of Kyburg and Morreau where the scales used in Barker's model are accordingly encoded as penumbral connections. Our aim is to elaborate under which circumstances predictions made by these models coincide.

DEFINITION 7 *Let C_0 be a context as defined by Barker and $\mathscr{P}$ be a precification space in the sense of Kyburg and Morreau. C_0 and $\mathscr{P}$ are called* corresponding models *if the following conditions are met:*

- *for each vague predicate p in C_0 there is predicate P in $\mathscr{R}$ and vice versa,*

- *for each individual* **a** *in C_0 there is an object a in $\mathscr{U}$ and vice versa,*

- *for each $m \in \mathscr{P}$ there exists $C = T_b^{-1} T_{km} m \subseteq C_0$ with $C \neq \emptyset$, and*

- *for each $C \subseteq C_0$ there exists $m = T_{km}^{-1} T_b C \in \mathscr{P}$.*

The notion of *corresponding* models of the two different approaches intuitively means that the same situation is modeled both using Barker's approach and using Kyburg and Morreau's one making the same assumptions. Therefore the last two requirements ensure that neither the penumbral connections on the partial interpretations are too strong, i.e. they forbid situations which are present in the other model, nor the initial set of possible worlds C_0 implicitly contains restrictions which are not reflected in the penumbral connections. These two requirements also imply that for each vague predicate under consideration the scale implicitly given in Barker's model is expressed in $\mathscr{P}$ via penumbral connections: if according to Barker, some individual is regarded as *tall* in all possible worlds, another individual with a higher degree of height is automatically also regarded as tall. If a precification space $\mathscr{P}$ according to Kyburg and Morreau fails to sanction such relationships via penumbral connections, then there will be precification points which cannot be translated to an according context as in Barker. Also note that, on the other hand, there are penumbral connections for Kyburg and Morreau's contexts which cannot—even implicitly—be expressed in Barker's approach. Therefore such penumbral connections have to be omitted when looking for a corresponding model following Barker. Take $D(P(a) \rightarrow P(b) \vee \neg P(b))$ as an example. Suppose, initially both $P(a)$ and $P(n)$ are undecided. Then, as soon as we add the new information $P(a)$ we also have to decide whether $P(b)$ or $\neg P(b)$. Using Barker this requires that among the possible worlds where **a** is P there are such worlds where also **b** is P and such worlds where **b** is not P. But when translating such a context to a partial interpretation of Kyburg and Morreau's model as described, this amounts to a precification point where a is in the extension of P while b's status of P-ness is left undecided. Therefore a context space with such a penumbral connection cannot correspond to one of Barker's contexts. Excluding such penumbral connections does, arguably, cause no harm since such a situation seems highly artificial and the ambiguity concerning the next precification point when updating with $P(a)$—whether $P(b)$ or $\neg P(b)$—would lead to confusion between the speaker and hearer in a real-life situation.

PROPOSITION 8 *Let C_0 and $\mathscr{P}$ be two corresponding models as in Definition 7 and let s be a proposition of the form "**a** is p", "**a** is not p", or "**a** is more p than **b**" such that $[\![s]\!](C_0) \neq \emptyset$.*
   Then there exists a unique, most general partial interpretation $m \in \mathscr{P}$ such that $P(a)$ is true at m, $P(a)$ is false at m, or $Per\_than(a,b)$ is true at m, respectively, and the translations to sets of complete interpretations $T_b([\![s]\!](C_0))$ and $T_{km} m$ coincide.

Proof Assume, no such unique, most general partial interpretation $m \in \mathscr{P}$ exists as described. This means that when adding s to the current knowledge base the penumbral connections enforce that also some other information is added but there are several ways to do so. Such a situation is, however, ruled out by the last two requirements of Definition 7 since it can not be equivalently modeled in a context as defined by Barker as exemplified above.

Let m_0 be the root of $\mathscr{P}$; by Definition 7 both $T_b^{-1}T_{km}m_0$ and $T_{km}^{-1}T_bC_0$ coincide and $c = T_{km}m_0 = T_bC_0$. When performing the update with s as described by Barker, the possible worlds of C_0 where s does not hold are filtered out to form the new resulting context: $C' = [\![s]\!](C_0) \subseteq C_0$. The according translation to sets of classical worlds $c' = T_bC'$ can therefore be equivalently obtained by removing those sets from c where s does not hold. Observe that because of Definition 7 there exists $m' = T_{km}^{-1}c' \in \mathscr{P}$. Since s holds at all classical worlds in c', it is also true at m'; e.g. if s is of the form "**a** is p" then $a \in l^+(p, m')$. Therefore, $m \leq m'$ and if m and m' are different, there exists a literal t such that t is true at m' but indefinite at m, hence $c_0 \supset T_{km}m \supset c$. However, as c denotes exactly the worlds in c_0 where s is true, $T_{km}m$ cannot lie between these two while satisfying s. Therefore m and m' coincide and thus $T_{km}m$ and T_bC coincide.   □

Note the requirement that $[\![s]\!](C_0) \neq \emptyset$. This means that the proposition s is not inconsistent with the context C_0. If it is, Barker's and Kyburg and Morreau's approaches differ significantly: While, using Barker, the empty context is returned for signaling a false or inconsistent proposition, Kyburg and Morreau describe how to update the context and still retaining as much information as possible as described in Section 3.2.

THEOREM 9 *Let C_0 and $\mathscr{P}$ with root m_0 be two corresponding models as in Definition 7 and consider a sequence $s_1, \ldots, s_n$ of propositions of the form "**a** is p", "**a** is not p", and "**a** is more p than **b**". Let the context and precification point obtained after updating C_0 and m_0 with all of s_1 to s_n be denoted as C and m, respectively. If $C \neq \emptyset$, then an additional proposition s is true at C if and only if s is true at m.*

Proof The theorem follows immediately from Proposition 8 by noting that after each update the resulting contexts can be translated into the same set of complete interpretations. Therefore also C and m can be translated to the same such set, and thus both approaches make the same predictions.   □

Informally, Theorem 9 tells us that both Barker's and Kyburg and Morreau's approaches are capable of making exactly the same predictions under three conditions: first, the assumptions made about the modeled situation must be such that they can be expressed in both models. Second, the uttered propositions are of the simple form as in the theorem. This is largely due to the fact that Kyburg and Morreau do not deal with measure phrases in their model. Third, all information must be consistent as described above. This is shown by describing how a context in either model can be translated to some intermediate representation (i.e. a set of classical worlds) without losing any information and vice versa how a context in either approach can be constructed from this intermediate representation. Finally, the important observation is that an utterance of a simple proposition has the same update effect on that intermediate representation of the context, no matter if we are using Barker's or Kyburg and Morreau's notion of context.

Conclusion and further work

Although scale and delineation based models seem fundamentally different at the first glance, we have seen that under certain preconditions they are capable of making the same predictions with regard to simple propositions. Barker's approach allows one to formulate predicate modifiers such as *very*, *definitely*, or *clearly* in a more fine grained manner than Kyburg and Morreau's since it explicitly models (possible) standards for vague predicates. Moreover, it straightforwardly allows for more complex propositions e.g. such as "*John is 2 cm taller than Jack*". On the other hand delineation models, and in particular Kyburg and Morreau's model, are clearly superior when it comes to inconsistent information and the shifting of vague standards. Their notion of context update builds on the well known and well elaborated theory of belief revision. However, there seems to be no fundamental reason why something similar should not be possible to be modeled for a scale based account; only the relationship to the AGM theory of belief revision will most probably be less direct than for Kyburg and Morreau's approach. Therefore such a treatment of inconsistent vague information within a scale based approach is left as a promising task for future research.

An advantage of the delineation approach other than accommodation of vague standards is that it seems computationally more feasible than scale based approaches. As we have seen, Barker initially presupposes a context space containing all possible standards of the vague predicates in question and all possible assignments from the relevant individuals to degrees. Constraints on these values such as relations between the vague standards of different predicates or the knowledge that some individual possesses some property to a higher degree than another individual are only implicit in the data and not modeled explicitly. Also scales for the vague gradable predicates under consideration are not modeled explicitly. For a delineation approach, on the other hand, initially only a partial interpretation together with a set of penumbral connections is sufficient and no degree values are needed.

One point where scale based and delineation approaches can be combined is Kyburg and Morreau's notion of context update. Remember the example in Section 3.2 where one out of the two individuals Jack and John was selected by the definite description "*the tall and bald guy*". There, we have to either revoke John's status of baldness or Jack's status of tallness. The only criterion that at as little information as possible shall be invalidated does not suffice in this situation to pick one of the two referents. It seems as in order to make (realistic) predictions about how humans handle such situations, we need more information, namely their degrees of height and tallness, respectively. Then the referent will be preferred for whom the standard has to be shifted by a lesser amount. It seems easier to remove the status of tallness from someone who is 1.70 m tall than from someone who is 1.90 m tall, although in some scenario both may not be described as tall at all. Kyburg and Morreau describe the use of *selection functions* for selecting one out of several ways to perform an update as described above. Such a selection function may be defined by means of Barker's model: perform an update in Barker's model for each way of updating and then make a choice such that as few possible worlds are filtered out as possible.

Another point of future research is the connection between Kyburg and Morreau's approach and Shapiro's account of vagueness in context. As we have seen, by dropping the completability requirement and using Shapiro's model instead of supervaluation allows for the formulation of more fine-grained penumbral connections especially when it comes to Sorites situations. Moreover, Shapiro's interpretation of partial precifications as model for contexts during a conversation and not just a technical vehicle arguably fits Kyburg and Morreau's purpose more closely.

BIBLIOGRAPHY

[1] C.E. Alchourrón, P. Gärdenfors, and D. Makinson. On the logic of theory change: Partial meet contraction and revision functions. *Journal of symbolic logic*, 50(2):510–530, 1985.

[2] C. Barker. On the dynamics of second-order vagueness. preliminary report.

[3] C. Barker. The dynamics of vagueness. *Linguistics and Philosophy*, 25(1):1–36, 2002.

[4] M. Dummett. Wang's paradox. *Synthese*, 30(3):301–324, 1975.

[5] K. Fine. Vagueness, truth and logic. *Synthese*, 30(3):265–300, 1975.

[6] J. Groenendijk and M. Stokhof. Dynamic predicate logic. *Linguistics and Philosophy*, 14(1):39–100, 1991.

[7] I. Heim. File change semantics and the familiarity theory of definiteness. In *Formal semantics: The essential readings*, pages 223–248. Blackwell Publishers, 2008.

[8] I. Heim. On the projection problem for presuppositions. In *Formal semantics: The essential readings*, pages 249–260. Blackwell Publishers, 2008.

[9] H. Kamp. Two theories about adjectives. *Formal semantics of natural language*, pages 123–155, 1975.

[10] C. Kennedy. Projecting the adjective: The syntax and semantics of gradability and comparison. *The number sense*, 4(4):10, 1999.

[11] C. Kennedy. Vagueness and grammar: The semantics of relative and absolute gradable adjectives. *Linguistics and Philosophy*, 30(1):1–45, 2007.

[12] E. Klein. A semantics for positive and comparative adjectives. *Linguistics and Philosophy*, 4(1):1–45, 1980.

[13] E. Klein. The interpretation of adjectival comparatives. *Journal of Linguistics*, 18(01):113–136, 1982.

[14] E. Klein. Comparatives. In A. von Stechow and D. Wunderlich, editors, *Semantics*, pages 673–691. Berlin: de Gruyter, 1991.

[15] A. Kyburg and M. Morreau. Fitting words: Vague language in context. *Linguistics and Philosophy*, 23(6):577–597, 2000.

[16] D. Lewis. General semantics. *Synthese*, 22(1):18–67, 1970.

[17] D. Lewis. Scorekeeping in a language game. *Journal of philosophical logic*, 8(1):339–359, 1979.

[18] R. Rooij. Vagueness and linguistics. *The Vagueness Handbook, to appear*.

[19] S. Shapiro. *Vagueness in context*. Oxford University Press, 2006.

[20] S. Shapiro. Reasoning with slippery predicates. *Studia Logica*, 90(3):313–336, 2008.

Christoph Roschger
Vienna University of Technology
Favoritenstr. 9-11/E1852
1040 Wien, Austria
Email: roschger@logic.at

Comments on *Comparing Context Updates Delineation and Scale Based Models of Vagueness* by Christoph Roschger

DAVID RIPLEY

In 'Comparing Context Updates in Delineation and Scale Based Models of Vagueness', Christoph Roschger argues that two frameworks, due respectively to Kyburg & Morreau and Barker, bear important similarities to each other in certain respects. Roschger begins by summarizing the respective frameworks, which I will not repeat, and proceeds to define four mappings: for each framework, he provides a mapping both to and from subsets of the space of classical possible worlds. By composing these mappings, Roschger uses these subsets as intermediaries, to move from one framework to the other and back again. This note will be spent reviewing these mappings. My goal is to clarify how they do their respective jobs, and to correct some errors in Roschger's work.

1 Reviewing the mappings

This section steps through the mappings Roschger defines between three spaces: the space of partial interpretations, used by Kyburg & Morreau, the space of Barker-contexts, as I will call the contexts used in Barker's framework, and the space of sets of classical possible worlds, used by Roschger as an intermediate between these other spaces. Note that the worlds appearing in Barker-contexts are more richly structured than classical possible worlds; they include thresholds on scales for various predicates. I'll call these worlds "Barker-worlds" to avoid confusion with the classical possible worlds Roschger uses.

Notation: I use $\mathfrak{P}$ for the set of all partial interpretations; any precisification space $\mathscr{P}$ is thus a subset of $\mathfrak{P}$. Similarly, I use $\mathfrak{S}$ for the set of all possible worlds; any set S of worlds is a subset of $\mathfrak{S}$. Roschger takes possible worlds to be consistent and complete sets of literals; I'll extend a similar approach to partial interpretations, taking them to be consistent sets of literals (let $\mathscr{L}_{\text{lit}}$ be the set of literals). I write $w \Vdash A$ to indicate that the possible world or the Barker-world w satisfies the sentence A.

For the mappings T_b and T_b^{-1}, a crucial notion will be that of a Barker-world *agreeing atomically* with a classical possible world. This happens when they satisfy all the same atomic sentences as each other. For classical worlds, atomic satisfaction is handled via membership, and for Barker-worlds, it is handled via the scale structure; nonetheless, these two approaches may produce the very same results. I write $c \mathscr{A} s$ to mean that the Barker-world c agrees atomically with the classical possible world s.[1]

---

[1] Note that if there is some c such that $c \mathscr{A} s$ and $c \mathscr{A} s'$, then $s = s'$ (possible worlds are individuated by the atomic sentences that hold there), while there might be distinct c, c' such that for some s, $c \mathscr{A} s$ and $c' \mathscr{A} s$ (distinct Barker worlds can agree on all atomic sentences).

The rest of the notation will follow Roschger. To save space I skip the proofs below, except for counterexamples to some of Roschger's claims; none of the omitted proofs is anything but routine.

1.1 T_{km} and T_{km}^{-1}

$T_{km}\colon \mathfrak{P} \mapsto \wp(\mathfrak{S})$ takes a partial interpretation as input and returns a set of possible worlds. In particular, $T_{km}(p) = \{s \in \mathfrak{S} \mid \forall A \in p\colon s \Vdash A\}$; T_{km} returns the set of possible worlds that satisfy every literal in p. Conversely, $T_{km}^{-1}\colon \wp(\mathfrak{S}) \mapsto \mathfrak{P}$ takes a set of possible worlds and yields a partial interpretation: $T_{km}^{-1}(S) = \{A \in \mathscr{L}_{\mathrm{lit}} \mid \forall s \in S\colon s \Vdash A\}$, including all and only the literals that every member of S agree in satisfying. While partial interpretations may occur in precisification spaces, nothing in either of these definitions pays attention to any precisification space that p occurs in. All that matters is p itself.

The spaces $\mathfrak{P}$ and $\wp(\mathfrak{S})$ these maps move between are both ordered by $\subseteq$, and both maps are antitone: if $p \subseteq p'$, then $T_{km}(p') \subseteq T_{km}(p)$, and if $S \subseteq S'$, then $T_{km}^{-1}(S') \subseteq T_{km}^{-1}(S)$. A more complete partial interpretation imposes more requirements, and so corresponds to a more restricted set of worlds.

T_{km}^{-1} really does reverse T_{km}; that is, for any p, $p = T_{km}^{-1}(T_{km}(p))$. On the other hand, it is not the case that $S = T_{km}(T_{km}^{-1}(S))$ for every S, despite Roschger's claim in his Proposition 4.[2] For a counterexample, consider any case in which $T_{km}^{-1}(S) = T_{km}^{-1}(S')$ while $S \neq S'$ (Roschger provides one such case immediately after his Proposition 4). Since $T_{km}^{-1}(S) = T_{km}^{-1}(S')$, $T_{km}(T_{km}^{-1}(S)) = T_{km}(T_{km}^{-1}(S'))$. This cannot be identical to both S and S', since $S \neq S'$, so either S or S' must provide a counterexample (in fact, both might). One direction of the claim does hold, however: $S \subseteq T_{km}^{-1}(T_{km}(S))$.

It follows from the above that T_{km} and T_{km}^{-1} form a(n antitone) Galois connection between $\mathfrak{P}$ and $\wp(\mathfrak{S})$: $p \subseteq T_{km}^{-1}(S)$ iff $S \subseteq T_{km}(p)$. These maps thus preserve a fair amount of the structure of the two spaces. Moreover, T_{km} is perfectly reversible: one can recover p from $T_{km}(p)$.

1.2 T_b and T_b^{-1}

T_b and T_b^{-1} tie their respective spaces together slightly less tightly. Throughout this section, everything should be considered relative to some fixed Barker-context C_0; every Barker-context C will be taken to be a subset of C_0.

$T_b\colon \wp(C_0) \mapsto \wp(\mathfrak{S})$ takes a Barker context C and maps it to a set of possible worlds as follows: $T_b(C) = \{s \in \mathfrak{S} \mid \exists c \in C\colon c\mathscr{A}s\}$. Conversely, $T_b^{-1}\colon \wp(\mathfrak{S}) \mapsto \wp(C_0)$ takes a set of classical possible worlds and maps it to a subset of C_0 in a similar way: $T_b^{-1}(S) = \{c \in C_0 \mid \exists s \in S\colon c\mathscr{A}s\}$. Again, the spaces involved in these mappings are naturally ordered by $\subseteq$; this time, the mappings are both monotone: if $C \subseteq C'$, then $T_b(C) \subseteq T_b(C')$, and if $S \subseteq S'$, then $T_b^{-1}(S) \subseteq T_b^{-1}(S')$.

Unlike the Kyburg & Morreau case, here T_b^{-1} is not a true inverse of T_b; we can have C such that $C \neq T_b^{-1}(T_b(C))$. This is because T_b and T_b^{-1} pay attention only to which atomic sentences a given Barker-world satisfies, but there may well be a Barker-

---

[2]The claim does hold for sets S that are themselves $T_{km}(p)$ for some partial interpretation p; in these cases, it follows from the fact that $p = T_{km}^{-1}(T_{km}(p))$, by applying T_{km} to both sides.

context C that differentiates between Barker-worlds that agree on all atomics. However, we do have one direction: $C \subseteq T_b^{-1}(T_b(C))$. We also do not have $S = T_b(T_b^{-1}(S))$; for a particular $s \in S$, there might be no $c \in C_0$ such that $c \mathscr{A} s$; when this happens, $s \notin T_b(T_b^{-1}(S))$. Again, we have one direction: $T_b(T_b^{-1}(S)) \subseteq S$.

T_b and T_b^{-1} form a Galois connection (this time monotone) between $\wp(\mathfrak{S})$ and $\wp(C_0)$: the above facts guarantee that $C \subseteq T_b^{-1}(S)$ iff $T_b(C) \subseteq S$. Again, a considerable amount of structure is preserved by the mappings. This time, though, neither mapping is perfectly reversible.

2   How the mappings interact

The goal of Roschger's paper, though, is not just to map Kyburg & Morreau's machinery and Barker's machinery into a common space. It is to map each of them into the other, using $\wp(\mathfrak{S})$ as an intermediary. For a given C_0, we have $T_b^{-1} \circ T_{km} : \mathfrak{P} \mapsto \wp(C_0)$ and $T_{km}^{-1} \circ T_b : \wp(C_0) \mapsto \mathfrak{P}$ connecting the two approaches. For brevity, I'll write K for $T_{km}^{-1} \circ T_b$ and B for $T_b^{-1} \circ T_{km}$. From the above, it is quick to see that B and K themselves form a(n antitone) Galois connection between $\mathfrak{P}$ and $\wp(C_0)$; that is, $p \subseteq K(C)$ iff $C \subseteq B(p)$.

Roschger defines *correspondence*: a precisification space $\mathscr{P}$ corresponds to a Barker-context C_0 iff: 1) they have the same domain, and interpret the same atomic predicates; 2) for every $p \in \mathscr{P}$, there is a nonempty $C \subseteq C_0$ such that $C = B(p)$ (relative to C_0); and 3) for every $C \subseteq C_0$, there is a $p \in \mathscr{P}$ such that $p = K(C)$.

One immediate problem with this definition is that condition 3 is not meetable with only consistent partial valuations: $K(\emptyset)$ must be the absolutely inconsistent interpretation (the interpretation that satisfies *every* literal), but $\emptyset \subseteq C_0$ for any C_0. Since Roschger gives no suggestion of allowing inconsistent partial valuations, I assume this is a problem. Corresponding to the restriction to nonempty C in condition 2, then, I'll assume a weakened condition 3, allowing that there may be no $p \in \mathscr{P}$ such that $p = K(\emptyset)$. If this modification is not made, then there are no corresponding models.

Note as well that condition 2 is very weak. $B(p)$ is the set of Barker-worlds in C_0 that are compatible with p, and there is always some such set, although it may be empty. But for there to be a nonempty such set, all it takes is a single Barker-world in C_0 compatible with p. This world, though, might decide a huge variety of propositions that p remains silent on.

One might hope that in corresponding models $p = K(B(p))$ and $C = B(K(C))$, for every p and nonempty C. But one would be disappointed; the connection between corresponding models can be less tight than this. There is no guarantee in general that $p = K(B(p))$, only that $p \subseteq K(B(p))$; the move from a partial interpretation to a Barker-context and back again can result in a *gain* in information, even in corresponding models. Similarly, there is no guarantee that $C = B(K(C))$, only that $C \subseteq B(K(C))$; the move from a Barker-context to a partial interpretation and back again can result in a *loss* of information.

Whether these connections between corresponding models are tight enough or not depends on the goal in play. The key goal here, I take it, is embodied in Roschger's

Theorem 9, which depends on Proposition 8: that for any corresponding $\mathscr{P}$ and C_0 and any update of a certain form consistent with C_0, there is a unique most general $m \in \mathscr{P}$ such that the update is true at m and, where C is the result of applying the update to C_0, $T_{km}(m) = T_b(C)$.

What to make of this proposition, and the theorem that depends on it, is an interesting question; I won't explore it here, since unfortunately they are both false. Begin with Proposition 8: it can be that there is no such m. A simple example of this involves a precisification space $\mathscr{P}$ with three partial interpretations and a Barker-context C_0 with two Barker-worlds. Assume a language with a single predicate P and three names referring to three distinct things in the domain; let Pa, Pb, and Pd be the three resulting atomic sentences. Now let $\mathscr{P} = \{p_0, p_1, p_2\}$, where $p_0 = \{Pa\}$, $p_1 = \{Pa, Pb, \neg Pd\}$, and $p_2 = \{Pa, \neg Pb, Pd\}$. Let $C_0 = \{c_1, c_2\}$, where $c_1 \Vdash Pa, Pb$, and $\neg Pd$, and $c_2 \Vdash Pa, \neg Pb$, and Pd. (The scales can be set up any which way, so long as these satisfaction relations result.) These are corresponding models, by the above (modified) definition: every $p \in \mathscr{P}$ has some nonempty $B(p) \in C_0$ and every nonempty $C \subseteq C_0$ has some $K(C) \in \mathscr{P}$.[3]

Now, update these models with an assertion of Pa. C_0 updated in such a way is just C_0 itself, but there is no $m \in \mathscr{P}$ such that $T_{km}(m) = T_b(C_0)$. The best candidate for such an m would be p_0, but $T_{km}(p_0)$ will include the worlds $\{Pa, Pb, Pd\}$ and $\{Pa, \neg Pb, \neg Pd\}$; neither of these worlds is in $T_b(C_0)$. The argument Roschger gives for Proposition 8 assumes that $S = T_{km}(T_{km}^{-1}(S))$, but this is the mistaken Proposition 4.[4]

Theorem 9 is supposed to establish that corresponding models make equivalent predictions when given matching inputs. The above counterexample to Proposition 8 is also a counterexample to Theorem 9, as the proposition $\neg(Pb \wedge Pd)$ holds at C_0 but not at p_0.[5] I think the best way to understand the failure of Theorem 9 is as undermining the interest of Roschger's notion of *corresponding models*. It may yet be the case that there is a relation that can hold between a Kyburg & Morreau model and a Barker model such that when it holds the models make equivalent predictions. That would be an interesting and valuable discovery. Roschger's relation of correspondence, despite his claims, is not such a relation.

---

[3] In particular, $B(p_0) = C_0, B(p_1) = \{c_1\}$, and $B(p_2) = \{c_2\}$, while $K(C_0) = p_0$, $K(\{c_1\}) = p_1$, and $K(\{c_2\}) = p_2$. In this pair of models, then, we have $K(B(p)) = p$ and $B(K(C)) = C$; they are even more intimately related than corresponding models are required to be.

[4] Although this is a counterexample to Proposition 8 in its present form, it might be thought that Proposition 8 is meant to hold only for assertions that *add* to the current context, rather than simply reiterating something— Pa in the above example—already in the context. But there are counterexamples to this weakened claim as well. For example, start from the C_0 in the counterexample above, and add one more Barker-world c_3, such that $c_3 \Vdash \neg Pa, Pb$, and Pd, to yield C_0'. Then let $\mathscr{P}' = \{K(C) \mid C \subseteq C_0' \text{ and } C \neq \emptyset\}$. $\mathscr{P}'$ and C_0' correspond to each other, and again satisfy the extra conditions that $p = K(B(p))$ and $C = B(K(C))$. However, an assertion of *any* of Pa, Pb, or Pd in this case will both add information and yield a counterexample even to the weakened Proposition 8. (An assertion of Pa, in particular, results in narrowing C_0' down to C_0, and moving to a subtree of $\mathscr{P}'$ that is just like $\mathscr{P}$; then the counterexample given in the main text works as it does there. Assertions of Pb or Pd work similarly.)

[5] If Theorem 9 is weakened to a claim only about atomic propositions, it still fails, although the counterexample is a bit more complex: add to the main-text counterexample an additional proposition Pe, and let Pe hold at every partial interpretation in $\mathscr{P}$ as well as every Barker-world in C_0. Now add one additional partial interpretation p_3 to $\mathscr{P}$, at which only Pa holds. It can be verified that the resulting models are still corresponding, although they no longer satisfy $K(B(p)) = p$, as $K(B(p_3)) = p_0$. An assertion of Pa is now sufficient to guarantee Pe in the Barker model, but not in the Kyburg & Morreau model.

In sum, I think Roschger has made a compelling case that there are important similarities between the frameworks of Kyburg & Morreau and Barker, but that he has not succeeded in describing just what those connections are. More work will be necessary to gain an understanding of the relations between these frameworks. The questions driving Roschger's paper are about the similarity or possible equivalence of predictions made by these two frameworks; but the formal and structural situation needs to be clarified before these questions can be properly addressed. I hope this note contributes something towards that clarification, as a step towards the important questions that remain.

David Ripley
Department of Philosophy
University of Melbourne
Old Quad, Parkville
Victoria 3010, Australia
Email: davewripley@gmail.com

Reply to David Ripley's Comments on *Comparing context updates in delineation and scale based models of vagueness*

CHRISTOPH ROSCHGER[1]

In his comments to my contribution 'Comparing Context Updates in Delineation and Scale Based Models of Vagueness' David Ripley points out some severe technical flaws. As he shows by a counter-example, the main result of the paper does not hold. The goal of this reply is to explain where exactly the source of the problem lies and to point out a possible way to solve it.

In the paper I take two contextual approaches to vagueness both describing the notion of context update very precisely, namely one by Kyburg and Morreau and one by Barker. Besides analyzing strengths and weaknesses of these approaches I try to prove that they both make the same predictions, once the same situation is modeled twice using each approach. This is done by introducing an 'intermediate representation' of contexts and showing how contexts as defined by each approach can be translated into this representation and also the other way round. Finally, once this connection is established one can observe that a context update (with consistent information) has exactly the same effect on the intermediate representation in either approach. However, as Ripley points out, these translation functions are not perfectly reversible, they rather form antitone and monotone Galois connections between contexts and their intermediate representations. In order to illustrate this I will stick to the same notation as in the paper and in Ripley's comment: the mappings from Kyburg and Morreau's models into the intermediate representation and back will be denoted as T_{km} and T_{km}^{-1}, and T_b as well as T_b^{-1} for Barker's models. For directly translating between Kyburg and Morreau's and Barker's contexts I use the mappings $K = T_{km}^{-1} \circ T_b$ and $B = T_b^{-1} \circ T_{km}$. Assume two corresponding models, one according to Kyburg and Morreau and the other one according to Barker, let the initial contexts be denoted as p_0 and C_0, respectively, and let the resulting contexts after a (successful) update be called p and C. Theorem 8 then states that the intermediate representations of p and C coincide: $T_{km}(p) = T_b(C)$. As Ripley shows by giving a counter-example this claim does not hold due to the non-reversibility of these mappings. However, it is still true—at least for his example—that $K(C) = p$ and that $B(p) = C$. One might be tempted to reformulate Theorem 8 in such a way that it does not directly refer to the intermediate representation but makes use of these connections instead and thus try to save Theorem 9. As it turns out, this does not suffice; one has to go deeper and rethink the notion of *corresponding models*. Intuitively, two models of the same situation, one as defined by Kyburg and Morreau and the other as

---

[1] Supported by Eurocores-ESF/FWF grant I143-G15 (LogICCC-LoMoReVI).

defined by Barker, are called *corresponding* if they are constructed 'by making the same assumptions'. This entails that penumbral connections—explicit restrictions on the context space—in the first kind of model correspond to the (scalar) data in Barker's models. As the definition is formulated in the paper, it relies on the presented mappings between contexts and their intermediate representations, but it fails to capture this intuitive notion of correspondence. Ripley points to this deficiency in his counter-example to the Theorem 8: whereas in the context C_0 the proposition $\neg(Pb \wedge Pd)$ is true, it does not hold at context p_0, but they both fulfill the technical definition of corresponding contexts. This objection however is only partially valid: Kyburg and Morreau define *truth* at an incomplete precification point in a supervaluationist manner and in this case the proposition holds at all complete precifications of p_0. Nevertheless his observation is right that the definition is not strong enough to capture the intended notion.

In the following I will sketch how to change the relevant definitions of the paper to remedy this situation. First, let us recapitulate the mapping T_b from Barker's contexts to sets of classical worlds. It is beneficial to think of T_b as the partition of a context induced by $\mathscr{A}$.[1] The translation can be viewed as an *abstraction* of the context away from concrete degree values. This point of view makes it immediate that there cannot—in general—exist an inverse mapping T_b^{-1} and enables us to concentrate on the relationship between Kyburg and Morreau's notion of context and on this abstraction. There is one subtle problem with the mapping T_{km} as defined in the paper, namely its ignorance of penumbral connections. As already seen by Ripley's counter-example to Theorem 8 this inclusion of precification points violating penumbral connection leads to the failure of the theorem. Therefore we suggest another definition for T_{km}:

DEFINITION 1 *Let $\mathscr{P}$ be a precification space and $p \in \mathscr{P}$ a partial interpretation. Then the translation from p to a set of classical worlds, denoted as $T_{km}p$, is defined as the set of all complete precifications of p.*

$$T_{km}p =_{DEF} \{S_q \mid q \in \mathscr{P}, p \leq q, \text{ and } q \text{ is complete}\},$$

where S_q is defined as the smallest set such that $R(u) \in S_q$ iff $u \in l^+(R, q)$ and $\neg R(u) \in S_q$ otherwise for all predicates $R \in \mathscr{R}$ and all objects $u \in \mathscr{U}$.

In the paper, I gave an example why this definition of T_{km} is not fruitful: this way one cannot distinguish between different precification points which share the same set of complete precifications. However, since Kyburg and Morreau define truth at an incomplete point in a supervaluationist style, and not as local truth at a point, this loss of information does not seem to do any harm here. Incidentally, this revised version of T_{km} also sheds new light on the use of Shapiro's contextual approach to vagueness instead of supervaluation for Kyburg and Morreau's models as advocated in the paper. As T_{km} now heavily relies on complete precification points and in Shapiro's approach such precification points are not required to exist, this already gives hints to what respect Shapiro's approach may be more expressive than Kyburg and Morreau's as well as Barker's.

---

[1] As defined by Ripley, $c_1 \mathscr{A} c_2$ if and only if c_1 and c_2 agree on all atomic propositions.

Finally, the definition of *corresponding* contexts should be reformulated:

DEFINITION 2 *Let C_0 be a context as defined by Barker and $\mathscr{P}$ be a precification space in the sense of Kyburg and Morreau. C_0 and $\mathscr{P}$ are called* corresponding models *if the following conditions are met:*

- *for each vague predicate p in C_0 there is predicate P in $\mathscr{R}$ and vice versa,*

- *for each individual **a** in C_0 there is an object a in $\mathscr{U}$ and vice versa,*

- *for each $m \in \mathscr{P}$ there exists $C \subseteq C_0$ such that $T_{km}m = T_bC$, and*

- *for each non-empty $C \subseteq C_0$ there exists $m \in \mathscr{P}$ such that $T_bC = T_{km}m$.*

Note that now there is no reference to the inverse mappings in the definition of corresponding models and also note that this definition implies $T_{km}p_0 = T_bC_0$ for corresponding models. On the one hand this definition strictly ensures that all penumbral connections present in Kyburg and Morreau's model are enforced in each possible context in Barker's model and on the other hand the third clause forces Barker's model to be large enough to account for all possible complete precifications. Ensuring that penumbral connections are always in force nicely demonstrates why explicit penumbral connections in Kyburg and Morreau's approach are more expressive than the implicit ones in Barker's model. Consider, e.g., one predicate P, three objects a, b, and c, and the set $\mathscr{P}$ of precifications:

$$\{\{Pa\}, \{Pa, \neg Pb, Pc\}, \{Pa, Pb, \neg Pc\}, \{\neg Pa\}, \{\neg Pa, Pb, Pc\}, \{\neg Pa, \neg Pb, \neg Pc\}, \{\}\}.$$

Such a situation cannot be expressed in Barker's approach: there have to be possible Barker-style worlds corresponding to all of the four complete precifications. An update with Pb singles out the third and the fifth world, but there is no precification point (except the root) which has just these two as its complete precifications.[2]

Equipped with these new definitions of corresponding models and translations let us again take a look at Theorem 8. Let $\mathscr{P}$ and C_0 be two corresponding models and s a (consistent) proposition; initially, we have $T_bC_0 = T_{km}p_0$. It is now easy to see that in Barker's model all possible worlds not fulfilling s are filtered out, which amounts to all classical worlds $c \in T_bC_0$ which do not satisfy s being filtered out; let the resulting context be denoted as C. On the other hand, also in Kyburg and Morreau's model surely—as s is consistent with the current context—s will hold in all complete precifications of the new precification point p reached. However we still need to check that indeed $T_{km}p = T_bC$. We first show $T_{km}p \supseteq T_bC$: assume there exists a classical world $w \in T_bC$ such that $w \notin T_{km}p$. But then, by the definition of corresponding models, there exists a precification point $p_1 \geq p_0$ such that $w \in T_{km}p_1$ and s true at p_1. As $T_{km}p$ has been obtained just by updating with s and nothing else, $p_1 \geq p$ holds, but due to the monotony constraint on partial precifications this yields a contradiction to $w \notin T_{km}p$. The other direction, $T_{km}p \subseteq T_bC$ is analogous.

---

[2] Also, for Kyburg and Morreau's approach this situation is not entirely unproblematic: the update with Pb results in one of the respective two precifications, but it is not well-defined which one.

Summing up, I hope I have convincingly shown how to straighten out the errors made in my paper. In any case, there is a strong correspondence between these two approaches that seem to be so fundamentally different at the first glance.

Finally, I would like to thank David Ripley for the valuable feedback he gave me through his comments in this book and personally during this year's ESSLLI in Ljubljana, Slovenia. Fortunately I had the possibility to go there thanks to a travel grant by the LogICCC programme.

Standpoint Semantics:
A Framework for Formalising the
Variable Meaning of Vague Terms

BRANDON BENNETT[1]

Overview

The paper develops a formal model for interpreting vague languages in a setting similar to that of *supervaluation* semantics. Two modes of semantic variability are modelled, corresponding to different aspects of vagueness: one mode arises where there can be multiple definitions of a term involving different attributes or different logical combinations of attributes. The other relates to the threshold of applicability of a vague term with respect to the magnitude of relevant observable values.

The truth of a proposition depends on both the possible world and the *precisification* with respect to which it is evaluated. Structures representing both possible worlds and precisifications are specified in terms of primitive functions representing observable measurements, so that the semantics is grounded upon an underlying theory of physical reality. On the basis of this semantics, the acceptability of a proposition to an agent is characterised in terms of a combination of the agent's beliefs about the world and their attitude to admissible interpretations of vague predicates.

1 Introduction

The terminology of natural language is highly affected by vagueness. Except in specialised circumstances, there are no generally agreed criteria that precisely determine the applicability of our conceptual vocabulary to describing the world. This presents a considerable problem for the construction of a knowledge representation language that is intended to articulate information of a similar kind to that conveyed by natural language communication.

The fundamental idea of the *supervaluationist* account of vagueness, is that a language containing vague predicates can be interpreted in many different ways, each of which can be modelled in terms of a precise version of the language, which is referred to as a *precisification*. If a classical semantics is used to give a denotational valuation of expressions for each of these precise versions, the interpretation of the vague language itself is given by a *supervaluation*, which is determined by the collection of these classical valuations.

---

[1]Partial support of the *Co-Friend* project (FP7-ICT-214975, www.cofriend.net) and the EU Framework 7 is gratefully acknowledged. The paper has been enhanced by suggestions made in the detailed comments of two anonymous reviewers.

The view that vagueness can be analysed in terms of multiple senses was proposed by Mehlberg [16], and a formal semantics based on a multiplicity of classical interpretations was used by van Fraassen [18] to explain 'the logic of presupposition'. It was subsequently applied to the analysis of vagueness by Fine [8], and thereafter has been one of the more popular approaches to the semantics of vagueness adopted by philosophers and logicians. In the current paper we introduce a logic based on the essential idea of supervaluation semantics, but different in several respects from previous systems.

A major strength of the supervaluation approach is that it enables the expressive and inferential power of classical logic to be retained (albeit within the context somewhat more elaborate semantics) despite the presence of vagueness. In particular, necessary logical relationships among vague concepts can be specified using classical axioms and definitions. These analytic interdependencies (referred to by Fine as *penumbral* connections) will be preserved, even though the criteria of correspondence between concepts and the world are ill-defined and fluid.

Investigation of supervaluation semantics in the philosophical literature tends, as one might expect, to be drawn towards subtle foundational questions, such as those concerning the *sorites* paradox and second-order vagueness. By contrast, the purpose of the current paper is to flesh out the details of a particular variant of supervaluation semantics and to develop an expressive formal representation language that could be employed within information processing applications.

The development of the supervaluation idea in the current paper also departs somewhat from that proposed by Fine. In Fine's theory, precisifications vary in their level of precision, so that one precisification may be a more precise version of another. This gives rise to a partial order on precisifications. Fine then proposes a semantics that takes account of this ordering and defines a notion of *super-truth* in terms of the precisification structure as a whole: super-truth corresponds to truth at all maximally precise and *admissible* precisifications (where 'admissible' means that a precisification is considered a reasonable interpretation of the language and is taken as a primitive notion). Moreover, Fine suggests that 'truth' in a vague language may be identified with this notion of super-truth.

By contrast, in the current paper, we take each precisification to be a maximally precise version of the language. And we consider truth primarily as a property of propositions that is relative to a particular precisification, rather than determined by the whole set of possible precisifications. However, we will also introduce the notion of a proposition holding relative to a *standpoint*, which is associated with a set of precisifications considered acceptable by some agent. Formally, this notion is somewhat akin to 'super-truth', except that instead of assuming a fixed set of admissible precisifications, we consider the set of admissible precisifications to be determined relative to a particular agent in a particular situation.

Like supervaluation semantics, standpoint semantics may be regarded as a rival to the *fuzzy logic* approach to semantic indeterminacy [19]. Whereas fuzzy logic explores this indeterminacy in terms of degrees of truth and non-classical truth functions, standpoint semantics focuses on truth conditions rather than truth values, and employs a notion of truth that is close to the classical view, although relativised to account for a variety of possible interpretations. Nevertheless, we believe that strong correspondences between standpoint semantics and fuzzy logic can be established. By introducing a probability distribution over the space of precisifications, degrees of *acceptability* can be introduced, and it can be shown that the acceptability of vague conjunctions is governed by certain of the T-norms commonly used in fuzzy logic. Results in this area are beyond the scope of the present work, where we focus on the core model theory and employ a much simpler model of an agent's attitude to precisifications.

The formalism developed in the current paper takes ideas from previous theories proposed by Bennett [2, 4] and Halpern [9] and elaborates material presented in [5]. Halpern's paper analyses vagueness in terms of the subjective reports of multiple agents, but these play a similar role in his semantics to precisifications in the semantics proposed in this paper. Our approach also has some commonality with that of [13] and [14].

In [4] the semantics of vague adjectives is characterised in terms of their dependence on *relevant objective observables* (e.g. 'tall' is dependent on 'height'). One of the primary aims of the current paper is to provide a rigorous foundation for the notion of precisification, in which the interpretation associated with a precisification is explicitly defined in terms of choices made in imposing distinctions with regard to continuously varying properties manifest in possible states of the world. Bennett [2] proposed a two-dimensional model theory, in which the interpretations of propositions are indexed both by precisifications and possible worlds. Whereas a somewhat *ad hoc* relation of relevance between between vague predicates and observables was introduced in [4], the current paper makes a much more specific connection, in which thresholds occur explicitly in definitions of vague predicates. A concrete example of the use of this approach in an implemented computer system for processing geographic information can be found in [17] and [6].

The structure of the paper is as follows: in the next section we give an overview of the formal theory that will be developed, and consider some examples illustrating different kinds of vagueness. In Section 3 we specify a formal language that makes explicit the structure of both possible worlds and precisifications in terms of possible values of observable measurements. Section 5 gives a formal model of an agent's *standpoint* with respect to possible worlds that the agent considers plausible and precisifications that the agent considers admissible. We end with a consideration of further work and conclusions.

2 Preliminaries

Before getting into the details of our formal language and its semantics, we first clarify some aspects of our approach.

2.1 Comparison classes

To avoid confusion we briefly consider a phenomenon that is often associated with vagueness but will not be considered in the current paper. This is the relativity of the interpretation of vague adjectives to a given *comparison class*. For instance, when describing an object or creature as tall, we make a judgement based on the height of that object or creature. But in judging that a woman is tall we employ a different threshold of tallness from when describing a giraffe as tall. As in this example, the relevant comparison class is often determined by the count noun used to refer to the object, but it may sometimes be determined by the particular set of objects present in a given situation.

However, comparison class relativity is a side-issue that is not essential to vagueness itself. Even if we restrict attention to a definite class of individuals (say, adult males in Belgium) the adjective 'tall' is still vague. Similar remarks could be made about more general issues of context variability of the interpretation of terminology. If required, an explicit model of comparison class dependency of vague adjectives (perhaps similar to that given in [4]) could be incorporated into an extended version of our theory.

2.2   Distinguishing conceptual and sorites vagueness

An important feature of the proposed theory is that it makes a clear distinction between two forms of vagueness.

One type of vagueness arises where there is ambiguity with regard to which attributes or conditions are essential to the meaning of a given term, so that it is controversial how it should be defined. We call this *conceptual vagueness* (or 'deep ambiguity'). A good example of conceptual vagueness is the concept of *murder*. Although in most cases there will be general agreement as to whether a given act constitutes murder, the precise definition is subtle and controversial. Judicial systems vary as to the stipulations they make to characterise the crime of murder. Thus one may debate whether murder requires malice or intent, whether the murderer must be sane, whether the victim must be unwilling etc. Moreover, even where conditions are stipulated in great detail, cases may arise that defy simple judgement.

A somewhat different kind of vagueness occurs when the criteria for applicability of a term depend on placing a threshold on the *required magnitude* of one or more variable attributes. For instance, we may agree that the appropriateness of ascribing the predicate 'tall' to an individual depends on the height of that individual, but there is no definite height threshold that determines when the predicate is applicable. We refer to this as *sorites vagueness*, since the essence of the sorites paradox is the indeterminacy in the number of grains required to make a heap.

So to summarise: in the case of *conceptual vagueness* there is indeterminism regarding which property or logical combination of properties is relevant to determining whether a concept is applicable, whereas with *sorites vagueness* the relevant properties are clear, but the degree to which these properties must be present is indefinite.[2]

2.2.1   Combined modes of vagueness

It should be emphasised that the two kinds of vagueness I have identified are not exclusive—a single word or phrase may be, and often is, imbued with both conceptual and sorites vagueness.

For example, [11] considers the conditions under which one might describe a person as 'clever'. Here it is not clear what parameter or parameters are relevant to the attribution of cleverness. As Kamp suggests, quick wittedness and problem solving ability are both indications of cleverness, although one person might be considered more quick witted that another and yet less capable of problem solving.

Even the adjective 'tall', which is almost a paradigm case of sorites vagueness, is also to some extent affected by conceptual vagueness. This is because there is no universally agreed specification of exactly how a person's height should be measured.

---

[2]This distinction was identified and analysed in [3], but no formal semantics was presented.

Perhaps we can agree that shoes should not count towards height and that hair should also be excluded; but what about a wart on the top of a person's head? What if a person stretches their neck or hunches their shoulders? Of course such factors rarely impinge on actual uses of the word 'tall', and if we really wanted an objective measure of height we could legislate that a particular measurement regime be used. Nevertheless, the very fact that one might need to carry out such legislation in order to get a reliable objective measurement of tallness, demonstrates that the natural language adjective 'tall' is subject to conceptual ambiguity.

The adjective 'bald' and the count noun 'heap', which are also ubiquitous in discussions of the sorites paradox clearly suffer from considerable conceptual ambiguity as well as threshold indeterminacy. Baldness is not only judged by the number of hairs on a head, but also where they are located—it is a matter of coverage, not only numerical quantity. Likewise, a heap is not just any collection of grains. Intuitively, heap-hood requires particular structural properties; but the exact nature of these is difficult to pin down.

Despite their close connection, there are significant differences in the type of semantic variability involved in the two kinds of vagueness—to reiterate: conceptual vagueness is indeterminacy in the attribute or combination of attributes that must be present, whereas sorites vagueness is indeterminacy in the degree to which a continuously varying attribute (or attributes) must be present. Hence, we believe that a semantics for vague languages is most clearly specified by separating the two modes.

2.3 Predication, observables and thresholds

Our semantics explicitly models the applicability of vague predicates in terms of thresholds applied to relevant observable measurements. In the simplest case we assume that our judgement of whether a predicate ϕ applies to object x depends only on the value of a single measurement $f(x)$—the higher the value of $f(x)$, the more we are inclined to judge that $\phi(x)$ is true. Let $\tau(\phi)$ denote some reasonable threshold that we might set for the applicability of ϕ. Then $\phi(x)$ is judged to be true if $f(x)$ is greater than $\tau(\phi)$ and false if $f(x)$ is less than $\tau(\phi)$.

The case where we have $f(x) = \tau(\phi)$ presents a technical issue, in that there is no obvious basis to decide between assigning truth or falsity. This will be avoided by restricting the semantics so that a threshold value may not have the same value as any observable function.

2.4 Relating precisifications to cognitive attitudes

As well as relating precisifications to states of the world, we also model their relationship to the cognitive states of agents. We give an account of an agent's attitude to vague propositions in terms of a formalised notion of *standpoint*, which describes the agents belief state as well as the range of interpretations of vague terminology that they consider admissible. A *standpoint* will be modelled by a structure $\langle B, A, \Psi \rangle$, where: B is the set of possible worlds compatible with the agent's beliefs; A is the set of precisifications that are acceptable to the agent; and Ψ is a set of definitional theories that specify different ways in which the meaning of vague predicates can be represented in terms of some logical combination of threshold constraints. Hence, A models an agent's standpoint with respect to sorites vagueness, while Ψ models the standpoint in relation to conceptual vagueness.

As is usual in supervaluation-based approaches, we assume that when describing a particular situation or appraising a given set of propositions, a language user employs a choice of thresholds that is consistent across usages of all concepts. Thus, where two or more concepts have some semantic inter-dependence, this will be maintained by consistent usage of thresholds. For example 'tall' and 'short' are (in a particular context) mutually exclusive and are dependent on the objective observable of height. Thus the height threshold above which a person to be considered 'tall' must be greater than the height threshold below which a person is considered 'short'. However, we do not assume that an agent's point of view is determined by a single precisification but rather by a set of accepted thresholds (or, as in our further work, by a probability distribution over the set of all precisifications).

3   A language of precise observables and vague predicates

In this section we define a general-purpose formal language that (despite bearing only a coarse correspondence to the structure and meaning of natural language) is intended to exhibit some fundamental principles that govern the phenomenon of vagueness.

A key idea underlying the construction of this formalism is that the language should contain two types of vocabulary:

- A precise vocabulary for describing the results of precise objective measurements of the state of the world.

- A vague vocabulary which is defined in terms of the precise vocabulary, relative to a valuation of certain *threshold parameters*, which may occur in the definitions.

3.1   Measurement structures

At the base of the semantics is a structure that represents the state of a *possible world* in terms of a valuation of *measurement functions*, which specify the results of observations applied to the entities of some domain.[3]

An *n-ary measurement function* over domain D is a function $\mu : D^n \to \mathbb{Q}$, with $\mathbb{Q}$ being the set of rational numbers. Thus, $\mathbb{Q}^{D^n}$ is the set of all n-ary measurement functions and $\bigcup_{n \in \mathbb{N}} \mathbb{Q}^{D^n}$ is the set of all measurement functions of any arity (with domain D).

A *measurement structure* is a tuple $\langle D, M, v_M, w \rangle$, where:

- D is a domain of entities;

- $M = \{\dots, f_i, \dots\}$ is a set of measurement function symbols;

- $v_M : M \to \mathbb{N}$, is a mapping from the symbols in M to the natural numbers, giving the arity of each function;

- $w : M \to \bigcup_{n \in \mathbb{N}} \mathbb{Q}^{D^n}$, such that if $v_M(f) = m$ then $w(f) \in \mathbb{Q}^{D^m}$, is a function mapping each n-ary function symbol to a measurement function from D^n to $\mathbb{Q}$.

---

[3]Credit is given to one of the anonymous reviewers for suggestions leading to a more precise formulation of measurement structures than had been given in the originally submitted version of this paper.

Since each assignment function w characterises the domain and function symbols, as well as determining a valuation of the measurement functions over the domain, we regard each w as representing a *possible world*. A possible world in this sense is an *arbitrary* valuation of the function symbols over the domain. The valuation need not respect physical laws with regard to possible combinations of measurable values, so, in so far as the observable functions are intended to correspond to actual kinds of measurements, such worlds could be physically impossible.

Given a domain D, a set of measurement function symbols M, and an arity specification function v_M, the set of worlds that can be specified in terms of these elements can be defined by:

$$\text{Worlds}(D, M, v_M) = \{w \mid \langle D, M, v_M, w \rangle \text{ is a measurement structure}\} .$$

This definition assumes that we have the same set of entities present in every possible world—i.e. we have *constant domains*. There are strong arguments that this condition is unrealistic for a domain of real physical objects. However, this issue is complex and tangential to the main concerns of this paper, and will not be addressed here.

A *measurement frame* is a structure that specifies all possible worlds determined by a given measurement structure:

$$\langle D, M, v_M, W \rangle ,$$

where $W = \text{Worlds}(D, M, v_M)$.

3.2 A language of measurements and thresholds

Let us now consider the definition of a predicative language that can be interpreted relative to a measurement structure.

Let $\mathscr{L}(M, v_M, T, V)$ be the set of formulae of a first-order logical language[4] whose non-logical symbols consist of: a finite set of measurement function symbols $M = \{f_1, \ldots, f_k\}$, a finite set, $T = \{t_1, \ldots t_l\}$, of *threshold parameter* symbols, strict and non-strict inequality relations ($<$ and $\leq$), and a denumerable set $V = \{\ldots, x_i, \ldots\}$ of variable symbols. Every atomic formula of $\mathscr{L}(M, v_M, T, V)$ takes one of the forms:

A1. $f_j(x_1, \ldots, x_n) \leq f_k(y_1, \ldots, y_m)$

A2. $t_i \leq t_j$

A3. $t_i < f_j(x_1, \ldots, x_n)$

A4. $f_j(x_1, \ldots, x_n) < t_i$

where $n = v_M(f_j)$ and $m = v_M(f_k)$. Nested measurement functions are not allowed, since they operate on entities and their values are real numbers. Complex formulae are formed from atomic formulae by means of the standard truth-functional connectives and quantifiers over the variables (but not over the threshold parameters). $\mathscr{L}(M, v_M, T, V)$ includes formulae with free variables.

---

[4]In fact, this account does not depend on the specific details the language. I choose standard first-order logic for definiteness, but there could be reasons to use a more expressive language.

A realistic theory of observable measurements would model the fact that only certain measurements can be usefully compared. This could be achieved by classifying the observable functions into sorts according to the type of quantity that they designate and then restricting the syntax so that only observable values of the same type can be compared by means of the $\leq$ relation, thus restricting the syntax of atoms of the form **A1**. If the observables correspond to the kinds of measurement used in Newtonian physics, then the sorts of observable measurement could be classified in terms the fundamental dimensions of *length* (L), *time* (T) and *mass* (M), and also combinations of these basic dimensions formed by products and reciprocals (for example *area* has type $L \times L$ and *velocity* has type L/T). But the classification and comparability of measurement types is tangential to our primary aim of formalising modes of vagueness; so, for present purposes, we make the simplifying assumption that all measurements are comparable.

Although the syntactic specification of our language $\mathscr{L}(M, v_M, T, V)$ allows arbitrary logical combinations of atoms, the different forms of atoms express different kinds of information, which one would not normally mix within the same proposition. In applying the language to formalising the semantics and use of particular observables, one would typically employ formulae of the following forms, which are homogeneous with respect to the kinds of atoms they contain:

Constraints on observables Formulae containing only atoms of the form **A1** (i.e. those that do not contain threshold parameters) can be regarded as expressing constraints on the physical structure of the world. However, the language considered here is too limited to express a fully-fledged physical theory. To specify such a theory we would need operators designating mathematical functions that govern the relationships between observables (for instance $\forall x[density(x) = mass(x)/volume(x)]$). This would require the language to be extended with an appropriate vocabulary of mathematical functions to operate upon and combine values of the observables.

Threshold constraints Formulae of the form **A2** express ordering constraints between thresholds. A typical example would be t_short $\leq$ t_tall, stating that the threshold below which an individual is considered short is less than the threshold above which and individual is considered tall. Atoms of the form **A2** will not normally occur within more complex formulae. In applying our representation to describing the semantics of vague predicates, we have found many cases where it seems appropriate that a strict ordering be imposed between two different but related thresholds. In certain cases more complex ordering constraints may be required (such as in the specification for the colour purple, given below in Section 4).

Judgements A third class comprises those formulae containing atoms of forms **A3** and **A4**, by which the value of an observable measurement function is compared to a threshold parameter. These are perhaps the most significant type of formulae in the language as they play a crucial role in our account of vagueness. Simple examples include t_tall $< height(x)$ and $weight(x) <$ t_heavy. These express judgements that a given measurable property of an object lies above or below a given threshold. In the next section we shall see how these thresholds are linked to vague predicates.

3.3 Predicate definitions

Each formula of $\mathscr{L}(M, v_M, T, V)$ defines a predicate of arity n, where n is the number of free variables in the formula. Hence, we can extend L by defining new predicate symbols by means of formulae of the form

PG. $\forall x_1, \ldots, x_n [R(x_1, \ldots, x_n) \leftrightarrow \Phi(t_1, \ldots, t_m, x_1, \ldots, x_n)]$,

where $\Phi(t_1, \ldots, t_m, x_1, \ldots, x_n)$ is any formula in $\mathscr{L}(M, v_M, T, V)$ incorporating parameters $t_1, \ldots, t_m$ and with free variables $x_1, \ldots, x_n$.

For instance, $\forall x [\mathsf{Tall}(x) \leftrightarrow (\mathsf{t\_tall} \leq height(x))]$ is a typical example of a predicate defined in this way. Here, *height* is a measurement function and $\mathsf{t\_tall}$ is a threshold parameter. An informal interpretation of this formula is that an entity is tall just in case its height is greater than or equal to the value of the parameter $\mathsf{t\_tall}$.

3.4 An extended language including defined predicates

The language $\mathscr{L}(M, v_M, T, V)$ of measurements and thresholds will serve as a basis for an extended language incorporating symbols for vague predicates.

Let $\mathscr{L}(M, v_M, T, V, R, v_R, N)$ be the language obtained by supplementing the vocabulary of $\mathscr{L}(M, v_M, T, V)$ with a set of predicate symbols R, such that the arity of each symbol is given by the function $v_R \colon R \to \mathbb{N}$ and a set of constant symbols N (which will denote objects of the domain). The set of atomic formulae is extended to include those of the form

A5. $R_i(\alpha_1, \ldots, \alpha_n)$,

where each $\alpha_i \in (V \cup N)$. The complete set of formulae of $\mathscr{L}(M, v_M, T, V, R, v_R, N)$ includes all formulae constructed from this extended set of atomic formulae by application of Boolean connectives and quantification over variables in V.

3.5 Predicate grounding theories

Given a language $\mathscr{L}(M, v_M, T, V, R, v_R, N)$, a *predicate grounding theory* for this language is a set of formulae of the form **PG**, containing one formula for each relation $R_i \in R$. Thus, the predicate grounding theory *defines* every relation in R in terms of a formula of the sub-language $\mathscr{L}(M, v_M, T, V)$.

Let Θ be the set of all predicate grounding theories for $\mathscr{L}(M, v_M, T, V, R, v_R, N)$. Since each of these grounding theories includes a definition of every predicate in the language, we can define a function,

$$\mathsf{Def} \colon \Theta \times R \to \mathscr{L}(M, v_M, T, V),$$

such that $\mathsf{Def}(\theta, R)$ is a formula with $v_R(R)$ free variables, which gives a possible definition of the relation R.

3.6 Parameterised precisification models

We now define a model structure to provide a semantics for $\mathscr{L}(M, v_M, T, V, R, v_R, N)$. The model incorporates a measurement frame together with mappings from the language symbols onto elements of the frame. Specifically, a *parameterised precisification model* is a structure

$$\mathfrak{M} = \langle \mathcal{M}, R, v_R, N, V, T, \Theta, \kappa, \xi, P \rangle,$$

where

- $\mathcal{M} = \langle D, M, v_M, W \rangle$ is a measurement frame;

- R is a set of predicate symbols;

- $v_R \colon R \to \mathbb{N}$ gives the arity of each predicate symbol;

- N is a set $\{\ldots, n_i, \ldots\}$ of nominal constants;

- V is a set $\{\ldots, x_i, \ldots\}$ of variable symbols;

- T is a finite set $\{\ldots, t_i, \ldots\}$ of threshold parameter symbols;

- $\Theta = \{\ldots, \theta_i, \ldots\}$, where each θ_i is a predicate grounding theory for the language;

- $\kappa \colon N \to D$ maps nominal constants to entities of the domain;

- $\xi \colon V \to D$ maps variable symbols to entities of the domain;

- $P = \{p \mid p \colon T \to (\mathbb{R} \setminus \mathbb{Q})\}$, is the set of all mappings from threshold parameters to *irrational* numbers. (P is the set of precisifications.)

The assignment of irrational numbers to threshold parameters is primarily a technical means to ensure that every observable value is either greater or smaller than any threshold parameter. However, it can be motivated by regarding the values of thresholds as *cuts* (in roughly the same sense as in *Dedekind cut*) between two sets of rational numbers, where all values in one set are strictly lower than all values in the other set. (On the other hand, it may be preferable to specify the domains of observables and thresholds as constituting disjoint sub-domains of the rationals.)

3.7   Interpretation function

The semantic interpretation function, $[\![\chi]\!]_{\mathfrak{M}}^{w,p,\theta}$, gives the denotation of any formula or term χ of the language relative to a given model $\mathfrak{M}$, a possible world $w \in W$, a predicate grounding theory $\theta \in \Theta$ and a precisification $p \in P$. The θ index models semantic indeterminacy arising from conceptual vagueness, whereas the p index models indeterminacy due to sorites vagueness.

To specify the interpretation function, the following auxiliary notations will be used:

- $\mathfrak{M} \overset{x}{\sim} \mathfrak{M}'$ means that models $\mathfrak{M}$ and $\mathfrak{M}'$ are identical except for their variable assignment functions ξ and ξ'. And moreover, these assignment functions are identical, except that they may differ in the value assigned to the variable x.

- $\mathrm{Subst}([x_1 \Rightarrow \alpha_1, \ldots, x_n \Rightarrow \alpha_n], \phi)$ refers to the formula resulting from ϕ after replacing each variable x_i by α_i.

The interpretation function can now be specified. The Boolean connectives and quantifier have their standard classical interpretation:

- $[\![\neg\phi]\!]_{\mathfrak{M}}^{w,p,\theta} = \mathbf{t}$ if $[\![\phi]\!]_{\mathfrak{M}}^{w,p,\theta} = \mathbf{f}$, otherwise $= \mathbf{f}$;

- $[\![\phi \wedge \psi]\!]_{\mathfrak{M}}^{w,p,\theta} = \mathbf{t}$ if $[\![\phi]\!]_{\mathfrak{M}}^{w,p,\theta} = \mathbf{t}$ and $[\![\psi]\!]_{\mathfrak{M}}^{w,p,\theta} = \mathbf{t}$, otherwise $= \mathbf{f}$;

- $[\![\forall x[\psi]]\!]_{\mathfrak{M}}^{w,p,\theta} = \mathbf{t}$ if $[\![\psi]\!]_{\mathfrak{M}'}^{w,p,\theta}$ for all $\mathfrak{M}'$ such that $\mathfrak{M} \overset{x}{\sim} \mathfrak{M}'$, otherwise $= \mathbf{f}$.

The inequality relations are interpreted as follows, where γ_i and γ_j may each be either a threshold parameter or a measurement function term:

- $[\![\gamma_i \leq \gamma_j]\!]_{\mathfrak{M}}^{w,p,\theta} = \mathbf{t}$ if $[\![\gamma_i]\!]_{\mathfrak{M}}^{w,p,\theta}$ is less than or equal to $[\![\gamma_j]\!]_{\mathfrak{M}}^{w,p,\theta}$, otherwise $= \mathbf{f}$;

- $[\![\gamma_i < \gamma_j]\!]_{\mathfrak{M}}^{w,p,\theta} = \mathbf{t}$ if $[\![\gamma_i]\!]_{\mathfrak{M}}^{w,p,\theta}$ is strictly less than $[\![\gamma_j]\!]_{\mathfrak{M}}^{w,p,\theta}$, otherwise $= \mathbf{f}$.

The value of measurement functions depends on the possible world in which the measurement is made; and hence, their interpretation depends on the w index:

- $[\![f(\alpha_1,\ldots,\alpha_n)]\!]_{\mathfrak{M}}^{w,p,\theta} = w(f)(\langle\delta(\alpha_1),\ldots,\delta(\alpha_n)\rangle)$,
  where $\delta(\alpha) = \kappa(\alpha)$ if $\alpha \in N$ and $\delta(\alpha) = \xi(\alpha)$ if $\alpha \in V$.

Interpretation of the threshold parameters depends on the precisification index, p:

- $[\![\mathsf{t}]\!]_{\mathfrak{M}}^{w,p,\theta} = p(\mathsf{t})$;

Finally, the interpretation of the defined predicate and relation symbols is dependent upon the grounding theory θ:

- $[\![R(\alpha_1,\ldots,\alpha_n)]\!]_{\mathfrak{M}}^{w,p,\theta} = [\![\mathsf{Subst}([x_1 \Rightarrow \alpha_1,\ldots,x_n \Rightarrow \alpha_n],\mathsf{Def}(\theta,R))]\!]_{\mathfrak{M}}^{w,p,\theta}$.

On the basis of the interpretation function, a semantic satisfaction relation can be defined by

$$\mathfrak{M}, \langle w, p, \theta \rangle \Vdash \phi \quad \text{iff} \quad [\![\phi]\!]_{\mathfrak{M}}^{w,p,\theta} = \mathbf{t}.$$

This says that formula ϕ is true in model $\mathfrak{M}$, at world w and precisification p, with respect to predicate grounding theory θ.

The *interpretation set* of a proposition relative to a model $\mathfrak{M}$ is given by:

$$[\![\phi]\!]_{\mathfrak{M}} = \{\langle w, p, \theta \rangle \mid (\mathfrak{M}, \langle w, p, \theta \rangle \Vdash \phi)\}.$$

This is the set of world/precisification/grounding theory triples for which formula ϕ is evaluated as true.

We have now established the main result of this paper: we have defined a first-order language with a semantics that gives a special status to observable measurements and threshold parameters. The interpretation function for this language is such that each valuation of observable measurements corresponds to a possible world, and each valuation of threshold parameters corresponds to a precisification. In terms of this semantics, each propositional formula is interpreted as the set of possible world/precisification/grounding theory triples at which the proposition is considered to be true.

4   Penumbral connections

A major selling point of supervaluation-based accounts of vagueness is that they provide
a framework within which one can model dependencies among vague predicates—i.e.
penumbral connections. To use an example of Fine, there is a vague borderline demar-
cating the applicability of the terms 'pink' and 'red' but the terms are exclusive in that
one would not normally describe an object as both pink and red. A primary motivation
for the development of standpoint semantics was to refine and make more explicit the
nature of such interdependencies.

The phenomenon of penumbral connection is of course controversial and is one
of the key points of contention between supervaluationist approaches and fuzzy logics.
Fuzzy logicians tend to the view that an object can be both pink and red to some de-
gree, and consequently a proposition of the form $(\mathsf{Pink}(x) \wedge \mathsf{Red}(x))$ may also be true
to some degree. By contrast, a supervaluationist would say that an object may be pink
according to one precisification and red according to another but there is no precisification according to which the object is both pink and red, and hence the proposition
$(\mathsf{Pink}(x) \wedge \mathsf{Red}(x))$ must be false (indeed *super-false*). In the present account, we lean
more towards the supervaluationist account, although we do have leeway to accom-
modate some facets of the fuzzy viewpoint. Since our interpretation function evaluates
propositions with respect to a predicate grounding theory (as well as a precisification) we
may weaken dependencies between predicates by allowing that some grounding theories
do not enforce them. But in the present paper we do not consider this possibility in detail.

Within the language $\mathscr{L}(M, v_M, T, V, R, v_R, N)$, penumbral connections are made explicit by predicate grounding definitions, and also by specifying ordering constraints
between threshold parameters. We conjecture that this approach, is adequate to describe
most, if not all, dependencies between vague predicates. In the case of predicates 'tall'
and 'short', which have provided most of our examples, so far, their penumbral connect-
ion is straightforwardly represented by the definitions $\forall x[\mathsf{Tall}(x) \leftrightarrow (\mathsf{t\_tall} \leq height(x))]$
and $\forall x[\mathsf{Short}(x) \leftrightarrow (height(x) \leq \mathsf{t\_short})]$ and the threshold constraint $\mathsf{t\_short} < \mathsf{t\_tall}$.

As a more tricky example, we consider the vague colour terms *red, orange, pink* and
peach. We may describe this four-fold categorisation in terms of divisions based on two
threshold parameters, one concerning the observed *hue* of an object and the other concerning the *saturation* of the object's observed colour (low saturation being characteristic of *pastel* colours such as pink and peach). However, a problem arises concerning the
hue of a colour. Hue is normally measured in terms of a cyclical scale which runs from
red, through the rainbow to violet and then back to red. This measure corresponds well
with our perceptual experience of colour, in that we perceive colours as if they form a
circle in which there is a continuous transition from blue through violet to red. In order to
circumvent this we can adopt a measurement of hue which forms a linear scale based on
the physical frequency spectrum of light. Thus, *hue*(x) would give the value corresponding to the frequency within the visible spectrum that is most strongly reflected by object
x. Using this measurement of hue, the colour predicates may be defined as follows:

$$\mathsf{Red}(x) \leftrightarrow (\ (hue(x) < \mathsf{t\_red\text{-}orange}) \wedge (\mathsf{t\_pastel} < saturation(x))\ )$$

$$\mathsf{Orange}(x) \leftrightarrow (\ (\mathsf{t\_red\text{-}orrange} < hue(x)) \wedge (hue(x) < \mathsf{t\_orange\text{-}yellow})$$
$$\wedge (\mathsf{t\_pastel} < saturation(x))\ )$$

$$\text{Pink}(x) \leftrightarrow (\ (hue(x) < \text{t\_red-orange}) \wedge (saturation(x) < \text{t\_pastel})) \ )$$

$$\text{Peach}(x) \leftrightarrow (\ (\text{t\_red-orange} < hue(x)) \wedge (hue(x) < \text{t\_orrange-yellow})$$
$$\wedge (saturation(x) < \text{t\_pastel}) \ )$$

And the threshold constraint (t_red-orange < t_orange-yellow) should also be specified.

This analysis faces a further complication if we consider a colour such as purple, where the boundary between a purple hue and a red hue could be interpreted as lying either near the high end of the scale or at the low end of the scale (if some reddish hues are regarded as purple). To account for this we must allow that the blue-purple threshold boundary can be either lower or higher than the purple-red boundary. In the first case the hue of a purple object must lie both above the blue-purple threshold *and* below the purple-red threshold. But in the second case (where the range of purples is regarded as wrapping round from the high end to the low end of the hue scale) an object will count as purple if its hue is *either* higher than the blue-purple threshold *or* lower than the purple-red threshold. Thus, we would get the following grounding definition (with no additional constraint on the ordering of t_blue-purple and t_purple-red):

$$\text{Purple}(x) \leftrightarrow (\ (\ (\text{t\_blue-purple} < \text{t\_purple-red}) \wedge$$
$$(\text{t\_blue-purple} < hue(x)) \wedge (hue(x) < \text{t\_purple-red}) \ )$$
$$\vee$$
$$(\ (\text{t\_purple-red} < \text{t\_blue-purple}) \wedge$$
$$((\text{t\_blue-purple} < hue(x)) \vee (hue(x) < \text{t\_purple-red}))$$
$$) \ )$$
$$\wedge (\text{t\_pastel} < saturation(x))$$

5   Standpoints and proposition evaluation

In order to take account of an agent's comprehension of propositional information, we need to relate the agent's cognitive state to our formal semantics of propositions, which gives the meaning of a proposition in terms of an interpretation set. Two aspects of the cognitive state are clearly relevant: what the agent believes about the state of the world, and what the agent regards as an acceptable usage of terminology (especially vague predicates). Whether the agent considers a proposition to be true will depend on both these aspects.

Beliefs may be modelled either syntactically in terms of formulae expressing facts and theories that an agent regards as true, or semantically in terms of possible states of the world that an agent considers plausible. In the framework of classical logic, where each predicate has a definite meaning, the two perspectives are tightly linked, since any set of formulae determines a fixed set of possible worlds that satisfy that set. But if propositions can vary in meaning, according to different interpretations of vague predicates, the correspondence is more fluid: different interpretations will be true in different sets of possible worlds. Thus, in order to separate an agent's beliefs about the world from their attitude to linguistic meanings, the beliefs must be modelled in a way that is not affected by linguistic variability. Hence, our model of belief is primarily based on sets of plausible possible worlds rather than theories. Of course the structure of a possible world will still be determined relative to a formal language, but this will be the limited language of observable measurement functions, which contains no predicates other than precise ordering relations.

In accordance with the interpretation function, $[\![\chi]\!]_{\mathfrak{M}}^{w,p,\theta}$, specified above, the agent's attitude to the meanings of vocabulary terms is modelled in terms of both the predicate grounding definitions and the choices of threshold values that the agent considers to be acceptable.

5.1   A formal model of a standpoint

We represent an agent's attitude by a structure that we call a *standpoint*, which characterises the range of possible worlds and linguistic interpretations that are plausible/acceptable to the agent. Formally, a standpoint is modelled by a tuple,

$$\langle B, A, \Psi \rangle,$$

where:

- $B \subseteq W$ is the agent's *belief set*—i.e. the set of possible worlds that are compatible with the agent's beliefs,

- $A \subseteq P$ is the agent's *admissibility set*—i.e. the set of precisifications that the agent considers to make reasonable assignments to all threshold parameters, and hence to be *admissible*,

- $\Psi \subseteq \Theta$ is a set of predicate grounding theories that characterises all possible definitions of ambiguous predicates that the agent regards as acceptable.

In this model, the belief state of an agent is characterised in purely *de re* fashion—that is in terms of states of the world rather than in terms of linguistic propositional expressions that are accepted as true. This belief model (due to Hintikka [10]) is relatively simple and clear, although may be criticised on the grounds that it treats agents as *logically omniscient*—they always believe all logical consequences of their beliefs. In further development it might be useful to introduce a richer belief theory within which one can distinguish an agent's *de re* beliefs, from explicit propositional belief (along the lines of [7]).

In order that A adequately models the set of precisifications that are acceptable to an agent, we may want to place restrictions on which subsets of P are regarded as legitimate admissibility sets. One plausible requirement is that the set of acceptable values that could be assigned to any given threshold parameter ought to lie in a range that is convex with respect to the ordering relation on the value domain. In other words, the possible values of a parameter include all intermediate values that lie between other possible values. For example, if one sometimes uses language on the basis of a threshold for tallness of 180 cm and at other times on the basis of 185 cm being the threshold, then one may argue that 182 cm or 183 cm must also be reasonable threshold choices. Counter to this, one might object that, in describing a particular state of the world involving specific individuals, it may be natural to divide tall from short individuals only at certain points, because of the distribution of their heights—i.e. such a break is more natural if it falls in a gap in the height distribution of the individuals under consideration. The question of what conditions should be placed on A is a subject of ongoing work. But, even without any further constraints, our semantics already captures significant aspects of the interpretation of vague predicates.

The Ψ component of a standpoint allows one to model an agent's ambivalence with regard to the appropriate grounding definition for certain predicates. Thus, rather than specifying each grounding theory $\theta \in \Psi$ separately it would be more feasible to give a range of possible definitions for each conceptually vague predicate (or group of inter-dependent group of predicates). An acceptable grounding theory then corresponds to a selection for each predicate of a particular definition from a set of possible alternatives.

5.2 Truth with respect to a standpoint

For any given model $\mathfrak{M}$, we can now formally define the condition that a formula ϕ holds with respect to a particular standpoint $\langle B, A, \Psi \rangle$. Specifically, we define:

- $\mathfrak{M}, \langle B, A, \Psi \rangle \Vdash \phi$ iff $(B \times A \times \Psi) \subseteq \llbracket \phi \rrbracket_{\mathfrak{M}}$.

So ϕ holds for a standpoint if it is true at all worlds in the belief set for all admissible precisifications and all acceptable predicate grounding theories. In other words, the agent considers that, for any reasonable interpretation of ambiguous predicates and all choices of threshold parameters, ϕ is true in all possible worlds consistent with the agent's beliefs.

5.3 Weaker forms of assertion relative to a standpoint

Our standpoint semantics also enables us to specify a number of modal-like operators by means of which we can describe more ambivalent and/or less confident attitudes that an agent may have to a given proposition:

- $\mathfrak{M}, \langle B, A, \Psi \rangle \Vdash \mathsf{CouldSay}(\phi)$ iff $(B \times \{p\} \times \{\theta\}) \subseteq \llbracket \phi \rrbracket_{\mathfrak{M}}$,
  for some $p \in A$ and some $\theta \in \Psi$.

- $\mathfrak{M}, \langle B, A, \Psi \rangle \Vdash \mathsf{CouldBe}(\phi)$ iff $(\{w\} \times A \times \Psi) \subseteq \llbracket \phi \rrbracket_{\mathfrak{M}}$, for some $w \in B$.

- $\mathfrak{M}, \langle B, A, \Psi \rangle \Vdash \mathsf{CouldBeSay}(\phi)$ iff $\langle w, p, \theta \rangle \in \llbracket \phi \rrbracket_{\mathfrak{M}}$,
  for some $w \in B$, $p \in A$ and $\theta \in \Psi$.

$\mathsf{CouldSay}(\phi)$ asserts that for all worlds in the agent's belief set, ϕ is true in some admissible precisification for some acceptable grounding theory. This operator is used to characterise an assertion made in a context where an agent is fully confident that their beliefs relevant to ϕ are correct, but is unsure about the choice of words used to express ϕ. By contrast, $\mathsf{CouldBe}(\phi)$ means that, for all reasonable interpretations of predicate definitions and thresholds, there is some world compatible with the agent's beliefs where ϕ is true. In this case the interpretation of the words used to express ϕ is taken to be uncontroversial, but the state of reality, which would determine whether ϕ is true, is uncertain. Finally, $\mathsf{CouldBeSay}(\phi)$ indicates that there is some combination of acceptable predicate definitions, threshold choices and a world state compatible with the agent's beliefs, according to which ϕ would be interpreted as true.

This distinction between the operators CouldBe and CouldSay is closely related to distinctions made by J.L. Austin [1], in his analysis of different ways in which the sense of a predicate may be related to the properties of an object to which it is applied. He introduced the idea of the *onus of match* between the sense of a word and the corresponding property of the object, and suggested that in some speech situations one is clear about the meaning of the word but unsure whether the object possesses the appropriate property, whereas in others one is clear about the properties of the object but unsure about whether the word adequately describes the object.

A number of other modalities could be defined. In the specifications for CouldSay(ϕ) and CouldBeSay(ϕ), the indices giving the precisification p and grounding theory θ are both allowed to vary (independently). But we could, for instance, define a modality M such that M(ϕ) is true iff $(B \times A \times \{\theta\}) \subseteq [\![\phi]\!]_{\mathfrak{M}}$ for some particular $\theta \in \Psi$—i.e. there is some acceptable grounding theory, relative to which ϕ holds for every admissible precisification. Such a modality does not have an obvious informal interpretation, since in ordinary language we tend to conflate conceptual and sorites variability within the general phenomenon of vagueness; however, it may still provide an informative characterisation of an agent's attitude to a proposition.

6 Further work and conclusions

We have given an overview of a semantic framework within which various significant aspects of vagueness can be articulated. Although the theory developed so far is already quite complex, there are still many loose ends that would need to be tied up in order to provide a solid foundation for representing and reasoning with information expressed in terms of vague predicates. As such, the framework is intended to provide a platform upon which more practical knowledge representation languages can be developed. Such development would most likely involve both simplification of some parts of the formalism and elaboration of others.

In the current work, the focus has been on semantics. Although the syntax of a formal representation has been specified, nothing has been said about the proof theory governing valid inference within this system. In fact, since the basic language is essentially a variant of first-order logic, standard proof systems can be be applied. However, if (as suggested in Section 5.3) the language is extended by modal operators to express the ambivalent truth status of vague propositions, then additional inference rules will be needed in order to take account of these operators. Investigation of the proof theory of such extended languages is the subject of ongoing work.

An obvious major extension to the theory would be to add probability distributions over the belief set and/or the set of admissible precisifications to model the relative plausibility of different possible worlds and the relative acceptability of different precisifications. Indeed, work has already been carried out on such an extension. Initial investigations seem to be fruitful and indicate that this approach may be fruitful as a means to explain the famous *sorites paradox* and related phenomena.

Another interesting direction for further work would be to study the assimilation of new information in terms of the transformation from an agent's initial standpoint to a modified standpoint. Here the issue arises that when an agent receives information that is incompatible with their current standpoint, they must choose whether to modify their beliefs or to try to interpret the information from the point of view of a different standpoint. This study could extend to more general aspects of the exchange of information between two agents in the presence of vagueness. The notion of *context* is likely to be relevant to such an investigation.

For practical applications it may be convenient to replace the somewhat elaborate model theory we have given with a more standard first-order semantics. This would require that the semantic indices (worlds and precisifications) were in some way incorporated into the object language. This could be achieved in a similar way to how temporal logics are often treated within AI formalisms (e.g. by a Situation Calculus [15] style formulation such as $\mathsf{Holds}(\phi, \langle w, p, \theta \rangle)$).

In summary, this paper has outlined the structure of a formal semantics for interpreting vague languages, that models both the definitional ambiguity of conceptual terms and the variability of thresholds used to determine their applicability. The framework characterises an explicit link between the thresholds governing predicate applicability and observable properties of the world. This link provides a basis for detailed semantic modelling of the modes of variability in the meanings of particular vague predicative terms. It also enables specification of complex penumbral connections between related terms. Additionally, the paper has suggested a model of the cognitive standpoint of an intelligent agent incorporating both a belief state and an attitude towards the interpretation of vague terms.

BIBLIOGRAPHY

[1] John L. Austin. How to talk: some simple ways. *Proceedings of the Aristotelian Society*, 1953. Also in J.L. Austin Philosophical Papers, Clarendon Press, 1961.

[2] Brandon Bennett. Modal semantics for knowledge bases dealing with vague concepts. In Anthony G. Cohn, Leonard Schubert, and S. Shapiro, editors, *Principles of Knowledge Representation and Reasoning: Proceedings of the 6th International Conference (KR-98)*, pages 234–244. Morgan Kaufman, 1998.

[3] Brandon Bennett. Modes of concept definition and varieties of vagueness. *Applied Ontology*, 1(1): 17–26, 2005.

[4] Brandon Bennett. A theory of vague adjectives grounded in relevant observables. In Patrick Doherty, John Mylopoulos, and Christopher A. Welty, editors, *Proceedings of the Tenth International Conference on Principles of Knowledge Representation and Reasoning*, pages 36–45. AAAI Press, 2006.

[5] Brandon Bennett. Possible worlds and possible meanings: A semantics for the interpretation of vague languages. In *Commonsense 2011: Tenth International Symposium on Logical Formalizations of Commonsense Reasoning*, AAAI Spring Symposium, Stanford University, 2011. AAAI.

[6] Brandon Bennett, David Mallenby, and Allan Third. An ontology for grounding vague geographic terms. In C. Eschenbach and M. Gruninger, editors, *Proceedings of the 5th International Conference on Formal Ontology in Information Systems (FOIS-08)*. IOS Press, 2008.

[7] Ronald Fagin and Joseph Y. Halpern. Belief, awareness, and limited reasoning. *Artificial Intelligence*, 34:39–76, 1988.

[8] Kit Fine. Vagueness, truth and logic. *Synthèse*, 30:263–300, 1975.

[9] Joseph Y. Halpern. Intransitivity and vagueness. In *Principles of Knowledge Representation: Proceedings of the Ninth International Conference (KR-2004)*, pages 121–129, 2004.

[10] Jaakko Hintikka. *Knowledge and Belief: An Introduction to the Logic of the Two Notions.* Cornell University Press, Ithaca, N.Y., 1962.

[11] Hans Kamp. Two theories about adjectives. In E.L. Keenan, editor, *Formal Semantics of Natural Language*. Cambridge University Press, Cambridge, England, 1975.

[12] Rosanna Keefe and Peter Smith. *Vagueness: a Reader.* MIT Press, 1996.

[13] Jonathan Lawry. Appropriateness measures: an uncertainty model for vague concepts. *Synthse*, 161:255–269, 2008.

[14] Jonathan Lawry and Yongchuan Tang. Uncertainty modelling for vague concepts: A prototype theory approach. *Artificial Intelligence*, 173(18):1539–1558, 2009.

[15] John McCarthy and Patrick J. Hayes. Some philosophical problems from the standpoint of artificial intelligence. In B. Meltzer and D. Mitchie, editors, *Machine Intelligenge*, volume 4, pages 463–502. Edinburgh University Press, 1969.

[16] Henryk Mehlberg. *The Reach of Science*. University of Toronto Press, 1958. Extract on Truth and Vagueness, pages 427–55, reprinted in [12].

[17] Paulo Santos, Brandon Bennett, and Georgios Sakellariou. Supervaluation semantics for an inland water feature ontology. In Leslie Pack Kaelbling and Alessandro Saffiotti, editors, *Proceedings of the 19th International Joint Conference on Artificial Intelligence (IJCAI-05)*, pages 564–569, Edinburgh, 2005. Professional Book Center.

[18] Bas C. van Fraassen. Presupposition, supervaluations and free logic. In Karel Lambert, editor, *The Logical Way of Doing Things*, Chapter 4, pages 67–91. Yale University Press, New Haven, 1969.

[19] Lofti A. Zadeh. Fuzzy logic and approximate reasoning. *Synthese*, 30:407–428, 1975.

Brandon Bennett
School of Computing
University of Leeds
Leeds, LS2 9JT, UK
Email: B.Bennett@leeds.ac.uk

Comments on *Standpoint Semantics: A Framework for Formalising the Variable Meaning of Vague Terms* by **Brandon Bennett**

PETER MILNE

Introduction

Brandon Bennett [1] offers us a fragment of a first-order theory of the precisification of vague predicates, a theory that applies in the case when there is a (measurable) physical magnitude underlying the vague predicate, as height underlies 'tall'. The basic thought is that vague predicates are precisified through the specification of thresholds, e.g., a height above which an individual counts as tall; the vagueness of a term such as 'tall' is reflected in the fact that various thresholds are acceptable to a speaker of English.

1   Degrees and modality

Let's start with a very simple thought: whatever sorites vagueness—to use Bennett's terminology[1]—there may be regarding 'tall', there is none associated with the comparatives 'at least as tall' and 'taller'. With heights in the background, we, of course, have these two equivalences:

$$x \text{ is at least as tall as } y \text{ iff } height(x) \geq height(y)$$

$$x \text{ is taller than } y \text{ iff } height(x) > height(y),$$

but the important point is that these equivalences are not definitional of their left-hand sides. In fact, in the theory of measurement, we arrive at the magnitude *height* and the properties of scales for the measurement of height from comparisons on a sufficiently rich domain [9, 4].

However one chooses to precisify the word 'tall', in any *finite* domain in which something or someone counts as tall, there *has* to be an individual d_{tall_1} such that

$$x \text{ is tall iff } x \text{ is at least as tall as } d_{tall_1}$$

and an individual d_{tall_2} such that

$$x \text{ is tall iff } x \text{ is taller than } d_{tall_2},$$

---

[1] Bennett writes (p. 264), 'A somewhat different kind of vagueness occurs when the criteria for applicability of a term depend on placing a threshold on the *required magnitude* of one or more variable attributes. For instance, we may agree that the appropriateness of ascribing the predicate 'tall' to an individual depends on the height of that individual, but there is no definite height threshold that determines when the predicate is applicable. We refer to this as *sorites vagueness*, since the essence of the sorites paradox is the indeterminacy in the number of grains required to make a heap.'

for under the precisification there is a (possibly jointly) least tall tall individual and a (possibly jointly) tallest non-tall individual. Of course, neither of these conditions need hold in an infinite domain: there could be an infinite sequence of non-tall individuals, each taller than its predecessor in the sequence, *and* an infinite sequence of tall individuals, each taller than its successors in the sequence, and no individual taller than the ones in the first sequence but not as tall as any of the ones in the second. Nonetheless, even in these circumstances, it's true, given a precisification of 'tall', that *either*

x is tall iff x is taller than each the individuals in the first sequence

or

x is tall iff x is at least as tall as one of the individuals in the second sequence.

Vagueness in the use of the term 'tall' with respect to a fixed domain of individuals is reflected in differing choices for the distinguished individual/set of individuals.

To be sure, what we have here is, for a very good reason, an unnatural way of thinking about our use of a vague predicate. What it does serve to show is that a "pure" theory of precisification of vague predicates in application to a fixed domain can be developed without appeal to an underlying physical magnitude and its values as measured on some scale.[2]

Why is this approach so unnatural? Because of a feature of our use of adjectives such as 'tall'. It is not just that, as it happens, say,

x is tall iff x is at least as tall as d_{tall}

but

x *would be* tall if x *were* at least as tall as d_{tall} *is.*

Notice that this last is an 'if', *not* an 'if, and only if', for it simply does not follow that x would be tall *only if x were* at least as tall as d_{tall} is. It might be that, while being at least as tall as d_{tall} is is, as it happens, not just sufficient but also necessary (in the logician's weak, extensional, non-definitional sense of these terms) given the actual heights of the denizens of the domain, our precisified understanding of 'tall' is such that an individual *could be* tall without being as tall as d_{tall} is.

Talk of degrees such as heights comes naturally when we try to say what is going on in such comparisons. Consider Russell's example and, more particularly, his commentary:

> I have heard of a touchy owner of a yacht to whom a guest, on first seeing it, remarked, "I thought your yacht was larger than it is"; and the owner replied, "No, my yacht is not larger than it is". What the guest meant was, "The size that I thought your yacht was is greater than the size your yacht is"; the meaning attributed to him is, "I thought the size of your yacht was greater than the size of your yacht". [8, p. 489]

---

[2]It is sometimes suggested that 'tall' means taller than average (with respect to some contextually given reference class) e.g., [10, p. 60] or—better, perhaps—taller than most. The notion of an average would seem to presuppose the availability of some suitably structured scale but, in any case, there are sound reasons on which to reject both these analyses—see, e.g., [3, p. 126].

It is hard to see how we can explain such locutions without recourse to lengths/sizes/ heights/ *etc.*, in a word *degrees*. Counterpart theory may offer a way to avoid them—'*x* could be taller than it is' translates into '*x* has a counterpart in some world which is taller than *x*'—but within anything like Kripkean semantics for modal logic, in which the same individual may inhabit different worlds and to which Bennett is committed when he makes his worlds share a common domain, it seems that we need degrees— see [6]. (There are strong modal principles associated with our use of degrees; we "export" scales from this world to others. When we say '*x* could be 5 cm taller than *y*', on its most obvious reading we treat '5 cm' as rigidly designating the same amount as in this world, just as much as we do when we say '*x* could be 5 cm taller than it is', albeit that we know the unit of measurement could have been fixed differently.)

These considerations go a long way to ground Bennett's project. They indicate why the account of precisification is best carried out in terms of degrees. Whether the degrees associated with a comparative are susceptible of numerical representation and, if so, what structure they have varies. On the face of it, what was said above regarding comparisons applies as much to 'funnier' and 'funny' as to 'taller' and 'tall' despite the fact that there is no SI unit of funniness, funniness is not a physical magnitude/Lockean primary quality, and, much more obviously than 'tall', 'funny' exhibits both conceptual and sorites vagueness. Nonetheless, following Russell's lead, analysing the two meanings of 'I thought you were funnier than you are' will lead us to degrees (or extents) of funniness. — And whatever the exact structure of degrees of funniness, we can envisage precisifications of the vague predicate 'funny' being made using them.

If what I have just said is on the right track, we are left with a conceptual conundrum: we happily make "cross-world" modal comparisons of the '*x* could be taller than it is' form, which we understand in terms of heights, but, according to the theory of measurement, we arrive at heights, and the properties of scales of measurement for height, from a foundation of comparisons—non-modal comparisons, to be sure, but only so thanks to the fiction that we have a well-enough stocked domain. We flesh out the fiction by supposing that there *could be* individuals whose heights fall between those of extant individuals, *i.e.* individuals taller than some who exist, shorter than others, and not the same height as any existing individuals.

2   The basic idea and its representation

In the simplest case, whether a vague one-place predicate ϕ under a precisification holds of an object is taken to be determined by whether a relevant, measurable, physical quantity f, possessed by the object, exceeds some threshold value t. Measured values of physical quantities are taken to be rational numbers; for convenience, threshold values are taken to to be non-rational reals.[3] Thus whether x is ϕ is determined by whether $f(x) > t$. This is *one* precisification of the vague predicate ϕ.

---

[3]While there are good reasons for taking *measured* values of physical quantities to be rational, there is nothing in physical theory that precludes possessed values being non-rational real numbers. Why Bennett is concerned only with measured values, 'the results of observations applied to the entities of some domain' (p. 266), and not possessed values is left unexplained, and is all the odder since a possible world in the sense of his theory is 'an arbitrary valuation of the function symbols over the domain', consequently 'the valuation need not respect physical laws with regard to possible combinations of measurable values, so, in so far as the observable functions are intended to correspond to actual kinds of measurements, such worlds could be

2.1   Measurement functions and measurement frames

Bennett says (p. 266),

> At the base of the semantics is a structure that represents the state of a *possible world* in terms of a valuation of *measurement functions*, which specify the results of observations applied to the entities of some domain.

A *measurement structure* is a quadruple $\langle D, M, v_M, w \rangle$ where

- D is a domain of entities,

- $M = \{f_1, f_2, \ldots, f_i, \ldots\}$ is a set of measurement function symbols,

- $v_M : M \to \mathbb{N}$ is a mapping from the symbols in M to the natural numbers, giving the arity of each function,

- $w : M \to \bigcup_{n \in \mathbb{N}+} \mathbb{Q}^{D^n}$ is a function mapping each n-ary function symbol to a measurement function from D^n to $\mathbb{Q}$, *i.e.* $w(f_i) \in \mathbb{Q}^{D^{v_M(f_i)}}$.

From the perspective of orthodox model theory, this is unusual in that measurement functions are functions from D^n to $\mathbb{Q}$, for appropriate n, not into the domain D, but this is merely unusual, not something to balk at. What is much, much odder is that "measurement structures" are a mashup of syntax, interpretation, and signature. M is certainly syntax; w interprets the members of M; depending on the text one follows, M [2, p. 4], v_M [5, p. 6], or the pair $\langle M, v_M \rangle$ [7, p. 3] is the signature of the structure $\langle D, w(f_1), w(f_2), \ldots, w(f_i), \ldots \rangle$.

On Bennett's formulation, the syntax that is to be interpreted in the measurement structure $\langle D, M, v_M, w \rangle$ is itself specified by that structure, *i.e.*, by the structure that interprets it. So one and the same measurement structure cannot interpret two distinct sets of measurement function symbols. This is a perverse and unmotivated restriction, for it rules out by fiat the possibility that sentences of different languages have the same interpretation.

The *measurement frame* associated with the triple of domain D, set of measurement symbols M, and arity assignment v_M is the quadruple $\langle D, M, v_M, W \rangle$ where $W = \{w : \langle D, M, v_M, w \rangle$ is a measurement structure$\}$. I'm not sure what the point of taking it to be a quadruple is. Nothing is lost, as far as I can see, if, instead, we think of it as—as I'd like to put it—the set of all structures with domain D and signature v_M (it being understood that the range of the functions is $\mathbb{Q}$, not D).

2.2   Parameterised precisification models

As Bennett defines it, a *parameterised*[4] *precisification model* $\mathfrak{M}$ is, in effect, a 13-tuple comprising

- a domain D,

- a collection M of measurement function symbols,

---

physically impossible' (p. 267). The restriction is not essential to the development of his theory: simply replace all occurrences of $\mathbb{Q}$ with $\mathbb{R}$.

[4] I'd prefer 'parametrised', in analogy with 'parametric'.

- an assignment v_M of arities to the measurement function symbols,

- the set, W, of all assignments to the measurement function symbols in M of functions from n-tuples (n as specified by v_M) of D to rational numbers,

- a set R of predicate symbols (to be thought of as vague predicates of natural language),

- an assignment v_R of arities to these predicate symbols,

- a set N of constants (thought of as referring to members of the domain D),

- a set V of variables (thought of as ranging over elements of the domain D),

- a second set T of constants (*threshold parameter symbols*, thought of as referring to non-rational real numbers that serve as thresholds),

- a set Θ of predicate grounding theories,

- a function κ mapping members of the set N of constants to members of the domain, D,

- an assignment ξ mapping the variables in V to members of the domain, D,

- the set, P, of *all* mappings of the set T of constants to non-rational real numbers.

Even without saying what a predicate grounding theory is, we see, again, the same ghastly mélange of syntax, interpretation, and signature. What's worse, this is an incomplete specification since it leaves out of account the symbols '$<$' and '$\leq$' which are to be given their standard interpretation in the structure $\langle \mathbb{R}, \leq \rangle$ of the real numbers.

Let us try to impose some model-theoretic order. First, syntax: we have a language with vocabulary $N \cup T \cup R \cup \{<, \leq\} \cup M \cup V$. We are told that every atomic formula built up from the vocabulary $T \cup \{<, \leq\} \cup M \cup V$ takes one of the forms

- $f_i(x_1, x_2, \ldots, x_{v_M(f_i)}) \leq f_j(y_1, y_2, \ldots, y_{v_M(f_j)})$

- $t_i \leq t_j$

- $t_j < f_i(x_1, x_2, \ldots, x_{v_M(f_i)})$

- $f_i(x_1, x_2, \ldots, x_{v_M(f_i)}) < t_j.$

In company with ξ, each pair of functions $\langle w, p \rangle$ with $w \in W$ and $p \in P$, furnishes these formulas with interpretations in the structure $\langle \mathbb{R}, \leq \rangle$.

A *predicate grounding theory* θ associates with each predicate ϕ in R a sentence of the form

$$\forall x_1 \forall x_2 \ldots \forall x_{v_R(\phi)} \left[\phi(x_1, x_2, \ldots, x_{v_R(\phi)}) \leftrightarrow \Phi(t_1, t_2, \ldots, t_m, x_1, x_2, \ldots, x_{v_R(\phi)}) \right]$$

where $t_1, t_2, \ldots, t_m \in T$ and $\Phi(t_1, t_2, \ldots, t_m, x_1, x_2, \ldots, x_{v_R(\phi)})$ is *any* formula in the language with vocabulary $T \cup \{<, \leq\} \cup M \cup V$ in which $x_1, x_2, \ldots, x_{v_R(\phi)}$ occur free.

Predicates in R are not assigned extensions. Rather, atomic formulas in the language with vocabulary $N \cup R \cup V$ are determined as satisfied or not by means of κ, ξ, p, *w and* a predicate grounding theory. The quadruple $\langle \xi, \kappa, p, w \rangle$ determines which substitution instances, possibly involving constants in N, of $\Phi(t_1, t_2, \ldots, t_m, x_1, x_2, \ldots, x_{v_R(\phi)})$ are satisfied in $\langle \mathbb{R}, \leq \rangle$. The cognate substitution instances of $\phi(x_1, x_2, \ldots, x_{v_R(\phi)})$, atomic formulas in the language with vocabulary $N \cup R \cup V$, are then determined as satisfied, the rest not.

2.3 Interpretation

There are three dimensions of variability, parametrised by w, p and θ. Bennett says (p. 270), 'The θ index models semantic indeterminacy arising from conceptual vagueness, whereas the p index models indeterminacy due to sorites vagueness.' If this were true, varying θ while keeping p and w constant should make no odds to sorites vagueness, the vagueness due to indeterminacy of threshold values. Bennett's first example of a predicate-grounding clause is

$$\forall x [\text{tall}(x) \leftrightarrow (t_{\text{tall}} < height(x))].$$

Don't let the occurrence of the subscript 'tall' on 't' fool you. Nothing in what he says about predicate grounding theories requires a fixed association between threshold parameters and predicates. So sorites vagueness is not merely confined to the choice of threshold values determined by p; predicate grounding theories can affect it and, depending on just what they say, might be solely concerned with it.

The three parameters are not treated equally in a model $\mathfrak{M}$. On the modal and sorites dimensions of variability, we are, apparently, required to allow *all* logically possible worlds (W) and assignments of threshold values (P), whereas Θ can be any (non-empty) set of predicate grounding theories.

3 Standpoints

Bennett recognizes that not all assignments of values to threshold parameter symbols are on a par but makes this a feature of the possibly idiosyncratic attitudes of an agent, not the semantics of the language. In a model $\mathfrak{M}$ an agent's *standpoint* is a triple comprising (i) a subset of the set of worlds, (ii) a subset of the set of assignments of values to threshold parameter symbols, and (iii) a subset of the set of predicate grounding theories. It's common enough practice to take an agent's beliefs about the way things are to be modelled by a set of worlds, intuitively the worlds that, for all the agent believes, may be actual. Borrowing a term from supervaluationist semantics, Bennett says (p. 274) of the second element that it

> is the agent's *admissibility* set—i.e. the set of precisifications that the agent considers to make reasonable assignments to all threshold parameters, and hence to be *admissible*,

and, similarly, the third element in the standpoint comprises

> a set of predicate grounding theories that characterises all possible definitions of ambiguous predicates that the agent regards as acceptable.

As Bennett says,

> a standpoint [...] characterises the range of possible worlds and linguistic interpretations that are plausible/acceptable to the agent,

which, in a way, is just fine and dandy, but unless he is committed to the primacy of idiolects and the authoritativeness of agents regarding their own idiolects, the agent's beliefs regarding precisifications of the vague predicates of her language have no part to play in providing a semantics of vague terms, not that Bennett suggests otherwise, despite calling his paper 'Standpoint semantics'. Speakers of a language can have all sorts of beliefs, *including mistaken beliefs*, about the meanings of expressions in their (native and other) languages. In one sense, these beliefs are distinct from how they take the world to be—represented by some subset of W. But for most, if not all, of what we have beliefs about, there are standards of correctness, albeit perhaps transcending all possibility of verification. When Bennett offers us a predicate grounding theory for the colour terms *red, orange, pink, peach* and *purple*, he presents it for all the world as though he were making *approximately correct* observations about English usage. He does *not* report it *merely* as part of his idiosyncratic standpoint (and, frankly, if he had, I doubt I'd have been interested in it).

In addition to the set of precisifications an agent considers to make reasonable assignments to all threshold parameters and the set of predicate grounding theories that characterises all possible definitions of ambiguous predicates that the agent regards as acceptable, there are the set of precisifications of vague predicates in English that make assignments to all threshold parameters and the set of predicate grounding theories that characterises definitions of ambiguous predicates in English *compatible with English usage*. It is these that determine whether the agent's idiosyncratic beliefs about the reasonableness of precisifications and the acceptability of predicate grounding theories are right or wrong. It is these that, conceivably, play a role in the semantics of the vague predicates of English. And, of course, there is undoubtedly an element of vagueness in the determination of which are compatible with English usage.

BIBLIOGRAPHY

[1] B. Bennett, 'Standpoint Semantics: a framework for formalising the variable meaning of vague terms', *this volume*.
[2] W. Hodges, *Model Theory, Encyclopedia of Mathematics and its Applications*, vol. 42, Cambridge: Cambridge University Press, 1993.
[3] J.A.W. Kamp, 'Two theories about adjectives', in E. L. Keenan (ed.), *Formal Semantics of Natural Language*, Cambridge: Cambridge University Press, 1975, pp. 123–155.
[4] D.H. Krantz, R.D. Luce, P. Suppes and A. Tversky, *Foundations of Measurement*, Vol. I, *Additive and Polynomial Representations*, San Diego and London: Academic Press, 1971.
[5] M. Manzano, *Model Theory*, Oxford: Oxford University Press, 1999.
[6] P. Milne, 'Modal Metaphysics and Comparatives', *Australasian J. of Philosophy* 70 (1992): 248–262.
[7] P. Rothmaker, *Introduction to Model Theory*, OPA (Overseas Publishers Association) N.V./Gordon and Breach Science Publishers, 2000.
[8] B. Russell, 'On Denoting', *Mind* 14 (1905): 479–493.
[9] S.S. Stevens, 'On the Theory of Scales of Measurement', *Science* 103 (1946): 677–680.
[10] A. von Stechow, 'Comparing Semantic Theories of Comparison', *Journal of Semantics* 3 (1984): 1–77.

Peter Milne
Department of Philosophy
University of Stirling
Stirling FK4 9LA, United Kingdom
Email: peter.milne@stir.ac.uk

Reply to Peter Milne's Comments on *Standpoint Semantics: A Framework for Formalising the Variable Meaning of Vague Terms*

BRANDON BENNETT

In his comments on my paper, Peter Milne raises a number of interesting points about my semantics, and also makes a number of less interesting and somewhat misleading comments regarding my notation. I shall address what I regard as Milne's most significant observations in more or less the sequence that they occur in his commentary. Luckily this means I shall start by considering one of the more interesting points.

In his Section 1, entitled 'Degrees and modality', Milne draws attention to the fact that, in founding the theory of measurements, strong arguments can be made in favour of the view that all measurement systems must originate from comparative observations of the relative properties of individuals of a domain (e.g. 'John is taller than Mary'), rather than from intrinsic absolute properties of objects (e.g. 'John is 6′ tall'). Nevertheless, as Milne agrees, it is often natural to think in terms of the degree to which a particular individual exhibits some property—i.e. the magnitude of some observable associated with the individual. The idea that the state of the world (and indeed any possible world) can be fully described in terms of such magnitudes is fundamental to my semantics, since I explicitly identify possible worlds with valuations of measurement functions.

Milne finds it puzzling that articulating a semantics in terms of magnitudes should appear natural and attractive, whereas the theory of measurements apparently requires that comparative relations should be prior to magnitudes. I am no expert on theories of measurement, and should really learn more about them,[1] but it seems to me that, even though comparisons may be epistemologically prior to magnitudes, this need not necessarily bear direct correspondence to the structure of a semantic model. I see the situation as somewhat analogous to that of Euclidean geometry, where our perceptions of geometrical configurations of points are typically described by relational terminology (such as 'point x lies between points y and z'), whereas the standard Cartesian model associates each point with a tuple of real numbers.

I now consider Milne's Section 2, where he recapitulates my representation. One point that he picks up on concerns my stipulation that the values of measurement functions should be rational numbers, whereas the values of threshold parameters must be irrational. I originally took this approach for purely technical reasons because I wanted to avoid the possibility that a measurement value should exactly coincide with a thresh-

---

[1] From my cursory reading of Milne's references, they seem to be an excellent starting point for studying this topic.

old which would lead to an awkward complication in the specification of the truth conditions of vague predications. It is likely that the semantics could be formulated differently, such that measurement functions and thresholds both have $\mathbb{R}$ (or perhaps both have $\mathbb{Q}$) as their value domain. However, I am still inclined to the view that separating the domains is both natural and technically advantageous. Moreover, I think that many physicists would reject the idea that physical objects have intrinsic properties whose values are real numbers, and are possessed independently of any actual measurement.

In the remainder of Section 2, Milne proceeds at some length to take issue with some minor aspects of my notation. If these criticisms were justified, I would describe them as pedantic. But, as it happens the criticisms are both unjustified and misleading. Milne's main bone of contention seems to be that in specifying a structure to support the semantic interpretation of a logical language, I often present the structure in terms of a tuple, in which I include not only interpretation functions but also the symbol set or sets that are to be interpreted. This enables me to specify the interpretation functions (which form the meat of the semantic structure) in a self-contained way, since their domains are explicit in the tuple rather than given in some external specification of the vocabulary.

Milne considers this to be mixing syntax and semantics, which of course would not be a good idea. But Milne's use of the term 'syntax' is sloppy and confusing. Symbol sets are *vocabulary* not syntax. Syntax concerns the ordering of symbols into meaningful expressions, and semantics concerns the meaning of these symbols and expressions. Many well known and highly rigorous logic texts[2] present formal semantics in a style similar to my own—i.e. without the use of 'signatures' and with symbols of the object language incorporated into the model structures. Typically, in expositions of this kind, the vocabulary sets are not specified as top-level elements of a model tuple but are instead referred to as domains of the interpretation functions in the tuple. But the symbols of the vocabulary are none the less included in the model, since these functions will correspond to sets of pairs, with a symbol being the first element of each pair. Moreover, in presenting algebras and algebraic semantics, it is very common to incorporate the signature explicitly into the model structure specification.

Just to check that my notation is not hopelessly antiquated and out of line with current thinking, I re-read the beginning of Wilfred Hodges excellent 'A Shorter Model Theory' (1997, Cambridge University Press). On page 2, in his definition of 'structure' Hodges makes it very clear that he considers the symbols to be interpreted as essential ingredients of a structure. Then on page 4 we find the following remarks about the particular way a structure should be formalised:

> Exactly what is a structure? Our definition said nothing about the way in which the ingredients ... are packed into a single entity. But this was a deliberate oversight—the packing arrangements will never matter to us... The important thing is to know what the symbols and the ingredients are, and this can be indicated in any reasonable way.

---

[2] To take just one classic example, Hughes and Cresswell's 'An Introduction to Modal Logic', 1969, Methuen.

Hodges follows this by an example of a structure $\langle \mathbb{R}, +, -, \cdot, 0, 1 \leq \rangle$, saying that $+$, $-$, $\cdot$, 0, 1, and $\leq$ are symbols naming functions, constant elements and relations over the domain $\mathbb{R}$. In Milne's terminology this would be described as a "ghastly mélange of syntax, interpretation and signature".

Milne (who seems to have a very broad idea of perversion) claims further that my notation is perverse because "it rules out the possibility that sentences of different languages have the same interpretation". Of course this is true, since a measurement structure gives an interpretation for a particular set of function symbols. But this is normal in model theory. As Hodges says [p4]: "We shall assume that the signature of a structure can be read off uniquely from the structure", and indeed, Hodges usually refers to any particular structure as an L-structure, with L being its signature. Of course we may still want to say that two languages have isomorphic interpretations, where the isomorphism is characterised by a bijection between symbols of the two languages. Indeed the notion that sentences of different languages could have the same interpretation only makes sense in relation to a particular translation establishing a correspondence between the symbols of each language. (Such bijections can be specified by means of signatures, but there are other ways to do this.)

It is true that one can separate language vocabulary from semantics by regarding a language *signature* as providing an enumeration of symbols of each syntactic category. An interpretation can then be cast in terms of these enumerations (i.e. as a mapping from natural numbers to denotations), rather than the symbols themselves. This formulation of semantics may be advantageous for certain purposes, but such technicalities bear little relevance to the points I was trying to make in the exposition of my semantic framework.

I now return to more substantial issues. In his Section 3.2 Milne examines the three dimensions of variability in the interpretation of vague predicates that are modelled my system. He notes that the grounding theory parameter θ, which is supposed to model vagueness of the conceptual ambiguity variety, could potentially impact upon variability that one would normally regard as sorites vagueness. This is true. However, as Milne also notes, the θ parameter is not intended to range over arbitrary predicate grounding theories but only some particular non-empty set Θ of grounding theories. Perhaps I did not make it clear enough that I am assuming that the theories in Θ are carefully constructed in order that the semantics only allows a range of 'reasonable' groundings for each vague predicate. It is Θ that enforces the specific semantics (what Montague would call 'meaning postulates') of the system.

Finally, we come to Section 3 of Milne's commentary, concerning my notion of 'Standpoint'. Milne suggests that a standpoint may be regarded as characterising an agent's idiolect, i.e. their personal attitude to language and its semantics, and rightly points out that the view that semantics is determined primarily by idiolects is untenable, since the expressions of a natural language must have meaning independently of any particular agent's personal beliefs and idiosyncratic attitude to the meaning of terms.

It seems I did not sufficiently explain my notion of standpoint, since I do not intend standpoints to correspond to the idiolects of particular agents. What I call a 'standpoint' corresponds not to the general linguistic dispositions of an agent, but to a particular attitude held at a particular time in a particular situation. Thus an agent can and often will change their standpoint depending on the situation at hand and the kind of information they wish to convey. Answering the question of when and why an agent would adopt a particular standpoint in a particular context is of course crucial if one wants to move beyond my standpoint-relative semantics, to a broader account of the semantics of vague terms. In fact I have already directed considerable attention to this question, and have made some progress in formulating a more general framework, within which the standpoint of a particular agent in a particular situation can be evaluated in relation to a corpus of linguistic acts representative of the patterns of vocabulary usage in a community of agents sharing a common language. This generalised standpoint semantics involves the introduction of a level statistical machinery on top of the semantics that I have presented in my contribution to this volume.

Handling Borderline Cases Using Degrees: An Information Processing Perspective

HENRI PRADE AND STEVEN SCHOCKAERT[1]

Overview

Although linguistic vagueness is generally related to the existence of borderline cases, the main theories of vagueness are not primarily aimed at handling borderline cases explicitly. As a result, these theories are able to avoid the use of truth degrees, e.g. by focusing on truth value gaps or by taking the epistemic point of view that there is an unknown but sharp boundary between truth and falsity. We argue that, on the other hand, in information processing settings, borderline cases usually are a matter of degree, or at least of ranking, although such degrees may serve different purposes. To support our claim, this paper discusses a number of information processing scenarios, in relation with their use of degrees to handle borderline cases. First, we consider the use of fuzzy labels, contrasting the role of (graded) borderline cases in three different situations: (i) allowing for flexibility when specifying and evaluating fuzzy requests, (ii) allowing for abstraction when describing precise information, and (iii) allowing for uncertainty when stating imprecise information. Second, we discuss the idea of degrees of typicality in the setting of formal concept analysis, seeing e.g. penguins or kiwis as borderline cases of birds. Finally, we illustrate how degrees of similarity may be useful for maintaining consistency, taking advantage of a flexible understanding of linguistic terms, seeing e.g. civil unions as borderline cases of marriages.

1 Introduction

Vagueness already has a long history in modern philosophy, and there are different, somewhat rival, views of vagueness [24, 23, 41, 43]. The supervaluation view [44, 17], for instance, prefers to admit a truth value *gap*: borderline statements have no truth value, but a compound statement involving vague terms may be true if it is true for every possible way in which these vague terms can be precisified (where a vague term is thus viewed as the collection of all its possible sharpened versions). In contrast, the epistemic view [48] rather presupposes the existence of a unique, precise border between truth and falsity, but considers "vagueness as a kind of ignorance", inasmuch that "there really is a grain of sand whose removal turns a heap into a non-heap, but we

[1] This paper develops the content of an extended abstract entitled "About vagueness, typicality and similarity" by the first author, presented at the Logical Models of Reasoning with Vague Information Conference (LoMoReVI), on Sept. 14–17, 2009 at Čejkovice, Czech Republic. Steven Schockaert is a postdoctoral fellow of the Research Foundation – Flanders (FWO).

cannot know which one it is". However, despite the lack of a unified view on vagueness, it is generally agreed that "a term is vague to the extent that it has borderline cases" [42], hence vagueness might be equated with the idea that a vague concept partitions the universe of discourse (sometimes implicitly) into more than two parts; see e.g. [9] for a detailed discussion on the kind of informational scenarios that give rise to such a situation. Nonetheless, the study of vagueness has mainly concentrated on the difficulty of reasoning with vague statements in general, rather than on the explicit handling of borderline cases in practical applications.

In contrast, while the representation of vagueness has not been so much of an issue in Artificial Intelligence (AI) and Pattern Recognition, these fields have progressively built methods that allow to explicitly handle borderline cases in different information processing settings, using degrees in one way or another to distinguish between different levels of being borderline. The field of AI, for instance, has focused on the representation of incomplete and uncertain information, or on the introduction of flexibility when dealing with soft constraints. In that respect, the development of fuzzy logic [49]—assigning intermediary truth values to borderline statements—has primarily been motivated by the need to handle gradual properties in approximate reasoning, rather than offering an alternative theory of vagueness, even if a treatment of sorites using fuzzy logic has been proposed very early [20] (see also [40]). Another example is the development of non-monotonic reasoning approaches for handling exceptions under incomplete information [25], which often rely on plausibility orderings between interpretations to determine what is true in the most normal worlds. For instance, given that typical birds can fly while penguins cannot, penguins are seen as exceptional birds, and are in this sense borderline. Along the same lines, AI uses orderings to represent user preferences, or to encode priorities when revising knowledge bases, while Pattern Recognition has found it advantageous to allow elements to have a graded membership in a given cluster [4].

Thus there seems to be a gap between the philosophical views on vagueness (e.g. supervaluation semantics), and practical methods for handling borderline cases (e.g. based on fuzzy set theory). In this respect, it is interesting to note that a refinement of supervaluation semantics, called standpoint semantics [3], has recently been proposed which seems to bridge this gap to a large extent. Essentially, standpoint semantics adds structure to supervaluation semantics by restricting the possible precisifications of a vague term to those that correspond to a *standpoint*, i.e. a given choice of threshold values for a fixed set of parameters. A fuzzy set can then be seen as an approximate representation of the possible standpoints that can be taken regarding some vague term, sacrificing some structure for better tractability. Note that this view on fuzzy sets is similar to the view of a fuzzy set as the approximation of a random set. The transition from supervaluation semantics to standpoint semantics also seems to support the view that in practical applications, handling borderline cases often requires the use of degrees in one form or another, including intermediary truth values, rankings, or threshold values (i.e. standpoints).

In this paper, we further elaborate on the role of degrees when dealing with borderline cases. By zooming in on a number of basic situations in which borderline cases are encountered, we illustrate how degrees may serve different purposes, and why they are important in applications. In Section 2, we discuss the different uses of fuzzy labels, where degrees are used to model gradualness, allowing for a continuous transition from objects that perfectly satisfy some criterion to objects that do not satisfy it at all. We especially contrast three different uses of fuzzy labels. First, fuzzy labels may be used to express requests, in which case the degrees associated with borderline cases express levels of flexibility. Second, fuzzy labels may be used to describe precise information in a more abstract way (e.g. categorization), in which case degrees express levels of compatibility. Third, fuzzy labels may be used for the imprecise description of ill-known cases, in which case degrees express levels of uncertainty. Subsequently, Section 3 considers statements such as "Tweety is a bird". While "bird" does not correspond to a fuzzy label, birds which lack some typical properties such as "being able to fly" or "having feathers" (e.g. kiwis) may be considered as borderline. Note that tacitly assuming that "Tweety is a typical bird" when all we know is that "Tweety is a bird" is often done in commonsense reasoning. Borderline cases of birds may be graded by asserting that birds are typical (i.e. not borderline) to the extent that they satisfy all the important properties. We discuss the practical use of such degrees of typicality in the context of formal concept analysis. In particular, we focus on the question of how to assess the degree to which some known entity is a typical bird, as well as on the question of how to model the uncertainty that arises when all we know is that "Tweety is a typical bird". Finally, in Section 4, we consider assertions such as "John is married", which may require a more permissive understanding than what the term "married" actually means. For instance, when a source tells us that John is married, it is still somewhat plausible that John is, in fact, in a civil union. Concepts which are similar to marriages, such as a civil union, may thus be seen as borderline cases, even if civil unions do not correspond to special cases of marriages. This view is close to the idea of verisimilitude, i.e. the idea that some false statements are closer to the truth than others. Indeed, the assertion "John is married" is intuitively less false when John is in a civil union than when he is single. We discuss how such a similarity-based treatment of statements can be a useful tool for maintaining consistency in a knowledge representation setting.

In some sense, the information processing setting illustrates the difference between a vague term and the vague understanding of a term. Indeed, the use of fuzzy labels allows for a non-vague understanding of vague terms, while Sections 3 and 4 are concerned with the vague understanding of non-vague terms.

In all of the considered scenarios, we find that degrees play a key role in the practical handling of borderline cases. At first glance, this observation seems at odds with the limited attention that has been given to degrees in most philosophical treatments of vagueness. However, one may argue that, despite the focus on borderline cases, strictly speaking, none of the scenarios we discuss is really concerned with vagueness as it is usually understood, but rather with related notions such as fuzziness, typicality and similarity. Indeed, borderline cases between compatible and incompatible; typical and atypical; similar and dissimilar; etc., are different in nature from borderline cases between truth and falsity. It is tempting to speculate that this subtle difference may be responsible for much of the controversy on the use of degrees in theories of vagueness.

2   On the different uses of fuzzy labels

A fuzzy set A is a mapping from some universe of discourse U to the unit interval $[0, 1]$. For any u in U, $A(u)$ is called the membership degree of u in A, and reflects the extent to which object u satisfies some underlying property. This property is usually described by means of a possibly vague, linguistic label. We use the term fuzzy label to denote such a linguistic description whose interpretation is explicitly specified as a fuzzy set. It is important to note that by providing a fuzzy set as the interpretation of a linguistic description, any vagueness that may have resided in the linguistic description is resolved. What remains is the idea of gradualness, captured by the associated fuzzy set representation: some objects are more compatible than others with a fuzzy label. Indeed, Zadeh himself already considered that vagueness should not be confused with fuzziness. He wrote (in a footnote p. 396 in [49]): "Although the terms fuzzy and vague are frequently used interchangeably in the literature, there is, in fact, a significant difference between them. Specifically, a proposition p is fuzzy if it contains words which are labels of fuzzy sets; and p is vague if it is both fuzzy and insufficiently specific for a particular purpose." So he associates the idea of vagueness with situations where the information at hand is insufficient for some particular use. This may be viewed as putting vagueness closer to generality, or even to ambiguity, two other notions that are classically distinguished from vagueness (see, e.g., [42]). More interestingly, it is noticeable that in Zadeh's view, vagueness is not a feature which is intrinsically attached to a statement (as fuzziness is), but is rather associated to a proposition in the context of a particular purpose. In fact, acknowledging the use of fuzzy labels when modeling vagueness would for instance amount to adapt the supervaluation view such that the possible delineations of a vague term may be fuzzy sets rather than classical sets. This is beyond the scope of this paper.

We may think of very different circumstances in which fuzzy labels or fuzzy sets may be used. There are uses of fuzzy sets as a device for compact encoding that are motivated by technical needs, e.g. using Łukasiewicz multi-valued logic to encode linear optimization problems [21] or to deal with aspects of coding theory [5], using fuzzy description logics for handling data on continuous domains in multimedia information retrieval [31], and using fuzzy answer set programming to find strong Nash equilibria [37]. In this paper, however, we focus on the cognitive uses. Fuzzy sets are useful when expressing desires or requests, when categorizing situations, or when interpreting received information. These three cognitive tasks, which are discussed in more detail below, favor different representation capabilities of fuzzy sets: respectively the encoding of a preference ordering, the embedding of a notion of similarity, and the expression of an uncertainty distribution [11].

Fuzzy labels expressing preference

Consider the situation in which some user is looking for an apartment to let, and attempts to express her desires as a query to some database. In such a case, it may be difficult to come up with a good query which only uses hard constraints, because there is a risk to over-constrain (in which case there would be no matches) or under-constrain (in which case there would be many suboptimal matches) the request. To cope with this, the user may come up with an under-constrained query, together with additional information about her preferences, which could be used to rank the objects matching the actual query. This can easily be accomplished using fuzzy labels. For instance, the user may ask for an apartment that is "rather cheap" and "close" to downtown. This request may be translated into a query by assuming a very liberal understanding of the terms "rather cheap" and "close", while a fuzzy set representation of these terms may be used to subsequently rank the matching apartments.

When expressing desires, fuzzy sets are thus used to encode which are the more or less acceptable values, the fully acceptable values, and the fully excluded values of the relevant attributes. In case the underlying attribute values are ordered on a continuum, processing the query basically amounts to building a membership function representation for each linguistic term, and choosing appropriate operations on fuzzy sets to combine the elementary requirements (e.g. generalizations of set complementation, union and intersection). If the underlying attribute domain is discrete and unordered, a direct assessment of acceptability levels would be required for every attribute value. In such a case, it may be appropriate to use a *scale* for the membership degrees which is different from the real unit interval, the latter being appropriate especially for numerical attributes.

Note that, in principle, fuzzy sets representing preferences are not necessarily associated with a label. Labels are useful here only if the user needs to communicate about what she is looking for, or if the queries are expressed in a prescribed fuzzy vocabulary that has been defined in advance. Since all linguistic terms in such a fuzzy vocabulary have been given a precise meaning, through the specification of fuzzy sets, there is no vagueness in the query itself. However, the vagueness of the associated linguistic terms helps us to get an intuitive grasp of the kind of flexibility that is offered by a fuzzy request. Hence, instead of being a culprit, the vagueness of language is actually advantageous here.

Fuzzy labels expressing similarity

For humans, it is often straightforward to provide natural language descriptions of numerical information. By abstracting away from the actual numbers, the main conclusions that can be drawn from available data may then be easier to see. There is a discrepancy, however, between the continuum of values for attributes such as "age", and the finite (and generally small) number of natural language terms that are at our disposal to describe them. When interfacing numerical domains with natural language terms, it may be beneficial to represent these terms as fuzzy sets. The gradualness of predicates such as "young", viewed as a fuzzy label, then enables us to avoid the use of precise threshold values, which would to a large extent be arbitrary. In other words, the purpose of using fuzzy labels is to allow for flexible threshold values. The decision of which is the most appropriate label to describe a given situation or object can then be postponed, which may allow us to take additional information into account. Note that the final label that is used to describe some situation may also be a compound label (e.g. "old but not very old"), which is obtained using linguistic connectives (e.g. "but") and hedges (e.g. "very"). Note that this use of fuzzy labels is rather different from its use in the specification of queries. Here, the underlying fuzzy set representations essentially convey a notion of similarity: the ages that are somewhat compatible with the predicate "young" are those that are *similar* to ages which are perfectly compatible with it. The need to qualify a particular situation or object, using a linguistic label, may arise for instance in categorization, as is done by fuzzy symbolic sensors [29]. Another application is when a natural language generation system has to build a minimal description designating (in a non-ambiguous manner) an object in a scene, using a limited vocabulary referring for instance to size, location, or color (see [15] for a study of this problem).

The qualification of a particular case, as described above, should be contrasted with the description of *generic* situations. Given a database (whose attribute values are precisely known), one may for instance be interested in providing some partial summaries of its content through aggregates and association rules. Using fuzzy labels, we may state assertions such as "the average salary of *young* people in the company is *about* 1500 euros" or "more than 90% of *young* people have a salary less than …". Without fuzzy labels, precise thresholds need to be used, as in "the average salary of people below 30 …", or "93% of people below 35 have a salary less than …". The main advantage of using fuzzy labels, here, is that they may cover a larger portion of the data. The flexible thresholds that are introduced by using fuzzy labels thus work at our advantage: as several labels may be more or less acceptable to describe a given situation, there is more freedom to come up with informative and useful rules, while staying sufficiently close to what the data actually conveys. However, in order for such statements with fuzzy categories to make sense, it is desirable that for any acceptable precisification of these categories, the value of the average (or any other considered measure) does not vary too much, and remains in a prescribed (fuzzy) range. See [10] and [14] for database aggregates and association rules respectively, on this issue.

Fuzzy labels expressing uncertainty

In the previous two settings, fuzzy labels were used w.r.t. perfectly known information, resp. to convey desires and to provide linguistic descriptions. Here we consider the setting where one receives a piece of information which is expressed linguistically, such as "Bob is young". In this case, we do not have access to any precise information, and we thus remain uncertain about the actual age of Bob. Such a statement of the form X *is A*, where X refers to a single-valued attribute (here the age) is *fuzzy* if A is represented as a fuzzy set. Similarly, the statement X *is A* is *imprecise* as soon as the extension of the set (or fuzzy set) representing A is not a singleton of the universe of discourse U, as in the statement "John is between 20 and 30 years old" (assuming for instance that U is some subset of the set of positive integers). In both cases, we are *uncertain* about the precise age of the person, although we do know that some ages are impossible, because they are not compatible at all with the given (fuzzy) label. Moreover, given a fuzzy label such as "young", it is clear that the more a given age can be considered as young, the more it is compatible with the asserted information, and hence the more it should be considered as a possible value. This leads us to take the *degree of possibility* that $age(Bob)$ is 25 to be the degree of membership of 25 in the fuzzy set representing "young" [49]. More generally, it is postulated that

$$\pi_X(u) = \mu_A(u), \ \forall u \in U$$

where $\pi_X(u)$ represents the degree to which u is considered as a possible value of X and $\mu_A(u)$ represents the membership degree of u in the fuzzy set corresponding with the label A. This means that a value u is all the more possible ($\pi_X(u)$ is all the higher) as u is considered to be more consistent with the fuzzy meaning conveyed by A. *But*, this does not mean that the predicate "young" is vague, or involve any uncertainty in *itself*, at least as long as there is no disagreement about the membership function representing this predicate in the considered context. What may be uncertain is not the piece of information in itself (in fact, it is fully certain that "Bob is young", inasmuch as the source that provides the information is reliable), but e.g. the truth of a statement such as "Bob is less than 25", when all we know is that "Bob is young".

The three uses of fuzzy labels discussed in this section illustrate the role which is played by graded borderline cases in settings where vague linguistic terms are precisiated using fuzzy sets. As we illustrate in the next two sections, graded borderline cases may also play a central role when there is no vagueness, strictly speaking, in the considered descriptions. Indeed, even for a term with a well-defined meaning, in some situations, it is of interest to consider a more restrictive, or on the contrary, a more liberal view of the extension of the term, as we are going to see in Sections 3 and 4 respectively.

3   Introducing typicality in formal concept analysis

The idea of a concept, for which there exist different views, is difficult to define, although it is clear that concepts play a crucial role in categorization tasks [28, 30]. Classically, categorical membership differs from typicality, and both notions may even refer to different sets of features. Moreover typicality is not directly linked with vagueness, while categorical membership is. Still, it is interesting to examine how these aspects interact in the setting of formal concept analysis, even if formal concepts are an idealized and simplified view of the idea of a concept. In this section, we provide an illustration of the use of degrees for handling borderline cases with respect to the notion of a formal concept.

Formal concept analysis (FCA) [47] is a mathematical theory that defines a formal concept as a pair of two sets: i) a set of objects, called the extension of the formal concept, and ii) a set of properties, called its intension. Thus, for instance, a set of animal species (playing the role of the objects) is considered together with a set of properties (e.g. 'laying eggs', 'flying', 'having fur', etc.). In particular, FCA starts from the notion of a (formal) context, which is represented by a binary relation $R \subseteq Obj \times Prop$ that encodes which objects satisfy which properties. In other words, the pair (x,y) is an element of R if and only if object x has property y. Then, the concept 'bird' can be defined in a context which links animal species to relevant properties for describing animals.

What makes FCA theory attractive is its ability, when objects have known properties, to jointly identify the extension and the intension of formal concepts. Moreover, the set of formal concepts induced by a formal context is organized in a double lattice structure (w.r.t. objects and properties), which is exploited by data mining algorithms [34]. Despite the general attractiveness of FCA, however, typicality has not been considered in this setting, with the exception of a very recent proposal [7] that we discuss now, after recalling some basic notions.

Given a context, the extension and intension of a concept are supposed to mutually determine each other. We denote by $R(x)$ the set of properties possessed by object x, and by $R^{-1}(y)$ the set of objects having properties y. One can define

- the set of objects $R^{-1}(Y)$ having all the properties of some subset $Y \subseteq Prop$ as $R^{-1}(Y) = \{x \in Obj \mid Y \subseteq R(x)\}$, and dually,

- the set of properties $R(X)$ possessed by all the objects in some subset $X \subseteq Obj$ as $R(X) = \{y \in Prop \mid X \subseteq R^{-1}(y)\}$.

Then, a formal concept is an (extension, intension)-pair (X,Y), such that

(1) $X = R^{-1}(Y)$ and $Y = R(X)$

with respect to a context R. Thus, in a formal concept, the objects in the extension have all the properties in the intension, and conversely the properties in the intension are possessed by all the objects in the extension.

Table 1 provides a toy example of a formal (sub)context, where the objects and properties relate to birds:

$Obj = \{sparrow, parrot, penguin, kiwi\}$

$Prop = \{\text{'laying eggs'}, \text{'having two legs'}, \text{'flying'}, \text{'having feathers'}\}$

The symbol + in a cell of Table 1 indicates that the corresponding object has the corresponding property. Both of the following pairs are examples of formal concepts:

$(\{sparrow, parrot\}, \{\text{'laying eggs'}, \text{'having two legs'}, \text{'flying'}, \text{'having feathers'}\})$

$(\{sparrow, parrot, penguin, kiwi\}, \{\text{'laying eggs'}, \text{'having two legs'}\})$

Note that since $(Obj, Prop)$ does not constitute a formal concept in itself, either some properties or some objects need to be left out. The first case corresponds to the (unique) formal concept whose intention contains all properties. Likewise, the second case corresponds to the (unique) formal concept whose extension is the set of all objects. Generally speaking, it can be shown that a formal concept (X,Y) is such that $X \times Y \subseteq R$ holds. Note that this Cartesian product visually gives birth to a rectangle made of + (maybe after a proper reordering of the lines and/or the columns) in the table.

Degrees can be introduced in two different ways in FCA. First, we may consider the relation describing the formal context to be fuzzy [1], with the aim of acknowledging the gradualness of properties. Then, the extent to which (x,y) is an element of R is a matter of degree that reflects to what extent object x has property y, and $R^{-1}(y)$ is the fuzzy set of objects having property y to some degree. By extending the definition of a formal concept in a natural way, formal fuzzy concepts can then be introduced. However, such fuzzy concepts have nothing to do with typicality.

The second type of degrees that may be considered in FCA are obtained by keeping R crisp (i.e. binary-valued), and by relating degrees of typicality of objects to degrees of importance of properties, as we are going to see. Let us consider a particular subcontext, corresponding to a set of objects $X^{sc} \subseteq Obj$ and a set of associated properties $Y^{sc} \subseteq Prop$. Then, the basic idea is to equip Y^{sc} with degrees of importance and X^{sc} with degrees of typicality, and to put the *important* properties of the subcontext in relation with its *typical* objects, via a mutual characterization similar to the one provided by Equation (1). This can be summarized by the two following principles:

(A) An object x is all the more normal (or typical) w.r.t. a set of properties Y^{sc} as it has all the properties $y \in Y^{sc}$ that are sufficiently important;

(B) A property y is all the more important w.r.t. a set of objects X^{sc} as all the objects $x \in X^{sc}$ that are sufficiently normal have it.

Let us illustrate this idea on the example of Table 1, and let us assume the following typicality levels: $X_{typ}^{sc}(sparrow) = X_{typ}^{sc}(parrot) = 1$, $X_{typ}^{sc}(penguin) = \alpha < 1$ (since penguins do not fly), and $X_{typ}^{sc}(kiwi) = \beta$, with $1 > \alpha > \beta$ (since kiwis do not fly and have no feathers). Note that the levels used here are purely symbolic, and are just supposed to belong to an ordinal scale.

Table 1.

R	eggs	2 legs	feather	fly
sparrow	+	+	+	+
parrot	+	+	+	+
penguin	+	+	+	
kiwi	+	+		

To compute the fuzzy set of important properties according to principle (B) above, we need to evaluate the degree of inclusion of a fuzzy set of typical objects into the set of objects having property y. This can be accomplished using a multiple-valued implication connective $\rightarrow$ as follows:

$$(2) \quad Y_{imp}^{sc}(y) = min_x(X_{typ}^{sc}(x) \rightarrow R(x,y))$$

where $Y_{imp}^{sc}(y)$ is the degree of importance of property y. Moreover, as R is a crisp relation, we either have $R(x,y) = 1$ (when x has property y) or $R(x,y) = 0$ (otherwise). The implication connective satisfies $a \rightarrow 1 = 1$ as any multiple-valued implication, and should be chosen such that $a \rightarrow 0 = 1 - a$. This choice expresses the idea that the more a bird is considered typical, the less the properties that it does not have are assumed to be important in the definition of the concept *bird*. Note that in the case where (X^{sc}, Y^{sc}) would be a classical formal concept, $Y^{sc}(y) = min_x X^{sc}(x) \rightarrow R(x,y)$ is nothing but $Y^{sc} = R(X^{sc})$.

Let us now compute the fuzzy set (with membership function μ) of typical objects according to principle (A) above by

$$(3) \quad \mu(x) = min_y(Y_{imp}^{sc}(y) \rightarrow R(x,y))$$

We get $\mu(sparrow) = \mu(parrot) = 1$; $\mu(penguin) = \alpha$; $\mu(kiwi) = \beta$ (since $(1 - a) \rightarrow 0 = a$). As can be observed, we have $\forall x$, $\mu(x) = X_{typ}^{sc}(x)$. In fact, the equations (2)–(3) are the counterparts of the definition of a formal concept, given in (1), taking into account the graded interrelation between important properties and typical objects [7]. Thus, in the example of Table 1, the pair of fuzzy sets $(X_{typ}^{sc}, Y_{imp}^{sc})$ constitutes a generalized formal concept, since the fuzzy sets of important properties and of typical objects are in agreement.

More generally, typicality has been addressed in the setting of prototype theory. The idea, noticed by Wittgenstein, that things covered by a term often share a family resemblance may be seen as being at the basis of prototype theory [36], where categorization is understood in terms of similarity (see [28]). Then, a sparrow appears to be a more typical bird than a kiwi, inasmuch as a sparrow has more of the constituent properties of a bird prototype than a kiwi. This is also acknowledged in the approach presented above.

In this context, it is useful to refer to the critical discussion of a fuzzy set-based approach to prototype theory made by Osherson and Smith [33] when dealing with conceptual combination (see Zadeh [50] for a reply). This discussion is centered around the problem of compound concepts, noticing e.g. that the set of all typical red birds is not the intersection of the set of typical red animals with the set of typical birds. In our setting, this phenomenon can be accounted for noting that typical red birds would be defined on the basis of an explicit representation of important properties for red birds, which cannot be obtained from the important properties for red animals and those for birds. As a result, a fuzzy set of typical red birds, in our setting, will not necessarily correspond to the fuzzy set combination of a fuzzy set of typical red animals and a fuzzy set of typical birds.

This approach enables us to relate a typicality preordering among objects to an importance preordering among properties. It has some common flavor with the approach proposed, in a different perspective, by Freund, Desclés, Pascu and Cardot [16], which starts from the commonly accepted idea that a (proto)typical object in a category is an object that satisfies any *normally expected* property from the category (e.g., "birds fly"), and uses a *non-monotonic* reasoning view for performing contextual inferences about typical objects. However, our focus here is not inference, and we have rather tried to embed typicality in the setting of formal concept analysis. Besides, Freund [18, 19] proposes a qualitative model where the typicality associated with a concept is described using an ordering that takes into account the characteristic features of the concept. The approach uses a "salience" (partial) order between features, just as we use an importance ordering between properties. However, the salience ordering is not associated with a typicality ordering in the way proposed here, even if the relation with FCA is also discussed in [18] (when typicality is not graded).

Interestingly enough, the view proposed here leads to a representation of statements such as "Tweety is a bird" in terms of the certainty with which Tweety has each of the considered properties, just as in possibilistic logic [13] (which also provides a way for processing non-monotonic reasoning [2]).

Indeed, representing a statement such as "Tweety is a bird" amounts to state that i) it is fully possible that Tweety has the (Boolean) properties that a bird may have, and ii) the *possibility* that Tweety does *not* have the property y is all the greater as y is less important for birds,

$$\forall y \in Y^{bird}, \pi_{y(Tweety)}(yes) = 1 \text{ and } \pi_{y(Tweety)}(no) = 1 - Y^{bird}_{imp}(y)$$

where Y^{bird}_{imp} is the fuzzy set of *important properties* for birds. Equivalently, the *certainty* that Tweety has property y is all the greater as y is more important for birds, and is equal to $Y^{bird}_{imp}(y)$.

One might think of another representation of "Tweety is a bird" that would perfectly parallel the one used for restricting the possible values of a single-valued attribute (e.g., representing "Bob is young" by $\pi_{age(Bob)}(u) = \mu_{young}(u)$). Namely, one may also represent "Tweety is a bird" as a possibility distribution over a set of mutually exclusive species of birds

$$\forall x \in X^{bird}, \pi_{type(Tweety)}(x) = X^{bird}_{typ}(x).$$

This would also enable us to conclude, using the subcontext R in Table 1, that indeed the certainty that Tweety has property y is equal to $Y_{imp}^{bird}(y)$. But, the representation in terms of more or less certain properties is generally more compact in practice than the one in terms of objects (e.g., in our example, we have considered only four types of birds for simplicity!).

As typicality has allowed us in this section to restrict the extension of a concept, the next section addresses the converse concern, namely *enlarging* the meaning of a term to *close* terms having *similar* meanings. For instance, the term "married" may be understood strictly, or may sometimes be interpreted in a flexible way by replacing it by a (possibly weighted) disjunction such as "married or in a civil union".

4 Flexible understanding of linguistic terms for maintaining consistency

When a statement involving a vague term is asserted, its precise meaning may differ depending on the context in which it is used and on the person who is asserting it. As a result, upon receiving such a statement, we are often uncertain about its precise meaning. In some scenarios, this uncertainty may be intended by the speaker. Indeed, vagueness may among others be used to help the listener focus on what is relevant in the given context, it may soften complaints or criticisms, or it may be used to deliberately put the listener on the wrong tracks without the risk of being accused of lying [22]. This latter aspect of communication is also stressed in [27], where a bipolar view on assertability is put forward, distinguishing between situations in which a statement is definitively assertable, situations in which it is merely acceptable to assert it, and situations in which it cannot be asserted without condemnation; see [26] for a Bayesian treatment of this issue. A similar view on vagueness in dialogues is also suggested by Wahlster [45], giving the example of a dialogue between a hotel owner and a customer, who wants to know whether the room he is considering to rent is 'large'. Clearly, when the owner subsequently claims that the room is 'quite large', it is not at all certain that the customer would agree when seeing the room. Note that in the latter case, a vague term is used even though the hotel owner may know the exact surface of the room. In addition to the problem of finding the most appropriate linguistic label to describe a precisely known state of affairs, the goal of using vague language may also be to cope with a lack of precise knowledge, as already discussed in Section 2.

In general, successful communication depends on the ability of the participants to establish a common ground which is sufficiently specific. The required alignment between speaker and listener may happen explicitly, e.g. through clarification requests and reformulations, but also implicitly. In the latter case, the listener may for instance revise earlier assumptions on the meaning of assertions when they turn out to be inconsistent with subsequent assertions. It is important to note that these considerations do not only apply to vague terms: natural language terms with a precise and unambiguous meaning are often used in a flexible way, encompassing situations that are not normally associated with the term. For instance, suppose we initially believe that John is married, while later we notice that he answers negatively to the question *Are you married?* on a web form. We may then revise our earlier belief by assuming a more liberal understanding of the term *married*, viz. we take our earlier beliefs to mean that John is either married or in a civil union, and thus, given our new observation, that he is in a civil union. Note that there is a certain duality between this idea of flexibly using a precise term and the idea of typicality which was discussed in the previous section. Indeed, when we reinterpret statements about birds as statements about typical birds, we tighten our understanding of some well-defined concept, while in the marriage example, we enlarge our understanding of a well-defined concept.

In a computational setting, where knowledge is encoded in some logic and is provided to us by a number of different sources, assumptions need to be made about what the considered terms, e.g. associated with atomic propositions, mean. As sources may have used some terms in a slightly unexpected way, when integrating knowledge from different sources, we may end up with a knowledge base that is logically inconsistent. This observation suggests a view on maintaining consistency in a knowledge representation setting based on a flexible reading of propositions. Indeed, when a knowledge base turns out to be inconsistent with an observation, we may restore consistency by getting rid of the *less entrenched* formulas, but also by weakening some formulas, assuming a more tolerant reading of the terms underlying it. For the ease of presentation, in the following we assume a scenario involving two agents: the *listener*, whose initial knowledge includes all relevant integrity constraints (e.g. indicating which properties are mutually exclusive), and the *speaker*, which corresponds to an external source that provides us with new information. We also assume that the listener has background knowledge about how the terms used by the speaker should be understood, i.e. some form of alignment is assumed between the listener and the speaker.

To deal with inconsistencies that are due to flexible language usage, it is useful to notice that the exact meaning of an atomic property p as it is understood by the speaker may not necessarily be expressible in the language of the listener. For instance, what the speaker calls 'cold weather' may have a more narrow meaning than how the listener understands this term, and there may be no other term whose understanding by the listener exactly corresponds to the speaker's understanding of 'cold weather'. Let us write p_{speak} and p_{list} to denote the understanding of the atomic property p by the speaker and listener respectively. We may then consider the weakest formula α_{list}^- which is expressible in the language of the listener and which entails p_{speak}, and the strongest formula α_{list}^+ which is expressible in the language of the listener and which is entailed by p_{speak}. Conversely, p_{list} may not be expressible in the language of the speaker and we may need to consider entailing and entailed statements α_{speak}^- and α_{speak}^+.

The two agents are perfectly aligned when for each atomic property p, the four corresponding formulas α_{list}^-, α_{list}^+, α_{speak}^- and α_{speak}^+ are known. Note in particular that modeling the (mis)alignment between speaker and listener due to flexible language does not, as such, require the use of degrees. However, in most situations, we will only have incomplete knowledge about how the understanding of a given term by the speaker is related to its understanding by the listener. It may thus be useful to introduce degrees to discriminate between more and less plausible alignments. In practice, e.g. our information about α_{list}^- may be encoded in a graded way, differentiating between formulas α which definitely entail p_{speak} and formulas that plausibly entail it. As a form of plausible reasoning, we may initially make some rather strong assumptions on the alignment between both sources (e.g. assuming α^-_{list} to be a rather weak formula), and then revise these assumptions (e.g. assuming α^-_{list} to be a stronger formula) when inconsistencies arise. For example, if the speaker tells us that it is warm outside, we may initially take this to mean that the temperature is above $30°C$, and later revise this to "above $25°C$". As another example, suppose that the speaker tells us that John is married, then we may model the resulting knowledge, in the language of the listener, using the following possibilistic logic knowledge base:

$$K = \{(married_{list}, 0.5), (married_{list} \vee civil\text{-}union_{list}, 0.75),$$
$$(married_{list} \vee civil\text{-}union_{list} \vee cohabitation_{list}, 1)\}$$

where the certainty weights are interpreted in a *purely ordinal* fashion, as lower bounds on the necessity that the corresponding proposition is satisfied [13]. The knowledge base K models the fact that we are certain that $married_{speak}$ entails $married_{list} \vee civil\text{-}union_{list}$ $\vee cohabitation_{list}$, and somewhat certain that it entails $married_{list} \vee civil\text{-}union_{list}$; with even more limited certainty we believe that it entails $married_{list}$. In other words, the idea is to progressively weaken what is claimed by the speaker, and believe the resulting propositions with increasing certainty. This way of modeling the alignment between speaker and listener can be generalized to a setting where information is provided by multiple sources. It can be used as a basis for merging propositional information coming from different sources, by treating conflicts among these sources as evidence for misalignment [38, 39]. The degrees that are used can also be given a probabilistic flavor, or we may avoid the use of numerical degrees altogether and rely on symbolic, partially ordered certainty scores [39]. Moreover, it should be stressed that, as for degrees of typicality, the degrees we consider here are not directly related to categorical membership. Indeed, degrees are used to encode what we know about the alignment; their purpose is to allow us to find the most likely alignment between speaker and listener which does not lead to logical inconsistency.

Essentially, the approach outlined above deals with inconsistencies by assuming that when somebody asserts some proposition, we may (only) deduce (with complete certainty) that something similar to that proposition is the case, where we do not only consider the logical models of that proposition as possible worlds, but also those worlds that can be related to models by assuming a flexible understanding of the underlying terms. Such a similarity-based view on logical consequence may also be studied in an abstract way by considering similarity-based consequence operators of the form $\models^\lambda$, where $p \models^\lambda q$ means that all models of p are similar to some model of q and λ is a tolerance parameter on the required strength of similarity [8]. This idea stands in contrast to non-monotonic consequence relations where p entails q when the most typical models of p are also models of q [25]. Finally, note that a similarity-based view in this spirit was also put forward in [35], in the context of belief revision.

5 Conclusion

In this paper, we have contrasted the notion of borderline cases as they relate to linguistic vagueness, with scenarios in information processing where borderline cases need to be explicitly handled. We have, in particular, emphasized that the introduction of degrees may be useful in the latter case—or even required—to appropriately deal with borderline cases. To illustrate this point, we have discussed three different scenarios, in which degrees refer to fuzziness, typicality, and similarity respectively.

Specifically, we have first considered the use of fuzzy labels, focusing on cognitive uses such as expressing flexible requests, describing known states of fact, or summarizing or classifying situations. By interpreting the meaning of linguistic terms as fuzzy sets, the vagueness of these terms becomes a useful feature, as it e.g. provides an intuitive way to convey that a given piece of information should be understood with some tolerance. Note that such uses of fuzzy sets remain in general distinct from their use to compactly encode (crisp) information, which was very early recognized in the case of multiple-valued truth-functional logics by de Finetti [6]. Second, within the framework of formal concept analysis, we have discussed how the degree to which an object is a typical instance of some class can be related to the importance of properties in the definition of this class. Finally, we have addressed the importance of similarity, as the basis for a flexible understanding of properties, for inconsistency management.

While borderline cases play a central role in each of the scenarios we discussed, it is important to notice that the associated degrees are not degrees of truth. We have left aside classical issues related to vagueness such as approximate truth (e.g., [46, 32]) which would deserve longer developments, and should not be confused with uncertainty about binary truth [12].

BIBLIOGRAPHY

[1] Bělohlávek, R. Fuzzy Galois connections. *Math. Logic Quart.*, 45, 497–504, 1999.
[2] Benferhat, S., Dubois, D., Prade, H. Practical handling of exception-tainted rules and independence information in possibilistic logic. *Applied Intelligence*, 9, 101–127, 1998.
[3] Bennett, B. Spatial vagueness. In: *Methods for Handling Imperfect Spatial Information*, (R. Jeansoulin, O. Papini, H. Prade, S. Schockaert, eds.), vol. 256 in Studies in Fuzziness and Soft Computing series, Springer-Verlag, 15–47, 2010.
[4] Bezdek, J.C., Keller, J., Krisnapuram, R., Pal, N.R. Fuzzy Models and Algorithms for Pattern Recognition and Image Processing. Kluwer Acad. Publ., 1999.
[5] Czyzowicz, J., Mundici, D., Pelc, A. Ulam's searching game with lies. *J. of Combinatorial Theory*, Series A, 52, 62–76, 1989.
[6] De Finetti, B. La logique de la probabilité, *Actes Congrès Int. de Philos. Scient.*, Paris, 1935, Hermann et Cie Editions, Paris, IV1–IV9, 1936.
[7] Djouadi, Y., Dubois D., L., Prade, H. Graduality, uncertainty and typicality in formal concept analysis. In: *35 years of Fuzzy Set Theory: Celebratory Volume Dedicated to the Retirement of Etienne E. Kerre*, (C. Cornelis, G. Deschrijver, M. Nachtegael, S. Schockaert, Y. Shi, eds.), vol. 261 in Studies in Fuzziness and Soft Computing series, 127–147, Springer Verlag, 2010.
[8] Dubois, D., Esteva, F., Garcia, P., Godo, L., Prade, H. A logical approach to interpolation based on similarity relations, *International Journal of Approximate Reasoning*, 17, 1–36, 1997.
[9] Dubois, D., Esteva, F., Godo, L., Prade, H. An information-based discussion of vagueness: six scenarios leading to vagueness. In: *Handbook of Categorization in Cognitive Science*, (H. Cohen, C. Lefebvre, eds.), Chapter 40, 891–909, Elsevier, 2005.
[10] Dubois, D., Prade, H. Measuring properties of fuzzy sets: a general technique and its use in fuzzy query evaluation. *Fuzzy Sets and Systems*, 38, 137–152,1990.
[11] Dubois, D., Prade, H. The three semantics of fuzzy sets. *Fuzzy Sets and Systems*, 90, 141–150, 1997.
[12] Dubois, D., Prade, H. Possibility theory, probability theory and multiple-valued logics: A clarification. *Annals of Mathematics and Artificial Intelligence*, 32, 35–66, 2001.
[13] Dubois, D., Prade, H. Possibilistic logic: a retrospective and prospective view. *Fuzzy Sets and Systems*, 144, 3–23 2004.
[14] Dubois, D., Prade, H., Sudkamp, T. On the representation, measurement, and discovery of fuzzy associations. *IEEE Trans. on Fuzzy Systems*, 13, 250–262, 2005.

[15] Farreny, H., Prade, H. On the best way of designating objects in sentence generation. *Kybernetes*, 13 (1), 43–46, 1984.

[16] Freund, M., Desclés J.-P., Pascu, A., Cardot, J. Typicality, contextual inferences and object determination logic. *Proc. of the 17th Inter. Florida Artificial Intelligence Research Society Conf.* (FLAIRS), (V. Barr, Z. Markov, eds.), Miami Beach, Fl, USA, 5 p., 2004.

[17] Fine, K., Vagueness, truth and logic. *Synthese*, 54, 235–259, 1975. Reprinted in *Vagueness: A Reader*, (R. Keefe and P. Smith, eds.), MIT Press, Cambridge,119–150, 1996.

[18] Freund, M. On the notion of concepts. I. Artificial Intelligence, 172, 570–590, 2008.

[19] Freund, M. On the notion of concepts. II. Artificial Intelligence, 173, 167–179, 2009.

[20] Gaines, B.R., Foundations of fuzzy reasoning. *Int. J. Man-Machine Studies*, 8, 623–668, 1976.

[21] Hähnle, R. Proof theory of many-valued logic – linear optimization – logic design: connections and interactions. *Soft Computing*, 1, 107–119, 1997.

[22] Jucker, A. H., Smith, S.W., Lüdge, T. Interactive aspects of vagueness in conversation, *Journal of Pragmatics*, 35 (12), 1737–1769, 2003.

[23] Keefe R. *Theories of Vagueness*. Cambridge University Press, 2000.

[24] Keefe R., Smith, P. (eds.) *Vagueness: A Reader*. MIT Press, Cambridge, 1996.

[25] Kraus, S., Lehmann, D., Magidor, M. Nonmonotonic reasoning, preferential models and cumulative logics, *Artificial Intelligence*, 44, 167–207, 1990.

[26] Kyburg, A.: When vague sentences inform: A model of assertability. Synthese 124,175–192, 2000.

[27] Lawry, J. Imprecise bipolar belief measures based on partial knowledge from agent dialogues. *Proc. of the 4th Inter. Conf. on Scalable Uncertainty Management*, LNAI 6379, Springer, 205–218, 2010.

[28] Margolis, E., Laurence, S. Concepts. In: *The Stanford Encyclopedia of Philosophy* (Fall 2008 Edition), E.N. Zalta (ed.), http://plato.stanford.edu/archives/fall2008/entries/concepts.

[29] Mauris, G., Benoit, E., Foulloy, L. Fuzzy symbolic sensors – From concept to applications. *Measurement*, 12, 357–384, 1994.

[30] Medin, D. L., Rips, L. J. Concepts and categories: Memory, meaning and metaphysics. In: The Cambridge Handbook of Thinking and Reasoning, Chapter 3, (K.J. Holyoak, R.G. Morrison (Jr.), eds.), 37–72, 2005.

[31] Meghini, C., Sebastiani, F., Straccia, U. A model of multimedia information retrieval. *J. of the ACM*, 48, 909–970, 2001.

[32] Niiniluoto, I. *Truthlikeness*. D. Reidel, Dordrecht, 1987.

[33] Osherson, D. N., Smith, E. E. On the adequacy of prototype theory as a theory of concepts. *Cognition*, 9, 59–72, 1981.

[34] Pasquier, N., Bastide, Y., Taouil, R., Lakhal, L. Efficient mining of association rules using closed itemset lattices. *Inf. Syst.*, 24(1): 25–46, 1999.

[35] Rodriguez, R., Garcia, P., Godo, L., Relating similarity-based models, counterfactuals and theory change. *Proc. of the 3rd Europ. Congress on Intelligent Techniques and Soft Computing* (EUFIT'95), Aachen, Aug. 28–31, 230–234, 1995.

[36] Rosch, E., Mervis, C. Family resemblances: Studies in the internal structure of categories. *Cognitive Psychology*, 7, 573–605, 1975.

[37] Schockaert, S., Janssen, J., Vermeir, D., De Cock, M. Answer sets in a fuzzy equilibrium logic. *Proc. of the 3rd Inter. Conf. on Web Reasoning and Rule Systems*, 135–149, 2009.

[38] Schockaert, S. and Prade, H. An inconsistency-tolerant approach to information merging based on proposition relaxation, In:*Proc. of the 24th AAAI Conf. on Artificial Intelligence*, 363–368, 2010.

[39] Schockaert, S., Prade, H. Solving conflicts in information merging by a flexible interpretation of atomic propositions. Artificial Intelligence, to appear.

[40] Shramko, Y., Wansing, H., Truth Values, *The Stanford Encyclopedia of Philosophy* (Summer 2010 Edition), (E.N. Zalta, ed.), http://plato.stanford.edu/archives/sum2010/entries/truth-values.

[41] Smith, N. J. J. Vagueness as closeness. *Australasian J. of Philosophy*, 83, 157–83, 2005.

[42] Sorensen, R. Vagueness. *The Stanford Encyclopedia of Philosophy* (Fall 2008 Edition), (E.N. Zalta, ed.), http://plato.stanford.edu/archives/fall2008/entries/vagueness/.

[43] Sorensen, A. *Vagueness and Contradiction*. Oxford University Press, 2001.

[44] van Fraassen, B. C. Presuppositions, supervaluations and free logic. In: *The Logical Way of Doing Things*, (K. Lambert, ed.), Yale University Press, 67–91, 1969.

[45] Wahlster, W. Implementing fuzziness in dialogue systems. In: *Empirical Semantics*, (B. Rieger, ed.), Brockmeyer, Bochum, 1980.

[46] Weston, T. Approximate truth. *J. of Philosophical Logic*, 16, 203–227, 1987.

[47] Wille, R. Restructuring lattice theory: an approach based on hierarchies of con- cepts. In: *Ordered Sets*, (I. Rival, ed.), Reidel, Dordrecht, 445–470, 1982.

[48] Williamson, T. *Vagueness*. Routledge, London, 1994.

[49] Zadeh, L. A. PRUF: A meaning representation language for natural languages. *Int. J. of Man-Machine Studies*, 10, 395–460, 1978.

[50] Zadeh, L. A. A note on prototype theory and fuzzy sets. *Cognition*, 12, 291–297, 1982.

Henri Prade

IRIT – Institut de Recherche en Informatique de Toulouse

University of Toulouse

118 route de Narbonne

31062 Toulouse Cedex 09, France

Email: prade@irit.fr

Steven Schockaert

Ghent University

Department of Applied Mathematics and Computer Science

Krijgslaan 281, 9000 Gent, Belgium

Email: steven.schockaert@ugent.be

Comments on *Handling Borderline Cases Using Degrees: An Information Processing Perspective* by Henri Prade and Steven Schockaert

Lluís Godo

The paper discusses, in an information processing setting, different situations where explicit graded representation of borderlines cases may be advantageous rather than a problem. In the first part of the paper, the authors consider the use of fuzzy labels in three different cognitive tasks (specification of preferences, categorization, representation of incomplete knowledge) which lead to three different semantics for membership degrees in fuzzy sets, namely in terms of preference, similarity, and uncertainty, respectively. Then the authors focus on two further applications of using degrees as a flexible representation tool for borderline cases. The first one is in the field of formal concept analysis, where one can attach typicality degrees to objects. It is shown that the typicality ordering on objects induces in turn a gradation of the properties describing concepts involving typical objects in terms of the importance of these properties. Finally, they show how an approximate understanding of a non-vague property may help in dealing with possible inconsistencies in an information exchange process. In this short note, rather than formulating critical comments I just want to offer a few additional, complementary remarks to some aspects addressed in the paper.

The authors make an interesting distinction between dealing with non-vague understanding of vague terms on the one hand and vague understanding of non-vague terms on the other. The use of fuzzy labels, as described in Section 2, falls into the first scenario, since fuzzy labels (as considered by the authors) are explicitly specified by corresponding fuzzy sets, i.e. by precise real-valued functions.[1] Lawry's label semantics[2] offers an alternative model where, instead of associating a fuzzy set to a fuzzy label, one attaches to each object x a probability distribution P_x over a set $\mathscr{L}$ of fuzzy labels covering the domain of some variable. Moreover, the probability $P_x(L)$ measures the appropriateness with that a label $L \in \mathscr{L}$ applies to x. One could discuss advantages and problems of such an approach, but in any case it in fact amounts to an even sharper example of a non-vague, degree-based understanding of fuzzy labels. Notice that this approach has also been extended to include elements of prototype theory into the picture.[3]

About the extension of formal concept analysis described in Section 3, it is indeed interesting to further refine the model in order to allow restricting the extension of a

---

[1] This point is further discussed in the paper by Didier Dubois in this volume.

[2] J. Lawry, A framework for linguistic modelling, Artificial Intelligence 155 (2004) 1–39.

[3] J. Lawry and Y. Tang, Uncertainty modeling for vague concepts: A prototype theory approach. Artificial Intelligence 173 (2009), 1539–1558.

concept to those elements that are more typical. A small remark here is that a typicality ordering on objects is something that depends in turn on the target formal concept to be characterized. For instance a penguin is a less typical bird than a sparrow, but it is also a more typical animal-living-in-cold-areas than a sparrow. This concept dependent ordering is at variance with the traditional fuzzy approach to formal concept analysis, where the relation R in a formal context expresses the degrees with which a set of objects satisfy a set of properties, independently of the concept being characterized. However these two kinds of orderings are not incompatible, one could easily imagine an approach allowing degrees in both the satisfaction of properties by objects and in the context dependent typicality of objects.

In the final part of the paper, the authors claim that artificially introducing vagueness, and thus borderline cases, in some situations may indeed help to resolve inconsistencies related to different understandings of the meaning of the same expression by two agents. The idea is to assume similar but more imprecise meanings, in order to provide some room for making them compatible to some extent. Although the basic notion at work in this approach seems to be that of closeness or similarity, in the communication example developed in the paper the weakening of the proposition asserted by the speaker is represented by a set of propositions standing for the possible meanings of the original assertion, ranked according to the degree of certainty with which they are satisfied. This may be viewed as a set of graded borderline propositions. So, in a sense, the underlying similarity on propositions is turned into an (ordinal) uncertainty mapping. Actually, from a technical point of view, given the proposition asserted by the speaker, a similarity relation on the set of possible worlds allows one to define the (fuzzy) set of worlds that are close or similar to those satisfying the proposition. Taking this as the available (incomplete) information, a possibility distribution is induced, as explained in the section on fuzzy labels expressing uncertainty. From that one can infer the degree of certainty with which different propositions of interest are believed to hold. Therefore, although similarity-based reasoning and truthlikeness have different motivations regarding uncertain reasoning, there are situations where concrete bridges can be established.

Lluís Godo
IIIA, Artificial Intelligence Research Institute
CSIC, Spanish Scientific Research Council
Campus de la Universitat Autònoma de Barcelona s/n
08193 Bellaterra, Spain
Email: godo@iiia.csic.es

Reply to Lluís Godo's Comments on
Handling Borderline Cases Using Degrees: An Information Processing Perspective

HENRI PRADE AND STEVEN SCHOCKAERT

We thank Lluís Godo for his accurate summary of our contribution and for his additional comments. In the following, we briefly come back to some of these comments.

Indeed, our paper considers different situations in knowledge representation where borderline cases exist. Borderline cases may be simply distinguished from cases considered as central or normal.[1] But, it is often beneficial to use degrees (which belong to a scale that may be only ordinal) for handling them. For instance, a penguin is a less typical representative of the concept of bird than a sparrow. However as noticed in the comments, a penguin is a quite typical Antarctic bird, and thus typicality is context-dependent. This should not be surprising. Since 'bird' and 'Antarctic bird' are different concepts, they may have different typicality ordering. Here we also have a non-monotonic reasoning situation, since one of the concepts is a subconcept of the other. This dependency of the typicality ordering on the context might also be put in parallel with the fact that fuzzy set representations of gradual properties depend on the context as well: a 'large butterfly' is certainly smaller than a 'large elephant'. Still in such a case, the word 'large' has a different meaning depending on the context, while in the previous example, it is not the representation of 'bird' that differs, it is the concept 'bird' itself which is replaced by a more specific one, strictly speaking.

The last part of our paper deals with what may be regarded as a vague, or at least flexible, understanding of non-vague terms, interpreting, e.g., 'married' as 'married (in a strict juridical sense)', but also possibly as 'married or living in a marital way', which may be useful for solving apparent inconsistency between reports. Interestingly enough, in such a case the person who receives the information 'married' is faced with a situation of uncertainty in meaning,[2] while it is rather a matter of preference for the person who labels a situation with a word (or an expression) rather than with another one; moreover, the words or expressions between which one hesitates have somewhat similar meanings. This illustrates the fact that in practice, uncertainty, or preferences, may be related to similarity, although these three notions should be distinguished and can be associated with degrees which should not be handled in the same way in general.

---

[1] Such an idea was first proposed by Y. Gentilhomme in "Les ensembles flous en linguistique. Cahiers de Linguistique Théorique et Appliquée (Bucarest), 5, 47–63, 1968".

[2] See, e.g., Schefe, P. On foundations of reasoning with uncertain facts and vague concepts. Int. J. of Man-Machine Studies, 12, 35–62, 1980.

Have Fuzzy Sets Anything to Do with Vagueness?

DIDIER DUBOIS[1]

1 Introduction

From their inception, fuzzy sets were introduced by Zadeh [55] with a view to formalize human knowledge in engineering problems. This implies fuzzy sets had somehow to come to grip with some aspects of natural language modeling, and in particular, with the concept of vagueness, i.e., the idea that the extension of some natural language predicates lacks clear truth conditions. The claim that fuzzy sets are a basic tool for addressing vagueness of linguistic terms has been around for a long time. For instance, Novák [38] insists that fuzzy logic is tailored for vagueness and he opposes vagueness to uncertainty.

Nevertheless, in the last thirty years, the literature dealing with vagueness has grown significantly, and much of it is far from agreeing on the central role played by fuzzy sets in this phenomenon. Following Keefe & Smith [42], vague concepts in natural language display three features:

- **The existence of borderline cases**: That is, there are some objects such that neither a concept nor its negation can be applied to them. For a borderline object, it is difficult to make a firm decision as to the truth or the falsity of a proposition containing a vague predicate applied to this object, even if a precise description of the latter is available. The existence of borderline cases is sometimes seen as a violation of the law of excluded middle.

- **Unsharp boundaries**: The extent to which a vague concept applies to an object is supposed to be a matter of degree, not an all-or-nothing decision. It is relevant for predicates referring to continuous scales, like *tall, old*, etc. This idea can be viewed as a specialisation of the former, if we regard as borderline cases objects for which a proposition is neither totally true nor totally false. In the following, we shall speak of "gradualness" to describe such a feature. Using degrees of appropriateness of concepts to objects as truth degrees of statements involving these concepts goes against the Boolean tradition of classical logic.

- **Susceptibility to Sorites paradoxes.** This is the idea that the presence of vague propositions make long inference chains inappropriate, yielding debatable results. The well-known examples deal with heaps of sand (whereby, since adding a grain

[1]The author wishes to thank the referees for their careful reading of the preliminary drafts, for their suggestions and additional references.

of sand to a small heap keeps its small, all heaps of sand should be considered small), young persons getting older from one day to the next, bald persons that are added one hair, etc.

Since their inception, fuzzy sets have been controversial for philosophers, many of whom are reluctant to consider the possibility of non-Boolean predicates, as it questions the usual view of truth as an absolute entity. A disagreement opposes those who, like Williamson, claim a vague predicate has a standard, though ill-known, extension [53], to those who, like Kit Fine, deny the existence of a decision threshold and just speak of a truth value gap [19]. However, the two latter views reject the idea of gradual truth, and concur on the point that fuzzy sets do not propose a good model for vague predicates. One of the reasons for the misunderstanding between fuzzy sets and the philosophy of vagueness may lie in the fact that Zadeh was trained in engineering mathematics, not in the area of philosophy. In particular, vagueness is often understood as a defect of natural language (since it is not appropriate for devising formal proofs, it questions usual rational forms of reasoning). Actually, the vagueness of linguistic terms was considered as a logical nightmare for early 20th century philosophers. In contrast, for Zadeh, going from Boolean logic to fuzzy logic is viewed as a positive move: it captures tolerance to errors (softening blunt threshold effects in algorithms) and may account for the flexible use of words by people [54]. It also allows for information summarisation: detailed descriptions are sometimes hard to make sense of, while summaries, even if imprecise, are easier to grasp [56].

However, the epistemological situation of fuzzy set theory itself is far from being clear. Fuzzy sets and their extensions have been understood in various ways in the literature: there are several notions that are appealed to in connection with fuzzy sets, like similarity, uncertainty and preference [17]. It is indeed natural to represent incomplete knowledge by sets (e.g. of possible models of a knowledge base or error intervals). This is also connected to modal logic accounts of reasoning about knowledge [29], and to possibility theory [58, 15]. So not only does vagueness interact with fuzzy sets, but both interact with notions of uncertainty as well, even within fuzzy set theory, to wit:

- A fuzzy set may account for epistemic uncertainty since it extends the notion of a set of possible values understood as an epistemic state.

- Epistemic uncertainty is gradual since belief is often a matter of degree.

- Sometimes, membership functions may account for an ill-known crisp boundary (the random set view of fuzzy sets [25]) and can then be seen as modeling vagueness in agreement with the excluded middle law.

- Higher order fuzzy sets, such as interval-valued or type 2 fuzzy sets (see [12] for a bibliography) are supposed to capture ill-known membership functions of linguistic categories. This seems to refer again, perhaps more convincingly, to a form of vagueness (this will become clearer in Section 4).

Nevertheless, in his works, Zadeh insists that fuzziness is not vagueness. The term fuzzy is restricted to sets where the transition between membership and non-membership is gradual rather than abrupt. Zadeh [54] argues as follows:

Although the terms fuzzy and vague are frequently used interchangeably in the literature, there is, in fact, a significant difference between them. Specifically, a proposition, p, is fuzzy if it contains words which are labels of fuzzy sets; and p is vague if it is both fuzzy and insufficiently specific for a particular purpose. For example, "Bob will be back in a few minutes" is fuzzy, while "Bob will be back sometime" is vague if it is insufficiently informative as a basis for a decision. Thus, the vagueness of a proposition is a decision-dependent characteristic whereas its fuzziness is not.

Of course, the distinction made by Zadeh may not be so strict as he claims. While "in a few minutes" is more specific than "sometime" and sounds less vague, one may argue that there is some residual vagueness in the former, and that the latter does not sound very crisp after all.

The basic aim of this paper is to tentatively clarify the positioning of fuzzy sets in studies about vagueness. Our thesis is that the issue of gradual membership has little to do with the issue of vagueness of words in natural language. Vagueness refers to some uncertainty of meaning, but the fact that the extension of a predicate is not crisp is distinct from the idea that this predicate is tainted with vagueness. We only admit that a gradual predicate is more likely to be vague than a Boolean one, simply because providing a formal model and a protocol to compute gradual truth values precisely is more difficult than when only truth or falsity is to be decided. In fact we can use fuzzy sets (gradual membership functions) or non-dichotomous representations of sets in contexts where natural language is absent. Membership functions can be constructed from fuzzy clustering procedures, from imprecise statistics, or they can represent utility functions, without requesting interpretations in natural languages.

The rest of the paper is organised as follows: first we revisit the information-oriented view of non-dichotomous representations of sets, previously devised with Esteva, Godo and Prade [11], that enables some form of classification of situations where properties are not perceived to be all-or-nothing. In Section 3, we point out that the gradualness of predicates is perhaps not intrinsic. It may depend on whether we take the point of view of agents asserting statements involving non-Boolean predicates, or receiving them. This kind of contextualisation may be relevant for the study of vagueness. In Section 4, we shall then propose a tentative solution to some controversies about vagueness and the role of fuzzy sets, considering that the gradualness of predicates is distinct from, even if sometimes related to, the issue of uncertainty of meaning. So, epistemic and truth value gap approaches apply as much to membership functions of gradual predicates as to Boolean concepts. We also discuss the situation of Nick Smith's blurry sets and fuzzy plurivaluationism in this framework.

2   An information-oriented setting for non-dichotomous representations of sets

We consider the issue of describing objects by means of properties, a core issue in information sciences. There are a number of situations in which a property or a set of properties lead to a non-dichotomous partition of a set of objects [11]. These situations interfere with the issue of vagueness, but not all of them are motivated by it. Notations adopted are as follows. Consider:

- A finite set of objects or entities, denoted by $\mathcal{O}$

- A finite set $\mathcal{A}$ of attributes $a : \mathcal{O} \to D_a$ each with domain D_a

- A property or predicate P referring to attribute a

For binary attributes and in the case of a clear-cut property P, $D_a = \{y_a, n_a\}$, and the extension of P is $Ext(P) = \{o \in \mathcal{O}, a(o) = y_a\}$. More generally, for a many-valued attribute domain, there is a non-empty subset $Y_P \subset D_a$, called positive domain of P, such that $Ext(P) = \{o \in \mathcal{O}, a(o) \in Y_P\}$.

If $\neg P$ denotes the opposite property let $Ext(\neg P) = \{o \in \mathcal{O}, a(o) \in N_P\}$ for some subset N_P of D_a. Then a property is classical if the two following laws hold:

- the excluded-middle law (EML): $Y_P \cup N_P = D_a$, so that $Ext(P) \cup Ext(\neg P) = \mathcal{O}$;

- the non-contradiction law (NCL): $Y_P \cap N_P = \emptyset$, so that $Ext(P) \cap Ext(\neg P) = \emptyset$.

We consider non-classical properties where EML does not seem to apply (nor possibly NCL). Six scenarii have been considered where properties share the set of objects under concern into three subsets [11]. Here, we refresh this classification into three categories:

1. Gradual properties: dropping the bivalence assumption;

2. Bivalent views of the vagueness of linguistic terms where truth conditions are ill-defined (creating truth value gaps) or ill-known (due to partial ignorance on the position of the threshold between true and false);

3. Limited perception of the human mind whereby some objects and/or attribute values are indiscernible.

For each scenario, we consider whether vagueness is at stake or not.

2.1 Gradual properties

Many properties in natural languages P like *tall, young,* etc. and concepts as well (like *bird, chair*) seem to define an implicit (sometimes complete) ordering on the attribute domain D_a and /or the set of objects they pertain to. No matter how narrow the considered context, there does not seem to exist an arbitrarily precise threshold dictating whether a male human height corresponds to the expression *tall man* or not. As people can be tall *to some extent*, it always seems to be a matter of degree. A gradual property P is defined by a pair $(D_a^P, \geq_P)$, where $D_a^P \subset D_a$ is the support of P, and $\geq_P$ is a partial order on D_a such that

- $a(o) \geq_P a(o')$ means that P applies to o is at least as much as to o';

- $u = a(o) \in D_a^P$ means that o is somewhat P: $\forall u \in D_a^P, v \notin D_a^P, u >_P v$

- $u = a(o) \notin D_a^P$ means that P is clearly false for o, and $\forall u, v \notin D_a^P, u =_P v$

An opposite ordering relation $\geq_{\neg P}$ on D_a referring to the negation of P can be defined by $u \geq_{\neg P} v$ if and only if $v \geq_P u$, where $D_a^{\neg P} = D_a \setminus \{u, \nexists u' >_P u\}$ (the prototypical values for $a(o)$ relative to P are ruled out for $\neg P$). It is not clear whether the ordering $\geq_P$ should be total. Some objects may be incomparable in terms of property P. This is especially true with complex concepts that underlie several dimensions. For instance, if P means *comfortable*, two chairs may be somewhat comfortable to some extent for different reasons (one has a soft back but is too low, the other has a perfect seat height but has a hard back), without leading to preferring one to the other.

Nevertheless, the role of the membership function μ_P of P is to provide a representation of this possibly partial ordering on a totally ordered scale (incomparabilities may be solved by a final choice to buy one of the two chairs). A membership function is a mapping from the attribute scale D_a to a bounded totally ordered set L (with top 1 and bottom 0), $\mu_P(u)$ representing the degree to which object o such that $a(o) = u$ satisfies P. In other words, $a(o) >_P a(o')$ implies $\mu_P(a(o)) > \mu_P(a(o'))$. In particular, D_a^P is the support of the fuzzy set defined by μ_P: $D_a^P = \{u, \mu_P(u) > 0\}$. An early example of membership function was suggested by the American philosopher Max Black in 1937 [1], who called them "consistency profiles" in order to "characterize vague symbols." The generalization of the traditional binary characteristic function has been first considered by H. Weyl [52], who explicitly replaces it by a continuous characteristic function to the unit interval. The same kind of generalization was further proposed in 1951 by Kaplan and Schott [31]. See Dubois et al. [13] for details on these works pioneering the notion of fuzzy sets.

There are some reasons for the presence of gradualness in natural language:

- Some predicates refer to an underlying continuous measurement scale D_a for the attribute (*tall*: height; *young*: age). Such terms behave as if there were no threshold on the real line separating the P's from the non$P$'s (if there were such a threshold, it would be too precise to be cognitively relevant). A natural test for detecting this kind of predicates is to check whether the phrase *very P* makes sense. The property is gradual when the answer is yes. The hedge *very* sounds odd when applied to Boolean properties, like *single* or *major* applied to a person. This hedge test clearly makes sense for predicates referring to the extremities of a measurement scale (like *tall* and *small*) but may fail on predicates like *medium*.[2] Gradual predicates of that kind are simple in the sense that the underlying measurement scale is crystal clear. Then, the use of the unit interval as a truth set L is a just a way of rescaling the attribute domain D_a according to the meaning of P. Truth-functionality for complex propositions involving such fuzzy predicates is mathematically consistent (thus yielding algebraic structures different from a Boolean algebra, as seen in mathematical fuzzy logic [26]) even if not compulsory.

- Some concepts like *Bird, Chair*, underlie a typicality ordering on the set of objects. For instance, a penguin is a less typical bird than a swallow. So when someone speaks of birds in general, people do not think that penguins are being referred to in the first place. In this case, the corresponding sets of attributes is less clear,

---

[2] As pointed out by a referee. But for those terms, perhaps another hedge like *more or less*, may be used.

and there is no obvious numerical measurement scale that can account for them. So it is much more difficult to come up with a numerical membership function. A mere ordering relation $\geq_P$ may make sense, or, at best, a coarse classification of objects into typical, borderline and clearly unsuitable items. Such concepts are better described by a list of (possibly Boolean) properties, the satisfaction of part of which ensures partial membership of an object to the concept extension. These properties may have levels of priority, some being more important than others for defining the concept. This kind of framework comes close to Formal Concept Analysis [21] and has been studied in detail by Freund [20] who proposes a methodology for deriving a partial ordering $\geq_P$ from the knowledge of a set Δ_P of more or less important properties that make up a concept. A similar idea is outlined in [8], where importance degrees belong to a totally ordered scale. Freund actually considers two orderings of objects relative to a concept: a membership ordering, and a typicality ordering where typicality is viewed as stronger than mere membership and relies on a subset of more or less characteristic properties in Δ_P.

How can the extension of P be defined in such framework?

- One may assume that there is no Boolean extension but a gradual one $\tilde{E}xt(P)$ with membership function μ_P.

- Or one may define $Ext(P)$ to be the set of prototypes of P, i.e. $Prot(P) = \{o \in \mathscr{O} \mid a(o) \text{ maximal according to } \geq_P\}$.

- Or yet one may define $Ext(P) = \{o \in \mathscr{O}, a(o) \in D_a^P\}$, only excluding the clearly irrelevant objects for P.

A precise boundary separating objects such that P holds from those where $\neg P$ holds *does not exist* under the gradual view. Depending on the choice of connectives, EML and CL may hold or not [26]. The two last options lead to a trichotomy of the set of objects. In the second one, there are the prototypes of P, the prototypes of $\neg P$, i.e., $Prot(\neg P) = \{o \in \mathscr{O}, a(o) \notin D_a^P\}$ and the set of borderline cases $\mathscr{O} \setminus (Prot(P) \cup Prot(\neg P))$. In the third option, the borderline cases are objects that are both P and $\neg P$.

The third option can be obtained when the domain D_a is equipped with a distance function $d_a : D_a \times D_a \to [0, +\infty)$. In that case, there is a notion of similarity between objects that leads to a form of gradualness understood as limited deviation from full truth [11]. A similarity relation expressing closeness between objects can be defined as a mapping $S : \mathscr{O} \times \mathscr{O} \to [0,1]$ such that $S(o,o) = 1$ (reflexivity), $S(o,o') = S(o',o)$ (symmetry) and $S(o',o) = 1 \implies o = o'$ (separability). An example is of the form $S(o,o') = \frac{1}{1+d_a(a(o),a(o'))}$. $S(o_1,o_2) > S(o_1,o_3)$ means that o_1 is more similar to o_2 than to o_3. Given a Boolean predicate P pertaining to attribute a, one can propose the following computation of membership degrees: $\mu_P(a(o))$ is the extent to which o is close or similar to some object in $Ext(P)$ (Ruspini [43]). By means of the similarity relation, it is possible to declare a gradual property $\tilde{P}$ all the more satisfied by objects as they are closer to being P according to S. We can proceed similarly for $Ext(\neg P)$ (which is equal to $Ext(P)^c$, since P is Boolean). More precisely:

$$\mu_{\tilde{P}}(a(o)) = \sup_{o' \in Ext(P)} S(o,o') \qquad \mu_{\widetilde{\neg P}}(a(o)) = \sup_{o' \notin Ext(P)} S(o,o').$$

By construction $\mu_{\tilde{P}}(a(o)) = 1, \forall o \in Ext(P)$ and $\mu_{\neg P}(a(o)) = 1, \forall o \notin Ext(P)$. Noticing that $D_a^{\tilde{P}} = \{u, \mu_{\tilde{P}}(u) > 0\}$, it is clear that $\{o, a(o) \in D_a^{\tilde{P}} \cap D_a^{\neg P}\}$ forms a generally non-empty set of borderline cases, i.e. the law of contradiction fails while the excluded middle law holds. This view may be related to Weston [51]'s idea of approximate truth as reflecting a distance between a statement and the ideal truth. It is also related to the notion of truthlikeness of Niiniluoto [37] and of similarity-based reasoning as surveyed in [22]. It also emphasizes a prototype-based view of fuzzy sets (considering the membership function of a gradual predicate as induced by a set of prototypes and a similarity relation. See Osherson and Smith [39] for a critical discussion and Zadeh's [59] reply. This view of fuzzy sets is not truth-functional since $\widetilde{P \cap Q}$ will generally differ from $\tilde{P} \cap \tilde{Q}$ (for instance, if $P \cap Q = \emptyset, \widetilde{P \cap Q} = \emptyset$ but $\tilde{P} \cap \tilde{Q}$ may be non-empty).

Under the above view, gradualness, not vagueness specifically, is caused by closeness (the presence of a distance between attribute values making objects with very close descriptions possible). This view conflicts with Smith's claim that closeness is the essence of vagueness [47]. The present thesis is that closeness is a natural source of gradualness (related to a continuous measurement scale for the concerned attribute), and that the increased measurement difficulty for numerical membership grades, compared with Boolean ones, results in a higher propensity of gradual predicates to being perceived as vague. As pointed out earlier, typicality is another source of (ordinal) gradualness not especially accounted for by metric structures, even if relative closeness between objects with respect to their adequacy to a gradual predicate could be rendered by means of preference-difference measurement techniques [2].

Even if the presence of intermediate truth values is considered to be a feature of vague propositions, gradualness understood as above clearly does not cover all issues debated about vagueness. Especially, insofar as a precise membership function is obtained for the property and one admits that there is no underlying ill-known boundary, the gradual extension is perfectly defined and there is no uncertainty about the meaning of property P. In that sense a membership function is a more accurate description of a gradual predicate than a regular characteristic function. While vagueness is a defect, gradualness is an enrichment of the Boolean representation. Likewise a metric space is a richer description than a mere set, so that the use of similarity-based degrees of truth makes a logical description finer: it does not create an anomaly nor a defect, contrary to what vagueness is supposed to do, according to many philosophers. Especially the argument against membership functions, whereby it is a paradox to use precise membership grades, works if the gradual model of the non-Boolean concept under concern is meant to account for uncertainty about membership. Insofar as gradual concepts just display gradualness, the membership function model makes sense. However, the latter is of course an ideal view tailored for gradual properties defined on simple linear measurement scales, and many have pointed out the difficulty to actually come up with the precise membership function, if any, of a gradual property. But the use of a membership function is often a good enough working assumption for information engineers, with no pretence to address philosophical issues, but for the suggestion that for some propositions, truth may intrinsically be a matter of degree. This point also indicates that there is more to vagueness than gradualness.

2.2 Ignorance and truth value gaps

Another point of view on non-classical properties is to admit that there are some objects that for sure satisfy them, others that for sure don't, and still other objects for which it is hard or even impossible to assign a clear-cut truth value. This situation, that is considered as a feature of vagueness, also leads to partition the set of objects into three subsets: $\mathscr{C}(P), \mathscr{C}(\neg P), \mathscr{B}(P)$ forming a partition of $\mathscr{O}$, where $\mathscr{C}(P)$ consists of objects for which P is definitely true, $\mathscr{C}(\neg P)$ of objects for which P is definitely false, and the set $\mathscr{B}(P)$ consists of borderlines cases.

As it seems there are two main views of this kind of paradigm: the truth value gap view of Fine [19] and the epistemic view of Williamson [53].

According to Fine, a proposition o *is* P is said to be supertrue if it is true in all ways of making P classical (sharpenings, or precisiations of P). This approach is non-classical in the sense that a proposition can be neither supertrue nor superfalse. A precisiation of P is a clear-cut property $P^{\mathscr{S}}$ with extension $\mathscr{S} \subset \mathscr{O}$, in agreement with P on all objects that clearly satisfy P and all objects that clearly falsify it. Hence $Ext(P^{\mathscr{S}})$ is a subset $\mathscr{S}$ of objects such that $\mathscr{C}(P) \subseteq \mathscr{S} \subseteq \mathscr{C}(P) \cup \mathscr{B}(P)$. So o *is* P is super-true if o *is* $P^{\mathscr{S}}$ is true for all $\mathscr{S}$ in this family. Clearly it is equivalent to requiring that o *is* $P^{\mathscr{C}(P)}$ is true.

According to Williamson, a proposition o *is* P is either true or false in borderline cases, it is just that we are not in a position to find out which truth value the proposition takes. The main difference between Fine and Williamson seems to be in some sense metaphysical: whether or not there is a true classical extension. For Fine, this true extension does not exist, and this is precisely the characteristic of vagueness: if o is borderline, i.e., $o \in \mathscr{B}(P)$, there is no truth value for the proposition o *is* P. There is a truth value gap. In contrast, for Williamson, the true classical extension $Ext(P)$ that provides the precise meaning of P exists, but it is ill-known. Vagueness thus consists in this uncertainty of meaning. All that is known is that $\mathscr{C}(P) \subseteq Ext(P) \subseteq \mathscr{C}(P) \cup \mathscr{B}(P)$.

There is in fact yet another view in the same vein called *plurivaluationism* [4]. It accepts Boolean representations of vague concepts, but contends that any sharp definition of the extension of P lying between $\mathscr{C}(P)$ and $\mathscr{C}(P) \cup \mathscr{B}(P)$ is equally good to represent P. Under this view the thick boundary between P accounts for the idea that in practice, there is no need to bother being more precise.

Kit Fine's truth value gap approach is based on so-called "*supervaluations*", first proposed by van Fraassen [49] in the context of incomplete information logics, whereby *supertrue* means true in all complete information states compatible with the available knowledge. Van Fraassen criticizes the loss of the excluded middle and contradiction law in logics of incomplete information like partial logic, where interpretations are changed into partial interpretations. This view is closely related to possibility theory (as discussed in [9]). Define a Boolean possibility distribution $\pi : 2^{\mathscr{O}} \to \{0,1\}$ over possible extensions of P, such that $\pi(\mathscr{S}) = 1$ if and only if $\mathscr{C}(P) \subseteq \mathscr{S} \subseteq \mathscr{C}(P) \cup \mathscr{B}(P)$. The level of certainty that o *is* P is $N(o \in Ext(P)) = \inf_{\mathscr{S}:o \notin \mathscr{S}} 1 - \pi(\mathscr{S})$ [15]. Then, P being supertrue is equated to o *is* P having full certainty, that is, $N(o \in Ext(P)) = 1$. Indeed the latter reduces to

$$\{\mathscr{S}, \mathscr{C}(P) \subseteq \mathscr{S} \subseteq \mathscr{C}(P) \cup \mathscr{B}(P)\} \subseteq \{\mathscr{S}, o \in \mathscr{S}\},$$

which holds only if o *is* P is supertrue (i.e., again $o \in \mathscr{C}(P)$).

Supervaluation was introduced to cope with incomplete information, not vagueness. As a complete state of information refers to a precise description of the actual world, it is clear that in the original supervaluation framework, the correct complete state of information exists, so that it sounds coherent with Williamson's ideas. Interestingly, Kit Fine seems to borrow the supervaluation machinery while doing away with this assumption.

These approaches, including plurivaluationism, may be viewed as attempts to reconcile vagueness and the laws of classical logic. For supervaluationists and plurivaluationists, the latter hold for each sharpening of P; for epistemicists, they hold for the "real" extension of P. By construction, the proposition o is P or not P is, accordingly, supertrue or certainly true as, whatever the choice of $\mathscr{S}$ as a substitute for $Ext(P)$, $\mathscr{S} \cup \neg\mathscr{S} = \mathcal{O}$. Likewise, o is P and not P is superfalse or certainly false.

This kind of view can go along with the presence of a membership function, even if its meaning will be different from the case of the gradual setting. For instance one can explain the truth value gap by the disagreement between people as to what is the true extension of P.

Suppose we get different crisp representations of P provided by a set of n agents. Each agent i provides a partition (Y_P^i, N_P^i) of D_a. Then the trichotomy $\mathscr{C}(P), \mathscr{C}(\neg P), \mathscr{B}(P)$ is retrieved letting

- $\mathscr{C}(P) = \{o \in \mathcal{O}, a(o) \in \cap_{i=1,\dots,n} Y_P^i\}$

- $\mathscr{C}(\neg P) = \{o \in \mathcal{O}, a(o) \in \cap_{i=1,\dots,n} N_P^i\}$

"o is P" is super-true (false) if it is true (false) for all agents. Otherwise the Boolean truth value is not defined. Instead, one may define a membership function of the form:

$$\mu_P(o) = \frac{|\{i, a(o) \in Y_P^i\}|}{n}.$$

This kind of fuzzy sets clearly expresses variability across agents and will not be truth-functional. This membership function is the one-point-coverage function of a random set, and is not meant to express gradualness.

The above protocol may be hard to follow as people may be reluctant to provide clear-cut subsets of the attribute scale, or even to exhaustively describe the extension of a predicate. There have been some more realistic experiments carried out to identify membership functions of gradual or vague predicates by asking individuals in a group to classify objects as being P or not, enforcing a clear-cut reply. The membership grade $\mu_P(u)$ is then interpreted as a conditional probability [28]:

$$\mu_P(u) = Prob(\text{asserting "o is P"}|o(a) = u).$$

Again it represents variability, not gradualness [30]. Nevertheless, if a property is intrinsically gradual, and a clear-cut decision is artificially enforced in the experiment, one may assume that the more o is P (in the gradual view) the more likely (in the probability sense) o will be classified as P by agents. At the theoretical level, this is also the path followed by Scozzafava and his group [3] to interpret membership functions. The two above approaches are compatible if each agent i declares "o is P" whenever $u \in Y_P^i$.

Recently, Lawry [34] has built an extensive theory of what he calls "label semantics", based on the voting approach and the bivalence assumption that for each voting individual a label P (the name of a property on an attribute domain) applies or not to a given object. It also obviates the need to use attribute domains and extensions. Given an object o and a set of labels Λ, a mass function m_o in the sense of the transferable belief model of Smets [45] is defined on Λ. The mass $m_o(T)$ of a set of labels $T \subseteq \Lambda$ is the proportion of individuals that consider the object o to be properly qualified by the set of labels T. The appropriateness (membership grade) of label P to object o is then defined as $\sum_{P \in T} m_o(T)$. This view of vagueness is clearly in agreement with Williamson's idea of an unknown crisp extension of vague predicates, but it is agreed that this crisp description may vary across individuals and is not a presupposed objective entity. More recently, Lawry and Gonzalez-Rodriguez [35] have extended the label semantics, moving from binary to three-valued truth (individuals decide between true, false and borderline) while keeping the same experimental setting. Their work emphasises the point that the three truth values are a matter of representation convention and should not be confused with the uncertainty due to vagueness, the latter being expressed by a hesitation between the three truth values in the three-valued framework.

2.3 Limited perception

Numerical measurement scales and continuous mathematical models often provide formal representation settings that are much more refined than what human perception can handle. Measurement scales are often assumed to be arbitrarily precise, and the unit interval chosen as the set of possible membership grades is a good example such an excessively refined modeling choice. The continuity assumption is in contradiction with the limited perception capabilities of the human mind. Hence, for gradual properties with continuous attribute scales, one may argue that people cannot distinguish between very close attribute values, hence between objects whose description is almost the same. Some philosophers like R. Parikh [40] argue that one reason for vagueness maybe the difficulty to perceive the difference between close values in D_a: if $d_a(u,v) \leq \varepsilon$ then u is perceived as being the same value as v. Even if there is an actual standard extension of property P, two objects o and o' such that $o \in Ext(P), o' \in Ext(\neg P)$ will be perceived as borderline for P whenever $d_a(a(o), a(o')) \leq \varepsilon$, where ε is the perception threshold in D_a. Even if the boundary of the extension of P exists, it will be perceived as a thick area of borderline objects (of width 2ε).

In other words, there is a reflexive and symmetric indiscernibility relation I on D_a hence on $\mathcal{O}$, defined by uIv if and only if $d_a(u,v) \leq \varepsilon$. So the continuous scale D_a is not the proper space for describing properties pertaining to attribute a. Each element $u \in D_a$ is actually perceived as the subset $G_a(u) = \{v, uIv\}$ of elements that cannot be told apart from u. Each subset $G_a(u)$ is called a granule around u. The perceived attribute scale is a subset of the set of possible granules of D_a, that is a family $\mathcal{G}_a \subset \{G_a(u), u \in D_a\}$, that forms a covering of D_a (and oftentimes, just a partition).

This perception limitation induces indiscernibility on the set $\mathcal{O}$ of objects. Any object o cannot be told apart from objects in $[o]_a = \{o', a(o') \in G_a(a(o))\}$, and even, using a granular scale, $\mathcal{G}_a$, from objects whose attribute value belongs to the same granule in $\mathcal{G}_a$. As a consequence any standard predicate on D_a corresponds to an ill-defined subset of objects in $\mathscr{O}$, that can be modelled as follows:

- The set $\mathscr{C}(P) = Ext(P)_* = \{o \in \mathscr{O}, [o]_a \subseteq Ext(P)\}$ is the set of objects that are clearly P.

- The set $\mathscr{P}(P) = Ext(P)^* = \{o \in \mathscr{O}, [o]_a \cap Ext(P) \neq \emptyset\} \supseteq \mathscr{C}(P)$ is the set of objects that are possibly P.

- The set $\mathscr{B}(P) = \mathscr{P}(P) \setminus \mathscr{C}(P)$ is the set of borderline objects for P.

- The set $\mathscr{C}(\neg P) = Ext(\neg P)_* = (Ext(P)^c)_* = (Ext(P)^*)^c$, i.e., the complement of $Ext(P)^*$ is the set of objects that are clearly not P.

This approach was formalised by Williamson [53, appendix] in his logic of clarity. It is also a special case of imprecise information handling in the representation of objects [14, 5]. Namely, one may define a multivalued mapping Γ from $\mathscr{O}$ to D_a, namely, $\Gamma(o) = G_a(a(o))$, and it is easy to see that $\mathscr{C}(P)$ is the lower inverse image, via Γ, of the positive domain of P in the sense of Dempster [7]: $\mathscr{C}(P) = \{o \in \mathscr{O}, \Gamma(o) \subseteq Y_P\}$, where $\Gamma(o)$ is the set of possible values of o. The set $\Gamma(o)$ represents what is known about the attribute value $a(o)$. Here the lack of knowledge is due to limited perception.

Note that in the case of modeling vagueness due to indiscernibility, one can have access to $\mathscr{C}(P)$ and $\mathscr{C}(\neg P)$ (individuals can point out objects that are definitely P or not), but not to the real extension of P (nor the positive domain Y_P). Moreover in this interpretive setting, there is a reductio ad infinitum effect because it is clear that the crisp boundary of $\mathscr{C}(P)$ cannot be precisely perceived either, since $(Ext(P)_*)_* \subset Ext(P)_*$, generally. This is because the reflexive and symmetric relation I is not transitive. It is transitive if the granulation of the attribute scale D_a is done via quantization, that is using a partition of D_a whose elements are perceived as distinct. This is a very common method for interfacing numerical attribute scales and symbolic ones. Then I is an equivalence relation, and the approximation pair $(Ext(P)_*, Ext(P)^*)$ defines a rough set [41], such that $(Ext(P)_*)_* = Ext(P)_*$. Halpern [27] tries to reconcile, in a modal logic framework, the intransitivity of reported perceptions (by sensors), and the transitivity of subjective perceptions, noticing the former are based on measurements of the real state of the world, while the perceived appropriateness of vague predicates depends on the state of the perceiving agent at the moment of the perception experiment.

The limited perception approach can actually go along with gradual truth if we admit that two attribute values may be distinguishable to a degree, all the higher as the values are far away from one another. In this case, the indiscernibility relation on the attribute scale is a fuzzy symmetric and reflexive relation, an example of which is: $I(u, v) = \min(1, \frac{\varepsilon}{d_a(u,v)})$. Note that the separability property of similarity relations used in Section 2.1 does not hold since the stress here is on limited perception. See Klawonn [33] for a detailed overview of this approach. In that case, indistiguishability granules become gradual, with membership values $\mu_{G_a(u)}(v) = I(u, v)$, and the set $\mathscr{P}(P)$ becomes the gradual extensional hull of the crisp extension $Ext(P)$: its membership function becomes $\mu_{\mathscr{P}(P)}(a(o)) = \sup_{o':a(o') \in Ext(P)} I(a(o), a(o'))$.

2.4 Connectives

Boolean connectives can be extended to the gradual setting and remain truth-functional, extending truth tables to more than two truth values, including the unit interval.
The price paid is clearly a loss of properties with respect to the Boolean algebra [26].
When the gradualness of properties is due to some tolerance, modelled by a distance
function, and applied to basically Boolean properties, the crisp sets are the "real" things
while the fuzzy sets are their relaxed representations. One can observe a lack of truth-
functionality as indicated in Section 2.1. This is because in this case there are not more
so-generated fuzzy sets than crisp sets, so that the underlying algebra is Boolean, and
truth-functionality on a continuous truth-set is at odds with the Boolean structure. Connectives are not truth-functional either under the epistemic and truth value gap or plurivaluationist semantics, but the Boolean nature of extensions (or precisiations) is retained.
This is not surprising because truth-functionality is always lost under partial ignorance
(see [9] for a detailed discussion). The third approach based on limited perception is a
also a case of incomplete information due to indiscernibility between close values. The
truth-functionality is then again lost. In other words truth-functionality is maintained
only if the extension of properties is considered intrinsically gradual and no reference is
made to an underlying Boolean property either made flexible so as to cope with closeness, or blurred due to limited perception. Most models of vagueness pointed out above
lead to a loss of truth-functionality, but for the pure gradualness situation.

2.5 How to tell vagueness from gradualness?

Even though the above discussion points out a distinction, and possibly some independence, between the idea of vagueness and the idea of gradualness of concepts, it is
noticeable that the three features of vagueness considered by Keefe and Smith and recalled in the introduction are of little avail to tell one from the other. Clearly, among
these three key-features, the first one, i.e., the presence of borderline cases, seems to
suggest a three-valued logic; besides, admitting gradual truth leads to consider as borderline cases situations where fuzzy propositions take truth values different from true
and false. The second property seems to directly propose that truth might come by degrees. But several approaches, recalled above, view borderline cases as an effect of the
partial knowledge of a crisp boundary, or derive numerical membership functions that
represent uncertainty about Boolean truth, and not intrinsic gradualness of concepts. The
presence of the Sorites paradox does not seem to solve the dispute between bivalence and
multivalence. Indeed, the Sorites paradox has been given plausible explanations both in
the setting of fuzzy logic (originally by Goguen [24]) via a graceful degradation of the
truth values of the conclusion, and by the epistemic, yet Boolean, approach to vagueness
(as discussed by Williamson [53]) as a result of uncertainty pervading the meaning of
concepts. One way out of this difficulty consists in acknowledging a difference of nature between vagueness and gradual truth. The gradualness of concepts may perhaps be
observed (a person can rank objects in terms of their appropriateness as instances of a
concept), but gradual truth is a representation convention: we decide to define a property
as liable to have two or more truth values when applied to object for a reason of modeling convenience. Gradual truth looks natural and easy to quantify for some concepts
(like *tall*), natural but more difficult to quantify for other ones (like *beautiful* or *bird*)

and very debatable for yet others (like *single*). In contrast, vagueness is a phenomenon observed in the way people use language, and is characterized by, as Halpern [27] says, variability in the use of some concepts both between and within speakers. It may be that one cause of such variability is the gradual perception of some concepts or some words in natural language. However, one should consider gradual truth more as a modeling assumption than as an actually observable phenomenon (it makes no sense to ask people for numerical membership grades, or truth degrees).

3　Is there a threshold underlying a gradual concept?

At this point we are led to the question whether some properties are intrinsically gradual so as to lead to a notion of gradual truth for statements involving such properties. The advocates of the truth value gap and the epistemic view deny the possibility of gradual predicates, and consider their approaches as undermining the arguments in favor of many-valued truth. Yet, it is hard to believe that, talking about the height of people there is an infinitely precise (but unknown) threshold dividing the height range between tall heights and non-tall heights (assuming the context is made precise enough). Instead of taking sides, it sounds more reasonable to try and reconcile the epistemic and the gradual views on fuzzy concepts. In fact, what is embarrassing about the claims made on all sides is that they seem to consider the meaning of vague properties and the existence or not of classical extensions *in abstracto*, regardless of the way people use such properties. We suggest that the choice between an ill-known crisp extension and a gradual extension of a vague property (say *tall*) depends on the role of the agent with respect to a statement containing this vague property (say *Jon is tall*). It is interesting to consider two very distinct situations:

- **Asserting a gradual statement**: the case when an agent declares "*Jon is tall*". This claim is unambiguous so the utterer must use an implicit decision threshold.

- **Receiving a gradual statement**: the case when an agent receives a piece of information of the form "*Jon is tall*". There is no need for any threshold if the gradualness of the meaning is acknowledged by the receiver.

3.1　Asserting a gradual statement

The fact of asserting a statement "*o is P*" is a Boolean event (the agent asserts it or not) whether the statement is vague, gradual, or not. In the case where P is a gradual property, everything occurs as if the decision of asserting P were made by means of a clear-cut positive domain $Y_P \subset D_a$, whereby "*o is P*" is asserted because $a(o) \in Y_P$. For instance, if an agent declares that *Jon is tall*, and *tall* is a gradual predicate on the human height scale, say a real interval D_a, then there must be a threshold α in $[0,1]$ such that statement "*Jon is tall*" was asserted because $\mu_P(Jon) \geq \alpha$. This is equivalent to claim that everything happens as if there were a threshold $\theta \in D_a$ such that $height(Jon) \geq \theta$. We say "everything happens as if" because we certainly do not have access to this threshold when we are told that *Jon is tall* (if we know the actual height $height(Jon) = h$, all we know is that $\theta \leq h$). Even more, it is not clear whether the utterer is aware of this threshold. It may vary with time (the next time the same individual utters the same statement, another threshold may be used), let alone with the identity of the utterer, and some other kind of circumstances (the people that were seen before Jon showed up) that makes the perception of tallness a subjective matter, and not only a function of height [27]. In any case this threshold (that makes a gradual property P temporarily crisp) is ill-known, utterer-dependent, possibly time-dependent. It is not intrinsic.

This model somewhat goes along with the epistemic view, while putting it in a very pragmatic setting. The threshold view seems to have been adopted by linguists like Kennedy [32]. The latter studies adjectives gradable on a numerical scale and comments at length on the nature of such a threshold. In the basic model, it is supposed to reflect "the average degree to which the objects in the comparison class possess the property", and the author considers more general kinds of context-sensitive thresholds acting as comparison standards justifying the utterance of gradual propositions. Kennedy makes the distinction between absolute gradable adjectives (like *open* and *closed* for a door) that admit minimum and maximal standards, and relative ones (like *tall* for a man). When asserting *the door is open* we just need a minimal aperture of the door; when asserting *the door is closed* we generally mean fully closed. Representing *open* and *closed* by membership functions, it is clear that the decision threshold in these cases are respectively such that $\mu_{open}(\theta) = 0$ (the statement is uttered for doors inside the support of the fuzzy set), resp. $\mu_{close}(\theta) = 1$ (resp. inside the core). For those adjectives, the similarity-based explanation of gradual membership degrees (tolerance with respect to a norm) looks plausible. Kennedy indicates that absolute gradable adjectives do not trigger the Sorites paradox. The threshold generally corresponds to another cut level $\mu_P(\theta) = \alpha \neq 0, 1$ for relative gradable adjectives, and the variability of this threshold explains the perceived vagueness of such adjectives.

In practice, when asserting a gradual statement, gradual truth can be temporarily dispensed with, and membership degrees may then just reflect the probability that a label is appropriate to an object for the agent (like in the voting paradigm) [34, 3]. Note that the Boolean quality of the asserted proposition is only a convention adopted by the utterer. We may ask for a more refined convention, asking the agent to choose between true, false and borderline, like Lawry and Gonzalez-Rodriguez [35]. However, as said earlier, it does not look sensible to ask questions referring to a finer classification, let alone to request numbers between 0 and 1.

The implicit threshold involved in the utterance of a statement involving a gradual predicate like *tall* is more likely to be subject to variability among and within agents than the threshold used to define a crisp predicate, as the latter is often part of the definition of the concept (for instance *major* is defined by a legal age threshold). This variability is characteristic of gradual predicates understood as being vague.

3.2 Receiving a gradual statement

Generally people have a good idea whether a property is gradual or not, as suggested in Section 2.1. The predicate *tall* is clearly gradual since an individual can be more or less *tall*. Hence, taking the point of view of the receiver, the latter, upon hearing that *Jon is tall* has been asserted, already knows that this property P is gradual. Its acceptance as a valid information presupposes that the receiver believes the utterer, but it does not require any decision, on the side of the receiver, pertaining to an underlying threshold separating *tall* and *non-tall*. The only decision made by the receiver is that of accepting the statement as reliable enough (if any threshold is involved in the receiver's decision to take the utterer's statement for granted, it is a reliability threshold pertaining to the source of information). Since the receiver acknowledges the gradualness of the property, one may assume, insofar as he knows the meaning of P and the attribute scale is clear and simple (like the height scale), that this meaning can be approximated by a membership function. It can be done by pointing out prototypes of P and $\neg P$ and a simple interpolation is often enough for practical purposes. Another assumption is needed for the receiver to understand the information conveyed by the utterer properly: the receiver must assume that his/her membership function of P is close enough to the one of the emitter (which means, of course, the receiver is aware of the context in which the statement is uttered).

If these assumptions are met, the information about the height of Jon boils down to a set of more or less possible values modelled by the membership function μ_P on D_a. This membership function is interpreted as a possibility distribution π, whereby $\pi(u)$, the degree of possibility that $height(Jon) = u$ is equated to the membership grade $\mu_P(u)$ [58]. This possibility distribution represents the epistemic state of the receiver only knowing that *Jon is tall*. In this view, saying that the statement *Jon is tall* is true for the receiver means that the latter considers it as a totally safe assertion that can be fully trusted. It does not mean that for the receiver, $\mu_P(height(Jon)) = 1$; it means $\pi = \mu_P$. In case the receiver does not trust the utterer, one may model this kind of unreliability by means of certainty-qualification [15], for instance $\pi = \max(\mu_P, 1 - r)$, where $r \in [0, 1]$ is the degree of the receiver's certainty that the information is reliable. This is similar to the discounting of testimonies in Shafer's theory of evidence [44].

This piece of information may be used to expand or revise the prior epistemic state of the receiver [16]. Note that even the absolute gradable adjectives in the sense of Kennedy [32] can be interpreted in a gradual way, by introducing some tolerance. The major interest for the receiver to interpret statements of the utterer in a gradual way could be to eventually solve conflicts in the information thus collected: conflicts between gradual representations can be gradual too, and lead to a compromise solution, while inconsistent bodies of crisp representations of gradual propositions are harder to handle. In other words, the use of membership functions of fuzzy sets to represent gradual properties, as proposed by Zadeh [58], makes sense and is even quite useful from the point of view of receiving and processing information, not so much from the point of view of asserting propositions involving gradual predicates. Also, note the opposite nature of the respective situations of the emitter and the receiver. The emitter has enough knowledge about the height of Jon to be able to assert *Jon is tall*, making this statement true in the Boolean sense. In contrast, the information item *Jon is tall* maybe the only one obtained so far by the receiver (who thus has no prior idea of the actual height of Jon nor about the threshold used by the utterer to make his statement). Viewed from the receiver, the "truth" of the utterer's statement means that he is ready to adopt the membership function μ_P as a possibility distribution representing his epistemic state about the height of Jon. So, the receiver does not even handle degrees of truth, but only possibility degrees: $\mu_P(u)$ is the degree to which the receiver, accepting the information item, considers $Height(Jon) = u$ plausible.

One way to cope with some controversies between fuzzy set theory advocates and vagueness philosophers is to consider they do not study the same problem at all. The latter are interested in how people decide to use vague predicates when they speak, the former are concerned with the modeling and the storing of information coming from humans. In that sense, the vagueness and the gradualness of natural language terms can be viewed as orthogonal concerns.

4   Toward a reconciliation of some views of vagueness

In this section, we suggest another reason why the epistemic and truth value gap approaches to vagueness should be seen as compatible with a non-bivalent view of some properties or predicates. Indeed, there seems to be a strong historical tradition for Bivalence in logic. The status of truth in philosophy is so prominent that it is taken as an objective notion, whose perfection cannot go along with shades of truth. Especially, the existence of a decision threshold in the epistemic view sounds like a "realistic" point of view a la Plato. Yet, as pointed out by De Finetti [6] in an early paper discussing Łukasiewicz logic, the bivalence of propositions can be viewed as a representational convention, not at all a matter of actual fact:[3]

> Propositions are assigned two values, true or false, and no other, not because
> there "exists" an a priori truth called "excluded middle law", but because
> we call "propositions" logical entities built in such a way that only a yes/no
> answer is possible

Hence, we may infer that more generally, truth values are always a matter of convention. Gradual truth is another convention, different from the bivalent one. It is instrumental in the faithful representation of the meaning of some terms in natural language pertaining to numerical attribute scales, in order to process information. So adopting gradual truth as the proper convention for representing predicates like *tall*, *old* and the like, one may again consider the issue of vagueness as the presence of cases where truth values can hardly be assigned to propositions applied to some objects. But instead of considering borderline cases as those where it is not clear whether a vague proposition is true of false, one may consider that in borderline cases, not only truth is gradual but the assignment of a gradual truth value is difficult or impossible.

4.1   Ill-known fuzzy sets and gradual truth value gaps

Adopting this stance, the existence of intrinsically gradual properties no longer contradicts the epistemic view of vagueness. The epistemic thesis assumes that vague predicates have clear-cut extensions even if there is some limited knowledge about them. Consider the claim made by Williamson [53, p. 201]:

> Bivalence holds in borderline cases. It is just that we are in no position to
> find out which truth value the vague utterance has.

The last part of the claim may hold for gradual properties, without requesting bivalence as a prerequisite. Even if a gradual predicate should rather be modelled by a fuzzy set

---

[3]Our translation from the French.

than a crisp set, its membership function has little chance to be well-known. A *gradual epistemic view* could postulate that the membership function of a gradual predicate exists but one is partially ignorant about it, hence the vagueness phenomenon.

As it looks much more difficult to define membership functions of gradual predicates precisely than crisp extensions of clearly bivalent ones, it is natural that most gradual concepts sound more usually vague than crisp ones. In other words, the vagueness of a fuzzy concept could be modelled via intervals of truth values, or even fuzzy sets thereof, the latter representing knowledge about an albeit precise but ill-known gradual truth value [57]. In a nutshell, we could argue that vagueness is due to partial ignorance about the meaning of categories irrespective of their being considered as gradual or not. This thesis disentangles the issue of gradual propositions from the problem of vagueness.

The way interval-valued fuzzy sets (IVFs, for short) are used in the fuzzy set community ([50], for instance) seems to be at odds with the epistemic view of vagueness, even with the above non-bivalent stance. An interval-valued fuzzy set *IF* is defined by an interval-valued membership function: $IF(u) = [\mu_*(u), \mu^*(u)], \forall u \in D_a$. Under the epistemic view, there exists a real membership function $\mu \in IF$, i.e., $\mu_*(u) \leq \mu(u) \leq \mu^*(u)$.

However, interval-valued fuzzy sets are construed truth-functionally. The union, intersection and complementation of IVF's are obtained by canonically extending fuzzy set-theoretic operations to interval-valued operands in the sense of *interval arithmetics*. For instance, restricting to the most commonly used connectives, with $IF(u) = [\mu_*(u), \mu^*(u)], IG(u) = [v_*(u), v^*(u)]$:

$$IF \cap IG(u) = [\min(\mu_*(u), v_*(u)), \min(\mu^*(u), v^*(u))];$$

$$IF \cup IG(u) = [\max(\mu_*(u), v_*(u)), \max(\mu^*(u), v^*(u))];$$

$$IF^c(u) = [1 - \mu^*(u), 1 - \mu_*(u)].$$

IVFs are then viewed as special case of L-fuzzy sets in the sense of Goguen [23] where L is a set of intervals on [0, 1]. Hence, interval-valued fuzzy sets have a weaker structure than the fuzzy set algebra of precise values they extend. However, just as the epistemic view on vague predicates insists that they remain bivalent whether truth or falsity can be decided or not, so that the properties of classical logic should be preserved, the epistemic view on vague gradual predicates maintains that the algebraic structure of precise truth values should be preserved even if ill-known. For instance, if the conjunction of fuzzy sets is performed using the minimum, the weak form of the contradiction law $(\min(\mu(u), 1 - \mu(u)) \leq 0.5)$ should hold for gradual propositions, while it does not hold for IVFs with the above definition of intersection and negation of interval-valued fuzzy sets (see [10] for a more detailed discussion). In this approach, truth values are precise but ill-known. The price for preserving the tautologies of the underlying many-valued logic is as usual a loss of truth-functionality. This would allow a non-truth-functional epistemic approach to gradual concepts, such that propositions have precise gradual truth values, however pervaded with uncertainty. A logical approach to this view is described by Lehmke [36], for instance.

Likewise, the supervaluationism of Kit Fine could be accommodated in a gradual setting: for instance we could define a vague statement to be super-α-true if it is at least

α-true in all of its gradual precisiations (precise membership functions). Restricting the truth set to three values, one may likewise consider propositions that are "super-borderline" (i.e., they are neither totally true nor totally false in all three-valued precisiations of the membership function). In this approach, no assumption is made about the existence of a "true" membership function. However, in the same way as in the classical approach, where all classical models compatible with the non-classical supervaluationist model must be used to check super-truth, all membership functions $\mu \in IF$ are to be used for checking super-α-truth, even if none of them is the true one. In the interval-fuzzy set setting, one may say that o is F is

- super-α-true when $\mu_*(u) \geq \alpha$,

- super-α-false when $\mu^*(u) \leq 1 - \alpha$.

The supervaluationistic approach to vagueness proposed by Kit Fine could thus extend to gradual truth values, making it closer to Smith's fuzzy plurivaluationism [48]. In the latter view though, in contrast with the former, all precise membership functions are equally acceptable, and one lacks reason for choosing between them due to semantic indecision, or as Smith puts it "the meaning-determining facts" preventing us from choosing a unique intended model. Both fuzzy supervaluationism and fuzzy plurivaluationism would again lead to a non-truth-functional calculus of IVFs in order to preserve the algebraic properties of the underlying set of precise membership functions.

4.2 Blurry sets

At this point, it is interesting to examine the positioning of the so-called blurry set approach to vagueness proposed by Nick Smith [46]. Smith advocates the idea that if a property is gradual, propositions referring to it should have gradual truth values. However, like in this paper, he considers simple membership functions valued on the unit interval are insufficient to account for vagueness. More precisely, for him, numerical values are only approximations of actual truth values. Smith proposes to represent truth values by means of so-called degree functions, which are probability-like kinds of fractal constructs. The idea is that if someone says *Jon is tall is 0.6 true*, we call assertion A_1, then we should allow degrees of truth for assertion A_1, say an assertion A_2 of the form A_1 *is 0.3 true* to make sense, and so on, ad infinitum. However, rather than seeing this construction as a hierarchy of assignments of simple numerical truth values, Smith views it as the *single assignment* of a complex truth value consisting of a so-called *degree function*.

Roughly speaking a degree function is a mapping f from arbitrary sequences of real values in the unit interval to the unit interval. For instance if f pertains to the statement *Jon is tall*, $f(0.6, 0.3) = 0.5$ means: *It is 0.5 true that it is 0.3 true that it is 0.6 true that Jon is tall*. Moreover each of these degrees is viewed as a scalar approximation of a more complex entity, degrees at lower levels being fixed. Namely, there is a density function $\delta_{f(a_1,\ldots,a_n)}(x)$ on $[0, 1]$ representing the blurry region of more or less appropriate values of the degree of truth at level $n + 1$, whose approximation is then understood as the mean-value of the probability measure having this density. In the paper [46], the density is supposed to be normal, with a variance small enough to fit the narrow gauge of the unit interval. Under these restrictions, a degree function is an infinite sequence of elements of the unit interval, the constant sequence of 1's standing for *utterly true*, the constant sequence of 0's standing for *utterly false*. Then, standard fuzzy set connectives can be extended to degree functions, by applying them componentwise to sequences of numbers in the unit interval.

This extension of fuzzy sets, and the context in which it is devised calls for several comments:

- First, Smith seems to endorse an objectivist view of degrees of truth, whereby, in his words [46, p. 169], "each vague sentence is assigned a unique degree function as its unique truth value". This is a first point of disagreement with the positioning of fuzzy sets with respect to the vagueness problem adopted here. In the view advocated in the present discussion, there is no such thing as the actual truth value of a vague statement. The use of membership function (and the unit interval) and of a precise truth value is viewed as a pure convention that helps representing knowledge. The reason why a statement like *Jon is tall is 0.6 true* may be debatable is not because, as Smith says "it is a first approximation of the actual truth value of the vague statement". Fair enough, a membership function is an approximate rendering of a meaning. But what is problematic in Smith's construct is to assume that any sensible person will ever make a statement of the form *Jon is tall is 0.6 true*. The utterer may declare at best *Jon is more or less tall*, for instance, and this statement is considered (fully) true by the receiver who takes it for granted. The 0.6 degree plays a role in the emitter-receiver framework outlined above. However it may be seen as follows: what the receiver models is a membership function for *tall*, which is supposed to be a good enough representation. Then, if the height of Jon eventually gets to be known by the receiver, say 1.7 meters high, the degree of membership $\mu_P(1.7) = 0.6$ (say) can be obtained, and acts as an encoding of the idea that John is tall to some extent. However this figure is a mathematical representation and cannot be naturally produced (let alone interpreted) in communication between persons (even if people can easily outline whole membership functions on simple continuous measurement scales).

- Another difficulty is the extreme mathematical complexity of what Smith considers to be an actual truth value, and the fact that at the same time the author has to resort to ad hoc tricks like approximately fitting a Gaussian density to the unit interval. One may admit such approximations if empirical tests are made to generate sequences of numbers in the unit interval prescribed by the theory. Given the lack of intuition of what a degree of truth can be for lay-people (and even very educated ones), as opposed to other concepts such as utility, probability, cost or similarity, it is unlikely that this theory can be empirically tested. Now if the notion of degree function is to be taken as the basis of a mathematical theory of vagueness, then it could be useful to see if the theoretical results obtained are still valid beyond Gaussians squeezed on the unit interval, i.e. whether this ad hoc restriction is needed at all.

- Finally it is surprizing to see probability density functions and averages playing a key-role in this construction, while never being given any uncertainty-driven interpretation. The author says (p. 172) that the degree of truth of a statement should be represented as a blurry region stretching between 0 and 1. The idea is accommodated by regarding the curve as the graph of a density function. What this density function stands for is not very clear: does it account for variability of the truth value people would use (if they were forced to)? is it a representation of subjective belief about the truth value? In contrast, if a precise value cannot be assigned due to a lack of information, why not use a possibility distribution? Why should the blurry region have a symmetric shape at all (especially for small and for large membership values?). The use of averages also looks partially debatable: if the precise approximation of the truth value corresponds to the one that stands out in the blurry region, a modal value looks more plausible than an average value. In a nutshell, the extreme sophistication of the representation seems to go along with a number of degrees of freedom in the choice of definitions and parameters, both at the interpretive and the mathematical level, which deserves more scrutiny.

Overall, beyond their impressive mathematical and conceptual construction, blurry sets seem to be an idealistic view of gradual vagueness, whose adequacy to concrete data looks very difficult to validate. We suggest here that the use of simple membership functions cannot by itself account for the vagueness phenomenon (and we claim it was not the original intention of the founder of fuzzy sets either, let alone the one of the many users of fuzzy set theory since then). From this point of view, we are not better off by making the notion of truth value very complex, and considering it as a real entity. One reason is that it does not directly fit with the point that vagueness is to a large extent due to uncertainty of meaning. It is the human incapacity to represent gradual predicates by precise membership functions that should be modelled (be it due to their contextual nature, lack of knowledge or lack of definiteness). Instead, the theory of blurry sets seems to bypass this kind of uncertainty by means of a new kind of higher order truth value. The fact that blurry sets are compositional just like fuzzy sets (and interval-valued fuzzy sets) should act as a warning on the fact that this construction is not tailored for uncertainty due to vagueness. But then, what do these blurry regions of the unit interval represent? The fuzzy plurivaluationistic approach later developed by Smith [48] looks simpler and more convincing, even if the present paper suggests, contrary to Smith, that the vagueness phenomenon is related to the fact that several membership functions are possible, and not to the gradual nature of propositions considered vague.

5   Conclusion

It should be clear from the above discussion that fuzzy sets, as explained by Zadeh, have no ambition to grasp the philosophical issue of vagueness, and that gradualness does not always imply the presence of uncertainty: some membership functions only encode the idea of degrees as a substitute to Boolean representations. In fact, some gradual functions do not even encode fuzzy sets [18]. Fuzzy sets refer to sets with gradual boundaries, while vagueness results in a lack of capability to assign truth values to linguistic statements (whether modelled in a bivalent setting or not). If this separation between gradualness and vagueness is taken for granted, vagueness appears as a form of uncertainty in meaning, hence does not lend itself to compositionality. It seems that many controversies between fuzzy set theory scholars and philosophers of vagueness come from the presupposition that fuzzy set theory is a full-fledged approach to vagueness, which turns out not to be the case. Fuzzy sets can be useful in many areas not concerned with the study of natural language, and the vagueness phenomenon is at best facilitated by the presence of gradual predicates, since gradual representations look more cognitively demanding than Boolean ones. We also claim that the study of vagueness may benefit from the choice of the point of view in a dialogue: whether the vague statement is asserted or received seems to matter. Moreover, just as Smith did for pluri-valuationism, we argue that neither the epistemic view to vagueness nor supervaluations are incompatible with the idea of gradual predicates.

BIBLIOGRAPHY

[1] M. Black. Vagueness. *Philosophi of Science*, 4:427–455, 1937.

[2] D. Bouyssou and M. Pirlot: Following the traces: An introduction to conjoint measurement without transitivity and additivity. *European Journal of Operational Research*, 163(2):287–337, 2005

[3] G. Coletti and R. Scozzafava. Conditional probability, fuzzy sets and possibility: a unifying view. *Fuzzy Sets and Systems*, 144:227–249, 2004.

[4] R.T. Cook Vagueness and mathematical precision. *Mind*, 111:225–247, 2002.

[5] I. Couso and D. Dubois. Rough sets, coverings and incomplete information. *Fundamenta Informaticae*, 108:223–247, 2011.

[6] B. De Finetti. La logique de la probabilité. In *Actes Congrès Int. de Philos. Scient., Paris*, pages 1–9, Hermann et Cie Editions, Paris, 1936.

[7] A.P. Dempster. Upper and lower probabilities induced by a multivalued mapping. *Annals of Mathematical Statistics*, 38:325–339, 1967.

[8] Y. Djouadi, D. Dubois, and H. Prade. Graduality, uncertainty and typicality in formal concept analysis. In C. Cornelis, G. Deschrijver, M. Nachtegael, and S. Schockaert, editors, *35 years of Fuzzy Sets Theory*, pages 127–147. Springer, Berlin, 2010.

[9] D. Dubois. On ignorance and contradiction considered as truth-values. *Logic Journal of the IGPL*, 16(2):195–216, 2008.

[10] D. Dubois. Degrees of truth, ill-known sets and contradiction. In B. Bouchon-Meunier, L. Magdalena, M. Ojeda-Aciego, and J.-L. Verdegay, editors, *Foundations of Reasoning under Uncertainty,*, volume 249 of *Studies in Fuzziness and Soft Computing*, pages 65–83. Springer-Verlag, 2010.

[11] D. Dubois, F. Esteva, L. Godo, and H. Prade. An information-based discussion of vagueness: six scenarios leading to vagueness (Chapter 40) . In H. Cohen and C. Lefebvre, editors, *Handbook of categorization in cognitive science* , pages 891–909. Elsevier, Amsterdam, 2005.

[12] D. Dubois, S. Gottwald, P. Hájek, J. Kacprzyk, and H. Prade. Terminological difficulties in fuzzy set theory - the case of "intuitionistic fuzzy sets". *Fuzzy Sets and Systems*, 156(3):485–491, 2005.

[13] D. Dubois, W. Ostasiewicz, and H. Prade. Fuzzy sets: History and basic notions. In D. Dubois and H. Prade, editors, *Fundamentals of Fuzzy Sets* , The Handbooks of Fuzzy Sets Series, pages 21–124. Kluwer Academic Publishers, Boston, 2000.

[14] D. Dubois and H. Prade. Twofold fuzzy sets and rough sets: Some issues in knowledge representation. *Fuzzy Sets and Systems*, 23:3–18, 1987.

[15] D. Dubois and H. Prade. *Possibility Theory*. Plenum Press, New York, 1988.

[16] D. Dubois and H. Prade. Belief change and possibility theory. In P Gärdenfors, editor, *Belief Revision*, pages 142–182. Cambridge University Press, Cambridge, UK, 1992.

[17] D. Dubois and H. Prade. The three semantics of fuzzy sets. *Fuzzy Sets and Systems*, 90:141–150, 1997.

[18] D. Dubois and H. Prade. Gradual elements in a fuzzy set. *Soft Computing*, 12:165–175, 2008.

[19] K. Fine. Vagueness, truth and logic. *Synthese*, 30:265–300, 1975.

[20] M. Freund. On the notion of concept I. *Artificial Intelligence*, 172(4–5):570–590, 2008.

[21] B. Ganter and R. Wille. *Formal Concept Analysis, Mathematical Foundations*. Springer-Verlag, 1999.

[22] L. Godo and R. O. Rodriguez. Logical approaches to fuzzy similarity-based reasoning: an overview. In *Preferences and Similarities*, volume 504 of *CISM Courses and Lectures*, pages 75–128. Springer, 2008.

[23] J. A. Goguen. *L*-fuzzy sets. *Journal of Mathematical Analysis and Applications*, 18:145–174, 1967.

[24] J. A. Goguen. The logic of inexact concepts. *Synthèse*, 19:325–373, 1969.

[25] I. R. Goodman. Some new results concerning random sets and fuzzy sets. *Information Sciences*, 34:93–113, 1984.

[26] P. Hájek. *Metamathematics of Fuzzy Logic*. Kluwer, Dordrecht, 1998.

[27] J. Halpern. Intransitivity and vagueness. In D. Dubois, C.A. Welty, and M.-A. Williams, editors, *Proceedings of the Ninth International Conference on Principles of Knowledge Representation and Reasoning*, pages 121–129. AAAI Press, 2004.

[28] H.M. Hersh, A. Caramazza, and H.H. Brownell. Effects of context on fuzzy membership functions. In M.M.Gupta, R.R. Ragade, and Yager R.R., editors, *Advances in Fuzzy Set Theory and Applications*, pages 389–408. North-Holland, Amsterdam, 1979.

[29] J. Hintikka. *Knowledge and Belief*. Cornell University Press, Ithaca, 1962.

[30] E. Hisdal. Are grades of membership probabilities? *Fuzzy Sets and Systems*, 25:325–348, 1988.

[31] A. Kaplan and H.F. Schott. A calculus for empirical classes. *Methods*, III:165–188, 1951.

[32] C. Kennedy. Vagueness and grammar: the semantics of relative and absolute gradable adjectives. *Linguistics and Philosophy*, 30:1–45, 2007.

[33] F. Klawonn. Fuzzy points, fuzzy relations and fuzzy functions. In V. Novák and I. Perfilieva, editors, *Discovering the World with Fuzzy Logic*, pages 431–453. Springer, Berlin, 2000.

[34] J. Lawry. *Modelling and Reasoning with Vague Concepts*, volume 12 of *Studies in Computational Intelligence*. Springer, 2006.

[35] J. Lawry and I. González Rodríguez. Generalised label semantics as a model of epistemic vagueness. In Claudio Sossai and Gaetano Chemello, editors, *ECSQARU*, volume 5590 of *Lecture Notes in Computer Science*, pages 626–637. Springer, 2009.

[36] S. Lehmke. Degrees of truth and degrees of validity. In *Discovering the World with Fuzzy Logic*, pages 192–237. Physica Verlag, Heidelberg, 2001.

[37] I. Niiniluoto. *Truthlikeness*. D. Reidel, Dordrecht, 1987.

[38] V. Novák. Are fuzzy sets a reasonable tool for modeling vague phenomena? *Fuzzy Sets and Systems*, 156(3):341–348, 2005.

[39] D.N. Osherson and E.E. Smith. On the adequacy of prototype theory as a theory of concepts. *Cognition*, 9:59–72, 1981.

[40] R. Parikh. The problem of vague predicates. In R.S. Cohen and M.W. Wartopsky, editors, *Language, Logic and Method*, pages 241–261. D. Reidel, Dordrecht, The Netherlands, 1983.

[41] Z. Pawlak. *Rough Sets - Theoretical Aspects of Reasoning about Data*. Kluwer Academic Publ., Dordrecht, The Netherlands, 1991.

[42] P. Smith and R. Keefe. *Vagueness: A Reader*. MIT Press, Cambridge, MA, 1997.

[43] E.H. Ruspini. On the semantics of fuzzy logic. *International Journal of Approximate Reasoning*, 5:45–88, 1991.

[44] G. Shafer. *A Mathematical Theory of Evidence*. Princeton University Press, Princeton, 1976.

[45] Ph. Smets. The transferable belief model for quantified belief representation. In D.M. Gabbay and Ph. Smets, editors, *Handbook of Defeasible Reasoning and Uncertainty Management Systems*, volume 1, pages 267–301. Kluwer, Doordrecht, The Netherlands, 1998.

[46] N.J.J. Smith. Vagueness and blurry sets. *Journal of Philosophical Logic*, 33:165–235, 2004.

[47] N.J.J. Smith. Vagueness and closeness. *Australasian Journal of Philosophy*, 83:157–183, 2005.

[48] N.J.J. Smith. Vagueness and Degrees of Truth. Oxford University Press, Oxford, UK, 2008.

[49] B.C. van Fraassen. Singular terms, truth-value gaps, and free logic. *Journal of Philosophy*, 63:481–495, 1966.

[50] B. van Gasse, C. Cornelis, G. Deschrijver, and E.E. Kerre. Triangle algebras: A formal logic approach to interval-valued residuated lattices. *Fuzzy Sets and Systems*, 159(9):1042–1060, 2008.

[51] T. Weston. Approximate truth. *Journal of Philosophical Logic*, 16:203–227, 1987.

[52] H. Weyl. The ghost of modality. In *Philosophical essays in memory of Edmund Husserl*, pages 278–303. Cambridge, MA, 1940.

[53] T. Williamson. *Vagueness*. Routledge, London, 1994.

[54] L.A. Zadeh. PRUF - a meaning representation language for natural languages. *International Journal of Man-Machine Studies*, 10:395–460, 1978.

[55] L.A. Zadeh. Fuzzy sets. *Information and Control*, 8:338–353, 1965.

[56] L.A. Zadeh. Outline of a new approach to the analysis of complex system and decision processes. *IEEE Transactions on Systems, Man and Cybernetics*, 3:28–44, 1973.

[57] L.A. Zadeh. The concept of a linguistic variable and its application to approximate reasoning, part I. *Information Sciences*, 8:199–249, 1975.

[58] L.A. Zadeh. Fuzzy sets as a basis for a theory of possibility. *Fuzzy Sets and Systems*, 1:1–28, 1978.

[59] L.A. Zadeh. A note on prototype theory and fuzzy sets. *Cognition*, 12:291–297, 1982.

Didier Dubois
IRIT – Institut de Recherche en Informatique de Toulouse
CNRS and University of Toulouse
118 route de Narbonne
31062 Toulouse Cedex 09, France
Email: dubois@irit.fr

Comments on *Have Fuzzy Sets Anything to do with Vagueness?* by Didier Dubois

LLUÍS GODO

The paper by Didier Dubois discusses the controversial relationship between Zadeh's fuzzy sets and vagueness. The author explores the issue from different perspectives and critically examines the role of fuzzy sets in studies of vagueness. Contrary to a common opinion within the fuzzy set community, he claims that fuzziness (in the sense of properties with gradual membership) has little in common with vagueness. The proposed thesis is that vagueness refers to uncertainty or variability in the meaning of predicates, regardless of whether they are Boolean or gradual. In this sense, a fuzzy set, taken as the representation of the meaning of a gradual predicate, is not actually a vague object at all but a very precise one.

Actually the latter view is, in a sense, in accordance with the usual criticism raised by philosophers of vagueness against degree-based approaches, in particular those based on fuzzy sets. The criticism focuses on the artificial precision imposed by a real-valued membership function when chosen as the meaning a gradual vague predicate.[1] Although I basically agree with most of the ideas expressed by the author, still I would like to comment on a few questions.

- One of the main arguments developed by Dubois is to differentiate gradualness from vagueness; the key observation being that vagueness entails some sort of indeterminacy or uncertainty about the meaning of the relevant predicate, while gradualness does not. This is based on the assumption (as far as I understand) that gradual properties can be unambiguously described by a membership function, and hence, once this is accepted, any uncertainty on the meaning of gradual predicates is ruled out. This is justified from an information engineering point of view in Section 2.1 by the empirical fact that in many applications only a fuzzy set approximating the meaning of a predicate is needed. While this may be an acceptable assumption in such a restrictive context, where gradualness in that sense may be felt as different from vagueness, in a more general perspective it seems hardly reasonable to assume a unique one-to-one correspondence between gradual properties and fuzzy sets, and that gradual properties do not suffer from meaning indeterminacy. So, in my opinion, there is no intrinsic difference in general between gradual and vague predicates other than the fact that the former ones are related to measurement variables while the latter may be of a more abstract nature.

---

[1] See the paper by Nick Smith in this volume for a very clear statement of the problem of what he calls the basic fuzzy theory of vagueness.

- The author proposes some bridges that might reconcile fuzzy sets and theories of vagueness, in particular the idea of extending the epistemic stance to gradual predicates, e.g., by using sets of fuzzy sets as a way to account for a form of epistemic uncertainty about the meaning of gradual predicates: we don't know which is the interpretation (in terms of a membership function) of a gradual property, rather we only know that it belongs to a given set of possible functions. In such a case, this is usually specified with a lower and upper bound of the membership degree for each object to the extension of the predicate. This fuzzy epistemic view, although it may be seen as an improvement, does not completely solve the above mentioned artificial precision problem since it transfers it to the membership functions delimiting the set of acceptable interpretations. Exactly the same problem appears when adopting other, more refined representations than simply sets for modeling partial ignorance about the intended interpretation of a gradual predicate, like higher-order fuzzy sets, probability distributions on families of fuzzy sets, etc.

- I would also like to comment on two questions that arise in Nick Smith's paper in this volume that I think are relevant in connection with this discussion. The first one is that fuzzy sets also appear, as models or interpretations of gradual predicates, in the framework of Mathematical fuzzy logic (MFL) and in the different formal systems of many-valued logics therein. But when reasoning in a given system of MFL one is not committed to choose a particular (precise) interpretation of the predicates, but one rather reasons about a whole set of interpretations of the given theory. In other words, in this logical framework one does not explicitly deal with precise, real-valued degrees of truth: those are only implicit in the models. In this sense, very similar to the spirit of the supervaluationistic approach, the models (of a given theory in a given formal fuzzy logic) can be understood as the set possible precisiations of the meaning of the formulas in your theory, but only what is common to all those interpretations is relevant for making derivations. Of course, the price paid for getting rid of the artificial precision problem in this framework, at least using plain systems of MFL, is the failure of capturing sorites-like inference schemes in full generality.

The second and final comment, still in connection with the degree-based approach to vagueness by Smith, is on the role played by similarity or closeness as a distinguishing feature of vagueness. Basically, Smith argues that a predicate P is vague if, for any objects a and b, the truth-degrees of $P(a)$ and $P(b)$ are very similar whenever a and b are very similar in all respects relevant to the application of P. This required condition between similarity of objects and similarity of truth-degrees, when P is considered a gradual property in the sense of this paper (i.e. with some associated membership function representing its meaning), it may actually induce some constraints on the kind of acceptable fuzzy set chosen to represent P. Indeed, simplifying much and in the setting of properties related to some measurement variable, that condition is requiring that two values very close on the measurement scale cannot have very different membership degrees. In other words, it is not acceptable for a membership function to have sudden changes within a region of close enough objects. In a MFL setting, if $\approx_P$ denotes a predicate encoding a graded similarity relation on pairs of objects in relation to P, then the above condition is indeed requiring that P must be extensional with respect to $\approx_P$. This can be easily captured by an axiom like $(\forall x, y)(\approx_P (x,y) \to P(x) \leftrightarrow P(y))$, which may be used to further constrain the set of acceptable models for a given theory. Notice that, in semantical terms, that axiom simply expresses that the more true it is that x and y are similar, the closer the truth-value of $P(x)$ is to the the truth-value of $P(y)$.

Lluís Godo
IIIA, Artificial Intelligence Research Institute
CSIC, Spanish Scientific Research Council
Campus de la Universitat Autònoma de Barcelona s/n
08193 Bellaterra, Spain
Email: godo@iiia.csic.es

Reply to Lluís Godo's Comments on
Have Fuzzy Sets Anything to Do with Vagueness?

DIDIER DUBOIS

In the following I briefly reply to the points made by Lluís Godo in his comment. Some of them reflect familiar objections made to the representation of vague categories by precise membership functions.

- Outside the need for a simple practical representation of verbal pieces of gradual information in information engineering areas, it is clear that I did not claim the possibility of having a one-to-one correspondence between gradual properties and membership functions in the absolute. For one, if the consensus on the meaning of words across people is often sufficient for words to be useful in communication between them, it is far from a perfect consensus. Worse, even for a single person the meaning of words is not fully stable across circumstances of their usage. Finally, membership functions are clearly an idealisation of some complex reality that is quite hard to grasp, and that is called vagueness. To be fair, membership functions are especially useful for predicates referring to measurable scales. Beyond this framework (which is nevertheless instrumental in applications) it is not clear they can be easily defined at all.

- The point whereby replacing membership functions by set-valued ones that capture imprecision on the actual membership values is paradoxical, since it transfers artificial precision to the membership functions delimitating the set of acceptable interpretations, is questionable. It makes sense if one admits that a membership grade is then replaced by a set that represents a new kind of membership grade more adapted to the vagueness situation. Then indeed the difficulty to be precise about the original membership function becomes the difficulty to describe a set-valued one precisely, and so forth ad infinitum with higher order representations. However the set-valued function used does not represent a membership function, it is not a substitute to it. It only represents what we know of the membership grades that are assumed to be precise (in the adopted model, if not in reality). So the precision on upper and lower bounds is not crucial: they are just upper and lower bounds. It is always possible to widen the sets if the set-valued function is viewed too narrow to be trusted. This is the same situation as when guessing the value of some quantity x which is incompletely known. Then we write $x \in [a,b]$ where a,b are precise. In case of doubt we can always decrease a and increase b, instead of trying to figure out precise values of a and b, and modeling them in turn by intervals. The point is that if the actual objective value of x

exists, there is no real value for the upper and lower bounds. Likewise, as already we can question the existence of membership functions (we have argued elsewhere they are just convenient fictions [1]) we can definitely claim that the existence of membership functions delimitating the set of acceptable representatives is even more elusive, and thus the question of their precision is arguably meaningless.

- I agree that in mathematical fuzzy logic, degrees of truth are internalized and thus the issue of measuring membership or truth-values is irrelevant in that setting. On the contrary in more explicit use of fuzzy sets the question of obtaining membership functions in a simple and relevant manner remains an important issue.

- I am also sympathetic to the idea that some extensionality property seems to be at work when modeling gradual concepts by membership functions. Especially if the measurement scale is continuous, it comes down to avoiding thresholding effects. Gradualness should come along with a form of continuity of membership functions enabling a graceful degradation when moving away from prototypes of a gradual concept. Requiring more than mere continuity, namely some kind of smoothness, by constraining the derivatives of the membership function, or exploiting similarity conditions (the more x and y are similar, the more the truth-value of $P(x)$ is close to the truth-value of $P(y)$) then becomes a natural issue to study.

BIBLIOGRAPHY

[1] D. Dubois, H. Prade: Fuzzy sets—A convenient fiction for modelling vagueness and possibility, comments on a paper by Laviolette and Seaman. *IEEE Transactions on Fuzzy Systems*, 2(1):16–21, 1994.

Many-Valued Semantics for Vague Counterfactuals

MARCO CERAMI AND PERE PARDO[1]

1 Introduction

This paper is an attempt to provide a formal semantics to counterfactual propositions that involve vague sentences as their antecedent or consequent. The initial work on counterfactuals, due to Lewis ([8]), was based on Classical Logic and thus it focused on crisp sentences. Lewis proposed a semantics based on the notion of possible worlds that captures alternative ways a world could be, including here our reality i.e., the world we live in (henceforth: the actual world, or our world). In Lewis' work, possible worlds can be seen as classical Boolean valuations, each valuation corresponding to a possible world.

Our aim is to generalize Lewis' system of spheres semantics based on Classical Propositional Logic, to a similar semantics based on many-valued logics. On the one hand, as long as the authors know, the claim that Lewis' systems of spheres provide a good semantics for counterfactual propositions does not seem to be controversial. On the other hand, however, many-valued logics are not universally accepted to be a good semantics for vague sentences (see [4] and [5] for an overview on different approaches to the subject). Even though this is not the right place to discuss whether many-valued logics are suitable tools for reasoning in presence of vagueness, we find necessary to spend a few lines in order to justify at least why our approach is based on this framework to formalize vague sentences.

Despite no general agreement exists on what a vague sentence is, there does not seem to be any problem in admitting that sentences involving predicates like *bald, young, near, tall* are vague sentences. A common feature of the above predicates seems to be the fact that they admit *borderline cases*, that make it not an easy matter to decide whether the sentences where they appear are either true or false. In our opinion the claim that every sentence has a truth-value (true or false) is a too strong claim indeed. Similarly for the claim that our inability to assign some truth-value (*true* or *false*) to some sentence must be a matter of *ignorance*, even when we happen to know the exact number of hair in a man's head, somebody's exact age and so on.

An important point in the defense of classical logic as the only tool for formalizing reasoning is usually that it is a very powerful tool. This is certainly true, but it is not a

[1]With partially support by Spanish MICINN projects FFI2008-03126-E/FILO (Eurocores-LogICCC Project LoMoReVI FP006), Consolider project AT (CSD2007-022), and ARINF TIN2009-14704-C03-03; by the Generalitat de Catalunya grant 2009-SGR-1434; and CSIC grant JAE Predoc 074. The authors wish to thank the two anonymous reviewers, Lluís Godo and Ondrej Majer for their helpful comments.

reason not to use, in some contexts, more refined tools: a chainsaw is a very powerful cutting tool, but this does not mean that somebody uses one to cut his nails.

On the other hand, t-norm based many-valued semantics is a robust and enough refining tool to handle vague propositions for several reasons. We report some of them:

1. It is simple and mathematically formalizable and this makes it suitable to be used in practical applications.

2. It does not presuppose ignorance, like epistemic theories on vagueness do, even when we have complete knowledge of the object under observation.

3. It gives an elegant solution to the famous Sorites paradox (see [7]) and this, for a theory, is a necessary condition to be a theory about vagueness.

4. Sentences that in other theories are considered as borderline cases can be handled like every other sentence.

In our context, then, vague sentences will be handled as many-valued sentences so we accept that there are sentences that can be neither (totally) true nor (totally) false.

As can be already seen from the classical definition of counterfactual, the antecedent of a counterfactual is false and not true at the same time. In a many-valued context where sentences can take intermediate values between true (1) and false (0), in contrast, a sentence can be not totally true (< 1) without being totally false (0). For this reason we prefer to generalize the definition of a counterfactual and define it as a conditional sentence whose antecedent is not 1-true. The present paper is an investigation on the consequences of this assumption with the aim of providing a semantics for vague counterfactuals.

As we will see later on, one immediate consequence of this new definition is a plurality of choices among possible definitions of truth-conditions for sentences like *If I were rich, I would be happy*. The requirement that the antecedent is not 1-true in the actual world forces us to choose among different sets of worlds where the antecedent is true enough to trigger counterfactual reasoning. This plurality of choices gives rise to different semantics depending on whether we demand that the antecedent is absolutely true (i.e. it has truth value 1) or relatively true (i.e. it has truth value >0) in other possible worlds (where, again, this antecedent must be more true than it actually is).

In the literature, the study of counterfactuals falls within the more general area of non-monotonic reasoning. Among related work, counterfactuals have been approached from distinct perspectives: uncertainty (see [10] for a probabilistic approach) and similarity (see [6]), but as far as we know, the present approach is the first study on counterfactuals from a fuzzy reasoning perspective. A main difference with the referred papers is that we focus on counterfactuals involving many-valued propositions, instead of just two-valued (or crisp) propositions.

The paper is structured as follows. In preliminary Section 2, we recall basic notions of Lewis' possible world semantics as well as the many-valued semantics based on the prominent t-norms: Łukasiewicz, Gödel and Product, with truth-values in the real unit interval $[0, 1]$. In Section 3, we introduce vague counterfactuals and discuss general issues about them. We also present the basic language we will make use of.

The next sections introduce the different semantics for counterfactuals according to the three basic t-norms, as well as reducibility results among these semantics (within each basic t-norm) and interdefinability results in the Łukasiewicz case. In Section 4, we define a direct generalization of Lewis' semantics to the many-valued case, where antecedents are required to be 1-true, i.e. true to degree 1 within the real unit interval of truth-values $[0, 1]$ generalizing the set $\{0, 1\}$ for *false* and *true* in classical logic.

Then in Section 5 we consider a more general semantics requiring the weaker condition that the truth-value of the antecedent attains a fixed truth-degree higher than the actual one (its truth-value in our actual world). Finally, we present in Section 6 what we call *more than actual* semantics, requiring that the antecedent attains an arbitrary value higher than the actual one.

After these semantic results, we show in Section 7 the consequences of expanding the language with Baaz' projection operator Δ and truth-constants for degrees of truth (introduced in [1] and [9, 2, 3], respectively). In particular, we prove that these expansions may endow some semantics with the expressive power of any member of a more general class of semantics, of which the former is a particular instance. These results may be used to simplify the truth-conditions given by any semantics in the latter class.

2 Preliminaries

In this preliminary section, we introduce classical counterfactuals and t-norm based semantics for propositional fuzzy logics.

2.1 Counterfactuals and Lewis' semantics

As commonly understood in the literature, *counterfactuals* (like: if it were the case that φ it would be the case that ψ) are conditional sentences whose antecedent is assumed to be false. In contrast with classical material implication, where a false antecedent makes the implication vacuously true, a counterfactual with an actually false antecedent can still be false. Hence, material implication cannot model reasoning about how things would be like if the world was different.

The need to establish a semantics for counterfactual conditionals arises from the fact that there are contingent sentences. These are sentences that, though they might be actually false, they do not express impossible or contradictory facts. As such, we can think of a state of affairs, not much different from the actual one, where such sentences are contingently true. This can be done because their truth would not violate too much fundamental laws valid in the actual world. When these contingent sentences occur as antecedents (or consequents) of some material implication, their contingency makes the implication contingent as well. However, we may want to capture the intuitive correctness of conditional sentences between contingent facts: for instance, *If there were no carbon on Earth, there would be no life either.* The truth of this counterfactual is not established by their actual truth-values. But it can indeed be established on the basis of other considerations.

Two forms of counterfactuals occur as expressions in the natural language, here called *would-* and *might*-counterfactuals:

- would-counterfactuals: *if it were the case that* φ, *it would be the case that* ψ; this form expresses a necessity statement concerning any relevant world where φ is true; for the counterfactual to be true, ψ must hold at all these worlds.

- might-counterfactuals: *if it were the case that* φ, *it might be the case that* ψ; this is a possibility statement concerning relevant worlds where φ is true; a single such world making ψ true will account for this possibility thus making this counterfactual true.

One of the main attempts to provide a semantics for the truth-conditions of a counterfactual conditional has been David Lewis' [8]. In order to give a semantics for counterfactuals, Lewis imagines that we can think about *possible worlds*.[2] The possibility of talking about possible worlds arises from the fact that we can represent our world by means of contingent sentences which express facts surrounding us: "the sky is blue", "water is composed of oxygen and hydrogen" are examples of such sentences. A possible world is a consistent set of facts or propositions (also called a state of affairs), possibly with some of these facts not holding in our world (i.e. with sentences expressing these propositions being actually false). Mathematical or logical truths do not express contingent propositions (they hold across possible worlds -no matter how much different they are from our world), and hence these are not seen as expressing propositions that constitute possible worlds. We will denote the set of propositions that are believed to hold in our world by the expression *actual world*, while every other maximally consistent set of propositions will be considered as a possible world. The set of possible worlds will be denoted by W. The elements of W can be distributed into subsets of worlds which are more or less similar with respect to the world selected as the actual world. Lewis suggests to organize the set of possible worlds into *spheres*, or subsets of W. These spheres are totally ordered by inclusion, with outer spheres containing inner spheres. The actual world is located at the innermost sphere, also called the center. Outer spheres contain inner spheres plus those worlds that are different enough (w.r.t. the actual world) to be located in these inner spheres. This gives an account of the difference of possible worlds with respect to the actual world.

The definitions in this subsection are taken from Lewis [8].

DEFINITION 1 *A* system of spheres *on the set of possible worlds W, denoted by $, is a subset of the power set of W which is totally ordered by inclusion, closed under arbitrary unions and non-empty intersections.*

It is possible to define several kinds of systems of spheres. In particular, Lewis considers the following additional properties of systems of spheres:

- *universal*: for every $w \in W$, there exists $S \in \$$ such that $w \in S$; i.e. every possible world is at least in one sphere. Equivalently, $\bigcup \$ = W$.

---

[2]Actually Lewis maintains that possible worlds do exist, but a long and tedious philosophical debate would be needed to define the meaning of the word *exist* in this context. We only will maintain that we can think about possible worlds and can use such idea for reasoning about counterfactuals or similar notions: in fact, conditional reasoning does not need the *real* existence of objects called "possible worlds".

- *centered*: there exists $w \in W$ such that $\{w\} = \bigcap\{S \in \$\}$; i.e. there is a unique world in the inner sphere. We will denote such a system by $\$^w$.

Intuitively, the elements of inner spheres are worlds not much different from the world(s) lying on the center of that system, while the elements of the outer spheres can be very different from the world(s) at the center.

The truth-value of a counterfactual in a system of spheres is defined in terms of the truth conditions of the formulas occurring in it. Boolean formulas are evaluated in a given world (taken as a propositional evaluation) in the usual way.

DEFINITION 2 *Consider the language* $L = \{\top, \bot, \neg, \wedge, \rightarrow\}$ *and the set* $\mathrm{Fm}(L)$:

$$\mathrm{Fm}(L) \quad := \quad \mathrm{Var} \cup \{\top, \bot\} \quad | \quad \neg\varphi \quad | \quad \varphi \wedge \psi \quad | \quad \varphi \rightarrow \psi$$

Let W *be a set of worlds* w. *For each* w, *we define a* propositional evaluation e_w *as a homomorphism* $e_w \colon \mathrm{Var} \rightarrow \{0,1\}$, *which assigns value 1 to each* $p \in \mathrm{Var}$ *iff* p *is true in world* w. *As usual,* e_w *can be inductively extended to every formula in* $\mathrm{Fm}(L)$. *We define the set of possible worlds satisfying* φ, *called* φ-worlds,

$$
\begin{array}{rcl}
[\top] & = & W \\
[\bot] & = & \emptyset \\
[p] & = & \{w \in W \mid e_w(p) = 1\}, \textit{ for each } p \in \mathrm{Var} \\
[\varphi \wedge \psi] & = & [\varphi] \cap [\psi] \\
[\varphi \rightarrow \psi] & = & (W \smallsetminus [\varphi]) \cup [\psi] \\
[\neg\varphi] & = & W \smallsetminus [\varphi]
\end{array}
$$

The two former definitions are related by the equivalence: $e_w(\varphi) = 1 \iff w \in [\varphi]$. *We will consider the binary connective* $\equiv$ *as a connective defined by:*

$$\varphi \equiv \psi \quad := \quad (\varphi \rightarrow \psi) \wedge (\psi \rightarrow \varphi)$$

With such a semantics and notion of system of spheres, Lewis proceeds to define the truth conditions for counterfactuals as follows:

DEFINITION 3 *Consider the language* $L_{\square\rightarrow} = \{\top, \bot, \neg, \wedge, \rightarrow, \square\rightarrow, \diamond\rightarrow\}$ *and the set* $\mathrm{Fm}(L_{\square\rightarrow})$:

$$\mathrm{Fm}(L) \quad := \quad \mathrm{Fm}(L) \quad | \quad \varphi \square\rightarrow \psi \quad | \quad \varphi \diamond\rightarrow \psi$$

A would counterfactual $\varphi \square\rightarrow \psi$ *is true at world* w *(according to system* $\$$) *iff either*

(1) no φ-world belongs to any sphere $S \in \$$, or

(2) some sphere $S \in \$$ does contain at least one φ-world, and $\varphi \rightarrow \psi$ holds at every world in S.

A might counterfactual $\varphi \diamond\rightarrow \psi$ *is true at world* w *(according to system* $\$$) *iff both*

(1) some φ-world belongs to some sphere $S \in \$$, and

(2) every sphere $S \in \$$ that contains at least one φ-world contains at least one world where $\varphi \wedge \psi$ holds.

In this paper we will assume that systems of spheres are universal and centered. We will denote by $\$^w$ the system of spheres centered on the world w. Moreover, our actual world will be denoted by $w^\star$. Another possibility discussed by Lewis is that the intersection of a set of spheres is empty. This is the case when there is a non-well-founded decreasing sequence of spheres whose intersection is not an element of the sequence. Even if this case is not often found in the classical framework, Lewis proposes a new condition to exclude it. The *Limit Assumption* stipulates that, if a φ-world exists, then there always exists a closest sphere $S \in \$$ containing a φ-world, for any $\varphi \in \mathrm{Fm}(L_{\square\to})$. In order to apply this assumption to the many-valued case, we present it in a more general form: If some sphere in $\$$ exists with some property P, then there exists a sphere $S \in \$$ having P such that for each other $S' \in \$$ having P, $S \subseteq S'$.

Indeed, in Definition 3 below, Lewis avoids relying on the Limit Assumption, that he considers somehow unnatural. But the cost of this move is to renounce to define a counterfactual as a conditional proposition that is true in the *closest* φ-sphere. Lewis presents another semantics to recover this notion of closest sphere (based on *selection functions*), though these produce unintuitive truth values for counterfactuals when the Limit Assumption fails (see p. 58 of [8]). In contrast, the semantics based on the notion of closest sphere (with the Limit Assumption) seems to be the most intuitive way to solve this issues, since it captures the idea of evaluating a counterfactual in the most similar worlds.

Finally consider counterfactuals nested in other counterfactual: *If it were the case that φ, then if it were the case that ψ then χ would be the case.* In the end, this composite counterfactual is evaluated w.r.t. the actual world, while the inner counterfactual, *If it were the case that ψ then χ would be the case*, is evaluated w.r.t. some φ-world(s). Thus, composite counterfactuals require different systems of spheres centered on different worlds, defined on the same universe W (and w.r.t. a fixed similarity relation among worlds). See Figure 1 for an illustration.

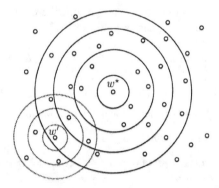

Figure 1. The semantics of counterfactual $\psi \,\square\!\!\to\, \chi$, nested in $\varphi \,\square\!\!\to\, (\psi \,\square\!\!\to\, \chi)$, takes place in each closest φ-world, e.g. in w'.

Despite Lewis directly takes $\square\!\!\to$ as primitive, defines $\diamond\!\!\to$ from the former and negation, interdefinability can be proved from Definition 3.

LEMMA 4 ([8]) *Let* φ, ψ *be formulas, then the following formulas are tautologies:*

$$\varphi \mathbin{\square\!\!\rightarrow} \psi \;=\; \neg(\varphi \mathbin{\diamondsuit\!\!\rightarrow} \neg\psi)$$

$$\varphi \mathbin{\diamondsuit\!\!\rightarrow} \psi \;=\; \neg(\varphi \mathbin{\square\!\!\rightarrow} \neg\psi)$$

Next we prove an equivalent characterization of the truth-conditions in Definition 3, suggested by Lewis (without proof). This is used later on to show that classical counterfactuals are a particular case of many-valued ones.

LEMMA 5 *Let W be a set of possible worlds with $w \in W$, and $\$$ a system of spheres satisfying the Limit Assumption. Then:*

(a) *A counterfactual $\varphi \mathbin{\square\!\!\rightarrow} \psi$ is true in world w, iff either $[\varphi] = \emptyset$ or $w' \models \psi$, for every $w' \in [\varphi] \cap \bigcap\{S \in \$^w \mid S \cap [\varphi] \neq \emptyset\}$.*

(b) *A counterfactual $\varphi \mathbin{\diamondsuit\!\!\rightarrow} \psi$ is true in world w, iff both $[\varphi] \neq \emptyset$ and $w' \models \psi$, for some $w' \in [\varphi] \cap \bigcap\{S \in \$^w \mid S \cap [\varphi] \neq \emptyset\}$.*

Proof To prove the right-to-left implication of (a) suppose that $\varphi \mathbin{\square\!\!\rightarrow} \psi$ is true in w. Then, by Definition 3, it holds either that (1) no φ-world belongs to any sphere $S \in \$$, or (2) some sphere $S \in \$$ does contain at least one φ-world, and $\varphi \rightarrow \psi$ holds at every world in S. The former (1) implies clause $[\varphi] = \emptyset$ and we are done. In case (2), let S' be a sphere (i) containing a φ-world and (ii) making $\varphi \rightarrow \psi$ true everywhere in S'. Since spheres are ordered by inclusion, by the Limit Assumption there exists a sphere S^* such that (i) $S^* \cap [\varphi] \neq \emptyset$, (ii) $S^* \subseteq [\varphi \rightarrow \psi]$ and (iii) S^* is $\subseteq$-minimal w.r.t. (i) and (ii). Now observe that $S^* = \bigcap\{S \in \$ \mid [\varphi] \cap S \neq \emptyset\}$:

($\subseteq$) Let S be such that (i) $[\varphi] \cap S \neq \emptyset$. Note that it cannot be the case that $S \subsetneq S^*$, because otherwise $S \subseteq S^* \subseteq [\varphi \rightarrow \psi]$, since S contains a φ-world and this is jointly incompatible with $\subseteq$-minimality of S^* w.r.t. (i) and (ii).

($\supseteq$) Let $w \in \bigcap\{S \in \$ \mid [\varphi] \cap S \neq \emptyset\}$. For any S'' with (i), (ii) and (iii) above, we have $S'' \in \{S \in \$ \mid [\varphi] \cap S \neq \emptyset\}$. In particular $S^* \in \{S \in \$ \mid [\varphi] \cap S \neq \emptyset\}$, so that $w \in S^*$.

Now, let $w' \in [\varphi] \cap S^*$. Since, by definition, $S^* \subseteq [\varphi \rightarrow \psi]$, we have $w' \in [\varphi] \cap [\varphi \rightarrow \psi]$. By modus ponens, $w' \in [\psi]$. Thus, it holds that, for every $w' \in [\varphi] \cap \bigcap\{S \in \$^w \mid S \cap [\varphi] \neq \emptyset\}$, we have $w' \models \psi$.

To prove the converse implication of (a) assume that, for every w', $w' \models \psi$ is implied by $w' \in [\varphi] \cap \bigcap\{S \in \$ \mid S \cap [\varphi] \neq \emptyset\}$ (since the assumption that $[\varphi] = \emptyset$ trivially implies the claim). Let $S^* = \bigcap\{S \in \$ \mid S \cap [\varphi] \neq \emptyset\}$. By the Limit Assumption, we have S^* is a sphere. Let $w \in S^*$. If, on the one hand, $w \in [\varphi]$, then by assumption $w \in [\psi]$ so that $w \in [\varphi \rightarrow \psi]$. If, on the other hand, $w \notin [\varphi]$. Then trivially $w \in [\varphi \rightarrow \psi]$. In either case, we have both $S^* \cap [\varphi] \neq \emptyset$ and $S^* \subseteq [\varphi \rightarrow \psi]$, so we are done.

For (b), we have $\varphi \mathbin{\diamondsuit\!\!\rightarrow} \psi$ is true at w iff $\neg(\varphi \mathbin{\rightarrow\square\!\!\rightarrow} \neg\psi)$ is true at w (by Lemma 4). This is equivalent to: it is not the case that either $[\varphi] = \emptyset$ or $w' \models \neg\psi$, for every $w' \in [\varphi] \cap \bigcap\{S \in \$^w \mid S \cap [\varphi] \neq \emptyset\}$. Thus, in other words, both $[\varphi] \neq \emptyset$ and for some $w' \in [\varphi] \cap \bigcap\{S \in \$^w \mid S \cap [\varphi] \neq \emptyset\}$ we have $w' \notin [\neg\psi]$. Therefore we know that $w' \in [\psi]$ for some $w' \in [\varphi] \cap \bigcap\{S \in \$^w \mid S \cap [\varphi] \neq \emptyset\}$, and so the proof is done. $\square$

Informally, this characterization reads as follows. A counterfactual $\varphi \mathbin{\Box\!\!\rightarrow} \psi$ is true in w iff either φ is false in every world in W, or ψ is true in every φ-world lying in the closest sphere containing a φ-world. A $\varphi \mathbin{\Diamond\!\!\rightarrow} \psi$ counterfactual is true in w iff both φ is true in some world in W and ψ is true in some φ-world lying in the closest sphere containing a φ-world.

Lewis refuses the idea that a possible world is merely a propositional evaluation of sentences, as in the tradition of frame-based semantics for Modal Logic. Nevertheless, he makes use of such notion of possible world when he defines the syntactical calculus of counterfactuals. Since our approach is more a formal than a philosophical one, we will consider a possible world to be just a propositional evaluation of sentences. As we will see, in our case sentences need not be evaluated simply as true or false, but they can take intermediate values.

2.2 Vague sentences and Fuzzy Logic

During the last century there has been a great deal of work in the field of *Propositional Fuzzy Logics*, which are suitable to model reasoning with vague propositions (see Fermüller [4] for an overview of other formalisms). We give below a brief account of such logics (see [7] for details).

We consider a *vague sentence* as a sentence that, by the nature of its meaning, cannot be understood as merely true or false. As an example, if we fix that a tall man is a man whose height is greater or equal to 1.80m̃, we cannot consider a man who is 1.79 m tall as a short man, even if he is not tall. This is related to the well-known Sorites paradox. A way to overcome this paradox is to consider *fuzzy sets*.

As defined in [11] by L.A. Zadeh, a fuzzy set C is a set whose characteristic function,[3] χ_C is a function which returns a real value between 0 and 1, i.e. $\chi_C(a) \in [0,1]$. Intuitively, if C is the set of tall men and a is a man who is 1.79 m tall, then $\chi_C(a) = 0.98$.

The last example shows that, in contrast to classical frameworks where *false* and *not true* are equivalent, the distinction between these two notions becomes fundamental in many-valued frameworks. In the context of predicate sentences, i.e. sentences of the form a is C, we can directly adapt the tool of fuzzy sets to give a value (between 0 and 1) to *a being an element of C*. We can also consider the sentence "*a* is C" as a whole propositional sentence p, and say that its value lies between 0 and 1. The former approach is known as predicate or first order calculus and the latter approach, propositional calculus. Following the literature on counterfactuals, we will follow the approach which considers atomic propositions as the minimal language entities.

Giving a sentence a propositional value, however, is not a trivial issue: it often depends on the meanings of the predicate and the individuals occurring in it. In the context of natural language, the same predicate, say *high*, may ask for the use of different systems of reference, e.g. depending on whether we want to talk about a high mountain or a high skyscraper. In the former case, we can fix that the membership of a mountain to the set of high mountains has value 1 if the mountain height is greater than or equal to 6000 m, it has value 0 if its height is less or equal to 2000 m, and it has a value between 0 and 1 if its height falls between the given values. In the latter case, we can fix that the

---

[3] In the classical framework, a *characteristic function* of set C is a function χ_C such that for an individual a, $\chi_C(a) = 1$ if $a \in C$ and $\chi_C(a) = 0$ otherwise.

membership of a skyscraper to the set of high skyscrapers has value 1, if its height is greater or equal to 150 m, has value 0, if its height is less or equal to 60 m, and a value between 0 and 1, if its height falls between the given values.

DEFINITION 6 *A t-norm is a binary operation* $*\colon [0,1]^2 \to [0,1]$ *such that:*

1. $*$ *is commutative and associative,*

2. $*$ *is non-decreasing in both arguments,*

3. *for every* $x \in [0,1]$, *it holds that* $1*x = x$.

If, $*$ *is a continuous mapping from* $[0,1]^2$ *to* $[0,1]$, *we talk about a* continuous *t-norm.*

A t-norm is normally understood as the function giving the truth value of conjunction in a propositional calculus. The basic examples of continuous t-norms are:

1. *Łukasiewicz t*-norm (denoted by Ł), defined by: $x*y = max(0, x+y-1)$,

2. *Gödel t*-norm (denoted by G), defined by: $x*y = min(x,y)$,

3. *Product t*-norm (denoted by Π), defined by: $x*y = x \cdot y$.

Given a continuous t-norm $*$, we can define its residuum (i.e. the function which gives the semantics for the implication):

DEFINITION 7 *Let* $*$ *be a continuous t-norm, then its residuum is a binary operation* $\Rightarrow_*\colon [0,1]^2 \to [0,1]$ *such that, for every* $x,y \in [0,1]$:

$$x \Rightarrow_* y = \sup \{z \in [0,1] \mid x*z \leq y\}$$

Now we define the logic of some continuous t-norm over a propositional language.

DEFINITION 8 *Let* $*$ *be continuous t-norm. The language of a propositional t-norm based logic,* $\mathrm{Fm}(L_*)$ *is defined as follows. Given a countable set* Var *of propositional variables and the connectives in* $\{\bot, \wedge_*, \to_*\}$, *the set* Fm *of formulas is defined as*

$$\mathrm{Fm}(L_*) \quad = \quad \mathrm{Var} \cup \{\bot\} \mid \varphi \wedge_* \psi \mid \varphi \to_* \psi$$

where φ *and* ψ *are formulas.*

We will consider the binary connective $\equiv_*$ *as a connective defined by:*

$$\varphi \equiv_* \psi \quad := \quad (\varphi \to_* \psi) \wedge_* (\psi \to_* \varphi)$$

REMARK 9 *Negation is defined within the language as*

$$\neg \varphi = \varphi \to_* \bot$$

A negation $\neg$ *is* involutive *iff* $\neg\neg\varphi \to \varphi$ *is valid. Among the three basic t-norm based logics, the only logic having an involutive negation is Łukasiewicz logic.*

Under a syntactical point of view, there is a set of axioms[4] for each of the basic continuous t-norms. A t-norm based propositional fuzzy logic is defined as usual:

---

[4]For reasons of space, we do not report here the set of axioms proper of each t-norm based propositional fuzzy logic. The axiomatization of the logics based on the three basic continuous t-norms can be found in [7].

DEFINITION 10 *Let* $* \in \{Ł, G, \Pi\}$, *a* $*$-*based propositional fuzzy logic (denoted by* L_*) *is the least set of formulas which includes the axioms of such logic and is closed under Modus Ponens.*

The *evaluation* of a formula is also defined as usual:

DEFINITION 11 *Let* $*$ *be a t-norm with* $* \in \{Ł, G, \Pi\}$ *and let* φ, ψ *formulas in* $\mathrm{Fm}(L_*)$. *The* propositional evaluation *is a mapping* $e : \mathrm{Var} \to [0,1]$ *defined inductively as follows:*

- $e(\perp) = 0$,

- $e(\top) = 1$,

- $e(\varphi \wedge_* \psi) = e(\varphi) * e(\psi)$,

- $e(\varphi \to_* \psi) = e(\varphi) \Rightarrow_* e(\psi)$.

REMARK 12 *According to the definition of negation (Remark 9) the semantics of negation in each basic t-norm based logic is computed as follows:*

For Łukasiewicz logic,[5] *we have* $e(\neg_Ł \varphi) = 1 - e(\varphi)$

For Gödel and Product logics, we have $e(\neg_G \varphi) = e(\neg_\Pi \varphi) = \begin{cases} 1 & \text{if } e(\varphi) = 0, \\ 0 & \text{otherwise} \end{cases}$

In [7], completeness results are provided for each of these basic propositional calculus w.r.t. the corresponding semantics.

3   Vague counterfactuals

By a *vague counterfactual* we understand a counterfactual involving vague sentences, i.e. sentences that are not merely true or false, but are evaluated in $[0,1]$. Actually, the fact that the involved sentences are evaluated in $[0,1]$ implies that the counterfactual, as a formula, is evaluated in $[0,1]$ as well.

The most widely accepted definition of a (classical) counterfactual is that of a conditional with an actually false antecedent. While in the classical framework there is no difference between *false* and *non-true* antecedents, in a many-valued framework non-true is not necessarily false but it can take another value < 1. For example, by sentence: "If a were tall, a would reach the roof", we mean that, within the actual world, individual a is not tall in degree 1. Though this does not mean that a is tall in degree 0, because we can think that a is not tall without thinking that a is short. In this case, we have different choices (now excluding the trivial case where the antecedent nowhere holds):

- the simplest case is to require that the antecedent takes value one (what we call 1-semantics, see Section 4 below),

- more generally, we may consider the value of the antecedent to be at least r, for some r higher than the actual value of the antecedent (called ($\geq r$)-semantics, see Section 5).

---

[5] Note that this negation turns out to be involutive, because $e(\neg \neg \varphi) = 1 - (1 - e(\varphi)) = e(\varphi)$.

A different approach is needed for sentences like: "If Prague was nearer, I could have arrived by feet". Now the antecedent must indeed be false (i.e. its evaluation, within the actual world, will be 0), since Prague cannot (in the actual world) be nearer than it is. In this case, we can look at possible worlds where the antecedent has an arbitrary value > 0. In this case we can

- look at possible worlds where the antecedent takes a value higher than in the actual world (see Section 6 below).

Clearly the worlds where it assumes the maximum value will be a subset of this set of worlds.

Before going on with a formalization of such truth conditions, it must be pointed out that such a semantics do not perfectly fit in with the framework of each basic t-norm based connective. Indeed we will devote more efforts to explain the case of the Łukasiewicz t-norm, because negation, in the other basic t-norms, presents some shortcomings w.r.t. interdefinability for counterfactual connectives and negated antecedents. We extend the propositional language Fm of a given t-norm based logic L_* with symbols for counterfactual connectives $\Box\!\!\to_*, \Diamond\!\!\to_*$.

DEFINITION 13 *Let $*$ be a basic t-norm. We define the language for vague counterfactuals $L_{\Box\!\!\to_*}$ as the least set of sentences containing $\mathrm{Fm}(L_*)$ and all the expressions of the form $\varphi \Box\!\!\to_* \psi$ and $\varphi \Diamond\!\!\to_* \psi$, where $\varphi, \psi \in \mathrm{Fm}(L_{\Box\!\!\to_*})$:*

$$\mathrm{Fm}(L_{\Box\!\!\to_*}) \quad = \quad \mathrm{Fm}(L_*) \mid \varphi \Box\!\!\to_* \psi \mid \varphi \Diamond\!\!\to_* \psi$$

We will consider vague counterfactuals as counterfactuals involving vague sentences in the language of some t-norm based logic L_*. So we proceed to define a semantics where the truth of the counterfactual $\varphi \Box\!\!\to_* \psi$ depends on the truth of the non-modal implication $\varphi \to_* \psi$ in the appropriate possible worlds, where now the implication admits values between 0 and 1.

We present first a direct generalization of Lewis' proposal to the fuzzy case, where we only consider worlds making the antecedent 1-true. We prove that the classical semantics is a particular case of the many-valued one. The scope of this semantics, though, is restrictive with respect to the use of vague counterfactuals in the natural language. The reason is that it ignores the case where the truth-value of the antecedent could be greater than in the actual world, but not being 1-true. For all these semantics, interdefinability results for *would* and *might* counterfactuals are proved for the case of Łukasiewicz logic.

4   1-semantics for vague counterfactuals

In the classical case considered by Lewis, any formula can only be either true or false. This is true as well for two-valued counterfactuals $\varphi \Box\!\!\to \psi$ in a given world w. Moreover, by definition of counterfactual, the antecedent φ must be false in the actual world. According to the theory of counterfactuals, we must then evaluate ψ in every closest world where the value of φ is different than its value in the actual world. In the classical case, such a difference necessarily yields the value *true*. Thus, in the classical case, the maximum change in the value of φ is already attained in the closest sphere where this

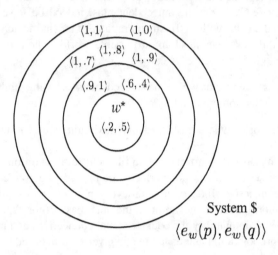

Figure 2. System of spheres from Example 16.

value changes. Outer spheres may contain worlds where many other things change, but
the value of φ will be either the actual value (i.e. false) or will remain the same than in
the relevant worlds on the closest sphere.

In contrast, as a system of spheres we now consider the set $\mathrm{Mod}(L_{\square\to*})$ of valuations[6] $e_w \colon \mathrm{Var} \to [0,1]$. As we said, the system of spheres is centered on the actual
world $w^\star$ i.e. $\{e_{w^\star}\} \subseteq S$, for any $S \in \$$. So, in outer spheres, the antecedent of a coun-
terfactual may have a value different both than that in the actual world and that in the
closest sphere where its value changes.

The semantics for non-counterfactual connectives is as usual. Before we define
the semantics for counterfactual connectives we recall a well-known result relating in-
fima and suprema (inf and sup) when the internal negation is involutive (that is, in
Łukasiewicz logic). This auxiliary lemma is extensively used later on for several interdefinability results between *would* and *might* counterfactuals.

LEMMA 14 *Let $X \subseteq [0,1]$ be a set of values. Then*

$$1 - \inf(X) = \sup(1 - X) \quad and \quad 1 - \sup(X) = \inf(1 - X)$$

where $1 - X = \{1 - x \mid x \in X\}$.

We define first a simple generalization of the semantics for the classical case, now
defining φ-worlds as worlds w where φ is 1-true: $e_w(\varphi) = 1$. The other semantics will
consider instead φ-worlds to be defined by some weaker condition, e.g. $e_w(\varphi) \geq r$ (for
some chosen value $r \in [0,1]$).

---

[6]We will use indistinctively the possible-world notation w and the algebraic one e_w.

DEFINITION 15 *Let $*$ be a basic t-norm and φ a formula. Let*

$$\mathbb{K}^1_\varphi = \{w' \in W \mid e_{w'}(\varphi) = 1 \text{ and } w' \in \bigcap\{S \in \$ \mid \exists w'' \in S \text{ such that } e_{w''}(\varphi) = 1\}\}$$

Then the 1-semantics of would and might counterfactuals $\varphi \mathbin{\Box\!\!\rightarrow}_* \psi$ and $\varphi \mathbin{\Diamond\!\!\rightarrow}_* \psi$ is defined by:

$$e^1_w(\varphi \mathbin{\Box\!\!\rightarrow}_* \psi) = \begin{cases} 1, & \text{if } \{w' \mid e_{w'}(\varphi) = 1\} = \emptyset \\ \inf\{e_{w'}(\varphi \rightarrow_* \psi) \mid w' \in \mathbb{K}^1_\varphi\} & \text{otherwise} \end{cases}$$

$$e^1_w(\varphi \mathbin{\Diamond\!\!\rightarrow}_* \psi) = \begin{cases} 0, & \text{if } \{w' \mid e_{w'}(\varphi) = 1\} = \emptyset \\ \sup\{e_{w'}(\varphi \wedge_* \psi) \mid w' \in \mathbb{K}^1_\varphi\} & \text{otherwise} \end{cases}$$

We assume, as a convention that, whenever $\{w' \in W \mid e_{w'}(\varphi) = 1\} \neq \emptyset$ and $\bigcap\{S \in \$ \mid \exists w'' \in S \text{ such that } e_{w''}(\varphi) = 1\} = \emptyset$, the value of the counterfactual is undefined.

In cases where there is no φ-world, we take the counterfactual to be *vacuously true*. If we assume Lewis' Limit Assumption, the value of any counterfactual is always defined. Recall that we consider only systems of spheres that satisfy the Limit Assumption.

EXAMPLE 16 *Let $*$ be any basic t-norm. Let $p = $ I am rich and $q = $ I am happy. Consider the system of spheres $\$$ from Figure 2. We identify each world w with a pair of truth-values $\langle e_w(p), e_w(q) \rangle$. For example, the actual world $w^\star$ is such that I am rather not rich but moderately happy. The 1-semantics for the would counterfactual $p \mathbin{\Box\!\!\rightarrow}_* q$, i.e. If I were rich, I would be happy, considers worlds in the third sphere $S = \{\langle 1, 0.7 \rangle, \langle 1, 0.8 \rangle, \langle 1, 0.9 \rangle\}$, giving*

$$e^1_{w^\star}(p \mathbin{\Box\!\!\rightarrow}_* q) = \inf\{1 \Rightarrow_* 0.7, 1 \Rightarrow_* 0.8, 1 \Rightarrow_* 0.9\} = \inf\{0.7, 0.8, 0.9\} = 0.7,$$

so that this counterfactual is quite true. The same sphere S is where the truth-value for the might counterfactual $p \mathbin{\Diamond\!\!\rightarrow}_* q$ is computed, now giving

$$e^1_{w^\star}(p \mathbin{\Diamond\!\!\rightarrow}_* q) = \sup\{1 \wedge_* 0.7, 1 \wedge_* 0.8, 1 \wedge_* 0.9\} = \sup\{0.7, 0.8, 0.9\} = 0.9,$$

so that If I were rich, I might be happy is highly true.

Restricting the set of truth-values to $\{0, 1\}$ makes our 1-semantics from Definition 15 and Lewis' semantics from Lemma 5 equivalent. In other words, Lewis' semantics for counterfactuals is a particular case of the preceding semantics under the condition that the evaluations are restricted to $\{0, 1\}$ as in classical logic.

PROPOSITION 17 *Let $*$ be a basic t-norm. Let $e^c_w(\cdot)$ denote Lewis' semantics and W a set of classical possible worlds (i.e. $W \subseteq \{e^c_w : \text{Var} \rightarrow \{0, 1\}\}$). For any classical system of spheres $\$$ and any world $w \in W$, the 1-semantics $e^1_w(\cdot)$ definition gives:*

$$e^c_w(\varphi \mathbin{\Box\!\!\rightarrow} \psi) = e^1_w(\varphi \mathbin{\Box\!\!\rightarrow}_* \psi)$$

$$e^c_w(\varphi \mathbin{\Diamond\!\!\rightarrow} \psi) = e^1_w(\varphi \mathbin{\Diamond\!\!\rightarrow}_* \psi)$$

Proof $(\mathbin{\Box\!\!\rightarrow})$ We have $e^c_w(\varphi \mathbin{\Box\!\!\rightarrow} \psi) = 1$ iff either $[\varphi] = \emptyset$ or or $w' \models \psi$, for every $w' \in [\varphi] \cap \bigcap\{S \in \$^w \mid S \cap [\varphi] \neq \emptyset\}$. This is equivalent to the fact that either $\mathbb{K}^1_\varphi = \emptyset$ or the infimum of $e^1_{w'}(\varphi \rightarrow_* \psi)$, for each such world w', is 1. But this is just $e^1_w(\varphi \mathbin{\Box\!\!\rightarrow}_* \psi) = 1$.

($\Diamond\to$)   We have $e_w^c(\varphi \Diamond\to \psi) = 1$ iff both $[\varphi] \neq \emptyset$ and $w' \models \psi$, for some world $w' \in [\varphi] \cap \bigcap \{S \in \$^w \mid S \cap [\varphi] \neq \emptyset\}$. This is equivalent to the fact that both $\mathbb{K}_\varphi^1 \neq \emptyset$ and the supremum of the values of $\varphi \wedge_* \psi$ is 1 in such a sphere, which is the definition of 1-semantics for might counterfactuals; hence, we have that $e_w^c(\varphi \Diamond\to \psi) = 1$ iff $e_w^1(\varphi \Diamond\to_* \psi) = 1$.   □

In the particular case of Łukasiewicz, we also have that classical interdefinability of *would* and *might* counterfactuals is preserved.

PROPOSITION 18 *Let W be a set of possible worlds, $w \in W$ and let $\neg_Ł$ be Łukasiewicz negation, then:*

$$e_w^1(\varphi \Diamond\to_Ł \psi) = e_w^1(\neg_Ł(\varphi \Box\to_Ł \neg_Ł \psi))$$
$$e_w^1(\varphi \Box\to_Ł \psi) = e_w^1(\neg_Ł(\varphi \Diamond\to_Ł \neg_Ł \psi))$$

Proof Let $\$$ and $w \in W$ be given, then $e_w^1(\neg_Ł(\varphi \Box\to_Ł \neg_Ł \psi)) =$

$$
\begin{array}{llr}
= & 1 - e_w^1(\varphi \Box\to_Ł \neg_Ł \psi) = & \text{Remark 12} \\
= & 1 - \inf\{e_{w'}^1(\varphi \to_Ł \neg_Ł \psi) \mid w' \in \mathbb{K}_\varphi^1\} = & \text{Definition 15} \\
= & 1 - \inf\{e_{w'}^1(\varphi \to_Ł (\psi \to_Ł \bot)) \mid w' \in \mathbb{K}_\varphi^1\} = & \text{Remark 9} \\
= & 1 - \inf\{e_{w'}^1((\varphi \wedge_Ł \psi) \to_Ł \bot) \mid w' \in \mathbb{K}_\varphi^1\} = & \text{Definition 7} \\
= & 1 - \inf\{e_{w'}^1(\neg_Ł(\varphi \wedge_Ł \psi)) \mid w' \in \mathbb{K}_\varphi^1\} = & \text{Remark 9} \\
= & 1 - \inf\{1 - e_{w'}^1(\varphi \wedge_Ł \psi) \mid w' \in \mathbb{K}_\varphi^1\} = & \text{Remark 12} \\
= & 1 - (1 - \sup\{e_{w'}^1(\varphi \wedge_Ł \psi) \mid w' \in \mathbb{K}_\varphi^1\}) = & \text{Lemma 14} \\
= & \sup\{e_{w'}^1(\varphi \wedge_Ł \psi) \mid w' \in \mathbb{K}_\varphi^1\} = & \text{Double neg. law} \\
= & e_w^1(\varphi \Diamond\to_Ł \psi) & \text{Definition 15}
\end{array}
$$

Hence, by Definition 15, we have exactly the definition of $e_w^1(\varphi \Diamond\to_Ł \psi)$:

$$e_w^1(\neg_Ł(\varphi \Box\to_Ł \neg_Ł \psi)) = \begin{cases} \neg_Ł 1 = 0, & \text{if } \{w' \mid e_{w'}(\varphi) = 1\} = \emptyset \\ \sup\{e_{w'}(\varphi \wedge_Ł \psi) \mid w' \in \mathbb{K}_\varphi^1\}, & \text{otherwise} \end{cases}$$

For the second equivalence it is enough to apply twice the Double Negation law to obtain: $e_w^1(\varphi \Box\to_Ł \psi) = e_w^1(\neg_Ł\neg_Ł(\varphi \Box\to_Ł \neg_Ł\neg_Ł \psi))$, and then by the former equivalence we have $e_w^1(\neg_Ł\neg_Ł (\varphi \Box\to_Ł \neg_Ł\neg_Ł \psi)) = e_w^1(\neg_Ł(\varphi \Diamond\to_Ł \neg_Ł \psi))$.   □

5   *r*-semantics for vague counterfactuals.

Having, in a many-valued framework, truth-values other than 0 and 1, permits us to look at worlds satisfying the antecedent φ of a counterfactual in a fixed degree r, with r lying between the actual truth-value of φ and 1: $e_{w^*}(\varphi) \leq r \leq 1$. (See Figure 3.)

Figure 3. Possible truth-values for antecedent φ in *r*-semantics.

We define next the corresponding semantics, called *r*-semantics, in terms of the set of worlds w with $e_w(\varphi) \geq r$.

DEFINITION 19 *Let $*$ be a basic t-norm and φ a formula. For a given $r > 0$, let*

$$\mathbb{K}_\varphi^r = \{w' \in W \mid e_{w'}(\varphi) \geq r \text{ and } w' \in \bigcap\{S \in \$ \mid \exists w'' \in S \text{ such that } e_{w''}(\varphi) \geq r\}\}$$

Then we define the r-semantics of $\square\!\!\rightarrow$ and $\diamondsuit\!\!\rightarrow$ as follows:

$$e_w^r(\varphi \,\square\!\!\rightarrow_* \psi) = \begin{cases} 1, & \text{if } \{w' \mid e_{w'}(\varphi) \geq r\} = \emptyset \\ \inf\{e_{w'}(\varphi \rightarrow_* \psi) \mid w' \in \mathbb{K}_\varphi^r\}, & \text{otherwise} \end{cases}$$

$$e_w^r(\varphi \,\diamondsuit\!\!\rightarrow_* \psi) = \begin{cases} 0, & \text{if } \{w' \mid e_{w'}(\varphi) \geq r\} = \emptyset \\ \sup\{e_{w'}(\varphi \wedge_* \psi) \mid w' \in \mathbb{K}_\varphi^r\}, & \text{otherwise} \end{cases}$$

We assume, as a convention that, whenever $\{w' \in W \mid e_{w'}(\varphi) \geq r\} \neq \emptyset$ and $\bigcap\{S \in \$ \mid \exists w'' \in S(e_{w''} \text{ such that } \varphi \geq r)\} = \emptyset$, the value of the counterfactual is undefined.

The Limit Assumption on systems of spheres excludes counterintuitive examples, and makes counterfactuals' truth-values always to be defined. The first result for this semantics is that for the particular case $r = 1$, it collapses to the previous 1-semantics.

PROPOSITION 20 *Let $*$ be a basic t-norm. Setting $r = 1$ for a given system of spheres $\$$ and world w, r-semantics collapses to the 1-semantics.*

$$e_w^1(\varphi \,\square\!\!\rightarrow_* \psi) = e_w^{r=1}(\varphi \,\square\!\!\rightarrow_* \psi)$$
$$e_w^1(\varphi \,\diamondsuit\!\!\rightarrow_* \psi) = e_w^{r=1}(\varphi \,\diamondsuit\!\!\rightarrow_* \psi)$$

Proof $(\square\!\!\rightarrow_*)$ Obvious, since the set of worlds in Definition 15 is identical to $\mathbb{K}_\varphi^1$ (because $e_w(\cdot) \geq 1 \iff e_w(\cdot) = 1$). $\qquad\square$

Moreover, in the two-valued case, Proposition 17 above makes Lewis' semantics (Definition 3) a particular case of the r-semantics for $r = 1$.

COROLLARY 21 *Let $*$ be a basic t-norm. Let W a set of classical possible worlds (i.e. $W \subseteq \{e_w^c : \text{Var} \rightarrow \{0, 1\}\}$). For any classical system of spheres $\$$ and any world $w \in W$, the r-semantics $e_w^r(\cdot)$ definition gives:*

$$e_w^c(\varphi \,\square\!\!\rightarrow \psi) = e_w^r(\varphi \,\square\!\!\rightarrow_* \psi) \text{ and } e_w^c(\varphi \,\diamondsuit\!\!\rightarrow \psi) = e_w^r(\varphi \,\diamondsuit\!\!\rightarrow_* \psi)$$

Proof If the evaluation is in $\{0, 1\}$, then the r-semantics reduces to $r = 1$ case. We apply Propositions 20 and 17. $\qquad\square$

Finally we prove that, in the r-semantics, $\square\!\!\rightarrow_*$ and $\diamondsuit\!\!\rightarrow_*$ can also be defined from each other for the Łukasiewicz case: $* = \text{Ł}$.

PROPOSITION 22 *Let W be a set of possible worlds, $w \in W$ and let $\neg_Ł$ be Łukasiewicz negation, then:*

$$e_w^r(\varphi \,\diamondsuit\!\!\rightarrow_Ł \psi) = e_w^r(\neg_Ł(\varphi \,\square\!\!\rightarrow_Ł \neg_Ł \psi))$$
$$e_w^r(\varphi \,\square\!\!\rightarrow_Ł \psi) = e_w^r(\neg_Ł(\varphi \,\diamondsuit\!\!\rightarrow_Ł \neg_Ł \psi))$$

Proof We have the following $e_w^r(\neg_{\text{Ł}}(\varphi \mathbin{\square\!\!\rightarrow}_{\text{Ł}} \neg_{\text{Ł}} \psi)) =$

$$
\begin{aligned}
&= \quad 1 - e_w^r(\varphi \mathbin{\square\!\!\rightarrow}_{\text{Ł}} \neg_{\text{Ł}} \psi) = && \text{Remark 12}\\
&= \quad 1 - \inf\{e_{w'}(\varphi \rightarrow_{\text{Ł}} \neg_{\text{Ł}} \psi) \mid w' \in \mathbb{K}_\varphi^r\} = && \text{Definition 19}\\
&= \quad \sup\{1 - e_{w'}(\varphi \rightarrow_{\text{Ł}} \neg_{\text{Ł}} \psi) \mid w' \in \mathbb{K}_\varphi^r\} = && \text{Lemma 14}\\
&= \quad \sup\{1 - e_{w'}(\varphi \rightarrow_{\text{Ł}} (\psi \rightarrow_{\text{Ł}} \bot)) \mid w' \in \mathbb{K}_\varphi^r\} = && \text{Remark 9}\\
&= \quad \sup\{1 - e_{w'}((\varphi \wedge_{\text{Ł}} \psi) \rightarrow_{\text{Ł}} \bot) \mid w' \in \mathbb{K}_\varphi^r\} = && \text{Definition 7}\\
&= \quad \sup\{1 - e_{w'}(\neg_{\text{Ł}}(\varphi \wedge_{\text{Ł}} \psi)) \mid w' \in \mathbb{K}_\varphi^r\} = && \text{Remark 9}\\
&= \quad \sup\{e_{w'}(\neg_{\text{Ł}} \neg_{\text{Ł}}(\varphi \wedge_{\text{Ł}} \psi)) \mid w' \in \mathbb{K}_\varphi^r\} = && \text{Remark 12}\\
&= \quad \sup\{e_{w'}(\varphi \wedge_{\text{Ł}} \psi) \mid w' \in \mathbb{K}_\varphi^r\} = && \text{Double Neg. Law}\\
&= \quad e_w^r(\varphi \mathbin{\Diamond\!\!\rightarrow}_{\text{Ł}} \psi) && \text{Def. 19}
\end{aligned}
$$

Hence, by Definition 19, we have exactly the definition of $e_w^r(\varphi \mathbin{\Diamond\!\!\rightarrow}_{\text{Ł}} \psi)$:

$$
e_w^r(\neg_{\text{Ł}}(\varphi \mathbin{\square\!\!\rightarrow}_{\text{Ł}} \neg_{\text{Ł}} \psi)) =
\begin{cases}
\neg_{\text{Ł}} 1 = 0, & \text{if } \{w' \mid e_{w'}(\varphi) \geq r\} = \emptyset\\
\sup\{e_{w'}(\varphi \wedge_{\text{Ł}} \psi) \mid w' \in \mathbb{K}_\varphi^r\}, & \text{otherwise}
\end{cases}
$$

The second equivalence is proven applying to the first the double negation law. $\qquad\square$

EXAMPLE 23 *Recall the system* \$ *from Figure 2. As before, let* $p = $ I am rich, $q =$ I am happy *but now we consider the Łukasiewicz t-norm* $*_{\text{Ł}}$ *only. The r-semantics with* $r \geq 0.5$ *is as follows. For the would counterfactual* $p \mathbin{\square\!\!\rightarrow}_{\text{Ł}} q$, If I were rich, I would be happy, *we look at worlds in the second sphere* $S = \{\langle 0.9, 1\rangle, \langle 0.6, 0.4\rangle\}$, *giving*

$$
e_{w^*}^{0.5}(p \mathbin{\square\!\!\rightarrow}_{\text{Ł}} q) = \inf\{0.9 \Rightarrow_{\text{Ł}} 1, 0.6 \Rightarrow_{\text{Ł}} 0.4\} = \inf\{1, 0.8\} = 0.8
$$

so that this counterfactual is very true. The same sphere S *is selected for evaluating the might counterfactual* $p \mathbin{\Diamond\!\!\rightarrow}_{\text{Ł}} q$, *now giving*

$$
e_{w^*}^{0.5}(p \mathbin{\Diamond\!\!\rightarrow}_{\text{Ł}} q) = \sup\{0.9 \wedge_{\text{Ł}} 1, 0.6 \wedge_{\text{Ł}} 0.4\} = \sup\{0.9, 0\} = 0.9
$$

so that If I were rich, I might be happy *is highly true.*

6   More-than-actual semantics

In the previous sections, we presented different semantics for counterfactuals $\varphi \mathbin{\square\!\!\rightarrow}_* \psi$ where relevant worlds assigned φ a fixed value higher than that of the actual world w^*. A weaker, yet perhaps more intuitive, semantics for counterfactuals will consider worlds assigning φ a value that is *minimally* higher than that of w^*. We will call this semantics *more-than-actual* semantics. See Figure 4 for the set of possible truth values for antecedent φ in relevant worlds.

Figure 4. Possible truth-values for antecedent φ in *more-than-actual* semantics.

There is a noticeable difference between the finite-valued case and the infinite-valued one. In the finitely-valued case, say $\{0 = r_0, r_1, \ldots, r_{k-1}, r_k = 1\}$ with $r_m < r_{m+1}$, we could simply set the lower bound r for the value of the antecedent to be *minimally* higher than the actual value: so, if $e_{w^*}(\varphi) = r_m$, then the designed value to be considered should be r_{m+1}. Each such case is a particular instance of the r-semantics considered above. In contrast, if the set of truth-values is dense, the notion of a next-degree does not make sense; so we cannot apply a r-semantics, because there is not any minimal value higher than r and, by definition of counterfactuals, we cannot set $r = e_{w^*}(\varphi)$ either.

In order to capture this notion of more-than-actual semantics, we propose a definition based both on the r-semantics and the notion of limit lim. As usual, $\lim_{x \to c^+} f(x)$ denotes the limit of $f(x)$ as x approaches to c from the right, i.e. as x decreases its value, while remaining strictly greater than c.

DEFINITION 24 *Let* $*$ *be a basic t-norm,* φ, ψ *formulas and r ranges on all values* $> e_w(\varphi)$. *The* more than actual *semantics* $e^*(\cdot)$ *for would and might counterfactuals is:*

$$e_w^*(\varphi \,\Box\!\!\rightarrow_* \psi) \;=\; \lim_{r \to e_w(\varphi)^+} e_w^r(\varphi \,\Box\!\!\rightarrow_* \psi)$$

$$e_w^*(\varphi \,\Diamond\!\!\rightarrow_* \psi) \;=\; \lim_{r \to e_w(\varphi)^+} e_w^r(\varphi \,\Diamond\!\!\rightarrow_* \psi)$$

We have that $e_w^*(\varphi \,\Box\!\!\rightarrow_* \psi)$ *is undefined iff for all $r > e_w(\varphi)$,* $e_w^r(\varphi \,\Box\!\!\rightarrow_* \psi)$ *is undefined.*

It is obvious that the finite-valued case is a particular instance of this definition:

$$e_w^*(\varphi \,\Box\!\!\rightarrow_* \psi) \;=\; e_w^{r_{m+1}}(\varphi \,\Box\!\!\rightarrow_* \psi), \qquad \text{where } r_m = e_w(\varphi)$$

It is interesting to observe the behavior of function $f(r) := e_w^r(\varphi \,\Box\!\!\rightarrow_* \psi)$ in comparison to the actual value of the (non-modal) residuated implication $e_{w^*}(\varphi \to_* \psi)$. We may have examples where the limit of $f(r)$ (for counterfactuals) coincides with that of the implication, and examples where these two values do not coincide:

EXAMPLE 25 *Consider the comparative counterfactual* If I were richer, I would be happy. *We assume a continuous system of spheres, with sphere S_r containing the most similar worlds where I am rich* ($= \varphi$) *in degree r, for any $r > e_{w^*}(\varphi)$. That is, worlds in S_r are minimal w.r.t. changes in propositions other than φ. The distance of worlds in sphere S_r is $r - e_{w^*}(\varphi)$. In the case that a small increase (say less than 1 cent) did not make a difference, the previous semantics gives a function $f(r)$ whose limit coincides with the actual value of the residuated implication $\varphi \to_* \psi$. In this case,* $e_{w^*}^*(p \,\Box\!\!\rightarrow_* q)$ $= e_{w^*}(p \to_* q)$. *See Figure 5 (left). In contrast, consider the following situation: you have \$10, and you want to buy a music CD, which is sold for \$10 plus some (obligatory but arbitrary) tip. Buying this CD would make you happier. The limit of function $f(r)$ does not coincide now with the implication $e_{w^*}(\varphi \to_* \psi)$. See Figure 5 (right).*

As before, we can prove for the Łukasiewicz t-norm that $\Box\!\!\rightarrow_{\text{Ł}}$ and $\Diamond\!\!\rightarrow_{\text{Ł}}$ are interdefinable according to the *more-than-actual*-semantics.

PROPOSITION 26 *Let W be a set of possible worlds, $w \in W$. Then:*

$$e_w^*(\varphi \,\Diamond\!\!\rightarrow_{\text{Ł}} \psi) \;=\; e_w^*(\neg_{\text{Ł}}(\varphi \,\Box\!\!\rightarrow_{\text{Ł}} \neg_{\text{Ł}}\psi))$$

$$e_w^*(\varphi \,\Box\!\!\rightarrow_{\text{Ł}} \psi) \;=\; e_w^*(\neg_{\text{Ł}}(\varphi \,\Diamond\!\!\rightarrow_{\text{Ł}} \neg_{\text{Ł}}\psi))$$

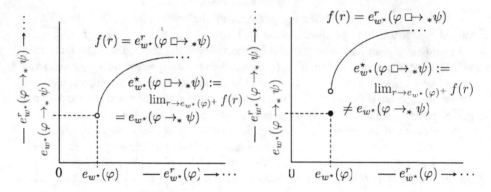

Figure 5. The limit of function $f(r)$ and the actual truth-value of $\varphi \rightarrow_* \psi$ coincide (left) and do not coincide (right). In both graphics, w_r denotes an arbitrary world in sphere S_r.

Proof We show the former claim $e_w^*(\varphi \Diamond\!\!\rightarrow_Ł \psi) = e_w^*(\neg_Ł(\varphi \Box\!\!\rightarrow_Ł \neg_Ł \psi))$, since the proof of the other is analogous. We have $e_w^*(\neg_Ł(\varphi \Box\!\!\rightarrow_Ł \psi)) =$

$$
\begin{aligned}
&= \lim_{r \to e_w(\varphi)^+} e_w^r(\neg_Ł(\varphi \Box\!\!\rightarrow_Ł \neg_Ł \psi)) = && \text{Definition 24} \\
&= \lim_{r \to e_w(\varphi)^+} e_w^r(\varphi \Diamond\!\!\rightarrow_Ł \neg_Ł \psi) = && \text{Proposition 22} \\
&= e_w^*(\varphi \Diamond\!\!\rightarrow_Ł \psi) && \text{Definition 24} \qquad \Box
\end{aligned}
$$

We give some examples of (non-)tautologies for the semantics presented above:

EXAMPLE 27 *For any of the above semantics, and any basic t-norm* $*$, *counterfactuals of the following form are tautologies (in systems* $\$$ *that are universal, centered and satisfying the Limit Assumption):*

$$
\varphi \Box\!\!\rightarrow_* (\psi \rightarrow_* \varphi), \qquad (\varphi \wedge_* \psi) \Box\!\!\rightarrow_* \varphi
$$

In contrast, these expressions are not tautologies for all φ, ψ:

$$
\varphi \Box\!\!\rightarrow_* (\psi \Box\!\!\rightarrow_* \varphi), \qquad \varphi \rightarrow_* (\psi \Box\!\!\rightarrow_* \varphi)
$$

Proof: About the first tautology: this follows from the fact that for any t-norm, any fuzzy model e_w satisfies: $e_w(\varphi \rightarrow_* (\psi \rightarrow_* \varphi)) = 1$. Hence, whatever be $r \in [0, 1]$, and $w \in \mathbb{K}^r$, the r-semantics assigns this counterfactual the value 1. Finally, for the more-than-actual semantics, say $> r = e_{w*}(\varphi)$, we just have the limit of r-semantics is again 1, for any $r' > r$.

The reasoning about the second tautology in similar, using that $(\varphi \wedge_* \psi) \rightarrow_* \varphi$ is a tautology in any model e_w, for an arbitrary t-norm.

For the first non-tautology we show it for Łukasiewicz t-norm and r-semantics with $r = 0.7$. Consider a set of possible worlds W and $w^*, w', w'' \in W$ such that $e_{w*}(\varphi) = 0.3$, $e_{w'}(\varphi) = 0.7$, $e_{w''}(\varphi) = 0.2$, and $e_{w''}(\psi) = 0.7$. Let it be a similarity relation that induces a system of spheres $\$^{w^*}$ in which $e_{w*}(\varphi \Box\!\!\rightarrow_* (\psi \Box\!\!\rightarrow_* \varphi)) = \inf\{e_w(\varphi \rightarrow_* (\psi \Box\!\!\rightarrow_* \varphi)) \mid w \in \mathbb{K}^{0.7}\} = e_{w'}(\varphi \rightarrow_* (\psi \Box\!\!\rightarrow_* \varphi))$ and a system of spheres $\$^{w'}$ in which $e_{w'}(\psi \Box\!\!\rightarrow_* \varphi)$

$= \inf\{e_w(\psi \to_* \varphi)) \mid w \in \mathbb{K}^{0.7}\} = e_{w''}(\psi \to_* \varphi) = 0.5.$ So, $e_{w^*}(\varphi \Box\!\!\to_* (\psi \Box\!\!\to_* \varphi)) = \inf\{e_w(\varphi \to_* (\psi \Box\!\!\to_* \varphi)) \mid w \in \mathbb{K}^{0.7}\} = e_{w'}(\varphi \to_* (\psi \Box\!\!\to_* \varphi)) = 0.7 \Rightarrow_* 0.5 = 0.8 < 1.$

For the second non-tautology we show it for Łukasiewicz t-norm and r-semantics with $r = 0.7$. Consider a set of possible worlds W and $w^*, w' \in W$ such that $e_{w^*}(\varphi) = 0.6$, $e_{w'}(\psi) = 0.8$ and $e_{w'}(\varphi) = 0.1$. Let it be a similarity relation that induces a system of spheres $\$^{w^*}$ in which $e_{w^*}(\psi \Box\!\!\to_* \varphi) = \inf\{e_w(\psi \to_* \varphi) \mid w \in \mathbb{K}^{0.7}\} = e_{w'}(\psi \to_* \varphi) = 0.8 \Rightarrow_* 0.1 = 0.3.$ So, $e_{w^*}(\varphi \to_* (\psi \Box\!\!\to_* \varphi)) = 0.6 \Rightarrow_* e_{w^*}(\psi \Box\!\!\to_* \varphi) = 0.6 \Rightarrow_* 0.3 = 0.7 < 1.$

7 Expanding the language

It is usual in the literature on fuzzy propositional logic, to study expansions of the language by some set of truth-constants or Baaz' operator Δ. In this section we study the expressivity of the language of counterfactuals when expanded in some of these ways. Informally, expanding the language by truth-constants permits to talk about truth-values within formulas, thus making possible to express that some formula is true *at least* (*at most, exactly*) in a certain degree. On the other hand, the Delta operator Δ allows us to distinguish whether a formula is 1-true or not.

7.1 Expanding the language with Δ

The Δ operator was introduced by Baaz in [1]. The semantics for this operator is:

$$e(\Delta\varphi) = \begin{cases} 1 & \text{if } e(\varphi) = 1 \\ 0 & \text{otherwise} \end{cases}$$

For instance, for $e(\varphi) = 0.9$, we have $e(\Delta\varphi) = 0$, while if $e(\varphi) = 1$, then $e(\Delta\varphi) = 1$.

Thus, this operator requires that the formula under its scope is absolutely true. In our context, this operator has the following consequences:

- If Δ is applied to the antecedent of a counterfactual $\varphi \Box\!\!\to_* \psi$, i.e. for $\Delta\varphi \Box\!\!\to_* \psi$, then the r-semantics collapses to the 1-semantics (the latter in a language without Δ).

- If, in addition, Δ is also applied to the consequent, i.e. $\Delta\varphi \Box\!\!\to_* \Delta\psi$, then each of our semantics collapse to the classical case of Lewis (applied to a language with Δ).

These claims are shown by the following propositions:

PROPOSITION 28 *Let $W, w \in W$ and $\$$ be given, and let $*$ be a basic t-norm. For any formulas φ, ψ, and a fixed $r > e_w(\varphi)$,*

$$e_w^r(\Delta\varphi \Box\!\!\to_* \psi) = e_w^1(\varphi \Box\!\!\to_* \psi)$$

Proof We have $e_w^r(\Delta\varphi \Box\!\!\to_* \psi) =$

$\begin{aligned}
&= \inf\{e_{w'}(\Delta\varphi \to_* \psi) \mid w' \in \mathbb{K}_\varphi^r\} = &&\text{Definition 19} \\
&= \inf\{e_{w'}(\Delta\varphi \to_* \psi) \mid w' \in \mathbb{K}_\varphi^1\} = &&\text{since } e_{w'}(\Delta\varphi) \geq r \Leftrightarrow e_{w'}(\Delta\varphi) = 1 \\
&= \inf\{e_{w'}(\varphi \to_* \psi) \mid w' \in \mathbb{K}_\varphi^1\} = &&\text{since } e_{w'}(\Delta\varphi) = 1 \Leftrightarrow e_{w'}(\varphi) = 1 \\
&= e_w^1(\varphi \Box\!\!\to_* \psi) &&\text{Definition 15} \quad\Box
\end{aligned}$

PROPOSITION 29 *Let $e_w^c(\cdot)$ denote Lewis' semantics and W a set of multi-valued possible worlds. For any system of spheres \$, any world $w \in W$ and any $r > 0$, the r-semantics $e_w^r(\cdot)$ definition gives:*

$$e_w^c(\varphi \mathbin{\Box\!\!\rightarrow} \psi) \;=\; e_w^r(\Delta\varphi \mathbin{\Box\!\!\rightarrow}_* \Delta\psi)$$

$$e_w^c(\varphi \mathbin{\Diamond\!\!\rightarrow} \psi) \;=\; e_w^r(\Delta\varphi \mathbin{\Diamond\!\!\rightarrow}_* \Delta\psi)$$

Proof We prove the result just for the would counterfactual $\Box\!\!\rightarrow_*$, since the prove for the other operator is analogous. We have that $e_w^c(\varphi \mathbin{\Box\!\!\rightarrow} \psi) = 1$ iff either $[\Delta\psi] = \emptyset$ or each φ-world w' in the \$-closest sphere S containing a φ-world, is a ψ-world. This is equivalent to the infimum of $e_{w'}^r(\Delta\varphi \rightarrow_* \Delta\psi)$ being 1. But this is just $e_{w'}^r(\Delta\varphi \mathbin{\Box\!\!\rightarrow}_* \Delta\psi) = 1$ for each such world w'.   □

Hence, in counterfactuals with Δ in the antecedent and the consequent, there is no need for many-valued truth conditions since these counterfactuals cannot take values besides 0 and 1.

This language expansion permits to define truth-conditions for the following examples: (1) If I were absolutely rich, I would be happy, $\Delta\varphi \mathbin{\Box\!\!\rightarrow}_* \psi$, and (2) If I were absolutely rich, I would be absolutely happy, $\Delta\varphi \mathbin{\Diamond\!\!\rightarrow} \Delta\psi$.

7.2 Expanding the language with truth-constants

Truth-constants were introduced by Pavelka (in [9]; see also Hájek [7]) for the case of Łukasiewicz t-norm (for other t-norms, see [2] and [3]). This formalism consists in introducing a suitable set of truth-constants into the language propositional fuzzy logic. By *suitable* we mean a subset C of the set of truth-values, closed under the operations of the truth-value algebra. Each new constant $\bar{r}$ can only take the truth-value r in any evaluation: $e(\bar{r}) = r$, for any e. For any t-norm $*$, it is always true that $\bar{r} \wedge_* \bar{s} \Leftrightarrow \overline{r * s}$ and $\bar{r} \rightarrow_* \bar{s} \Leftrightarrow \overline{r \Rightarrow_* s}$. As an example, $e(\overline{0.4} \rightarrow_* p) = 1$ iff $e(p) \geq 0.4$. An *evaluated formula*, as defined in [2], is a formula of the form $\bar{r} \rightarrow_* \varphi$, or $\varphi \rightarrow_* \bar{r}$, or $\varphi \equiv_* \bar{r}$, where φ contains no truth-constant but $\bot$ or $\bar{1}$. In the following, we assume that the set of formulas expanded by truth-constants is restricted to evaluated formulas of the form $\bar{r} \rightarrow_* \varphi$.

In our context, this operator has the following consequences:

- If evaluated formulas (of the mentioned kind) occur only in the the antecedent of a counterfactual, i.e. $(\bar{s} \rightarrow_* \varphi) \mathbin{\Box\!\!\rightarrow}_* \psi$, then the 1-semantics captures the r-semantics, for any $r > 0$.

- The r-semantics (without truth-constants) collapses to the classical semantics of Lewis applied to counterfactuals whose antecedent and consequent are evaluated formulas of the mentioned kind.

These claims are proved next:

PROPOSITION 30 *Let W, w and \$ be given, and let $*$ be a basic t-norm. For any formulas φ, ψ, and a fixed $r > e_w(\varphi)$,*

$$e_w^r(\varphi \mathbin{\Box\!\!\rightarrow}_* \psi) \;=\; e_w^1((\bar{r} \rightarrow_* \varphi) \mathbin{\Box\!\!\rightarrow}_* \psi)$$

Proof We have $e_w^1((\bar{r} \to_* \varphi) \Box\!\!\to_* \psi) =$

$$
\begin{aligned}
&= \ \inf\{e_{w'}((\bar{r} \to_* \varphi) \to_* \psi) \mid w' \in \mathbb{K}_\varphi^1\} = && \text{Definition 15}\\
&= \ \inf\{e_{w'}(\varphi \to_* \psi) \mid w' \in \mathbb{K}_\varphi^r\} = && \text{since } e_{w'}(\bar{r} \to_* \varphi) = 1 \Leftrightarrow e_{w'}(\varphi) \geq r\\
&= \ e_w^r(\varphi \Box\!\!\to_* \psi) && \text{Definition 19} \quad \Box
\end{aligned}
$$

PROPOSITION 31 *Let $e_w^c(\cdot)$ denote Lewis' semantics and W a set of many-valued possible worlds. For any system of spheres \$ and any world $w \in W$,*

$$
e_w^r(\varphi \Box\!\!\to_* \psi) \geq s \quad \Longleftrightarrow \quad e_w^c((\bar{r} \to_* \varphi) \Box\!\!\to_* (\bar{s} \to_* \psi)) = 1
$$

$$
e_w^r(\varphi \Diamond\!\!\to_* \psi) \geq s \quad \Longleftrightarrow \quad e_w^c((\bar{r} \to_* \varphi) \Diamond\!\!\to_* (\bar{s} \to_* \psi)) = 1
$$

Proof We will prove the result just for the would counterfactual $\Box\!\!\to$, since the proof for the other operator is analogous.

We have that $e_w^r(\varphi \Box\!\!\to_* \psi) \geq s$ if and only if each world w' which gives φ a value greater or equal than r in the \$-closest sphere S containing a world w'' which gives φ a value greater or equal than r, gives $\varphi \to_* \psi$ a value greater or equal than s. So, w' is a world such that (i) gives the formula $\bar{r} \to_* \varphi$ value 1, (ii) is an element of the \$-closest sphere S containing a world w'' giving the formula $\bar{r} \to_* \varphi$ value 1, and (iii) gives the formula $\bar{s} \to_* \psi$ value 1. $\qquad\Box$

The next examples illustrate instances of natural language expressions that can be expressed in a language expanded by truth-constants.

EXAMPLE 32 *Assume we interpret truth at degree (at least) 0.8 as* very *true. Then the following sentences:*

(1)   If I were very rich, I would be happy. $(\overline{0.8} \to_* \varphi) \Box\!\!\to \psi$
(2)   If I were very rich I would be quite happy. $(\overline{0.8} \to_* \varphi) \Diamond\!\!\to (\overline{0.7} \to_* \psi)$

8   Conclusions

We have addressed the problem of generalizing Lewis' system of spheres semantics to the many-valued case, making use of t-norm based semantics. This permits to provide truth-conditions for vague counterfactuals in a faithful way. Due to the plurality of truth-values, we do not obtain a unique semantics as a result. We define several semantics, each one meaningful in a different context a vague counterfactuals can be uttered.

For the case of Łukasiewicz t-norm, we prove that would and might counterfactuals are interdefinable just like in the classical case. Then, we also show for which pairs of semantics, one can be reduced to the other (including here semantics defined on expanded languages). See the scheme in the next figure for a summary of this reducibility.

BIBLIOGRAPHY

[1] Mathias Baaz: Infinite-valued Gödel logics with 0-1-projections and relativizations. In Gödel '96 (Brno, 1996), Springer, 1996, pp. 23–33.
[2] Francesc Esteva, Joan Gispert, Lluís Godo and Carles Noguera: Adding truth-constants to logics of continuous t-norms: Axiomatization and completeness results. Fuzzy Sets and Systems, 2007 (158), pp. 597–618.

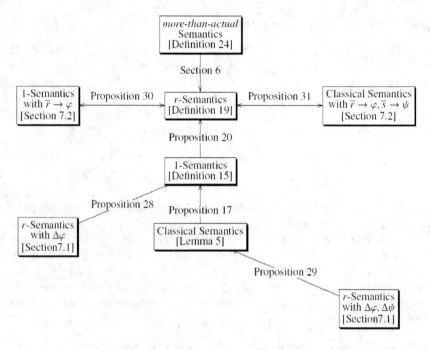

Figure 6. Reducibility relations among semantics for vague counterfactuals.

[3] Francesc Esteva, Lluís Godo and Carles Noguera: Expanding the propositional logic of a t-norm with truth-constants: completeness results for rational semantics. Soft Computing, 2010 (14), pp. 273–284.

[4] Christian G. Fermüller: Theories of Vagueness versus Fuzzy Logic: can logicians learn from philosophers? Neural Network World, 2003 (5), pp. 455–466.

[5] Christian G. Fermüller: Fuzzy logic and vagueness: can philosophers learn from Petr Hájek? In P. Cintula, Z. Haniková and V. Švejdar (eds.) *Witnessed years: Essays in Honour of Petr Hájek*, College Publications, 2009, pp. 373–386.

[6] Lluís Godo and Ricardo O. Rodríguez: Graded Similarity-based semantics for nonmonotonic inferences. Annals of Mathematics and Artificial Intelligence, 2002 (34), pp. 89–105.

[7] Petr Hájek: *Metamathematics of Fuzzy Logic*. Kluwer Academic Publisher, 1998.

[8] David Lewis: *Counterfactuals*. Oxford Basil Blackwell 1973.

[9] Jan Pavelka: On fuzzy logic I, II, III. Zeitschrift für Mathematische Logik und Grundlagen der Mathematik, 1979 (25), pp. 45–52, 119–134, 447–464.

[10] Judea Pearl: Causality: models, reasoning and inference. Cambridge University Press, 2000.

[11] Lofti A. Zadeh: Fuzzy Sets. *Information and Control*, 1965 (8), pp. 338–353.

Marco Cerami and Pere Pardo

Institut d'Investigació en Intel·ligència Artificial (IIIA – CSIC)

Campus UAB s/n 80193, Bellaterra, Catalunya

Email: {cerami, pardo}@iiia.csic.es

Comments on *Many-Valued Semantics for Vague Counterfactuals* by Marco Cerami and Pere Pardo

ONDREJ MAJER

As the title suggests, the authors propose a framework for analyzing vague counterfactuals in the framework of fuzzy logics. Although both subjects have been studied for quite a long time, Cerami and Pardo present one of the first attempts combining them (this topic is also independently studied by Běhounek and Majer).

1 Counterfactual conditionals

Many philosophers have attempted to provide logical analysis of counterfactuals (or natural language conditionals in general), most prominently Nelson Goodman, Robert Stalnaker and David Lewis. The most widely accepted solution currently is the Lewis-Stalnaker semantics, which is also the starting point for the authors.

There are several specifications of counterfactual conditionals based on grammatical form (subjunctive) and logical form (false antecedent). The authors specify the notion of counterfactual as conditional sentences whose antecedent is assumed to be false. This is certainly in accordance with the generally accepted convention, but it should be pointed out that there is no universally accepted criterion (sometimes we also use the subjunctive form for the situations which are not "contrary to the fact"). We also might not be sure about truth/falsity of the antecedent, as Lewis himself points out, and hence an adequate logical analysis of counterfactuals to also cover this case (the antecedent happens to be true after all).

The authors start with an exposition of the Lewis' sphere semantics, which is based on a standard possible-worlds semantics used in modal logics. Lewis assumes that a universe of possible worlds is equipped (on the top of existing structures like accessibility relation)with an ordering representing the similarity of a given world to the actual world (or a world which plays the role of the actual world). Formally, the similarity ordering can be represented by a system of spheres—a system of subsets of the universe which are nested (linearly ordered by inclusion), closed under unions and centered around the actual world. Although the sphere semantics is the one mostly referred to, Lewis provides several formalizations of the similarity relation in the terms of comparative possibility, selection functions (mentioned by the authors), degrees of similarity and some other notions and proves that each of them is equivalent to (some version of) the sphere semantics.

Lewis starts with the definition of a counterfactual saying that the counterfactual $A \mathbin{\Box\!\!\rightarrow} C$ is true at a given world, iff either there are no A-worlds (worlds in which A is true) or there is an AC-world, which is closer to the actual world than any $A\neg C$-world.

Another definition also discussed by Lewis employs the notion of the closest antecedent permitting sphere:

$A \ \Box\!\!\rightarrow C$ is true at a given world   iff   either there are no A-worlds or
the material conditional $A \rightarrow C$ holds in
the closest sphere containing an A-world.

This idea was formalized by Robert Stalnaker using selection functions and for many (including the authors) it seems to be more intuitively appealing than the Lewisian definition. However, the definition is less general as it relies on an assumption that many authors (including Lewis) consider restrictive and not very well justified. It is called the Limit assumption (LA) and requires that if a formula A is true in some world, then there always exists a closest sphere containing an A-world. In other words there is no non-well founded sequence of A-permitting spheres.

Cerami and Pardo argue in favor of the Limit assumption and claim that the case of non-well founded sequences "... is not often found in the classical framework, ...", but this does not seem to be quite justified. One can find sentences from everyday communication which do not satisfy LA. Consider the sentence "If I were (strictly) taller than 2 meters, I would play basketball" (or any other sentence using strict ordering)— even if we reason classically, there is no closest world in which I am strictly taller than 2 m. From this point of view it seems quite natural to avoid the Limit assumption and the price to be paid—not using the notion of the closest antecedent-permitting sphere—does not seem to be too high.

In the discussion about the Limit assumption the authors say: "Another possibility discussed by Lewis is that the intersection of a set of spheres is empty." This might be misleading as Lewis allows an empty intersection just for a set of spheres, each of which is A-permitting (contains some A-world) for a particular formula A. The intersection of all spheres is always non-empty (centering condition), it either contains just the actual world (Strong centering according to Lewis) or it might contain some other worlds as well (Weak centering).

Lewis provides an axiomatization for several counterfactual logics. Different properties of the similarity relation are characterized by different axioms, the only exception is the Limit assumption. It is usually referred to in the literature as 'the Lewis' system of counterfactuals', having in mind his basic system VC but, it should be stressed, that this is not the only one.

The authors intentionally concentrate on the semantics and neither provide an axiomatization of vague counterfactuals nor discuss the relation of their semantic framework to Lewis' axiomatic system.

When discussing Lewis' approach to possible worlds the authors say: "Lewis refuses the idea that a possible world is merely a propositional evaluation of sentences, as in the tradition of frame-based semantics for Modal Logic. Nevertheless, he makes use of such a notion of possible world when he defines the syntactical calculus of counterfactuals."

Both claims are disputable. In my opinion possible worlds semantics for modal logic neither speaks nor has to speak about propositional evaluations—a possible world is a primitive entity ('truthmaker') at which a formula takes a truth value (either bivalent or multivalued) and is not straightforwardly identified with a propositional evaluation. It can perfectly happen in a modal frame that two worlds agree on all values, but they are still two different possible worlds. Strictly speaking Lewis does not use the notion of evaluation in the definition of syntactical calculus. In the completeness proof he builds canonical models over maximal consistent sets of sentences, but this is a purely technical use.

2   Vague counterfactuals

After introducing the necessary apparatus from fuzzy logic, the authors proceed to the definition of a counterfactual. In agreement with the standard view, they assume that the antecedent of a counterfactual is not true, which can be paraphrased in a many-valued setup as 'not completely true'. They provide several generalizations of the classical Lewisian approach based on this reading.

As in the classical case (with Limit assumption), the truth of a vague counterfactual $\phi \mathrel{\Box\!\!\rightarrow} \psi$ depends on the behavior of the conditional $\phi \rightarrow \psi$ at the worlds, at which ϕ is (in some degree) true and which are closest to the actual world. Depending on the truth condition for the antecedent they provide three analyses:

1-*semantics* the closest worlds in which the antecedent is fully true

r-*semantics* the closest worlds in which the antecedent is true in the degree r

more than actual semantics the closest worlds in which the antecedent is more true, than in the actual world

The truth degree of the counterfactual in question is defined as the minimum of truth degrees of the conditional $\phi \rightarrow \psi$ in the closest worlds satisfying the corresponding condition.

1-semantics is a natural and intuitive generalization of the classical case; this is unlike the r-semantics, which seems to be of rather technical importance. The corresponding technical notion of an r-cut is used in mathematical fuzzy logic, but does not seem to have natural counterpart in natural language (we usually do not say "If I were at least 2/3-happy, life would be great."). I understood it rather as an auxiliary notion necessary for the *more than actual* semantics, defined as a limit of values of the counterfactual in question under r-semantics with r approaching the actual value.

The authors prove, that each of the proposed semantics correspond to the Lewisian one (more precisely to the system with Strong centering and Limit assumption). In particular, if the evaluation of propositions is bivalent, then the value of a counterfactual under the r-semantics (for the $r = 1$) coincides with the value in the sphere semantics.

3   Comments

Limit assumption From a formal point of view non well-founded sequences of truth values are a serious problem in the semantics of fuzzy logic (cf. the definition of the universal quantifier in predicate fuzzy logic and the problem of safe structures) so the Limit assumption seems to be a quite natural way to avoid them. However, the motivation for formalizing counterfactuals comes from natural language and its everyday use and from this point of view the Limit assumption is non-natural and restrictive, even in the classical bivalent case (see the discussion above). It would be interesting to observe if the Limit assumption is a necessary condition for the presented approach or if it is possible to avoid it (and still exclude the possibility that the truth value of some counterfactuals is undefined).

Crisp vs. vague approach to antecedent In the 1-semantics a counterfactual is evaluated with respect to the worlds, where the antecedent is strictly true (similarly true in the degree r in the r-semantics). On the other hand, one of the advantages of fuzzy solutions is that they are 'robust' in the sense that they take into account not only objects which (strictly) satisfy a certain condition (have a certain property), but also objects satisfying it 'roughly'. In the case of counterfactuals, not only the worlds where the antecedent is strictly true should count, but (to some extent) also the worlds in which it is almost true. Imagine an antecedent that is strictly true only in one world in the minimal sphere but in which there are several worlds which are true in the degree 0.99. Intuitively, they should also have some influence in determining the value of the vague counterfactual in question. Of course, a question then arises as to how to determine the dependence of the value of a vague counterfactual on the degree in which the antecedent is true. Similar reasoning can be applied to the minimality condition (strictly minimal vs. 'closed enough' to minimal).

The fuzzy paradigm seems to be reflected by *more than actual semantics*, where the 'close enough' worlds influence the value of a counterfactual via the notion of limit.

Comparisons with Lewis' approach The authors do compare their semantics with the sphere semantics, but it might be interesting to make a deeper comparison with the Lewisian approach.

Formal representation of counterfactuals is motivated by everyday use of conditionals, so an adequate formalization (either classical or many-valued) should reflect some common linguistic intuitions. Lewis thoroughly discusses the examples of use of conditional sentences, where some standard patterns of reasoning (valid for the material conditional) do not hold—he calls them counterfactual fallacies. His default examples are weakening (from $A \rightarrow C$ infer $A \wedge B \rightarrow C$), contraposition (from $A \rightarrow C$ infer $\neg A \rightarrow \neg C$) and transitivity (from $A \rightarrow B$ and $B \rightarrow C$ infer $A \rightarrow C$). Although the authors give some examples which illustrate their own solution, it would interesting to show how their system deals with Lewis' fallacies.

This is closely related to the last point—the authors focus on the semantics of counterfactuals and show the correspondence to the sphere semantics It would be interesting to know if their semantics corresponds to the Lewisian axiomatic system.

Ondrej Majer
Institute of Philosophy
Academy of Sciences of the Czech Republic
Jilská 1
110 00 Prague 1, Czech Republic
Email: majer@flu.cas.cz

Reasoning About Uncertainty of Fuzzy Events: An Overview

TOMMASO FLAMINIO, LLUÍS GODO, AND ENRICO MARCHIONI[1]

1 Introduction and motivations

Similarly to many areas of Artificial Intelligence, Logic as well has approached the definition of inferential systems that take into account elements from real-life situations. In particular, logical treatments have been trying to deal with the phenomena of vagueness and uncertainty. While a degree-based computational model of vagueness has been investigated through fuzzy set theory [88] and fuzzy logics, the study of uncertainty has been dealt with from the measure-theoretic point of view, which has also served as a basis to define logics of uncertainty (see e.g. [57]).

Fuzzy logics rely on the idea that truth comes in degrees. The inherent vagueness in many real-life declarative statements makes it impossible to predicate their full truth or full falsity. For this reason, propositions are taken as statements that can be regarded as partially true.

Measures of uncertainty aim at formalizing the strength of our beliefs in the occurrence of some events by assigning to those events a degree of belief concerning their occurrence. From the mathematical point of view, a measure of uncertainty is a function that assigns to each event (understood here as a formula in a specific logical language $\mathcal{LC}$) a value from a given scale, usually the real unit interval $[0,1]$, under some suitable constraints. A well-known example is given by probability measures which try to capture our degree of confidence in the occurrence of events by additive $[0,1]$-valued assignments.

Both fuzzy set theory and measures of uncertainty are linked by the need of intermediate values in their semantics, but they are essentially different. In particular, in the field of logics, a significant difference between fuzzy and probabilistic logic regards the fact that, while intermediate degrees of truth in fuzzy logic are compositional (i.e. the truth degree of a compound formula $\varphi \circ \psi$ only depends on the truth degrees of the simpler formulas φ and ψ), degrees of belief are not. In fact, for instance, the probability of a conjunction $\varphi \wedge \psi$ is not always a function of the probability of φ and the probability of ψ. Therefore, while fuzzy logics behave as (truth-functional) many-valued logics, probabilistic logics can be rather regarded as a kind of modal logics (cf. [50, 51] for instance).

[1]The authors thank the anonymous referees and Petr Cintula for their helpful remarks and suggestions. The authors acknowledge partial support from the Spanish projects ESF Eurocores-LogICCC/MICINN project (FFI2008-03126-E/FILO), TASSAT (TIN2010- 20967-C04-01), AT (CONSOLIDER CSD2007-0022, INGENIO 2010), ARINF (TIN2009-14704-C03-03) and the Marie Curie IRSES Project MATOMUVI. Flaminio and Marchioni also acknowledge partial support from the Juan de la Cierva Program of the Spanish MICINN.

The conclusion arising from the above mentioned differences is that the degree of truth of a formula cannot be understood, in general, as the degree of belief of the *same* formula. Still, we can interpret the degree of belief of a formula φ as the degree of truth of the modal formula $P\varphi$ that states that φ *is plausible* or *likely*.

This approach was first suggested by Hájek and Harmancová in [55], and later followed by Hájek, Esteva and Godo in [54, 52, 44, 45] where reasoning under uncertainty (modelled by probabilities, necessity and possibility measures, or even Dempster-Shafer belief functions) with classical propositions was captured in the framework of t-norm based logics. Indeed, given an assertion as "The proposition φ is plausible (probable, believable)", its degree of truth can be interpreted as the degree of uncertainty of the proposition φ. In fact, the higher our degree of confidence in φ is, the higher the degree of truth of the above sentence will be. In a certain sense, the predicate "is plausible (believable, probable)" can be regarded as a *fuzzy* modal operator over the proposition φ. Then, given a class of uncertainty measures, one can define modal many-valued formulas $\mathcal{M}\varphi$, whose interpretations are given by real numbers corresponding to the degree of uncertainty assigned to φ under measures μ of the given class. Furthermore, one can translate the specific postulates governing the behavior of particular classes of uncertainty measures into axioms on the modal formulas over a certain t-norm based logic, depending on the operations we need to represent.[2]

This logical approach to reason about uncertainty was also adopted to treat conditional probability in [71, 46, 47]; (generalized) conditional possibility and necessity in [67, 68]; and simple and conditional non-standard probability in [39]. A generalized treatment for both simple and conditional measures of uncertainty over Boolean events that covers most of the above ones was given by Marchioni in [69, 70].

Our aim, in this overview paper, is to give a comprehensive logical treatment of several generalizations of main classes of measures of uncertainty over fuzzy events. In particular, we will show how it is possible to represent and logically formalize reasoning about classes of measures such as probabilities, plausibility, possibilities and necessities over several classes of many-valued events. Fuzzy logics provide a powerful framework to handle and combine fuzziness and uncertainty. Indeed, in such logics the operations associated to the evaluation of the connectives are functions defined over the real unit interval $[0, 1]$, that correspond, directly or up to some combinations, to operations used to compute degrees of uncertainty. Then, such algebraic operations can be embedded in the connectives of the many-valued logical framework, resulting in clear and elegant formalizations.

This article is organized as follows. In Section 2, we provide the necessary logical background for the different fuzzy logics we will use throughout the paper. In Section 3, we introduce the basic concepts regarding some classes of measures over non-classical events. In Section 4, we deal with several modal expansions of particular fuzzy logics to treat classes of measures over fuzzy events. In Section 5, we study how to expand the language of those modal fuzzy logics by adding truth constants from the rational unit interval $[0, 1]$. In Section 6, we rely on those modal expansions to characterize, in purely logical terms, the problem of extending a partial uncertainty assignment over

---

[2]Needless to say, there are logics that are better suited than others to express the axioms of specific uncertainty measures, since some logics are not rich enough to capture the particular behavior of certain measures.

fuzzy events to a measure over the whole algebra they generate. We conclude with Section 7, where we discuss further and complementary readings about the topic of uncertainty measures over non-classical many-valued events.

2 Logical background

In this section, we introduce the background notions concerning the logic MTL [29], its extensions and expansions.

2.1 Core and Δ-core fuzzy logics

The language of MTL consists of a countable set $V = \{p_1, p_2, \ldots\}$ of propositional variables and a set of connectives $\mathcal{LC} = (\&, \rightarrow, \wedge, \bot)$ of type $(2, 2, 2, 0)$. The set Fm_V of formulas defined from the variables in V and the above connectives is built with the usual inductive clauses.

MTL has the following axiomatization:

(A1)	$(\varphi \rightarrow \psi) \rightarrow ((\psi \rightarrow \chi) \rightarrow (\varphi \rightarrow \chi))$	(A2)	$\varphi \& \psi \rightarrow \varphi$
(A3)	$\varphi \& \psi \rightarrow \psi \& \varphi$	(A4)	$\varphi \wedge \psi \rightarrow \varphi$
(A5)	$\varphi \wedge \psi \rightarrow \psi \wedge \varphi$	(A6)	$\varphi \& (\varphi \rightarrow \psi) \rightarrow \varphi \wedge \psi$
(A7a)	$(\varphi \rightarrow (\psi \rightarrow \chi)) \rightarrow (\varphi \& \psi \rightarrow \chi)$	(A7b)	$(\varphi \& \psi \rightarrow \chi) \rightarrow (\varphi \rightarrow (\psi \rightarrow \chi))$
(A8)	$((\varphi \rightarrow \psi) \rightarrow \chi) \rightarrow (((\psi \rightarrow \varphi) \rightarrow \chi) \rightarrow \chi)$	(A9)	$\bot \rightarrow \varphi.$

The only inference rule of MTL is modus ponens: from φ and $\varphi \rightarrow \psi$, infer ψ. A *proof* in MTL is a sequence $\varphi_1, \ldots, \varphi_n$ of formulas such that each φ_i either is an axiom of MTL, or follows from some preceding φ_j, φ_k $(j, k < i)$ by modus ponens. As usual, a set of formulas is called *a theory*. We say that a formula φ can be derived from a theory Γ, denoted as $\Gamma \vdash_{\text{MTL}} \varphi$, if there is a proof of φ from a set $\Gamma' \subseteq \Gamma$. A theory Γ is said to be consistent if $\Gamma \nvdash_{\text{MTL}} \bot$.

Other definable connectives are the following:

$\varphi \vee \psi$	is	$((\varphi \rightarrow \psi) \rightarrow \psi) \wedge ((\psi \rightarrow \varphi) \rightarrow \varphi),$
$\varphi \leftrightarrow \psi$	is	$(\varphi \rightarrow \psi) \& (\psi \rightarrow \varphi),$
$\neg \varphi$	is	$\varphi \rightarrow \bot,$
$\top$	is	$\neg \bot.$

We also use the following abbreviation: for all $n \in \mathbb{N}$, and for every $\varphi \in Fm_V$, φ^n stands for $\varphi \& \ldots \& \varphi$ (n-times).

DEFINITION 1 (1) *Let* $\varphi(p_1, \ldots, p_k)$ *be a formula in* Fm_V. *Then the* axiom schema *defined by* φ *is the set of all those formulas in* Fm_V *that can be defined from* φ *by substituting every propositional variable* p_i *occurring in* φ, *by a formula* $\psi_i \in Fm_V$.

(2) *A logic in the language* $\mathcal{LC}$ *is said to be a* schematic extension *of* MTL *if its axioms are those of* MTL *plus additional axiom schemas, with modus ponens as the unique inference rule.*

(3) *Consider a language* $\mathcal{LC}' \supset \mathcal{LC}$. *A logic axiomatized in the language* $\mathcal{LC}'$ *containing all the axioms and rules of* MTL *is said to be an* expansion *of* MTL.

An important expansion of MTL is the one obtained by expanding the language $\mathcal{LC}$ with the unary connective Δ (known in the literature as *Baaz's delta*, [6]), and adding the following axiom schemas:

($\Delta 1$) $\Delta\varphi \vee \neg\Delta\varphi$ ($\Delta 2$) $\Delta(\varphi \vee \psi) \rightarrow (\Delta\varphi \vee \Delta\psi)$

($\Delta 3$) $\Delta\varphi \rightarrow \varphi$ ($\Delta 4$) $\Delta\varphi \rightarrow \Delta\Delta\varphi$

($\Delta 5$) $\Delta(\varphi \rightarrow \psi) \rightarrow (\Delta\varphi \rightarrow \Delta\psi)$

along with the deduction rule of Δ-*necessitation*: from φ, deduce $\Delta\varphi$. The above logical system is called MTL$_\Delta$.

THEOREM 2   *Let* $\mathcal{L} \in \{\text{MTL}, \text{MTL}_\Delta\}$. *Consider the following properties for every set of formulas* $\Gamma \cup \{\varphi, \psi, \chi\}$ *in the language of* $\mathcal{L}$:

(*ldt*) $\Gamma, \varphi \vdash_{\mathcal{L}} \psi$ *iff there is an* $n \in \mathbb{N}$ *such that* $\Gamma \vdash_{\mathcal{L}} \varphi^n \rightarrow \psi$.

(Δdt) $\Gamma, \varphi \vdash_{\mathcal{L}} \psi$ *iff* $\Gamma \vdash_{\mathcal{L}} \Delta\varphi \rightarrow \psi$.

(*cong*) $\varphi \leftrightarrow \psi \vdash_{\mathcal{L}} \chi(\varphi) \leftrightarrow \chi(\psi)$.

Then, MTL *satisfies* (*ldt*) *and* (*cong*) *while* MTL$_\Delta$ *satisfies* (Δdt) *and* (*cong*).

Following [14], we say that a logic $\mathcal{L}$ is a *core fuzzy logic* if $\mathcal{L}$ expands MTL and satisfies (*ldt*) and (*cong*). A logic $\mathcal{L}$ is a Δ-*core fuzzy logic* if $\mathcal{L}$ expands MTL$_\Delta$ and satisfies (Δdt) and (*cong*).

An MTL-algebra is a structure $A = (A, \odot, \Rightarrow, \wedge, \vee, 0_A, 1_A)$ of type $(2,2,2,2,0,0)$ such that:

(1) The reduct $(A, \wedge, \vee, 0_A, 1_A)$ is a bounded lattice,

(2) The reduct $(A, \odot, 1_A)$ is a commutative monoid,

(3) The operations $\odot$ and $\Rightarrow$ form an adjoint pair:

$$\text{for all } x, y, z \in A, x \odot y \leq z \text{ iff } x \leq y \Rightarrow z.$$

(4) The prelinearity condition is satisfied:

$$\text{for all } x, y \in A, (x \Rightarrow y) \vee (y \Rightarrow x) = 1_A.$$

Since MTL and all (Δ-)core fuzzy logics are algebraizable in the sense of Blok and Pigozzi [7], we simply say that for any (Δ-)core fuzzy logic $\mathcal{L}$, the class (variety) of $\mathcal{L}$-algebras coincides with the equivalent algebraic semantics for $\mathcal{L}$. We refer to [14] for a more complete treatment.

Basic examples of MTL-algebras are obtained by equipping the real unit interval $[0,1]$ with a left continuous t-norm $*: [0,1] \times [0,1] \rightarrow [0,1]$ (cf. [52, 59]), its residuum $\Rightarrow_*: [0,1] \times [0,1] \rightarrow [0,1]$ and the usual lattice order of the reals. The main three examples of continuous t-norms are the Łukasiewicz t-norm ($x * y = \max(x + y - 1, 0)$), the product t-norm ($x * y = x \cdot y$) and the Gödel t-norm ($x * y = \min(x, y)$). These structures

$([0,1], *, \Rightarrow_*, \min, \max, 0, 1)$ are called *real* MTL-chains,[3] and they will play a crucial role in the rest of this paper. Of course, whenever we deal with particular expansions of MTL, we must take care of the standard interpretation of the symbols that expand the MTL-language. Recall that the standard interpretation of Baaz's delta is the following: for all $x \in [0,1]$, $\Delta(x) = 1$ if $x = 1$, and $\Delta(x) = 0$ otherwise.

An evaluation of Fm_V into a real MTL-chain is a map e from the propositional variables in V into $[0,1]$ that extends to formulas by truth-functionality. An evaluation e is a *model* for a formula φ if $e(\varphi) = 1$. An evaluation e is a model for a theory Γ, if $e(\psi) = 1$, for every $\psi \in \Gamma$.

Let now $\mathscr{L}$ denote any (Δ-)core fuzzy logic. Then we say that $\mathscr{L}$ enjoys:

- *Real completeness* (RC) if for every formula φ, $\vdash_{\mathscr{L}} \varphi$ iff for every evaluation e into a real $\mathscr{L}$-chain, $e(\varphi) = 1$.

- *Finite strong real completeness* (FSRC) if for every finite theory $\Gamma \cup \{\varphi\}$, $\Gamma \vdash_{\mathscr{L}} \varphi$ iff for every evaluation e into a real $\mathscr{L}$-chain that is a model for Γ, $e(\varphi) = 1$.

- *Strong real completeness* (SRC) if for every theory $\Gamma \cup \{\varphi\}$, $\Gamma \vdash_{\mathscr{L}} \varphi$ iff for every evaluation e into a real $\mathscr{L}$-chain that is a model for Γ, $e(\varphi) = 1$.

- *Strong hyperreal completeness* (SR*C) if for every theory $\Gamma \cup \{\varphi\}$, $\Gamma \vdash_{\mathscr{L}} \varphi$ iff for every evaluation e into a ultraproduct of real $\mathscr{L}$-chains that is a model for Γ, $e(\varphi) = 1$.

Jenei and Montagna proved in [58] that MTL enjoys SRC. We refer to [14] for a complete and in-depth study of such different notions of completeness for all the most prominent (Δ-)core fuzzy logics.

DEFINITION 3 *A (Δ-)core fuzzy logic $\mathscr{L}$ is said to be* locally finite *iff for every finite set V_0 of propositional variables, the Lindenbaum-Tarski algebra[4] Fm_{V_0} of $\mathscr{L}$ generated by the variables in V_0 is a finite algebra.*

2.2 Expansions with an involutive negation

As we pointed out above, in any (Δ-)core fuzzy logic, we can define a negation connective $\neg$, as $\neg \varphi := \varphi \to \bot$. This negation, in its standard interpretation, behaves quite differently depending on the chosen left-continuous t-norm and, in general, is not an involution, i.e. it does not satisfy the equation $\neg\neg x = x$.

A relevant expansion of a (Δ-)core fuzzy logic $\mathscr{L}$ is obtained by adding an involutive negation $\sim$ that does not depend on the chosen left-continuous t-norm [15, 30, 38]. In particular, we recall that MTL$_\sim$ is the logic obtained by expanding MTL$_\Delta$ with the unary symbol $\sim$, together with the following axioms:

(~1) $\sim\sim\varphi \leftrightarrow \varphi$
(~2) $\Delta(\varphi \to \psi) \to (\sim\psi \to \sim\varphi)$.

---

[3] In the literature of mathematical fuzzy logic, algebras over the real unit $[0,1]$ are also called *standard*.
[4] We remind the reader that, whenever we fix a language $\mathscr{LC}$, a set of variables V, and a logic $\mathscr{L}$ together with its consequence relation $\vdash_{\mathscr{L}}$, the Lindenbaum-Tarski algebra Fm_V is the quotient algebra of formulas modulo the equi-derivability relation. We invite the reader to consult [12] for further details.

MTL$_\sim$-algebras, the algebraic counterpart of MTL$_\sim$, are structures

$$(A, \odot, \Rightarrow, \wedge, \vee, \sim, \Delta, 0_A, 1_A)$$

of type $(2, 2, 2, 2, 1, 1, 0, 0)$ and are obviously defined. It is worth noticing that, as proved in [38], extensions of MTL$_\sim$ preserve (finite) strong standard completeness.

MTL$_\sim$ extensions are particularly interesting because, in each of their standard algebras, any operation $\oplus$ defined as: $x \oplus y := \sim(\sim x \odot \sim y)$ is interpreted as a t-conorm, thus making the system $(\odot, \oplus, \sim)$ a De Morgan triple [40]. We will see later that these structures allow to define a basic representation of possibility and necessity measures of fuzzy events (see Section 3.2.1).

2.3 Expansions with rational truth constants

Other notable expansions of a Δ-core fuzzy logic $\mathscr{L}$ are obtained by expanding its language with a set C of truth constants from $[0, 1]$. More precisely, let $*$ be any left continuous t-norm and $[0, 1]_*$ be the corresponding real algebra $([0, 1], *, \Rightarrow_*, \min, \max, 0, 1)$. Denote by $\mathscr{L}_*$ the algebraizable (in the sense of [7]) core fuzzy logic whose equivalent algebraic semantics is constituted by the variety $HSP([0, 1]_*)$, i.e. the variety generated by the standard algebra $[0, 1]_*$. The logic $\mathscr{L}_{*,\Delta}$ denotes as usual the expansion of $\mathscr{L}_*$ by the Baaz connective Δ.

Let C be a countable subset of $[0, 1]_*$. Then the logic $\mathscr{L}_{*,\Delta}(C)$ is the expansion of $\mathscr{L}_{*,\Delta}$ obtained by adding to its language the elements of C as constants and the following book-keeping axioms, where, for every $c \in C$, we denote its associated constant by $\overline{c}$ (notice that we still denote the top and bottom elements as 0 and 1):

(R1) $\overline{c_1} \,\&\, \overline{c_2} \leftrightarrow \overline{c_1 * c_2}$,
(R2) $\overline{c_1} \to \overline{c_2} \leftrightarrow \overline{c_1 \Rightarrow_* c_2}$,
(R3) $\Delta \overline{c} \leftrightarrow \overline{\Delta c}$.

For the logic $\mathscr{L}_{*,\Delta}(C)$, a different version of completeness has been introduced to interpret canonically the constant symbols [28]. In particular, we say that $\mathscr{L}_{*,\Delta}(C)$ has the *canonical* (finite) strong real-chain completeness iff $\mathscr{L}_{*,\Delta}(C)$ is (finitely) strong complete w.r.t. the real algebra $([0, 1], *, \Rightarrow_*, \min, \max, \{c\}_{c \in C})$, so that evaluations interpret every symbol $\overline{c}$ by the real number c (for all $c \in C$). Then, we have:

THEOREM 4 ([28, 31]) *Let* $* \in$ **CONT-fin**[5]$\cup$**WNM-fin**[6], *and let* $C \subset [0, 1]_*$ *be a suitable countable subalgebra. Then:*

(1) $\mathscr{L}_{*,\Delta}(C)$ *has the canonical finite strong real completeness.*

(2) $\mathscr{L}_{*,\Delta}(C)$ *has the canonical strong real completeness iff* $* \in$ **WNM-fin**.

---

[5]By the Mostert-Shields theorem [52, Theorem 2.1.16] every continuous t-norms $*: [0, 1] \times [0, 1] \to [0, 1]$ is an *ordinal sum* of the three basic t-norms: Gödel, product, and Łukasiewicz. **CONT-fin** denotes the class of all those continuous t-norms that are ordinal sums with finitely many components.

[6]Every nilpotent minimum t-norm $*$ (cf. [29]) is uniquely characterized by its associated weak negation $n_*: [0, 1] \to [0, 1]$. The t-norm $*$ is said to have a *finite partition* if its associated weak negation n_* is constant over finitely many intervals. **WNM-fin** denotes the class of all those weak nilpotent minimum t-norms having a finite partition. Notice that Gödel t-norm also belongs to this class.

For a given left-continuous t-norm $*$ and an involutive negation $n: [0,1] \to [0,1]$ closed over the rational unit interval $[0,1]_\mathbb{Q}$, let $\mathscr{L}_{*,n}([0,1]_\mathbb{Q})$ be the axiomatic extension of MTL$_\sim$ that is complete with respect to the variety of MTL$_\sim$-algebras generated by the real algebra $([0,1], *, \Rightarrow_*, n, \Delta, 0, 1)$. Then, $\mathscr{L}_{*,n}([0,1]_\mathbb{Q})$ is the expansion of $\mathscr{L}_{*,n}$ with truth-constants from the rational unit interval, together with the book-keeping axioms $(R1)$–$(R3)$ plus the following one for the involutive negation:

$(R4) \quad \sim \bar{c} \leftrightarrow \overline{n(c)}.$

Adopting the same techniques used in [38, Theorem 5.6, Theorem 5.13], it is not hard to show that the same conclusions of Theorem 4 can also be obtained for any $\mathscr{L}_{*,n}([0,1]_\mathbb{Q})$, whenever $* \in$ **CONT-fin** $\cup$ **WNM-fin**.

2.4 Łukasiewicz logics

Łukasiewicz logic Ł was introduced in [66], and has been widely studied by many authors both from the syntactical and algebraic point of view (cf. [8, 13, 52]). As a core fuzzy logic, Ł is obtained from MTL, by adding the following axioms:

(div) $\quad \varphi \wedge \psi \to (\varphi \,\&\, (\varphi \to \psi)),$
(inv) $\quad \neg\neg\varphi \to \varphi.$

Due to axiom (inv), the defined negation of Łukasiewicz logic is involutive. This allows us to define a connective of strong disjunction as follows: $\varphi \oplus \psi$ is $\neg(\neg\varphi \,\&\, \neg\psi)$.

For each $n \in \mathbb{N}$, the n-valued Łukasiewicz logic Ł$_n$ is the schematic extension of Ł with the axiom schemas:

$$(\text{Ł}_n 1) \quad (n-1)\varphi \leftrightarrow n\varphi, \qquad (\text{Ł}_n 2) \quad (k\varphi^{k-1})^n \leftrightarrow n\varphi^k,$$

for each integer $k = 2, \ldots, n-2$ that does not divide $n-1$, and where $n\varphi$ is an abbreviation for $\varphi \oplus \cdots \oplus \varphi$ (n times).

The algebraic counterpart for Łukasiewicz logic is the class of MV-algebras [11, 13]. These structures were introduced by Chang [11] using a different presentation that is equivalent to the one given as extensions of MTL-algebras. In its original language, an MV-algebra is a structure $\mathscr{A} = \langle A, \oplus, \neg, 0_A \rangle$ satisfying the following equations:

(MV1) $\quad x \oplus (y \oplus z) = (x \oplus y) \oplus z,$ (MV2) $\quad x \oplus y = y \oplus x,$
(MV3) $\quad x \oplus 0_A = x,$ (MV4) $\quad \neg\neg x = x,$
(MV5) $\quad x \oplus \neg 0_A = \neg 0_A,$ (MV6) $\quad \neg(\neg x \oplus y) \oplus y = \neg(\neg y \oplus x) \oplus x.$

As we stated, MV-algebras are MTL-algebras satisfying (see [13, 52]):

$$x \wedge y = x \odot (x \Rightarrow y); \qquad\qquad\qquad \text{(Divisibility)}$$
$$(x \Rightarrow 0_A) \Rightarrow 0_A = x. \qquad\qquad\qquad \text{(Involution)}$$

Indeed, in the signature $\langle \oplus, \neg, 0_A \rangle$, the monoidal operation $\odot$ can be defined as $x \odot y := \neg(\neg x \oplus \neg y)$, while the residuum of $\odot$ is definable as $x \Rightarrow y := \neg x \oplus y$. The top element is defined as $1_A := \neg 0_A$, and the order relation is obtained by defining $x \leq y$ iff $x \Rightarrow y = 1_A$, while the lattice operations are given by $x \wedge y := x \odot (\neg x \oplus y)$ and $x \vee y := (x \odot \neg y) \oplus y$. Moreover, we define the following useful abbreviation: for every natural n and $x \in A$, nx will denote $x \oplus \overset{n}{\cdots} \oplus x$, and x^n will denote $x \odot \overset{n}{\cdots} \odot x$.

For each $n \in \mathbb{N}$, an MV_n-algebra is an MV-algebra that satisfies the equations:

(MV7) $(n-1)x = nx$ (MV8) $(kx^{k-1})^n = nx^k$

for each integer $k = 2,\ldots,n-2$ not dividing $n-1$.

The class of MV-algebras (MV_n) forms a variety $\mathbb{MV}$ ($\mathbb{MV}_n$) that clearly is the equivalent algebraic semantics for Ł ($Ł_n$), in the sense of Blok and Pigozzi [7]. $\mathbb{MV}$ is generated as a quasivariety by the standard MV-algebra $[0,1]_{MV}$, i.e. the MV-algebra over the real unit interval $[0,1]$ with $x \oplus y = \min(x+y,1)$ and $\neg x = 1-x$.[7] Each $\mathbb{MV}_n$ is generated by the linearly ordered MV-algebra over the set $S_n = \{0,1/n,\ldots,(n-1)/n,1\}$ and whose operations are those of the MV-algebra over $[0,1]$, restricted to S_n.

Interesting examples of MV-algebras are the so-called Łukasiewicz *clans* of functions. Given a non-empty set X, consider the set of functions $[0,1]^X$ endowed with the pointwise extensions of the operations of the standard MV-algebra $[0,1]_{MV}$. Then a (Łukasiewicz) *clan* over X is any subalgebra $\mathscr{C} \subseteq [0,1]^X$, i.e. a set such that

(1) if $f,g \in \mathscr{C}$ then $f \oplus g \in \mathscr{C}$,

(2) if $f \in \mathscr{C}$ then $\neg f \in \mathscr{C}$,

(3) $\bar{0} \in \mathscr{C}$,

where $\bar{0}$ denotes the function constantly equal to 0. A clan $\mathscr{T}$ over X is called a (Łukasiewicz) *tribe* when it is closed with respect to a countable (pointwise) application of the $\oplus$ operation, i.e. if the following condition

$$\text{if } \{f_n \mid n \in \mathbb{N}\} \subseteq \mathscr{T} \text{ then } \bigoplus_{n\in\mathbb{N}} f_n \in \mathscr{T}$$

holds. Similarly, one can define an $Ł_n$-clan of functions over some set X to be any subalgebra $\mathscr{C} \subseteq (S_n)^X$.

The fact that $\mathbb{MV}$ is the equivalent algebraic semantics for Łukasiewicz logic Ł and is generated as a quasivariety by the standard MV-algebra $[0,1]_{MV}$ implies that Łukasiewicz logic enjoys FSRC. However Ł does not have SRC (cf. [14, 52]). On the other hand, for every $n \in \mathbb{N}$, the logic $Ł_n$ is strongly complete with respect to the MV-algebra S_n (cf. [34]).

Rational Łukasiewicz logic RŁ is a conservative expansion of Łukasiewicz logic introduced by Gerla in [42, 43], obtained by adding the set of unary connectives δ_n, one for each $n \in \mathbb{N}$, together with the following axioms:

(D1) $n\delta_n \varphi \leftrightarrow \varphi,$ (D2) $\neg \delta_n \varphi \oplus \neg(n-1)\delta_n \varphi.$

The algebraic semantics for RŁ is given by the variety of DMV-algebras (divisible MV-algebras), i.e. structures $\mathscr{A} = \langle A, \oplus, \neg, \{\delta_n\}_{n\in\mathbb{N}}, 0_A \rangle$ such that $\langle A, \oplus, \neg, 0_A \rangle$ is an MV-algebra and the following equations hold for all $x \in A$ and $n \in \mathbb{N}$:

($\delta_n 1$) $n(\delta_n x) = x,$ ($\delta_n 2$) $\delta_n x \odot (n-1)(\delta_n x) = 0_A.$

---

[7]Notice that there exist uncountably many MV-algebras whose universe is the real unit interval $[0,1]$, but they are all isomorphic to each other, and, in particular, to the standard MV-algebra.

An evaluation e of RŁ formulas into the real unit interval is just a Łukasiewicz logic evaluation extended for the connectives δ_n as follows: $e(\delta_n \varphi) = e(\varphi)/n$.

Notice that in RŁ all rationals in $[0,1]$ are definable (as truth constants) as:

- $\overline{1/n}$ is definable as $\delta_n \overline{1}$, and

- $\overline{m/n}$ is definable as $m(\delta_n \overline{1})$

since for any evaluation e: $e(\delta_n \overline{1}) = 1/n$ and $e(m(\delta_n \overline{1})) = (1/n) \oplus \overset{m}{\cdots} \oplus (1/n) = m/n$.

As shown in [43], the variety of DMV-algebras is generated as a quasivariety by the standard DMV-algebra $[0,1]_{\text{DMV}}$ (i.e. the expansion of $[0,1]_{\text{MV}}$ with the δ_n operations), and consequently RŁ enjoys FSRC. However, since it is a conservative expansion of Ł, RŁ does not have SRC.

We also introduce here a logic simpler than RŁ that we will make use of later in the paper. For every $n \in \mathbb{N}$, we denote by $Ł_n^+$ the expansion of $Ł_n$ obtained by expanding its language with the truth constant $\overline{1/n}$ together with the axioms:

$(n1)$ $n(\overline{1/n})$,
$(n2)$ $\neg(\overline{1/n} \& (n-1)\overline{1/n})$.

It is not difficult to see that the logic $Ł_n^+$ is strongly complete with respect to its related algebraic semantics, i.e. the MV-algebra over S_n expanded with a truth constant $\overline{1/n}$ satisfying the two equations corresponding to axioms $(n1)$ and $(n2)$.

THEOREM 5 ([13]) *The logics Ł and RŁ are not locally finite. For every $n \in \mathbb{N}$, the logics $Ł_n$ and $Ł_n^+$ are locally finite.*

3   Uncertainty measures over non-classical events

In this section we introduce the basic concepts regarding uncertainty measures over non-classical events. We start by introducing the definition of those uncertainty measures over Boolean algebras that we will later generalize for weaker structures. The modal logics we will present in Section 4 will be based on these generalizations.

3.1   The classical case

Classical representations of uncertainty are based on a set of *possible situations* (or worlds), sometimes called a *sample space* or a *frame of discernment*, which represents all the possible outcomes. A typical example is the toss of a die. In this case, the sample space is given by six different situations, each of them corresponding to a certain outcome. An event can be simply regarded as a subset of the sample space corresponding to the set of those situations in which the event is true. In the case of the toss of a die, for instance, the event "the outcome will be an even number" corresponds to the set given by $\{2,4,6\}$. Complex events can be seen as Boolean combinations of subsets of the sample space. For instance, the event "the outcome will be an even number and it will be strictly greater than 4" is nothing but the intersection of the sets $\{2,4,6\}$ and $\{5,6\}$. Measures of uncertainty are classically defined over the Boolean algebra generated by subsets of a given sample space.

An event can be also identified with the proposition whose meaning is the set of situations that make it true. From a logical point of view, we can associate to a proposition the set of classical evaluations in which the proposition is true. Each of those evaluations, in fact, corresponds to a possible situation.

In what follows we will use the words "event" and "proposition" with the same meaning, and they will refer to a set of situations, or equivalently to a set of classical evaluations. Given that measures are defined over the Boolean algebra of subsets of a sample space, we can consider measures as defined over the Boolean algebra of provably equivalent classical propositions.

In general, measures of uncertainty aim at formalizing our degree of confidence in the occurrence of an event by assigning a value from a partially ordered bounded scale. In its more general sense, this is encoded by the concept of plausibility measure introduced by Halpern (see [57]).[8] Given a partially ordered set $\langle L, \leq, 0, 1 \rangle$, an *L-valued plausibility measure* on a Boolean algebra $\mathscr{B} = (B, \wedge, \vee, \neg, 0_B, 1_B)$ of events is a mapping $\rho : B \to L$ satisfying the following properties:

i. $\rho(0_B) = 0$, and $\rho(1_B) = 1$,

ii. for every $x, y \in B$ with $x \leq y$, $\rho(x) \leq \rho(y)$, where $x \leq y$ denotes the order relation between elements of B.

The first two conditions mean that the certain event 1_B and the impossible event 0_B have measure 1 and 0, respectively.[9] Indeed, the certain event is satisfied in every possible situation, while the impossible event never occurs. The third condition corresponds to monotonicity, i.e. if the situations in which an event can occur are included in those that support another event, then the degree of uncertainty of the former is smaller than the degree of uncertainty of the latter.

Uncertainty measures are usually defined as real valued functions where the partially ordered scale is identified with the real unit interval $[0, 1]$. Plausibility measures of this kind are also known as *fuzzy measures*, and were first introduced by Sugeno in [87]. Thus, (classical) fuzzy measures are in fact plausibility measures assigning values from $[0, 1]$ to elements of the Boolean algebra of events.

Besides such common properties, each class of fuzzy measures basically differs from the others in how the measure of compound propositions or events is related to the measure of their components. In other words, what specifies the behavior of a fuzzy measure is how from assessments of uncertainty concerning different events we can determine the measure of (some of) their combinations. In a certain sense, we can say that classes of fuzzy measures are characterized by the satisfaction of some compositional properties. However, it is well-known that a proper fuzzy measure μ cannot be fully compositional.[10]

---

[8]We want to warn the reader not to confuse *plausibility measures* in the sense of [57] with *plausibility functions* in the sense of Dempster-Shafer theory, cf. [84].

[9]From now on, when no danger of confusion is possible, we will omit the subscripts of the bottom and top elements of the Boolean algebra 0_B and 1_B respectively, and we will simply write 0 and 1.

[10]In the sense that there do not exist functions $f_\wedge, f_\vee : B \times B \to L$ and $f_\neg : B \to L$ such that, for every $x, y \in B$, $\mu(x \wedge y) = f_\wedge(\mu(x), \mu(y))$, $\mu(x \vee y) = f_\vee(\mu(x), \mu(y))$, $\mu(\neg x) = f_\neg(\mu(x))$.

THEOREM 6 ([25]) *Let* $\mu: B \to L$ *be any L-valued fuzzy measure. If* μ *is fully compositional then it collapses into a two-valued function, i.e. for all* $x \in B$, $\mu(x) \in \{0,1\}$.

Typical examples of classes of fuzzy measures are probability measures, and possibility and necessity measures.[11]

(Finitely additive) probability measures, first introduced from a measure-theoretic perspective by Kolmogorov in [60], are fuzzy measures defined over a Boolean algebra $\mathscr{B}$ that satisfy the law of finite additivity:

for every $x, y \in B$ such that $x \wedge y = 0_B$, $\mu(x \vee y) = \mu(x) + \mu(y)$.

Any probability measure μ over a finite Boolean algebra $\mathscr{B}$ is uniquely determined by a corresponding probability distribution p on the (finite) set of atoms $\{a_i\}_{i \in I}$ of $\mathscr{B}$: by defining $p(a_i) = \mu(\{a_i\})$, so that $\sum_{i \in I} p(a_i) = 1$, it holds that, for any $x \in \mathscr{B}$, $\mu(x) = \sum_{a_j \leq x} p(a_j)$.

Possibility measures (introduced by Zadeh in [90], and deeply studied by Dubois and Prade [22, 24]) are a class of fuzzy measures satisfying the following law of composition w.r.t. the maximum t-conorm:

$$\mu(x \vee y) = \max(\mu(x), \mu(y)).$$

Similarly, necessity measures [22] are fuzzy measures satisfying the following law of composition w.r.t. the minimum t-norm:

$$\mu(x \wedge y) = \min(\mu(x), \mu(y)).$$

Possibility and necessity measures are dual in the sense that, given a possibility measure Π (a necessity measure N), one can derive its dual necessity measure as follows:

$$N(x) = 1 - \Pi(\neg x) \qquad [\Pi(x) = 1 - N(\neg x)].$$

Similarly to probability measures, any possibility measure Π over a finite Boolean algebra $\mathscr{B}$ is uniquely determined by a possibility distribution π on the set of atoms $\{a_i\}_{i \in I}$ of $\mathscr{B}$. Indeed, by defining $\pi(a_i) = \Pi(\{a_i\})$, one has $\sup_{i \in I} \pi(a_i) = 1$, and $\Pi(u) = \sup_{a_j \leq u} \pi(a_j)$ for any $u \in \mathscr{B}$. As for the dual necessity measure, we have $N(u) = \inf_{a_i \nleq u} 1 - \pi(a_i)$.

3.2 Non-classical events

In the literature, there seems not to be a general definition of the notion of a fuzzy measure defined over structures weaker than Boolean algebras. Generalized treatments have just covered specific cases, as we will see below, such as probability and necessity / possibility measures. Since those treatments study measures over particular subclasses of MTL-algebras, it seems natural to give a definition for those kinds of structures.

DEFINITION 7 *Given an* MTL-*algebra* $\mathscr{A}$, *a generalized fuzzy measure on* $\mathscr{A}$ *is a mapping* $\mu: A \to [0,1]$ *such that* $\mu(0_A) = 0$, $\mu(1_A) = 1$, *and for* $x, y \in A$, $\mu(x) \leq \mu(y)$ *whenever* $x \leq y$.

---

[11]Notice that we do not discuss here the appropriateness of a class of measures w.r.t. uncertainty phenomena and we do not compare them to each other. For such an analysis the reader is referred e.g. to papers by Smets [85, 86], Halpern's book [57] and the references therein.

In what follows, we are going to study particular classes of generalized fuzzy measures that are extensions of those introduced for the Boolean case.

3.2.1 Possibility and necessity measures

In this section we give a definition of generalized possibility and necessity measures over MTL-algebras (although we only make use of the underlying lattice structure). Notice that, even if the real unit interval $[0,1]$ is the most usual scale for all kinds of uncertainty measures, any bounded totally ordered set can be actually used (possibly equipped with suitable operations), especially in the case of non-additive measures of a more qualitative nature like possibility and necessity measures.

DEFINITION 8 *Let $\mathscr{A}$ be an* MTL-*algebra and let $\mu : A \to [0,1]$ be a generalized fuzzy measure over $\mathscr{A}$. Then:*

- *μ is called a* basic possibility measure *when for all $x,y \in A$*

$$\mu(x \vee y) = \max(\mu(x), \mu(y)),$$

- *μ is called a* basic necessity measure *when for all $x,y \in A$*

$$\mu(x \wedge y) = \min(\mu(x), \mu(y)).$$

For the case of $\mathscr{A}$ being a lattice of $[0,1]$-valued functions on a set X (i.e. a lattice of fuzzy sets), say $A = [0,1]^X$, several extensions of the notions of possibility and necessity measures for fuzzy sets have been proposed in relation to different logical systems extending the well-known Dubois-Lang-Prade's Possibilistic logic to fuzzy events, see e.g. [22, 21, 48, 4, 3, 5]. Actually, the different proposals in the literature arise from two observations. First of all, contrary to the classical case, $[0,1]$-valued basic possibility and necessity measures $\Pi, N : [0,1]^X \to [0,1]$ are not univocally determined by a possibility distribution π on the set X. The second observation is that, in the classical case, the expressions of possibility and necessity measures of subsets of X in terms of a possibility distribution on X can be equivalently rewritten as

$$\Pi(f) = \sup_{x \in X} \min(\pi(x), f(x)), \quad N(f) = \inf_{x \in X} \max(1 - \pi(x), f(x))$$

where $f : X \to \{0,1\}$ is two-valued function, which can be obviously identified with a subset of X. Therefore, natural generalizations of these expressions when $f : X \to [0,1]$ is a fuzzy subset of X are

$$\Pi(f) = \sup_{x \in X} \pi(x) \odot f(x), \quad N(f) = \inf_{x \in X} \pi(x) \Rightarrow f(x) \tag{*}$$

where $\odot$ is a t-norm and $\Rightarrow$ is some suitable fuzzy implication function.[12] In particular, the following implication functions have been discussed in the literature as instantiations of the $\Rightarrow$ operation in (*):

---

[12] The minimal properties required for a binary operation $\Rightarrow : [0,1] \times [0,1] \to [0,1]$ to be considered as a fuzzy counterpart of the classical $\{0,1\}$-valued implication truth-function are: $0 \Rightarrow 0 = 1$, $1 \Rightarrow 0 = 0$, $\Rightarrow$ is non-increasing in the first variable and non-decreasing in the second variable.

(1) $u \Rightarrow_{KD} v = \max(1 - u, v)$ (Kleene-Dienes implication)

(2) $u \Rightarrow_{RG} v = \begin{cases} 1, \text{if } u \leq v \\ 1 - u, \text{otherwise} \end{cases}$ (reciprocal of Gödel implication)

(3) $u \Rightarrow_{\text{Ł}} v = \min(1, 1 - u + v)$.   (Łukasiewicz implication)

All these functions actually lead to proper extensions of the above definition of necessity over classical sets or events in the sense that if f describes a crisp subset of X, i.e. f is a function $f : X \to \{0, 1\}$, then (*) gives $N(f) = \inf_{x: f(x)=0} 1 - \pi(x)$.

Moreover, if Π and N are required to be dual with respect to the standard negation, i.e. $\Pi(f) = 1 - N(1 - f)$, then one is led to consider the fuzzy implication $\Rightarrow$ defined as $x \Rightarrow y = (1 - x) \uplus y$ where $\uplus$ is the t-conorm dual of $\odot$. These kinds of fuzzy implications are commonly known as *strong implications*. Notice that $\Rightarrow_{KD}$ is the strong implication for $\odot = \min$ and $\Rightarrow_{\text{Ł}}$ is the strong implication for the Łukasiewicz t-norm.

Interestingly enough, these two notions of generalized possibilistic measures can be understood as a special kind of *fuzzy integrals*, called (generalized) *Sugeno integrals* [87]. Indeed, given a fuzzy measure $\mu : 2^X \to [0, 1]$, the *Sugeno integral* of a function $f : X \to [0, 1]$ with respect to μ is defined as

$$\oint_S f \, d\mu = \max_{i=1,\ldots,n} \min(f(x_{\sigma(i)}), \mu(A_{\sigma(i)}))$$

where σ is a permutation of the indices such that $f(x_{\sigma(1)}) \geq f(x_{\sigma(2)}) \geq \cdots \geq f(x_{\sigma(n)})$, and $A_{\sigma(i)} = \{x_{\sigma(1)}, \ldots, x_{\sigma(i)}\}$. When μ is a (classical) possibility measure on 2^X induced by a (normalized) possibility distribution $\pi : X \to [0, 1]$, i.e. $\mu(A) = \max\{\pi(x) \mid x \in A\}$ for every $A \subseteq X$, then the above expression of the Sugeno integral becomes (see e.g. [10])

$$\oint_S f \, d\pi = \max_{x \in X} \min(\pi(x), f(x)).$$

When the above minimum operation is replaced by an arbitrary t-norm $\odot$, we obtain the so-called generalized Sugeno integral [87]

$$\oint_{S,\odot} f \, d\mu = \max_{i=1,\ldots,n} f(x_{\sigma(i)}) \odot \mu(A_{\sigma(i)}),$$

which, in the case of μ being the possibility measure on 2^X defined by a possibility distribution π, becomes

$$\oint_{S,\odot} f \, d\pi = \max_{x \in X} \pi(x) \odot f(x).$$

The next theorem offers an axiomatic characterization of those measures for which there exists a possibility distribution that allows a representation in terms of a generalized Sugeno integral. The formulation we provide here is very general and makes only use of the structure of De Morgan triples[13] over the real unit interval.

---

[13] A De Morgan triple (see e.g. [40]) is a structure on the real unit interval $(\odot, \uplus, \neg)$ where $\odot$ is a t-norm, $\uplus$ a t-conorm, $\neg$ a strong negation function such that $x \uplus y = \neg(\neg x \odot \neg y)$ for all $x, y \in [0, 1]$.

THEOREM 9 *Let X be a finite set, let $(\odot, \uplus, 1-x)$ be a De Morgan triple, and let $N, \Pi: [0,1]^X \to [0,1]$ be a pair of dual basic necessity and possibility measures. Then, N satisfies the following property for all $r \in [0,1]$*

$$N(\bar{r} \uplus f) = r \uplus N(f)$$

$$\text{(or equivalently, } \Pi(\bar{r} \odot f) = r \odot \Pi(f))$$

if, and only if, there exists $\pi: X \to [0,1]$ such that $\Pi(f) = \max_{x \in X} \pi(x) \odot f(x)$ and $N(f) = 1 - \Pi(1-f) = \min_{x \in X}(1 - \pi(x)) \uplus f(x)$.

Proof Suppose N is such that $N(\bar{r} \uplus f) = \bar{r} \uplus_L N(f)$ for every $f \in [0,1]^X$ and $r \in [0,1]$. It is easy to check that every $f \in [0,1]^X$ can be written as

$$f = \bigwedge_{x \in X} \mathbf{x}^c \uplus \overline{f(x)},$$

where $\mathbf{x}^c: X \to [0,1]$ is the characteristic function of the complement of the singleton $\{x\}$, i.e. $\mathbf{x}^c(y) = 1$ if $y \neq x$ and $\mathbf{x}^c(x) = 0$, and $\overline{f(x)}$ stands for the constant function of value $f(x)$.

Now, by applying the axioms of a basic necessity measure and the assumption that $N(\bar{r} \uplus f) = \bar{r} \uplus N(f)$, we obtain that

$$N(f) = N\left(\bigwedge_{x \in X} \mathbf{x}^c \uplus \overline{f(x)} \right) = \min_{x \in X} N\left(\mathbf{x}^c \uplus \overline{f(x)} \right) = \min_{x \in X} N(\mathbf{x}^c) \uplus f(x).$$

Finally, by putting $\pi(x) = 1 - N(\mathbf{x}^c)$, we finally get

$$N(f) = \min_{x \in X} (1 - \pi(x)) \uplus f(x),$$

which, of course, by duality implies that

$$\Pi(f) = \max_{x \in X} \pi(x) \odot f(x)$$

The converse is easy.   □

This type of integral representation can be easily generalized when we replace the real unit interval $[0,1]$ as the scale for the measures by more general algebraic structures, for instance by residuated lattices with involution. The details are out of the scope of this paper.

3.2.2   Finitely additive measures

The classical notion of (finitely additive) probability measure on Boolean algebras was generalized in [74] by the notion of *state on MV-algebras*.

DEFINITION 10 ([74]) *By a state on an MV-algebra $\mathscr{A} = \langle A, \oplus, \neg, 0_A \rangle$ we mean a function $s: A \to [0,1]$ satisfying:*

(i) $s(1_A) = 1$,

(ii) *if $u \odot v = 0_A$, then $s(u \oplus v) = s(u) + s(v)$.*

The following proposition collects some properties that states enjoy.

PROPOSITION 11 ([74]) *Let s be a state on an MV-algebra A. Then the following hold properties hold:*

(*iii*) $s(\neg u) = 1 - s(u)$,

(*iv*) *if* $u \leq v$, *then* $s(u) \leq s(v)$,

(*v*) $s(u \oplus v) = s(u) + s(v) - s(u \odot v)$.

Moreover, a map $s \colon A \to [0,1]$ *is a state iff* (*i*) *and* (*v*) *hold.*

In [89], Zadeh introduced the following notion of probability on fuzzy sets. A fuzzy subset of a (finite) set X can be considered just as a function $f \in [0,1]^X$. Then, given a probability distribution $p \colon X \to [0,1]$ on X, the *probability* of f is defined as

$$p^*(f) = \sum_{x \in X} f(x) \cdot p(x),$$

where we have written $p(x)$ for $p(\{x\})$. Indeed, p^* is an example of state over the tribe $[0,1]^X$. The restriction of p^* over the S_n-valued fuzzy sets is also an example of state over $(S_n)^X$.

The notion of state on a clan can be applied to define what a state on formulas is. Let W and W_n be the set of $[0,1]_{MV}$-evaluations and S_n-evaluations respectively over the set of formulas $Fm(V)$ in the language of Łukasiewicz logic built from a set of propositional variables V. For each $X \subseteq W$, and each $\varphi \in Fm(V)$, let

$$\varphi_X^* \colon X \to [0,1]$$

be defined by $\varphi_X^*(w) = w(\varphi)$, where w is any $[0,1]_{MV}$-evaluation in X. Analogously, for any $Y \subseteq W_n$, define

$$\varphi_{Y,n}^* \colon Y \to S_n.$$

Then, both $Fm_X = \{\varphi_X^* \mid \varphi \in Fm(V)\}$ and $Fm_Y = \{\varphi_{Y,n}^* \mid \varphi \in Fm(V)\}$ are clans over W and W_n respectively. Then any state s on Fm_X (resp. on Fm_Y) induces a state on formulas $s' \colon Fm(V) \to [0,1]$ by putting $s'(\varphi) = s(\varphi_X^*)$ (resp. $= s'(\varphi_Y^*)$). Notice that $s'(\varphi) = s'(\psi)$ whenever $\varphi \leftrightarrow \psi$ is provable in Ł or in $Ł_n$ respectively.

Paris proved in [79, Appendix 2] that every state s on a finitely generated Fm_Y can be represented as an integral:

THEOREM 12 (Paris, [79]) *Let V_0 be a finite set of propositional variable, and let Y be the subset of W_n of all the evaluations of V_0 into S_n. Then for every state s on Fm_Y, there is a probability distribution p on Y such that, for every $\varphi_{Y,n}^* \in Fm_Y$,*

$$s(\varphi_{Y,n}^*) = \sum_{w \in Y} p(w) \cdot w(\varphi).$$

More general and sophisticated integral representation for states on MV-algebras were independently proved by Kroupa [63], and Panti [77]: for every MV-algebra $\mathscr{A}$, the set of all states on A is in one-to-one correspondence with the class of regular Borel probability measure on a compact Hausdorff space $\mathbb{X}$. In particular for every state s on A there is a regular Borel probability measure p on $\mathbb{X}$ such that s is the integral with respect to p. A discussion about this topic is beyond the scope of this paper (see [63, 77] for a detailed treatment).

4   Fuzzy modal logics for some classes of generalized plausibility measures

As seen in the previous section, generalized fuzzy measures assign to non-classical events values from the real unit interval $[0,1]$. As also mentioned in the introduction, the underlying idea of the fuzzy logic-based treatment of uncertainty is to introduce in a given fuzzy logic a modal operator $\mathcal{M}$, so that $\mathcal{M}\varphi$ denotes that φ *is likely, (plausible, probable, possible, etc.)*, where φ is a proposition denoting an event (classical or non-classical). Then, taking advantage of the real semantics of (Δ-)core fuzzy logics over the unit real interval $[0,1]$, particular truth-functions over $[0,1]$ can be used to express specific compositional properties of different classes of measures.

For instance, consider the class of generalized plausibility measures over an $\mathcal{L}$-algebra of events, for some (Δ-)core fuzzy logic $\mathcal{L}$. Recall that this class is characterized by the normalization axioms, $\rho(1)=1$ and $\rho(0)=0$, and monotonicity: whenever $x\le y$, $\rho(x)\le\rho(y)$. These properties can be easily captured within $\mathcal{L}$ itself over a language expanded by a modal operator Pl by considering the axioms $Pl\top$ and $\neg Pl\bot$, together with the inference rule: from $\varphi\to\psi$ infer $Pl\varphi\to Pl\psi$. Indeed, for any evaluation e over any real $\mathcal{L}$-algebra, $e(Pl\varphi\to Pl\psi)=1$ iff $e(Pl\varphi)\le e(Pl\psi)$. Therefore, we can say that any (Δ-)core fuzzy logic $\mathcal{L}$ is *adequate* for the class of generalized fuzzy measures over $\mathcal{L}$-algebras of events.

However, if we then want to rely on a certain logic to represent a particular subclass of fuzzy measures, we need to take into account whether the operations needed in the definition of the subclass can be defined in that logic.

To be more specific, consider a (Δ-)core fuzzy logic $\mathcal{L}$ which is complete with respect to a class $\mathcal{C}$ of real $\mathcal{L}$-algebras. Then any formula $\varphi(p_1,\dots,p_n)$ over propositional variables $p_1,\dots,p_n$ in the language of $\mathcal{L}$ defines a function $t_\varphi^A\colon[0,1]^n\to[0,1]$ for every real algebra $\mathcal{A}\in\mathcal{C}$, by stipulating $t_\varphi^A(a_1,\dots,a_n)=e(\varphi)$, where e is the $\mathcal{L}$-interpretation such that $e(p_1)=a_1,\dots,e(p_n)=a_n$. Then we say that a certain function $f\colon[0,1]^n\to[0,1]$ is *definable* in a (Δ-)core fuzzy logic $\mathcal{L}$ if:

(1)   there exists a class $\mathcal{C}$ of real algebras for which $\mathcal{L}$ is complete, and

(2)   there exists an $\mathcal{L}$-formula $\varphi(p_1,\dots,p_n)$ such that, for all $\mathcal{A}\in\mathcal{C}$, $t_\varphi^A(a_1,\dots,a_n)=f(a_1,\dots,a_n)$ for all $a_1,\dots,a_n\in A$.

For instance, the formulas $p_1\wedge p_2$ and $p_1\vee p_2$ define over any class of real MTL-chains the min and max functions respectively.

Informally speaking, we say that a (Δ-)core fuzzy logic $\mathcal{L}$ is *compatible with* a given subclass of fuzzy measures if the algebraic operations or relations playing a role in the axiomatic postulates of the given class of measures can be expressed by means of functions definable in $\mathcal{L}$.

We give an example to clarify this notion of compatibility.

EXAMPLE 13 *Consider the class of (finitely additive) probability measures on, say, classical events. In this case not every (Δ-)core fuzzy logic $\mathcal{L}$ is suitable to axiomatize a logic to reason about probabilities. In fact, the operation of (bounded) sum is necessary* *to express the law of finite additivity, and this operation is not present in all real algebras of all logics, but it is present, for instance, in the standard algebra $[0,1]_{MV}$ of Łukasiewicz logic Ł, and in the standard algebra of some of its expansions like Rational Łukasiewicz logic RŁ. These logics, therefore, allow to axiomatize a modal logic to reason about probability (also remember that Ł has an involutive negation), by allowing to express the additivity with the connective $\oplus$, whose standard interpretation is the truncated sum (recall Section 2.4, and see Section 4.4): $P(\varphi \vee \psi) \leftrightarrow P\varphi \oplus P\psi$, in case $\vdash \neg(\varphi \wedge \psi)$ over Classical Logic. In contrast, it is easy to observe that, for instance, a probability logic cannot be axiomatized over Gödel logic since the (truncated) addition cannot be expressed by means of Gödel logic truth-functions.*

In the rest of this section, we consider different fuzzy modal logics (in a restricted sense that will be clarified in the following definitions) axiomatizing reasoning about several classes of fuzzy measures. We introduce the fundamental syntactical and semantical frameworks that we will specifically enrich in the following subsections to deal with the distinguished classes of measures we have already recalled.

Unless stated otherwise, for the rest of this section we always consider $\mathscr{L}_1$ to be a (Δ-)core fuzzy logic used to represent events, and $\mathscr{L}_2$ to be a (Δ-)core fuzzy logic compatible with the specific class of measures we are going to reason about. As a matter of notation, let us denote by $\mathcal{M}$ any class of fuzzy measures as those we axiomatized in the first part of this section. We introduce the basic framework to formalize reasoning about fuzzy measures in $\mathcal{M}$. The syntactical apparatus built over $\mathscr{L}_1$ and $\mathscr{L}_2$ is denoted by $FM(\mathscr{L}_1, \mathscr{L}_2)$.

Syntax. The syntax of $FM(\mathscr{L}_1, \mathscr{L}_2)$ comprises a countable set of propositional variables $V = \{x_1, x_2, \ldots\}$, connectives from $\mathscr{L}_1$ and $\mathscr{L}_2$ [14] and the unary modality $\mathcal{M}$. Formulas belong to two classes:

EF: The class of formulas from $\mathscr{L}_1$. They are inductively defined as in Section 2, and will be used to denote events. The class of those formulas will be denoted by $\mathscr{E}$.

MF: The class of modal formulas is defined inductively: for every formula $\varphi \in \mathscr{E}$, $\mathcal{M}\varphi$ is an atomic modal formula, all truth-constants of $\mathscr{L}_2$ are also atomic modal formulas, and, moreover, compound formulas are defined from the atomic ones and using the connectives of $\mathscr{L}_2$. We will denote by $\mathcal{MF}$ the class of modal formulas.

Note that connectives appearing in the scope of the modal operator $\mathcal{M}$ are from $\mathscr{L}_1$, while those outside are from $\mathscr{L}_2$.

Semantics. [15] Let $\mathcal{C}_1$ be a class of $\mathscr{L}_1$-chains over a same universe U_1 for which $\mathscr{L}_1$ is complete, and let $\mathscr{A}_2$ be real $\mathscr{L}_2$-chain and such that it is compatible with $\mathcal{M}$. A semantics with respect to $\mathcal{C}_1$ and $\mathscr{A}_2$ for the language $FM(\mathscr{L}_1, \mathscr{L}_2)$ is defined as follows: a *real* $\{\mathcal{C}_1, \mathscr{A}_2\}$-$\mathcal{M}$ *model* is a triple $\langle W, e, \rho \rangle$ where:

- W is a non-empty set whose elements are called *nodes* or *possible words*.

---

[14] We will not distinguish the connective symbols of both logics since it will become clear form the context.

[15] The semantical framework we adopt here is inspired by the approach of [82] in the general setting of two-layered fuzzy modal logics. We thank Petr Cintula for bringing this work to our knowledge.

- $e \colon \mathscr{E} \times W \to U_1$, where U_1 is the common universe of the chains in $\mathcal{C}_1$, is a map such that, for every fixed $w \in W$, the map $e(\cdot, w) \colon \mathscr{E} \to U_1$ is an evaluation of non-modal formulas over a particular algebra $\mathscr{A}_w \in \mathcal{C}_1$

- $\rho \colon Fm_W(V) \to [0,1]$ is an $\mathcal{M}$-fuzzy measure, where $Fm_W(V)$ is defined as follows. For every formula $\varphi \in \mathscr{E}$, define the map $f_\varphi \colon W \to U_1$ such that, for every $w \in W$, $f_\varphi(w) = e(\varphi, w)$. Then $Fm_W(V)$ is the $\mathscr{L}_1$-algebra of all the functions defined in this way, with the pointwise application of the operations in the $\mathscr{A}_w$'s.

Let $M = \langle W, e, \rho \rangle$ be a $\{\mathcal{C}_1, \mathscr{A}_2\}$-$\mathcal{M}$ model, let w be a fixed node in W, and let ϕ be a formula of $FM(\mathscr{L}_1, \mathscr{L}_2)$. Then, the truth value of ϕ in M at the node w (we will denote this value by $\|\phi\|_{M,w} \in [0,1]$) is inductively defined as follows:

- If ϕ is a formula in $\mathscr{E}$, then $\|\phi\|_{M,w} = e(\phi, w)$.

- If ϕ is an atomic modal formula of the form $\mathcal{M}\psi$, then $\|\mathcal{M}\psi\|_{M,w} = \rho(f_\psi)$.

- If ϕ is a compound modal formula, then $\|\phi\|_{M,w}$ is computed by truth functionality and using the operations of $\mathscr{A}_2$.

Notice that when ϕ is modal, its truth value $\|\phi\|_{M,w}$ does not depend on the chosen world w, hence in these cases we will simplify the notation by dropping the subscript w, and we will write $\|\phi\|_M$. M will be called a *model* for ϕ when $\|\phi\|_M = 1$, and will be called a model for a modal theory Γ (i.e. $\Gamma \subseteq \mathcal{M}\mathscr{F}$) when it is a model for each formula in Γ.

In the remaining part of this section, it will be useful to consider $\{\mathcal{C}_1, \mathscr{A}_2\}$-$\mathcal{M}$ models $\langle W, e, \rho \rangle$, where the measure ρ takes values in an $\mathscr{L}_2$-chain $\mathscr{A}_2$ whose domain coincides with a non trivial ultrapower $^*[0,1]$ of $[0,1]$. Those models will be called *hyperreal*. Evaluations into a hyperreal $\{\mathcal{C}_1, \mathscr{A}_2\}$-$\mathcal{M}$ model are defined accordingly.

REMARK 14 (1) *To simplify the reading, and without danger of confusion, we will henceforth avoid mentioning the class of chains $\mathcal{C}_1$ and the algebra $\mathscr{A}_2$ when referring to the models introduced above. We will simply say that a triple $\langle W, e, \rho \rangle$ is a (real or hyperreal) $\mathcal{M}$-model. The class $\mathcal{C}_1$ and the algebra $\mathscr{A}_2$ will be always clear by the context.*

(2) In the following subsections, we will axiomatize particular classes of fuzzy measures. Case by case we will adopt a notation consistent with the class of measures we will deal with. Therefore, we will denote by $\mathcal{PL}$ the class of generalized plausibility measures, by Π the class of possibility measures, and so forth. For example, we will denote by $FPL(\mathscr{L}_1, \mathscr{L}_2)$ the logic for generalized plausibility and, also referring to what we stressed in (1), we will call its models the plausibilistic models. *Clearly the same notation (mutatis mutandis) will be also adopted for all the particular classes of fuzzy measures we are going to treat.*

4.1 A modal logic for generalized plausibility measures

In this section we take $\mathcal{M}$ to be the class of *generalized plausibility measures*, denoted as $\mathcal{PL}$, and let $\mathscr{L}_1, \mathscr{L}_2$ be two core fuzzy logics. Recall that any core fuzzy logic is compatible with $\mathcal{PL}$. The logic that allows to reason about generalized plausibility measures of over $\mathscr{L}_1$-events over the logic $\mathscr{L}_2$ will be called $F\mathcal{PL}(\mathscr{L}_1,\mathscr{L}_2)$, and its axioms and rules are the following:

Ax1 All axioms and rules of $\mathscr{L}_1$ restricted to formulas in $\mathscr{E}$.

Ax2 All axioms and rules of $\mathscr{L}_2$ restricted to modal formulas.

Ax3 Axiom for the modality Pl:

   Pl $\neg Pl(\bot)$,

M The rule of *monotonicity* for Pl: from $\varphi \rightarrow \psi$, deduce $Pl(\varphi) \rightarrow Pl(\psi)$.

(where $\varphi, \psi \in \mathscr{E}$)

N The rule of *necessitation* for Pl: from φ, deduce $Pl(\varphi)$.   (where $\varphi \in \mathscr{E}$)

Notice that nested modalities are not allowed, nor are formulas which contain modal formulas but also non-modal formulas that are not under the scope of any modality. That is to say that, for example, if $\varphi, \psi \in \mathscr{E}$, then neither $Pl(Pl(\varphi))$ nor $\psi \rightarrow Pl(\varphi)$ is a well-founded formula in our language.

The notion of *proof* in $F\mathcal{PL}(\mathscr{L}_1,\mathscr{L}_2)$ is defined as usual, and we denote by $\vdash_{\text{F}\mathcal{PL}}$ the relation of logical consequence. A *theory* is a set of formulas, and a *modal theory* is a set of modal formulas. For any theory Γ, and for every formula ϕ, we write $\Gamma \vdash_{\text{F}\mathcal{PL}} \phi$ to denote that ϕ follows from Γ in $F\mathcal{PL}(\mathscr{L}_1,\mathscr{L}_2)$.

PROPOSITION 15 *The logic* $F\mathcal{PL}(\mathscr{L}_1,\mathscr{L}_2)$ *proves the following:*

(1) *The modality Pl is normalized, that is* $\vdash_{\text{F}\mathcal{PL}} Pl(\bot) \leftrightarrow \bot$, *and* $\vdash_{\text{F}\mathcal{PL}} Pl(\top) \leftrightarrow \top$ *(where, as usual, $\top = \neg\bot$).*

(2) *The rule of* substitution of equivalents: $\tau \leftrightarrow \gamma \vdash_{\text{F}\mathcal{PL}} Pl(\tau) \leftrightarrow Pl(\gamma)$.

Proof (1)   Since in $\mathscr{L}_2$ the negation can be defined as $\neg\phi = \phi \rightarrow \bot$, the axiom **Pl** actually states that $Pl(\bot) \rightarrow \bot$. Moreover, $\bot \rightarrow Pl(\bot)$ trivially holds, and therefore $\vdash_{\text{F}\mathcal{PL}} Pl(\bot) \leftrightarrow \bot$. Finally, since $\vdash_{\text{F}\mathcal{PL}} Pl(\top)$, then $\vdash_{\text{F}\mathcal{PL}} Pl(\top) \leftrightarrow \top$.

(2)   As usual $\tau \leftrightarrow \gamma$ can be split in $\tau \rightarrow \gamma$ and $\gamma \rightarrow \tau$. Now, from $\tau \rightarrow \gamma$, and using (1), $\tau \rightarrow \gamma \vdash_{\text{F}\mathcal{PL}} Pl(\tau) \rightarrow Pl(\gamma)$. Similarly $\gamma \rightarrow \tau \vdash_{\text{F}\mathcal{PL}} Pl(\gamma) \rightarrow Pl(\tau)$.   □

As for the semantics, given a class $\mathcal{C}_1$ of real $\mathscr{L}_1$-algebras for which $\mathscr{L}_1$ is complete and a real $\mathscr{L}_2$-algebra $\mathscr{A}_2$ compatible with a generalized plausibility measure ρ, a $\{\mathcal{C}_1, \mathscr{A}_2\}$-$\mathcal{PL}$ model, for short a *plausibilistic model*, will be a triple $M = \langle W, e, \rho \rangle$ with the same definition and notation used above for the general case (see Remark 14).

REMARK 16 *The compatibility assumption of the algebra $\mathscr{A}_2$ with respect to the measure ρ is what guarantees that the logic $F\mathcal{PL}(\mathscr{L}_1,\mathscr{L}_2)$, and in particular its genuine modal axiom(s) and rule(s), is sound with respect to the class of plausibilistic models. The same observation applies to the other modal logics we will consider in the next subsections.*

DEFINITION 17 *Let* $\Gamma \cup \{\Phi\}$ *be a modal theory of* $\mathrm{FPL}(\mathscr{L}_1, \mathscr{L}_2)$. *Then we say that the logic* $\mathrm{FPL}(\mathscr{L}_1, \mathscr{L}_2)$ *is:*

- Finitely strongly complete *with respect to real plausibilistic models (real-FSC) if whenever* Γ *is finite, and* $\Gamma \nvdash_{\mathrm{FPL}} \Phi$, *there is a real plausibilistic model M for* Γ *such that* $\|\Phi\|_M < 1$.

- Strongly complete *with respect to real plausibilistic models (real-SC) if for every* Γ *such that* $\Gamma \nvdash_{\mathrm{FPL}} \Phi$, *there is a real plausibilistic model M for* Γ *such that* $\|\Phi\|_M < 1$.

- Strongly complete *with respect to hyperreal plausibilistic models (hyperreal-SC) if for every* Γ *such that* $\Gamma \nvdash_{\mathrm{FPL}} \Phi$, *there is a hyperreal plausibilistic model M for* Γ *such that* $\|\Phi\|_M < 1$.

Now we introduce a general way to prove (finite, strong) completeness for $\mathrm{FPL}(\mathscr{L}_1, \mathscr{L}_2)$ with respect to the class of real and hyperreal plausibility models. The same methods will be then applied in the following sections when we will study those extensions of $\mathrm{FPL}(\mathscr{L}_1, \mathscr{L}_2)$ that allow to deal with more specific uncertainty measures.

First, we define a translation mapping from the modal language of $\mathrm{FPL}(\mathscr{L}_1, \mathscr{L}_2)$ into the propositional language of $\mathscr{L}_2$. This translation works as follows: for every atomic modal formula $Pl(\varphi)$, we introduce a new variable p_φ in the language of $\mathscr{L}_2$. Then, we inductively define the translation $\bullet$ as follows:

- $(Pl(\varphi))^\bullet = p_\varphi$.

- $\perp^\bullet = \perp$.

- $(\star(\Phi_1, \ldots, \Phi_n))^\bullet = \star((\Phi_1)^\bullet, \ldots, (\Phi_n)^\bullet)$ for every n-ary connective $\star$ of $\mathscr{L}_2$.

For any modal theory Γ of $\mathrm{FPL}(\mathscr{L}_1, \mathscr{L}_2)$, in accordance with $\bullet$, we define

$$\Gamma^\bullet = \{\Psi^\bullet \mid \Psi \in \Gamma\}$$

$$\mathrm{FPL}^\bullet = \{\Theta^\bullet \mid \Theta \text{ is an instance of } \mathbf{Pl}\} \cup \{p_\varphi \mid \vdash_{\mathscr{L}_1} \varphi\} \cup \{p_\varphi \to p_\psi \mid \vdash_{\mathscr{L}_1} \varphi \to \psi\}.$$

LEMMA 18 *Let* $\Gamma \cup \{\Phi\}$ *be a modal theory of* $\mathrm{FPL}(\mathscr{L}_1, \mathscr{L}_2)$. *Then*

$$\Gamma \vdash_{\mathrm{FPL}} \Phi \text{ iff } \Gamma^\bullet \cup \mathrm{FPL}^\bullet \vdash_{\mathscr{L}_2} \Phi^\bullet.$$

Proof $(\Rightarrow)$ An $\mathrm{FPL}(\mathscr{L}_1, \mathscr{L}_2)$-proof $\Psi_1, \ldots, \Psi_n$ of Φ in Γ is made into an $\mathscr{L}_2$-proof of $\Phi^\bullet$ in $\Gamma^\bullet \cup FP^\bullet$ by deleting all $\mathscr{L}_1$-formulas and taking, for each modal formula Ψ_i, the $\mathscr{L}_2$ formula $\Psi_i^\bullet$.

$(\Leftarrow)$ Conversely, each $\mathscr{L}_2$-proof of $\Phi^\bullet$ has the form $\Psi_1^\bullet, \ldots, \Psi_n^\bullet$, where Ψ_i are modal formulas. Therefore the previous proof is converted into an $\mathrm{FPL}(\mathscr{L}_1, \mathscr{L}_2)$-proof of Φ in Γ, by adding for each Ψ_i of the form p_φ (φ being an $\mathscr{L}_1$-theorem) a proof in $\mathscr{L}_1$ of φ, and then applying a step of necessitation (**N**) in order to get $Pl(\varphi)$, and for each Ψ_j of the form $p_\varphi \to p_\psi$ a proof in $\mathscr{L}_1$ of $\varphi \to \psi$, and then applying a step of the monotonicity rule (**M**) in order to get $Pl(\varphi) \to Pl(\psi)$. $\square$

Now, assume $\Gamma \cup \{\Phi\}$ to be a finite modal theory over $F\mathcal{PL}(\mathcal{L}_1, \mathcal{L}_2)$, and let V_0 be the following set of propositional variables:

$$V_0 = \{v_i \mid v_i \text{ occurs in some } \varphi, P(\varphi) \text{ is a subformula of } \Psi, \Psi \in \Gamma \cup \{\Phi\}\},$$

i.e. V_0 is the set of all the propositional variables occurring in all the $\mathcal{L}_1$-formulas occurring in some modal formula of $\Gamma \cup \{\Phi\}$. Clearly V_0 is finite.

We can identify $\mathcal{F}_{\mathcal{L}_1}(V_0)$ with the Lindenbaum-Tarski algebra of $\mathcal{L}_1$ of formulas generated in the restricted language having V_0 as set of variables. Therefore, for every $[\varphi] \in \mathcal{F}_{\mathcal{L}_1}(V_0)$ we choose a representative of the class $[\varphi]$, that we will denote by $\varphi^\square$. Then, consider the following further translation map:

- For every modal formula Φ, let $\Phi^\square$ be the formula resulting from the substitution of each propositional variable p_φ occurring in $\Phi^\bullet$ by $p_{\varphi^\square}$,

- $(\star(\Phi_1, \ldots, \Phi_n))^\square = \star((\Phi_1)^\square, \ldots, (\Phi_n)^\square)$ for every n-ary connective $\star$ of $\mathcal{L}_2$.

In accordance with that translation, we define $\Gamma^\square$ and $F\mathcal{PL}^\square$ as:

$$\Gamma^\square = \{\Psi^\square \mid \Psi^\bullet \in \Gamma^\bullet\}$$

$$F\mathcal{PL}^\square = \{\Upsilon^\square \mid \Upsilon^\bullet \in F\mathcal{PL}^\bullet\}.$$

LEMMA 19 $\Gamma^\bullet \cup F\mathcal{PL}^\bullet \vdash_{\mathcal{L}_2} \Phi^\bullet$ iff $\Gamma^\square \cup F\mathcal{PL}^\square \vdash_{\mathcal{L}_2} \Phi^\square$.

Proof $(\Leftarrow)$ Let $\Gamma^\square \cup F\mathcal{PL}^\square \vdash_{\mathcal{L}_2} \Phi^\square$. Then, in order to prove the claim we have to show that $\Gamma^\bullet \cup F\mathcal{PL}^\bullet \vdash_{\mathcal{L}_2} \Phi^\bullet$ for each Φ such that its $\square$-translation is $\Phi^\square$. For instance, if $\Phi = Pl(\psi)$ then $\Phi^\square = p_{\psi^\square} = p_{\gamma^\square}$ for each $\gamma \in [\psi]$, therefore, if $\Gamma^\square \cup F\mathcal{PL}^\square \vdash_{\mathcal{L}_2} p_{\varphi^\square}$ we have to show that $\Gamma^\bullet \cup F\mathcal{PL}^\bullet \vdash_{\mathcal{L}_2} p_\gamma$ for each $\gamma \in [\varphi]$.

First, we notice that the following fact immediately follows from Proposition 15(2):

Claim 1 Let φ, ψ be $\mathcal{L}_1$-formulas. If $\vdash_{\mathcal{L}_1} \varphi \leftrightarrow \psi$, then $F\mathcal{PL}(\mathcal{L}_1, \mathcal{L}_2) \vdash Pl(\varphi) \leftrightarrow Pl(\psi)$ (and in particular $F\mathcal{PL}^\bullet \vdash_{\mathcal{L}_2} p_\varphi \leftrightarrow p_\psi$).

Let us now turn back to the proof of Lemma 19. Let Φ be a modal formula of $F\mathcal{PL}(\mathcal{L}_1, \mathcal{L}_2)$ and let $Pl(\varphi_1), \ldots, Pl(\varphi_k)$ be all the atomic modal formulas occurring in Φ. If $\Gamma^\square \cup F\mathcal{PL}^\square \vdash_{\mathcal{L}_2} \Phi^\square$, then, it easily follows from the above claim that $\Gamma^\bullet \cup F\mathcal{PL}^\bullet \vdash_{\mathcal{L}_2} \Phi^\bullet$ where $\Phi^\bullet$ is any $\mathcal{L}_2$-formula obtained by replacing each occurrence of a propositional variable p_{φ_i} with another p_{ψ_i} such that $\psi_i \in [\varphi_i]$. In fact, if $\psi_i \in [\varphi_i]$, then $\vdash_{\mathcal{L}_1} \psi_i \leftrightarrow \varphi_i$ and therefore, from Claim 1, $F\mathcal{PL}^\bullet \vdash_{\mathcal{L}_2} p_{\psi_i} \leftrightarrow p_{\varphi_i}$. Thus p_{φ_i} can be substituted with p_{ψ_i} without loss of generality in the proof. Therefore, in particular $\Gamma^\bullet \cup F\mathcal{PL}^\bullet \vdash_{\mathcal{L}_2} \Phi^\bullet$ and this direction is complete.

$(\Rightarrow)$ In order to prove the other direction let us assume $\Gamma^\bullet \cup F\mathcal{PL}^\bullet \vdash_{\mathcal{L}_2} \Phi^\bullet$ and let $\Psi_1^\bullet, \ldots, \Psi_k^\bullet$ be an $\mathcal{L}_2$-proof of $\Phi^\bullet$ in $\Gamma^\bullet \cup F\mathcal{PL}^\bullet$. For each $1 \leq j \leq k$ replace $\Psi_j^\bullet$ with $\Psi_j^\square$, the representative of its equivalence class in $\mathcal{F}_{\mathcal{L}_1}(V_0)$. Clearly $\Psi_1^\square, \ldots, \Psi_k^\square$ is an $\mathcal{L}_2$-proof of (a formula logically equivalent to) $\Phi^\square$. In fact, if $\Psi_k^\bullet = \Phi^\bullet$, then $\Psi_k^\square \leftrightarrow \Phi^\square$. Moreover, for each $1 \leq i < k$ one of the following holds:

(i) $\Psi_i^\square$ is (logically equivalent to) an axiom of $\mathcal{L}_2$,

(ii) $\Psi_i^\square \in \Gamma^\square \cup F\mathcal{PL}^\square$,

(iii) If $\Psi_t^{\bullet}$ is obtained by modus ponens from $\Psi_s^{\bullet} \to \Psi_t^{\bullet}$ and $\Psi_s^{\bullet}$, then we claim that $\Psi_t^{\square}$ is obtained by modus ponens from $\Psi_s^{\square} \to \Psi_t^{\square}$ and $\Psi_s^{\square}$. In fact we have just to note that $(\Psi_s \to \Psi_t)^{\square} = \Psi_s^{\square} \to \Psi_t^{\square}$ and thus the claim easily follows.

Moreover, since modus ponens is the only inference rule of $\mathscr{L}_2$ we have nothing to add, and our claim is settled. $\qquad\square$

Now, we are ready to state and prove our completeness theorem.

THEOREM 20 *Let $\mathscr{L}_1$ be a logic for events, and let $\mathscr{L}_2$ be a logic compatible with plausibility measures. Then the following hold:*

(1) *If $\mathscr{L}_1$ is locally finite, and $\mathscr{L}_2$ enjoys the FSRC, then $FPL(\mathscr{L}_1, \mathscr{L}_2)$ is real-FSC.*

(2) *If $\mathscr{L}_2$ has theSRC, then $FPL(\mathscr{L}_1, \mathscr{L}_2)$ is real-SC.*

(3) *If $\mathscr{L}_2$ has the FSRC, then $FPL(\mathscr{L}_1, \mathscr{L}_2)$ is hyperreal-SC.*

Proof (1)   Assume $\mathscr{L}_1$ to be locally finite and complete with respect to a class $\mathcal{C}_1 = \{L_i\}_{i \in I}$ of $\mathscr{L}_1$-chains over a same universe U_1. Let $\Gamma \cup \{\Phi\}$ be a modal theory of $FPL(\mathscr{L}_1, \mathscr{L}_2)$ such that $\Gamma \nvdash_{FPL} \Phi$. Then, by Definition 3, and by definition of $^{\square}$, it follows that $\Gamma^{\square} \cup FPL^{\square}$ is a finite theory of $\mathscr{L}_2$. Moreover, by Lemma 19, $\Gamma \nvdash_{FPL} \Phi$ iff $\Gamma^{\square} \cup FPL^{\square} \nvdash_{\mathscr{L}_2} \Phi^{\square}$. Since $\mathscr{L}_2$ enjoys FSRC, there is an evaluation v into a real $\mathscr{L}_2$-algebra $\mathscr{A}_2$ which is a model for $\Gamma^{\square} \cup FPL^{\square}$, but $v(\Phi^{\square}) < 1$.

Now consider the model $M = \langle W, e, \rho \rangle$ (cf. [82]), where:

- $W = \cup_{i \in I} W_i$ where W_i is the set of all evaluations on the algebra L_i.

- $e : V \times W \to U_1$ is defined as follows: for every $w \in W_i$, and every $p \in V$,

$$e(p, w) = \begin{cases} w(p) & \text{if } p \in V_0, \\ 0 & \text{otherwise.} \end{cases}$$

- $\rho : Fm_W(V_0) \to [0, 1]$ is defined as: for all $f_{\varphi} \in Fm_W(V_0)$,

$$\rho(f_{\varphi}) = v(Pl(\varphi)^{\square}).$$

Claim 2 *The model $M = \langle W, e, \rho \rangle$ is a plausibilistic model.*

Proof (*of the Claim 2*) We only need to prove that ρ is a plausibility measure. Then, recalling that $\bot^{\square} = \bot$, we have $\top^{\square} = \top$, and so $\rho(f_{\bot}) = v(\bot^{\square}) = v(\bot) = 0$. Analogously $\rho(f_{\top}) = 1$. To prove monotonicity, assume that $f_{\varphi} \leq f_{\psi}$ in $Fm_W(V_0)$. Now, $f_{\varphi} \leq f_{\psi}$ means that for every chain L_i and every evaluation w on L_i, $w(\varphi) \leq w(\psi)$, and by completeness of $\mathscr{L}_1$ with respect to $\mathcal{C}_1$, $\vdash_{\mathscr{L}_1} \varphi \to \psi$. By the monotonicity rule **M**, $\vdash_{FPL} Pl \varphi \to Pl \psi$. Hence $\top = (Pl \varphi \to Pl \psi)^{\square} = (Pl \varphi)^{\square} \to (Pl \psi)^{\square} \in FPL^{\square}$. Since v is a model of $FPL^{\square}$, we have $v(Pl(\varphi)^{\square} \to Pl(\psi)^{\square}) = 1$. But $v(Pl(\varphi)^{\square} \to Pl(\psi)^{\square}) = 1$ iff $v(Pl(\varphi)^{\square}) \leq v(Pl(\psi)^{\square})$ iff $\rho(f_{\varphi}) \leq \rho(f_{\psi})$. Therefore M is a plausibilistic model as required. $\qquad\square$

Let Ψ be any modal formula of $FPL(\mathscr{L}_1, \mathscr{L}_2)$. By induction on Ψ, it is now easy to show that $\|\Psi\|_M = v(\Psi^{\square})$, hence M is a plausibilistic model that satisfies every formula of Γ, and such that $\|\Phi\|_M < 1$ as required.

(2)   Let now $\Gamma \cup \{\Phi\}$ be any arbitrary modal theory of $FPL(\mathscr{L}_1, \mathscr{L}_2)$, and in particular assume Γ to be infinite. Therefore, independently from the fact that $\mathscr{L}_1$ is locally finite or not, the $\mathscr{L}_2$ propositional theory $\Gamma^\square \cup FPL^\square$ is infinite. Assume $\Gamma \nvdash_{FPL} \Phi$: from Lemma 19, $\Gamma^\square \cup FPL^\square \nvdash_{\mathscr{L}_2} \Phi^\square$. Since $\mathscr{L}_2$, by hypothesis, has strong real completeness, there exists, again, an evaluation v into a real $\mathscr{L}_2$-algebra such that v is a model of $\Gamma^\square \cup FPL^\square$, and $v(\Phi^\square) < 1$.

Then, the same plausibilistic model M we defined in the proof of (1) is appropriate for our purposes. Then, (2) is proved as well.[16]

(3)   Assume now Γ to be any arbitrary modal theory of $FPL(\mathscr{L}_1, \mathscr{L}_2)$. Assume that $\Gamma \nvdash_{FPL} \Phi$: so $\Gamma^\square \cup FPL^\square \nvdash_{\mathscr{L}_2} \Phi^\square$ by Lemma 19. By Definition 3, $\Gamma^\square \cup FPL^\square$ is not a finite theory of $\mathscr{L}_2$, but since $\mathscr{L}_2$ has FSRC, then by [34, Theorem 3.2], $\mathscr{L}_2$ has SR*C. Consequently, there is an evaluation v into a non-trivial ultraproduct of real $\mathscr{L}_2$-chains satisfying all the formulas in $\Gamma^\square \cup FPL^\square$, and $v(\Phi^\square) < 1$.

Again, the same strategy used in the proof of the claims (1) and (2) shows that the model $M = \langle W, e, \rho \rangle$, defined as in the proof of (1), evaluates into 1 all the modal formulas of Γ, and $\|\Phi\|_M < 1$. Notice that in this peculiar case, for every $f_\varphi \in Fm_W(V_0)$, $\rho(f_\varphi) = v(Pl(\varphi)^\square) \in {}^*[0,1]$, and M is in fact a hyperreal plausibilistic model. $\square$

4.2   Logics for generalized possibility and necessity

As we discussed in Section 3.2.1, possibility and necessity measures can be generalized to be defined on any lattice-ordered structure. Now, we show the logical counterpart of these measure-theoretical approaches introducing schematic extensions of $FPL(\mathscr{L}_1, \mathscr{L}_2)$ so as to capture these more peculiar mappings.

Since the formalisms we introduce are intended to deal with necessity and possibility measures, we are going to consider as $\mathscr{L}_1$, and $\mathscr{L}_2$ only those Δ-core fuzzy logics that are extensions of MTL$_\sim$. This will allow us to treat not only necessity but possibility measures as well, since they are definable as $\Pi(\varphi) := \sim N(\sim\varphi)$. With an abuse of notation, we denote by N (necessity) the modal operator of $FPL(\mathscr{L}_1, \mathscr{L}_2)$.

The logic $FN(\mathscr{L}_1, \mathscr{L}_2)$ is the schematic extension of $FPL(\mathscr{L}_1, \mathscr{L}_2)$ given by the basic axiom schema

FN $N(\varphi \wedge \psi) \leftrightarrow N(\varphi) \wedge N(\psi)$.

Necessity models for $FN(\mathscr{L}_1, \mathscr{L}_2)$ are particular plausibilistic models. Indeed, they are triples of the form $\langle W, e, N \rangle$, where W and e are defined as in the case of plausibilistic models, and where $N \colon Fm(\mathscr{L}_1)_W \to [0,1]$ is a necessity measure. Whenever N ranges over a non-trivial ultrapower $^*[0,1]$ of the unit interval $[0,1]$ we speak about *hyperreal necessity model*.

THEOREM 21 *Let $\mathscr{L}_1$ be a logic for events, and let $\mathscr{L}_2$ be a logic compatible with necessity measures. Then the following hold:*

(1) *If $\mathscr{L}_1$ is locally finite, and $\mathscr{L}_2$ has the FSRC, then $FN(\mathscr{L}_1, \mathscr{L}_2)$ is real-FSC.*

---

[16]In fact, in this case where $\mathscr{L}_2$ is assumed to have the SRC, the same result could have been obtained directly from the first translation $^\bullet$, i.e. without the further second translation $^\square$.

(2) *If $\mathscr{L}_2$ has the SRC, then* $\mathrm{FN}(\mathscr{L}_1, \mathscr{L}_2)$ *is real-SC.*

(3) *If $\mathscr{L}_2$ has the FSRC, then* $\mathrm{FN}(\mathscr{L}_1, \mathscr{L}_2)$ *is hyperreal-SC.*

Proof The claims can be easily proved by following the same lines of Lemmas 18 and 19, and Theorem 20. Indeed, using easy adaptations of Lemmas 18 and 19, one has to show that, given a modal theory Γ and a modal formula Φ, $\Gamma \vdash_{\mathrm{FN}} \Phi$ iff $\Gamma^\bullet \cup \mathrm{FN}^\bullet \vdash_{\mathscr{L}_2} \Phi^\bullet$ iff $\Gamma^\Box \cup \mathrm{FN}^\Box \vdash_{\mathscr{L}_2} \Phi^\Box$. The only point here is that when building the theory $\mathrm{FN}^\bullet$ one has to additionally consider countably many instances of the axiom **FN**. Then one has to show that the plausibilistic model $M = \langle W, e, N \rangle$ arising from the adaptation of the proof of Theorem 20, is indeed a necessity model. Adopting the same notation of the proof of Theorem 20, call v the $\mathscr{L}_2$-model of $\Gamma^\Box \cup FN^\Box$, and call $M = \langle W, e, N \rangle$ the plausibilistic model, where for every $f_\varphi \in Fm_W(V_0)$, we define $N(f_\varphi) = v(N(\varphi)^\Box)$. Then, since $\mathrm{FN}(\mathscr{L}_1, \mathscr{L}_2)$ is the basic schematic extension of $\mathrm{F}\mathscr{PL}(\mathscr{L}_1, \mathscr{L}_2)$ by the schema **FN**, for every $f_\varphi, f_\psi \in Fm_W(V_0)$,

$$N(f_\varphi \wedge f_\psi) = N(f_{\varphi \wedge \psi}) = v(N(\varphi \wedge \psi)^\Box) \text{ and } v((N(\varphi)^\Box \wedge N(\psi)^\Box) \leftrightarrow N(\varphi \wedge \psi)^\Box) = 1$$

because $(N(\varphi)^\Box \wedge N(\psi)^\Box) \leftrightarrow N(\varphi \wedge \psi)^\Box \in FN^\Box$ and v is a model of $FN^\Box$, and hence $N(f_\varphi \wedge f_\psi) = N(f_\varphi) \wedge N(f_\psi)$. Therefore N is a necessity and the claim is settled. $\square$

4.3 Logics for representable generalized possibility and necessity

For every t-norm $* \in \textbf{CONT-fin} \cup \textbf{WNM-fin}$, let $\mathscr{L}_1 = \mathscr{L}_2 = \mathscr{L}_*([0,1]_\mathbb{Q})$, as defined in Section 2.2. The logic $\mathrm{FN}^\mathbb{Q}(\mathscr{L}_1, \mathscr{L}_2)$ is the basic schematic extension of $\mathrm{FN}(\mathscr{L}_1, \mathscr{L}_2)$ given by the axiom schema

QN $N(\bar{r} \uplus \varphi) \leftrightarrow \bar{r} \uplus N(\varphi)$ for every $r \in [0,1] \cap \mathbb{Q}$,

and where $\varphi \uplus \psi$ stands for $\sim(\sim\varphi \mathbin{\&} \sim\psi)$ in $\mathscr{L}_*([0,1]_\mathbb{Q})$.

Notice that the logic $\mathrm{F}\Pi^\mathbb{Q}(\mathscr{L}_1, \mathscr{L}_2)$, where necessity measures are replaced by possibility measures, is in fact the same as $\mathrm{FN}^\mathbb{Q}(\mathscr{L}_1, \mathscr{L}_2)$, since the involutive negations of $\mathscr{L}_1$ and $\mathscr{L}_2$ allow the definition of possibility from necessity by duality. Therefore, we only focus on $\mathrm{FN}^\mathbb{Q}(\mathscr{L}_1, \mathscr{L}_2)$.

Homogeneous necessity models are necessity models $\langle W, e, N^\mathbb{Q} \rangle$ where

$$N^\mathbb{Q} \colon Fm_W(V) \to [0,1]$$

further satisfies: $N^\mathbb{Q}(\bar{r} \uplus \varphi) = r \uplus N^\mathbb{Q}(\varphi)$. Whenever the homogeneous necessity measure takes values in a non-trivial ultrapower $*[0,1]$ of the real unit interval, we speak, as usual, of *hyperreal homogeneous necessity models*. Unlike all the previously studied cases, it is now possible to introduce a stronger class of models. This is the class of *strong necessity models* of the form $M^\mathbb{Q} = \langle W, e, \pi \rangle$ where W and e are defined as above, and where $\pi \colon W \to [0,1]$ is a normalized possibility distribution, i.e. $\sup_{w \in W} \pi(w) = 1$. Evaluations in a strong necessity model are defined as usual, except for atomic modal formulas $N(\psi)$ that are now evaluated as follows:

$$\|N(\psi)\|_{M^\mathbb{Q}} = \inf_{w \in W} \left(\|\psi\|_{M^\mathbb{Q}, w} \uplus \pi(w) \right).$$

THEOREM 22 *Let* $\mathscr{L}_1 = \mathscr{L}_2 = \mathscr{L}_*([0,1]_{\mathbb{Q}})$ *for a t-norm* $* \in$ **CONT-fin** $\cup$ **WNM-fin**. *Then the following hold:*

(1) *If* $\mathscr{L}_1$ *is locally finite and* $\mathscr{L}_2$ *has FSRC, then the logic* $\mathrm{FN}^{\mathbb{Q}}(\mathscr{L}_1, \mathscr{L}_2)$ *is real-FSC with respect to the class of homogeneous necessity models, and the class of strong necessity models.*

(2) *If* $\mathscr{L}_2$ *has FSRC, then the logic* $\mathrm{FN}^{\mathbb{Q}}(\mathscr{L}_1, \mathscr{L}_2)$ *is hyperreal-SC with respect to the class of homogeneous necessity models.*

Proof An inspection of the proof of Theorem 20 and a similar technique used in the proof of Theorem 21, applied to **QN**, shows the first part of (1) and (2).

Take, now, a finite modal theory $\Gamma \cup \{\Phi\}$ such that $\Gamma \nvdash_{FN^{\mathbb{Q}}} \Phi$, and let $M = \langle W, e, N^{\mathbb{Q}} \rangle$ be the homogeneous necessity model satisfying all the formulas in Γ, and $\|\Phi\|_M < 1$.

$N^{\mathbb{Q}}$ is a homogeneous necessity measure on $Fm_W(V_0)$ and W coincides with the class of all $\mathscr{L}_1$-evaluations. Moreover, both $\langle W, *, \uplus, \sim \rangle$ and $\langle [0,1], *, \uplus, \sim \rangle$ are De Morgan triples, and, being M a model for **QN**, we have that $N^{\mathbb{Q}}(\bar{r} \uplus f) \leftrightarrow \bar{r} \uplus N^{\mathbb{Q}}(f)$ for every $r \in [0,1] \cap \mathbb{Q}$ and every $f \in Fm_W(V_0)$. Then, Theorem 9(1) ensures the existence of a normalized possibility distribution π on W such that, for every $f_\varphi \in Fm_W(V_0)$,

$$N^{\mathbb{Q}}(f_\varphi) = \bigwedge_{w \in W} \sim\pi(w) \uplus e(w, \varphi).$$

Thus $M^{\mathbb{Q}} = \langle W, e, \pi \rangle$ is a strong necessity model that satisfies Γ, but $\|\Phi\|_{M^{\mathbb{Q}}} < 1$. $\qquad \square$

REMARK 23 *An alternative modal-style treatment of (representable) possibility and necessity measure on many-valued events can be found in [20], where the authors rely on* $G_\Delta(\mathbb{Q})$ *(i.e. Gödel logic with* Δ *and truth constants from the rationals in* $[0,1]$*) as a logic for modal formulas. In fact, the only necessary ingredients to correctly axiomatize representable necessity and possibility modal formulas are the rational truth constants and the lattice operations. These requirements are fulfilled by* $G_\Delta(\mathbb{Q})$ *(i.e. in the present notation* $G_\Delta(\mathbb{Q})$ *is compatible with necessity and possibility over many-valued events).*

4.4 Logics for generalized probability

Now, we describe a logical treatment of probability measures. To keep the notation uniform, we denote by P the modal operator that interprets probability measures on fuzzy-events.

In what follows $\mathscr{L}_1$ stands for either Ł_k, or Ł, and $\mathscr{L}_2$ is any expansion of Łukasiewicz logic Ł. The logic $\mathrm{FP}(\mathscr{L}_1, \mathscr{L}_2)$ is the schematic extension of $\mathrm{FPL}(\mathscr{L}_1, \mathscr{L}_2)$ obtained by the following axioms:

P1 $P(\neg\varphi) \leftrightarrow \neg P(\varphi)$.

P2 $P(\varphi \oplus \psi) \leftrightarrow [(P(\varphi) \rightarrow P(\varphi \& \psi)) \rightarrow P(\psi)]$.

The notion of proof in $\mathrm{FP}(\mathscr{L}_1, \mathscr{L}_2)$ will be denoted by $\vdash_{\mathrm{FP}}$. Obviously the properties of normalization, and monotonicity we proved in Proposition 15, still hold for $\mathrm{FP}(\mathscr{L}_1, \mathscr{L}_2)$. In addition $\mathrm{FP}(\mathscr{L}_1, \mathscr{L}_2)$ satisfies the following:

PROPOSITION 24 *The modality P is finitely additive, that is, for every $\tau, \gamma \in \mathcal{E}$ it holds:*
$$\tau \& \gamma \to \bot \vdash_{\mathrm{F}\mathcal{P}} P(\tau \oplus \gamma) \leftrightarrow (P(\tau) \oplus P(\gamma)).$$

Proof Recall from Proposition 15, that $P(\bot) \leftrightarrow \bot$ holds in $\mathrm{F}\mathcal{P}(\mathcal{L}_1, \mathcal{L}_2)$. Now, since $\tau \& \gamma \to \bot$, we have $\tau \& \gamma \leftrightarrow \bot$, and by the rule of substitution of the equivalents (Proposition 15(2)), $P(\tau \& \gamma) \leftrightarrow \bot$. Therefore by **P2**, we get $\tau \& \gamma \to \bot \vdash_{\mathrm{F}\mathcal{P}} P(\tau \oplus \gamma) \leftrightarrow [(P(\tau) \to \bot) \to P(\psi)]$, and so $\tau \& \gamma \to \bot \vdash_{\mathrm{F}\mathcal{P}} P(\tau \oplus \gamma) \leftrightarrow (\neg P(\tau) \to P(\psi))$. □

Models for $\mathrm{F}\mathcal{P}(\mathcal{L}_1, \mathcal{L}_2)$ are special cases of plausibilistic models: a *(weak) probabilistic model* is a triple $M = \langle W, e, s \rangle$, where W and e are defined as in the case of plausibilistic models, and $s \colon Fm(\mathcal{L})_W \to [0,1]$ is a state. The evaluation of a formulas into a model M is defined as in the previous cases.

A probabilistic model is a *hyperreal probabilistic model*, whenever the measure s takes values from a non-trivial ultrapower $^*[0,1]$ of the unit interval $[0,1]$.

In analogy to the case of representable necessity and possibility measures, also for the case of probability, we can introduce the notion of *strong probabilistic model*. Indeed, strong probabilistic models are a triples $\langle W, e, p \rangle$ where W and e are as in the case of weak probabilistic models, and $p \colon W \to [0,1]$ is such that $W_0 = \{w \in W \mid p(w) > 0\}$ is countable, and $\sum_{w \in W_0} p(w) = 1$. Evaluations of (modal) formulas are defined as usual, with the exception of atomic modal formulas that are defined as follows: for every $P(\psi) \in \mathcal{M}\mathcal{F}$,

$$\|P(\psi)\|_M = \sum_{w \in W} p(w) \cdot \|\psi\|_{M,w}.$$

The following is, again, a direct consequence of Theorem 20.

THEOREM 25 *For every $k \in \mathbb{N}$, the logic $\mathrm{F}\mathcal{P}(\text{Ł}_k, \text{Ł})$ is real-FSC with respect to both the class of probabilistic models and the class of strong probabilistic models. Moreover, the logic $\mathrm{F}\mathcal{P}(\text{Ł}, \text{Ł})$ is hyperreal-SC.*

Proof Again, one starts by adapting Lemmas 18 and 19, by showing that, given a modal theory Γ and a modal formula Φ, $\Gamma \vdash_{\mathrm{F}\mathcal{P}} \Phi$ iff $\Gamma^\bullet \cup \mathrm{F}\mathcal{P}^\bullet \vdash_{\text{Ł}} \Phi^\bullet$ iff $\Gamma^\square \cup \mathrm{F}\mathcal{P}^\square \vdash_{\text{Ł}} \Phi^\square$, taking into account now that when building the theory $\mathrm{F}\mathcal{P}^\bullet$ one has to additionally consider instances of the axiom **P1** and **P2**. Then, the only necessary modification with respect to the proof of Theorem 20 regards the fact that we have to ensure that the measure $s \colon Fm_W(V_0) \to [0,1]$ of $M = \langle W, e, s \rangle$, defined as $s(f_\varphi) = v(P(\varphi)^\square) = v(p_{\varphi^\square})$, is a state. Following similar proofs in [52, Th. 8.4.9] and [35, Th. 4.2], it is easy to check that

$$s(f_\varphi \oplus f_\psi) = s(f_\varphi) + s(f_\psi) - s(f_\varphi \& f_\psi).$$

Therefore s is a state from Proposition 11.

To conclude our proof consider a finite modal theory $\Gamma \cup \{\Phi\}$ and assume $\Gamma \nvdash_{\mathrm{F}\mathcal{P}} \Phi$. From what we proved above, there is a probabilistic model $M = \langle W, e, s \rangle$ that is a model for Γ, and $\|\Phi\|_M < 1$. Adopting the same notation of Theorem 12, call Y the (finite) set of all the evaluations from V_0 into S_k. Then the state s is defined on the MV-algebra Fm_Y, hence, from Theorem 12, there exists a probability distribution p on Y such that for every $f_\varphi \in Fm_Y$, $s(f_\varphi) = \sum_{w \in Y} p(w) \cdot w(\varphi)$.

Now, we define $M' = \langle W_k, e, \hat{p} \rangle$ where W_k is the set of all the evaluations of variables in V into S_k, for every $w \in W_n$ and every variable q, $e(q, w) = w(q)$ and $\hat{p} \colon W_n \to [0, 1]$ satisfies:

$$\hat{p}(w) = \begin{cases} p(w) & \text{if } w \in Y, \\ 0 & \text{otherwise.} \end{cases}$$

Then M' is a strong probabilistic Łukasiewicz model, and it can be easily proved that for every modal formula Ψ of $F\mathcal{P}(\text{Ł}_k, \text{Ł})$, $\|\Psi\|_{M'} = \|\Psi\|_M$. Therefore M' is a model of Γ, and $\|\Phi\|_{M'} < 1$ as required. $\qquad\qquad\square$

5 Expansions with rational truth constants

In this section, we rely on basic schematic extensions of $F\mathcal{PL}(\mathcal{L}_1, \text{RŁ})$. Notice that the class $\mathcal{MF}$ of modal formulas of $F\mathcal{PL}(\mathcal{L}_1, \text{RŁ})$ is taken as closed under the operators δ_n, for every $n \in \mathbb{N}$, and therefore, for every modal formula Φ, $\delta_n \Phi$ is modal as well. We stress this fact because we adopt now the same notation we introduced in Section 2.4, and therefore, for every rational number $r = m/n \in [0, 1]$ with n, m being natural numbers, we write $\bar{r}$ or even $\overline{m/n}$ instead of $m\delta_n(\top)$.

We are going to study here plausibility measures from the general point of view, and so we consider only the modality Pl. The other cases involving (representable) necessity and possibility, and probability measures are similar and hence omitted. A complete treatment for those classes of measures can be found in [36, 35].

The logic $F\mathcal{PL}(\mathcal{L}_1, \text{RŁ})$ is significantly more expressive than a logic $F\mathcal{PL}(\mathcal{L}_1, \mathcal{L}_2)$ where $\mathcal{L}_2$ does not allow to define rational values. In fact it is now possible to deal with formulas like, for instance, $Pl(\varphi) \leftrightarrow \frac{1}{2}$ and $Pl(\psi) \to \frac{1}{3}$ whose intended interpretation is that *the plausibility of φ is $\frac{1}{2}$* and *the plausibility of ψ is at most $\frac{1}{3}$*, respectively.

Using Theorem 20, it is not difficult to prove that $F\mathcal{PL}(\mathcal{L}_1, \text{RŁ})$ is sound and (finitely strongly complete) with respect to the class of plausibilistic models. In fact RŁ has finite strong real completeness (see [43]). On the other hand, when we expand a logic by means of rational truth values, it is possible to define the notions of *provability degree* and *truth degree* of a formula ψ over an *arbitrary* theory Γ. For $F\mathcal{PL}(\mathcal{L}_1, \text{RŁ})$ they are defined as follows:

DEFINITION 26 *Let Γ be an $F\mathcal{PL}(\mathcal{L}_1, \text{RŁ})$ modal theory and let Φ be a modal formula. Then, the* provability degree *of Φ over Γ is defined as*

$$|\Phi|_\Gamma = \sup\{r \in [0, 1] \cap \mathbb{Q} \colon \Gamma \vdash_{\text{F}\mathcal{PL}} \bar{r} \to \Phi\},$$

and the truth degree *of Φ over Γ is defined as*

$$\|\Phi\|_\Gamma = \inf\{\|\Phi\|_M \mid M \text{ is a plausibilistic model of } \Gamma\}.$$

We say that $F\mathcal{PL}(\mathcal{L}_1, \text{RŁ})$ is Pavelka-style complete, *or that $F\mathcal{PL}(\mathcal{L}_1, \text{RŁ})$ enjoys the Pavelka-style completeness theorem iff for every modal theory $\Gamma \cup \{\Phi\}$,*

$$|\Phi|_\Gamma = \|\Phi\|_\Gamma.$$

Now we are going to show that $\mathrm{F}\mathcal{PL}(\mathcal{L}_1,\mathrm{R}Ł)$ is Pavelka-style complete. Just as a remark notice that, with respect to this kind of completeness, we are allowed to relax the hypothesis about the cardinality of the modal theory we are working with. In fact Γ is assumed to be an arbitrary (countable) theory, not necessarily finite. This is due to the fact that $\mathrm{R}Ł$ is indeed *strongly* Pavelka-style complete (cf. [43, Theorem 5.2.10]).

THEOREM 27 *Let Γ be a modal theory of $\mathrm{F}\mathcal{PL}(\mathcal{L},\mathrm{R}Ł)$, and let ϕ be a modal formula of $\mathrm{F}\mathcal{PL}(\mathcal{L},\mathrm{R}Ł)$. Then, the truth degree of ϕ in Γ equals the provability degree of ϕ in Γ:*

$$\|\phi\|_\Gamma = |\phi|_\Gamma.$$

Proof We are simply going to sketch the proof of Pavelka-style completeness for $\mathrm{F}\mathcal{PL}(\mathcal{L},\mathrm{R}Ł)$. The argument used is, in fact, routine, and more details can be found in [52, Theorem 8.4.9] for the case of Boolean events, and probability measure (but the same argument easily holds for our more general case).

Let $\Gamma \cup \{\Phi\}$ be an arbitrary modal theory of $\mathrm{F}\mathcal{PL}(\mathcal{L},\mathrm{R}Ł)$. Adopting the same notation of the above section, from Lemma 18, and Lemma 19, $\Gamma \vdash_{\mathrm{F}\mathcal{PL}} \Phi$ iff $\Gamma^\square \cup \mathrm{F}\mathcal{PL}^\square \vdash_{\mathrm{R}Ł} \Phi^\square$. Moreover, since the connectives of $\mathrm{R}Ł$ are all continuous, it is easy to show that

(1) $|\Phi|_\Gamma = |\Phi^\square|_{\Gamma^\square \cup \mathrm{F}\mathcal{PL}^\square}$.

We know from [43, Theorem 5.2.10], that $\mathrm{R}Ł$ is Pavelka-style complete, hence

(2) $|\Phi^\square|_{\Gamma^\square \cup \mathrm{F}\mathcal{PL}^\square} = \|\Phi^\square\|_{\Gamma^\square \cup \mathrm{F}\mathcal{PL}^\square}$.

A routine verification (see for instance the proof of Theorem 20) shows that from the map $\|\cdot\|_{\Gamma^\square \cup \mathrm{F}\mathcal{PL}^\square}$ evaluating the truth degree of formulas of the form $\varphi^\square$ into $[0,1]$, one can easily define a plausibilistic model capturing the same truth values of $\|\cdot\|_{\Gamma^\square \cup \mathrm{F}\mathcal{PL}^\square}$. Therefore

(3) $\|\Phi^\square\|_{\Gamma^\square \cup \mathrm{F}\mathcal{PL}^\square} = \|\Phi\|_\Gamma$.

Consequently, from (1), (2), and (3), we obtain $|\Phi|_\Gamma = \|\Phi\|_\Gamma$. $\square$

6   On the coherence problem

Take a finite set of events $\phi_1,\ldots,\phi_k \in \mathcal{E}$, and a map $\mathbf{a}: \phi_i \mapsto \alpha_i \in [0,1]$.

> *Can the map $\mathbf{a}$ be extended to an uncertainly measure on the algebra generated by the formulas $\phi_1,\ldots,\phi_k$?*

This problem generalizes a well-known and deeply-studied classical one. In fact, if we ask the above question in terms of classical events, and probability measures, then the above problem is known in the literature as *de Finetti coherence problem* [17, 18, 19].

We are now going to introduce a way to treat and characterize the above coherence criterion to deal with many-valued (and in general non-Boolean) events, and measures different from the additive ones.[17]

---

[17]De Finetti's coherence criterion has been recently studied for states and MV-algebras in [65, 75].

DEFINITION 28 *Let $\phi_1, \ldots, \phi_k$ be formulas in the language of $\mathscr{L}$ and let $\mathcal{M}$ be a class of generalized plausibility measures. Then a map $\mathbf{a}: \{\phi_1, \ldots, \phi_k\} \to [0,1]$ is said to be:*

(i) *A rational assignment, provided that for every $i = 1, \ldots, k$, $\mathbf{a}(\phi_i)$ is a rational number.*

(ii) *$\mathcal{M}$-Coherent if there is an uncertainty measure $\mu \in \mathcal{M}$ on the Lindenbaum-Tarski algebra Fm_V generated by the variables occurring in $\phi_1, \ldots, \phi_k$, such that, for all $i = 1, \ldots, n$, $\mathbf{a}(\phi_i) = \mu([\phi_i])$.*

Consider a finite set of $\mathscr{L}$-formulas $\phi_1, \ldots, \phi_k$, and a rational assignment

$$\mathbf{a}: \phi \mapsto \frac{n_i}{m_i}, \text{ (for } i = 1, \ldots, k\text{),}$$

where n_i and m_i are co-prime positive integers and such that $n_i \leq m_i$. Then, e.g. the following formulas are definable in the language of $FM(\mathscr{L}, R\L)$:

(4) $M(\phi_i) \leftrightarrow \overline{n_i/m_i}$.

The following theorem characterizes $\mathcal{M}$-coherent rational assignments in terms of consistency of the formulas defined in (4). Since the proof of the following theorem is similar for every class $\mathcal{M}$ of measures, we will concentrate on generalized plausibility measures, and we will omit the other cases (like necessity and probability).

THEOREM 29 *Let $\phi_1, \ldots, \phi_k$ be formulas in $\mathscr{L}$, and let*

$$\mathbf{a}: \phi_i \mapsto \frac{n_i}{m_i}$$

be a rational assignment. Then the following are equivalent:

(i) *$\mathbf{a}$ is $\mathcal{PL}$-coherent,*

(ii) *the modal theory $\Gamma = \{Pl(\phi_i) \leftrightarrow \overline{n_i/m_i} \mid i = 1, \ldots, k\}$ is consistent in $F\mathcal{PL}(\mathscr{L}_1, R\L)$ (i.e. $\Gamma \nvdash_{FP\mathcal{L}} \bot$).*

Proof $(i) \Rightarrow (ii)$. Let $\mathbf{a}$ be $\mathcal{PL}$-coherent, and let $\rho: \mathscr{F}_{\mathscr{L}_1}(V_0) \to [0,1]$ be a plausibility measure on the Lindenbaum-Tarski algebra of $\mathscr{L}_1$ defined from the set of variables V_0 occurring in $\phi_1, \ldots, \phi_k$, extending $\mathbf{a}$. Then, let W be defined as in the proof of Theorem 20 and consider the model $M = \langle W, e, \hat{\rho} \rangle$ where for every variable p and every $w \in W$, $e(p,w) = w(p)$, and where $\hat{\rho}: Fm_W(V) \to [0,1]$ is the plausibility measure such that for all $f_\varphi \in Fm_W(V)$, $\hat{\rho}(f_\varphi) = \rho([\varphi])$. Then M is a plausibilistic model for Γ. In fact, for every $i = 1, \ldots, k$,

$$
\begin{aligned}
\| Pl(\phi_i) \leftrightarrow \overline{n_i/m_i} \|_M &= 1 & \text{iff} \\
\| Pl(\phi_i) \|_M \leftrightarrow \| n_i/m_i \|_M &= 1 & \text{iff} \\
\| Pl(\phi_i) \|_M &= n_i/m_i & \text{iff} \\
\hat{\rho}(f_{\phi_i}) = \rho([\phi_i]) &= n_i/m_i.
\end{aligned}
$$

Therefore Γ has a model, and so $\Gamma \nvdash_{FP\mathcal{L}} \bot$.

$(ii) \Rightarrow (i)$. Assume, conversely, that $\Gamma \nvdash_{FPL} \bot$. Then, there exists a plausibilistic model $M = \langle W, e, \rho \rangle$ such that $\|\phi\|_M = 1$ for each $\phi \in \Gamma$. Consider the map $\hat{\rho} : Fm_W(V) \rightarrow [0,1]$ defined as follows: for every $[\psi] \in \mathscr{F}_{\mathscr{L}_1}(V)$,

$$\hat{\rho}([\psi]) = \|Pl(\psi)\|_M = \rho(f_\psi).$$

Then $\hat{\rho}$ is a generalized plausibility measure. In fact:

(i) $\hat{\rho}([\top]) = \|Pl(\top)\|_M = \|\top\|_M = 1$, and analogously $\hat{\rho}([\bot]) = 0$.

(ii) Assume that $[\varphi] \leq [\psi]$. Then $[\varphi \rightarrow \psi] = [\top]$, and hence, by the monotonicity rule one has $\|Pl(\varphi) \rightarrow Pl(\psi)\|_M = 1$ as well. But, this is equivalent to $\|Pl(\varphi)\|_M \leq \|Pl(\psi)\|_M$, i.e. $\hat{\rho}([\varphi]) \leq \hat{\rho}([\psi])$. Then $\hat{\rho}$ is monotone.

Moreover, for every $i = 1, \ldots, k$, $\hat{\rho}([\phi_i]) = \|Pl(\phi_i)\|_M = n_i/m_i$. In fact, by definition of Γ, $Pl(\phi_i) \leftrightarrow \overline{n_i/m_i} \in \Gamma$, hence $\|Pl(\phi_i) \leftrightarrow \overline{n_i/m_i}\|_M = 1$, i.e. $\|Pl(\phi_i)\|_M = n_i/m_i$. Consequently, $\hat{\rho}$ is a plausibility measure on $\mathscr{F}_{\mathscr{L}_1}(V)$ that extends **a**. Therefore, the claim is proved. $\square$

7 Conclusions and further readings

The monographs [57, 78] are standard references for a wide overview on classical uncertainty measures and reasoning under uncertainty. It is also worth mentioning the book [76] (consisting of two volumes) that offers a survey on measure theory with its many different branches, from the classical one to additive and non-additive measures on many-valued and quantum structures, along with many other related topics.

Normalized and additive maps on MV-algebras have been introduced by Kôpka and Chovanec in [61], and then by Mundici under the name of MV-algebraic states (or simply states) in [74]. More specifically, the notion of a state on MV-algebras is intimately connected with that of a state on an Abelian ℓ-group that can be found in Goodearl [49]. We also refer to the paper [26] for a comprehensive survey on the topic of states on MV-algebras and applications.

States have been also studied in a different framework than that of MV-algebras. The literature about this general approach includes several papers. In particular, we mention the work by Aguzzoli, Gerla and Marra [2] where they studied states on Gödel algebras, the paper [1] by Aguzzoli and Gerla where states were studied in the more general setting of Nilpotent Minimum algebras (cf. [29]). Dvurečenskij and Rachůnek studied in [27] probabilistic-style measures in bounded commutative and residuated ℓ-monoids. We also mention the work by Riečan on probability on BL-algebras, and IF-events [80, 81], and the paper by Mertanen and Turunen [72] dealing with states on semi-divisible residuated lattices.

Extensions of de Finetti's coherence criterion to deal with states on MV-algebras are studied in [79] for the case of events being (equivalence classes of) formulas of finitely valued Łukasiewicz logic. A first approach to the case of infinite valued Łukasiewicz logic was made by Gerla in [41], and subsequently characterized completely by Mundici [75]. In [65], Kühr and Mundici solved the problem of extending de Finetti's criterion to deal with formulas of any $[0,1]$-valued algebraic logic having connectives whose interpretation is given by continuous functions.

The problem of checking the coherence (in the sense of de Finetti) of a partial probabilistic assignment was shown to be NP-complete in [78]. This result was applied in [56] by Hájek and Tulipani to show that the satisfiability problem for a modal probabilistic logic for classical events is still NP-complete. The computational complexity of de Finetti's criterion for Łukasiewicz finitely valued events was studied by Hájek in [53], and a final NP-completeness result for the coherence problem of infinitely-valued Łukasiewicz events was proved by Bova and Flaminio in [9].

To conclude, we recall some fundamental papers on the topic of generalized measure on fuzzy events. In [73], Montagna studied de Finetti coherence criterion for conditional events in the sense of conditional states introduced by Kroupa in [62]. In [32], Fedel, Kreimel, Montagna and Roth characterized a coherent rationality criterion for non-reversible games on (divisible) MV-algebras by means of upper and lower probabilities. A multimodal based logical approach to upper and lower probability on MV-algebras was introduced in [33]. In [64, 37], the authors have begun a study of belief functions on particular classes of semisimple MV-algebras.

BIBLIOGRAPHY

[1] S. Aguzzoli and B. Gerla. Probability Measures in the Logic of Nilpotent Minimum. *Studia Logica* 94(2):151–176, 2010.

[2] S. Aguzzoli, B. Gerla, and V. Marra. De Finetti's No-Dutch-Book Criterion for Gödel logic. *Studia Logica* 90(1):25–41, 2008.

[3] T. Alsinet. *Logic Programming with Fuzzy Unification and Imprecise Constants: Possibilistic Semantics and Automated Deduction*. Monografies de l'Institut d'Investigació en Intel·ligència Artificial, Consejo Superior de Investigaciones Científicas, Barcelona, 2003.

[4] T. Alsinet, L, Godo, and S. Sandri. On the semantics and automated deduction for PLFC. In *Proc. of the 15th Annual Conference on Uncertainty in Artificial Intelligence* (UAI-99), K. Laskey and H. Prade (eds.), 3–12, Morgan Kaufmann, San Francisco CA, 1999.

[5] T. Alsinet, L. Godo, and S. Sandri. Two formalisms of extended possibilistic logic programming with context-dependent fuzzy unification: a comparative description. *Electronic Notes Theoretical Computer Science* 66(5), 2002.

[6] M. Baaz. Infinite-valued Gödel logics with 0-1-projections and relativizations. In P. Hájek, editor, *GÖDEL'96 – Logical Foundations of Mathematics, Computer Science and Physics*, Lecture Notes in Logic 6, 23–33, Springer-Verlag, Berlin, 1996.

[7] W. J. Blok and D. Pigozzii. Algebraizable logics. *Mem. Amer. Math. Soc.* 396(77), 1989.

[8] L. Borkowski. *J. Łukasiewicz. Selected Works*. Studies in Logic and the Foundations of Mathematics. North Holland, Amsterdam, 1970.

[9] S. Bova and T. Flaminio. The coherence of Łukasiewicz assessment is NP-complete. *International Journal of Approximate Reasoning* 51:294–304, 2010.

[10] T. Calvo, G. Mayor, and R. Mesiar (Editors). *Aggregation Operators: New Trends and Applications*, vol. 97 of Studies in Fuzziness and Soft Computing. Springer Verlag, 2002.

[11] C.C. Chang. Algebraic analysis of many valued logics. *Transactions of American Mathematical Society*, 88:456–490, 1958.

[12] C.C. Chang and H. J. Keisler. *Model Theory*. Studies in Logic and Foundation of Mathematics, vol. 73, 3rd edition, 1992.

[13] R. Cignoli, I.M.L. D'Ottaviano, and D. Mundici. *Algebraic Foundations of Many-valued Reasoning*. Kluwer, Dordrecht, 2000.

[14] P. Cintula, F. Esteva, L. Godo, J. Gispert, F. Montagna, and C. Noguera. Distinguished algebraic semantics for t-norm based fuzzy logics: Methods and algebraic equivalencies. *Annals of Pure Applied Logic* 160(1):53–81, 2009.

[15] P. Cintula, E. P. Klement, R. Mesiar, and M. Navara. Fuzzy Logic with an Additional Involutive Negation. *Fuzzy Sets and Systems*, 161(3):390–411, 2010.

[16] G. Coletti and R. Scozzafava. *Probabilistic Logic in a Coherent Setting*. Trends in Logic, vol. 15, Kluwer, 2002.

[17] B. de Finetti. Sul Significato Soggettivo della Probabilità, *Fundamenta Mathematicae* 17:298–329, 1931.

[18] B. de Finetti. La Prévision: ses Lois Logiques, ses Sources Subjectives, *Annales de l'Institut H. Poincaré* 7:1–68, 1937.

[19] B. de Finetti. *Theory of Probability, vol. I*, John Wiley and Sons, Chichester, 1974.

[20] P. Dellunde, L. Godo, and E. Marchioni. Exploring Extensions of Possibilistic Logic over Gödel Logic. In C. Sossai and G. Chemello (Eds.): *Proc. of ECSQARU 2009*, LNAI 5590, 923–934, 2009.

[21] D. Dubois, J. Lang, and H. Prade. Possibilistic Logic. In *Handbook of Logic in Artificial Intelligence and Logic Programming*, D. M.Gabbay et al. (eds), vol. 3, 439–513, Oxford University Press, 1994.

[22] D. Dubois and H. Prade. *Possibility Theory*. Plenum Press, New York, 1988.

[23] D. Dubois and H. Prade. The logical view of conditioning and its application to possibility and evidence theories. *International Journal of Approximate Reasoning*, 4:23–46, 1990.

[24] D. Dubois and H. Prade. Possibility theory: Qualitative and quantitative aspects. In *Handbook of Defeasible Reasoning and Uncertainty Management Systems*, D. M.Gabbay and Ph. Smets (eds), vol. 1, 169–226, Kluwer Academic Publisher, Dordrecht, The Netherlands, 1998.

[25] D. Dubois and H. Prade. Possibility Theory, probability theory and multiple- valued logics: A clarification. *Annals of Mathematics and Artificial Intelligence*, 32:35–66, 2001.

[26] A. Dvurečenskij. On states on MV-algebras and their applications. *Journal of Logic and Computation* 21(3):407–427, 2011.

[27] A. Dvurečenskij and J. Rachůnek. Probabilistic averaging in bounded commutative residuated ℓ-monoids. *Discrete Mathematics* 306(13):1317–1326, 2006.

[28] F. Esteva, J. Gispert, L. Godo, and C. Noguera. Adding truth-constants to logics of continuous t-norms: Axiomatization and completeness results. *Fuzzy Sets and Systems* 158(6):597–618, 2007.

[29] F. Esteva and L. Godo. Monoidal t-norm based logic: towards a logic for left- continuous t-norms. *Fuzzy Sets and Systems*, 124:271–288, 2001.

[30] F. Esteva, L. Godo, P. Hájek ,and M. Navara. Residuated Fuzzy Logics with an Involutive Negation. *Archive for Mathematical Logic* 39(2):103–124, 2000.

[31] F. Esteva, L. Godo ,and C. Noguera. On expansions of WNM t-norm based logics with truth-constants. *Fuzzy Sets and Systems*, 161(3):347–368, 2010.

[32] M. Fedel, K. Kreimel, F. Montagna, and W. Roth. Imprecise probabilities, bets and functional analytic methods in Łukasiewicz logic. To appear in *Forum Mathematicum*.

[33] M. Fedel and T. Flaminio. Non-revesible betting games on fuzzy events: complexity and algebra. *Fuzzy Sets and Systems* 169:91–104, 2011.

[34] T. Flaminio. Strong non-standard completeness for fuzzy logics. *Soft Computing* 12:321–333, 2008.

[35] T. Flaminio and L. Godo. A logic for reasoning about the probability of fuzzy events. *Fuzzy Sets and Systems* 158:625–638, 2007.

[36] T. Flaminio, L. Godo, and E. Marchioni. On the Logical Formalization of Possibilistic Counterparts of States over *n*-valued Łukasiewicz Events. *Journal of Logic and Computation* 21(3):429–446, 2011.

[37] T. Flaminio, L. Godo, and E. Marchioni. Belief Functions on MV-algebras of Fuzzy Events Based on Fuzzy Evidence. *ECSQARU 2011*, Weiru Liu (ed.), Lecture Notes in Artificial Intelligence, vol. 6717, Springer, pp. 628–639, 2011.

[38] T. Flaminio and E. Marchioni. T-norm based logics with an independent involutive negation. *Fuzzy Sets and Systems* 157(4):3125–3144, 2006.

[39] T. Flaminio and F. Montagna. A logical and algebraic treatment of conditional probability. *Archive for Mathematical logic* 44:245–262, 2005.

[40] P. Garcia and L. Valverde. Isomorphisms between De Morgan triplets. *Fuzzy Sets and Systems,* 30:27–36, 1987.

[41] B. Gerla. MV-algebras, multiple bets and subjective states. *International Journal of Approximate Reasoning* 25(1):1–13, 2000.

[42] B. Gerla. Rational Łukasiewicz logic and Divisible MV-algebras. *Neural Network World* 11:159–194, 2001.

[43] B. Gerla. *Many-valed Logics of Continuous t-norms and Their Functional Representation*. Ph.D. Thesis, University of Milan, 2001.

[44] L. Godo, F. Esteva, and P. Hájek. Reasoning about probability using fuzzy logic. *Neural Network World* 10(5):811–824, 2000.

[45] L. Godo, F. Esteva, and P. Hájek. A fuzzy modal logic for belief functions. *Fundamenta Informaticae* 57(2–4):127–146, 2003.

[46] L. Godo and E. Marchioni. Reasoning about coherent conditional probability in the fuzzy logic FCP(ŁΠ). In *Proc. of the Workshop on Conditionals, Information and Inference*, Ulm, 2004.

[47] L. Godo and E. Marchioni. Coherent conditional probability in a fuzzy logic setting. *Logic Journal of the IGPL* 14(3):457–481, 2006.

[48] L. Godo and L. Vila. Possibilistic Temporal Reasoning based on Fuzzy Temporal Constraints. In *Proc. of the 14th international joint conference on Artificial Intelligence* (IJCAI 95), vol. 2, 1916–1923, 1995.

[49] K.R. Goodearl. Partially Ordered Abelian Group with Interpolation. *AMS Mathematical Survey and Monographs* vol. 20, 1986.

[50] P. Hájek. On logics of approximate reasoning. *Neural Network World* 6:733–744, 1993.

[51] P. Hájek. On logics of approximate reasoning. In *Knowledge Representation and Reasoning under Uncertainty: Logic at Work* (M. Masuch and L. Polos, eds.), Lecture Notes in Artificial Intelligence 808, Springer-Verlag, 17–29, 1994.

[52] P. Hájek. *Metamathematics of Fuzzy Logic*. Kluwer Academy Publishers, 1998.

[53] P. Hájek. Complexity of fuzzy probability logics II. *Fuzzy Sets and Systems* 158(23):2605–2611, 2007.

[54] P. Hájek, L. Godo, and F. Esteva. Fuzzy Logic and Probability. In *Proc. of the 11th. Conference Uncertainty in Artificial Intelligence* (UAI'95), 237–244, 1995.

[55] P. Hájek and D. Harmancová. Medical fuzzy expert systems and reasoning about belief. Technical Report V-632, Prague, 1994.

[56] P. Hájek and S. Tulipani. Complexity of fuzzy probabilistic logics. *Fundamenta Informaticae*, 45:207–213, 2001.

[57] J.Y. Halpern. *Reasoning about Uncertainty*. The MIT Press, Cambridge Massachusetts, 2003.

[58] S. Jenei and F. Montagna. A proof of standard completeness for Esteva and Godo's logic MTL. *Studia Logica* 70:183–192, 2002.

[59] E.P. Klement, R. Mesiar, and E. Pap. *Triangular Norms*. Kluwer Academy Publishers, 2000.

[60] A.N. Kolmogorov. *Foundations of the Theory of Probability*. Chelsea Publishing Company, New York, 1960.

[61] F. Kôpka and F. Chovanec. D-posets. *Mathematica Slovaca* 44:21–34, 1994.

[62] T. Kroupa. Conditional probability on MV-algebras. *Fuzzy Sets and Systems,* 149:369–381, 2005.

[63] T. Kroupa. Every state on semisimple MV-algebra is integral. *Fuzzy Sets and Systems* 157:2771–2782, 2006.

[64] T. Kroupa. Belief Functions on Formulas in Łukasiewicz Logic. In *Proc. of 8th Workshop on Uncertainty Processing WUPES'09*. 2009.

[65] J. Kühr and D. Mundici. De Finetti theorem and Borel states in [0, 1]-valued algebraic logic. *International Journal of Approximate Reasoning* 46(3):605–616, 2007

[66] J. Łukasiewicz. O logice trówartosciowej (On three-valued logic). *Ruch Filozoficzny*, 5:170–171, 1920. English translation in [8].

[67] E. Marchioni. Possibilistic conditioning framed in fuzzy logics. *International Journal of Approximate Reasoning*, 43(2):133–165, 2006.

[68] E. Marchioni. A logical treatment of possibilistic conditioning. In *Proc. of the 8th European Conference on Symbolic and Quantitative Approaches to Reasoning with Uncertainty (ECSQARU 2005)*, Lecture Notes in Artificial Intelligence 3571, 701–713, Springer-Verlag, Berlin-Heidelberg, 2005.

[69] E. Marchioni. *Functional Definability Issues in Logics Based on Trangular Norms*. Monografies de l'Institut d'Investigació en Intel·ligència Artificial, CSIC, 2007.

[70] E. Marchioni. Uncertainty as a modality over t-norm based logics. In *Proc. of 5th Conference of the European Society for Fuzzy Logic and Technology*, Ostrava, 169–176, 2007.

[71] E. Marchioni and L. Godo. A logic for reasoning about coherent conditional probability: A modal fuzzy logic approach. In *Proc. of 9th European Conference on Logics in Artificial Intelligence (JELIA'04)*, Lecture Notes in Artificial Intelligence 3229, 213–225, Springer-Verlag, Berlin Heidelberg, 2004.

[72] J. Mertanen and E. Turunen. States on semi-divisible residuated lattices. *Soft Computing* 12:353–357, 2008.

[73] F. Montagna. A Notion of Coherence for Books on Conditional Events in Many-valued Logic. *Journal of Logic and Computation*, 21(5):829–850, 2011.

[74] D. Mundici. Averaging the truth-value in Lukasiewicz logic. *Studia Logica* 55(1):113–127, 1995.

[75] D. Mundici. Bookmaking over infinite-valued events. *International Journal of Approximate Reasoning* 43:223–240, 2006.

[76] E. Pap (editor). *Handbook of Measure Theory*, vols. I and II, Elsevier, 2002.

[77] G. Panti. Invariant measures in free MV-algebras. *Communications in Algebra* 36(8):2849–2861, 2008.

[78] J.B. Paris. *The Uncertain Reasoner's Companion, a mathematical prospective*, vol. 39 of Cambridge Tracts in Theoretical Computer Science. Cambridge University Press, 1994.

[79] J.B. Paris. A note on the Dutch Book method. In *Proc. of the Second International Symposium on Imprecise Probability and their Applications*, Cornell University, Ithaca NY, 2001.

[80] B. Riečan. On the probability on BL-algebras. *Acta Mathematica Nitra* 4, 3–13, 2000.

[81] B. Riečan. Probability Theory on IF-Events. In *Algebraic and Proof-theoretic Aspects of Non-classical Logics, Papers in Honor of Daniele Mundici on the Occasion of his 60th Birthday*, S. Aguzzoli et al. (eds.), Lecture Notes in Artificial Intelligence 4460, Springer, 290–308, 2007.

[82] P. Rusnok. *Probability in formal fuzzy logic*. Master's thesis, Czech Technical University in Prague, Faculty of Nuclear Sciences and Physical Engineering, Prague, 2008.

[83] D. Scott and P. Krauss. Assigning Probabilities to Logical Formulas. In *Aspect of Inductive Logic*, J. Hittikka and P. Suppes (eds.), North-Holland, Amsterdam, 219–264, 1966.

[84] G. Shafer. *A Mathematical Theory of Evidence*, Princeton University Press, 1976.

[85] P. Smets. Imperfect information: Imprecision – Uncertainty. In *Uncertainty Management in Information Systems. From Needs to Solutions*. A. Motro and Ph. Smets (eds.), Kluwer Academic Publishers, 225–254, 1997.

[86] P. Smets. Numerical representation of uncertainty. In *Handbook of Defeasible Reasoning and Uncertainty Management Systems*, vol. 3: Belief Change, D. Gabbay and P. Smets (Series Eds). D. Dubois and H. Prade (vol. Eds.), Kluwer, Doordrecht, 65–309, 1998.

[87] M. Sugeno. *Theory of fuzzy integrals and its applications*. Phd. Dissertation, Tokyo Institute of Technology, Tokyo, Japan, 1974.

[88] L.A. Zadeh. Fuzzy sets. *Information Control* 8, 338–353, 1965.

[89] L.A. Zadeh. Probability measures of fuzzy events. *Journal of Mathematical Analysis and Applications* 23:421–427, 1968.

[90] L.A. Zadeh. Fuzzy sets as a basis for a theory of possibility. *Fuzzy Sets and Systems* 1:3–28, 1978.

Tommaso Flaminio, Lluís Godo, and Enrico Marchioni
IIIA, Artificial Intelligence Research Institute
CSIC, Spanish Scientific Research Council
Campus de la Universitat Autònoma de Barcelona s/n
08193 Bellaterra, Spain
Emails: {tommaso, godo, enrico}@iiia.csic.es

Comments on *Reasoning About Uncertainty of Fuzzy Events: An Overview* by Tommaso Flaminio, Lluís Godo, and Enrico Marchioni

Tomáš Kroupa

The presented contribution deals with formal logical models capturing both *vagueness* and *uncertainty*. The vagueness facet of such models is represented by fuzzy events (many-valued events) which are measured by degrees of uncertainty (belief). Therefore, any logic for fuzzy events under uncertainty must have a sufficient expressive power to model inference on the side of the fuzzy events as well as to reproduce reasoning with degrees of uncertainty associated with those events. In particular, the logic chosen should be versatile enough to include in its language virtually any of the approaches to uncertainty processing, such as probability theory, possibility/necessity, Dempster-Shafer theory etc. The meaning of fuzzy events and their associated uncertainty degrees is usually rendered through de Finetti coherence criterion.

The authors provide a solid motivation for their approach and a historical summary of the similar investigations in Section 1. Discussing two components (vagueness and uncertainty) of the reasoning, they single out a crucial difference between *degrees of truth* and *degrees of belief:* intermediate truth degrees are compositional, whereas degrees of belief are not. For example, the truth degree of a conjunction $\varphi \wedge \psi$ is a two-place function depending only on the truth degrees of φ and ψ. On the other hand, the probability of $\varphi \wedge \psi$ is not, in general, a two-place function of the two corresponding probabilities of φ and ψ. The conclusion: since the role of the two degrees is essentially different, a variant of *modal logic* should be employed for expressing the degree of belief of φ as the degree of truth of the modal formula $P\varphi$ whose intended meaning is "φ is plausible". This direction was first pursued by Hájek and Harmancová.

Section 2 contains the necessary background on the logical apparatus used. The authors introduce the logic MTL of Esteva and Godo together with its algebraic semantics based on MTL-algebras. After discussing their basic properties and several types of completeness criteria, they discuss a few expansions of MTL:

- expansions with the involutive negation,

- expansions with rational truth constants,

- Łukasiewicz logic.

The importance of the last mentioned expansion cannot be overestimated in the studied context. Indeed, measure theory of fuzzy events based on *Łukasiewicz clans (tribes)* has already become a sound platform for developing several deep mathematical problems ranging from generalized measure theory and MV-probability (Butnariu, Navara, Riečan) over piecewise-linear homeomorphisms and geometry of unimodular triangulations (Mundici, Panti) to conditioning and de Finetti-type theorems (Fedel, Flaminio, Keimel, Montagna). This fact is not surprising since the Łukasiewicz disjunction has a straightforward arithmetic meaning. On the contrary, Gödel logic, which is another expansion of MTL, provides no connectives enabling to model the standard addition of reals.

Important classes of uncertainty measures are discussed in Section 3. The authors divide the content into the case of classical events and the case of fuzzy events, where the former case naturally motivates a very general definition of an uncertainty measure introduced in the latter case. Specifically, a *generalized fuzzy measure* is defined to be a monotone normalized $[0, 1]$-valued function on an MTL-algebra. This general concept is meant to cover special classes of measures, which are included in the section: possibility/necessity measures and finitely additive probabilities/states (the Dempster-Shafer's belief functions are not considered in this paper). It is known that every state is just an integral (a sum) of fuzzy events with respect to the classical probability measure. Along the same lines, the authors develop representation of necessities by generalized Sugeno integrals over fuzzy events with respect to classical necessity measures. This result is of chief importance in justifying the usual "min-preserving" definition since it shows that generalized necessities are extensions of classical necessities.

The core of the authors' contribution lies in Sections 4–5, where they present fuzzy modal logics for the previously mentioned classes of generalized fuzzy measures. Only expansions of MTL *compatible* with a given subclass of fuzzy measures are admissible, that is, the axioms of the given class of measures must be expressible by means of functions definable in the expansion of MTL. For example, Gödel logic is not compatible with the class of probabilities since probabilistic degrees of belief cannot be reproduced faithfully in this logic. The fundamental logical framework introduced by the authors consists of logic $\mathscr{L}_1$ (an expansion of MTL representing fuzzy events) and logic $\mathscr{L}_2$ (an expansion of MTL compatible with a specific class of uncertainty measures). Consequently, one can distinguish formulas from $\mathscr{L}_1$ (denoting fuzzy events) and modal formulas inductively defined over the formulas in $\mathscr{L}_1$ by considering the modality $\mathscr{M}$. Thus expression like $\mathscr{M}(\varphi \vee \psi)$ reads as "φ or ψ are plausible". Neither formulas such as $\varphi \wedge \mathscr{M}\psi$ nor nested modalities are allowed in the language. The semantics based on the set of possible worlds is adopted. The authors proceed with discussion of modal logic for generalized plausibility measures, logics for (representable) generalized possibility/necessity, logics for generalized probability, and their corresponding expansions with rational truth constants. The axioms and inference rules are introduced together with several completeness results (hyperreal completeness as well, in particular). Needless to say, these results witness that the program of formalizing uncertainty reasoning under vagueness is both feasible and successful.

Section 6 is devoted to a generalization of the well-known de Finetti coherence problem. In the framework of fuzzy events and their (rational) uncertainty assessments, this problem can be stated in the following way: given finitely-many formulas and their $[0, 1]$-valued rational assessment, is there an uncertainty measure extending the assessment to the Lindenbaum-Tarski algebra generated by the variables occurring in the formulas? This definition of a coherence problem is fairly general in allowing the uncertainty measure to belong to any class of uncertainty measures. It is shown that the coherence of a rational assessment is equivalent to consistency (in a relevant expansion of rational Łukasiewicz logic) of a certain modal theory naturally associated with the given set of fuzzy events. Finally, Section 7 concludes with a summary of state-of-the-art approaches to the topic, mentioning many relevant papers and books devoted to vagueness/uncertainty formalization.

The steadily expanding area of reasoning under both uncertainty and vagueness attracts researchers from a number of scientific fields: mathematics, logic, philosophy etc. The authors of this paper, who count among the experts in logic, made their exposition accessible to anyone with background knowledge in modern mathematical many-valued (fuzzy) logics. The view towards different uncertainty theories respects contemporary trends in uncertainty processing. In my opinion, the presented contribution is a valuable piece in the ever growing mosaic of logical formalizations of uncertainty reasoning with vague information.

Tomáš Kroupa
Institute of Information Theory and Automation
Academy of Sciences of the Czech Republic
Pod Vodárenskou věží 4
182 08 Prague, Czech Republic
Email: kroupa@utia.cas.cz

A Conversation About Fuzzy Logic and Vagueness

CHRISTIAN G. FERMÜLLER AND PETR HÁJEK[1]

Chris Fermüller: At the LoMoReVI conference, last September, in Čejkovice you gave an interesting presentation entitled *Vagueness and fuzzy logic—can logicians learn from philosophers and can philosophers learn from logicians?* ...

Petr Hájek: ... but I pointed out that my title in fact just added '*and can philosophers learn from logicians?*' to a title of an earlier paper of yours!

CF: I am flattered by this reference to my own work. But we should let our intended audience know a bit a more about the background of those two contributions. I still remember that I imagined to be quite bold and provocative by submitting a paper to a workshop on *Soft Computing*—organized by you, by the way, in 2003—that suggested already in the title that logicians should not just presume that the are properly dealing with vagueness when they investigate fuzzy logics, but should pay attention to the extended discourse on so-called 'theories of vagueness' in philosophy to understand the various challenges for correct reasoning in face of vagueness. I was really surprised when my submission was not only accepted, but when you even decided to make me an invited speaker, which entailed a longer presentation. A version of the contribution soon afterwards appeared as [7], again on your invitation.

PH: Don't forget that I also want to ask the reverse question: '*Can philosophers learn from logicians?*' I think that philosophers are often badly informed about what fuzzy logic in the narrow sense of formal development of many-valued calculi, often called just mathematical fuzzy logic, has to offer.

CF: I agree with you, of course, but my original audience consisted people working in fuzzy logic. I saw no point in explaining to them how philosophers could profit from a better knowledge of their field. But the LoMoReVI conference was an excellent opportunity to ask the 'reverse question', since we had experts from quite different areas: logic, mathematics, cognitive science, linguistics, but also philosophy. So what are the main features of fuzzy logic, that you think philosophers should learn about?

PH: First of all one should recall the distinction between fuzzy logic in the broad and in

---
[1]Christian G. Fermüller was supported by the grant I143-G15 of the Austrian Science Foundation (FWF) Petr Hájek was supported by the grant ICC/08/E018 of the Czech Science Foundation (both these grant are part of ESF Eurocores-LogICCC project FP006). Petr Hájek also acknowledges the support of the Institutional Researc Plan AV0Z10300504.

the narrow sense as presented by several authors, among them Wang who writes in [25]:

> Fuzzy logic in the narrow sense is formal development of various logical
> systems of many-valued logic. In the broad sense it is an extensive agenda
> whose primary aim is to utilize the apparatus of fuzzy set theory for devel-
> oping sound concepts, principles and methods for representing and dealing
> with knowledge expressed by statements in natural language.

I want to focus on fuzzy logic in the narrow sense, often called just mathematical fuzzy logic.

CF: Your monograph [13], published in 1998, has been and to a large extent still is *the* major source for research in mathematical fuzzy logic. In preparation for this conversation I checked the corresponding `google.scholar` entry, where it is currently listed as cited 2133 times—quite an achievement for a book entitled "Metamathematics of Fuzzy Logic" and that is certainly not a student textbook nor amounts to easy reading. I am glad that I had the chance to witness the evolution of its major concepts in the mid and late 1990's, when various collaborations, in particular also the *COST Action 15* on "Many-valued Logics for Computer Applications", gave ample opportunity to present and discuss what one can call the t-norm based approach to deductive logic. Let us try to summarize the essential ingredients very briefly.

PH: Well, a binary operation $*$ on the real unit interval $[0,1]$ is a t-norm if it is commutative $(x*y = y*x)$, associative $(x*(y*z) = (x*y)*z)$, non-decreasing in both arguments $(x \leq y$ implies $x*z \leq y*z$ and consequently $z*x \leq z*y)$, and where 1 is the unit element $(x*1 = x)$. I suggest to consider *any continuous t-norm* as a candidate of a truth function for conjunction.

CF: Sorry for interrupting already at this stage, but I think the intended general audience should take note of a few 'design decisions' that are implicit in choosing this starting point. First of all we have decided to consider not just 0 for 'false' and 1 for 'true' as formal truth values, but also all real numbers in between. In other words we have decided to allow for arbitrarily many intermediate truth values and insist that those values are densely linearly ordered. Moreover we stipulated that the semantics of conjunction as a logical connective can be modeled by some function over those 'degrees of truth'. This means that the semantic status of a conjunctive proposition $A\&B$, i.e. its degree of truth depends only on the degrees assigned to A and B, respectively, but not on any material relation between the propositions A and B. In other words we stipulate *truth functionality*. This move alone implies that whatever 'degrees of truth' are, they must be something very different from 'degrees of belief' and from probabilities that certainly do not propagate functionally over conjunction.

PH: Sure, but regarding the choice of $[0,1]$ as sets of truth value one should point that in investigations of mathematical fuzzy logic one frequently makes a move that is obvious to mathematicians, namely *generalizing* to algebraic structures that are less particular than $[0,1]$ equipped by the standard arithmetical operations and order. This gives the so-called *general semantics* of the logic in question. Regarding truth functionality, we can agree with the following critical statement of Gaifman [11]:

> There is no denying the graded nature of vague predicates—i.e. that the aptness of applying them can be a matter of degree—and there is no denying the gradual decrease in degree. More than other approaches degree theory does justice to these facts. But from this to the institution of many-valued logic, where connectives are interpreted as functions over truth degree there is a big jump.

However, I want to point out that various detailed suggestions on how to deal with truth functionality have been made. For example, Jeff Paris [22] investigates conditions that justify truth functionality. Also the philosophers N.J.J. Smith in has monograph "Vagueness and Degrees of Truth" [24] on vagueness is positive on truth degrees and on truth functionality under some conditions.

CF: Let us go further down the list of 'design choices' made by mathematical fuzzy logic. So far we have only mentioned possible truth functions of conjunction. But a considerable part of the mathematical beauty of the t-norm based approach that you have developed consists in the fact that one can derive truth function from all other logical connectives from given t-norms by quite straightforward assumptions on their relation to each other.

PH: A central tenet of this approach is to observe that any continuous t-norm has a unique residuum that we may take as corresponding implication. This is derived from the principle that $\|A \& B\| \leq \|C\|$ if and only if $\|A\| \leq \|B \to C\|$, where $\|X\|$ denotes the truth value assigned to proposition X. Thus the truth function of implication is given by $x \to y = \max_z\{x * z \leq y\}$, where $*$ is the corresponding t-norm. Negation, in turn, can be defined by $\neg A = A \to \bot$, where $\bot$ always receives the minimal truth value 0. Disjunction can be derived in various ways, e.g., by dualizing conjunction. Moreover, the popular choice of min for conjunction arises in two ways. First min is a one of three fundamental examples of a t-norm. The corresponding residual implication is given by $\|A \to B\| = 1$ for $\|A\| \leq \|B\|$ and $\|A \to B\| = \|B\|$ otherwise. The corresponding truth function for disjunction, dual to conjunction ($\vee$), is max, of course. This logic is called Gödel logic in our community, because of one of those famous short notes of Kurt Gödel from the 1930s, where he essentially defines these truth functions. But the logic is so fundamental that has been re-discovered and re-visited many times. Furthermore min as conjunction—or 'lattice conjunction' as our algebraically minded colleagues like to call it—arises in the t-norm based approach is the fact that it is *definable* in *all* those logics. i.e., even if we have chosen a another continuous t-norm as truth function for conjunction (&), min-conjunction ($\wedge$) is implicitly presented, e.g., by taking $A \wedge B$ to abbreviate $A \& (A \to B)$. In this sense all t-norm based logics—except Gödel logics, of course—have two conjunctions.

Having defined Gödel logics explicitly, we should also mention two other fundamental logics: namely, Łukasiewicz logic, arising from the continuous t-norm $a * b = \max(0, a + b - 1)$, and Product logic [16, 18], arising from standard multiplication over $[0, 1]$ as underlying t-norm. Moreover, the three mentioned logics can be combined into a single system, called $\text{Ł}\Pi\frac{1}{2}$ [6].

CF: But probably the most characteristic move that you have made in establishing t-norm based fuzzy logic as a rich research field is to ask: which logic arises if we do not fix any particular t-norm, but let conjunction vary over all continuous t-norms? You understandably call the resulting logic of all continuous t-norms "basic logic" [13, 4]. But since also other logics can and have been called "basic" in different contexts, it is best known as "Hájek's BL" nowadays. In this context one should probably also mention the logic MTL [5], that arises if one generalizes continuity to left-continuity, which is still sufficient to guarantee the existence of unique residua for corresponding t-norms.

We could indeed spend many hours discussing interesting and important results of mathematical fuzzy logic. At least one more basic fact should be mentioned: also first order versions, as well as various kinds of extensions, e.g., including modal operators, for the mentioned logics are well investigated by now.

But we should return to our motivating question: can fuzzy logic contribute to theories of vagueness as investigated by philosophers? "Theories of Vagueness", as you know, is in fact the title of a book [20] by the philosopher Rosanna Keefe, who is very critical about degree based approaches to vagueness. I don't think that pointing out that Keefe has not been aware of contemporary developments in mathematical fuzzy logic when she wrote her book suffices to deflect the worries that she and others have voiced about fuzzy logic in this context.

PH: Keefe characterizes the phenomena of vagueness quite neutrally focusing on so-called borderline cases, fuzzy boundaries, and susceptibility to the sorites paradox. I find it very acceptable, when she writes

> Vague predicates lack well-defined extensions. [They] are naturally described as having fuzzy, or blurred boundaries. Theorists should aim to find the best balance between preserving as many as possible of our judgments or opinions of various different kinds and meeting such requirements on theories as simplicity. There can be disputes about what is in the relevant body of opinions. Determining the counter-intuitive consequences of a theory is always a major part of its assessment.

Regarding the intermediary truth values of fuzzy logic she writes later in [20]:

> ... perhaps assignment of numbers in degree theory can be seen merely as a useful instrumental device. But what are we to say about the real truth-value status of borderline case predictions? The modeler's approach is a mere hand waving ... surely the assignment of numbers is central to it? Only order is important?

My comment here is, that we can indeed say that truth degrees are just a "model": the task is not to assign concrete numerical values to given sentences (formulas); rather the task is to study the notion of consequence (deduction) in presence of imprecise predicates. One should not conflate the idea that, in modeling logical consequence and validity, we *interpret* statements over structures where formulas are evaluated in $[0, 1]$ with the much stronger claim that we actually single out a particular such interpretation as the "correct" one, by *assigning* concrete values to atomic statements.

CF: I see a rather fundamental methodological issue at play here. Philosophers often seem to suppose that any proposed theory of vagueness is either correct or simply wrong. Moreover, all basic features of a "correct" model arising from such a theory are required to correspond to some feature of the modeled part of "the real world". An exception to this general tendency is Stewart Shapiro, who in his book "Vagueness in Context" [23] has a chapter on the role of model theory, where he leaves room for the possibility that a model includes elements that are not intended to directly refer to any parameter of the modeled scenarios. Truth values from the unit interval are explicitly mentioned as an example. Nevertheless Shapiro finally rejects fuzzy logic based models of vagueness for other reasons.

PH: In [14] I have taken Shapiro's book as a source for investigating some of the formal concepts he introduces in his contextualist approach to vagueness. No philosophical claims are made, but I demonstrate that Shapiro's model, that is based Kleene's three valued logic, can be rather straightforwardly generalized to BL as an underlying many valued logic.

CF: As you indicate yourself, this leaves open the question how to interpret the role of intermediate truth values. After all truth values from $[0, 1]$ or from some more general algebraic structure are the central feature of any fuzzy logic based model.

PH: Let me point out an analogy with subjective probability here. By saying "Probably I will come" you assume that there is some concrete value of your subjective probability without feeling obliged to "assign" it to what you say.

By the way, "probably" may be viewed as fuzzy modality, as explained in [13], Section 8.4, and in [12], as well as in many follow-up papers by colleagues. But, whereas the semantics of the logic of "probably" is specified truth functionally, probability itself of course is not truth functional. There is no contradiction here. Two levels of propositions are cleanly separated in the logic: the boolean propositions that refer to (crisp) sets of states measured by probabilities, and the fuzzy propositions that arise from identifying the probability of A with the truth value of "Probably A".

CF: The analogy with subjective probability is indeed illuminating. It also provides an occasion to recall a central fact about logical models of reasoning that is shared with probability theory. Quite clearly, the aim is not to model actually observed behavior of (fallible) human reasoners in face of vague, fuzzy, or uncertain information. As is well known, human agents are usually not very good in drawing correct inferences from such data and often behave inconsistently and rather unpredictably when confronted with such tasks.

While studying systematic biases and common pitfalls in reasoning under uncertainty and vagueness is a relevant topic in psychology with important applications, e.g., in economics and in medicine, the task of logic, like that of probability theory is quite different in this context: there is a strong *prescriptive* component that trumps *descriptive* adequateness. Thus, in proposing deductive fuzzy logic as a model of reasoning with vague expressions—at least of a certain type, namely gradable adjectives like "tall" or "expensive" when used in a fixed context—one does not predict that ordinary language users behave in a manner that involves the assignment of particular values to elementary propositions or the computation of truth values for logically complex sentence using particular truth functions. Rather fuzzy logic (in the narrow sense) suggests that we obtain a formal tool that generalizes classical logic in a manner, that allows one to speak of preservation of degrees of truth in inference in a precise and systematic manner. Such tools are potentially useful in engineering contexts, in particular in information processing. Whether the resulting "models" are also useful in philosophy and linguistics is a different question. Linguists seem to be unhappy about a naive application of fuzzy logics, because empirical investigations suggest that no truth function matches the way in which speakers tend to evaluate logically complex sentences involving gradable or vague adjectives. (See, e.g., Uli Sauerland's and Galit Sasson's contributions to this volume.)

Indeed, I think that, given the linguists' findings, truth functionality is best understood as a feature that it is *prescribed*, rather than "*predicted*" (to use a linguistic keyword). This actually already applies to classical logic. While we arguably *ought* to respect classical logic in drawing inferences, at least in realms like classical mathematics, logicians don't claim that ordinary language use of words like "and", "or", "implies", "for all" directly corresponds to the formal semantics codified in the corresponding truth tables, whether classical or many-valued.

Note that, if I am right about the prescriptive aspect of logic, this does not at all exclude the usefulness of truth functional logics also in the context of descriptive models. However it implies that, in order to arrive at a more realistic formal semantics of vague natural language, fuzzy logic will certainly have to be supplemented by various intensional features and also by mechanism that model the dynamics of quickly shifting contexts, as described, e.g., by Shapiro [23] but also by many linguists investigating vagueness, e.g., [1]. Actually much work done in the context of LoMoReVI is of this nature, namely *combining* deductive fuzzy logics with other types of logical models.

But then again, the role of classical logics in linguistics is analogous: it is routinely extended by intensional features, concepts from type theory and lambda calculus, generalized to so-called dynamic semantics, etc. Experts agree that there is no naive and direct translation from natural language into classical logic if we want to respect the apparent complexity of natural language expressions. Of course, the same applies to fuzzy logic. In any case, albeit the influential criticism of Kamp [19] and others, I'd say that the question of whether fuzzy logic can be usefully employed in linguistics is still open.

PH: Your terms "prescribed" and "predicted" are new for me; I find them interesting but cannot say much about this distinction. I think that the relation of mathematical fuzzy logic to natural language is very similar to that of classical mathematical logic and its relation to natural language: both deal with symbolic sentences (formulas), not with sentences of a natural language.

You say that the question of whether fuzzy logic can be usefully employed in linguistics is still open. My formulation would be "how far" instead of "whether" since I think that to some extent it has been shown already, e.g., by [24], that fuzzy logic can be usefully applied to the analysis of vague natural language.

CF: Indeed, Nick Smith [24] develops a theory of vagueness that puts fuzzy logic in its very center. Although he mainly addresses his colleagues in philosophy, I agree that it is also of direct relevance to linguistics.

However we have also mentioned that Rosanna Keefe in "Theories of Vagueness" [20] prominently criticizes an approach to vagueness that involves functions on degrees of truth as models for logical connectives. You have shortly discussed some of Keefe's objections in [15]. Since those objections are not only advanced by Keefe, but are rather widespread in philosophical discussions about fuzzy logic, I suggest to briefly look again into some concrete issues.

PH: One of the things Keefe complains about—in the sense of judging it to be counter-intuitive—is that, if A is a perfectly "half-true" proposition, i.e., if $\|A\| = 0.5$ then we have $\|A \to A\| = \|A \to \neg A\| = 1$, assuming the Łukasiewicz truth functions for implication ($\|A \to B\| = \min(1, 1 - \|A\| + \|B\|)$) and negation ($\|\neg A\| = 1 - \|A\|$). But I think that this ceases to be problematic if we view a "half-true" statement as characterized by receiving the same truth value as its negation and remember that, like in classical logic, we declare $\|A \to B\|$ to be 1 whenever $\|A\| \le \|B\|$.

CF: Still, I understand why Keefe thinks that modeling implication in this way clashes with some intuitions about the informal meaning of "if ... then ...". I guess that she would point out that it is hard to accept, previous to exposure to fuzzy logic, that "If it is cold then it is not cold" has the same semantic status as "If it is cold then it is cold" in a borderline context with respect to temperature. This, of course, is a consequence of truth functionality and of the rather innocent assumption that the truth value of a perfect "half-truth" is identical to that of its negation.

I think that the reliance on pre-theoretic intuitions is at least as problematic here as it is in the case of the so-called paradoxes of material implication for classical logic. That the formula $A \to B$ is true according to classical logic, whenever A is false or B is true, only emphasizes the well known fact that there is a mismatch between (1) the precise formal meaning of $\to$ as stipulated by the corresponding truth function and (2) the conditions under which an utterance of the form "If ... then ..." successfully conveys information among speakers of English. We have to keep in mind that *material* implication is not supposed to refer to any content-related dependency between its arguments, but only refers to the (degrees of) truth of the corresponding sub-formulas.

Your reply to Keefe's criticism points out that it is perfectly coherent to *define* the meaning of the connective "$\to$" in the indicated manner, if we are prepared to abstract away from natural language and from pre-formal intuitions. The main motivation for doing so is to arrive at a mathematically robust and elegant realm of logics that we can study in analogy to classical logic, right?

PH: Right. Let me once more emphasize that the metamathematics that arises from this particular generalization of classical logic is deep and beautiful indeed, as not only my book [13], but dozens, if not hundreds of papers in contemporary mathematical fuzzy logics can testify.

CF: I certainly agree. But this still leaves room for the possibility that mathematical fuzzy logic is just a niece piece of pure mathematics without much relevance for how we actually reason or should reason with vague notions and propositions.

PH: Well, then let us consider some sentences from natural language that may illustrate some properties of fuzzy logic.

Compare "I love you" with "I love you and I love you and I love you". Clearly the latter implies the former; but not necessarily conversely. If we model "and" by a non-idempotent t-norm then indeed a A is not equivalent to $A\&A$, matching the indicated intuition.

Moreover: "Do I like him? Oh, yes and no". Doesn't this mean that the truth value of "I like him" is neither 1 nor 0? Why shouldn't it be one half (0.5) in such a case?

CF: You might remember from earlier conversations that I actually have a different opinion about these examples. Let me briefly spell it out here once more.

As to repetition: I think that this is better analyzed as a pragmatic and not as a semantic phenomenon. To repeat a statement in the indicated manner is a way to *emphasize* the corresponding assertion. I don't think that conjunctive repetition in natural language entails the idea that the conjunction of identical statements may be less true than that the unrepeated statement. Note that linguists take it for granted that by asserting a declarative sentence S (in usual contexts) a speaker wants to convey that the proposition p_S expressed by S is true in the given context. Emphasis, hesitation, doubt, etc., about p_S may be expressed explicitly or implicitly by different means, but the impact of such qualifications should better not be conflated with the semantic status, i.e., the asserted truth of p_S itself.

As to "Yes and No": it is indeed not unusual to provide such an answer to the question whether (or to the suggestion that) a statement A holds. But it seems to me that this answer is a short form of expressing something like: "Yes, in some respect (i.e., in some relevant interpretation of the used words) A is indeed true; but in another, likewise relevant respect A is not true." If I am correct in this analysis, then degrees of truth do not enter the picture here. At least not in any direct manner.

PH: What about hedges like "very", "relatively", "somewhat", "definitely" etc.? Extending standard first order fuzzy logics, one may consider, e.g., "very" as a predicate modifier. Syntactically this amounts to the stipulation that for every sentence $P(a)$, where P is a fuzzy predicate and a is an individual, $very(P)(a)$ is also a well-formed sentence. Semantically, the extension of the predicate $very(P)$ is specified as a fuzzy set that can be obtained from the fuzzy set that represents the extension of the predicate P. This can be done in a simple and uniform manner, for example by squaring the membership function for P $(\mu_{very(P)}(a) = (\mu_P(a))^2$. Obviously there is great flexibility in this approach and one can study the logic of such "truth stressers", and similarly "truth depressors", over given fuzzy logics, like BL or MTL, both proof theoretically and from an algebraic point of view (see, e.g., [2, 3]).

CF: These are certainly good examples of research in contemporary fuzzy logic that is inspired by looking at words like "very", "relatively" etc. I have to admit that I am fascinated, but also a bit puzzled by the fact that one can retrieve literally hundreds of papers in fuzzy logic by searching for "linguistic hedges" in `google.scholar`. (Actually more than 27,100 entries are listed in total.) But if one looks at linguistic literature on the semantics of such words one finds quite different models. While gradability of adjectives and properties of corresponding order relations are investigated in this context, a methodological principle seems to be in place—almost universally accepted among linguists—that at the level of truth conditions one should stick with bivalent logic. I think that there are indeed good reasons, mostly left implicit, for sticking with this principle. If I understand linguists correctly, then a very important such reason is that their models should always be checked with respect to concrete linguistic data. But those data usually only allow to categorize linguistic expressions as being accepted or not accepted by competent language users. Indeed, it is hard to imagine how one could use a standard linguistic corpus to extract information about degrees of acceptability in connection with logical connectives.

My remarks are not intended to imply that there can't be a role for fuzzy logic in linguistics. In recent work with Christoph Roschger [9] we explicitly talk about potential bridges between fuzzy logic and linguistic models. But these "bridges" do not directly refer to deductive t-norm based fuzzy logics. We rather looked at ways to systematically extract fuzzy sets from given contextual models, as they are used in so-called dynamic semantics. Of course, one could also generalize the underlying bivalent models to fuzzy ones. But the price, in terms of diminished linguistic significance, is hardly worth paying, unless one can show that mathematical structures arise that are interesting enough to be studied for their own sake.

A direct role for logics like Łukasiewicz, Gödel, Product logic, and more fundamental deductive fuzzy logics, like BL and MTL, in linguistic contexts may arise if we insist on the linguistic fact, that "true" itself is sometimes used as gradable adjective, just like "tall", "clever", "heavy" etc. The various fuzzy logics then correspond to (prescriptive) models of reasoning that take perfectly comprehensible talk about statements being only "somewhat true", "more true" than others, or "definitely true" at face value. Of course, we thereby abstract away from individual utterances and idealize actual language use in a manner that is familiar from classical logic.

PH: Your last remark may bring us back to philosophy. There the *sorites* paradox is considered whenever one discusses the role of logic in reasoning with vague notions. In [17] an analysis of *sorites* is offered using a hedge *At*—"almost true". Consider the axioms: $bold(0)$ and $(\forall n)(bold(n) \to At(bold(n+1)))$, where $(bold(n))$ represents the proposition that a man with n hears on his head is bold. This is augmented by further natural axioms about *At*. Based on basic logic BL we obtain a simple and clear degree based semantics for *At* and for *bold* that does not lead to contradiction or to counterintuitive assumptions.

CF: This is indeed a nice example of how fuzzy logic can be used as a *prescriptive* tool of reasoning. The paradox simply disappears, which of course implies that the model is not be understood *descriptively*. If people actually find themselves to be in a sorites like scenario, they will feel the tendency to end up with contradicting assumptions. In other words they do not use fuzzy logic to start with. After all we ("competent speakers") do understand that such a scenario can is "paradoxical". Your models show that one can avoid or circumvent the difficulty by considering "near-truth" in a systematic manner.

Shapiro [23] offers an alternative analysis that moves closer to observable behavior of speakers. He invites us to imagine a community of conversationalists that are successively confronted with members of a sorites series, e.g., a series of 1000 men, starting with Yul Brynner and ending with Steve Pinker, where each man is indistinguishable from his neighbors in the series in respect of boldness. Shapiro's model predicts, that if the conversationalists are forced to judge the boldness of each of those men one by one, they will try to maintain consistency with their earlier (yes/no) judgments. However at some point they will realize that this is not possible if they don't want to call Steve Pinker bold, which is absurd, as anyone that has ever seen a picture of Pinker can testify. Thus they will retract earlier judgments made along their forced march through the sorites series and thereby "jump" between different (partial) truth assignments. Shapiro uses precisification spaces based on Kleene's three valued logic to model the resulting concept of inference formally.

As you have already mentioned, you have shown in [14] how Shapiro's model can be generalized to placing fuzzy instead of of a three valued interpretations at its core. In [8] I indicate that this can be understood as abstracting away from a concretely given sorites situation towards a model that summarizes in a static picture what can be observed about the overall dynamics of many individual instances of forced marches through a sorites series. In that interpretation degrees of truth emerge as measures of likelihood of "jumps", i.e., of revisions of binary judgments. Truth-functionality is preserved, because for complex statement we don't consider the likelihood of, say, judging $A\&B$ to be true, but rather the (properly regulated) degree of truth of the statement "A is likely to be judged true and B is likely to be judged true". (There is some similarity to the earlier mentioned logic of "probably" as a fuzzy modality.)

PH: We should not give the wrong impression that fuzzy logic in its broader sense of dealing with problems and applications arising from a graded notion of membership in a set is mainly used to analyze vague language. The areas of fuzzy controlling, soft computing, and inference using "fuzzy if-then rules" have not only attracted a lot of research, but can point to many interesting applications in engineering, decision making, data mining, etc. (see, e.g., [25]). The simple idea to model an instruction like "If the pressure is rather high. then turn the valve slightly to left" by reference to fuzzy sets rather than to fixed threshold values has proved to be effective and useful.

With hindsight it is hard to understand why Zadeh's proposal to generalize the classical notion of a set ("crisp set") to a fuzzy set by allowing intermediate degrees of membership [21] has been met with so much resistance from traditional mathematics and engineering. Presumably many found it unacceptable to declare that vagueness is not necessarily a defect of language, and that it may be adequate and useful to deal with it mathematically instead of trying to eliminate it. There is a frequently encountered misunderstanding here: fuzzy logic provides precise mathematical means to talk about impreciseness, but it does not advocate imprecise or vague mathematics.

CF: As Didier Dubois in his contribution to this volume reminds us, Zadeh insisted that a proposition is vague if, in addition to being fuzzy, i.e., amenable to representation by fuzzy sets and relations, "it is insufficiently specific for a particular purpose" [26]. I am not sure that this characterization of vagueness is robust enough to assist useful formal models. But in any case, it is clear that fuzziness and vagueness are closely related and might not always be distinguishable in practice. At the very least there is some kind of dependency: fuzzy notions systematically give rise to vague language.

PH: Let us finally return to our two-fold question: can logicians learn from philosophers and can philosophers learn from logicians? I think we both agree that the answer should be "yes".

CF: Certainly. Moreover, thanks also to the activities in LoMoReVI and our sister Log-ICCC project VAAG, we may include linguists in the circle of mutual learning regarding appropriate theorizing about vagueness.

BIBLIOGRAPHY

[1] Barker C.: The dynamics of vagueness, *Linguistics and Philosophy* 25(1):1–36, 2002.

[2] Bělohlávek R., Funioková T., and Vychodil V.: Fuzzy closure operators with truth stressers, *Logic Journal of IGPL* 13(5):503–513, 2005.

[3] Ciabattoni A., Metcalfe G., and Montagna F.: Algebraic and proof-theoretic characterizations of truth stressers for MTL and its extensions. *Fuzzy Sets and Systems* 161(3):369–389, 2010.

[4] Cignoli R.L.O., Esteva F., Godo L., and Torrens A.: Basic logic is the logic of continuous t-norms and their residua, *Soft Computing* 4:106–112, 2000.

[5] Esteva F., Godo L.: Monoidal t-norm based logic, *Fuzzy sets and systems* 124:271–288, 2001.

[6] Esteva F., Godo L., and Montagna F.: The ŁΠ and ŁΠ$\frac{1}{2}$ logics: Two complete fuzzy systems joining Łukasiewicz and product logic', *Archive for Mathematical Logic* 40:39–67, 2001.

[7] Fermüller C.G.: Theories of vagueness versus fuzzy logic: can logicians learn from philosophers?', *Neural Network World* 13:455–465, 2003.

[8] Fermüller C.G.: Fuzzy logic and vagueness: can philosophers learn from Petr Hájek? In P. Cintula, Z. Haniková, and V. Švejdar (eds.), *Witnessed Years: Essays in Honour of Petr Hájek*, College Publications, 373–386, 2009.

[9] Fermüller C.G. and Roschger C.: Bridges Between Contextual Linguistic Models of Vagueness and T-norm Based Fuzzy Logic. In T. Kroupa, J. Vejnarova (eds.), Proceedings of 8th WUPES, 69–79, 2009.

[10] Fine K.: Vagueness, truth and logic. *Synthese* 30:265–300, 1975.

[11] Gaifman H.: Vagueness, tolerance and contextual logic. *Synthese* 174:5–46, 2010.

[12] Godo L., Esteva F., and Hájek P.: Reasoning about probability using fuzzy logic, *Neural Network World* 10(5):811–824, 2000.

[13] Hájek P.: *Metamathematics of Fuzzy Logic*, Kluwer, 1998.

[14] Hájek P.: On Vagueness, Truth Values and Fuzzy Logics. *Studia Logica* 91:367–382, 2009.

[15] Hájek P.: Deductive systems of fuzzy logic. A. Gupta, R. Parikh, and J. van Benthem (eds.), Logic at the crossroads: an interdisciplinary view, 60–74. Allied publishers PVT, New Delhi 2007.

[16] Hájek P., Esteva F., and Godo L.: A complete many-valued logic with product conjunction. *Archive for Mathematical Logic* 35:198–208, 1996.

[17] Hájek P., Novák V.: The Sorites paradox and fuzzy logic, *Int. J. of General Systems* 32:373–383, 2003.

[18] Horčík R., Cintula P.: Product Łukasiewicz logic, *Arch. Math. Log.* 43:477–503, 2004.

[19] Kamp H.: Two theories of adjectives. In Edward Keenan (eds.) *Formal Semantics of Natural Languages*. Cambridge University Press, 1975.

[20] Keefe R.: *Theories of Vagueness*, Cambridge University Press, 2000.

[21] Klir G.J., Yuan B., (eds.) *Fuzzy sets, fuzzy logic and fuzzy systems: Selected papers by Lotfi A. Zadeh.* World Scientific Singapore 1996.

[22] Paris J.B.: *The uncertain reasoner's companion: a mathematical perspective.* Cambridge Tracts in Theoretical Computer Science 39, Cambridge University Press, 1994.

[23] Shapiro S.: *Vagueness in Context,* Oxford University Press, 2006.

[24] Smith N.J.J.: *Vagueness and truth degrees* Oxford Uiv. Press 2008

[25] Wang P., Da Ruan, and Kerre E.E. (eds.): *Fuzzy logic – a spectrum of theoretical and practical issues.* Springer 2007.

[26] Zadeh L.A.: PRUF—a meaning representation language for natural languages. *International Journal of Man-Machine Studies* 10(4):395–460, 1978.

Christian G. Fermüller
Vienna University of Technology
Favoritenstr. 9–11/E1852
A-1040 Wien, Austria
Email: chrisf@logic.at

Petr Hájek
Institute of Computer Science
Academy of Sciences of the Czech Republic
Pod Vodárenskou věží, 2
182 07 Prague, Czech Republic
Email: hajek@cs.cas.cz

Comments on *A Conversation About Fuzzy Logic and Vagueness* by Christian G. Fermüller and Petr Hájek

Nicholas J.J. Smith

Introduction

In the spirit of this enlightening conversation and indeed of this entire volume—promoting mutual understanding and learning between philosophers, logicians and linguists working on vagueness related issues—I shall in these comments consider three points, which if not kept in mind have significant potential to promote misunderstanding between practitioners of these three disciplines. All three points are discussed by Fermüller and Hájek: I do not take myself to be adding points that have been overlooked; I simply focus on these three points and discuss each in a little more detail—at the expense of not mentioning many other interesting issues covered in this fascinating and wide-ranging conversation.

1 Models

On p. 408, Hájek comments:

> the task is not to assign concrete numerical values to given sentences (formulas); rather the task is to study the notion of consequence (deduction) in presence of imprecise predicates. One should not conflate the idea that, in modeling logical consequence and validity, we *interpret* statements over structures where formulas are evaluated in $[0, 1]$ with the much stronger claim that we actually single out a particular such interpretation as the "correct" one, by *assigning* concrete values to atomic statements.

When Hájek talks about 'the task' here, he means the task for (mathematical fuzzy) logicians. Philosophers and linguists are often interested in different tasks (still connected with vagueness). Realising that they are (sometimes) interested in different tasks is the first point that must be kept in mind if philosophers, logicians and linguists are not to misunderstand one another.

To help fix ideas, I shall focus here on the different roles that *models* (structures, interpretations) play in relation to different tasks. First, consider the task mentioned by Hájek: modelling logical consequence. When this task is approached from a model-theoretic (rather than purely deductive or proof-theoretic) point of view, models play a role. Indeed, *all* models (of the relevant sort: classical models; fuzzy models of one or another precisely specified kind; and so on) play an equal role: α is a logical consequence of Γ just in case there is *no model at all* on which every $\gamma \in \Gamma$ has degree of truth 1 and α does not, or on which α's degree of truth is lower than the infimum of the degrees of truth of members of Γ, and so on (depending upon the particular notion of consequence in play).

Other tasks also involve models, but not in this even-handed way: some models are more important than others. For example: suppose we want to know whether a particular piece of reasoning (involving vague terms) is *sound*. What we want to know is whether the argument is *valid* (the task considered above) *and* whether the premisses are true. What we mean by 'true' here is really, actually true. To capture this idea, we need a notion of a special, designated model. Real, actual truth is then truth relative to *this* model. Consider a second example. A claim is made, involving vague terms, which is considered by competent speakers to be 'out of order' in some way: not the right thing to say in the circumstances. We want to know whether the claim is false, or true but unassertible. Again, what we mean by 'true' ('false') here is really, actually true (false)—and to capture this idea, we need a notion of a special, designated model.[1]

Yet other tasks involve models in even more subtle ways. For example, suppose we want to know the *truth conditions* of some statement involving vague terms. There are various things that could be meant by this—here is one: we want to know what a *possible world* would have to be like for the statement to come out true relative to that possible world. For concreteness, let's suppose that we are concerned with the statement 'Bob is tall', represented as Tb in a formal language, and that we are working with fuzzy models, each of which comprises a domain (set of objects), an assignment of an individual in that domain to b, and an assignment of a fuzzy subset of that domain (mapping from the domain to $[0, 1]$) to T. In this setting, one thing that will serve as a specification of the truth conditions of Tb is an assignment of an *intension* to each of T and b, where the intension of a symbol α is a function from possible worlds to values (extensions): that is, things of the kind α gets assigned in a model. Thus, in our case, the intension of T will be a function from worlds to fuzzy sets, and the intension of b will be a function from worlds to objects. Together, these determine a truth value for Tb relative to each world. Note that an assignment of intensions to T and b does not involve models *directly*: neither all models equally, nor some special models in particular. At the same time, an assignment of intensions to T and b *yields* a model, when combined with a particular possible world. Furthermore, one of these models in particular will often be of special interest: the one obtained by combining the given intensions with the *actual* world.[2]

I have discussed only a small selection of tasks in which philosophers, logicians and linguists working on vagueness related issues might be engaged. Problems facing those working on one task might pose no obstacle to those working on another;[3] results from one investigation may not be (directly) useful in a different investigation. I would say that the first item of business, when a practitioner of one discipline looks at another discipline, is to understand what task is being attempted: it may well be quite different from the tasks typically undertaken in one's home discipline.

---

[1] For further discussion, see §1 of my 'Fuzzy Logic and Higher-Order Vagueness' (this volume).

[2] For a more detailed discussion of the relationships between models and assignments of intensions, see Smith [6, Ch. 11].

[3] See for example the discussion of the problem of artificial precision in §1 of my 'Fuzzy Logic and Higher-Order Vagueness' (this volume).

2   Propositions, sentences and well formed formulas

On p. 410, Hájek comments:

> I think that the relation of mathematical fuzzy logic to natural language is
> very similar to that of classical mathematical logic and its relation to natural
> language: both deal with symbolic sentences (formulas), not with sentences
> of a natural language.

and on p. 412 Fermüller comments:

> Note that linguists take it for granted that by asserting a declarative sen-
> tence S (in usual contexts) a speaker wants to convey that the proposition
> p_S expressed by S is true in the given context.

Realising that, although they may use typographically similar expressions, they may
nevertheless (sometimes) be interested in different kinds of entities—sentences (of natural language), propositions (expressed by the utterance of such sentences in contexts)
and well formed formulas (sentences of a formal language)—is the second point that
must be kept in mind if philosophers, logicians and linguists are not to misunderstand
one another.

For the sake of simplicity and concreteness, let us proceed in terms of the following
set of basic distinctions. By producing a *token* of a certain *sentence type* in a particular
context, a speaker may express a certain *proposition*. Sentence types (and their component expressions) have *meanings*, which play a role in determining which proposition is
expressed when a token of the sentence is produced in a certain context. Propositions
(and their components, if they are taken to be structured entities) have *contents*, which
play a role in determining their *truth values* relative to given *possible worlds*. Now
consider some different tasks in which one might be interested:

1. One might want to investigate the meanings of natural language expressions. In
   this case one might employ a formal language whose symbols represent natural
   language expression types. (This is, I think, one reasonable construal of what is
   going on in some of the *linguistics* literature on formal semantics; cf. e.g. Heim
   and Kratzer [4].)

2. One might want to investigate the truth conditions of propositions expressed by
   utterances of natural language sentences. In this case one might employ a formal
   language which looks just like the language employed in case (1), except this time
   the guiding idea is quite different: the symbols of the formal language represent
   components of (structured) propositions. (This is, I think, one reasonable construal of what is going on in some of the *philosophical* literature on formal logic;
   cf. e.g. Smith [6].)

3. One might want to investigate various notions of logical consequence. In this
   case one might employ a formal language which again looks just like the language employed in cases (1) and (2), except this time the symbols of the formal
   language are not taken to represent anything else—or at least, whether or not

they represent anything else (e.g. components of natural language sentences, or of propositions) is beside the point: as far as one's investigations of logical consequence are concerned, the well formed formulas (and sets, multisets, sequences etc. thereof) are themselves the objects of interest—the relata of the consequence relation. (This is, I think, one reasonable construal of what is going on in some of the pure/mathematical *logic* literature; cf. e.g. Hájek's comment quoted above.)

There is one area in particular where the issues just mentioned play an important role—and this is discussed in some detail in the conversation (pp. 7–11). The days are long gone when anyone would be convinced by a simple argument of the form 'Such-and-such a conditional would sound quite wrong when uttered in such-and-such a context; therefore it is incorrect to represent natural language indicative conditionals as material conditionals'. Since Grice [1], it is widely appreciated that there are many moving parts in between judgements of assertibility and assignments of truth values, and that there is no simple, direct argument from the former to the latter. The point seems to be less well remembered when it comes to discussions of fuzzy approaches to vagueness. In this context, surprisingly, arguments of this simple form do seem to have convinced many philosophers, linguists and logicians that truth-functional fuzzy logics cannot provide an adequate account of the phenomena of vague language use. I think that at least part of the problem here may be a tendency to jump freely between seeing (e.g.) $Tb \wedge \neg Tb$ as a representation of the natural language sentence type 'Bob is tall and Bob is not tall', and seeing it as a representation of the proposition expressed by some utterance of this sentence type in some particular context. It may be a commitment of some version of fuzzy logic that the proposition $Tb \wedge \neg Tb$ can have a degree of truth as high as 0.5; but this in no way conflicts with the claim that the sentence 'Bob is tall and Bob is not tall' can be used to express a proposition which cannot be true to a degree greater than 0.[4]

3 'Fuzzy' logic

On p. 414, Hájek comments:

> With hindsight it is hard to understand why Zadeh's proposal to generalize the classical notion of a set ("crisp set") to a fuzzy set by allowing intermediate degrees of membership has been met with so much resistance from traditional mathematics and engineering. Presumably many found it unacceptable to declare that vagueness is not necessarily a defect of language, and that it may be adequate and useful to deal with it mathematically instead of trying to eliminate it. There is a frequently encountered misunderstanding here: fuzzy logic provides precise mathematical means to talk about impreciseness, but it does not advocate imprecise or vague mathematics.

This is the final potential misunderstanding I want to focus on: the idea that fuzzy logic involves making logic or mathematics vague. It is useful to recall that one reason why this idea persists is the multiplicity of uses of the term 'fuzzy logic'. One standard

---

[4]For related discussion, see Smith [5, §5.5].

use of the term is to pick out logics where the set of truth values is $[0,1]$. There is nothing inherently vague or imprecise about such logics. However, Zadeh himself uses a different terminology, according to which $[0,1]$-valued logic is *nonfuzzy*, and the term 'fuzzy logic' is reserved for a more elaborate view [7, pp. 409–10]. Now consider the following well-known and influential passages from Haack:

> Fuzzy logic, in brief, is not just a logic for handling arguments in which vague terms occur essentially; it is *itself* imprecise. It is for this reason that I said that Zadeh's proposal is much more radical than anything previously discussed; for it challenges deeply entrenched ideas about the characteristic objectives and methods of logic. For the pioneers of formal logic a large part of the point of formalisation was that only thus could one hope to have *precise* canons of valid reasoning. Zadeh proposes that logic compromise with vagueness. [2, p. 167]

> Zadeh offers us not only a radically non-standard logic, but also a radically non-standard conception of the nature of logic. It would scarcely be an exaggeration to say that fuzzy logic lacks every feature that the pioneers of modern logic wanted logic *for* ... it is not just a logic of vagueness, it is—what from Frege's point of view would have been a contradiction in terms—a vague logic. [3, p. 441]

Haack notes explicitly that she is concerned with fuzzy logic in Zadeh's elaborate sense and *not* with $[0,1]$-valued logics. Nevertheless, the mistaken view that $[0,1]$-valued logics are inherently vague seems to persist—along with the mistaken attribution of this view to Haack. (For further discussion, see Smith [5, §5.7].)

BIBLIOGRAPHY

[1] Paul Grice. *Studies in the Way of Words*. Harvard University Press, Cambridge MA, 1989.
[2] Susan Haack. *Philosophy of Logics*. Cambridge University Press, Cambridge, 1978.
[3] Susan Haack. Do we need "fuzzy logic"? *International Journal of Man-Machine Studies*, 11:437–45, 1979.
[4] Irene Heim and Angelika Kratzer. *Semantics in Generative Grammar*. Blackwell, Malden MA, 1998.
[5] Nicholas J.J. Smith. *Vagueness and Degrees of Truth*. Oxford University Press, Oxford, 2008.
[6] Nicholas J.J. Smith. *Logic: The Laws of Truth*. Princeton University Press, Princeton, forthcoming.
[7] Lotfi A. Zadeh. Fuzzy logic and approximate reasoning. *Synthese*, 30:407–28, 1975.

Nicholas J.J. Smith
Department of Philosophy
Main Quadrangle A14
The University of Sydney
NSW 2006 Australia
Email: njjsmith@sydney.edu.au

www.ingramcontent.com/pod-product-compliance
Lightning Source LLC
LaVergne TN
LVHW012326060326
832902LV00011B/1747